EMPIRES OF THE SILK ROAD

EMPIRES OF THE SILK ROAD

A History of Central Eurasia

from the Bronze Age

to the Present

CHRISTOPHER I. BECKWITH

PRINCETON UNIVERSITY PRESS

Princeton and Oxford

Published by Princeton University Press, 41 William Street, Princeton, New Jersey 08540
In the United Kingdom: Princeton University Press, 6 Oxford Street, Woodstock,
Oxfordshire OX20 1TW
press.princeton.edu

Seventh printing, and first paperback printing, 2011
Paperback ISBN 978-0-691-15034-5

The Library of Congress has cataloged the cloth edition of this book as follows
Beckwith, Christopher I., 1945–
Empires of the Silk Road : a history of Central Eurasia from
the Bronze Age to the present / Christopher I. Beckwith.
p.   cm.
Includes bibliographical references and index.
ISBN 978-0-691-13589-2 (hardcover : alk. paper)
1. Asia, Central—History.   2. Europe, Eastern—History.   3. East Asia—History.
4. Middle East—History.   I. Title.
DS329.4.B43 2009   958—dc22
2008023715
British Library Cataloging-in-Publication Data is available
This book has been composed in Minion Pro.
Printed on acid-free paper. ∞
Printed in the United States of America
5   7   9   10   8   6

CONTENTS

—◆—

PREFACE

This book presents a new view of the history of Central Eurasia and the other parts of the Eurasian continent directly involved in Central Eurasian history. Originally I planned to write a sketch of the essential topical elements of a history of Central Eurasia, without much of a chronological narrative. Having in mind the French tradition of writing professionally informed but readable essays for an educated general audience, with minimal annotation, I imagined it with the title *Esquisse d'une histoire de l'Eurasie centrale*. In the actual writing, the people and events insisted on following their proper order and I found myself giving a basic outline of the political and cultural history of Central Eurasia within the context of a history of Eurasia as a whole, sometimes with extensive annotation, only occasionally involving reexamination of primary sources.[1]

Nevertheless, I have kept my original main goal foremost in my mind: to clarify fundamental issues of Central Eurasian history that to my knowledge have never been explained correctly or, in some cases, even mentioned. Without such explanation, it would continue to be impossible to understand the ebb and flow of history in Eurasia as anything other than the fantasy and mystery that fill most accounts. Mysteries are intriguing, and sometimes they must remain unsolved, but enough source material is available to explain much of what has been mysterious in Central Eurasian history without resorting to the "usual suspects."

In this connection there is a widespread opinion that few sources exist for Central Eurasian history and consequently little can be said about it. That is a misconception. An immense body of source material exists on the history of Central Eurasia, especially in its connections with the peripheral civilizations.[2] Because that history covers a span of four millennia, and as there is a

---

[1] On the meaning of "primary sources" in the history of premodern periods, see endnote 1.

[2] The history of Central Eurasian interaction with the Indian subcontinent (and, to a slightly lesser extent, the pre-Islamic history of Persia and southern Central Asia) is very poorly documented until fairly recent times. Due partly to this fact, and partly to my own failings (including lack of interest in South Asia), I have paid less attention to the topic. However, much important and interesting work is currently being done on the history of the region from Mughal times to the nineteenth century, and it is to be hoped that more will soon be learned about the earlier periods as well.

correspondingly large secondary literature on some of the topics within that area and period, to do it any sort of justice would require a series of massive tomes that could be produced only by a team of scholars, not by one writer working alone with attendant limitations on knowledge, skills, energy, and time. The only way a single individual could manage to produce a book on such a huge topic would be by pulling back and taking a big-picture approach— a very broad perspective—which, as it happens, is what interests me.

In general, therefore, this book is not a highly focused treatment of any specific topics, individuals, political units, periods, or cultures (not even of the Central Eurasian Culture Complex, which deserves a book of its own), with the partial exception of those that are of particular interest to me. It is also not an exhaustive account of events, names, and dates, though the observant reader will note that I have tried to provide that information for all important events and people, even though I sometimes have had to go to surprisingly great lengths to find it. Finally, it is not a source study or a comprehensive annotated bibliography. In recent years a number of excellent studies have been published on some of the most notable people, places, periods, and other topics, with full annotation and references, and I recommend them to interested readers.

What I have done is to reexamine the more or less unitary received view of Central Eurasians and Central Eurasian history and attempt to revise it. The notes are therefore largely devoted to discussion of selected points I felt needed further comment or investigation. Whatever detail I have been able to squeeze into the narrative or the topical sections is there mostly because it seemed important to me at the time and I did not want to leave it out. That means I have left out many things that are undoubtedly important but did not seem crucial to me at the time, or that I simply overlooked. I originally did not intend to include more than absolutely minimal annotation, to keep my focus on the argument. As one can see, it did not end up quite that minimal. Habits are difficult to repress, and apparently I *like* notes that go into detail on interesting topics. (Some long notes, which are mainly of interest to specialist scholars, would cause congestion in the main text, so I have placed them in a separate notes section at the end.)

However, this book does not go to the other logical extreme either. It is not a general theory of history, and I do not intend to imply any such theory in it. There are many recent works of this type, but my book is not one of them. I also do not examine in any detail the many theories—or, rather, variants of the one current theory—of Central Eurasian state formation that have been published in the past few decades, though they are discussed briefly in the epilogue. Neither my interpretation nor my terminology derives from such theoretical or metatheoretical works. My intention has been to let my interpretations arise naturally from straightforward presentation and analysis of what I consider to be the most relevant data known to me. I may not have succeeded in this attempt, but in any case I have intentionally left the book free of overt and covert references to world-historical theories and metatheories, most of which I know little about.

With respect to the data and history writing in general, some comment on my own approach is perhaps necessary, especially in view of the recent application of the "Postmodernist" approach to history, the arts, and other fields. According to the Modernist imperative, the old must always, unceasingly, be replaced by the new, thus producing permanent revolution.[3] The Postmodernist point of view, the logical development of Modernism, rejects what it calls the positivist, essentially non-Modern practice of evaluating and judging problems or objects according to specific agreed criteria. Instead, Postmodernists consider all judgments to be relative. "In our postmodern age, we can no longer take recourse to [sic] the myth of 'objectivity,'" it is claimed.[4] "Suspicions are legitimately aroused due to the considerable differences in the opinions of the foremost authorities in this area."[5] History is only opinion. Therefore, no valid judgments can be made. We cannot know what happened or why, but can only guess at the modern motivations for the modern "construction of identity" of a nation, the nationalistic polemics of anti-intellectuals and nonscholars, and so on. All manuscripts are equally valuable, so it is a waste of time to edit them—or worse, they are said to be important mainly for the information they reveal about their scribes and their cultural milieux, so producing critical editions of them eliminates this valuable information. Besides, we cannot know what any author really

[3] See the discussion of Modernism and related topics in chapters 11 and 12.
[4] Bryant (2001). The same kinds of claims are made in other fields, including archaeology: "Postmodernism has impacted archaeology under the rubric of post-processualism, which holds that every reading or decoding of a text, including an archaeological text, is another encoding, since all truth is subjective" (Bryant 2001: 236). Having weighed different claims, some made by professional scholars of high reputation, some made by nationalistic politicians, Bryant (2001: 298–310) finally concludes that one cannot clearly decide between solid scholarship and the alternative. On the topic dealt with by his book, see appendix A.
[5] Bryant (1999: 79); see appendix A.

intended to say anyway, so there is no point in even trying to find out what he or she actually wrote.[6] Art is whatever anyone claims to be art. No ranking of it is possible. There is no good art or bad art; all is only opinion. Therefore it is impossible, formally, to improve art; one can only change it. Unfortunately, obligatory constant change, and the elimination of all criteria, necessarily equals or produces stasis: no real change. The same applies to politics, in which the Modern "democratic" system allows only superficial change and thus produces stasis. Because no valid judgments can be made by humans—all human judgments are opinions only—all data must be equal. (As a consequence, Postmodernists' judgment about the invalidity of judgments must also be invalid, but the idea of criticizing Postmodernist dogma does not seem to be popular among them.) In accordance with the Postmodernist view, there is only a choice between religious belief in whatever one is told (i.e., suspension of disbelief) or total skepticism (suspension of both belief and disbelief). In both cases, the result, if followed resolutely to the logical extreme, is cessation of thought, or at least elimination of even the possibility of critical thought.[7] If the vast majority of people, who are capable only of the former choice (total belief), are joined by intellectuals and artists, all agreeing to abandon reason, the result will be an age of credulity, repression, and terror that will put all earlier ones to shame. I do not think this is 'good'. I think it is 'bad'. I reject Modernism and its hyper-Modern mutation, Postmodernism. They are anti-intellectual movements that have wreaked great damage in practically all fields of human endeavor. I hope that a future generation of young people might be inspired to attack these movements and reject them so that one day a new age of fine arts (at least) will dawn.

Paleontology, a kind of history, is actually a hard science, so it has been largely immune to the anti-intellectualism of Postmodernist scholars.[8] Al-

---

[6] Of course, anyone who wishes to examine the original manuscripts is free to do so. The point of producing a critical edition is to establish the archetype, the closest possible approximation to the original text, so as to eliminate corruptions that do not belong to the original, and to reveal the intended meaning of the author or authors to the extent possible. Critical edition is criticized as "positivist" because it is to some extent a scientific method and postmodernists reject science as "positivism."

[7] This result was well understood by the Skeptics, philosophers of Antiquity who overtly aimed at this cessation. Their goal was to achieve happiness by eliminating the discontent arising from too much critical thought.

[8] The followers of fundamentalism (an extreme type of Modernism) object even to the results of paleontology.

though I am interested in dinosaurs, this book is not about their history but about human history; in my view, though, the same rules apply, and the Postmodern view is literally nonsense (literal nonsense being, in part, the goal of the view's proponents). I do not think that my own experience of the world is a meaningless miasma of misperceptions simply because it has been experienced by me and is therefore subjective. It is certainly true that everything is to some degree uncertain—including science, as scientists know very well—and all scholars must, of course, take uncertainty and subjectivity into account. I do not think history is a science in the modern Anglo-American sense, but I do think it must be approached the same way as science, just as all other fields of scholarly endeavor should be. Because the Postmodern agenda demands the abandoning not only of science but of rationality, I cannot accept it as a valid approach for scholars or intellectuals in general.

I also believe it is important to recognize the forces behind human motivations, especially as concerns sociopolitical organization, war, and conceptualizations of these and other fields of human activity, such as the arts. Although this book is not a study of ethology or anthropology, whether concerning primates or humans, in writing a history on such a big scale I noticed that human behavior seems to be remarkably consistent. This is not to claim that history per se repeats itself, but rather that humans do tend to do the same things, repeatedly, while, on the other hand, true coincidences are extremely rare. People also tend to copy other people. For example, the wagon, with its wheels, seems to have been invented only once; it is a gradual, secondary development from prewheeled "vehicles," and it took a long time to finally become the true wagon; but when it did so, it was very quickly copied by the neighbors of those who had developed it. The consistency of human behavior over such great expanses of space and time can clearly be due only to our common genetic heritage. Viewed from the perspective of Eurasian history over the past four millennia, there does not seem to me to be any significant difference between the default underlying human sociopolitical structure during this time period—that is, down to the present day—and that of primates in general. The Alpha Male Hierarchy is our system too, regardless of whatever cosmetics have been applied to hide it. To put it another way, in my opinion the Modern political system is in fact simply a disguised primate-type hierarchy, and as such it is not essentially different from any other political system human primates have dreamed up. If recognition of a problem is the first step to a cure, it is long past time for this particular problem to be recognized and a cure for it be found, or at least a medicine for it to be developed, to keep it under control before it is too late for humans and the planet Earth.

From the preceding statements readers can draw their own conclusions about my approach in this book, but I hereby state it explicitly, as simply and clearly as I can: my aim has been to write a realistic, objective view of the history of Central Eurasia and Central Eurasians, not to repeat and annotate the received view or any of the Postmodern metahistorical or antihistorical views.[9]

The origins of this book ultimately go back almost exactly two decades, when I wrote a paper on the idea of the *barbarian* (on which see the epilogue) and considered writing an overarching history of all of Central Eurasia. My return to the topic is in part the result of a conversation I had some years ago with Anya King, who remarked about the widespread personal use of silken goods by Central Eurasian nomads. Following up on this observation, I did some calculation and concluded that the trade in luxury goods must have constituted a very significant part of the internal economy within Central Eurasia. Subsequently, while teaching my Central Eurasian History course, I noticed that the appearance, waxing and waning, and disappearance of Silk Road commerce paralleled that of the native Central Eurasian empires chronologically. I began to seriously rethink my views on the history of the Silk Road and the nomad empires, and in turn my ideas about Central Eurasian history as a whole. I gave the first public presentation of my new interpretation of Central Eurasian history as a paper, "The Silk Road and the Nomad Empires," in the Silk Road Symposium organized by the Staatliche Museen zu Berlin on June 3, 2004.

My understanding of the topic continued to change significantly while I worked on the book. In fact, very little in the finished text has much to do with my original plan. Not only the particulars but the vision as a whole changed while I was writing it, in turn causing me to revise my presentation of the particulars. I could probably keep on revising and rewriting in this way indefinitely if I were so inclined, but I have other interests I would like to pursue, so the volume you hold in your hands represents essentially the state of my ideas when I finished the near-final draft early in 2007.

---

[9] On the need for a scholarly encyclopedic work on Central Eurasian history, see endnote 2.

I have attempted to pay special attention to the underlying cultural elements that formed the Central Eurasian Culture Complex, which I believe to be important for understanding the narrative of what happened, why, and to what effect in the history of Central Eurasia and—to some extent—in the rest of Eurasia. In my coverage of the modern period, I have paid special attention to the phenomenon of Modernism, which is responsible for the cultural devastation of Central Eurasia in the twentieth century, both in political life and in the arts, which have yet to recover from its grip. I hope that some of the points I have noticed, and the arguments I have made, will lead to a better understanding of it and maybe even point the way to improving the human condition today.

As noted, this book is about Central Eurasia in general, over the entire historical period. Because of the scale involved, many topics are barely mentioned. Yet, even if I had been able to cover all fields of scholarship in Central Eurasian studies, I would not have been able to find much published research on many of them—including important topics in history, linguistics, anthropology, art, literature, music, and practically all other fields—despite the undoubted progress that has been made recently by young scholars of Central Eurasian studies. While other areas of the world—particularly Western Europe and North America—receive, if anything, too much attention, most major topics of Central Eurasian studies have been neglected, some almost completely. Some major sources—such as Hsüan Tsang's *Hsi yü chi* 'Account of the Western Regions'—still do not have a scholarly critical edition and modern annotated translation. Others have not even been touched.

Indeed, one cannot find a single book or major research article, good or bad, on many of those topics. Just to take poetry, how many new books are published every year on, say, *Janghar* (the Kalmyk national epic), Rudaki (the earliest great poet to write in New Persian), or Li Po (one of the two or three greatest poets who wrote in Chinese)? In English, the count has hovered between zero (*Janghar* and Rudaki) and less than one (Li Po) for decades. How about the history of the Avar, Türk, or Junghar empires, or linguistic studies of Kalmyk, Bactrian, or Kirghiz (Kyrgyz)? It is rare that even an article is published on any of these major topics in Central Eurasian studies. To be sure, outstanding works, many of them listed in the bibliography, have been published on history topics in the past decade, and even some in linguistics, a model being Clark's 1998 book on Turkmen. Nevertheless, the examples given here of topics that have *not* been treated well, or at all, are only a tiny fraction of the major topics of Central Eurasian studies—including art and architecture, history, language and linguistics, literature, music, philosophy, and many others—most of which remain little studied or almost completely ignored.

By contrast, every year many hundreds of books are published, and many thousands of conference papers given, on Chaucer, Shakespeare, and other early English writers, as well as countless thousands more on modern English-language writers, as well as on Anglo-American history, English linguistics, and Anglo-American anything else. We do not really need more of them for the time being.

In short, rather than writing yet another overconceptualized, overspecialized work on topics that have been, relatively speaking, studied into the ground, consider contributing just one article, or even a small book, on one of the countless neglected topics of Central Eurasian studies. Some of them are mentioned, all too briefly, in these pages.

In conclusion, much needs to be done, from every approach imaginable, on the subject of Central Eurasian history. I wish everyone well in their efforts to fill the many lacunae that remain.

Note to the Paperback Edition

I am pleased that this book has been well enough received to merit a paperback edition, and have taken the opportunity to correct a number of errors of different kinds in the text. I would like to thank Nicola Di Cosmo, Gisaburo N. Kiyose, Andrew Shimunek, and Endymion Wilkinson for kindly sending me their comments and corrections. Unfortunately, all of the changes could not be made in this paperback edition, but they will most definitely be incorporated into a future edition of this book. I am of course responsible for any errors, old or new, that remain.

C. I. Beckwith
Tokyo, 2010

ACKNOWLEDGMENTS

In support of the research and writing of this book I was awarded an Indiana University Summer Faculty Fellowship (2004); a Fulbright-Hays Faculty Research Abroad Fellowship (2004–2005), tenure taken in Tokyo, Japan; and a Guggenheim Foundation Fellowship (2004–2005), tenure taken in 2005–2006 in Bloomington and in Dénia, Spain. In Dénia I completed the first full draft and then totally rewrote it, producing the essence of the final book minus much checking and correction of details, editing, and bibliographical additions. I am grateful to the granting institutions for their generous support.

I would also like to thank all those who advised me on my applications, wrote letters of recommendation for me, or helped me in other ways. In particular, I am indebted to E. Bruce Brooks of the Warring States Working Group at the University of Massachusetts at Amherst; Nicola Di Cosmo of the Institute for Advanced Study at Princeton; Denis Sinor of Indiana University; Tatsuo Nakami of the Institute for Languages and Cultures of Asia and Africa at Tokyo University of Foreign Studies; and Roxana Ma Newman, Toivo Raun, and Rose Vondrasek of Indiana University. Without their support I would not have had the time to write this book. I also would like to thank the staff at Princeton University Press, including Rob Tempio, senior editor; Sara Lerner, production editor; Chris Brest, cartographer; Dimitri Karetnikov, illustration specialist; Tracy Baldwin, cover designer; Brian MacDonald, copyeditor; and all others who worked on the book, for their efforts to make it turn out well.

I would have made many more mistakes without the help of my teachers, colleagues, students, and friends. I am especially grateful to Peter Golden and Cynthia King, who not only read the entire manuscript carefully and offered many comments and corrections, but also suggested numerous significant improvements and spent a great deal of time discussing problems of detail with me. I am deeply indebted as well to Ernest Krysty, who very kindly calligraphed the Old English text of the epigraph to chapter 4 and the Tokharian text of the epigraph to chapter 6. In addition, I would also like to thank Christopher Atwood, Brian Baumann, Wolfgang Behr, Gardner Bovingdon, Devin DeWeese, Jennifer Dubeansky, Christian Faggionato, Ron

Feldstein, Victoria Tin-bor Hui, György Kara, Anya King, Gisaburo N. Kiyose, John R. Krueger, Ernest Krysty, Edward Lazzerini, Wen-Ling Liu, Bruce MacLaren, Victor Mair, Jan Nattier, David Nivison, Kurban Niyaz, David Pankenier, Yuri Pines, Edward Shaughnessy, Eric Schluessel, Mihály Szegedy-Maszák, Kevin Van Bladel, and Michael Walter for their generous help, ranging from reading all or part of the manuscript or discussing various topics I treat in it to giving advice or providing answers to particular questions. Despite all their advice, which I have sometimes not heeded, probably unwisely, I am sure that I have committed errors of fact or interpretation or omission. I hope that other scholars will point them out so they can be corrected in any future revised edition. In any case, I am ultimately responsible for any mistakes or misinterpretations that remain. In particular, I would like to say that because this book is intended to revise the received view of Central Eurasia and Central Eurasians, I have often had to point out what I believe to be errors in the works of many scholars—and I include myself among those who have at one time followed one or another old view that I now consider to be wrong—but this does not mean I do not respect their learning. Specialists in Central Eurasian history have produced many fine works of scholarship. I could not have written anything without the help of all the scholars who have worked on the topics treated in this book before me, and I am grateful to them for their contributions.[1]

Most of all I thank my wife, Inna, for her support and encouragement. To her I dedicate this book.

---

[1] The final manuscript of this book was finished and accepted by the publisher in 2007. After it was finished I learned of numerous publications, some recent and some old, which either I had overlooked or I had known about but was unable to obtain by that time. In a very few cases where I felt corrections had to be made on the basis of new information, I managed to make minor additions or changes before the copyediting process was finished in spring 2008, but in general I was unable to take most of the new publications into account, and have therefore omitted them from the bibliography, which is intended to include only works I have cited. Accordingly, some highly relevant new works, such as David W. Anthony's book *The Horse, the Wheel, and Language: How Bronze-Age Riders from the Eurasian Steppes Shaped the Modern World* (Princeton, 2007), are not discussed or cited. I regret that I have not been able to take into account and cite all of the important works by so many excellent scholars that have come to my attention since the manuscript was finished.

Bax.	William H. Baxter. *A Handbook of Old Chinese Phonology.* Berlin: Mouton de Gruyter, 1992.
CAH	I.E.S. Edwards, C. J. Gadd, and N.G.L. Hammond, eds. *The Cambridge Ancient History.* Vol. I, part 2: *Early History of the Middle East.* 3rd ed. Cambridge: Cambridge University Press, 1971.
CS	Ling-hu Te-fen. 周書 (*Chou shu*). Peking: Chung-hua shu-chü, 1971.
CTS	Liu Hsü et. al. 舊唐書 (*Chiu T'ang shu*). Peking: Chung-hua shu-chü, 1975.
CUP	Henricus Denifle. *Chartularium Universitatis Parisiensis.* Paris, 1899. Reprint, Brussels: Culture et Civilisation, 1964.
*E.I.*₂	H.A.R. Gibb et al., eds. *The Encyclopaedia of Islam.* New ed. Leiden: Brill, 1960–2002.
EIEC	J. P. Mallory and D. Q. Adams, eds. *Encyclopedia of Indo-European Culture.* London: Fitzroy Dearborn, 1997.
GSE	*Great Soviet Encyclopedia: A Translation of the Third Edition.* New York: Macmillan, 1973–1983.
HS	Pan Ku et al. 漢書 (*Han shu*). Peking: Chung-hua shu-chü, 1962.
HHS	Fan Yeh. 後漢書 (*Hou Han shu*). Peking: Chung-hua shu-chü, 1965.
HTS	Ou-yang Hsiu and Sung Ch'i. 新唐書 (*Hsin T'ang shu*). Peking: Chung-hua shu-chü, 1975.
HYC	Hsüan Tsang. 大唐西域記 *Ta T'ang Hsi yü chi.*
MChi	Middle Chinese.
NMan	New Mandarin (Modern Standard Chinese).
OChi	Old Chinese (unperiodized reconstruction).
PIE	Proto-Indo-European.
Pok.	Julius Pokorny. *Indogermanisches etymologisches Wörterbuch.* I. Band. Bern: Francke Verlag, 1959.

Pul.   Edwin G. Pulleyblank. *Lexicon of Reconstructed Pronuncia-*
            tion in Early Middle Chinese, Late Middle Chinese, and Early
            Mandarin. Vancouver: UBC Press, 1991.

q.v.   *quod vide* (which see).

SKC   Ch'en Shou. 三國志 (*San kuo chih*). Peking: Chung-hua
            shu-chü, 1959.

Sta.   Sergei A. Starostin. Реконструкция древнекитайской
            фонопогической системы. Moscow: Nauka, 1989.

Tak.   Tokio Takata. 敦煌資料による中國語史の研究 :
            九・十世紀の河西方言. (*A Historical Study of the Chinese*
            Language Based on Dunhuang Materials). Tokyo: Sôbunsha,
            1988.

TCTC   Ssu-ma Kuang. 資治通鑑 (*Tzu chih t'ung chien*). Hong Kong:
            Chung-hua shu-chü, 1956.

TFYK   Wang Ch'in-jo et al., eds. 册府元龜 (*Ts'e fu yüan kuei*).
            Hong Kong: Chung-hua shu-chü, 1960.

TSFC   Hui Li. 大慈恩寺三藏法師傳 (*Ta tz'u en ssu San Tsang fa*
            shih chuan). Ed. Sun Yü-t'ang and Hsieh Fang. Peking:
            Chung-hua shu-chü, 2000.

Wat.   Calvert Watkins. *The American Heritage Dictionary of*
            Indo-European Roots. 2nd ed. Boston: Houghton Mifflin,
            2000.

*   (at the beginning of a word) a linguistically reconstructed
            form.

☆   (at the beginning of a word) a form reconstructed according
            to Chinese *fan-ch'ieh* spellings and/or rhymes.

INTRODUCTION

Central Eurasia[1] is the vast, largely landlocked area in between Europe, the Middle East, South Asia, East Asia,[2] and the sub-Arctic and Arctic taïga-tundra zone. It is one of the six major constituent world areas of the Eurasian continent.

Because geographical boundaries change along with human cultural and political change, the regions included within Central Eurasia have changed over time. From High Antiquity to the Roman conquests by Julius Caesar and his successors, and again from the fall of the Roman Empire to the end of the Early Middle Ages, Central Eurasia generally included most of Europe north of the Mediterranean zone. Culturally speaking, Central Eurasia was thus a horizontal band from the Atlantic to the Pacific between the warmer peripheral regions to the south and the Arctic to the north. Its approximate limits after the Early Middle Ages (when Central Eurasia was actually at its height and reached its greatest extent) *exclude* Europe west of the Danube, the Near or Middle East (the Levant, Mesopotamia, Anatolia, western and southern Iran, and the Caucasus), South and Southeast Asia, East Asia (Japan, Korea, and China proper), and Arctic and sub-Arctic Northern Eurasia. There are of course no fixed boundaries between any of these regions or areas—all change gradually and imperceptibly into one other—but the central points of each of the peripheral regions are distinctive and clearly non–Central Eurasian. This traditional Central Eurasia has shrunk further with the Europeanization of the Slavs in the Western Steppe during the Middle Ages[3] and the settlement of Manchuria and Inner Mongolia by Chinese in the nineteenth and twentieth centuries.

---

[1] On other terms for Central Eurasia, and the usage and meaning of 'Central Asia' today, see endnote 3.

[2] Southeast Asia, which is not much discussed in this book, is usually treated as an extension of South Asia or East Asia, but in truth it is a subregion of its own, much as the Arabian Peninsula is. Like Western Europe and Northeast Asia (consisting of Japan and Korea in the usual usage, plus southern Manchuria in premodern times), Southeast Asia is geographically broken up by mountains, rivers, and the sea. While I do not by any means embrace geographical determinism without reserve, it is difficult not to see a great deal else in common in the historical development of these areas.

[3] See Rolle (1989: 16–17).

What may be called "traditional Central Eurasia" after the Early Middle Ages thus included the temperate zone roughly between the lower Danube River region in the west and the Yalu River region in the east, and between the sub-Arctic taïga forest zone in the north[4] and the Himalayas in the south. It included the Western (Pontic) Steppe and North Caucasus Steppe (now Ukraine and south Russia); the Central Steppe and Western Central Asia, also known together as West Turkistan (now Kazakhstan, Turkmenistan, Uzbekistan, Tajikistan, and Kirghizstan); Southern Central Asia (now Afghanistan and northeastern Iran); Jungharia and Eastern Central Asia or the Tarim Basin, also known together as East Turkistan (now Xinjiang); Tibet; the Eastern Steppe (now Mongolia and Inner Mongolia); and Manchuria. Of these regions, most of the Western Steppe, Inner Mongolia, and Manchuria are no longer culturally part of Central Eurasia.

Central Eurasian peoples made fundamental, crucial contributions to the formation of world civilization, to the extent that understanding Eurasian history is impossible without including the relationship between Central Eurasians and the peoples around them. A history of Central Eurasia therefore necessarily also treats to some degree the great peripheral civilizations of Eurasia—Europe, the Middle East, South Asia, and East Asia—which were once deeply involved in Central Eurasian history.

Traditional Central Eurasia was coterminous with the ancient continental internal economy and international trade system misleadingly conceptualized and labeled as the Silk Road. It has often been distinguished from the Littoral zone maritime trade network, which also existed in some sense from prehistoric times and steadily increased in importance throughout Antiquity and the Middle Ages, but the sources make no such distinction. The continental and maritime trade routes were all integral parts of what must be considered to have been a single international trade system. That system was resoundingly, overwhelmingly, oriented to the Eurasian continental economy (and its local economies) based in the great political entities of Eurasia, all of which were focused not on the sea but on Central Eurasia. The Littoral System, as a distinctive economy of major significance, developed only after the Western European establishment of regu-

---

[4] This area should properly be called Northern Eurasia, but this term has unfortunately been used by some as a near-synonym for Central Eurasia.

lar open-sea trade between Europe and South, Southeast, and East Asia, as discussed in chapter 10; it became completely separate from the Silk Road only when the latter no longer existed.

The cultural-geographical area of Central Eurasia must be distinguished from the Central Eurasian *peoples* and from Central Eurasian *languages*, all of which have been variously defined. While the topic of this book is the history of Central Eurasia, it is really about the Central Eurasian peoples. It therefore includes the history of Central Eurasians who left their homeland for one of the other regions, carrying with them their Central Eurasian languages and the Central Eurasian Culture Complex (on which see the prologue). To some extent, the history of Eurasia as a whole from its beginnings to the present day can be viewed as the successive movements of Central Eurasians and Central Eurasian cultures into the periphery and of peripheral peoples and their cultures into Central Eurasia.

Modern scholars have done much to correct some of the earlier misconceptions about Central Eurasia and Central Eurasians, and they have added significantly to the store of data concerning the area and its peoples. Unfortunately, the corrections that have been made have not been adopted by most historians, and very many fundamental points have not been noticed, let alone corrected. In particular, the general view of Central Eurasians and their role in the history of Eurasia, even in studies by Central Eurasianists, contains a significant number of unrecognized cultural misperceptions and biases. Some of them are recent, but others are inherited from the Renaissance, and still others—especially the idea of the *barbarian*—go back to Antiquity. The following is only a brief summary of some of the main points, which are discussed in detail in the epilogue.

Most modern historians have implicitly accepted the largely negative views about Central Eurasians expressed in peripheral peoples' historical and other literary sources without taking into serious consideration the positive views about Central Eurasians expressed in the very same peripheral culture sources, not to speak of the views held by Central Eurasians about the peripheral peoples. Although works by peripheral peoples provide more or less our only surviving record of many Central Eurasians until well into the Middle Ages, when sources in local Central Eurasian languages began to be written, most works by peripheral peoples are not by any means as one-sided as historians have generally made them out to be. The antipathy felt by Central

Eurasians for the peripheral peoples is noted by historians and travelers from the periphery as well as by the Central Eurasians themselves in cases where sources in their languages are preserved—for example, by the Scythians for the Greeks and Persians, by the Hsiung-nu for the Chinese, and by the Turks for both the Chinese and the Greeks. The sensationalistic descriptions by Herodotus and other early historians should long ago have been corrected through the positive evaluations given by Greeks, Chinese, and others living among Central Eurasians as well as by the substantial amount of neutral, purely descriptive information provided by travelers and the same early writers themselves.

The received view of premodern Central Eurasia is almost exclusively a stereotype based on a misconstruing of only one segment of Central Eurasian society: the peoples of the steppe zone who have been widely believed to be "pure" nomads, distinct and isolated from settled Central Eurasians. Leaving aside the very serious problem that, ethnolinguistically speaking, the nomads cannot be clearly distinguished historically or archaeologically from urbanite and agriculturalist Central Eurasians,[5] it is important to recognize and understand the stereotypes and misconceptions that fill the modern view of the Central Eurasian nomads:[6]

- The Central Eurasian nomads were warlike—fierce and cruel natural warriors—due to their harsh environment and difficult way of life. This natural ability was much aided by their skills in horseback riding and hunting with bow and arrow, which were easily translated into military skills.

- The Central Eurasian nomads' life-style left them poor, because their production was insufficient for their needs. They therefore robbed the rich peripheral agricultural peoples to get what they needed or wanted. This "needy nomad" theory is related to the "extortion and booty" model and "greedy barbarian" model of Central Eurasian relations with the peripheral states.

[5] It is also necessary to abandon the idea that the urban Sogdians were "natural merchants," despite the sources' fondness for saying so. Recent scholarship (Grenet 2005; cf. Moribe 2005 and de la Vaissière 2005a) reveals that the Sogdians were as much warriors as anyone else in Central Eurasia.

[6] Aspects of all of these points have been criticized astutely by one or another contemporary scholar, but the ideas persist and most of them call for a great deal more criticism.

- Because Central Eurasians were natural warriors—and, as nomads, constantly moving—they were hard to defeat. They were a permanent military threat to the peripheral peoples, whom they regularly attacked and defeated. Central Eurasians thus dominated Eurasia militarily down to early modern times.

Despite some comments found in historical sources that appear to support these ideas, careful reading of the same sources flatly contradicts them. The falseness of these views is also demonstrated by simple examination of uncontested historical fact. They are ultimately all direct descendants, little changed, of the constituent elements of the ancient Graeco-Roman idea, or fantasy, of the *barbarian*. Pastoral nomadic Central Eurasians were no more "natural warriors" than urban Central Eurasians were "natural merchants," or agricultural Central Eurasians were "natural farmers." Both nomad-founded states and those founded by sedentary peoples were complex societies. Although most people in the nomad sector of the former type of state were typically skilled at riding and hunting—a fact that never failed to impress non-nomadic peoples, who comment on it repeatedly—the far more populous and rich peripheral sedentary societies included very many people who were professional soldiers trained exclusively for war. This gave them the advantage over Central Eurasians in most conflicts.

The nomads also were not poor. To be precise, some nomads were rich, some were poor, and most were somewhere in between, just as in any other culture zone, but the rank-and-file nomads were much better off in every way than their counterparts in the peripheral agricultural regions, who were slaves or treated little better than slaves. The nomads did want very much to trade with their neighbors, whoever they were, and generally reacted violently when they were met with violence or contempt, as one might expect most people anywhere to do. The biggest myth of all—that Central Eurasians were an unusually serious military threat to the peripheral states—is pure fiction. In short, neither Central Eurasia nor Central Eurasian history has anything to do with the fantasy of the *barbarian* or the modern covert version of it discussed at length in the epilogue.

Central Eurasian history concerns many different peoples who practiced several different ways of life. Each Central Eurasian culture consisted of countless individuals, each of whom had a distinct personality, just as in the rest of the world. Central Eurasians were strong and weak, enlightened and depraved, and everything in between, exactly like people of any other area or culture. Practically everything one can say about Central Eurasians, as people, can be said about every other people in Eurasia. It is necessary to at least *attempt* to be neutral in writing history.

But what about the *barbarians*? If the historical record actually tells us Central Eurasians were not *barbarians*, what were they? They were dynamic, creative people. Central Eurasia was the home of the Indo-Europeans, who expanded across Eurasia from sea to sea and established the foundations of what has become world civilization. Central Asia in the Middle Ages was the economic, cultural, and intellectual center of the world, and Central Asians are responsible for essential elements of modern science, technology, and the arts. The historical record unambiguously shows that Central Eurasians were people who fought against overwhelming—indeed, hopeless—odds, defending their homelands, their families, and their way of life from relentless encroachment and ruthless invasion by the peripheral peoples of Eurasia. The Central Eurasians lost almost everything, eventually, but they fought the good fight. This book is thus ultimately about the continent-wide struggle between the Central Eurasians and the peripheral peoples,[7] leading to the victory of the latter, the destruction of the Central Eurasian states, and the reduction of Central Eurasian peoples to extreme poverty and near extinction before their miraculous rebirth, in the nick of time, at the end of the twentieth century.

One may still wish to ask, was not the history of Central Eurasia, dominated by states founded by nomadic or partly nomadic people, unique in its tendencies and outcomes? No. The struggle of the vastly outnumbered nations of Central Eurasia against the inexorable expansion of their peripheral neighbors was paralleled by that of the American Indian nations against the Europeans and their ex-colonial clients, the European-American states, who pursued a policy of overt or covert genocide in most countries of the Americas. In North America, the Indians fought to save their lands, their nations, and their families, but they lost. Their fields of corn were burned, their families were massacred, and the few survivors were transported by force to

---

[7] The dichotomy was not by any means always in operation everywhere. Some important exceptions are discussed by Di Cosmo (2002a) and others. The point is that, over the long duration of Eurasian history, the inexorable trend was the reduction of Central Eurasian territory and the Central Eurasian peoples' loss of power, wealth, and, in countless cases, life.

desert lands where they were left to die. Up until a few decades ago, the Indians were condemned by the unjust, genocidal victors as "savages." Finally, when they had almost disappeared, some among the victor peoples had a twinge of conscience and realized that the historical treatment of the Indians was exactly the reverse of the truth. Recognition of the struggles of the Central Eurasian peoples against the more than two-millennia-long mistreatment by their peripheral neighbors is long overdue. The warriors of Central Eurasia were not *barbarians*. They were heroes, and the epics of their peoples sing their undying fame.

EMPIRES OF THE SILK ROAD

PROLOGUE

—ᐠᘏᓚ—

The Hero and His Friends

Эртиин экн цагт һаргсн,
Тэк Зула хаани үлдл,
Таңсг Бумб хаани ач,
Үзң алдр хаани көвүн
Үйин өнчи Җаңһр билэ.
Эркн хө мөстэдэн
Догшн маңһст нутган дээлүлҗ,
Өнчн бийэр үлдгсн;
һун оргч насндан,
Арнзл Зеердиннь үрэ цагт
Көл өргҗ мордгсн,
һүрвн ик бээрин ам эвдгсн,
һульҗң ик маңһс хааг номдан орулсн.
                                        —*Җаңһр*

> Born in a bygone age long ago,
> Descendant of the wild horse, Zûla Khan,
> Bûmba's grandson, the gentle khan,
> Son of Üzeng, the famous khan:
> Janghar the matchless he was.
> When he reached the tender age of two
> A cruel dragon invaded his homeland
> And he was left an orphan.
> Attaining the age of three, up onto
> Auburn—his charger in his third year—he
> Scrambled and mounted,
> Smashed the gates of three great fortresses, and
> Subdued the great dragon, the ruthless one.
> —From *Janghar*[1]

The First Story

The Lord of Heaven above impregnated the daughter of the Lord of the Waters below, and a son was miraculously born.

But an evil king killed the prince's father and enslaved the prince's mother, and the orphaned prince was cast into the wilderness at birth.

---

[1] In this selection from the Kalmyk national epic (Anonymous 1990: 10) I have omitted the unusually long, stylistically odd second line, which seems to be an intrusive editorial addition perhaps intended to mollify strict Buddhist readers.

—ᐠᘏᓚ—

*There, instead of harming him, the wild beasts took care of him. He sur-
vived and became wily and powerful.*

*The marvelous child was brought to the royal court, where he was raised by
the king almost like one of his sons.*

He grew up strong, skilled with horses, and an expert with the bow.

*Despite his talents, he was sent to work in the stables. When an enemy at-
tacked the kingdom, the stableboy defeated them with his powerful bow. His
heroic reputation spread far and wide.*

*The king and his sons were afraid of the hero, and the sons convinced the
king to employ a stratagem to have him murdered. But the prince was warned
in time and miraculously escaped.*

*He acquired a following of courageous young warrior friends. They at-
tacked and killed the evil king, freed their women, and established a righteous
and prosperous kingdom.*

*Bards sang the story of the prince and his companions to the heroes them-
selves and at the courts of other princes and heroes, in their time and long afterward. They had achieved undying fame.*

Central Eurasian National Origin Myths

In myth and legend, if not in fact, the Central Eurasian founders of many
great realms followed this heroic model from protohistorical and early historical times on, including the Bronze Age Hittites[2] and Chou Chinese; the
Classical period Scythians, Romans, Wu-sun, and Koguryo; the medieval
Turks and Mongols; and the Junghars and Manchus[3] of the late Renaissance
and Enlightenment.

---

[2] On Hittite myths and similarities with foundation myths of other peoples, see endnote 4. The
Hittites also had an institutionalized guard corps that seems to have been a comitatus, q.v.
below.

[3] No Junghar origin myth seems to be preserved in historical sources, though various of the
Oirat constituent peoples are said to have origin myths. However, the beginning of the epic of
Janghar, the national hero of the Junghars and their Oirat relatives, among whom the best
known today are the Kalmyks, is a version of the First Story; see the quotation at the chapter
head.

During the Shang Dynasty[4] Lady Yüan of the Chiang[5] clan offered sacrifice so that she would no longer be childless. Afterward she stepped in the footprint of the King of Heaven and became pregnant. She gave birth to Hou Chi 'Lord Millet'.

The baby was left in a narrow lane, but the sheep and cattle lovingly protected him. He was left in a wide forest, but woodcutters saved him. He was placed on the freezing ice, but birds protected him with their wings. When the birds left, Hou Chi began to cry. His mother then knew he was a supernatural being, and she took him back and raised him.

When he grew up, he served Emperor Yao, who appointed him Master of Horses. He also planted beans, grain, and gourds, and all grew abundantly.[6] He founded the Chou Dynasty, which overthrew the evil last ruler of Shang.[7]

The son of the god of Heaven[8] was herding his cattle near the lands of the daughter of the god of the Dnieper River, and he let his horses graze while he was sleeping. The river god's daughter stole the horses and made him lie with her before she would give the horses back to him. Three sons were born to her.

When the three sons were grown up, their mother, following their father's directions, presented the sons with his great bow. Whoever could draw the bow would become king. Each boy tried it, but only the youngest could pull the bow.

---

[4] The date of the Chou conquest of Shang is controversial; the dates 1046 or 1045 BC now dominate scholarly discussion.

[5] The Chiang 姜 NMan *jiâng* are generally believed to be related to the Ch'iang 羌 NMan *qiâng*, the main enemies of the Shang Dynasty, who were skilled in the use of chariots. See appendix B. I generally cite modern Mandarin words first in the traditional Wade-Giles system, sans tone marks, then in the pinyin system. The first of the above words would be transcribed fully as *chiang¹* in Wade-Giles. Some pinyin printing styles write *jiâng* as *jiāng*, but in this book, as in many others, the circumflex is generally used as the equivalent of the macron except in direct quotations and Old Chinese forms (where the macron indicates length).

[6] On founders as agricultural fertility gods, see endnote 5.

[7] The story presented here is a conflation of two texts, the version preserved in the *Shih ching*, Ode 245 "Sheng Min" (Legge 1935: 465–472) and the version in the *Lun Heng* (Yamada 1976: 146).

[8] On the Scythian gods according to Herodotus, see endnote 6.

Three marvelous golden objects fell to earth from Heaven: a plow and yoke, a sword, and a cup. Each of the three sons attempted to pick up the golden objects. When the oldest son approached them, they blazed up with fire, so he could not take them. The same thing happened to the middle son. When the youngest son tried it, he had no difficulty taking them.

The youngest son, Scythês,[9] therefore became king of his people, who called themselves Scythians after his name.

The Scythians were attacked by the Massagetae, and fleeing from them crossed the Araxes River into Cimmeria, which they made their home. Relying on their skill with horses and the bow they became a great nation.

The brothers Numitor and Amulius were descendants of Aeneas, who had led the Trojan refugees to Italy. Numitor, the rightful king, was deposed by Amulius, who forced Numitor's daughter Rhea Silvia to become a celibate Vestal Virgin so that she would not bear any successors to Numitor. But one night the god Mars came and raped Rhea Silvia, who then gave birth to beautiful twin boys, Romulus and Remus. Amulius had Rhea Silvia imprisoned and ordered the twins to be killed.

The servant who had been told to expose them could not carry out the order and left them in their cradle beside the Tiber River, which overflowed and carried the cradle downstream to a sheltered spot. There the twins were nursed by a she-wolf and fed by a bird[10] until a herdsman discovered them and took them home. He and his wife raised them as their own children.

They grew up strong and noble, skilled in hunting and herding. When they were taken to the royal court, Amulius attempted to have them killed, but they escaped, and with the oppressed shepherds and other people they finally put the unjust king to death. Numitor, the grandfather of Romulus and Remus and the rightful ruler, was restored as king.

The twins then left with their followers to found a new city. They argued about the city's location, and the argument turned into a battle in which Romulus and his personal bodyguard of 300 mounted warriors, the Celeres, killed Remus. Romulus then founded the circular city of Rome.[11]

---

[9] See appendix B on the names of the Scythians, Sakas, and other Northern Iranians.

[10] It is specifically said to have been a woodpecker; see below.

[11] This summary largely follows Plutarch's (Perrin 1998: 94 et seq.) long version, which does not actually differ, in its fundamental elements, from his principle alternate version and the ver-

—◁◆▷—

*Tumen,[12] the first great ruler[13] of the Hsiung-nu,[14] built a strong nation in the Eastern Steppe. He had a son named Mo-tun,[15] who was the crown prince. Later, *Tumen had a son by his favorite consort and wanted to get rid of Mo-tun so he could make his new son the crown prince. He made a treaty with the *Tok^war (Yüeh-chih)[16] and sent Mo-tun to them as a hostage to guarantee the treaty, as was the custom. After Mo-tun arrived, *Tumen attacked the *Tok^war. The *Tok^war wanted to execute Mo-tun according to the terms of the treaty, but he stole one of their best horses and escaped back home.[17] *Tumen praised his strength and made him a myriarch, the commander of ten thousand mounted warriors.[18]

Mo-tun then made a whistling arrow with which to train his riders to shoot. He ordered them to obey him, saying, "Whoever does not shoot what the whistling arrow shoots will be decapitated." They went hunting, and as Mo-tun said, he cut off the head of whoever did not shoot what he shot with the whistling arrow. Then Mo-tun used the whistling arrow to shoot his best horse. Some of his men were afraid to shoot it. Mo-tun immediately decapitated them. Next he shot his favorite wife. Some of his men were terrified and did not dare to shoot her. He cut their heads off like the others. Again he went hunting, and used the whistling arrow to shoot the king's best horse. All of his men shot it. Then Mo-tun knew they were ready. He went hunting with his father the king and shot him with the whistling arrow. His men, following the whistling arrow, shot and killed *Tumen. Mo-tun then executed all officials

---

sion in Livy (Foster 1988: 16 et seq.). The Celeres, the mounted bodyguard of Romulus mentioned in Livy (Foster 1988: 56–57), was certainly a comitatus, at least in origin. One intriguing detail in Plutarch's first, shorter, version is the name of the evil king, Ταρχέτιος Tarchetius, which is strikingly similar to the name Ταργιτάος Targitaus, the legendary royal father of the first Scythian ruler in one of Herodotus's versions of the Scythian origin myth; this would seem unlikely to be coincidental.

[12] On T'ou-man 頭曼 NMan *tóumàn* < MChi *təu (Tak. 346–347; Pul. 311 *dəw) -*man (Pul. 207), see endnote 10.

[13] On his Hsiung-nu title, see endnote 7.

[14] On the Old Chinese pronunciation of Mandarin Hsiung-nu (*xiôngnú*), see endnotes 51 and 52.

[15] On the name Mo-tun, see endnote 8. Although the heroic founder ruler in the story is Mo-tun, not *Tumen (the actual founder), all the essential elements of the First Story are present except for the divine birth and exposure.

[16] The name of this people, written in Chinese 月氏 (also written 月支), which is read in modern Mandarin Yüeh-chih, was in Old Chinese pronounced *Tok^war-(*Tog^war-)kē. See appendix B. This version follows the *Han shu* (HS 94a: 3749). See endnote 9.

[17] On the *Shih chi* version of the story, see endnote 9.

[18] On the name *Tumen and proposed etymologies for it, see endnote 10.

—◁◆▷—

and family members who would not obey him, and he himself became king.[19]

⸻

The *Aśvin (Wu-sun) and the *Tokʷar both lived between the Ch'i-lien "Heavenly" Mountains (located in what is now Central Kansu) and Tun-huang.[20] The *Aśvin were a small nation. The *Tokʷar attacked and killed their king and seized their land. The *Aśvin people fled to the Hsiung-nu. The newborn *Aśvin prince, the K'un-mu, was taken out into the grassland and left there.[21] A wolf was seen suckling him, and a crow holding meat in its mouth hovering by his side.[22] The boy was thought to be a supernatural being and brought to the Hsiung-nu king, who liked him and raised him.

When the K'un-mu grew up, the king put him in charge of the *Aśvin people and made him a general in the army. The K'un-mu won many victories for the Hsiung-nu. At that time the *Tokʷar, who had been defeated by the Hsiung-nu, had moved west and attacked the Sakas. The Sakas in turn moved away, far to the south, and the *Tokʷar occupied their territory. The K'un-mu had become strong and asked the Hsiung-nu king for permission to avenge his father. He then launched a campaign to the west against the *Tokʷar, crushing them in 133–132 BC.[23] The *Tokʷar fled further west and south, into the territory of Bactria. The K'un-mu settled his people in the former Saka lands vacated by the defeated *Tokʷar, and his army became still stronger. When the Hsiung-nu king died, the K'un-mu refused to serve his successor. The Hsiung-nu sent an army of picked warriors against the K'un-mu, but they were unable to conquer him. Then, even more than be-

---

[19] HS 94a: 3749. On Mo-tun's comitatus and Hsiung-nu burial customs, see endnote 11.

[20] See appendix B on the name *Aśvin and the reading of the title of their king. The gloss of the Ch'i-lien Mountains' non-Chinese name is in the Shih chi (Watson 1961, II: 268). The Wu-sun origin myth is discussed by Golden (2006).

[21] This is the version in the Han shu (HS 61: 2691–2692), which is surely correct. In the Shih chi (Watson 1961, II: 271; cf. Di Cosmo 2002a: 176) and the Lun heng (Yamada 1976: 147), the Hsiung-nu are the attackers, and the Hsiung-nu king is the one who considers the marvelous infant K'un-mu to be a supernatural being (神 NMan shén) and therefore adopts him. The Shih chi version does not make any sense in the context of the whole story. Cf. Benjamin (2003).

[22] This story is very close to that of Romulus and Remus. For discussion of the birds involved, see endnote 12.

[23] Benjamin (2003).

⸻

fore, the Hsiung-nu considered him to be a supernatural being, and they avoided him.[24]

In the northern land of *Saklai[25] a prince was miraculously born. Though his father was the sun god and his mother was the daughter of the River Lord, the king[26] of the country took the child and cast him to the beasts. But the pigs and horses and birds of the wilderness kept him warm, so the boy did not die.

Because the king could not kill the boy, he allowed his mother to raise him. When the prince was old enough, he was ordered to serve the king as a horse herder. He was an excellent archer and was given the name *TümeN.[27]

The king was warned by his sons that *TümeN was too dangerous and would take over the kingdom. They plotted to kill him, but *TümeN's mother warned him in time, and he fled southward.

Reaching a river that he could not ford, he struck the river with his bow and called out, "I am the son of the sun and the grandson of the River Lord. My enemies are upon me. How can I cross?" The alligators[28] and soft-shelled turtles floated together to make a bridge. When *TümeN had crossed over they dispersed, so his enemies could not reach him.

He built Ortu, his capital, and established a new kingdom. His realm was divided into four constituent parts, with one lord (*ka) over each of the four directions.[29]

[24] Based on the report of Chang Ch'ien to the Han emperor Wu-ti in his biography (HS 61: 2691–2692). The Wu-sun origin myth is discussed by Golden (2006).

[25] On the transcriptions of the name *Saklai and the lack of critical editions of Chinese texts, see endnote 13.

[26] On later versions of the story, see endnote 14.

[27] On the Koguryo etymology (perhaps a folk etymology) of the name, see endnote 15.

[28] None of the attested versions have alligators here, but the White Rabbit of Inaba story in the Kojiki, which is a version of the river-crossing motif, has for the helpful animals wani, which are described in early Japanese sources as alligators or crocodiles, and the parallel in the ancient Bamboo Annals has alligators and turtles (Beckwith 2007a: 30–31). Although alligators do not live in Korea or Japan, Alligator sinensis is native to North China and was once widespread there (q.v. endnote 16). It seems clear that the Puyo-Koguryoic version of the story changed the unknown river creatures, alligators, to known ones, fish. The alligators would seem to date to the earlier Common Japanese-Koguryoic period, when the unified ancestral people lived at least as far south as the Yellow River basin and knew about alligators.

[29] Beckwith (2007a: 29–30). The earliest recorded version is in the Lun heng, by Wang Ch'ung, a first-century AD text, followed by the the Wei lüeh, a lost work quoted in the annotations to

Persia was under the rule of Ardawân (Artabanus V), the evil last Parthian ruler. The governor of Pars, Pâbag, employed a shepherd, Sâsân, to tend his horses and cattle. Pâbag did not know the shepherd was a descendant of the great King of Kings, Darius, but one night he had a dream in which he saw the sun shining from the head of Sâsân, lighting the whole world. He then gave his own daughter to Sâsân in marriage. She bore him a son, whom they named Ardaxšêr (Ardashîr), and Pâbag raised the boy as his own child.

When Ardaxšêr was a youth, he was so wise and skilled at riding that King Ardawân heard about him and ordered him to come to court to be raised with his own sons, the princes. But Ardaxšêr was a better rider and hunter than the sons of Ardawân, and he killed an onager with a single powerful arrow shot from his bow. When the king asked who had done the marvelous deed, Ardaxšêr said, "I did it." But the crown prince lied to his father, claiming, "No, it was me." Ardaxšêr angrily challenged the prince. The king was displeased with Ardaxšêr because of this and sent him to the stables to tend the horses and cattle. He no longer treated Ardaxšêr as the equal of his own sons, the princes.

Ardaxšêr then met the king's favorite maiden and had a liaison with her. Having made their plans together, they fled the court of Ardawân on horseback. The king pursued them with his army, but Ardaxšêr reached the sea before Ardawân and his army, and thus escaped.[30] The king turned back, leaving Ardaxšêr free of his enemies. Ardaxšêr gathered an army of his own and killed Ardawân in battle. Ardaxšêr then married the daughter of the dead king and became ruler in his stead, founding the great Sasanid Dynasty.[31]

The child who was the ancestor of the Türk people was abandoned in the wilderness to die, but he was saved by a she-wolf, who nursed him. Later

---

the *San kuo chih*, a third-century AD text. The earliest version written by the Koguryo themselves is found in the King Kwanggaet'o memorial inscription of 414.

[30] The text does not explain why Ardaxšêr would escape if he reached the sea before Ardawân. This detail would appear to reflect the element of water—usually a water deity or water crossing—that appears at one point or another in most versions of the First Story. On the water crossing in the Turkic and Mongolic versions see de Rachewiltz (2004: 231–233).

[31] Horne (1917, VII: 225–253), Arkenberg (1998), Grenet (2003), Čunakovskij (1987).

the wolf, pregnant with the boy's offspring, escaped her enemies by crossing the Western Sea to a cave in a mountain north of Qocho, one of the cities of the Tokharians.[32] The first Turks subsequently moved to the Altai, where they are known as expert ironworkers, as the Scythians are also known to have been.[33]

Toward the middle of the sixth century the Türk under their leader *Tumïn[34] were subjects of the Avars or Jou-jan,[35] a people of unknown origin whose nomad warrior kingdom ruled the Eastern Steppe. *Tumïn had become a great lord in his own right, and had entered into diplomatic and commercial relations with the T'o-pa (Toba) Wei Dynasty in China.

When an enemy, the T'ieh-le, threatened the Avar Empire, *Tumïn led his men to attack them. He defeated them and subjugated the entire nation.[36] Buoyed by his victory, *Tumïn requested an alliance with the Avars as recognition of his merit—this meant taking the hand of the daughter of the Avar kaghan in marriage.

But the kaghan, Anagai, refused his request. He sent an emissary to *Tumïn to rebuke him, saying, "You are my blacksmith slave. How dare you utter these words?" *Tumïn himself now became angry and killed the emissary. He cut off relations with the Avars and successfully sought a marriage alliance with the Chinese instead. The following year *Tumïn attacked the Avars and crushed them in a great battle. Anagai committed

[32] See also the detailed discussion of the Turkic origin myth(s) by Golden (2006); cf. Sinor (1982). There are several different myths. In one of them the first Türk is nursed by a wolf, exactly as in the Roman myth of Romulus and Remus, in which a wolf nurses the twins in the wilderness. (The wolf was sacred to the god of war, Mars, who was the twins' father.) In one of the Turkic versions the wolf subsequently escapes—across the Western Sea—to a cave in the mountains, where she gives birth to a generation of "proto-Turks," thus making the Türk the descendants of a she-wolf (CS 50: 909). Cf. de Rachewiltz (2004: 231–233), who discusses the relationship between the Turkic and Mongol versions of the story. The Türk banner was topped with a golden wolf's head, and the warriors of the Türk comitatus were called böri 'wolves'. In both Greek and Chinese sources the Türk are said to be descended from the Sakas; cf. endnote 52. I follow the customary use of the spelling Türk to refer specifically to the early, more or less unified Turkic people, especially under the "dynastic" Türk of the first two Türk empires. The spelling Turk is used as a generic term for Turkic peoples, languages, and so on, including all Turks after the Türk empires.

[33] See Rolle (1989: 119–121) on an excavated Scythian city in which large-scale iron smelting and forging, weapon manufacturing, and general metalsmithing in iron, gold, and other metals took place. The iron was obtained from the same deposits used by the well-known modern iron and steel works in the area of Krivoi Rog.

[34] On Bumïn, the form of the name *Tumïn found in the Old Turkic inscriptions, see endnote 17.

[35] On the problem of the Chinese name of the Avars, see endnote 18.

[36] CS 50: 908.

suicide in spring of 552, and his son fled to China.[37] *Tumïn then took the title of kaghan.

Though he died shortly afterward, *Tumïn's successors chased any Avars who did not submit to them across the length and breadth of Eurasia, from China in the East to Constantinople in the West,[38] and became rulers of the entire steppe zone.

The Mongols were descended from a heavenly blue-gray wolf and a fallow doe. They crossed a great body of water to reach a safe land—an enclosed valley in the mountains—where they produced the progenitors of the later Mongols.

In the Eastern Steppe in the twelfth century, a remarkable son was born to the Mongol tribal chief, Yesügei. The boy Temüjin was the great-grandson of Khabul Khan, who had been captured and killed by the Tatars, the allies of the Jurchen of North China. Yesügei had named his son Temüjin ('Iron-smith') after a Tatar leader he had captured. When Temüjin was still a child, Yesügei was murdered by the Tatars. His subjects were taken by his kinsmen the Taičighut, who left Temüjin's mother and her children behind with nothing.

They were poor, and suffered greatly. Temüjin and his brothers caught fish in the Onon River, while his mother wandered in the steppe searching for wild onions, crabapples, and whatever else she could find to feed her children. They thus survived on their wits and grew up.

Slowly men recognized Temüjin's leadership, and he acquired a personal following of four great warriors. He unified all the peoples of the Eastern Steppe, who acclaimed him Chinggis Khan ('universal ruler').[39] He conquered the Tatars, defeated the Jurchen, and went on to pacify the peoples of the four directions.

---

[37] CS 50: 909.

[38] The remnant of the Avars who appeared exactly at this time on the eastern frontier of the Byzantine Empire were given refuge there, and despite the warm relations that soon developed between the Turks and the Byzantine Greeks when the Turks reached Constantinople, the refugees were not handed over. They eventually established a new kaghanate in Pannonia (the area of modern Hungary), which lasted until it was destroyed by the armies of Charlemagne's Franks between 791 and 802 (Szádeczky-Kardoss 1990: 217–219).

[39] See endnote 83 on this title.

No one can say that the heroes who accomplished these deeds for their people did not do them. The Chou Dynasty of China, the Roman Empire, the Wu-sun Kingdom, and the Hsiung-nu Empire are all historical facts, as are the realms of the Koguryo, the Türk, the Mongols, and others. How these nations really were founded is obscured by the mists of time, in which the merging of legendary story and history is nearly total. Even the relatively late, more or less historical accounts of the foundation of the Mongol Empire contain legendary or mythical elements that are presented as facts along with purely historical events. Yet that is unimportant. What really mattered was that the unjust overlords who suppressed the righteous people and stole their wealth were finally overthrown, and the men who did the deed were national heroes.

In each case the subject people lived for a time under the unjust rule of their conquerors, and as their vassals they fought for them. By fighting in their conquerors' armies, the subject people acquired the life-style of steppe warriors. They also learned from their rulers the ideal of the hero in the First Story, which was sung in different versions over and over from campfire to campfire around the kingdom along with other heroic epics that told stories almost as old, with a similar moral.

After the subject people had thoroughly assimilated their overlords' steppe way of life, military techniques, political culture, and mythology, they eventually rebelled. If successful, they followed the ideal pattern told in the stories and became free, replacing their overlords as rulers of the steppe.

In their successful campaign to establish their power over the land, the former vassal people, now the rulers of their own kingdom, inevitably subjugated other peoples, one of whom would serve them, learn from them, and eventually overthrow them in exactly the same way. This cycle began at least as early as the foundation of the Hittite Empire in the seventeenth century BC and can be traced historically in Central Eurasia itself over a period of some two millennia from the first known large, organized state of the steppe zone, the Scythian Empire, which was established in the seventh century BC, down to the Junghars and Manchus in early modern times.

These legendary accounts—nearly always presented as history by the people who preserved them—attest to the fact that nation after nation in

Central Eurasia attempted to substantiate its belief in the First Story by following the state-formation model it prescribes.

The essential elements of the First Story, which may appear incompletely or in a slightly different order in the actual attested versions, are:

A maiden is impregnated by a heavenly spirit or god.
The rightful king is deposed unjustly.
The maiden gives birth to a marvelous baby boy.
The unjust king orders the baby to be exposed.
The wild beasts nurture the baby so he survives.
The baby is discovered in the wilderness and saved.
The boy grows up to be a skilled horseman and archer.
He is brought to court but put in a subservient position.
He is in danger of being put to death but escapes.
He acquires a following of oath-sworn warriors.
He overthrows the tyrant and reestablishes justice in the kingdom.
He founds a new city or dynasty.

This looks very much like a schematic folktale, not history, at least when presented as a list. It may be difficult for historians and other scholars today to accept that people of the early second millennium BC would believe such stories to be actual history, or perhaps idealized history, but the theory that human societies sometimes base far-reaching actions on ideological or religious beliefs should be no surprise to medievalists, or indeed to anyone living in the late twentieth and early twenty-first centuries AD. The mythological beliefs in the First Story belong to the collection of cultural elements shared by the peoples of premodern Central Eurasia that goes back to the Proto-Indo-Europeans. It is called here the Central Eurasian Culture Complex.

The Comitatus

The most crucial element of the early form of the Central Eurasian Culture Complex was the sociopolitical-religious ideal of the heroic lord and his *comitatus,* a war band of his friends sworn to defend him to the death. The essential features of the comitatus and its oath are known to have existed as early as the Scythians and seem difficult to separate clearly from the oath of blood brotherhood to death, which is attested from ancient sources on the Scythians through the medieval *Secret History of the Mongols*. Lucian (second century AD) has his Scythian character Toxaris say:

> Friendships are not formed with us, as with you, over the wine-cups, nor are they determined by considerations of age or neighbourhood. We wait till we see a brave man, capable of valiant deeds, and to him we all turn our attention. Friendship with us is like courtship with you: rather than fail of our object, and undergo the disgrace of a rejection, we are content to urge our suit patiently, and to give our constant attendance. At length a friend is accepted, and the engagement is concluded with our most solemn oath: "to live together and if need be to die for one another." That vow is faithfully kept: once let the friends draw blood from their fingers into a cup, dip the points of their swords therein, and drink of that draught together, and from that moment nothing can part them.[40]

The core comitatus consisted of a small number of warriors, who are called or referred to as friends.[41] Chinggis Khan himself had four: Khubilai, Jelme, Jebe, and Sübedei, whom Jamukha characterizes as the four fierce wolves or dogs of Chinggis. The characterization of the comitatus warriors as wolves or other fierce animals goes all the way back to Proto-Indo-European times. The core group—usually a small number of men[42]—committed ritual suicide (or was executed) to accompany the lord if he predeceased the group, and each man was buried "armed to the teeth" for battle in the next world.[43] The comitatus warriors took their oath freely and, in doing so, broke their original connections to their clan or nation.[44] They became as close or closer than family to

---

[40] The Lucian passage is from Fowler and Fowler (1905). Rolle (1989: 61–63) includes an excavated portrayal of two Scythians drinking the draft of blood brotherhood. Their practice accords closely with accounts of the early Germanic peoples.

[41] In Mongol *nökör*, plural *nököd*. For the Russian equivalent see note 44 in this chapter.

[42] However, the full comitatus had structure and rank, and practice varied from place to place. In Central Asia, especially, the number of men interred with their lord could be very large.

[43] As amply shown by archaeological finds (Rolle 1989: 64 et seq.).

[44] By contrast, the units of the regular army were organized according to "nations" and clans. This point is made most clearly by Vladimirtsov in his discussion of the Mongol system, in which he uses the Russian term дружинники 'comitatus warriors', members of a дружина 'comitatus'; these terms are translated into French as *les antrustions* and *la truste*, respectively (Vladimirtsov 1948: 110 et seq.; 2002: 382 et seq.). On the Indo-European "wolves," see *EIEC* 631–636 and the illuminating analyses of Bruce Lincoln (1991: 131–137). On the four "wolves" of Chinggis, see Vladimirtsov (1948: 115–116; 2002: 386–387). Vladimirtsov's treatment

their lord, they lived in their lord's house with him, and they were rewarded lavishly by him in return for their oath. The comitatus is attested archaeologically in burials, historically in descriptions of cultures from all parts of Central Eurasia, and in early literary texts. The most famous are perhaps the *Rig Veda* hymns to the deified comitatus of Indra, the *Marut* chariot warriors. A vivid example is found in a dialogue between the lord and his warrior friends where *Ahi* is the snake-demon enemy, the dragon of many Central Eurasian heroic epics:[45]

> *Indra speaks:*
> Where, O Maruts, was that custom with you, when you left me alone in the killing of Ahi? I indeed am terrible, powerful, strong; I escaped from the blows of every enemy.
>
> *The Maruts speak:*
> Thou hast achieved much with us as companions. With equal valour, O hero! Let us achieve then many things, O thou most powerful, O Indra! Whatever we, O Maruts, wish with our mind.
> [*Indra boasts and complains some more. The Maruts then praise him.*]
>
> *Indra speaks:*
> O Maruts, now your praise has pleased me, the glorious hymn which you have made for me, ye men—for me, for Indra, for the joyful hero, as friends for a friend.

The lord and his comitatus formed the heart of every newborn Central Eurasian nation.[46] In Central Asia the warriors of a typical ruler's full comita-

---

forms part of his analysis of what he calls Mongol feudalism; despite some irrelevant theoretical background, the comparison with European medieval feudalism is not only apt but historically relevant, as argued in the present work. The Mongol comitatus is discussed by Allsen (1997: 52–55, 79, 103–104).

[45] From book I, hymn 165 (Müller 1891: 180–181). I have made minor changes of punctuation and capitalization.

[46] Although many refer to the social subunits that made up larger states and empires as tribes, there has been growing awareness in recent years that the traditional idea of a tribe is not applicable to premodern Central Eurasia. The Chinese term for these subunits, 部 *bù*, literally means 'part, subdivision', as does the Old Tibetan term, *sde*. See Lindner (1982: 701). These terms are close in usage to that of Latin *natio*, plural *nationes* (which has been used recently by a number of Central Eurasianists). I have found no good equivalent term in English. In most cases where a term of some kind is unavoidable, I have used *people*, in others *nation*.

tus, even that of a mere governor, numbered in the thousands and was extremely expensive to maintain. In the Middle Ages, the comitatus and ideas of rulership gradually changed with the adoption of world religions, which frown on suicide or ritual murder, but they otherwise continued down to the conquest of Central Eurasia by peripheral powers. The traditional heroic ideal of the lord and his comitatus was celebrated by bards in chanted or sung epic poems such as *Beowulf, Janghar, Manas,* and *Gesar,* which have been preserved down to the present as written or oral literature. The tradition was long maintained even among peoples who had left Central Eurasia proper centuries earlier. Both Attila the Hun and Charlemagne were praised by their bards and patronized the regular performance of heroic epic poems.

The comitatus is attested directly or indirectly in historical sources on the Hittites, the Achaemenid Persians,[47] the Scythians, the Khwarizmians,[48] the Hsiung-nu, the ancient and early medieval Germanic peoples, the Sasanid Persians,[49] the Huns,[50] the Hephthalites,[51] the Koguryo, the early dynastic Japanese,[52] the Turks (including at least the Türk, Khazars,[53] and Uighurs),

---

[47] The Achaemenids had an elite royal bodyguard of 10,000 Median and Persian warriors called the "corps of immortals," who wore "garments adorned with cloth of gold" (Allsen 1997: 79). The same institution existed at the time of the Sasanids, though generally under a different name (Zakeri 1995: 77); see below.

[48] In 328 BC, the King of Khwarizmia, Pharasmanes, visited Alexander the Great in Bactria with "his retinue of 1,500 cavalrymen" (Bosworth 1997: 1061). These men were certainly his comitatus. There are many medieval Khwarizmian examples as well, indicating the system was practiced there for at least a millennium.

[49] On the question of the existence of a Sasanid comitatus, see endnote 19.

[50] The Greek sources refer to the members of Attila's comitatus as λογάδες (logades) 'picked men', who are also sometimes called ἐπιτήδειοι 'close associates' (Thompson 1996: 108, 179). It was the job of the λογάδες to "guard Attila's person, and each of them accompanied his master in arms for a specified part of the day, a fact which gave them ready access to his person and conversation. Although they regarded this task as δουλεία 'slavery', they were capable of the greatest loyalty in carrying it out.... We know further that a sort of hierarchy existed among them, which was indicated by the seats allotted to them when they sat down to feast with their master: Onegesius sat at Attila's right hand and Berichus at his left.... The λογάδες owed their allegiance to Attila alone, but they gave it to him solely because he could provide ... gifts on a larger scale than anyone else" (Thompson 1996: 181–182, 192). Despite Thompson's anti-Hun bias, and his apparent unawareness of the existence of the comitatus among them—he nowhere mentions it, at least not in connection with his much-discussed λογάδες—the Hun comitatus in his description is remarkable for its closeness to the pattern known from medieval sources.

[51] According to Procopius; see below.

[52] See chapter 4.

[53] Golden (2001; 2002: 141; 2002–2003; 2004; 2006).

the Sogdians, the Tibetans, the Slavs,[54] the Khitans,[55] the Mongols,[56] and others.[57] It was adopted briefly by the Byzantines and Chinese,[58] and especially by the Arabs, who, after adapting it to Islam, made it a permanent feature of Islamic culture down to early modern times.[59]

In the early form of the Central Eurasian Culture Complex, the highly trained warrior members of a lord's comitatus—a guard corps loyal not to the government but to the lord personally—took an oath to defend him to the death. The core members of the comitatus, his sworn friends, committed suicide, or were ritually executed, in order to be buried with him if he happened to predecease them. The peripheral cultures' historical sources explicitly say so, time and again, as Ibn Faḍlân remarks about the Vikings on the Volga, who were known as Rus:[60]

> One of the customs of the king of the Rus is that with him in his palace he has four hundred men from among his most valiant and trusted men. They die when he dies and are killed for his sake.

Why would anyone willingly do this?

There was a very good reason. The lord in turn rewarded his comitatus, especially the core group of friends, by treating them as his own family, sharing his habitation and worldly goods with them, and bestowing much wealth upon them. Warriors belonging to a comitatus were rewarded with almost unimaginable wealth and honor in their societies, not just once but over and over throughout their lives, as long as they served their lord, and in the afterlife as well.[61] They wore silken clothes embroidered with gold, or cloth of gold, decorated with gems, pearls, and gold ornaments; they lived in the same palatial quarters together with their lord; and they ate and drank

---

[54] Christian (1998: 342, 358, 363–364, 390).

[55] On the Khitan and Kereit comitatus, see endnote 20.

[56] The *kešig*, usually translated as 'Royal Guard', 'personal bodyguard', or the like, q.v. below.

[57] For example, the Romans, as noted above.

[58] On the Byzantine and Chinese cases, see endnote 22.

[59] On the comitatus in general, see Beckwith (1984a). On the transmission of the Sogdian and Turkic comitatus to the Arabs, see further de la Vaissière (2005a, 2007).

[60] Frye (2005: 70–71), who gives the name in its Arabic form "Rusiya" in his translation here.

[61] For numerous examples of lords bestowing wealth, especially silk, gold, and other luxurious goods, upon their comitatus members, see Allsen (1997). According to al-Ṭabarî, in 738 the Türgiš ruler every month bestowed on each of his 15,000 men "one piece of silk, which was at that time worth twenty-five dirhams" (Allsen 1997: 55), thus totaling 4.5 million dirhams a year.

the same food and drink with him.[62] They were his companions in life and in death. Ibn Faḍlân says of the ruler of the Khazars,

> When he is buried the heads of those who buried him are struck off.... His grave is called "Paradise," and they say, He has entered paradise. All the chambers are spread with silk brocade interwoven with gold.[63]

The reward for absolute loyalty unto death was clear to those who belonged to the comitatus. The punishment for those who were not loyal to their lord was also clear:

> You shall have no joy   in the homeland you love,
> Your farms shall be forfeit,   and each man fare
> alone and landless   when foreign lords
> learn of your flight,   your failure of faith.
> Better to die   than dwell in disgrace.[64]

According to a story in the *Secret History*, a comitatus warrior abandoned his defeated Kereit lord, who could no longer provide him with good food, gilt clothing, and high status, and he went to serve the victor—Chinggis Khan—instead. Chinggis rightly declared that the man had abandoned his liege lord and could not be trusted to become a companion (*nöker*); he ordered him to be executed.[65]

There are descriptions of the early form of the comitatus system, or mention of its members, from the North Sea to the Japan Sea and from the sub-Arctic to the Himalayas—in other words, throughout Central Eurasia and among all well-described Central Eurasian peoples from at least the Hittites down to the adoption of world religions in the Middle Ages. By contrast, the true comitatus is unknown among non–Central Eurasian peoples, who tend to express astonishment in their descriptions of it.

The earliest clear account of the comitatus (and first usage of the term *comitatus* to refer to it) is in the *Germania* (completed in AD 98), where

---

[62] Tacitus (Mattingly 1970: 113) says, "Their meals, for which plentiful if homely fare is provided, count in lieu of pay." He also comments on the constant demands made by comitatus members on their lord for valuable gifts.

[63] Quoted in Dunlop (1954: 112). On the remarks of observers, see endnote 21.

[64] *Beowulf*, lines 2886–2891 (Dobbie 1953: 89), translation of Sullivan and Murphy (2004: 81, their lines 2539–2543).

[65] Allsen (1997: 53).

Tacitus describes its basic elements among the early Germanic peoples in the West. Of the lord, he says, "Both prestige and power depend on being continually attended by a large train of picked young warriors, which is a distinction in peace and a protection in war." Of the comitatus structure he notes that there are "grades of rank" within it, and of its members he says, "to leave a battle alive after their chief has fallen means lifelong infamy and shame." He also remarks, "They are always making demands on the generosity of their chief."[66] This characterization is equally true of the Mongol comitatus of Chinggis Khan, which included the small core comitatus group—his *nöker*s or 'friends'—and the extended comitatus, mainly a large imperial bodyguard, the *kesig* or *kesigten*, which numbered 10,000 by the end of his life. It is described quite accurately by Marco Polo, who provides the additional detail that the comitatus of Khubilai, which numbered 12,000 horsemen, was divided into four units with one "captain" over each.[67]

The comitatus survived well into the Middle Ages in Europe. In England it is referred to as late as in *Beowulf*,[68] which includes references to the comitatus oath and the lord's payment of wealth to his companions, who lived in the same hall with him. In Scandinavia and the steppe zone, it lasted longer still.[69]

One of the crucial elements of the comitatus was that it was the lord's personal guard corps. The warriors stayed near him day and night, no further than the door of his splendid golden hall or yurt,[70] which stood in the center of the *ordo*, the camp of the ruler's comitatus and capital of the realm.[71]

The specific day-to-day duties of the comitatus of the Huns, the Turks, and other Central Eurasian peoples, whose versions of the system were described and are therefore known to a certain extent, are virtually identical

---

[66] Mattingly (1970: 112–113); cf. Hutton (1970: 151–152).

[67] Latham (1958: 135). Allsen (1997) cites copious material that fully corroborates Marco Polo's account. Di Cosmo (1999b: 18) notes that "the *kesik*, instituted in 1203–1204, initially comprised only 80 day guards and 70 night guards." The consistent specification of a subdivision of the guard corps into day guards and night guards (among other subdivisions) from the Hittites on is interesting and worth further investigation.

[68] In Old English the comitatus is called the *weored* (among other spellings) or, more frequently, *gedryht*, on which see endnote 24.

[69] See Lindow (1976) for a detailed examination of the terminology and some analysis of the structure of the comitatus in Scandinavia.

[70] See note 29 in chapter 6 for discussion of famous medieval examples of the "golden dome" or "golden domed-tent (yurt)" of various rulers.

[71] For discussion of the Mongol terms, see endnote 23.

to those of the Mongols, about whom more is known than any other premodern steppe people. Chinggis Khan's comitatus was carefully structured and regulated by ordinances decreed by the khan himself.

Chinggis khan organized his armies on the decimal system, [and] also created a personal bodyguard (*kesig*). As originally constituted, the guard consisted of a day watch (*turgha'ud*) of seventy men, a night watch (*kebte'üd*) of eighty, and a detachment of braves (*ba'aturs*) numbering one thousand. The *kesig* ... was recruited from his *nökers*[72] ... guardsmen (*kesigten*) served simultaneously as protectors of the khan's person and as domestics who tended his private needs and looked after his possessions. In this latter capacity, *kesigten* held appointments as chamberlains (*cherbi*), stewards (*ba'urchi*), quiver bearers (*khorchi*), doorkeepers (*e'ütenchi*), and grooms (*aghtachi*). The guards, moreover, supervised the activities of the female attendants and minor functionaries such as camel herders and cowherds; took care of the khan's tents, carts, weapons, musical instruments, and regalia; and prepared his food and drink.... And because the guard/household establishment provided both personal service and the machinery through which Chinggis khan administered his rapidly multiplying subjects, territories, and economic interests, it accompanied him wherever he went—on a campaign or on a hunting trip.[73]

The detail available about the Mongol comitatus allows inferences to be made about the system as practiced among Central Eurasian peoples who are much less well known.[74]

Scattered remarks in ancient Chinese and Greek sources, and the distribution of the comitatus system all over Central Eurasia, demonstrate that it was a fundamental feature of the Central Eurasian Culture Complex. Procopius says of the Hephthalites on the northeastern frontier of the Sasanid Persian Empire:[75]

---

[72] I have modified Allsen's text, which has "*ba'atud*," the Mongol plural of *ba'atur* 'hero', and "*nököd*," the Mongol plural of *nöker* or *nökör* 'friends'.

[73] Allsen (1994: 343–344).

[74] It might be profitable for a Hittite specialist to reexamine the text known as the "Hittite Instruction for the Royal Bodyguard" (Güterbock and van den Hout 1991) with this in mind.

[75] He calls them "the Ephthalite Huns, who are called White Huns." However, they seem not to have been Huns; their ethnolinguistic connections are unknown. The Persian name of their

Moreover, the wealthy citizens are in the habit of attaching to themselves friends to the number of twenty or more, as the case may be, and these become permanently their banquet-companions, and have a share in all their property, enjoying some kind of a common right in this matter. Then, when a man who has gathered such a company together comes to die, it is the custom that all these men be borne alive into the tomb with him.[76]

Of the early Tibetan Empire the Chinese sources say:

The lord and his ministers—five or six persons called "common-fated ones"—make friends with each other. When the lord dies, they all commit suicide to be buried with him, and the things he wore, trinkets he used, and horses he rode, all are buried with him.[77]

These reports are reminiscent of the accounts in the *Secret History of the Mongols* in which Temüjin and a *nöker* 'friend' swear to "share one life." The centrality of friendship is attested to in the names of several well-known variants of the system, including the Slavic *družina* 'comitatus' (Russian *drug* 'friend' and *družba* 'friendship'),[78] and the Mongol *nöker* 'friend; core comitatus member'.[79] Similarly, Marwazî describes the comitatus of the kaghan of the Uighur Empire in the Eastern Steppe:

Their king is named Toghuz Qaghan, and he has many soldiers. Of old their king had a thousand *châkar*s, and four hundred maidens. The *châkar*s would eat meals at his place three times each day, and they would be given drink three times after the meal.[80]

The Chinese—like the Classical and later Greeks[81]—did not themselves have the comitatus tradition, but Central Eurasians in Chinese service con-

---

city, which he spells Γοργὼ Gorgô, is Gorgân, meaning 'Wolves'. See the comments above on comitatus members being called wolves.

[76] Procopius I, iii (Dewing 1914, I: 12–15).

[77] *HTS* 216a: 6063; *CTS* 196a: 5220; *TFYK* 961: 15r–15v; cf. Pelliot (1961: 3, 81–82). See further, Beckwith (1984a: 34).

[78] On the etymology of the Slavic and Germanic word or words for the comitatus and its members, see endnote 24.

[79] See de Rachewiltz (2004) on the *Secret History*; see Lindow (1976) on the Germanic and Slavic comitatus.

[80] Minorsky (1942: 18).

[81] However, the *early* Romans clearly did have the comitatus, which they called the Celeres, described as a company of 300 mounted warriors who accompanied Romulus, the first Roman king, at all times. See above.

tinued to practice it. Upon the death of T'ai-tsung, the second emperor of the T'ang Dynasty, several Turkic generals he had defeated, who had submitted to him, requested permission to commit suicide to be buried with him. Though they were denied permission, one did so anyway. The half-Sogdian, half-Turkic general An Lu-shan,[82] who rebelled against the T'ang in 755 and almost brought down the dynasty, had a personal comitatus of eight thousand warriors of Tongra (Turkic), Tatabï, and Khitan (Mongolic) origin, whom he treated as his own sons.[83]

The lords of the Central Eurasian states, whether nomadic like the Turkic kaghans or settled like the Sogdian princes, typically had thousands of *châkar*s, or comitatus warriors,[84] though it seems likely that, as in early Germanic Europe and the early Tibetan Empire, only a relatively small number of them were bound by a common-fate oath. Their continued loyalty and commitment[85] depended upon their lord sticking to his side of the bargain, which was to honor them and frequently give them great wealth, especially in the form of precious silk garments and gold objects that could be worn or otherwise easily transported. The descriptions of early Central Eurasian courts comment on the splendid silks worn by the companions of the lord.[86]

The Chinese monk Hsüan Tsang, who traveled from China to India via Central Asia in the early seventh century and wrote a detailed account of his journey, describes the nominal ruler of the Western Turks, Tung Yabghu Kaghan, wearing a green satin robe and a long band of white silk on his head. His "ministers," over 200 strong, all wore embroidered silk robes. The early Byzantine Greek visitors to the Western Turkic court describe with astonishment the Turks' wealth in gold and silk.[87]

---

[82] See chapter 6. He is said to have been an orphan, so his ethnicity is based on that of his adoptive parents. His actual ethnic background is thus unknown.

[83] On the foreign name of An Lu-shan's comitatus and Central Eurasian *châkar*s in China, see endnote 25.

[84] On the warlike ethos of the Sogdians, especially the nobility, see Grenet (2005).

[85] The *Secret History of the Mongols*, though not a history per se, is a rich source for the dynamics of Central Eurasians bound to each other by such oaths, of which there seem to have been several different kinds.

[86] There are also admonitions by Central Eurasian councillors (such as Toñukuk, in the Old Turkic inscriptions), who argue against the wearing of silk—indicating that the Türk were wearing it. See Allsen (1997) for examples and references.

[87] Blockley (1985: 115).

Marco Polo describes the silk robes bestowed on Khubilai Khan's twelve thousand bodyguards.[88] "To each of these he has given thirteen robes, every one of a different colour. They are splendidly adorned with pearls and gems and other adornments and are of immense value. . . . The cost of these robes, to the number of 156,000 in all, amounts to a quantity of treasure that is almost past computation."[89] Indeed, it must have required around a million yards of fine silk, plus vast quantities of gold and jewels, to make the robes. The tremendous quantity of them, many if not most of which were made of gold brocade, was noted by nearly every foreign traveler to the Mongol courts.[90]

Where did all the silk come from? There is a widespread misconception that Central Eurasians pillaged and plundered the poor innocent Chinese or Persians or Greeks in order to get the silk. (For an extensive discussion of this idea, see the epilogue.) At least from Han Dynasty times on, however, if not earlier, the Chinese had to import horses, which could not be raised in sufficient numbers and quality for their needs. In early medieval T'ang Dynasty times, once again they desperately wanted and needed horses in great numbers in order to build and maintain a huge empire. Chinese historical texts contain enough material on the trade in horses and silk between the Turks and Chinese to reveal that the recorded, official transactions were large, involving more than twenty thousand horses on the one hand and more than a million bolts of raw silk on the other. Although the Chinese historians rarely give an actual equation of such numbers, still there are a few instances, mostly not in the official histories, where prices were recorded anyway, so it is known that the normal price of an imported horse in China fluctuated between about twenty-five and thirty-eight bolts of raw silk.[91] The trade constituted a significant part of the Chinese economy in the early medieval period[92] and continued to be important until the Manchu conquest, when the entire Eastern Steppe and other horse-producing areas (such

---

[88] These were members of the *kesig* (or *kesigten*) 'bodyguard', which made up the bulk of the full comitatus. The number had grown from Chinggis Khan's time, and continued to grow.

[89] Latham (1958: 138, 140–141); cf. Allsen (1997: 19–20).

[90] Allsen (1997: 16–26) gives many detailed, colorful examples.

[91] For historiographical problems concerning the quality and price of Turk horses sold to the Chinese, see endnote 26.

[92] See Beckwith (1991); cf. Jagchid and Symons (1989), whose discussion of this topic is unfortunately marred by many mistakes of fact and interpretation.

as the Kokonor region) came under the control of the Ch'ing Empire. In short, it is known that the vast majority of the silk possessed by the Central Eurasians in the two millennia from early Hsiung-nu times[93] through the Mongols down to the Manchu conquest was obtained through trade and taxation, not war or extortion.[94]

> We normally think of nomadic states as stimulating long-distance exchange through the creation of a pax that provides security and transportation facilities; but in fact the process of state formation among the nomads in and of itself stimulates trade through an increased demand for precious metals, gems, and, most particularly, fine cloths. Politics, especially imperial politics, was impossible without such commodities.[95]

After Central Eurasian peoples converted to world religions in the Middle Ages, the practice of ritual suicide or execution of the core comitatus gradually ended, but the comitatus tradition otherwise continued within Central Eurasia[96] and still required the bestowal of silks and other treasure on its members.

The Islamicized Comitatus

The comitatus was among the Central Asian cultural elements introduced into the Near East from the very beginning of the Arab Empire's expansion there. 'Ubayd Allâh ibn Ziyâd, the first Arab to lead a military expedition into Central Asia, returned to Basra with a comitatus of two thousand Bukharan archers.[97] His second successor, Sa'îd ibn 'Uthmân, brought

---

[93] Hayashi (1984).

[94] For details on the Mongols' acquisition, production, and use of silks, especially brocades, and other precious fabrics, see Allsen (1997), whose discussion presents ample evidence that the Mongols did not use the putative "robbery" approach commonly ascribed to them and other Central Eurasians but employed, more or less exclusively, taxation and trade, and strongly encouraged the latter. See endnote 27 and the epilogue for further discussion.

[95] Allsen (1997: 104; cf. 103).

[96] In Western Europe the comitatus gradually disappeared as the Germanic peoples became Romanized (or "Europeanized"). On the Scandinavian development, see Lindow (1976). On the adoption of the Visigothic comitatus by the early Muslims of Spain, see Beckwith (1984a: 40–41 n. 52).

[97] Ṭabarî ii: 170; Beckwith (1984a: 36).

back fifty warriors, nobles' sons, from Samarkand, but when he settled them in Medina, he took away their beautiful clothes and treated them as slaves. They murdered him and then, true to their comitatus oath, committed suicide.[98] The most famous Arab governor-general of Central Asia, Qutayba ibn Muslim al-Bâhilî, had a large comitatus of Central Asian archers. This "group from among the sons of the kings of Sogdiana who refused to abandon him" fought to the death for him when he rebelled in 715.[99]

The Arab model came from Central Asia, where the importance of the comitatus was well known and recognized by both Arab and Chinese historians. The Chinese sources say of the Central Asians, "They enlist the brave and strong as *châkars*. *Châkars* are like what are called 'warriors' in Chinese."[100] Of the comitatus in Samarkand Hsüan Tsang remarks, "They have very many *châkars*. The men who are *châkars* are courageous and fierce by nature. They look upon death as returning home. In battle no enemy can withstand them."[101]

One of the most prominent local Central Asian leaders of the early eighth century was Al-Iskand, the king of Kišš (now Shahr-i Sabz) and Nasaf, who had lost his throne during the Arab invasion. With his comitatus, he campaigned against the Arabs across Central Asia for at least a decade and was known to the Chinese as "King of the *Châkars*."[102] In 741 the Arab governor Naṣr ibn Sayyâr pardoned Al-Iskand and his comitatus and allowed them to return to their homes. The following year, Naṣr acquired 1,000 *châkars*, armed them, and provided them with horses.[103]

Central Asian influence on the Arab Islamic world became more direct with the settlement of the great Abbasid army of Central Asians, or 'Khurasanis', around Baghdad after completion of the new capital, the City of Peace, begun in 762. Under the influence of Khālid ibn Barmak, the Central Asian circular royal palace-city plan of the Parthians and Sasanids was used as the model. It was the plan followed both for the former Sasanid capital of Ctesi-

---

[98] Beckwith (1984a: 36).
[99] Shaban (1970: 75).
[100] *HTS* 221b: 6244.
[101] *HYC* 1: 871c.
[102] *TFYK* 964: 20r; Chavannes (1903: 147); cf. Beckwith (1984a: 37 and nn. 34 and 39).
[103] Ṭabarî ii: 1765; cf. Beckwith (1984a: 38), q.v. for further examples.

phon, about thirty kilometers southeast of Baghdad, and for the Nawbahâr, a Buddhist monastery (Khālid's family home) that had originally been built as a Sasanid royal palace in the Central Asian city of Balkh.[104] The influence was reinforced half a century later when the civil war between the sons of Hârûn al-Rashîd was won by al-Ma'mûn, whose capital, the Central Asian city of Marw, became the capital of the caliphate for a decade. When he finally returned to Baghdad, followed by a large, Central Asianized court, he brought with him a comitatus. Although several Arab governors of Central Asia had previously acquired such a guard corps, al-Ma'mûn was the first caliph to do so. The Central Asian *châkars*—referred to in Arabicized form as *shâkiriyya* and later referred to as *mamlûks* or *ghulâms*—constituted a new imperial guard corps that was loyal to the ruler personally. Because the Arab soldiers who were the predecessors of the *shâkiriyya* were considered untrustworthy and unprofessional, they were dismissed. The continuation of this policy by al-Ma'mûn's successor al-Mu'taṣim (r. 833–842) is not surprising; the latter was the son of Hârûn al-Rashîd by his Sogdian wife Mârida and had begun acquiring a Central Asian comitatus long before becoming caliph.[105]

The Amîr al-Ḥakam ibn Hishâm (r. 796–822), the contemporary of al-Ma'mûn in the Umayyad Caliphate's continuation in Spain, acquired a comitatus of foreigners known as *al-Ḥaras* 'the Guard'. They were put under the command of the Visigothic chief of the Christians of Cordoba, *Comes* ('Count') Rabî', son of Theodulf, so the guard was literally a comitatus. The Visigoths had maintained the traditional early Germanic comitatus in which the guard corps warriors swore an oath to defend the lord to the death.[106]

The Central Eurasian comitatus system, Islamicized as the *mamlûk* or *ghulâm* system, became a fundamental feature of traditional Islamic polities, and remained so in some places down to modern times.[107]

---

[104] *Nawbahâr* is the Persianized form of Sanskrit *Nava Vihâra* 'the new *vihâra*'. For scholarship on the plan, see endnote 28.

[105] See de la Vaissière (2005a: 141).

[106] See Beckwith (1984a: 40–41 n. 52) for details and references.

[107] See de la Vaissière (2005b) and Beckwith (1984a). The Islamicized comitatus has been nearly universally misunderstood by Western scholars, who refer to it as a "slave soldier" system and argue that it is an "Arab" institution. For criticism of this mistaken view, see Beckwith (1984a) and de la Vaissière (2005b, 2005c, 2007).

The Comitatus and Trade

The rewards paid to a comitatus member were substantial. They included gold, silver, precious stones, silks, gilded armor and weapons, horses, and other valuable things, as vividly described in many sources. Comitatus members were buried with a great store of weaponry, plus horses (and chariots in the earliest times, when they were still used as military weapons). Much wealth was also buried with the deceased lord. Burials were generally covered with a huge earthen tumulus, though this varies from subregion to subregion and people to people. Within traditional Central Eurasia, such burials are attested among the Scythians and their immediate predecessors, the Iranian and pre-Turkic peoples of the Altai-Tien Shan region, the Huns, the Merovingian Franks, the Turks, the Tibetans, the Koguryo, and the Mongols. Outside Central Eurasia proper, such burials are found in Shang China and premedieval Japan as well as among the Anglo-Saxons and other Germanic peoples of northwestern Europe. The burials are signs that the Central Eurasian Culture Complex was at one time alive and functioning in these places.

Though some of this wealth was obtained by warfare[108] or tribute,[109] methods used by powerful states throughout Eurasia for the same purpose, the great bulk of it was accumulated by trade, which was the most powerful driving force behind the internal economy of Central Eurasia, as noted by foreign commentators from Antiquity through the Middle Ages. This commerce ranged from local trade in agricultural products and the products of animal husbandry to long-distance trade in silks, spices, and other goods.

In Central Eurasia, "rural people" included both agriculturalists living in the fertile irrigated areas near the cities and nomads living out in the grasslands; the agriculturalists produced and consumed mainly grains and other

---

[108] Lest it be thought that booty acquisition was an exclusively Central Eurasian practice, as many appear to believe, it must be pointed out that the accounts of, for example, Chinese and Arab victories over Central Eurasian peoples nearly always mention both the number of people decapitated (generally only the leaders were taken captive, to be pardoned or executed later) but also valuables captured, such as suits of armor and, especially, cattle, horses, sheep, and so on, which in some cases are said to have numbered more than a million head. On the scholarly treatment of the information on this, see endnote 29.

[109] When Chinese or Romans demanded payment from other nations it is called "tribute" or "taxation" by most historians, but when Central Eurasians demanded it, it is called "extortion."

vegetable products, whereas the nomads produced and consumed mainly meat, milk, wool, and other animal products.[110] The relationship was economically equivalent to that in the agricultural-urban society of China, in which the people—both in the cities and their surrounding agricultural areas and in the more distant purely agricultural areas—were in most cases ethnolinguistically more or less identical. The difference was that in Central Eurasia the *distal* rural people—the nomads—were usually distinct ethnolinguistically from the urban people of the city-states and their *proximal* rural people, with both of whom the nomads traded and over whom they usually exercised a loose kind of suzerainty maintained by taxation.

To the nomads, therefore, Chinese cities in or near their territory were—or should have been—just as open to trade with them as the Central Asian cities were. Throughout recorded Chinese history, the local Chinese in frontier areas were more than willing to trade with the nomads, but when the frontiers came under active Chinese central governmental control, restrictions often were placed on the trade, it was taxed heavily, or it was simply forbidden outright. The predictable result, time and again, was nomadic raids or outright warfare, the primary purpose of which (as repeated over and over in the sources) was to make the frontier trading cities—which were built in former pastureland that had been seized from the nomads—once again accessible.[111] From one end of Central Eurasia to the other, the nomads' peace terms with peripheral states regularly included trading rights of one kind or another.

---

[110] See Noonan (1997) on the Khazar economy.

[111] In the east much of the best pastureland had been captured by Chinese invasions beginning in the Warring States period. The territory was held by Chinese fortresses and walls built right through the steppe, including the Great Wall, which mainly connected earlier walls together and strengthened them. These walls were not built to protect the Chinese from the Central Eurasians but to hold Central Eurasian territory conquered by the Chinese (Di Cosmo 2002a: 149–158). That is, they were offensive works, not defensive ones. The purpose of the nomadic raids or warfare against the Chinese was undoubtedly mainly to remove the Chinese from the seized pastureland and restore it to nomadic control, as indicated by the fact that the nomads almost exclusively took animals and people as booty on these raids (cf. Hayashi 1984). The theories ultimately based on the idea of the Chinese as victims of Central Eurasian aggression, and the nomads as poverty-stricken barbarians greedy for Chinese silks and other products, are not only unsupported by the Chinese historical sources, they are directly contradicted by them, as well as by archaeology. The same applies all along the frontier between Central Eurasia and the periphery of Eurasia, from east to west. See further in the epilogue.

In short, the Silk Road was not an isolated, intrusive element in Central Eurasian culture, it was a fundamental, constituent element of the economy. Moreover, it seems not to be possible to separate out the international trade component from the local trade component, or local from long-distance cultural interchange. All of it together—the nomadic pastoral economy, the agricultural "oasis" economy, and the Central Asian urban economy—constituted the Silk Road. Its origins, and the formation of the Central Eurasian Culture Complex, go back to the Indo-European migrations four millennia ago.

1

———

The Chariot Warriors

युङ्गाध्वं हँय अरुषी रथे युङ्गाध्वं रथेषु रोहितः ।
युङ्गाध्वं हरी अजिरा धुरि वोळ्हवे वहिष्ठा धुरि वोळ्हवे ॥
उत सय वाज्य अरुषस तुविष्वणिर इह सम धायि दर्षतः ।
मा बो यामेषु मरुतश चिरं करत पर तं रथेषु चोदत ॥

> Harness the red mares to the chariot!
>   Harness to the chariots the ruddy ones!
> Harness the two fast yellow ones to the chariot pole,
>   fasten the best at pulling to the pole, to draw it.
> And was this thundering red charger
>   put here just to be admired?
> Don't let him cause you any delay, O Maruts
>   in your chariots! Spur him on!
>   —From the *Rig Veda*[1]

The First Central Eurasians

The Central Eurasian Culture Complex, which dominated much of Eurasia for nearly four millennia, developed among a people known only from historical linguistics: the Proto-Indo-Europeans. Because the precise location of their homeland is not known for certain, scholars working in various areas of cultural history have attempted to develop a model of the Indo-European homeland and of Indo-European culture based on information derived from historical linguistics. The words shared by the languages and cultures of Indo-European peoples in distant areas of Eurasia constitute evidence that the things they refer to are the shared inheritance of their Proto-Indo-European ancestors. Based on words referring to flora, fauna, and other things, as well as on archaeology and historical sources, it has been concluded that the Proto-Indo-European homeland was in Central Eurasia, specifically in the mixed steppe-forest zone between the southern Ural Mountains, the North Caucasus, and the Black Sea.[2]

---

[1] Text from http://www.sacred-texts.com/hin/rvsan/rv05056.htm, book 5, hymn 56.
[2] See appendix A.

*About four thousand years ago Indo-European-speaking people began mi-
grating from that homeland. They spread across most of the Eurasian continent during the second millennium BC and developed into the historically
attested Indo-European peoples by dominating and mixing with the native
peoples of the lands into which they migrated.*

*Their migration out of Central Eurasia proper appears to have taken place
in three distinct stages. The initial movement or first wave occurred at the very
end of the third millennium, and the third wave late in the second millennium
or beginning of the first millennium BC, but the most important was the
second wave, around the seventeenth century BC, in which Indo-European-
speaking people established themselves in parts of Europe, the Near East, India, and China, as well as within Central Eurasia itself. The migrations were
not organized and consisted not of mass movements of people but of individual clan groups or, perhaps more likely, warrior bands. They seem first to have
fought for their neighbors as mercenaries and only later took over. The
Indo-Europeans spoke more or less the same language, but in settling in their
new homes they took local wives who spoke non-Indo-European languages;
within a generation or two the local creoles they developed became new
Indo-European daughter languages.*

*By the beginning of the first millennium BC much of Eurasia had already
been Indo-Europeanized, and most of the rest of it had come under very heavy
Indo-European cultural and linguistic influence. This millennium-long movement constitutes the First Central Eurasian Conquest of Eurasia.*

The Indo-European Diaspora

Proto-Indo-European,[3] when still a unified language, was necessarily spoken in a small region with few or no significant dialect differences.[4] There
seems to be no linguistically acceptable reason to posit the breakup of the
language any earlier than shortly before the first Indo-European daughter
languages and their speakers are attested in the historical record about four
thousand years ago. The traditional idea, still generally believed, has the
breakup occurring due to glacially slow internal change over time from a

[3] See appendix A.
[4] On the recently growing failure to understand this necessity, and the implications thereof,
see endnote 30.

unity some six or seven millennia ago:[5] "In view of the great divergence among the languages of our earliest materials, we can scarcely place the community of speakers of proto-Indo-European later than the early part of the fourth millennium [BC]."[6] This would make Indo-European typologically unique among all the many thousands of known languages in the world. The idea must be rejected. By contrast, the view of the early Indo-Europeanists, who suggested a period around four millennia ago,[7] is supported by the available data, including typology, and also corresponds to the younger end of the dating ranges suggested by several proposals of Indo-Europeanist scholars.[8]

At the time of the Indo-Europeans' departure from their original homeland, it seems that there were still only minor dialect differences among the different tribal groups.[9] Their diaspora, or migrations away from the vicinity of their Central Eurasian homeland, can to some extent be reconstructed on the basis of the linguistic and cultural features they acquired along the way, also taking into account legendary material, such as the Old Indic and Old Iranian textual references to the conquest of foreign peoples and each other, as well as early historical data from the ancient Near East and the typology of ethnolinguistic change in Central Eurasia and vicinity in historically known periods. The following reconstruction represents an attempt to reconcile the linguistic facts with other data.[10]

[5] See, for example, Lehmann (1993). Mallory and Adams give "4000 BC" (2006: 106), but also "c. 4500–2500 BC" (2006: 449). Both works discuss the influence of local non-Indo-European languages on the Indo-European languages. Lehmann's (1993: 281–283) discussion of it actually supports the creolization theory, though it is not mentioned there and he elsewhere argues against it (see below). Mallory and Adams (2006: 463) cite the work of Johanna Nichols without discussion. Neither suggests creolization as the motivation for the formation of the daughter languages. Lehmann (1993: 263) implicitly argues against the idea: "Formerly, linguists and archaeologists ascribed change of dialects and languages to invasions of new peoples. . . . In time it became clear that in the fifth millennium [BC] tribal groups lacked the means and population to carry out such massive shifts." On the creolization theory, see also Garrett (1999, 2006), Beckwith (2006a, 2007c), and appendix A.
[6] Lehmann (1993: 266).
[7] They proposed the end of the third millennium BC (Lehmann 1993: 266).
[8] Mallory and Adams (1997: 297–299) discuss the main proposals.
[9] See Garrett (2006) and Beckwith (2006a). On the important historical implications of dialects, sociolects, and other aspects of variation in language, see Lehmann (1973), Labov (1982), and subsequent work.
[10] For discussion of other views, see Mallory (1989) and Mallory and Adams (1997, 2006). On the problem of Indo-Iranian, see endnote 31 and appendix A.

First of all, the Indo-European speakers spread, from somewhat further north,[11] up to the Caucasus and Black Sea regions, which were already occupied by non-Indo-European-speaking peoples. Those who continued on, going much further than the others, are the ancestors of the Tokharians and Anatolians, who share the Group A features[12] and constitute the only known members from what may be called the first wave of emigrants out of Central Eurasia. They are attested in the eastern Tarim Basin and Anatolian Plateau regions at the very end of the third or beginning of the second millennium BC[13] and in the nineteenth century BC, respectively. The Proto-Indo-Europeans are known to have had wagons, but the first wave seems to have left the proximal homeland either before the war chariot per se was developed, or before the Indo-Europeans had learned how to use chariots for war.[14]

Although the Indo-Europeans settled in new lands, in some cases (such as Greece) evidently by conquest, they did not always dominate the local people in the beginning. Instead, they often served the local peoples as mercenary warriors, or came under their domination in general. In either case, the Indo-European migrants—who were mostly men—married local women and, by mixing with them, developed their distinctive creole dialect features. The most influential of the new dialects was Proto-Indo-Iranian, the speakers of which appear to have been influenced linguistically by a non-Indo-European people from whom the Indo-Iranians borrowed their distinctive religious beliefs and practices. The locus of this convergence is increasingly thought to have been the area of the advanced, non-Indo-European-speaking Bactria-Margiana Culture[15] centered in what is now northwestern Afghanistan and southern Turkmenistan. The other Indo-Europeans developed different dialects and beliefs under the influence of other non-Indo-European languages and cultures.

---

[11] The middle Volga was already suggested as the homeland by Schrader in 1890 (Lehmann 1993: 279). Cf. endnote 32.

[12] Hock (1999a: 13); see also appendix A.

[13] See appendix A and Beckwith (2006a, 2007c), and the studies in Mair (1998); cf. Barber (1999) and Mallory and Mair (2000). Much further scholarship is needed on the Tarim Basin discoveries, which are of revolutionary importance for the archaeology and history of both the Proto-Indo-Europeans and the Proto-Chinese.

[14] See Hock (1999a: 12–13).

[15] On the theory that Indo-Iranian underwent a formative stage under its influence, see endnote 33.

After the Proto-Indo-Iranian dialect and culture had formed, the Greek, Italic, Germanic, and Armenian dialect speakers and some of the Indo-Iranians came under the influence of a non-Indo-European language with a significantly different phonological system,[16] which introduced the highly distinctive Group B features,[17] as well as the particular features that characterize Proto-Indic and distinguish it from Proto-Iranian.[18] When a long enough period had passed for the Group B linguistic features to have taken hold, the Indians and Iranians seem to have become enemies. The Indo-Europeans of Group B also either acquired the chariot or learned how to use their existing chariot-like vehicles for warfare, as did the Group A Hittites, whose home city, Kanesh, has the earliest archaeological (pictorial) evidence for a chariot-like vehicle in the ancient Near East. This weapon gave the Indo-European peoples a technological edge over their neighbors.[19]

The Iranians subsequently defeated the Indians and chased them to the extremities of Central Eurasia.[20] The second wave of migrations out of the steppe zone and its vicinity then began. It included the peoples who spoke the Group B dialects—Indic, Greek, Italic, Germanic, and Armenian. The Indo-Europeans of this group did have the war chariot, and when they moved into the areas of the peripheral civilizations in the mid-second millennium BC they had a revolutionary cultural and ethnolinguistic impact on them. They settled in their newly conquered lands and took local wives, whose non-Indo-European languages and cultures had an equally revolutionary impact on the Indo-Europeans, again producing new Indo-European creoles.[21] With the second wave, two more Indo-European peoples—the Old Indic speakers of Mitanni and the Mycenaean Greeks—enter actual recorded

---

[16] See appendix A. If further morphophonological features (especially loanwords) that are specific to Group B are isolated, it might be possible to identify the alien language. Witzel (2003) discusses such loanwords in Indo-Iranian.

[17] See appendix A.

[18] On Avestan and the Indo-Iranian problem, see appendix A; cf. endnotes 31 and 33.

[19] See the comments of Hock (1999a: 12–13).

[20] We know only that the Iranians did split the Indic-speaking peoples into a western group, who migrated (or had already migrated) into the Near East, and a southeastern group, who migrated (or had already migrated) into India. Cf. Bryant (2001: 134). The Avestan texts could perhaps belong to this period of complex interaction between Indic and Iranian speakers; see appendix A. The *Aśvin or Wu-sun people of ancient Jungharia and vicinity might have been remnants of an eastern Indic group; see appendix B.

[21] See appendix A.

history. The second wave had a much greater impact on the Eurasian world than the first wave.

Old Indic and Mycenaean Greek are both first attested in their earliest locations—upper Mesopotamia and the Greek Aegean, respectively—in the middle of the second millennium BC, in similar historical circumstances. The Old Indic linguistic materials are distinctively Indic, not Indo-Iranian, while the Shaft Grave culture of Greece, which appears precisely at this time, has been identified with the appearance of the Mycenaean Greeks. The particular closeness of Greek and Indic in certain respects as compared to other Group B languages suggests they may have remained together as a subgroup until shortly before they settled in their respective destinations,[22] but Group B had broken up by this date.

The second-wave period ended with Iranians dominating all of the Central Eurasian steppe zone and with Germanic peoples in temperate-zone Central Europe. Because the Germanic peoples largely retained the Central Eurasian Culture Complex, they effectively enlarged the Central Eurasian cultural area.[23]

Finally the third wave, or Group C, migrated. It consisted of the Celtic, Baltic, Slavic, Albanian,[24] and Iranian peoples, who had remained in the area of the homeland in Central Eurasia proper outside the region inhabited by the Group B peoples. The Celtic, Albanian, Slavic, and Baltic peoples moved westward, northwestward, and northward away from the Iranians, who nevertheless continued to expand and to dominate them (most strongly the Celts and Slavs). At the same time, the Iranians apparently pursued the Indians across the Near East to the Levant (the lands of the eastern Mediterranean littoral), across Iran into India,[25] and perhaps across Eastern Central Asia into China.

---

[22] According to the traditional view of the closeness of Old Indic (Vedic Sanskrit) and Avestan even after the Group B divergence, the formation and breakup of the group must have occurred in a very short time. This problem may be a chimera based on the mistaken understanding of Avestan; see appendix A. The very late attestation of the linguistically most archaic texts in Indic and Iranian is one of the many major problems of Indo-Iranian studies, a field in which too many facts do not fit the theories.

[23] The other second-wave languages, which are attested somewhat later, are Italic (from the early first millennium BC), Germanic (late first millennium BC), and Armenian (early first millennium AD).

[24] The Celtic and Iranian branches are attested in the first millennium BC, and Slavic by the middle of the first millennium AD, but Baltic and Albanian are only attested in the latter half of the second millennium AD. The development of Albanian is particularly obscure.

[25] Cf. Bryant (2001: 134), q.v. on the "Indo-Aryan migration debate." Most of the debate is founded upon the failure to understand linguistics and on political motivations having

The traditional theory that Indo-European developed into its attested daughter languages over many millennia in the Proto-Indo-European homeland is essentially impossible typologically. It has recently been contested, and a more likely "big-bang" type of split proposed instead, such as the one historically attested later for the spread of Turkic and Mongolic.[26] The old theory is essentially disproved also by the fact that, if the Indo-European daughter languages had already been fully developed before the migrations, there would be evidence of early Greek, for example, in Iran, or Russia; evidence of Germanic in India or Italy; evidence of Tokharian in Greece or Iran, and so on. But there is no such evidence. Leaving aside much later, historically attested migrations, Anatolian is known only from Anatolia, Greek only from Greece, Tokharian only from East Turkistan, Germanic only from northwestern Europe, Armenian only from Armenia, and so on. The only possible exception is Old Indic, which is attested first in upper Mesopotamia and the Levant, and later in India. Although it is assumed that the Iranian expansion into Persia is responsible for splitting the Old Indic–speaking people into the two attested branches, even in this case there is no evidence for Indic ever having been spoken in Europe, say, or northern Eurasia. Proto-Indo-European was spoken in the Central Eurasian homeland, while the attested daughter languages were spoken in their attested homelands outside it, where they developed as creoles almost instantaneously after their introduction there. The scenario presented here thus accords with typology, the recorded history of language development and spread, and with the actual attested situation of the Indo-European daughter languages.

The Early Peoples of Kroraina

The earliest Indo-Europeans discovered so far are directly known only from archaeology and palaeoanthropology. Although there is no way to know what language—let alone which dialect—was spoken by the people whose remains have been excavated, they are marked by specific physical anthropological

---

nothing to do with linguistics or history. On the scientific linguistic impossibility of the "indigenous Indo-Aryan" idea that is increasingly popular in India (Bryant 1999, 2001), see Hock (1999a).

[26] Nichols (1997a, 1997b), Garrett (1999, 2006), Beckwith (2006a).

CHAPTER 1

and cultural features, the lack of any other known long-distance migrants at that point in history, and the unusually clear continuity of their occupation down to historical times. The historical and linguistic evidence allows them to be identified as Proto-Tokharians.

Their mummified Caucasoid bodies, the earliest dated to around 2000 BC, have been found in great numbers in the eastern Tarim Basin in the area of ancient Kroraina, near Lop Nor, which is just west of the ancient pre-Chinese cultural zone. The best-reported site so far is Qäwrigul (*qävrigul* 'grave valley').

The people wore wool garments, both felted and woven, and were buried with baskets containing grains of wheat placed beside their heads, as well as branches of ephedra, the plant from which the intoxicating drink of the Vedas, *soma* (Iranian *haoma*), appears to have been made. The bodies typically have ochre applied to their faces. Remains of domestic cattle, sheep, goat, horse, and camel[27] show that the animals were raised by the Krorainian people, who also hunted wild sheep, deer, and birds, and caught fish.[28] This cultural assemblage is characteristic of the early Indo-Europeans.[29]

It has long been known that a language or dialect of Tokharian was spoken in the Kroraina area and neighboring regions in early Antiquity. It survived there long enough to leave loanwords in the third-century AD literary Prakrit documents from Kroraina, the region said by the Chinese to be the ancient home of the Yüeh-chih, who are in turn explicitly equated with Tokharians. The Tokharian language shares some features with Anatolian, the only other known Group A daughter language of Proto-Indo-European, and the earliest to be attested, in the nineteenth century BC. It is therefore possible to state fairly confidently that the early inhabitants of the Kroraina region—who are known to have been Yüeh-chih, which people are solidly identified both with the Tokharoi of Greek sources and with the

[27] The Late Bronze Age peoples of the Western Steppe, including the Cimmerians, the predecessors of the Scythians, bred cattle, sheep, goats, pigs, and horses. Their emphasis on cattle as their main domestic animal continues the state of affairs believed to have existed under the Proto-Indo-Europeans. This distribution changed dramatically in the Early Iron Age, when the main animals raised by steppe peoples became sheep and horses, though pigs continued to be raised in the forest and forest steppe zones, and the domestic cat and the donkey were added to the assemblage (Rolle 1989: 100–101).

[28] Mallory and Mair (2000: 138–139).

[29] Chinese-area relatives of wheat, domesticated sheep, and domesticated horses are known from paleobiological study to have been introduced from the west not long after 2000 BC. On the introduction of the domesticated horse, see endnote 34.

peoples of Kucha and Turfan (Qocho), who spoke West and East Tokharian respectively—were Proto-Tokharian speakers.[30]

The Anatolians

The pre-Anatolian origins of the Indo-European speakers who became the Anatolians are much debated, due to the ambiguous archaeological evidence. Their earliest linguistic and historical attestations are as names mentioned in Assyrian mercantile texts from nineteenth-century BC Kanesh.[31] From them stem the earliest certainly known Indo-European nation, the Hittites, who around 1650 BC[32] established a powerful state in the territory of the Hatti, the non-Indo-European people they supplanted and whose name they adopted.[33] The extant Hittite language texts were mostly written in the fourteenth and thirteenth centuries BC, but some are copies of originals as old as the seventeenth century BC.[34]

The history of the Hittite migration is unknown and must be inferred or reconstructed indirectly on the basis of suggestive details that are known. It is clear that the Hittites did not take power as an invading army—that is, by direct conquest from outside. They had lived in the area of Hatti long enough to be an established local people by the time of their conquest. It is unclear whether the Hittites had chariots when they first settled in Anatolia, but the fact that the earliest "Near Eastern" representations of what look like chariots are on seals from the Hittite home city of Kanesh[35] suggests that they did have

[30] See appendix B.
[31] *CAH* I.2: 833; cf. *EIEC* 13. There are "a few Hittite words (for example, *išhyuli*, 'obligation, contract') in Assyrian texts from Kanesh (modern Kültepe) dating from the nineteenth century" (Bryce 2005: 13, 21 et seq.), which are believed to indicate that "Indo-European languages were already in the Central Anatolian area at the beginning of the second millennium" (Melchert 1995: 2152). Bryce (2005: 23) cites occurrences of "the names of house-owners with Anatolian names, like Peruwa, Galulu, Saktanuwa, Suppiahsu" in the Kanesh texts. However, they do not in fact indicate that Indo-European speakers were there *before* the nineteenth century BC. See also endnote 35 on the earliest attestation of Indo-Europeans.
[32] Bryce (2005: 68).
[33] *EIEC* 15. Their original name is unknown. On their name and their language as a creole, see endnote 36.
[34] *CAH* 1.2: 831. The other known Anatolian languages (principally Luwian, Palaic, Lydian, and Lycian) are all attested later than Hittite. Though some have argued that the names mentioned in early Assyrian texts were specifically Luwian, this appears not to be the case.
[35] Drews (1988: 94).

chariots. In any case, they certainly did have and use them in their later conquest of Hatti and establishment of their empire. On the basis of numerous similar cases from Antiquity up through the Middle Ages, as well as the First Story model, it is likely that Central Eurasian–type warrior-merchants from a group of Anatolians were hired by the Hatti Kingdom to fight against other groups of invading Indo-Europeans and thus became established in the kingdom.

In view of the first Hittite rulers' cultural assimilation to the Hatti, they must have grown up learning Hatti customs and language. But as Indo-Europeans they belonged to a warrior-trader patriarchal culture and identified themselves primarily with their fathers' people. They retained their own language and kept at least some of their own beliefs and customs as well. The Hittite king had an elite personal bodyguard, the MEŠEDI, consisting of twelve warriors who accompanied and protected him at all times.[36] Considering their small number and very high status (similar to that of the Old Indic–speaking *maryannu* in the neighboring Mitanni Kingdom), it is likely that they were in fact his comitatus.[37] With the Hittites' Indo-European hero-worshiping ethos, and sympathy for themselves as downtrodden people whose cattle and women had unrightfully been stolen by their alien rulers, it was only a matter of time before they realized that they were in the position of subjects under unjust alien rulers. When they had the knowledge and means to do so, they overthrew the Hatti rulers and set up their own leader as king. This they did with their first fully historical king, Hattusili I, who established the Hittite Kingdom around 1650 BC with the great assistance of the most advanced weapon of the day, the war chariot,[38] which was just then spreading across the Near East.[39]

[36] See Bryce (2002: 21–23; cf. 2005: 109). On the similarity of Hittite and Scythian burial customs, see Rolle (1989: 34).

[37] Further work by Hittitologists could perhaps clarify this issue.

[38] Hittite does not seem to preserve the Proto-Indo-European words for 'wagon' and so forth, suggesting that the speakers acquired the chariot only after or during their immigration to Anatolia. Cf. Hock (1999a: 12). The real problem may be that we do not yet know enough about Hittite and the Hittites.

[39] Drews (1993: 106; 2004: 49). The people of Troy VI, who are thought to have been Anatolian speakers, also used chariots. "The men who founded Troy VI introduced horses to northwestern Anatolia, and so long as the city endured (ca. 1700–1225 BC) they used their horses not only to pull chariots but also to provide themselves with meat" (Drews 2004: 55). Because the consumption of horsemeat outside of Central Eurasia was extremely rare—it was virtually unknown in most of the ancient Near East—this suggests that the consumers came from Central Eurasia; cf. Drews (2004: 44).

Only with the establishment of a Hittite state did the Hittite people truly come into being as a nation—one that had Hatti mothers and cousins and uncles. They raided Syria and Mesopotamia, fought with the other great kingdoms of the day (including Egypt), and are mentioned in the Bible.

The Hittites' culture became radically changed by mixture with the Hatti and with other peoples, particularly the Mitanni—both their Old Indic–speaking *maryannu* rulers and their non-Indo-European Hurrian subjects—with whose kingdom in northern Mesopotamia, to the southeast of Hattusa, the Hittites were often at odds. The Hittites managed to maintain their language for half a millennium, but at the end of the Bronze Age in the early twelfth century BC their kingdom was overwhelmed by the convulsions traditionally ascribed to the little-known Sea Peoples, who overran and destroyed many realms in the Levant, particularly in Syria and Palestine, but also in Egypt and Greece.[40] A branch of the Hittite dynasty managed to survive for several more generations in Carchemish, but the Hittites as a people disappeared.[41] The monumental stone Lion Gate of the Hittite capital city still stands today at the entrance to the ruins of Hattusa[42] in Central Anatolia.

The Maryannu

The first Indo-European people of the second wave (Group B) who left clear records of their presence are the Old Indic–speaking chariot warriors known as the *maryannu*. They formed the ruling class of the Hurrian kingdom of Mitanni, the center of which was located in the area of northern Mesopotamia and northern Syria. The rulers of this kingdom have Old Indic names;[43] the names of the gods they worshiped are Old Indic; the root *marya-* of their

---

[40] Bryce (2005: 333–340), Drews (1993: 8–11), cf. Oren (2000).

[41] Bryce (2005: 347–355). Other Anatolian peoples survived well into the Classical Graeco-Roman period, but nevertheless remain less well known than the Hittites.

[42] Or Hattuša; now the village of Boğazköy (or Boğazkale), about 150 kilometers east of Ankara (formerly Angora, ancient Ancyra). See the map and photographs in Bryce (2005: 43, 45, 84), and Bryce (2002) for detailed coverage of the city itself.

[43] Burney (2004: 204) says, "Much attention has been devoted to a non-Hurrian element in Mitanni, on linguistic evidence clearly Indo-Aryan. Highly influential as this group was, they were undoubtedly a small minority among their Hurrian subjects. They included, however, the royal house, whose names were all Indo-Aryan." Rewriting his comments to remove the odd negative slant, this would read, "An important non-Hurrian element in Mitanni was

name *maryannu* 'chariot warrior' is Old Indic;[44] and words for chariots, horses, horse training, and other elements of their culture are Old Indic. Though the Mitanni texts are written in the local non-Indo-European language, Hurrian, which survived at the expense of the invaders' Old Indic language, the *maryannu* clearly spoke Indic, not Hurrian, at least in the beginning, and the Mitanni Kingdom must therefore have been Indic in origin.[45] How exactly they established their kingdom and maintained their Indic language long enough that it could be preserved as names and loanwords after it ceased to be spoken is unknown, but there is no question about their ethnolinguistic origins. The early Mitanni rulers must have spoken Old Indic, and they were chariot warriors—or, more likely, the Old Indic–speaking rulers had a large comitatus consisting of chariot warriors.[46]

Moreover, they must have brought chariots, the technology of chariot warfare, and the knowledge of horses with them to the Mitanni area. If they had not, and the Hurrians, the local non-Indo-European people, had possessed chariots and had known how to use them, first the Hurrians would probably have prevailed against the Old Indic invaders. Second, the Mitanni texts would not have Old Indic words for these things, and they would not have Old Indic names for their rulers;[47] they would have Hurrian words, or other local ancient Near Eastern ones. If the *maryannu* had learned about chariots, horses, and chariot warfare from the Hurrians, they would not have influenced the Hurrian language and culture in this way.

The reverse is also true. If the *maryannu* had *not* known about chariots, horses, chariot warfare, horse training, and so forth before entering Upper Mesopotamia, but learned them from the Hurrians or other ancient Near Eastern peoples after they arrived, the words for these things in the famous horse-training manual of Kikkuli would be in a non-Indo-European

---

on linguistic evidence clearly Indo-Aryan. Known as the *maryannu*, these people were highly influential and included the royal house, whose names were all Indo-Aryan."

[44] For the etymology of *marya* 'young (chariot-) warrior', *marut* 'chariot warrior', and their relatives, see endnote 37.

[45] Freu (2003).

[46] Many of the leading men of Central Eurasian states, not only the rulers, typically had a comitatus. The Mitanni comitatus of chariot-warrior archers is the clear predecessor of the mounted-archer comitatus known from the first millennium BC onward.

[47] Freu (2003: 19) notes, "tous les souverains ont porté des noms appartenant à l'onomastique védique, analysables par les seuls catégories du sanscrit."

language—either Hurrian or some other ancient Near Eastern language, such as Assyrian. But the Kikkuli text has Old Indic words for them, most of which are inherited from Indo-European, not Hurrian or other ancient Near Eastern words.[48] The "localist" Mitanni theory is impossible.[49]

By the same token, there are no words from Dravidian or Munda or other Indian subcontinent languages in the Mitanni material. If the *maryannu* had come from the Indian subcontinent, their language would have non-Indo-European words for the horse and chariot, as well as for cultural features known to have existed in earlier times in India, such as cattle, grain, and many other things. But Old Indic, both in Mitanni and in India, shares the same cultural vocabulary, which is Indo-European—and therefore Central Eurasian—in origin.

Because it is not possible to derive the Mesopotamian Indic subgroup from the subcontinental Indic subgroup or vice versa, both must have derived from one and the same ancestral Old Indic group. Their territory must have been invaded by the Iranians, who expanded southward into Iran at their expense, leaving the two subgroups separated from each other, as has long been argued on the basis of comparative studies of Indic and Iranian mythology.[50]

The Mitanni Kingdom was founded in the late sixteenth century BC and lasted as an independent realm until it was defeated by the Hittite king Suppiluliuma between 1340 and 1325 BC. Though the Mitanni shortly thereafter broke free of the Hittites, they soon came under the control of the Assyrians. King Šattuara II tried to reestablish the Mitanni state in about 1265, but he was defeated and driven from the realm around 1260 by the Assyrian king Salmanasar I (r. 1273–1244).[51]

---

[48] See the similar point made by Witzel (2001). There are also numerous other loanwords from Hurrian and other ancient Near Eastern languages.

[49] See the discussion of this issue in Freu's (2003) Mitanni history, which also gives extensive bibliographical references to the considerable literature on the Indic language of the Mitanni kings and chariot warriors and their relatives who left their names and scattered words all across the Levant in the second millennium BC. Cf. *EIEC* 306. Like some scholars of ancient East Asia who ignore or downplay the evidence of early Indo-European intrusion, some scholars of the ancient Near East (e.g., Van de Mieroop 2004: 112–117) similarly attempt to bury this material.

[50] As noted above, the name of the Wu-sun 烏孫 *Aśvin of ancient Jungharia and the Ili River region suggests they may have been a remnant nation of Old Indic speakers in Central Eurasia. Their names and titles should be reexamined with a possible Indic linguistic connection in mind. See appendix B.

[51] Freu (2003: 221–223); Van de Mieroop (2004: 121).

Northern India

The archaeological evidence for the migration of the Old Indic speakers into northwestern India remains unclear down to the present. Nevertheless, the Old Indic language unquestionably is intrusive in India, having entered the subcontinent from the northwest. Moreover, the appearance of the early Old Indic speakers in India is explicitly represented in the earliest legends of their descendants as an immigrant, conquering nation imposing itself on local peoples who were non-Indo-European in race, language, and culture.[52] This is absolutely clear in the most ancient text,[53] the *Rig Veda*, and continues in much later compositions such as the Indian national epic, the *Mahâbhârata*, especially in its oldest core sections. These early warlike immigrants herded cattle, fought from horse-drawn chariots, and had a highly patriarchal society. They were, simply put, Indo-Europeans.[54]

The Indo-European conquest of India did not end with the Vedas. It continued over a period of centuries, as the Old Indic–speaking people spread their language and culture across northern India and points beyond. At the same time, the local peoples of India heavily influenced the newcomers, who mixed with them in every way conceivable, eventually producing a distinctive new hybrid culture.[55]

Mycenaean Greece

The single most remarkable archaeological event in the protohistorical period of Greece is the appearance around 1600 BC of the monumental,

---

[52] The Old Indic intrusion into India is widely believed to have happened after the Harappan or Indus Valley civilization of northwestern India suddenly collapsed in the first half of the second millennium BC, and the Vedas are now considered to have been codified in the area of Punjab. However, the controversy about the events in question has become more or less completely politicized, and most of what is written about it is unreliable at best. See endnote 38 for a brief discussion and references.

[53] According to tradition the *Rig Veda* is the most ancient Old Indic text (or rather, collection of texts). It is not actually attested until around a millennium ago. See appendix A.

[54] See endnote 37 on the Old Indic words *marya* and *marut*, and cf. Witzel (2001).

[55] There was no retention of "pure" Indo-Aryan culture or "pure" local non-Indo-Aryan culture. They were both mixtures to start with, and they mixed with each other. It is that creole hybrid (along with successive rehybridizations) which has created Indian civilization.

treasure-filled burials known as the Shaft Graves. The weapons, golden grave goods, and other artifacts found in the grave circles at Mycenae are completely unprecedented in Greece and can only be explained as intrusive foreign cultural elements. In other words, these archaeological materials, which are now firmly identified with the Mycenaean Greeks, were introduced by them.[56] The Mycenaeans are the first Indo-Europeans known to have arrived in the area of the Greek Aegean, which had long been occupied by non-Indo-European-speaking peoples. This has received additional confirmation from linguistics, which has shown that Mycenaean Greek precedes all of the later known ancient Greek dialects.[57] The earliest texts date to the fourteenth century BC and include the palace archives of Knossos, Crete, in which numerous chariots and chariot parts are mentioned and catalogued. Moreover, Mycenaean artistic portrayals of war chariots have been found at Mycenae, from the sixteenth to fifteenth centuries BC.[58] It cannot be doubted that the Mycenaeans had and used chariots in their conquest of Greece.

The Yellow River Valley

The war chariot and some other elements of the Central Eurasian Culture Complex appeared in China[59] somewhat before the twelfth century BC. Burials in the royal necropolis found in the ruins of the late Shang capital at Anyang on the north bank of the Yellow River include numerous chariots

---

[56] Drews (1988: 21–24). James Muhly (quoted in Drews 1988: 23, n. 16) says, "The one dramatic transition in prehistoric Greece came towards the . . . latter part of the seventeenth century B.C., and is represented by the Shaft Graves at Mycenae. Nothing yet known from the impoverished Middle Helladic period prepares one for the wealth and splendor of Shaft Grave Mycenae."

[57] Garrett (1999). Mallory (1989: 66–71) somewhat similarly concludes that the "current state of our knowledge of the Greek dialects can accommodate Indo-Europeans entering Greece at any time between 2200 and 1600 BC to emerge later as Greek speakers." The Mycenaean Greek writing system, Linear B, was brilliantly deciphered by Michael Ventris in 1954. With this breakthrough, Ventris and Chadwick were able to begin reading Mycenaean texts. See Chadwick (1958). They contain, among other things, inventories of chariots and chariot parts, arrowheads, and other military equipment.

[58] On the archaeological controversy about the invention, earliest attestation, and use of the chariot, focusing on the Shaft Graves of the Mycenaean Greeks and the evidence from the Hittite home city of Kanesh, see endnote 39.

[59] On the origins, location, and extent of the earliest "Chinese" state, and the linguistic origins of Chinese, see endnote 40.

and their horses, often along with the chariot warriors and their weapons.[60] The chariots have many spokes rather than only four or six, the typical numbers used in the ancient Near East; they thus have extremely close analogues to contemporaneous chariots found in the Caucasus.[61] They are also often found together with "northern" type knives typical of the steppe zone.[62] It is now accepted that the chariot is an intrusive cultural artifact that entered Shang China from the north or northwest without any wheeled-vehicle precursors.[63] The practice of burying chariots along with their horses and young men with weapons who seem to be their drivers and archers[64] is a distinctive mark of the Central Eurasian Culture Complex, which at that time was undoubtedly still exclusively Indo-European. Such burials are frequently found at Shang sites, usually in association with the burial of high-ranking noblemen.[65] As noted, historical sources on Central Eurasia from Antiquity through the Early Middle Ages attest that the men who belonged to a lord's comitatus were buried together with him and their horses, weapons, and valuables. It is also significant that the first written Chinese texts, the Oracle Bone Inscriptions, began to be composed at about the same time. Although there seems to be no direct connection between this writing system and any other known system,[66] the as-yet-unidentified Indo-European

[60] Bagley (1999: 202 et seq.).
[61] Bagley (1999: 207). They have been found at Lchashen, southwest of the Caucasus Mountains near Lake Sevan in Armenia, and are dated to approximately the middle of the second millennium BC. See Barbieri-Low (2000: 38), who compares them to the remarkably similar Shang chariots. The historically earliest known chariots and chariot warriors in the ancient Near East were in the Hittite and Mitanni kingdoms directly to the west of Lchashen. Barbieri-Low (2000: 37–39) argues that the Near Eastern chariot was derived directly from a relative of the smaller steppe chariot represented by those found in burials of the Sintashta-Petrovka culture located in the southern Ural Mountain area in what is now northwestern Kazakhstan and southern Russia, while the larger Chinese chariot was derived from a relative of the Lchashen chariot.
[62] Bagley (1999: 208), Barbieri-Low (2000: 42–43).
[63] Piggott (1992: 63), Shaughnessy (1988). For a "local development" view, see endnote 41.
[64] Barbieri-Low (2000: 19 et seq.), who remarks on the "young male humans" buried with the chariots. The often stated idea that these young men were officials is belied by their youth and the presence of weapons with them.
[65] Barbieri-Low (2000: 22) notes, "In the majority of excavated examples, from one to three humans were also sacrificed and placed within the chariot pit . . . they are said to be invariably male (20–35 years old)." He adds, "These young men (age 20–35), who are often found in association with weapons, bronze rein-holders, and jade or bronze whip-handles, were probably the actual warriors and drivers who operated the chariots" (Barbieri-Low 2000: 32–33). On the Central Eurasian style of the weapons, see endnote 42.
[66] Although it is widely believed that important elements of bronze technology were introduced from the northwest in the second millennium BC, it is thought by some Sinologists that the

people who brought the chariots to China may well have brought the *idea* of writing[67] as well.

The introduction of the chariot and comitatus burial in China can only be due to the appearance of a Central Eurasian people there. "Anyang chariot burials thus seem to indicate a substantial interaction with northern neighbors beginning about 1200 B.C.: not an invasion, but not a border incident either. The mere capture of enemy chariots and horses would not have brought the skills required to use, maintain, and reproduce them. . . . The clearly marked advent of the chariot is a clue to an episode of cultural contact that deserves more attention than it has received."[68] Because all other known examples of chariot warriors at that time were Indo-Europeans, most of whom belonged to Group B, the newcomers must have been Indo-Europeans. Considering the intruders' significant impact on the culture of the Yellow River valley, they must have had a powerful linguistic impact also, one not limited to the words for the newly imported artifacts and practices. So far, their language has not yet been identified more specifically, but it is quite possible that it represents an otherwise unknown branch of Indo-European.[69]

The Chou Conquest of Shang China

The story of Hou Chi 'Lord Millet', the divine founder of the Chou Dynasty, is a typical Central Eurasian foundation myth, closely paralleled by the Roman myth, the Wu-sun (*Aśvin) myth, and the Puyo-Koguryo myth. How could the origin of the most revered Chinese dynasty be represented by such an alien foundation myth?

It might seem surprising that the Chou, the ideal model of a dynasty throughout Chinese history, is traditionally considered by Chinese scholars to have been non-Chinese in origin. This view is not so surprising upon examination of the data on which it is based. The Chou came from what

---

revolutionary changes in Chinese bronze metallurgy that took place in the fifteenth and fourteenth centuries BC were largely in the vastly expanded scale of the industry and skill of workmanship in bronze casting (Bagley 1999: 136–142 et seq.).

[67] On the structure and origins of the Chinese writing system, see endnote 43.

[68] Bagley (1999: 207–208).

[69] See Beckwith (2002a, 2006c).

was at the time the western frontier of the Chinese culture area. The mother of Hou Chi, Chiang Yüan, was by name a member of the Chiang clan. The Chiang are generally accepted to have been a non-Chinese people related to or more likely identical to the Ch'iang, who were the main foreign enemies of the Shang Dynasty.[70] The Ch'iang were evidently skilled chariot warriors in the Shang period, and were therefore necessarily well acquainted with horses and wheels. But it has been shown that the Tibeto-Burman words for 'horse', though ultimately Indo-European in origin, were borrowed from Old Chinese, not from Indo-European directly,[71] and the same appears to be true for the Tibetan word for 'wheel'.[72] For this and other reasons it is probable that the early Ch'iang were not Tibeto-Burman speakers (as widely believed), but Indo-Europeans, and Chiang Yüan belonged to a clan that was Indo-European in origin. The Central Eurasian myth about her and her son, the ancestor of the Chou line, is thus not surprising after all.

Yet the literary language of the Chou, preserved mainly in the Bronze Inscriptions (texts inscribed on ritual bronze vessels), is clearly the continuation of the Shang language of the Oracle Bone Inscriptions, and both are certainly ancestral to modern Chinese. In the traditional view, which still dominates the view of Sinological linguists, there is no room for any significant foreign influence on the development of Chinese.[73] Yet this cannot be correct. The mounting evidence against the isolationist position, especially from archaeology, indicates that the intrusive Indo-European people who brought the chariot had a powerful influence on Shang culture and may even have been responsible for the foundation of the Shang Dynasty (ca. 1570–1045 BC) itself. The Shang realm occupied only a rather small area in the Yellow River valley in what is now northern and eastern Honan (Henan), southeastern Shansi (Shanxi), and western Shantung (Shandong);[74] such a state could easily have been dominated by an aggressive Indo-European people armed with war chariots. Although there is no direct evidence for or

---

[70] On the names Chiang 姜 and Ch'iang 羌 and their etymology, see endnote 44 and appendix B.

[71] For the reconstruction of the Old Chinese dialect forms of the word for 'horse', see endnote 45.

[72] For the reconstruction of the Old Chinese and Old Tibetan words for 'wheel, chariot', see endnote 46.

[73] For criticism of the current dominant view, see Endnote 47.

[74] Keightley (1999: 277).

against any such political event, the existence of the intrusive chariot warriors, and their influence on Chinese material culture, cannot be denied.

The appearance of chariot warriors in East Asia coincides approximately with their appearance in Greece (Europe), Mesopotamia (the Near East, Southwest Asia), and northwestern India (South Asia).[75] In all of the non-East Asian cases, the chariot warrior people spoke an Indo-European language and had Central Eurasian culture. In the East Asian case the chariot warriors appear to have had the same Central Eurasian culture as the Indo-Europeans in the other regions of Eurasia. They should therefore have spoken an Indo-European language.

Linguistically, there are only two possible outcomes of this Indo-European intrusion. The Early Old Chinese language of the Oracle Bone Inscriptions is either a non-Indo-European language with an intrusive Indo-European element or an Indo-European language with an intrusive non-Indo-European element.[76] In both scenarios, the language of the Bronze Inscriptions, Classical Chinese, and the modern Chinese languages and dialects are clear continuations of Early Old Chinese, the language of the Oracle Bone Inscriptions, which was therefore already "Chinese." Recent linguistic research on Early Old Chinese supports the presence of numerous Indo-European elements that are clearly related to Proto-Indo-European already in the Shang period Oracle Bone Inscriptions. Their identification with a particular *branch* of Indo-European remains uncertain. However, it is possible that the language was close to Proto-Indo-European itself.

According to one current theory,[77] the most likely scenario is that a small group of Indo-European chariot warriors entered the pre-Chinese culture zone in the central Yellow River valley as mercenaries. They stayed and intermarried with the local people, with the result that either their language became creolized by the local language, exactly as happened to the other Indo-European daughter languages, or the local language was creolized or

---

[75] Any argument against the Indo-European affiliations of the intrusive people in Shang China must ignore this evidence and much else. Those who argue against the theory do indeed ignore the evidence. Unfortunately, no one has yet been able to reconstruct Old Chinese accurately enough to determine the extent of the influence.

[76] The theory of the mixed language (on which see endnote 48) has been disproved, leaving only two possibilities.

[77] Beckwith (2006a: 23–36); cf. Nichols (1997a, 1997b), Garrett (1999).

otherwise significantly influenced by Indo-European (as happened to the Indo-European *maryannu* of Mitanni). In either case, the Indo-European language material in the resulting language, Early Old Chinese, derives from generic late Proto-Indo-European, from a known Indo-European daughter language, or from an already independent Indo-European daughter language that is otherwise unknown.

It has recently been argued that the widely believed theory of a genetic relationship between Chinese and Tibeto-Burman—the so-called Sino-Tibetan theory—seems to be based on a shared Indo-European lexical inheritance.[78] Some of this material demonstrably entered Tibeto-Burman as loanwords via Chinese. For example, the words for 'horse', 'wheel', 'iron', and other things known to have been introduced into East Asia after the early second millennium BC, have been treated as Sino-Tibetan words, yet the things themselves, and thus the words for them, could not have been known many thousands of years earlier, at the time of the hypothetical Proto-Sino-Tibetan language, and their phonological shape reflects Old Chinese influence. Nevertheless, although some of the Indo-European element in Tibeto-Burman seems clearly to have entered via Chinese, in many other instances chronological considerations make such a pathway difficult, if not impossible. The most likely solution is that the Indo-European intrusion produced a creole not only with the pre-Chinese of the Yellow River valley but also with at least some of the pre-Tibeto-Burmans further to the southwest in the presumed home of Proto-Tibeto-Burman.[79]

Only further linguistic research will establish whether Early Old Chinese is a minimally maintained Indo-European language or a minimally maintained local East Asian language. Whichever way it turns out, it is certain that Indo-European speakers and their language had a strong influence on what became China and also, directly or indirectly, on the Tibeto-Burman peoples.[80]

---

[78] The lack of regular morphophonological or syntactic correspondences has also been noted (Beckwith 1996, 2006a).

[79] This scenario also neatly explains the transfer of the exonym Ch'iang 羌 'Indo-Europeans' to later mean 'Tibeto-Burmans'. The most serious problem at the moment, however, is the lack of any actual Proto-Tibeto-Burman reconstruction. The *Urtext* of Benedict's (1972) book, flawed as it is, remains the first and so far the only attempt to reconstruct Proto-Tibeto-Burman based on strictly linguistic sources and methods.

[80] On the typological issues involved, see Beckwith (2006a: 1 et seq.; 2007b: 189).

The Iranian Conquest of Central Eurasia

The early history of the Iranian domination of the Central Eurasian steppe zone as well as southern Central Asia (now Afghanistan), Iran, and Mesopotamia is extremely obscure. Proto-Indo-Iranian, the speakers of which have been archaeologically identified with the Andronovo culture, broke up into Proto-Indic and Proto-Iranian no later than the physical separation of Group B from the other Indo-European dialects. Old Indic, a Group B language, had thus become distinct from Proto-Iranian proper[81] no later than the time of the migration of the Indic speakers southward in connection with the breakup of Group B, which event must be dated to about 1600 BC. If the Iranian defeat of the Indians happened at this time, it is unclear why they took so long to pursue their presumed enemies to the south.

Iranian speakers did eventually replace Indic speakers in Iran. There is no further direct evidence of Indic in the area of Iran and the Near East after the end of the Bronze Age around the twelfth century BC. The earliest historical and linguistic evidence also unequivocally supports the archaeological evidence that the early peoples of the Central Eurasian steppe zone and the riverine agricultural regions of Central Asia were Iranian speakers.

Archaeologists are now generally agreed that the Andronovo culture of the Central Steppe region in the second millennium BC is to be equated with the Indo-Iranians. However, no matter how pastorally oriented these people's culture probably was, they were not nomads. They lived in permanent houses, not on wagons or in tents as the earliest nomads are known to have done. The division into Indic and Iranian took place no later than the sixteenth century BC, long before the development of mounted nomadism, which was an achievement of the steppe-dwelling Iranians who grew out of the Andronovo culture.[82] However, the entire Central Eurasian steppe had become an Iranian culture zone before the first mention of Iranians in historical sources: the Persians in 835 BC and the Medes in the eighth century BC.[83] Central Eurasian Iranians are first mentioned in the seventh century BC, when Greek and ancient Near Eastern sources record that the Iranian-speaking Medes were subjugated by the Scythians for a time in the seventh

---

[81] That is, not including Avestan, q.v. appendix A.

[82] Di Cosmo (1999a, 2002a), Mallory (1989), *EIEC* 308–311.

[83] *EIEC* 311.

century BC and that the Scythians moved into the Western Steppe from the east, an event confirmed by archaeology.[84]

The Horse and Chariot and the Indo-Europeans

The earliest archaeologically discovered chariot remains have been found in Central Eurasia, at the Sintashta site in the southern Ural-Volga steppe zone dated to circa 2000 BC.[85] The earliest historically known occurrences of chariots actually being used in war date to the mid-seventeenth century BC, when the Hittites under Hattusili I (r. ca. 1650–1620 BC) used them in the process of establishing their kingdom in Anatolia.[86] The *maryannu*, the Old Indic-speaking charioteers of the Mitanni, the Hittites' neighbors to the east and south, were experts in the training of chariot horses. The contemporaneous Mycenaean Greeks, the Hittites' neighbors to the west and the second Indo-European people to develop a written language, also used war chariots in their conquests. So did the Old Indic speakers who invaded northwestern India, apparently at about this time. These historical events are not coincidental.

War chariots are complex, sophisticated machines, the successful use of which required four inseparable elements: the chariots themselves, highly trained domesticated horses, drivers, and archers. Because the earliest known chariot warriors were all Indo-Europeans, it seems highly probable that the drivers and warriors originated in Central Eurasia. Where then did the horses and chariots come from?

The horse is native to Central Eurasia. Although wild horses did roam as far south as Palestine in the Pleistocene epoch, they subsequently disappeared, evidently due to hunting. Przewalski's horse, the wild horse of the Eastern Steppe north of the pre-Chinese cultural zone, is genetically distinct from domesticated horses, which were domesticated by about 2000 BC,

---

[84] *EIEC* 311.

[85] *EIEC* 309, 520–521.

[86] Burney (2004: 64–65). The Hittite chariot crew originally consisted of a driver and an archer, as in other early cultures' use of chariots, but this seems to have changed by the Battle of Kadesh in 1274 (if we assume that the depictions on the Egyptian reliefs portraying the battle are historically accurate), in which the crew consisted of a driver, an archer, and a shield bearer whose job was to defend the others (Bryce 2002: 111). Hittite charioteers are also listed in records of military personnel from the seventeenth century BC on (Burney 2004: 64).

or in any case earlier than their first use as draft animals for chariots. They could therefore hardly have been domesticated in the ancient Near East, where horses only appear, or reappear, together with the chariot.[87] Also, horses were adopted by local rulers much later than their attested use by Hittites, Mitanni, and Mycenaeans—for example, in New Kingdom Egypt, where the chariot is a known importation from Mitanni.[88] Studies of the materials used in preserved Egyptian chariots confirm that the Egyptians imported them from the Transcaucasus area.

The fully formed war chariot is known from archaeology to have been introduced into previously vehicle-less Shang China from the northwest no later than the twelfth century BC, and probably somewhat earlier, because the earliest examples found so far date to the thirteenth century and already have extensive local Shang decorative detail that presupposes a period of acculturation in China. The chariot was also used by foreign peoples in warfare with the Shang Chinese. The chariot horse must have come along with the chariot.[89] Domesticated horses were buried together with men and chariots in the Shang royal burial ground. The burial of chariots with their horses and charioteers is typical of the Central Eurasian Culture Complex, which seems to have been exclusively Indo-European down to the end of the second millennium BC.

Domesticated horses may have appeared in Anatolia, and possibly in the Near East proper, by 2000 BC—in which case the exporters necessarily were Central Eurasians—but they remained rare at best until the seventeenth century, when Indo-European chariot warriors, driving the perfected war chariot, seized control of preexisting cultures in Central Anatolia (the Hittites), Upper Mesopotamia (the *maryannu* of Mitanni), and the Greek Aegean (the Mycenaean Greeks). Most ancient Near Eastern words for 'horse' are borrowed from an Indo-Iranian language; in view of the early dates, well

---

[87] The mitochondrial DNA study of Jansen et al. (2002: 10910) concludes, "Although there are claims for horse domestication as early as 4500 BC for Iberia and the Eurasian steppe, the earliest undisputed evidence [is] chariot burials dating to 2000 BC from Krivoe Ozero (Sintashta-Petrovka culture) on the Ural steppe," and in view of the sudden spread of the chariot across Eurasia in the mid-second millennium BC, "the knowledge and the initially domesticated horses themselves would have spread, with local mares incorporated *en route*, forming our regional mtDNA clusters" along with the chariots. On scholarly arguments concerning the Sintashta-Petrovka chariot, the earliest so far discovered, see endnote 49.

[88] Burney (2004: 65).

[89] The Proto-Tokharians introduced the domestic horse several centuries earlier, probably as a food animal, as noted above.

before the attested appearance of Iranians outside Central Eurasia, that language can only be Old Indic. Literary evidence from the non-Indo-European kingdoms of the ancient Near East also explicitly attests that horses long remained rare and expensive imports there and that the local people were unaccustomed to handling horses for any purpose other than athletic daredevil displays.[90]

The earliest clear descriptions and portrayals of the chariot are of a machine used for shooting with the bow, not a vehicle for royal display. All hard evidence indicates that wherever it appeared it was a military weapon first and foremost, and only later did it come to be used for prestige activities such as parades.[91] This is also true for literary evidence. Even late references to chariots being used to transport warriors to battle, as in the *Iliad*, are warfare usages.[92] The chariot was undoubtedly also used from the beginning for hunting, perhaps because it was necessary to train the charioteers and their horses for battle, and to keep them in training. Hunting from chariots in a Central Eurasian context, particularly the *grande battue*, while it served the important purpose of gathering food, was conducted exactly the same as war.[93] But it seems that the ancient Central Eurasians did not distinguish clearly between an attack against enemy humans and an attack against animals.

The chariot's primary use as a military weapon accounts for the heroic qualities attached to the chariot warriors, and vice versa. There would hardly have been anything particularly heroic about driving a parade vehicle. It is also difficult to imagine that a ruler would allow a pure symbol of rulership to be used by anyone not from the royal family, let alone common soldiers. Chariot racing must have developed as a natural outgrowth of chariot warriors training to use the chariots in battle, and also of exercising the horses to keep them in good condition and prepared for the distractions of the battlefield.

[90] Drews (2004).

[91] Contra Littauer and Crouwel (2002). Another reason it is unlikely that the chariot was first used for royal display is that advances in military technology have consistently preceded use of the technology for other purposes.

[92] The poem's description of their use is not historically correct for the period before the end of the Bronze Age, during which chariots were still serious military weapons. See Drews (1988: 161 et seq.).

[93] Cf. Allsen (2006).

THE WAR CHARIOT

A very light two-wheeled wagon normally drawn by two horses and ridden by a driver and an archer, the chariot is the world's first complex machine,[94] and at the same time the first technologically advanced weapon. A true chariot is so light that an empty one can be lifted with one hand, and its wheels are so delicate that the chariot cannot be left standing for long. It has to be placed on a raised axle-rest when not in use to avoid deformation of the rims, or else the wheels need to be removed and stored separately from the body. It cannot be used to haul anything heavy or bulky.[95] It can hold two men at most,[96] and can barely hold those two—in all cases one must be the driver, and in nearly all historical cases the other person was an archer. Chariots thus had no practical use other than warfare, hunting, and, eventually, parades.

The chariot was designed to go fast, to carry its occupants into battle at high speed, so it was intended to be used with horses, the only domesticated animals capable of pulling it at high speed. Because cavalry had not yet been invented, there was nothing more frightening to an enemy than to face warriors traveling faster than anyone could imagine while shooting a constant stream of deadly arrows as they passed. This made the chariot the superweapon of the day.

By contrast, the earliest known vehicle, invented several thousand years previously, was incredibly heavy and slow. Its four wheels were made of solid wood sliced from tree trunks (evidently an artifact of the earlier use of solid tree trunks themselves as wheel-axle units). These wagons could only be pulled by teams of oxen, so they moved at a speed slower than that of walking cattle, which is slower than a human normally walks. The only thing such a vehicle was good for, practically speaking, was transporting heavy or

---

[94] Simply constructing a chariot involved many specialized crafts, most importantly, knowledge of the design and how to make it actually work. A chariot has spoked wheels and is practically the opposite of an oxcart. It is not even related closely to early two-wheeled oxcarts, which have a strikingly different design and the same drawbacks as the four-wheeled oxcart.

[95] Cf. Littauer and Crouwel (2002). Thus, *pace* Bryce (2002), chariots could not have been used to transport household goods in time of peace.

[96] Later, some chariots were enlarged and strengthened to hold three or even four men (Littauer and Crouwel 2002). These vehicles must have been slower and less maneuverable than the two-man chariot, and more like battle wagons.

bulky things, and that is exactly how such wagons continued to be used down to modern times.[97]

Yet the fact that a human sat or stood on the wagon to direct its course suggested power. The wagon became a symbol of royal majesty, and kings paraded slowly and majestically past their people in fancy oxcarts. The other peoples of the ancient Near East and vicinity very quickly learned about the oxcart and copied it and its uses. The Proto-Indo-Europeans, with their plentiful cattle, were no exception. The royal oxcart remained a symbol of kingship throughout the Indo-European world into the Middle Ages. The chariot did not replace it in this function, although the heroic attributes of chariot warriors became attributes of rulers when they had to become warriors and fight from chariots to defend their thrones against foreign kings who used chariots in warfare.

The physical and linguistic evidence, as well as most of the circumstantial evidence, points to the late Indo-Europeans as the inventors or perfectors of the chariot. The earliest known true, practical, war chariots have been found in the area of Transcaucasia directly to the east of the lands of the Hittites and Mitanni, who were the earliest known users of chariots in war.[98] The Egyptians were still importing chariots from Transcaucasia even in the Late Bronze Age. It is highly unlikely that the chariot has a non-Indo-European origin in the ancient civilizations of the Fertile Crescent, but in any case the identity and location of the domesticators of the horse and the inventors of the chariot are not really significant. What matters is that Indo-European peoples were the first to use the combination, the war chariot, effectively in war. They appeared along with it in Greece, the ancient Near East, India, and China between the seventeenth and fifteenth centuries BC. Before Indo-Europeans are known to have appeared in the ancient Near East, there is no evidence that true horse-drawn chariots were used in war there or anywhere else.

---

[97] Their use is regularly listed as an option in Pegolotti's (1936) manual for Silk Road merchants in the late Mongol period. He also records how much each form of transport could carry and how long each took to traverse a given leg of his itinerary.

[98] The archaeological connection of the Mycenaean Greek culture of the Shaft Graves with the culture of the North Caucasus Steppe explains the Greeks' early possession of chariots as well; see above.

THE CHARIOT WARRIORS

There is no reason to believe that any Indo-European speakers went any-where out of their homeland in Central Eurasia before about 2000 BC, and when the migrations began, they did not happen in isolation. Archaeology has shown that in every location in Eurasia where Indo-European daughter languages have come to be spoken, modern humans had already settled there long beforehand, with the sole exception of the Tarim Basin, the final destination of the people who are known to us as the Tokharians. Yet the Tokharians first migrated into the intervening regions, which were already inhabited by other peoples, before eventually moving on to the Tarim re-gion. No known early Indo-European people thus expanded into a linguis-tic and cultural vacuum in Eurasia; each had to deal with preexisting local inhabitants.

No evidence has been found for a frontal assault invasion of any part of Eurasia by Indo-Europeans. The reason is that they undoubtedly did not ac-complish their conquests that way. Yet they fought with their neighbors, as do all humans, whatever their culture. And in their conflicts with periph-eral peoples, the Central Eurasians used a new weapon, the chariot, which until then had not been used in warfare.[99]

The chariot was such a sophisticated, highly tuned machine, it was ex-tremely expensive to build or buy, to train its horses and drivers, and to main-tain. Its users had to be experts. Indo-European peoples of the second wave became the world's first experts in the maintenance and use of chariots and chariot horses, and they were the first to use them successfully in war. The unfamiliarity of non-Indo-European peoples of the ancient Near East with domesticated horses,[100] let alone in connection with chariots, is well known from textual evidence of different kinds until long after the second-wave peo-ples had already used them in war all across the ancient Near East.[101]

The ancient Near Eastern kingdoms, however, were highly organized, and many were literate; they did not take the Indo-European migrations

---

[99] Van de Mieroop (2004: 117).

[100] See the citations collected by Drews (1988: 74 et seq.).

[101] The same was clearly true of the Chinese chariot. As Barbieri-Low (2000: 47) and other spe-cialists have pointed out, the horse-drawn chariot was far too complicated a piece of machin-ery for uninitiates to operate, let alone copy.

into their territories lying down. Because they did not have chariots and the horses specially trained to pull them, or specially trained drivers to drive them and warriors who knew how to fight from them, at the beginning of this confrontation their only way of fighting against the Indo-European chariot warriors was to hire some of the same people to fight on their behalf against the other Indo-Europeans. The result of this practice was to prolong the Indo-European monopoly on expertise relating to horses and chariots. Although our primary evidence for the introduction of the chariot into China is archaeological,[102] it was undoubtedly accomplished in exactly the same way.

Eventually, the non-Indo-Europeans of the ancient Near East did acquire the skills involved in raising and training horses and in using chariots, if not in building them (the best-preserved Bronze Age chariot, from an Egyptian tomb, is constructed of materials from Transcaucasia, and was probably built there). The most detailed and best-preserved artistic depiction of the use of chariots in warfare is late, from an Egyptian wall relief celebrating Rameses II's self-proclaimed defeat of the Hittites at the battle of Kadesh in Syria in 1274 BC.[103] Yet it is certain that the Egyptians got the chariot, and learned how to use it, from non-Egyptians. Similarly, the Mesopotamians eventually overcame their fear of horses and chariots and adopted them for warfare, as attested by historical accounts as well as by later Assyrian wall reliefs and other artistic representations.[104]

The chariot became obsolete—as a war machine—in the Near East when the Sea Peoples and others participating in the destruction that ended the Bronze Age learned how to use javelins thrown by running warriors to disable horses, chariots, and charioteers.[105] Nevertheless, the vehicles long continued to be used for racing, and even in warfare, though usually not as archery platforms but as prestige vehicles for generals, great warriors, and other leaders. Although they were eventually replaced more or less com-

---

[102] See endnote 46 for some of the linguistic evidence.

[103] The battle was evidently a draw, but the Hittites, led by King Muwatalli, were the ultimate victors. On the battle and its aftermath, see Bryce (2005: 234–241).

[104] The chariot seems to have been too good an invention to completely abandon. Long after it had lost its usefulness as a weapon, it was still used as a military transport for high-ranking warriors, or as a military command post, as a parade vehicle for generals and kings, and for racing.

[105] Drews (2004).

pletely by horse riding, chariots continued to be used in places in Central Eurasia into late medieval times for rituals involving the imperial cultus, even in places where they had not been actually driven for many hundreds of years.[106]

---

[106] In Tibet, where vehicles were largely unknown until modern times, the deceased emperor was paraded around in a wagon before he was buried (Walter forthcoming), exactly like the deceased Scythian ruler. See Rolle (1989: 24–25) for discussion and a photograph of a Scythian funeral wagon being excavated. Benedict the Pole, who visited the camp of the Mongol khan Batu in 1245, says he saw "a chariot bearing a gold statue of the emperor, which it is their custom to worship." A similar object was seen by Carpini at the court of Güyüg in Mongolia (Allsen 1997: 62).

2

The Royal Scythians

τὸν ἱππευτάν τ' Ἀμαζόνων στρατὸν
Μαιῶτιν ἀμφὶ πολυπόταμον
ἔβα δι' ἄξεινον οἶδμα λίμνας,
τίν' οὐκ ἀφ' Ἑλλανίας
ἄγορον ἀλίσας φίλων,
κόρας Ἀρείας πέπλων
χρυσεόστολον φάρος,
ζωστῆρος ὀλεθρίους ἄγρας.
     — Εὐριπίδης, Ἡρακλῆς[1]

> Against the mounted army of the Amazons
>   on both sides of many-streamed Maeotis
> He coursed through the Sea, hostile swelling of water,
>   having mustered a host of friends
> From all over the lands of Hellas
>   to capture the gold-embroidered robe,
> The tunic of the martial maiden:
>   a deadly hunt for a war-belt.[2]
>   —Euripides, *Heracles*

The First Steppe Empire and Creation of the Silk Road

With the perfection of equestrian skills and development of the techniques and life-style of mounted horse nomadism around the beginning of the first millennium BC,[3] *the steppe zone core of Central Eurasia belonged to the Northern Iranians. In the middle of the millennium, the Scythians, the first historically well-known pastoral nomadic nation, migrated into the Western Steppe and established themselves there as a major power. Other steppe Iranians migrated eastward as far as China.*[4]

---

[1] Euripides, *Heracles*, Greek edition by Gilbert Murray (http://www.perseus.tufts.edu/cgi-bin/ptext?lookup-Eur.+Her. +408). My rendering is a little free, partly due to the crux in the text, for which various solutions have been proposed.

[2] Sarmatian women warriors (who seem to have been the inspiration for the Amazons), like Scythian and Sarmatian male warriors, had heavy iron-armored fighting belts, as did the early Greeks themselves. See Rolle (1989). The "gold-embroidered robe" is also Central Eurasian.

[3] Di Cosmo (2002a: 21–24).

[4] Large areas of Siberia, deep into Mongolia, were anthropologically Europoid in High Antiquity, and only gradually became Mongolic during the first millennium BC, the turning point

While the Scythians are best known as fierce warriors, their greatest accomplishment was the development of a trade system, described by Herodotus and other early Greek writers, that linked Greece, Persia, and the lands to the east and made the Scythians immensely wealthy. Their motivation was not greed, as historians from Antiquity up to the present have often attributed to Central Eurasians. From later periods about which more is known, it is clear that a major driving force behind their interest in trade was the need to support their sociopolitical infrastructure, which was built around the person of the ruler and his comitatus, or oath-sworn guard corps, whose members numbered in the thousands. A bustling land-based international commerce developed in Central Eurasia as a direct result of the trade interests of the Scythians, Sogdians, Hsiung-nu, and other early Central Eurasians. These interests are explicitly mentioned in the early Greek and Chinese sources. Although some long-distance trade had existed for millennia, it only became a significant economic force under the Scythians and other steppe Iranians and their successors. Because the Central Eurasians traded with people on their borders whoever they were, they traded with the civilizations of Europe, the Near East, South Asia and East Asia and indirectly connected the peripheral cultures to each other through Central Eurasia.

During the heyday of Scythian power, the peripheral city-state cultures of High Antiquity also reached their apogee. The fact that the classic philosophical works in the ancient Greek, Indic, and Chinese languages were produced at about the same time has long intrigued scholars, suggesting the possibility that there was some interchange of ideas among these cultures already in that period. The existence of Central Eurasian philosophers has generally been overlooked.

The Scythians' empire and trade network in the Western Steppe constituted a template for subsequent, increasingly powerful states based in Central Eurasia. The growth in wealth and power of Central Eurasians, and their increasing contact with peripheral cultures, led to invasions by peripheral states—usually justified by claims that the Central Eurasians had invaded them first. The earliest known invasions are by the Chou Dynasty Chinese, who defeated the people of Kuei-fang in two battles in 979 BC and captured

being around the fifth or fourth century BC (Rolle 1989: 56); Eastern Central Asia (East Turkistan) remained Europoid, and Indo-European in language, until late in the first millennium AD. On the early peoples of the Eastern Steppe, most of whom have not yet been identified ethnolinguistically, see Di Cosmo (2002a).

more than 13,000 people, including four chiefs (who were executed) and much booty.[5] The Chinese repeatedly invaded the Eastern Steppe at every opportunity from then on[6] down to modern times. The Achaemenid Persians under Darius conquered Bactria and Sogdiana and then invaded Scythia in circa 514–512 BC. The Macedonians and Greeks under Alexander invaded Central Asia in the late fourth century BC. The latter two conquests had very strong repercussions for the cultures of Central Asia.

Iranian State Formation in Central Eurasia and Iran

The Iranian domination of Central Eurasia must have begun before circa 1600 BC, when the Group B Indo-Europeans appeared in upper Mesopotamia and the Greek Aegean, and members of the same group also moved into India and China. Although the earliest evidence for simple steppe nomadism goes back to the third millennium BC, perhaps as an adaptation to the fact that the region is climatically unsuited to intensive agriculture, on the basis of archaeology, as well as the earliest historical and linguistic evidence, it is now agreed that the *horse-mounted* pastoral nomadic life-style was developed by the Iranians of the steppe zone early in the first millennium BC.[7] While this does not precede the earliest clear evidence for horse riding by anyone anywhere, the steppe Iranians do seem to be the first people who took to riding as a normal activity, not something undertaken only by daredevils and acrobats.[8] Despite the polemics by specialists in the ancient Near East, it is unusually difficult to believe that the Indo-Europeans—who probably first domesticated the horse and in any case are the first people

---

[5] Di Cosmo (1999a: 919).

[6] Di Cosmo details the wars against the Ti, who were divided into White Ti (Pai Ti) in the west and Red Ti (Ch'ih Ti) in the east, and comments, "The most vicious wars against the Ti were those waged by the state of Chin, bent on a campaign of annihilation that eventually paid off in 594 and 593 B.C., with the destruction of several Ch'ih Ti groups. This attack probably took place in conjunction with an internal crisis of the Ti, as there is evidence of famine and political dissent among them" (Di Cosmo 1999a: 947–951; Romanization changed to the modified Wade-Giles system used in this book and Di Cosmo's 2002a book). He also notes an invasion of the White Ti in 530 BC recorded in the *Ch'un-ch'iu* (Di Cosmo 2002a: 97 et seq.); other sources claim that the Ti were subjugated by Chin in 541 BC. However, they continued to exist and periodically regained independence, struggling with the Chinese down to the mid-third century BC (Di Cosmo 1999a: 948, 951).

[7] Di Cosmo (2002a: 21–24).

[8] See the excellent treatment by Drews (2004).

known from ancient Near Eastern sources to be expert in the use of horses—
were the last to learn how to ride them. The first people who are known to
have relied nearly exclusively on the mounted archer in warfare were Central Eurasian Iranians, who for centuries maintained their superiority in
this kind of warfare.[9]

Persians are mentioned in ninth-century BC Assyrian sources,[10] but the
first solid, clear historical accounts of Iranian-speaking peoples are in connection with the Medes and Scythians a century later.

In the late eighth century BC the Medes, an Iranian people, established a
kingdom in and east of the Elburz Mountains of northwestern Iran. They
were major opponents of the Assyrians in the early seventh century, but at
that point the Cimmerians and the Scythians invaded Media and dominated or actually took control of the kingdom.[11]

The Scythians were a Northern (or "East") Iranian people. According to
Herodotus (born 484 BC), who actually visited the city of Olbia (located at
the mouth of the Bug River) and other places in Scythia,[12] they called themselves *Scoloti*. They were called *Saka* by the Persians and, in Assyrian, *Iškuzai*
or *Aškuzai*. All of these names represent the same underlying name as the
Greek form *Scytha-*, namely Northern Iranian *Skuδa 'archer'.[13] It is the name
of all of the Northern Iranian peoples living between the Greeks in the West
and the Chinese in the East.

The Cimmerians, a little-known steppe people thought to have been Iranians, entered the ancient Near East in the late eighth century BC, where
they defeated Urartu in 714 BC. They then attacked the Phrygians to the west

---

[9] Arguments to the contrary are highly doubtful. However, more archaeological work is needed to
settle the problem of the periodization of the development of mounted warfare in Central Eurasia.

[10] The earliest apparent historical reference to Iranians "occurs in the ninth century when in 835
BC the Assyrian king Shalmaneser received tribute from the twenty-seven tribes of the
Paršuwaš, which is generally thought to indicate the Persians" (*EIEC* 311). The earliest *poten-
tial* references to Indo-Iranians are in Shang Chinese accounts of wars with the Ch'iang
people and in references to the Chou Chinese and their Chiang allies. Although the name
Ch'iang/Chiang could be a transcription of a Tokharian word (see appendix B), it could also
be a blanket category label for foreigners skilled with war chariots. The dates and the connection with chariots both suggest they were Indo-Europeans, perhaps of Group B—which
would rule out Iranians.

[11] On the Cimmerians according to Herodotus, see endnote 50.

[12] Rolle (1989: 12–13).

[13] Ultimately from Proto-Indo-European *skud-o 'shooter, archer' (Szemerényi 1980: 17, 21). See
appendix B.

and destroyed their kingdom in around 696 BC, but were subsequently defeated by the Assyrian king Esarhaddon (r. 681–669 BC). Although the Cimmerians next defeated and killed the Lydian king, Gyges, in battle in 652, they were themselves crushed shortly afterward by the Scythians under their king Madúês[14] in the 630s. According to Herodotus, the Scythians "invaded Asia in their pursuit of the Cimmerians, and made an end of the power of the Medes, who were the rulers of Asia before the coming of the Scythians."[15] This account sounds remarkably similar to that of later Central Eurasian state-foundation conflicts, including that of the Hsiung-nu versus the *Tok^war, the Huns versus the Goths, and the Turks versus the Avars.

The Scythians were involved in wars all across the ancient Near East, from Anatolia to Egypt, usually (perhaps always) in alliance with the Assyrians or others. "In Mesopotamia, Syria, and Egypt, in the sites of the 7th to the beginning of the 6th centuries B.C., particularly in the defensive walls of towns, bronze arrowheads of the Scythian type have been found—the direct result of invasions and sieges." The Scythians also left their arrowheads in the clay walls of the northern Urartian fortress of Karmir-Blur (near Yerevan), which they destroyed.[16] Finally the Medes crushed the Scythians around 585 BC.[17] The surviving Scythians retreated back north.

The Medes subsequently joined with the Babylonians in a successful attack on Assyria that led to the destruction of the Assyrian Empire. Shortly before 585 BC, the Medes destroyed the remnants of the Urartian state to their northwest and extended their realm as far as western Anatolia and northern Syria,[18] but they were in turn conquered in 553 or 550 BC by the Persian leader Cyrus (r. 559–530), who absorbed the whole Median kingdom and essentially merged his realm with it, founding the Persian Empire.[19] Under Cyrus the Persians took Iran and Anatolia and, in 539, at-

[14] In Herodotus, Μαδύης (r. 645–615?), son of Πρωτοθύης (Bartatua, r. 675–645?).

[15] Godley (1972: 198–199); cf. Rawlinson (1992: 58–59, 295).

[16] Melyukova (1990: 100). One Scythian alliance with the Assyrians is known in some detail; see Rolle (1989: 71–72).

[17] Szemerényi (1980: 6).

[18] Van de Mieroop (2004: 254–257).

[19] Unlike the Medes, who apparently did not develop a writing system for their own language or maintain archives in any other language, the Persians used Imperial Aramaic, a Semitic literary language, and Elamite, another local Near Eastern language. Under Darius, they also developed an alphabetic cuneiform writing system for their own language, Old Persian, and used it for monumental inscriptions. This Western Iranian language is quite different from

tacked the Babylonians, defeating them and incorporating the entire Near East except for Egypt and Arabia into the empire. Cyrus then invaded Central Asia, where he died in battle in 530 or 529 against the Massagetae, a North Iranian people whose queen, following steppe custom, made a trophy out of his skull.[20]

The Western Steppe: The Scythians and Sarmatians

The Cimmerians, who the Greeks say were the inhabitants of the Pontic Steppe before the Scythians, are mentioned in Near Eastern sources before and during the Scythian period there but are otherwise little known. After their defeat by the Medes, the Scythians retreated back into the North Caucasus Steppe. Having acquired from the Medes, Urartians, Assyrians, and other peoples in the ancient Near East much wealth, knowledge about absolute monarchy, and experience in war, they used their skills to subjugate the people there—probably including their own Iranian relatives—and establish an empire that soon stretched across the entire Western Steppe north of the Black Sea, from the Caucasus west as far as the Danube. The western part of this territory included vast agricultural lands farmed by Thracians.

From their base in the steppe, the Scythians further developed a long-distance trade network, described by Herodotus, that they found already in place. With their discovery that the Greeks living in their colonial towns on the Black Sea coast—and as far away as Greece—would pay gold for grain, the Scythians began an extremely profitable business.[21] Their appetite for luxuries, especially gold, grew rapidly. The Scythian royal burials were filled with beautifully crafted golden treasures in the Scythian animal style, some of which escaped tomb robbers and now grace the museums of Russia and Ukraine. Because gold is not native to the area of Scythia, all of it was

---

the putatively earliest Iranian language, Avestan, which is not actually localizable in place or time but is strikingly similar to Vedic Sanskrit. See appendix A.

[20] Rolle (1989: 96).

[21] Strabo (Jones 1924: 242–243) goes on at some length about the productivity of the land cultivated by the Scythian farmers (the Georgi) and the fabulous amounts of grain shipped to Greece during the great famine (ca. 360 BC). He also mentions the Greek importation of salted fish from Maeotis (the Sea of Azov).

imported, mostly from great distances, including as far as the Altai Mountains, as archaeology has revealed.[22] This particular gold route thus constituted a considerable part of early east-west transcontinental trade.

As mentioned earlier, the Scythians' sociopolitical practices included the comitatus, the apparent ritual sacrifice of which in one instance is vividly described by Herodotus and has been confirmed to some extent by archaeology.[23]

The Scythian Empire is said by Herodotus to have consisted of several peoples,[24] of which he gives differing accounts. The national origin myth he relates purports to explain the division of the Scythians into three branches:[25]

> There appeared in this country, being then a desert, a man whose name was Targitaus. His parents, they say … were Zeus and a daughter of the river Borysthenes [the Dnieper]. Such (it is said) was Targitaus' lineage; and he had three sons, Lipoxaïs, Arpoxaïs, and *Skoloxaïs,[26] youngest of the three. In the time of their rule (so the story goes) there fell down from the sky into Scythia certain implements, all of gold, namely, a plough, a yoke, a sword, and a drinking cup.[27] The eldest of them, seeing this, came near with intent to take them; but the gold began to burn as he came, and he ceased from his essay; then the second approached, and the gold did again as before; when these two had been driven away by the burning of the gold, last came the youngest brother, and the burning was quenched at his approach; so he took the gold to his own house. At this his elder brothers saw how matters stood, and made over the whole royal power to the youngest.[28]

> Lipoxaïs, it is said, was the father of the Scythian clan called Auchatae; Arpoxaïs, the second brother, of those called Katiari and Traspians;

---

[22] Rolle (1989: 52–53).

[23] Taylor (2003) remarks about one tumulus within Scythia, "The recent re-excavation and analysis demonstrates the existence of complex rituals around the edge of the mound, with a further grave (1/84) and concentrations of horse bones that should perhaps be seen in connection with a final rite of closure (or incorporation), as Herodotus so clearly described."

[24] Or nations; for the terminology see note 46 in the prologue.

[25] Godley 1972: 202–205; cf. Rawlinson (1992: 296–297).

[26] The received text has *Coloxaïs*; see appendix B.

[27] Godley has "flask" here; I have substituted the usual translation 'cup'.

[28] See the discussion of this myth in the prologue.

the youngest, who was king, of those called Paralatae. All these together bear the name of Skoloti, after their king *Skoloxaïs; "Scythians" is a name given them by Greeks.[29]

The explanation of the four implements given by Herodotus is undoubtedly
mistaken, based on his own text. Despite the youngest son's possession of
the gold objects, the four implements clearly correspond to the four peoples
subsequently divided up among the three sons. They also correspond to
the occupations of the four Scythian peoples given below in his own text:
the plow for the Plowing Scythians, the yoke for the Husbandmen, and the
sword for the Royal Scythians, which leaves the drinking cup for the
Nomad Scythians.[30]

Herodotus and all other sources agree that the nation as a whole was
ruled by the Royal Scythians, the warriors who controlled most of the
wealth. They were "the largest and bravest of the Scythian tribes, which
looks upon all the other tribes in the light of slaves." Below them were the
Nomad Scythians, who were perhaps simply the nomadic Scythians who
did not belong to the royal clan; the Husbandmen, called Borysthenites by
the Greeks; and the Plowing Scythians, agriculturalists who grew grain "not
for their own use, but for sale." The localization of these peoples on Scythian
territory, though described by Herodotus, is not well established, but the
Crimea and the region to the west of it (southern Ukraine), where the rich
soil has remained highly productive down to the present day, was occupied
primarily by agriculturalists, while the eastern part, which is still largely
open grassland, was occupied by the pastoral nomads.

In addition, Herodotus describes a great number of other peoples, Scythian, part-Scythian, and non-Scythian, living within the Scythian realm,
such as "the Callippedae, who are Scythian Greeks, and beyond them another tribe called Alazones; these and the Callippidae, though in other matters they live like the Scythians, sow and eat corn, and onions, garlic, lentils,

---

[29] This passage has generated much confusion about the name and identity of the Scythians; see
appendix B.
[30] Legrand, citing Benveniste, says, "Ces objets sont les symboles des trois classes des sociétés
iraniennes; la coupe, de celle des prêtres; la sagaris,—une sorte de hache (. . .),—de celle des
guerriers; la charrue et la joug réunis (le joug servant à atteler la charrue), de celle des agricul-
teurs" (Legrand 1949: 50). Rolle (1989: 123) says, based on "written sources," that the Scythians
had three kings who ruled simultaneously, one of them being a primus inter pares. However,
the historical accounts of Scythian rulers, who present them very clearly as sole monarchs, do
not support this.

and millet. Above the Alazones dwell Scythian tillers of the land, who sow corn not for eating but for selling; north of these the Neuri; to the north of the Neuri the land is uninhabited as far as we know."[31] Archaeological studies indicate that some of these and perhaps other peoples in the Scythian realm were not Northern Iranian in culture but Thracian, and probably spoke Thracian or other non-Iranian languages.

Despite the factual complexity, theoretically Scythian society was divided into four peoples plus the ruler: an ideal organization typical of Central Eurasian states at least as late as the Mongol Empire. It is also notable that the dominant people considered all the others as their "slaves."[32] This view was shared by other peoples in Central Eurasia later on as well.

Herodotus[33] describes the Scythians as "pure nomads":

I praise not the Scythians in all respects, but in this greatest matter they have so devised that none who attacks them can escape, and none can catch them if they desire not to be found. For when men have no established cities or fortresses, but all are house-bearers and mounted archers, living not by tilling the soil but by cattle-rearing and carrying their dwellings on waggons,[34] how should these not be invincible and unapproachable? This invention they have made in a land which suits their purpose and has rivers which are their allies; for their country is level and grassy and well watered and rivers run through it not much less in number than the canals of Egypt.

The account of Herodotus is the earliest surviving narrative description of any Central Eurasian nomadic people in any source, but already it contains elements of the misleading stereotype that has dominated histories of Cen-

[31] Godley (1972: 216–219); cf. Rawlinson (1992: 302).
[32] The sole English term 'slave' for what was a complex hierarchy—most of the members of which would not be considered slaves by English speakers—is loaded with early modern connotations. See Beckwith (1984a).
[33] Godley (1972: 241–242); cf. Rawlinson (1992: 314–315).
[34] Strabo (Jones 1924: 222–223, 242–243) remarks somewhat later that the tents "on the wagons in which they spend their lives" were made of felt. They had huge numbers of them; a Scythian who had only one was considered poor; a rich man might have eighty wagons. They were mostly pulled by oxen and moved at the slow speed of these grazing animals. For further discussion and pictures showing archaeologically recovered clay models (apparently toys) of these tent-wagons, see Rolle (1989: 114–115). Strabo also emphasizes that the nomads lived on the milk, meat, and cheese from their herds, "from time to time moving to other places that have grass." He explicitly notes that although they were warriors, the nomads were basically peaceful and only went to war when absolutely necessary. See the epilogue.

tral Eurasians down to the present day. Herodotus, like other peripheral culture authors of his time and later, was fascinated by nomadism. He does not say much about the extensive agriculture that went on in the Scythian realm. He also neglects to explain why the Scythians maintained the cities he comments on, in particular Gelonus, which was located at the northern edge of the steppe in the territory of the Budini, another of the many "Scythian nations" he describes:

The Budini are a great and numerous nation; the eyes of all of them are very bright, and they are red-haired. They have a city built of wood, called Gelonus. The wall of it is thirty furlongs [stadia] in length on each side of the city; this wall is high and all of wood; and their houses are wooden, and their temples; for there are among them temples of Greek gods, furnished in Greek fashion with images and altars and shrines of wood; and they honour Dionysus every two years with festivals and revels. For the Geloni are by their origin Greeks, who left their trading ports to settle among the Budini; and they speak a language half Greek and half Scythian. But the Budini speak not the same language as the Geloni, nor is their manner of life the same. The Budini are native to the country; they are nomads, and the only people in these parts that eat fir-cones; the Geloni are tillers of the soil, eating grain and possessing gardens; they are wholly unlike the Budini in form and in complexion. Yet the Greeks call the Budini too Geloni; but this is wrong. All their country is thickly wooded with every kind of tree; in the depths of the forests there is a great and wide lake and marsh surrounded by reeds; otters are caught in it, and beavers.[35]

The city of Gelonus, or one more or less exactly like it, has been excavated by archaeologists at Belsk (Bilsk), on the northern edge of the steppe. It is a forty-square-kilometer settlement, and "the commanding ramparts [which are 20.5 miles long][36] and remarkable extent of the site suggest a place of great importance. Strategically situated on the exact boundary of the steppe and forest-steppe, Gelonus could have controlled trade from

---

[35] Godley (1972: 308–309); cf. Rawlinson (1992: 339). For Godley's "ruddy" (referring to the Budini's hair) I have substituted "red-haired"; for his "native to the soil" I have substituted "native to the country."

[36] Rolle (1989: 119).

north to south. The presence of craft workshops and large amounts of imported Greek pottery, dating from the fifth and fourth centuries BC, suggest that it did."[37]

The attention of the Persians and Greeks was surely drawn by the prosperity of the Scythians, not their martial prowess, which would obviously have been a good reason for *not* invading them. It was hardly any desire for vengeance that induced Darius to consider the conquest of Scythia, as Herodotus claims, but the belief that Scythia was worth conquering.

Darius (r. 521–486) usurped the throne during the civil war between Cyrus's successor Cambyses and his brother. He greatly expanded the frontiers of the Persian Empire to include Egypt in the southwest, northwestern India in the southeast, and Central Asia in the northeast. He met resistance in the north from the steppe Iranians—the Sakas and Scythians[38]—and in the west from the Greeks. After defeating the Sakas or "Asian Scythians," and capturing their king, Skuka, in 520–519 BC,[39] he decided, against the advice of his counselors, to invade Scythia, home of the European Scythians, and subjugate it. Darius prepared by having a bridge of boats built across the Bosphorus to Thrace and ordered his Ionian Greek subjects to sail to the Danube and up the river to the point above where the mouths separate, and bridge it for him.

In 513–512 BC Darius marched a huge army—according to Herodotus, 700,000 men strong—across the Bosphorus and through Thrace, which he subdued as he went, until he reached the Danube.[40] He then crossed the river and marched eastward into Scythia, ordering his Ionian forces to guard the bridge until he returned. The Persians chased the Scythians across the empty steppe, seeking to do battle with them, but the Scythians used the classic Central Eurasian guerrilla warfare technique of feinting and withdrawing,[41] which forced the Persians to march deeper and deeper into

---

[37] Taylor (2003); cf. Rolle (1989: 117–122) on this and other Scythian urban sites.

[38] The Persians referred to all Northern Iranian peoples, including the Scythians, as *Saka* (q.v. appendix B). Modern scholars have mostly used the name Saka to refer to Iranians of the Eastern Steppe and Tarim Basin. I have usually followed this practice.

[39] Rolle (1989: 7).

[40] The dates and locations of the campaign(s) are disputed. According to Melyukova (1990: 101), the Persians crossed the Don and entered the territory of the Sarmatians, but this would seem to be unlikely on the basis of the account by Herodotus.

[41] It is now well known that the Scythians and other Central Eurasian steppe peoples wore armor in battle. It is attested both literarily and archaeologically. See Rolle (1989) for discussion and numerous pictures of Scythian armor.

Scythian lands, where they found no cities to conquer and no supplies to commandeer. In frustration, Darius sent a message to the ruler of the Scythians, Idanthyrsus, demanding that he stand and fight or simply surrender. The Scythian replied, according to Herodotus:

> It is thus with me, Persian: I have never fled for fear of any man, nor do I now flee from you; this that I have done is no new thing or other than my practice in peace. But as to the reason why I do not straightway fight with you, this too I will tell you. For we Scythians have no towns or planted lands, that we might meet you the sooner in battle, fearing lest the one be taken or the other wasted. But if nothing will serve you but fighting straightway, we have the graves of our fathers; come, find these and essay to destroy them; then shall you know whether we will fight you for those graves or no. Till then we will not join battle unless we think it good.[42]

Darius ended up retreating, having built a few fortresses in his progress across Scythia. He had accomplished nothing except the further strengthening of the Scythians' reputation as a great warrior nation.

The wars of Darius and his successors against the Greeks continued down to the time of the Macedonian prince Alexander the Great. After subduing the Levant and Egypt, Alexander turned to the Persian Empire in 334 BC. He finally defeated Darius III (r. 336–331 BC) and after the latter's death in 330 BC in Central Asia, Alexander had himself proclaimed Persian emperor. He had conquered the entire Persian Empire, including Bactria and Sogdiana. To cement his control of the Central Asian region, he married Roxana (Roxane), a Bactrian noblewoman, in 327.

Alexander does not seem to have planned an invasion of Scythia, perhaps due to the military difficulties involved. His army consisted largely of highly trained Macedonian and Greek foot soldiers, whose phalanx formation was difficult for any enemy to overcome, but his cavalry was small. The only way to subdue a fully mobile nomadic nation was with a full-sized nomadic-style cavalry. His limited mounted forces could not have taken on a large nomadic army fighting in its home territory. Despite the undoubted advantage that his cavalry gave him in flanking movements in sedentary Near Eastern battles, Alexander would have faced the same problem Darius encountered.

[42] Godley (1972: 326–328); cf. Rawlinson (1992: 346–347).

The successors of the Scythians, the Sarmatians (in Greek, Σαυρομάται 'Sauromatians'), spoke a Northern Iranian language akin to Scythian. They were notable for the great prominence of women in general and especially for the presence among them of women warriors. According to Herodotus they were called *Oiorpata* 'man slayers' in the Scythian language.[43] The unusual status of women, which was markedly different from the extremely androcentric Scythian and Greek cultures, was noticed by Herodotus and has received solid confirmation by archaeology. Although the tale he recounts about the Sarmatians' origin as a cross of Scythian boys and Amazon women is probably just an entertaining story, it is likely that the Greek legends about the race of Amazons are based on the real-life Sarmatian women warriors. In the last couple of centuries BC, the Sarmatians came into contact, and conflict, with the Romans.

The Eastern Steppe: The Hsiung-nu

At the eastern end of the steppe zone, in what is now Mongolia, former Inner Mongolia, and the eastern Tarim Basin, the nomadic-dominant form of the Central Eurasian Culture Complex became an established life-style between the eighth and seventh centuries BC,[44] chronologically parallel to its establishment in the Western Steppe. Archaeologists have established a solid chronology, confirmed by dendrochronology, for the spread of this Early Iron Age culture across the steppe zone of Central Eurasia from the Western Steppe north of the Black Sea to the eastern Altai region of the Mongolian Plateau.[45] Archaeology has also confirmed the conclusions of philologists and historians on the ethnolinguistic identity of the early peoples of the Eastern Steppe zone. The dominant people in the western part of it, from the Altai of western Mongolia[46] south through the Kroraina area around the Lop Nor to the Ch'i-lien Mountains, the northern outliers of the Tibetan Pla-

---

[43] Godley (1972: 310–311); Herodotus explains that "in Scythian a man is *oior* and to kill is *pata*." Scythian *oior* (the Greek transcription perhaps representing a Scythian [wior]) is an obvious cognate of Avestan *vīra* 'man; human', Sanskrit *vīrá*- 'hero; man; husband', Latin *vir* 'man', Old English *wer* 'man, husband', Gothic *waír* 'man', etc., all from Proto-Indo-European *wīr-or *wi-ro- 'man' (*EIEC* 366).

[44] Di Cosmo (2002a: 57, 65, 71).

[45] Di Cosmo (2002a: 36).

[46] Di Cosmo (2002a: 39).

teau, were Caucasoid in race; those in the northern region seem to have spoken North Iranian "Saka" languages or dialects, while those in the Kroraina area spoke Tokharian languages or dialects. The dominant peoples in the eastern part, including the central and eastern Mongolian Plateau, Inner Mongolia, and southwestern Manchuria, were racially Mongoloid peoples who spoke unknown languages.[47] The Chinese sources mention that the cities near the northern frontier of the Chinese cultural zone were involved in trade with the foreign peoples.

The Chinese invaded the Ti in the late seventh and early sixth centuries, but little more is known about them until the end of the Warring States period, when King Wu-ling (r. 325–299 BC) of the northern state of Chao ordered his people to adopt nomadic-style clothing and customs and to practice horsemanship.[48] He defeated the Central Eurasian peoples known as the Lin Hu[49] and Loufan and built a great wall from Tai at the foot of the Yin Shan (the mountain range on the north side of the great bend of the Yellow River) to Kao-ch'üeh, where he built the commanderies of Yün-chung, Yen-men, and Tai.[50] After defeating Chung-shan in 295 BC, Chao enclosed the entire great bend of the Yellow River in a ring of fortifications. The kingdom thus substantially expanded its territory and established control over the southern part of the Eastern Steppe, including the Ordos, the best pasturelands in the region.

Sometime shortly before the state of Ch'in conquered the last of the post–Chou Dynasty warring kingdoms and unified the Central States under the Ch'in Dynasty in 221 BC, the people who ruled the Eastern Steppe, including the Ordos, were known as the Hsiung-nu. The Ch'in general Meng T'ien attacked and crushed them in 215 BC, and the First Emperor of Ch'in built the Great Wall. He conscripted hundreds of thousands of Chinese, who linked together the many old walls built against each other and against their neighbors by the Chao, other Chinese, and non-Chinese. The wall and line of fortifications stretched from Lin-t'ao in Kansu to Liao-tung and enclosed the entire Yellow River valley, including the former Hsiung-nu homeland. The Hsiung-nu, under their first known leader and apparent founder, T'ou-man

---

[47] Di Cosmo (2002a: 39, 163–166).

[48] See the extensive discussion in Di Cosmo (2002a: 134–138). Other than the adoption of trousers, however, the perennial Chinese weakness with respect to horses and cavalry indicates that the king did not revolutionize China's military in the long run.

[49] This is one of the earliest datable uses of *Hu*, a term for foreigners of the north and west that seems originally to have been an ethnonym but became quasi-generic quite early.

[50] Di Cosmo (1999a: 961).

(*TumeN), fled north beyond the frontier into the Mongolian Plateau.[51] It is likely that his son, Mo-tun, rose to power in 209 BC as a consequence of this devastating defeat.[52]

The Hsiung-nu have often been identified with the Huns of Europe, despite the gap of several centuries between the periods in which the two flourished and the lack of any known direct connection.[53] Although some clever arguments have been made, mostly based on the apparent similarity of the names,[54] one of the basic problems is that their name, which is now pronounced Hsiung-nu in modern Mandarin Chinese, from Middle Chinese *χoŋnu or *χⁱoŋnu,[55] must have been pronounced quite differently at the time the Chinese on the northern frontier first learned of this people and transcribed their name. Among other possibilities, the name could correspond to a form of the name of the Northern Iranians,[56] eastern forms of which—Saka, Sakla, and so forth—are recorded in several guises in Chinese[57] accounts about a century younger[58] than the first references to the Hsiung-nu. Whatever the Hsiung-nu ended up becoming by the fall of the Hsiung-nu Empire, it is probable that they either learned the Iranian nomadic model by serving for a time as subjects of an Iranian steppe zone people, as in the First Story

---

[51] Di Cosmo (2002a: 174–176, 186–187).

[52] Yü (1990: 120). The overthrow of T'ou-man (*TumeN) took place only six years after his defeat by Meng T'ien. The actual history of Mo-tun's rise to power seems unlikely to have resembled the fascinating but largely legendary story related in the prologue, though his comitatus—his highly trained, personally loyal bodyguard—was certainly involved, as noted by Di Cosmo (2002a: 186).

[53] Although some tantalizing arguments have been made on the basis of archaeological artifacts, they do not solve the severe chronological and other problems.

[54] On the debate over the origins of the Hsiung-nu and their putative historical connection with the Huns, see endnote 51.

[55] Pulleyblank (1991: 346, 227) reconstructs 匈奴 Middle Chinese *χuawŋnɔ. Baxter (1992: 798, 779) has *χⁱowŋnu (based on homophones he cites), but Pulleyblank's reconstruction better reflects the "spellings" in the Ch'ieh-yün. As for Modern Standard Chinese (Mandarin), the name is spelled xiōngnú in the pinyin romanization system, but actually it is pronounced [ɕⁱuŋnu].

[56] The transcription of the name Hsiung-nu is early and was certainly done via an Old Chinese frontier dialect, so that the original *s- initial was probably transcribed before the change of Old Chinese *s- to *χ-. For details, see endnote 52.

[57] See appendix B. For forms of the name Saka in eastern Eurasia, see endnote 53.

[58] They evidently go back to the reports of the envoy and explorer Chang Ch'ien, who was sent to find the Yüeh-chih (*Tokʷar) in 139–138 BC but was caught and detained on the way there and again on the way back. He only escaped back to China in 126 BC, along with his Hsiung-nu wife and his former slave. For a translation of the account of his journey in the Shih chi, see Watson (1961, II: 264 et seq.).

model (the most likely scenario), or they included an Iranian component when they started out, and like many other peoples in Central Eurasia, such as the Tibetans, are known by a foreign name applied by others to them.[59]

The Ch'in conquest was short-lived. The Ch'in Dynasty collapsed shortly after the death of the First Emperor, and during the following civil war in China the conscripts who had been sent to the frontier abandoned their posts and returned home. The Hsiung-nu then returned to their homeland in the Ordos.

Chinese knowledge of the Eastern Steppe greatly increased during the following Han Dynasty, especially under the reign of Emperor Wu (r. 140–87 BC), who is responsible for the long-lasting expansion of the Chinese Empire into Central Eurasia.

Intellectual Development in Classical Antiquity

In the fifth and fourth centuries BC, at the same time as the emergence of the Silk Road and the early nomad states of Central Eurasia, the peripheral city-state cultures of High Antiquity reached their apogee and produced the classic philosophical and other literary works in the ancient Greek, Indic, and Chinese languages. Socrates (469–399 BC), Plato (427–347 BC), and Aristotle (384–322 BC) were—very roughly—the contemporaries of Gautama Buddha (perhaps fl. ca. 500 BC), Pāṇini (perhaps fifth century BC),[60] and Kauṭilya (fl. ca. 321–296 BC)[61] as well as Confucius (ca. 550–480 BC),[62] Lao-tzu (perhaps late fifth century BC), and Chuang Tzu (fourth century BC).[63] The idea of any cross-fertilization among these three cultures has generally been dismissed out of hand by historians, largely because it has been extremely difficult to demonstrate many *specific* borrowings back and forth. Nevertheless, there are some, and it must furthermore be considered odd if such distant areas as East Asia and the Aegean—in which the people evidently knew little

---

[59] The problem of the ethnolinguistic affiliation of the Hsiung-nu is still very far from settled.

[60] Coward and Kunjunni Raja (1990: 4).

[61] Bilimoria (1998: 220–222).

[62] This is my estimate, based on the discussion of his chronology given by E. Bruce Brooks (http://www.umass.edu/wsp/results/dates/confucius.html).

[63] Most of these dates are disputed. I have taken the unnoted dates from Audi (1999). Most of the texts involved are accretional, so only parts of them could have been composed by their nominal authors.

more about each other at the time than their predecessors had a millennium earlier when they acquired literacy—should suddenly have started arguing not only about their actual governments but about *government* in general, asking questions about their existence, and talking about logic and looking into the way the human mind works. Surely the contrast with the previous millennium is striking. That was a period when questions were asked about uncertainties such as whether the king's wife would conceive or not, whether the gods would look down with favor upon the sacrifices offered to them, or whether the next kingdom could be safely attacked or not. The asking of questions *about the questions themselves* was new, and it is difficult to find the precedents or motivation for the development in each case.

The three areas had some political features in common—notably, each culture was shared among a large number of small states, none of which could completely dominate the others. They also shared, indirectly, the effects of the increase in world trade brought about by the development of the nomadic empires. Growth of commerce virtually always entails growth of a commercial class and the spread of foreign ideas. As noted above, it has not yet been demonstrated that there was any significant direct intellectual relationship between early China and early Greece (or India). This is not surprising, because there seems not to have been any direct connection of any kind between those two cultures, and it is quite possible that none will ever be found. Yet the question must be asked: how did the philosophical period of Classical Antiquity happen? It would seem extremely unlikely that three distant cultures should virtually simultaneously have developed similar intellectual interests and have come up with similar answers in some instances. If a positive solution to this problem is conceivable, it must involve Central Eurasia.

The only means of contact among those three cultures at that time in history was overland. As shown throughout this book, however, Central Eurasia was not simply a conduit for goods to and from East Asia and Western Europe. It was an economy and world of its own, with many subregions, nations, states, and cultures. Confucius is said to have remarked that if a ruler has lost knowledge of good government, he should "study it among the foreign peoples of the four directions."[64] Alexander the Great's conquest and colonization of

---

[64] According to the *Tso-chuan*, in the seventeenth year of the Duke of Chao 昭 (Yang 1990: 1389). The whole quote runs: 吾聞之，天子失官，學在四夷. Although the standard *Tso-chuan* edition I cite here, by Yang Po-chün, has a doubled 官 character (i.e., his text has 吾聞之，天子失官，官學在四夷), which he supports with citations of early texts and commentaries,

Bactria in the fourth century BC introduced Greek culture, including Greek philosophy, into the heart of Central Asia. A recent careful study has shown that specific elements derived from the Greek philosophical tradition first appear in Chinese literature shortly after Alexander's conquest.[65]

Early Classical Greece, India, and China were at the time still merely small appendages outside the vast territory of Central Eurasian culture, which bordered on all three of them. In the sixth and early fifth centuries BC, more or less the entire northern steppe zone, and much of the southern, Central Asian zone, was Iranian-speaking. There were at least two important philosophers or religious thinkers from early Central Eurasia. Anacharsis the Scythian had a Greek mother and spoke and wrote Greek. According to Diogenes Laertius, in the 47th Olympiad (591–588 BC) he traveled to Greece, where he became well known for his abstemiousness and pithy remarks.[66] He was counted as one of the Seven Sages of Antiquity by the Greeks and is considered to be one of the early Cynics.[67] The famous Demosthenes, grandson of a rich Scythian woman, was often accused of being a *barbarian*.[68] Zoroaster, the founder of Zorastrianism, is widely believed to have come from the area of Khwarizmia, though some other Central Eurasian region inhabited by pastoral Iranians is perhaps just as likely. His dates are unknown, but he could well have been a contemporary of Confucius and Buddha.[69] Were there others? Did the Classical philosophers of the peripheral cultures reflect not only their own ideas but those of the philosophers of Central Eurasian Indo-Iranian peoples? According to one ancient Chinese text, Confucius believed the Central Eurasians had the answers, and some of the Greeks seem to have had similar opinions. Is there any basis for such opinions? Do the social and religious ideas of Central Eurasians, including the importance of friendship and the beliefs behind the comitatus, imply philosophical positions or interests, such as the quest for happiness, or the perfect state?

---

the result is an extremely odd *lectio difficilior* with irregular scansion. Yang's edition does not tell us which other versions of the text had or have only *one* 官; nor, so far as I noticed, does he say what any of these texts' positions are on the stemma. Once again, the lack of a true *critical edition* leaves us in the dark. For an example of a critical edition of a Chinese text—the only one I have ever seen—see the model work by Thompson (1979), and note especially Thompson's remarks in his preface.

[65] Brooks (1999).

[66] Hicks (1980, I: 104–111).

[67] Cancik and Schneider (1996: 639).

[68] Rolle (1989: 13).

[69] On one problem with the "high" dates for him, see appendix A, on Avestan.

The Nomadic Form of the Central Eurasian Culture Complex

The rise, flourishing, and disappearance of the famous transcontinental commercial system known collectively as the Silk Road chronologically parallels, exactly, the rise of the Scythians, the flourishing of the independent Central Eurasian empires, and the destruction of the Junghars. In that two-millennium-long period, most of Central Eurasia proper was dominated by nomad-warrior-ruled states that depended primarily on trade in order to accumulate wealth, as attested by ancient and medieval sources in the languages surrounding Central Eurasia.

Trade was important for both nomadic and non-nomadic cultures, but it was critical for the nomadic states. The crucial nature of trade was not, however, because of the supposed poverty of the nomads.[70] Nomads were in general much better fed and led much easier, longer lives, than the inhabitants of the large agricultural states. There was a constant drain of people escaping from China into the realms of the Eastern Steppe, where they did not hesitate to proclaim the superiority of the nomadic life-style. Similarly, many Greeks and Romans joined the Huns and other Central Eurasian peoples, where they lived better and were treated better than they had been back home. Central Eurasian peoples knew that it was far more profitable to trade and tax than it was to raid and destroy. Historical examples of the latter activity are the exception rather than the rule and are usually a consequence of open war.

The reason trade was so important to the nomadic peoples seems rather to have been the necessity of supporting the ruler and his comitatus, the cost of which is attested by archaeological excavations and by historical descriptions of the wealth lavished on comitatus members across Central Eurasia from Antiquity onward. The ruler-comitatus relationship was the sociopolitical foundation stone of all states throughout Central Eurasia, whatever their life-style, until well into the Middle Ages. Without it, the ruler would not have been able to maintain himself on the throne in this life and would have been defenseless against his enemies in the next life. The sumptuous burials of Central Eurasian rulers from the Scythians through

---

[70] For example, Hildinger (2001) claims that "historically, nomads have lived in appalling poverty, at the very margin of life, and this poverty can be mitigated only by contact with settled peoples." The exact opposite was true, as is pointed out in ancient and medieval travelers' accounts, many of which have been translated into English.

the Mongols display their belief in the afterlife and desire to enjoy it the same way they had this life.

Both the Greeks, especially through the *History* of Herodotus and the accounts of Alexander's campaigns, and the Chinese, beginning with the reports of Chang Ch'ien at the time of Emperor Wu, provide fairly accurate descriptions of Central Eurasian cities. Herodotus tells us that the main city of Scythia, Gelonus, was thirty kilometers square and the commercial center of the Scythian trade network. The city of Bactra, later Balkh, the greatest urban center of Bactriana and seat of the Achaemenid satrap,[71] was taken by Alexander in 329–327 BC,[72] two centuries before its conquest by the Tokharians. He also took Maracanda (Samarkand, the main city of Sogdiana) in 329 BC and established his power as far as Ferghana. Between 139 and 122 BC Chang Ch'ien traveled across Eastern Central Asia and visited many cities, which he or his successors describe in some detail. All of the Central Asian cities depended primarily on irrigated agriculture in the valleys and alluvial fans of the Central Asian rivers, most of which begin in the mountains and end in the desert. Yet, despite their urbanity, the peoples there were just as warlike or non-warlike as the nomads—who were just as interested in trade as the urban peoples—and each of the great lords among both peoples maintained a comitatus. The ancient Chinese travelers to Sogdiana found it an intensely cultivated agricultural region with many cities and huge numbers of warriors. The Sogdians, no less than the nomadic peoples around them, needed to trade to acquire the wealth to bestow on their comitatus members; it was clearly not the reverse. They needed their warriors for their internal political purposes, just as the nomads did. In the early medieval period, the comitatus was evidently more widespread among the Sogdians and other settled Central Asians than among any other Central Eurasian people, and the Sogdians were as involved in wars within Central Eurasia and in the peripheral states as the nomadic peoples were.[73] There is no reason to think the situation was any different in Antiquity.

---

[71] A number of documents from Bactria written in Imperial Aramaic, dating to the fourth century, have recently been discovered. They will shed much light on the local administration and other details of the culture in Bactria during this period (Shaked 2004).

[72] Hornblower and Spawforth (2003: 58).

[73] Grenet (2005), Moribe (2005), de la Vaissière (2005a).

3

Between Roman and Chinese Legions

漢細君公主

顧為黃鵠兮歸故鄉
居常土思兮心內傷
以肉為食兮酪為漿
穹廬為室兮旃為牆
遠托異國兮烏孫王
吾家嫁我兮天一方

> My family has married me off to the ends of the earth,
> To live far away in the alien land of the Aśvin king.
> A yurt is my dwelling, of felt are my walls;
> For food I have meat, with koumiss to drink.
> I'm always homesick and inside my heart aches;
> I wish I were a yellow swan and could fly back home.
> —Princess Hsi-chün of Han

The First Regional Empire Period in Eurasia

The central period of Classical Antiquity, from the third century BC to the third century AD, was marked most notably by the development of the Roman and Chinese empires. Agricultural, partly urbanized cultures, they expanded to great size until they dominated the western and eastern extremes of the Eurasian continent. Both expanded deep into Central Eurasia.

In the Western Steppe, the Sarmatians, the successors of the Scythians, gave way to their Iranian relatives, the Alans. In Western Central Asia, the migrating Tokharian confederation conquered the Greek state in Bactria, from which the Kushan Empire emerged and extended from Central Asia into northern India. Meanwhile, the new Persian Empire of the Parthians spread westward as far as the Greek city-states and contested the Near East with the Romans. The Tokharians' old enemies, the Hsiung-nu, continued to dominate the Eastern Steppe until they divided into northern and southern halves. With Chinese help, the southern half destroyed the north and left the Eastern Steppe open to the Mongolic confederation of the Hsien-pei, who moved in from the mountains of western Manchuria and replaced the Hsiung-nu.

The volume of trade with Central Eurasia—the Silk Road—grew to such an extent that Roman and Chinese writers, who normally disdain to mention commerce, actually discuss it. But despite the trade, and a few long-distance diplomatic contacts, the Romans and Chinese remained far apart both geographically and culturally. They knew extremely little about each other or about the rest of the world beyond their immediate neighbors, in whom they were not very much interested either. Late in the period the movement of ideas along the trade routes, particularly the Buddhist and Christian faiths, had a great effect on both center and periphery.

The Roman Empire and Central Eurasia

The Roman realm had actually expanded to imperial extent well over a century before it is generally considered to have become an empire under the successors of Julius Caesar (d. 44 BC). By 100 BC the Romans already ruled Italy, southern Gaul, Greece, Anatolia, and much of North Africa and were expanding into Spain as well. With the conquest of both Cisalpine and Transalpine Gaul, which were Celtic-speaking territories, Rome had already begun successfully expanding into Central Eurasia long before Caesar's conquest of the rest of Gaul (by 56 BC). Caesar even raided Britain in 55 and 54 BC and attacked the Germans in Germania.[1] His conquests were unprovoked, purely imperialistic expansion, in which resistance—for example, that of the Veneti in northwestern Gaul—was "crushed ferociously, their leaders executed and the population sold into slavery."[2]

After Julius Caesar, the Romans continued their attempts to subjugate the Germanic peoples on their northern and eastern borders. The nearer parts of Germania were subjugated, rebelled against the Romans, and were resubjugated repeatedly over the remaining centuries of the Western Roman Empire. However, some of the Germanic peoples living along the border were taken in as *foederati* 'federates' and served as auxiliaries on Roman campaigns against other Germanic peoples. In the process they were partly assimilated to Roman culture and eventually became more dedicated to the

---

[1] James (2001: 18–22). Britain was later largely conquered by his nominal great-grandson Claudius in AD 43.
[2] James (2001: 18).

survival of the Roman Empire than the increasingly decadent Romans themselves.

The first-century AD *Germania* by the Roman historian Tacitus gives the earliest detailed description of the Germanic peoples. In his account of their culture, he pays special attention to the comitatus and notes the existence of all of its essential elements: a large group of warriors permanently attached to a lord, who were supposed to die with him, so that leaving a battle alive after their chief had fallen resulted in permanent loss of honor and the status of, essentially, an outcast. Tacitus also notes the existence of "grades of rank" in the comitatus and the fact that maintaining one was extremely expensive: the members were "always making demands of their chief, asking for a coveted war-horse or a spear stained with the blood of a defeated enemy."[3]

The long-lasting importance of the comitatus among the Germanic peoples is notable. In addition to its presence in early Francia, it still existed in Visigothic Spain as late as the eighth century and continued to be practiced in Scandinavia for several centuries more. One reason that some early medieval chronicle writers believed that the Franks were related to the Turks, and give historical and etymological explanations for this belief,[4] is very likely that Franks had met Turks and the two peoples understood that their cultures were similar in some respects.[5]

The Frankish king Childeric I (d. 481–482), the father of Clovis, was the son of Merovech (d. 456/457), the posthumously designated founder of the Merovingian Dynasty who fought with the Roman general Aetius against Attila the Hun in the Battle of the Catalaunian Fields. His tomb is similar to those of the eastern Germanic kings of the Danube region. He was buried with sumptuous, golden grave goods in a barrow chamber under a tumulus

---

[3] Mattingly (1970: 113); cf. Hutton (1970: 152–153). See the discussion above in the prologue.

[4] See Beckwith (forthcoming-a).

[5] Scherman (1987: 102–103) notes that when most Franks had adopted the Roman fashion of short hair, members of the Merovingian royal family kept the old tradition of wearing their hair long and loose, and they took good care of it. The Turks and other Central Eurasians further to the east also wore their hair long, but (if later tradition reflects the earlier period correctly) in braids. The earliest remark on the Turks in a Greek text is an uncomplimentary remark of Agathias (Keydell 1967: 13) on their hair—"unkempt, dry and dirty and tied up in an unsightly knot" (Frendo 1975: 11)—in comparison with the beautiful hair of the Frankish kings, which the Greek writer greatly admired. It seems French stylistic elegance has a long tradition.

measuring twenty by forty meters.[6] At the perimeter of the tumulus are several burials of horses and men. Yet it is fairly certain that the Franks had been living along the northern border of the Roman Empire, serving as foederati, for a long time, and Childeric himself was buried with the symbol of a Roman governor of Belgium. The basic features of the Central Eurasian Culture Complex, including the comitatus, were thus found among the early Franks, but they were obviously not adopted from the Romans. So where did they come from?

The account of Tacitus and other early records reveal very clearly that the early Germanic peoples, including the ancestors of the Franks, belonged to the Central Eurasian Culture Complex, which they had maintained from Proto-Indo-European times, just as the Alans and other Central Asian Iranians of the time had done. This signifies in turn that ancient Germania was culturally a part of Central Eurasia and had been so ever since the Germanic migration there more than a millennium earlier.[7]

The Western Steppe

By the early first century AD, the Alans,[8] an Iranian-speaking people related to the Sarmatians and Scythians, had occupied the crucial steppe lands along the Don to the northeast of the Sea of Azov and, according to Josephus (AD 37–100), attacked and plundered Media from there. By the second century AD the Alans dominated the Pontic and North Caucasus regions and were the dominant people on the Western Steppe zone up to the southeastern Roman frontier.[9]

The Romans attacked the remnant Sarmatians and the Alans from Dacia (approximately modern Romania), which the emperor Trajan (r. AD 98–117) conquered with much brutality in AD 107, garrisoned, and settled with

---

[6] The cloisonné pieces are believed to be Byzantine in style. The tomb was discovered at Tournai, Belgium, in 1643 and has recently been reexcavated (Kazanski 2000). A photograph of one of the horse burials is available at http://www.ru.nl/ahc/vg/html/vg 000153.htm. Cf. Brulet (1997).

[7] The problem of the date of the pre-Germanic migration into Europe has so far defied all attempts at solution, despite frequent declarations to the contrary. See chapter 1, and cf. the careful, balanced treatment by Adams (*EIEC* 218–223).

[8] On their names and early history, see Golden (2006).

[9] Melyukova (1990: 113).

Roman colonists. Of the Dacians, "Many were forced into slavery, some committed suicide, and the Romans killed many to set an example for the rest of the provinces to fall in line. Trajan killed 10,000 men just in his gladiatorial games."[10]

Captive Alans were moved deep into the imperial domains in Roman Gaul, as far as Brittany, where they served in the Roman armies. They remained ethnically distinct for centuries, their descendants maintaining some steppe-Iranian traditions well after their linguistic assimilation, and they are thought to have had a significant influence on medieval European folklore.[11] Even fairly late into the Middle Ages, companies of mounted Alan archers are repeatedly noted for their exceptional effectiveness against all enemy forces.

In the second and third centuries AD, the Goths (Gothones), an East Germanic nation that in the time of Tacitus occupied the Baltic Sea around the Vistula River, expanded southward and eastward to the Black Sea. They thenceforth dominated at least the western part of the Pontic Steppe, though not as organized states but as independent groups, until the rise of Ermanaric, who created the Greutungi confederacy of Goths, who later came to be known as the Ostrogoths, the 'Goths of the Rising Sun' or 'East Goths'. He did this in the time-honored state-building method, conquering and subjugating the neighboring peoples. His realm had become a powerful kingdom by AD 370—*before* any attack by the Huns.

The Huns are first noted by Ptolemy in the second century. They lived in the eastern Pontic Steppe in Sarmatia, that is, east of the Sea of Azov and beyond the Don River. The next significant information about them concerns a war between the Huns and the Alans, which the Huns, under their leader Balamber, won. The Huns and the Alans then attacked the Ostrogoths, who occupied the steppe west of the Don River, and defeated them in turn.[12] In view of the earlier history of the Goths there, it seems probable that the Huns' march against the Goths, and their invasion of the Roman

---

[10] Lehmann (2006). On Dacia and the Roman conquest there, see endnote 54.

[11] Bachrach (1973). The name *Lancelot* and the story of the sword in the stone, among other elements of the story, are widely thought to be Alan in origin and to have modern reflexes in the language and folklore of the Ossetians, the Alans' modern descendants in the Caucasus region (Anderson 2004: 13 et seq.; Colarusso 2002; cf. Littleton and Malcor 1994).

[12] Ammianus says that Ermanaric, the king of the Ostrogoths, then committed suicide in or about 375 "rather than lead his own people into bondage to the Huns" (Burns 1980: 35).

Empire—evidently in pursuit of Goths and others who had not submitted to the Huns—was actually a direct consequence of Gothic attacks against the Huns by Ermanaric. Sarmatian, Alan, and Gothic power in the Western Steppe was broken by the Huns by 375. Large groups of Central Eurasians, mainly Goths, then approached the frontiers of the Eastern Roman Empire seeking asylum. Many of those defeated, along with numerous other peoples, submitted to the Hun leadership and joined them on their campaigns.[13]

The Parthian Empire

Alexander the Great (356–323 BC) had no heir[14] and left his vast conquests to his army. The generals divided the empire among themselves and established their own dynasties. In Persia, Seleucus I (r. 312–281 BC), who under Alexander's bidding had married Apame, the daughter of a Sogdian satrap, in 324 BC, established the Seleucid Dynasty, which essentially restored the realm of the Persian Empire from Syria to the Jaxartes. In 238 BC Parthia (present-day northeastern Iran and southern Turkmenistan) was invaded by the Parni, a people speaking a Northern Iranian dialect, led by Arsaces (r. ca. 247–ca. 217/214 BC), who established the independent Arsacid Dynasty in Parthia.[15] Seleucid rule in Persia ended in 129 BC when the Parthians defeated the Seleucids and killed Antiochus VII in battle. Just at that point in time the Parthians were suffering from an invasion of Sakas who may have been fleeing from the Tokharians (Τόχαροι, Yüeh-chih).[16] The latter killed Ardawân (Artabanus II or I, ca. 128–124/123 BC) in battle and conquered

---

[13] Sinor (1990c).

[14] His Central Asian wife Roxana (Roxane) gave birth to a son in August 323 BC—too late for the succession struggle, because Alexander had died on June 10, 323.

[15] Bivar (1983a: 28–29, 98).

[16] According to Chinese sources, the Yüeh-chih (*Tokʷar) attacked the Saka (Śaka in Indian sources) living near the Issyk Kul in 160 BC. In 128, when Chang Ch'ien was in the area, the Tokharians were based between Samarkand and the Oxus River, having already subdued Bactria. The Parthians are known in Chinese sources as An-hsi 安息 NMan ânxî, from MChi *ansik (Pul. 24, 330), from OChi *ansək or *arsək according to the usual reconstruction (Sta. 577, 552), but probably rather from OChi *arsək, that is, *arśák, a perfect transcription of the Parthian form of the dynastic name Aršak (written 'ršk).

Bactria. The Parthians recovered, however, and their empire was firmly established under Mithridates II (the Great, r. ca. 124/123–87 BC).

The Parthians established an energetic though rather decentralized dynasty. They maintained many Central Eurasian Iranian customs, including military dependence on mounted archers—they are famous for the Parthian shot[17]—and oral epic poetry, which unfortunately has not survived. Despite occasional reverses in the perennial struggle with the Romans for control of the Near East, the Parthians generally succeeded in maintaining traditional Iranian control over most of Iraq as well as Iran during the four centuries of their existence until the reign of Ardawân (Artabanus V or IV, r. ca. AD 213–224), who was killed by Ardaxšêr, founder of the Sasanid Dynasty.

The Tokharians and the Kushan Empire

In Central Asia, a remarkable sequence of events recorded in both Western and Eastern historical sources led to the creation of the Kushan Empire. Its beginnings lie ultimately in the first wave of the Indo-European migration, around 2000 BC, when the Group A dialect speakers who became Proto-Tokharians arrived in the area of Kansu and dwelled west of Tun-huang in an area that included Lop Nor and the later Kroraina Kingdom. Eighteen centuries passed. In the third century BC, the Tokharian people—called Yüeh-chih,[18] that is, *Tok^war—still lived in the area.

When the Hsiung-nu were in their early, expansive phase in the early second century BC, the *Tok^war were the great power to their west and south. The Hsiung-nu defeated them conclusively in 176 or 175 BC, drove them from their ancestral lands, and also subjugated the *Aśvin (Wu-sun)[19] and others in the vicinity.[20] Some of the *Tok^war, known as the Lesser Yüeh-chih, fled

---

[17] The Central Eurasian practice of shooting backward at one's pursuers while in flight on horseback.

[18] This is the modern Mandarin Chinese pronunciation of the characters used to transcribe the foreign people's name; for the reconstruction *Tok^war, see appendix B.

[19] See appendix B.

[20] The *Aśvin, according to all accounts, invaded Jungharia to attack the *Tok^war living in the former territory of the Sakas (cf. Bivar 1983b: 192). After their victory, the *Aśvin settled there themselves. That means they arrived in Jungharia after the *Tok^war, *pace* Christian (1998: 210) and many others.

south and took refuge among the Ch'iang people in the Nan Shan, but the main body of survivors, the Great Yüeh-chih, migrated to the west into Jungharia. It is not known if the ancestors of the speakers of the attested East Tokharian and West Tokharian languages had previously settled in the areas of Qocho and of Kucha and Karashahr, respectively (their later attested early medieval locations) or if they settled there at this time, during the Great Yüeh-chih migration. The *Tok^{w}ar drove the resident people, the Sakas, out of Jungharia,[21] but only a few years later they were themselves attacked and defeated by the *Aśvin. The *Tok^{w}ar then migrated west and south into Sogdiana, from which they attacked the Parthians and subjugated Bactria in 124 or 123 BC. They gradually crossed the Oxus and settled in Bactria proper, where they established a strong kingdom later known as Tokhâristân,[22] 'land of the Tokhar (*Tok^{w}ar)'.

In about 50 BC Kujula Kadphises, chief of the Kushan (Kuṣâna), subjugated the other four constituent chiefdoms of Tokhâristân and founded the Kushan Empire. He extended his realm southward into India as far as the mouth of the Indus, taking control of a maritime trade route that directly connected India with the Roman ports in Egypt, thus bypassing the Parthians and their taxes. The Kushans greatly profited from this trade. Their sway extended eastward into the Tarim region as well, where they left their mark in the name Küsän,[23] the local form of the name of the capital of the later Tokharian-speaking kingdom of Kucha. Records from their rule in the characteristic Kharoṣṭhî script they used have been found as far east as Kroraina (Lou-lan). The Kushans were the most important single people responsible for the spread of Buddhism into Parthia, Central Asia, and China. The empire reached its height under the fifth ruler, Kanishka (Kaniṣka, fl. ca. AD 150), who patronized Buddhism, among other religions.

The Kushan Empire is unfortunately little known except for its coinage and other material remains; to a great extent it remains a mystery. Ardaxšêr I, founder of the Sasanid Dynasty, attacked the Kushans and forced their submission to him in about AD 225.

---

[21] The Saka, or Śaka, people then began their long migration that ended with their conquest of northern India, where they are also known as the Indo-Scythians.

[22] The name is recorded in early Arabic accounts as Ṭukhâristân, representing a foreign Tukhâristân or Tokhâristân, in which the earlier syllable [k^{w}ar] ~ [χ^{w}ar] has become [χa:r].

[23] This is the Old Uighur form of the name; in Old Tibetan it is written Guzan, pronounced [küsan] or [küsän]. There is still a town between Kucha and Kashgar named Küsen.

CHAPTER 3

The Chinese Empire and Central Eurasia

The collapse of the Ch'in Dynasty in 210–206 BC led to the formation of a new, long-lasting dynasty, the Western Han (210 BC–AD 6). Under Emperor Wu (r. 141–87 BC), the Chinese once again set their sights on a vastly expanded empire. After several failed expeditions, between 127 and 119 BC they won several major victories over the Hsiung-nu, capturing the Ordos region in the north—thus once again forcing the Hsiung-nu to flee from their ancestral homeland and move northward far beyond the great bend of the Yellow River—and also striking west, taking the strategic Ch'i-lien Mountains in Lung-hsi (the area of modern Kansu). The frontier walls built by the three northern kingdoms of the late Warring States period, Ch'in, Chao, and Yen, which had been linked up by Ch'in to run from Tun-huang to Liao-tung to hold conquered Hsiung-nu territory, were repaired, and the fortresses reoccupied. Emperor Wu also sent out expeditions into the Western Regions in an attempt to take control of the Silk Road cities from the Hsiung-nu. The reports of Chinese envoys and generals supplied the Chinese geographers and historians with much firsthand information on Central Eurasia from the Eastern Steppe and Tarim Basin west as far as Iran, and some much less precise secondhand information on regions beyond, including the Parthian and Roman empires.

The most important and vivid accounts are those of Chang Ch'ien (d. 113 BC), who in 139 BC left on a mission to entice the *Tokʷar to return to their previous homeland in the region between Tun-huang and the Ch'i-lien Mountains. Chang was captured by the Hsiung-nu, among whom he lived for ten years before escaping and continuing his journey to the west. He was in Bactria in about 128 and returned home in 122 BC after another, shorter stay among the Hsiung-nu.[24] After being sent out again in 115, he returned and died two years later.[25]

The Han Dynasty histories' description of the Hsiung-nu—"pure" pastoral nomads who herd their flocks, following the pastures and water, and grow up riding and hunting, so that they are "natural warriors"[26]—is strik-

[24] Yü (1986: 458 n. 260).
[25] Loewe (1986: 164), Yü (1967: 135–136).
[26] For a translation of the *Shih chi* version, see Watson (1961, II: 155 et seq.). The *Shih chi* is dated earlier than the *Han shu*, but it has been demonstrated that both histories draw on the same

ingly similar to the description of the Scythian pastoral nomads by Herodotus. The two peoples shared the same mode of life, down to details, as archaeology and many studies have confirmed.

> They live on the northern frontier, wandering from place to place following the grass to herd their animals. The majority of their animals are horses, cattle, and sheep. . . . They have no walled cities where they stay and cultivate the fields, but each does have his own land. . . . The young boys can ride sheep and shoot birds and mice with bow and arrow; when they are somewhat grown they then shoot foxes and rabbits, which they eat. When they are strong and can pull a warrior's bow, they all become armored cavalrymen.[27]

Nevertheless, as with Herodotus, the most valuable information about the Hsiung-nu is to be found in other parts of the histories. A Chinese eunuch who had gone over to the Hsiung-nu and was treated with great favor by the Hsiung-nu emperor criticized the Central Eurasians' liking for Chinese silks and Chinese food.

> All the multitudes of the Hsiung-nu nation would not amount to [the population of] one province in the Han empire. The strength of the Hsiung-nu lies in the very fact that their food and clothing are different from those of the Chinese, and they are therefore not dependent upon the Han for anything.[28]

The Han armies and diplomats were eventually successful in reducing the power of the Hsiung-nu considerably and spreading Chinese culture into the steppe zone.

> In the territory beyond the Yellow River . . . the Han established irrigation works and set up garrison farms here and there, sending fifty or

---

archival material, so that the *Han shu* does not always simply copy the *Shih chi*. The fame of the *Shih chi* among Chinese is due not so much to the fact that it was the first "modern" history written in what had just become standard Classical Chinese, but rather to its literary style.

[27] HS (94a: 3743); cf. Watson (1961, II: 155). Note the explicit reference to armor.

[28] Watson (1961, II: 170). The eunuch goes on to urge the Hsiung-nu to spurn the foreign imports in favor of homely but sturdy, healthy local Hsiung-nu products and thus to stay independent of the Chinese. This dialogue would seem to betray Chinese prejudices about trade, as well as ignorance of its central importance to Central Eurasians such as the Hsiung-nu. In view of the similar statements in the Old Turkic inscription of Toñukuk, however, they may represent a traditional conservative current of thought within Central Eurasian states.

sixty thousand officials and soldiers to man them. Gradually the farms ate up more and more territory until they bordered the lands of the Hsiung-nu to the north.[29]

But the Hsiung-nu's experience with the Chinese had hardened them and they fought back, always attempting to regain their southern homeland and to retain their control of the Central Asian cities. In fact, despite major Han successes in both regions, the Hsiung-nu continued to exercise effective control over the Tarim Basin cities. Chinese policies could be peaceful and fair:

> When the present emperor [Wu] came to the throne he reaffirmed the peace alliance and treated the Hsiung-nu with generosity, allowing them to trade in the markets of the border stations and sending them lavish gifts. From the *Shan-yü*[30] on down, all the Hsiung-nu grew friendly with the Han, coming and going along the Great Wall.

The Chinese could also be treacherous and violent if they thought they could lure the Hsiung-nu into a trap so they could be massacred. Following just such a failed attempt to capture the Hsiung-nu ruler at the city of Ma-i, near the northeast bend of the Yellow River, in 124 BC, open war broke out:

> After this the Hsiung-nu . . . began to attack the border defenses wherever they happened to be. Time and again they crossed the frontier and carried out innumerable plundering raids. At the same time they continued to be as greedy as ever, delighting in the border markets and longing for Han goods, and the Han for its part continued to allow them to trade in the markets in order to sap their resources.
>
> Five years after the Ma-i campaign, in the autumn [129 BC], the Han government dispatched four generals, each with a force of ten thousand cavalry, to make a surprise attack on the barbarians at the border markets.[31]

[29] Watson (1961, II: 183).
[30] The reconstruction of the Hsiung-nu title for their ruler, *Ch'an-yü*, traditionally read *Shan-yü*, is uncertain; see endnote 7.
[31] Watson (1961, II: 177–178). On the mistranslation of Chinese words for foreigners as "barbarians," see the epilogue.

Despite their eventual division into two kingdoms in AD 49, the Northern Hsiung-nu, the stronger of the two, continued to dominate much of Central Asia. Their influence extended as far as Sogdiana, where they were still considered the nominal suzerains of the region.

The Chinese dynastic histories complain about the distance between China and Central Asia as a major factor in establishing and maintaining military control over the region. However, the main reason China did not achieve more than nominal control over the cities of Eastern Central Asia is certainly economic. The economies of the Central Asian cities were founded on the trade relationship between the urban and rural peoples that had developed over centuries. The Hsiung-nu pastoral economy was not distinct from the agricultural and urban economies of Central Eurasia, and the active presence of the nomads was vital for the economic and political health of both the Hsiung-nu and the peoples of the Tarim cities.

The Hsiung-nu insistence on being allowed to trade freely at the Han frontier towns was opposed by some of the Chinese court officials, but the Han usually saw the comparative benefit to be obtained. When they agreed to allow the Hsiung-nu to trade, that meant peace, and the Hsiung-nu then rarely "raided" the frontier. In this connection it cannot be forgotten that the frontier established by the Chinese extended deep into Central Eurasian territory, so that the "Chinese" market towns were in regions where many—perhaps the majority—of the people were not ethnic Chinese. Even at the height of their power, the Hsiung-nu conducted raids (as contrasted with attacks during full-scale war with China)[32] that penetrated only into the outer limits of former Hsiung-nu territory, places located in former Inner Mongolia, Manchuria, northern Shansi, Shensi, Kansu, and so on.[33]

The Hsien-pei in the Eastern Steppe

When Hsiung-nu power in the steppe declined, due partly to natural internal change and partly to Chinese attacks and political machinations, among

---

[32] Also, during Chinese civil wars, Central Eurasians living near the northern frontier of China often fought as mercenaries or allies of one or another Chinese faction.

[33] Yü (1986: 389).

other factors,[34] the steppe peoples who had been subjugated by the Hsiung-nu increasingly took the opportunity to establish themselves as rulers in their own right. By far the most important of these revolutions was that of the Hsien-pei, a Proto-Mongolic-speaking people who had lived in the eastern part of the Hsiung-nu realm, in what is now western Manchuria, and had been subjugated already by Mo-tun (r. 209–174 BC), the second great ruler of the Hsiung-nu.

The Northern Hsiung-nu Empire effectively collapsed between AD 83 and 87. In the latter year, the Hsien-pei crushed the Hsiung-nu in battle and killed their ruler. When the remainder of the Northern Hsiung-nu moved west into the Ili Valley region in 91, the Hsien-pei moved into their former lands, replaced the Hsiung-nu as rulers of the Eastern Steppe, and expanded as far as the *Aśvin in the west.[35]

The Japanese-Koguryoic Conquests

Some time before the early second century BC, the Proto-Japanese-Koguryoic people moved into the area of Liao-hsi (what is now western Liaoning and Inner Mongolia) from further south, where they seem to have been rice farmers and fishermen. The Wa, a remnant of the Proto-Japanese branch of the Japanese-Koguryoic-speaking people who were still living in the Liao-hsi area in the second century AD, were fishermen, and undoubtedly farmers too, not animal-herding steppe warriors. By contrast, their Koguryo relatives had become a mounted-warrior nation familiar with steppe warfare by AD 12, when they are first mentioned in historical sources as living in the Liao-hsi area.[36] The Koguryo, the Puyo, and other Puyo-Koguryo peoples had adopted all the major attributes of the Central Eurasian Culture Complex, including the origin myth (see the prologue), the comitatus, the burial

[34] Yü (1986: 404–405).

[35] Yü (1990: 148–149).

[36] According to the account (*HS* 99: 4130), the Chinese had wanted to force the Koguryo to attack the Hsiung-nu, but they refused. When the governor of Liao-hsi murdered the Koguryo ruler, the people "rebelled" against the Chinese and escaped from the governor by riding out into the steppe. From that point on, they began moving into Liao-tung and southern Manchuria. This account is the earliest historical notice of the Koguryo. The putatively earlier geographical evidence placing them near Korea is part of a later textual addition dating to the first century AD (Beckwith 2007a: 33–34 n. 12), which was perhaps intended to glorify the conquests of Emperor Wu.

of their rulers in large tumuli, and the theoretical division of their king-doms into four constituent geographically oriented parts.[37]

Partly as a result of the Hsien-pei expansion, and partly due to Chinese pressure under the rule of Wang Mang (r. AD 9–23), some of the Puyo-Koguryo began migrating into Liao-tung, where their Hui-Mo (or Hui and Mo) or Yemaek relatives had already moved by about 100 BC, at which time they are mentioned in the *Shih chi* as living in the region of Liao-tung and Ch'ao-hsien (then southeastern Manchuria).[38] They formed three kingdoms, the Koguryo Kingdom in southern Manchuria from the Liao River to the Yalu River, the Puyo Kingdom[39] in south-central Manchuria north of the Koguryo, and the Hui-Mo or Yemaek Kingdom[40] along the eastern coast of the Korean Peninsula, extending southward as far as the Korean-speaking realm of Chin Han in the southeastern corner of the peninsula. Although the Puyo-Koguryo dynasties were repeatedly disrupted, particularly by the Chinese and the Hsien-pei, their peoples remained firmly established in these locations.

Classical Central Eurasia

The golden age of Classical Antiquity in the West and the East had already passed before the Roman Empire conquered most of the Mediterranean lit-toral and began moving into the hinterland, and before the Chinese Empire similarly conquered the area to a great distance outward in all directions from the capital. The Classical tradition remained strong in the two empires, and in both of them that meant expansion to the greatest extent possible. Yet, although they did succeed in attaining their main goal—significantly

---

[37] The Koguryo elite warriors referred to in the sources were probably the king's comitatus; unfortunately, the sources are unclear on this point. However, the Japanese warriors who fought in the wars of the Three Kingdoms period on the Korean Peninsula acquired the full Central Eurasian Culture Complex, including the comitatus, and brought it with them when they returned to Japan, so the Puyo-Koguryo peoples from whom it is agreed they learned it must have had the comitatus themselves.

[38] They are mentioned in the chapter on the Hsiung-nu as well as in the "neutral" context of the chapter on commerce, "the Money-makers" (Watson 1961, II: 163, 185, 487).

[39] See Byington (2003).

[40] See Beckwith (2007a, 2006e, 2005a). 'Yemaek' is the Sino-Korean reading of the same charac-ters.

greater expanse of territory—their infrastructure was physically unable to hold it beyond a certain point.

At first, the Classical empires' relentless one-track-mind approach to Central Eurasian polities—divide, invade, and destroy—was successful. The Romans conquered deep into largely Germanic western Central Eurasia along a line running through the middle of Western Europe from the North Sea to the Black Sea. They sowed division and created weakness very effectively among those peoples they could not directly control. The Chinese were even more successful. Not only did they acquire and maintain fairly secure access halfway across Central Asia, despite their failure to completely eliminate Hsiung-nu suzerainty there (fortunately for the Central Eurasian economy), they also succeeded in dividing the Hsiung-nu into two hostile states: a southern realm, which was almost completely beholden to China, and a northern realm, which lasted only a few decades after the split. The long-lasting Southern Hsiung-nu state, though increasingly controlled by the Chinese over time, effectively kept northern China away from the Mongolic Hsien-pei, who replaced the Northern Hsiung-nu as rulers of the Eastern Steppe.

The aggressive foreign policy successes of the Chinese and Roman empires ultimately had disastrous consequences. The partial closing of the frontier to trade by both empires, and their destabilization of Central Eurasia by their incessant attacks, resulted in internecine war in the region. The serious decline in Silk Road commerce that followed—observable in the shrinkage of the areal extent of Central Asian cities—may have been one of the causes of the long-lasting recession that eventually brought about the collapse of both the Western Roman Empire and the Eastern Han Empire (and its eventual successor the Chin Dynasty), and with them the end of Classical civilization.[41]

---

[41] The following Central Eurasian migration covered not only the colonized Central Eurasian areas but even the peripheral states' homeland regions. In the Roman Empire, that meant not only Gaul, much of Germania, and Dacia, but virtually all of Western Europe south of Scandinavia, and even across the Mediterranean to North Africa. In China, the migration covered the colonized former Central Eurasian territories of the Ordos and Shensi, northern Shansi, and southern Manchuria, as well as some of the traditionally Chinese areas south of the eastern bend of the Yellow River and the dynastic home of the Chou, Ch'in, and Han dynasties in or around Ch'ang-an in the Kuan-chung region of the Wei River valley.

4

The Age of Attila the Hun

*Sēle hlīfade
hēah ond horngēap. heaðowylma bād
laðan līges, ne wæs hit lenge þa gēn
þæt se ecghete aþumswēorian
æfter wælniðe wæcnan scolde.*

*Ða se ellengǣst earfoðlīce
þrāge geþolode, sē þe in þȳstrum bād
þæt hē dōgora gehwām drēam gehȳrde
hlūdne in healle; þǣr wæs hearpan swēg
swutol sang scopes.*

> The hall towered up,
> high and wide-gabled:　　war-flame awaited,
> evil fire.　　Nor was it long after
> that the fatal struggle　　of the oath-sworn
> should awaken,　　after bloody slaughter.
> Then the mighty demon　　with difficulty
> the time endured,　　he that in darkness dwelt,
> as every day he　　heard the music
> loud in the hall:　　the sound of the harp,
> the bard's clear song.[1]
>
> —From *Beowulf*

The Great Wandering of Peoples

After the second century AD, *when the great empires of Classical Antiquity started breaking up, the peoples of northern Eurasia began migrating toward the south. This far-reaching historical event, known as the Great Wandering of Peoples, or Völkerwanderung, saw the movement of largely Germanic groups into the western half of the former Roman Empire; the little-known Chionites, Hephthalites, and others into the Central Asian territories of the Persian Empire; and mainly Mongolic peoples into the northern half of the former Chinese Empire. While the causes of the movement remain unknown and difficult to discover, its results were revolutionary for Western Europe, and ultimately for Eurasian and world civilization as a whole.*

---

[1] The quotation introduces Grendel, the monster defeated by the hero Beowulf. On the textual problem, see endnote 55.

One of the most remarkable migrations was that of a previously unknown people, the Huns, who seized control of the Western Steppe from the Alans and Goths in traditional steppe fashion. Pursuing those who did not submit led the Huns deep into Europe. The sudden influx of Alans, Goths, and Huns, among others, brought European observers into closer contact with steppe culture than ever before. Although the Huns' domination of the Western Steppe and parts of Western Europe did not last long, their rule left permanent impressions, both good and bad, on the European consciousness.

The Great Wandering of Peoples reestablished nearly all of Western Europe as part of the Central Eurasian Culture Complex, which spread at that time to Japan as well, thus covering the northern temperate zone of Eurasia from Britain to Japan. Politically and linguistically, the migrations established peoples speaking Germanic and Mongolic languages in the dominant position in much of the western and eastern extremes of Eurasia respectively. Demographically, the significance of the Germanic and Mongolic migration into the Roman and Chinese empires was the restoration of the normal state of affairs from the point of view of Central Eurasians: no borders between Central Eurasia and the periphery and the free movement of peoples from rural to urban areas and back, regardless of ethnolinguistic and political divisions. But the results were different in East and West, perhaps because of the much higher population of Chinese in North China compared to the relatively low population of Romans in the Western Roman Empire.

The Huns and the Fall of the Western Roman Empire

The Huns had taken up residence northeast of the Sea of Azov—in the eastern part of the Western Steppe—by about AD 200. They are otherwise unknown before that point and have no known historical, political, linguistic, or other connections.[2] In or around 370 the Huns entered the Pontic Steppe proper under their leader Balamber (or Balimber, fl. ca. 370–376).[3] It is highly probable that their movement was in response to an attack on them by Ermanaric during his attempted formation of an Ostrogothic empire

---

[2] Identification with the Hsiung-nu is still often argued (e.g., de la Vaissière 2005d), but there are many problems with the proposal. See the section on the Hsiung-nu in chapter 2, and endnotes 51 and 52.

[3] Unfortunately, nothing else is known about Balamber.

there.[4] The Huns pushed westward, crushing the Alans and Ostrogoths by 375, in which year Ermanaric committed suicide. In 376, fleeing from the Huns, the Visigoths (Tervingi) under their military leader Fritigern (fl. 376–378)[5] asked the Romans for refuge. They were then allowed to cross the Danube into the Eastern Roman Empire. They were supposed to settle in central Thrace, but even before they had arrived there, they were mistreated badly by their hosts, partly deliberately, partly as a result of the problems involved with bringing a large part of a foreign nation into the empire.

> The management of these problems and the opportunities to grow rich at the expense of the Gothic refugees and their amazing treasures overtaxed the moral and administrative abilities of the Romans in charge of the operation. Moreover, despite continuous use, the available transportation was not sufficient to ferry this mass of people across the Danube. Roman ideas about the order of embarkation destroyed or threatened the family and clan structure of the Goths. An inadequate supply of foodstuffs—a shortage that was not necessarily intentional—also did not help to calm the hungry tribe. Roman observers described the misery of the Tervingi and complained of their exploitation by dishonest officials and generals. Despair led to self-enslavement, to the separation of families, and the handing over even of noble children.[6]

Not surprisingly, Fritigern rebelled in 378. The Visigoths defeated the army of Emperor Valens (r. 364–378), who attacked them near Adrianople, and killed the Roman ruler in battle. Two years later the Romans offered the Goths, Alans, and evidently some Huns the territory of Pannonia (modern Hungary) to hold as *foederates*, or 'federates'. On October 3, 382, a new treaty between Romans and Goths was ratified. The new federates served in the Roman army as early as 388 and proved their worth by helping Emperor Theodosius I (379–395) defeat the rebel Maximus.[7]

---

[4] The known history of the wide-ranging expansionistic wars of Ermanaric cannot be ignored in any discussion of the coming of the Huns, yet modern histories still present the Hun attack against the Alans and Huns as unexpected and unprovoked. The sources do not tell us the Huns' motivations, but in the light of Ostrogothic history it is unlikely that the invasion was unprovoked. On Ermanaric's empire and the early Goths in general, see Wolfram (1988).

[5] Wolfram (1988: 133).

[6] Wolfram (1988: 119).

[7] Wolfram (1988: 135–136).

From that point on, the Huns worked for imperial pay more often than they fought against the Romans. They also evidently launched an invasion of the Persian Empire in 395–396 from the Pontic Steppe area, passing by the Caucasus Mountains into Armenia, Syria, Palestine, and northern Mesopotamia. While it is commonly believed that the Huns undertook this risky expedition into Persian territory for booty, a Syrian chronicler who records it gives as the cause of the invasion the tyrannical behavior of a Roman official.[8] On this expedition the Huns even assaulted, unsuccessfully, the Sasanid Persian capital at Ctesiphon, but the Persians defeated them and the Huns withdrew to focus their attention on Europe. The reason given by the chronicler for the invasion may well be incorrect—certainly the fact that the Huns invaded the Persians rather than the Romans is cause for doubt—in which case the reason for the invasion would actually be unknown. Nevertheless, it is irrelevant whether a tyrannical Roman official or someone or something else entirely was really the cause of the invasion. The significance of the chronicler's comment is that even the peripheral peoples who suffered from the invasion believed that there was a cause, and that it was a just cause. The Huns did not attack because they were ferocious barbarians and could not help themselves.[9]

The first Hun rulers known by name after the shadowy Balamber did not control the entire Hun realm. Hun treaties made with the Romans were thus essentially made with local leaders. When an attack of Huns occurred, the Romans blamed it on the Huns breaking the treaty, but this invariably seems to have been the action of one or another people or group that had not been signatory to the treaty and presumably had their own unknown reasons for the attack. It was only with the centralization of power attained under Ruga or Rua (d. 434) that a unified Hun nation began developing.

Upon Ruga's death, his nephews Bleda and Attila succeeded him. Bleda, the elder, ruled the eastern territories and Attila the western. Emperor Theodosius II of the Eastern Roman Empire then negotiated new peace terms with the Huns, promising that "there should be safe markets with equal

---

[8] Cf. Sinor (1990c: 182–183), who doubts this reason. However, when sufficient information about Hun attacks is available, they seem to have had just cause. See endnotes 56 and 57, and the epilogue.
[9] Sinor (1990c: 184). On the frequent confusion of the Huns with the Hephthalites and others, see endnote 56.

rights for Romans and Huns"[10] and agreeing to pay the Hun rulers 700 Roman pounds of gold a year. The treaty was good for both sides. "When they had made peace with the Romans, Attila, Bleda and their forces marched through Scythia [the Western Steppe] subduing the tribes there."[11]

When Theodosius II stopped regular payment of tribute to the Huns, Attila and Bleda launched a campaign against the Romans in 440 and 441. Crossing the Danube, they crushed the imperial forces, captured cities, and defeated a Roman army below the walls of Constantinople, which Theodosius had made the capital.[12] The emperor finally sued for peace again and agreed to Attila's demands, including cession of more territory, payment of the tribute in arrears, and the tripling of the former annual tribute amount to 2,100 Roman pounds of gold—which was actually still a pittance by Roman standards.[13]

Five years later, the Romans had given Attila cause to attack them again. In 447 he rode south, defeating the Roman army sent against him, and reached Thermopylae. The Romans began peace negotiations, accompanied by political intrigue and attempted assassination, as described in some detail by Priscus, a member of a Roman embassy sent to Attila's court in 448. In 450, while negotiations were still ongoing, Theodosius II died. He was succeeded by Marcian (r. 450–457), who stopped payment of tribute.

But Attila, who was sole ruler of the Hun Empire after his brother had died in or around 445, did not follow expectations and invade the Eastern Roman Empire in retaliation. He had gotten a justification, or excuse, to invade the Western Roman Empire when he received a letter from Honoria, sister of Valentinian III (r. 425–455), accompanied by her personal ring. She had been sent

---

[10] On Roman border officials' misbehavior as the cause of Hun complaints against the Romans, see endnote 57.

[11] Blockley (1983, II: 227).

[12] "Theodosius was the first of the emperors to make Constantinople his permanent residence . . . other emperors maintained the peripatetic lifestyle of so many of their predecessors" (Howarth 1994: 61).

[13] These peace settlements paid to the Huns in gold, though protested as onerous both in the sources and in virtually all modern accounts, were in fact a minuscule percentage of the imperial fisc. In another connection it is noted that "four thousand pounds of gold amounts to the yearly income of a senator of the wealthy, though not the wealthiest, class" (Wolfram 1988: 154). According to Treadgold (1997: 40, 145), Justinian changed the ratio of *nomismata* (Latin *solidi*), or gold coins, to 72 per Roman pound. He estimates the annual state budget in the years 450 to 457 to have amounted to about 7,784,000 *nomismata*. Because 2,100 pounds of gold would have equaled 151,200 *nomismata*, the indemnity paid to the Huns—a punishment that the Romans fully deserved—came to 1.9 percent of the imperial budget. The stories that the wealthy men of Constantinople were reduced to penury in order to pay the indemnity are fairy tales.

into captivity by her brother, who had executed her lover, and she asked Attila to help her. Attila took her request as an offer of marriage and marched west with a huge army, consisting mainly of Huns, Goths, and Alans, to free her and claim what he announced would be his dowry—half of the Western Roman Empire. Estimates in the sources have his forces at between 300,000 and 700,000 men, though the army was probably much smaller.

In 451 the Huns took and sacked the northern cities of the Western Roman Empire along the Rhine in Gaul and Germania. Turning to central Gaul, they then attacked Orleans, a strategic city in northwestern Gaul. But in the midst of the Huns' assault, the Roman general Flavius Aetius approached, commanding a large army consisting mainly of Romans, Franks, and Visigoths. Attila withdrew and prepared for battle.

It is commonly thought that the Huns swept into Europe on horseback and easily defeated the Romans, who were unaccustomed to fighting nomad armies. However, though the Huns did retain control of the Pontic Steppe— one of Attila's sons ruled over the peoples by the Black Sea[14]—within Western Europe there was little pasture for their horses. The relatively limited grassland of the Pannonian Plain could not support the vast herds the nomad pastoralists maintained in Central Eurasia. The Huns were able to keep only enough horses for an auxiliary cavalry force. As a result, they fought the Romans in Gaul and Italy almost entirely as infantry.[15]

On or around June 20, 451, the two armies met in the Battle of the Catalaunian Fields.[16] It was a fierce engagement and the losses on both sides were great—estimates in the sources are between 200,000 and 300,000 men killed. Partly through good generalship and firsthand knowledge of Hun tactics gained during his stay as a hostage among the Huns after the death of Stilicho in 408,[17] Aetius was the victor, though his main ally Theodoric, king of the Visigoths, was killed in battle. Despite the Romans' victory, their forces had suffered too, and the Visigoths withdrew, so Aetius did not pursue the Huns. Similarly Attila, though his army was still strong, withdrew to Pannonia.

---

[14] Blockley (1983, II: 275).

[15] For a detailed examination, see Lindner (1981).

[16] The exact location is unknown. It is widely thought to have been somewhere in the Champagne region near what is now Châlons, but this too is uncertain.

[17] A few years earlier Aetius had been a hostage among the Goths, so his knowledge of the tactics of these two peoples must have been unparalleled.

In 452, rather than attacking Gaul again, the Huns crossed the Alps and descended into Italy. They sacked the cities in the Po Valley and other places in northern Italy, then turned south toward Ravenna, which was at the time the capital of the Western Roman Empire. Emperor Valentinian III fled the city for Rome, much further to the south. A Roman delegation that included Pope Leo I went north to the Po River, where it met Attila and the pope tried to dissuade him from attacking Ravenna.

By that time Attila did not need much persuading. His troops were suffering due to the famine and plague in the region, and an army sent by Emperor Marcian had attacked the Huns' homeland in Pannonia. Attila withdrew and returned home. Early the following year, on the night of his marriage to a beautiful new bride, Ildico, he died from unknown causes.[18] He was buried in traditional steppe style.[19]

The three sons of Attila fought over the succession, but none managed to establish himself as sole ruler. The Germanic subjects of the Huns rose up in revolt. In 455 the king of the Gepids, Ardaric, defeated the Huns in Pannonia and killed many of them, including Attila's eldest son, Ellac. A great number of survivors fled southeastward back to the Black Sea region, where Ernac (or Irnik) took command. The Hun Empire was gone, but the Huns under Ernac's brother Dengizikh continued to be a power in southeastern Europe until his death in 469, while those under Ernac remained the dominant ethnic group on the Western Steppe for several generations before they finally disappeared as a people.[20]

Aetius, who had almost single-handedly saved the Western Roman Empire despite all the obstacles put in his way by the politicians of the day, was

[18] There are several suggested explanations. According to Priscus (from Jordanes, summarized in Theophanes), he choked to death in the night from a nasal hemorrhage (Blockley 1983, II: 316–319). The unusual nosebleed story would seem to have the ring of truth, but it has also been argued that Attila was assassinated. This may be so, but Babcock's (2005) theory that it was done by Attila's closest retainers, Edeco and Orestes, would seem highly unlikely.

[19] The men who were slain and buried with Attila according to Jordanes (Blockley 1983, II: 319) were certainly killed ritually (cf. Sinor 1990c: 197) and may well have been members of his comitatus. In view of the fact that the observers who described the burial were not killed, the executions were hardly done to hide the location.

[20] The Huns of the Western Steppe appear to have formed an element of the later Danubian Bulgars, a Turkic people who, under Asparukh, moved into the Balkans in 680 and founded a powerful kingdom there, which eventually became Bulgaria (Sinor 1990c: 198–199). Like the name Scythian up to the early medieval period, the name Hun became a generic (usually pejorative) term in subsequent history for any steppe-warrior people, or even any enemy people, regardless of their actual identity.

murdered in 454 by Emperor Valentinian III himself. The emperor was assassinated the following year by the supporters of Aetius, but the damage had already been done. There was no one left capable of leading the Romans.

By 473, when the Ostrogoths invaded Italy, the Western Roman Empire was little more than a fiction. Orestes, the Pannonian Roman who had been Attila's right-hand man, deposed the emperor Nepos in 475 and installed his own little son Romulus Augustulus as emperor. The boy was on the throne for little over a year when Odoacer, king of the Sciri people, deposed him in 476 and had himself declared king of Italy. Romulus Augustulus was thus the last Roman emperor of the West. Odoacer remained on his throne until 493, when he was killed by Theodoric the Ostrogoth, who had been sent by the Byzantines to depose him.[21] Taking the throne for himself, Theodoric established an Ostrogothic kingdom that eventually included Italy, Sicily, Dalmatia, and territories to the north. He accepted the nominal suzerainty of the Eastern Roman Empire, however, and, unlike Odoacer, he was a relatively cultured man. He brought peace and promoted both Roman and Gothic culture in the territory under his control.

The Early Germanic Kingdoms in Western Europe

Many Germanic peoples migrated into the lands of the Western Roman Empire, both before and after its fall.

In the far northwest, the former Roman colony in Britain had been abandoned militarily by 410, when the emperor Honorius told the beleaguered citizens there to defend themselves.[22] From the fourth century into the sixth century, during the Great Wandering of Peoples, Irish peoples crossed over and settled on the west coast of Britain, especially in Scotland, while Germanic peoples, primarily Angles, Saxons, and Jutes, crossed the English Channel and settled in Britain, bringing with them the latest continental version of the Central Eurasian Culture Complex.[23] The Germanic peoples soon became the dominant power in Britain.[24]

---

[21] Wolfram (1988).

[22] Blair (2003: 3).

[23] The Celts who had preceded them had already introduced an earlier form of the Central Eurasian Culture Complex, complete with war chariots, at the time of their migration to the British Isles.

[24] Blair (2003: 1–6).

The Vandals and others marched south through Gaul and Spain, devastating as they went, until they crossed over into North Africa, where they established a kingdom based in Carthage that survived until the Arab conquest in the mid-seventh century.

The Visigoths, following the Vandals, migrated into Aquitaine in Gaul and took control of the Iberian Peninsula. Gradually pushed to the southwest out of Gaul by the Franks, the Visigoths built a strong kingdom in Spain that lasted until the Arabs conquered them in the early eighth century.

Others, such as the Burgundians and the Langobards or Lombards, established kingdoms that survived long enough to leave their mark on the landscape but were eventually absorbed by larger states.

The most important of all the Germanic peoples in Western Europe were eventually to be the Franks, who are believed to have come from the territory immediately to the east of the Rhine River, but who are recorded as having believed that they had come from Pannonia or further east.[25] Under the dynamic early Merovingian king Childeric I (d. 481), and especially his son Clovis (r. 481–511), the Franks gradually spread their control over Gaul. During the Early Middle Ages they built the first agrarian-urban empire ever based in Europe north of the Mediterranean.[26] Their conquests, and those of the Goths, Anglo-Saxons, and other Germanic peoples, firmly reestablished the Central Eurasian Culture Complex in the former Roman domains in Europe north of the Mediterranean. But the Romans and other Romanized peoples stayed, and were very influential. The resulting cultural blending of the Central Eurasian Germanic peoples and their Romanized subjects laid the foundations of what eventually became a distinctive new European civilization.

Growth of the Eastern Roman and Sasanid Persian Empires

Although the Western Roman Empire declined very rapidly after the third century, and collapsed utterly in the fifth, it is a curious fact that the core of the Eastern Roman Empire did not decline economically and politically, but maintained itself rather successfully. The Eastern Roman (or Byzantine)

---

[25] Beckwith (forthcoming-a), Wood (1994: 33–35), Ewig (1997).
[26] Wood (1994: 38–42).

Empire became increasingly Greek in language, Near Eastern in its cultural orientation, and fixated on Persia in its foreign policy.

In 224 Ardaxšêr (Ardashîr I, r. 224–ca. 240) overthrew the Parthian ruler Ardawân (Artabanus V) and established the Sasanid Dynasty. He quickly took control of the traditional Persian territories—the Iranian Plateau and eastern Mesopotamia. But the Persians came into conflict with the Eastern Roman Empire, which had long contested the rule of Mesopotamia with the Parthians. The Sasanids were determined to reestablish the realm once ruled by the Achaemenids centuries before, including western Mesopotamia, Anatolia, and much of the rest of the Near East. They fought many wars with the Romans. The boundary between the two empires, usually somewhere in Mesopotamia, shifted back and forth several times.

The Sasanids also marched into the east. They attacked the Kushans, took Bactria and Transoxiana, and subjugated the remnants of the Kushan Empire.

In the fifth century the Hephthalites or 'White Huns' attacked the Central Asian territories of the Sasanid Empire, defeating the Persians in 483 and exacting tribute. The Hephthalites settled in the area of Bactria and Transoxiana and remained independent for about a century. They extended their power eastward as far as Turfan in the Tarim Basin and sent ambassadors to the Wei Dynasty in North China.[27]

The height of the Persian Empire under the Sasanids was reached under Khosraw I (Anushirvan the Just, r. 531–579), whose reign was largely peaceful after the successful conclusion of a protracted war with the Eastern Roman Empire in 561.[28]

Fall of the Chinese Empire and Hsien-pei Migration into North China

The Later or Eastern Han Dynasty (AD 25–220), which was the restored and reinvigorated continuation of the Former or Western Han Dynasty (202 BC–AD 9), finally collapsed from the usual internal dynastic causes. The territory of the empire was divided among several short-lived kingdoms that

---

[27] Millward (2007: 30–31). See endnote 56.
[28] Frye (1983: 153–160).

engaged in civil war for half a century, ending with the formation of the Chin Dynasty (265–419). The Chin was in virtually every respect a continuation of the Later Han, though weaker militarily.

As the Chin declined, the long-delayed reaction of the northern peoples to the aggressive, expansionistic policies of the former united Chinese Empire fell upon the dynasty. A branch of the Mongolic Hsien-pei people in southern Manchuria who had long been at war on and off with China expanded southward into Chin. They took the name *Taghbač (T'o-pa) 'Lords of the Earth',[29] and founded a new Chinese-style dynasty, the Northern Wei (386–ca. 550), which dominated North China for nearly two centuries.

During the period of the flourishing of the northern dynasties, the southern part of what had been Han China—essentially the region south of the Yangtze River—was divided among several states with ethnically Chinese dynasties. For two centuries the Chinese cultural area of East Asia remained divided into a number of kingdoms, with dynasties largely of foreign origin ruling over mostly ethnic Chinese in the north and ethnically Chinese dynasties ruling over Chinese and non-Chinese in the south.

The Avars and the Coming of the Turks

At the same time as the *Taghbač conquest of North China, the Avars[30] conquered the Eastern Steppe and built an empire stretching from Karashahr in the northwestern Tarim Basin to the borders of the Koguryo Kingdom in the east.[31] The ethnolinguistic relationships of the Avars, known to the Chinese as Jou-jan,[32] have not been determined.[33] The Chinese sources claim that the first Avar was a slave of the *Taghbač.[34] If the Avars had indeed been so subjugated, in their period of service they would have learned the steppe warrior variant of the Central Eurasian Culture Complex and,

---

[29] That is, *Taγβač; in Mandarin, T'o-pa; in Old Turkic metathesized into Taβγač. The language of this name is—or was understood to be—part Mongolic and part Indic (Beckwith 2005b; cf. Beckwith forthcoming-a).

[30] See endnote 18 on the controversy surrounding the names and the identification of the Jou-jan with the Avars.

[31] Sinor (1990c: 293).

[32] Also written Juan-juan and Ju-ju (in pinyin Rouran, etc.).

[33] On the ethnolinguistic identity of the Avars, who were probably not a Mongolic people, see endnote 58.

[34] Sinor (1990c: 293).

following the dynamic of the First Story, would gradually have become strong enough to overthrow their lords. During the rule of the founder of the T'o-pa Wei Dynasty, T'o-pa Kuei (r. 386–409), the Avars under their ruler She-lun established their empire in the Eastern Steppe and northern Tarim Basin.[35] They maintained their power, despite many serious reverses, including incursions by the *Taghbač and other peoples, for some two centuries. The Avars thus restored to some degree the former realm of the Hsiung-nu and brought under their sway many other peoples, including the Türk. After a long period of destabilization and division, in or around 524 Anagai became *kaghan* 'emperor'[36] of the Avars and began rebuilding their realm into that of a great power.

The Puyo-Koguryo Migration into the Korean Peninsula

During the first few centuries AD, the Puyo and Koguryo kingdoms maintained themselves in southern Manchuria, ruling over native people they treated as slaves. The Koguryo many times came into conflict with the Chinese Empire's easternmost commandery in Lolang in the northern Korean Peninsula. Nevertheless, despite the periodic flourishing of the Koguryo, the Chinese maintained themselves in the region even after the fall of the Han Dynasty, partly because of several wars between the Koguryo and the Mu-jung clan of the Hsien-pei to their west, who twice devastatingly defeated the Koguryo.

In the fourth century the Koguryo finally captured Lolang. Renaming it *Piarna 'level land' in their language (in Sino-Korean reading, *Pyong'yang*), they moved their capital there and, along with other Puyo-Koguryoic peo-

---

[35] Sinor (1990c: 293), who notes that little is known about the Avars (Jou-jan). Nevertheless, there is enough material in the Chinese sources for a good book on them.

[36] The Old Turkic form of the word, *qayan*, has a feminine equivalent, *qatun*, which has the same unusual morphological characteristics that are neither Mongolic nor Turkic. The title *qayan* is first attested in the mid-third century among one of the Hsien-pei peoples (Liu 1989), all linguistically identified members of which spoke Mongolic languages, but these particular words are not Mongolic in structure. The source of the words and their morphology remains unknown. Simple segmentation of the two words produces a root *qa-, the usual eastern Eurasian word for 'ruler' found earliest in the Korean Peninsula area in Late Antiquity and much later in early Mongolian sources (Khitan and Middle Mongolian); see Beckwith (2007a: 43–44, 46–47 n. 46). The Avars were undoubtedly heavily influenced by the Mongolic *Taghbač in the period when the latter ruled North China.

ples, proceeded to overrun most of the Korean Peninsula. The Kingdom of Paekche was established by the Puyo clan in the area of the former Ma Han realm in southwestern Korea, while another Puyo-Koguryo clan established a dynasty in the new Silla Kingdom in the area of the former Chin Han realm in the southeasternmost corner of Korea, though the kingdom remained Korean-speaking. The one area that seems to have escaped the nation building of the Puyo-Koguryo people, as well as the influence of their language, was the realm of former Pyon Han, in the central part of the south coast of the Korean Peninsula. It became known as Kara, or Mimana,[37] and never achieved political equality with the other kingdoms of the peninsula.[38] Little is known about Kara, but it was under heavy Japanese influence and at times was a Japanese tributary state, if not an outright colony. The period of the Three Kingdoms in Korea was one of demographic and cultural growth accompanied by almost constant warfare somewhere on the peninsula.

The Central Eurasian Culture Complex in Japan

At the far eastern end of Eurasia, the Wa—the Proto-Japanese speakers who emigrated to Japan and the southern end of the Korean Peninsula[39] from the Asian mainland (apparently from the Liao-hsi region)[40] at the inception of the Yayoi period (ca. fourth century BC to fourth century AD)[41]—clearly did not belong to the Central Eurasian Culture Complex. In Japan they gradually developed a distinctive culture of their own, partly under influences emanating from the Korean Peninsula.

The Wa conducted active trade and political relations with the states of the Korean Peninsula. Much of the trade centered on the acquisition of iron, the production of which was of great importance in the southern part of the peninsula. Following the migration of the Puyo-Koguryoic-speaking peoples

---

[37] It is possible that the name Kara is an exonym, suggesting that the "native" name was Mimana. The spelling Kaya is the modern Korean reading of the characters used to write the name; the pronunciation /kara/ (transcriptionally *kala) is certain (Beckwith 2007a: 40 n. 27).

[38] See Beckwith (2006c).

[39] On the modern controversy over the ethnolinguistic history of the early Korean Peninsula region, see endnote 59.

[40] Liao-hsi is their last *known* location on the Asian mainland (Beckwith 2007a).

[41] On the controversy over the dating of the Yayoi period, see endnote 60.

southward throughout the Korean Peninsula, the Japanese became deeply enmeshed in the internecine wars of the states that formed there.

In the course of the Japanese military experience in Korea, Japanese soldiers were defeated on many occasions by one or another of the kingdoms established there by the Puyo-Koguryo warriors, who belonged to the Central Eurasian Culture Complex.[42] Following the dynamic of the First Story, Japanese warriors fighting in the service of Puyo-Koguryo lords must have acquired their version of the steppe form of the Central Eurasian Culture Complex, in particular the comitatus, whose members are known in Old Japanese as *toneri*.[43] The early Japanese mounted archer warrior, the *bushi*, like the later samurai, his institutional descendant, "was merely one variant of the Asian-style mounted archer predominant in the Middle East and the steppe; similarities among all the fighting men of these early centuries of Japanese history far outweigh the differences."[44] The close warrior companions of a lord in early Japan also were expected to commit suicide to be buried with him (called *junshi* 'following in death') and regularly did so. When some of these Japanese warriors returned home from the Korean Peninsula area, along with natives of the peninsula, the result was the transmission of the Central Eurasian Culture Complex to Japan[45] and the revolution in Japanese culture and politics known as the Kofun period. It produced the Japanese imperial dynasty, which began its conquest and unification of Japan at that time.[46] The island country then increasingly looked to the continent for cultural input.

[42] Even in the fragmentary historical record that does exist, several disastrous defeats are recorded. Many more defeats, and victories as well, must have occurred, but no record of them has survived.

[43] *Toneri* is translated as 'royal retainers' by Farris (1995: 27–28). In at least one early case a *toneri* is called a 'slave' of his lord, as in continental Central Eurasian cultures where the comitatus warrior is often referred to as a 'slave' or the like.

[44] Farris (1995: 7).

[45] The introduction of Central Eurasian–style burials, and the great increase in the size and splendor of the burial mounds erected at this time are clear signs of this specific new influence (this Japanese archaeological-historical period takes its name from its distinctive, enormous *kofun* 'ancient tumuli'); another sign is the comitatus warriors' ritual suicide, or *junshi*, which, though later discouraged, continued to be practiced by samurai down to recent times; for a detailed study see Turnbull (2003).

[46] It is often argued that the imperial dynasty was ethnically Korean, sometimes specifically Paekche, in origin. These arguments are not really supportable by the sources, whether in Japanese or other languages. The old horserider theory of Egami Namio, published in English in 1964, has been pursued in a simplified form by others (e.g., Ledyard 1975), who argue that a continental Altaic steppe-warrior people conquered Japan and established the impe-

The Great Wandering of Peoples and Central Eurasia

The reason for the Central Eurasians' migrations into the remains of the Classical empires are unknown.[47] Only the fact of their migration is known. Yet that itself is significant. The normal situation within Central Eurasia with respect to migration was that it frequently occurred. Most steppe zone Central Eurasians were nomadic or seminomadic stockbreeders—effectively, farmers whose fields changed during the year and whose "crops," their animals, moved constantly. Though the people knew who "owned" the grazing rights and water rights to specific lands at specific times of the year, there were in general no markers between one people's pastures and those of the next. For these reasons, nonsedentary Central Eurasia was character-ized by a great deal of fluidity. Nations were defined by their people, who were bound together by oaths, not by the land they inhabited.

From the beginning of historical records, the entire territory of Eurasia, including all of Central Eurasia, was already occupied by one or another people. Although some peaceful political and demographic adjustments did occur, most have evidently not made it into the historical record, wherein war typically decides who rules the contested territory. Those among the ruling clan of the losers who were not killed or did not submit to the win-ning clan would flee; in some cases, they fled to a peripheral empire such as Rome or China and asked for, or demanded, refuge. But most of the ordi-nary people, the rank-and-file survivors of the defeated group, who were largely pastoralists (animal farmers) and agriculturalists, would normally merge with the members of the new nation. There was not necessarily any change at the local level, and many peoples maintained their languages and traditions for centuries despite the change of rulers. This pattern occurred over and over in Central Eurasia from the beginning of the historical record

---

rial dynasty. That particular idea has been disproved by archaeology (Hudson 1999), but it is undoubtedly true that the dynamic new nation-building dynasty was founded by warriors—returning Japanese—who had adopted the Central Eurasian Culture Complex in the Korean Peninsula. The lack of any support for the ethnic Korean conquest theories con-trasts with the substantial support—partly via the material presented very carefully by Egami (1964) himself in the very same work—for such a "conquest" of Japan by Central Eur-asianized Japanese. See Beckwith (2007a).

[47] The scenario presented here is one of a number of possibilities. On stereotypical, unlikely, or unfounded explanations for the *Völkerwanderung*, see endnote 61.

down to modern times; it is exactly the same process as the changes of government and expansions and contractions of territory that characterize the history of the peripheral agricultural-urban cultures of Europe and China.

All empire builders, whether ruled by nomadic or agrarian dynasties, attempted to expand as far as possible in all directions. As noted above, there were no physical barriers to prevent movement in the steppe zone, and from the Central Eurasian point of view borders were meaningless. As a consequence, when a winning clan was extraordinarily successful, the new nation could rapidly expand across the entire expanse of the Central Eurasian steppe zone up to the walls and fortresses of the peripheral empires. This happened at least three times in Central Eurasian history: under the Scythians (or Northern Iranians), the Turks, and the Mongols.

In the agrarian Eurasian periphery, by contrast, borders between nations were macrocosmic reflections of the borders between agricultural fields, the stable microcosms that made up the empires. Local, internal adjustments in the political order could not take place without an imperial response against the uprising. Adjustments across borders meant war between empires. The borders attracted merchants and other people from both cultural worlds to the trading cities, which were tightly controlled and taxed during periods when the peripheral states ruled over them. Many Central Eurasian groups developed half-Roman, half-Persian, or half-Chinese cultures in the border regions.

One specific factor that certainly helped drive the migrations, at least initially, was the economic decline of both Rome and China. The border areas of these empires were much more strongly affected by economic trouble than their more central areas, which had accumulated and retained more wealth. It must have been increasingly difficult to make a living as a foreign trader or immigrant worker when the frontier cities and villas of the wealthy imperials themselves were strapped for funds and shrinking, or were simply abandoned.

The economic troubles would also have entailed difficulties for the Central Eurasian rulers, who needed to continually acquire luxury goods and other forms of wealth to distribute to their comitatus members and allies. When the border markets collapsed, or were destroyed in the wars that became more and more devastating as the general situation worsened, it became imperative for men who needed to trade to move closer to localities where it was still possible to do business. The fact that the Eastern Roman Empire was located further "inside" Eurasia than the Western realm, and managed to survive, though much reduced in size, and that the Persian Empire was relatively little affected by the great migrations, mainly losing its colonial territories in Central Asia, would seem to confirm the principle on a larger scale.

When the Classical empires of Rome and China crumbled, the borders that had been officially closed for so long became porous. The local half-Romanized or half-Sinified Central Eurasians moved deeper inside the empires they had come to depend on, hoping to continue their way of life more securely. These first immigrants mostly admired the imperial cultures and wanted to preserve them.

In Europe, for example, they fought beside the Romans against others such as the Goths and Huns who came from further out in Central Eurasia. But the latter actually wanted the same thing: the Huns were explicit, consistent, and emphatic in their demand to be allowed to trade at Roman frontier markets.

When these adjustments in the *local* political and demographic order that had been prevented for so long took place, they allowed other adjustments deeper within Central Eurasia to follow like a chain reaction. Altogether they constituted the Great Wandering of Peoples. What was of revolutionary importance about the movement was its effect on Western Europe.

Re–Central Eurasianization of Europe and the Medieval Revolution

The long decline of the Western Roman Empire was accompanied by the gradual immigration of half-Romanized peoples from Northern and Eastern Europe. Although there was also considerable immigration into the Eastern Roman Empire, the larger population there and its greater economic vitality meant that the immigrants were mostly absorbed by the dominant Greek population. In the West, many of the new cities built by the Romans were near the northern limits of their conquests in what had been Germanic or Celtic territory, where the people belonged to the Central Eurasian Culture Complex, not the Mediterranean–Ancient Near Eastern "Hellenistic" culture out of which the Roman Empire had grown and developed over several hundred years. When the Western Empire weakened internally, the government was forced to withdraw imperial troops closer to the center of the realm—northern Italy and Rome itself. Despite the frontier peoples' semi-Romanized cultural development, their fundamental culture was still Central Eurasian: trade was absolutely necessary, and they were willing to fight if there was no other way to reach the markets. The decline of the cities in the West forced the Central Eurasians to move deeper into the empire to find viable markets. The inevitable result was conflict and retreat of the Romans still further south.

The move of the frontier peoples into the Western Roman Empire—which is thought to have been partly depopulated, for unknown internal reasons— in turn induced peoples further out in Central Eurasia to move west and south as well. The entire movement was accompanied by the efforts of various peoples to establish kingdoms or empires of their own in Central Eurasia or on the frontiers of the Roman Empire. The culmination was the mass movement of the Goths, Huns, and Franks in the fourth and fifth centuries, during which nearly all of Romanized Western Europe was overrun. By the end of the fifth century, the Central Eurasian Culture Complex was in place not only in previously non-Romanized Northern, Central, and Eastern Europe but in the formerly Romanized parts of North Africa, the Iberian Peninsula, England, France, Belgium, Switzerland, northern Italy, Germania, and most of the Balkans.

The famous, seductive argument of Henri Pirenne, to the effect that the Middle Ages and medieval civilization in Western Europe began not with the "barbarian conquests" but with Islamic conquest of the Mediterranean and the isolation and impoverishment of what had been the Western Roman Empire,[48] is based on several serious errors and has been totally disproved both in general and in great detail.[49] It nevertheless continues to be followed by most medievalists for a number of reasons, none of them good. As a result, the origins and development of medieval European culture now constitute a great historical mystery, and many proposals have been made to try and solve it.

[48] Pirenne (1939).
[49] This theory has been much discussed. Lyon (1972) carefully surveys all the critical literature and shows that no important element of the theory has withstood scientific examination. However, he unexpectedly concludes that the continuing broad acceptance of the major points of the Pirenne Thesis and its chronology for the beginning of the Middle Ages nevertheless indicates its validity. See Beckwith (1987a/1993: 173 et seq.) for detailed criticism.

The earlier belief of historians that the "barbarian conquests" were the turning point between Classical Antiquity and the Middle Ages—as the writers who lived in the age of the Great Wandering of Peoples themselves suggest—deserves to be reexamined in the light of the Central Eurasian Culture Complex. There is no question but that the Germanic form of it was reintroduced into Western Europe and became the dominant sociopolitical system there, developing gradually into what is now known as "medieval" culture, which included the "feudal" system or systems, the special status of trading cities, and the special status of the warrior class. The persistence of Graeco-Roman elements—most significantly the dominance of Latin as the common literary language of Western Europe—and the long survival of some pockets of rural Antiquity in the south, did not restore the ancient Mediterranean high culture anywhere in what had been the Western Roman Empire. But that culture did not disappear, either. Romans and Romanized peoples lived in the new Germanic kingdoms, and a merger of the two peoples began to take place almost from the outset. The primary result of the re–Central Eurasianization of Romanized Western Europe was the cultural revolution known prosaically as the Middle Ages.[50]

---

[50] The introduction during the High Middle Ages of Arab Islamic knowledge and techniques into the new European culture supercharged it and is clearly one of the elements responsible for initiating the beginnings of modern science, but it did not eliminate the Central Eurasian element in European culture. This is fully evident from the history of the Age of Exploration, q.v. chapter 9.

5

The Türk Empire

天馬來出月支窟
背為虎文龍翼骨
嘶青雲振綠髮
蘭筋權奇走滅沒
騰崑崙歷西極
李白 天馬歌

The heavenly horse sprang from a Tokharian cave:
Tiger-striped back, bones of dragon wing,
Neighing blue clouds, he shook his green mane.
An orchid-veined courser, he ran off in a flash
Up the Kunlun Mountains, vanishing over the Western horizon.
—Li Po, *The Song of the Heavenly Horse*

The Second Regional Empire Period in Eurasia

In the mid-sixth century the Persian and Eastern Roman empires were at war, while both East Asia and Western Europe were divided among feuding king-doms. In the Eastern Steppe, following the dynamics of the Central Eurasian Culture Complex myth, the Türk people overthrew their overlords, the Avars, and chased their remnants to the ends of Eurasia. In so doing, they linked up all the peripheral civilizations of Eurasia via its urbanized core, Central Asia, which quickly became the commercial-cultural heart not only of Central Eur-asia but of the Eurasian world as a whole. Because of the Turks' eagerness to trade, their military power that helped encourage other peoples to trade with them, and their rule over most of Central Asia, the Central Eurasian economy—the Silk Road—flourished as never before.

By the end of the sixth century, China was reunited by the short-lived Sui Dynasty and attempted to expand into Central Eurasia again. The collapse of the dynasty, and the collapse of the Persian and Eastern Roman empires shortly thereafter, was followed by the establishment of new imperial realms both there and in other previously marginal regions: the Franks in Western Europe; the Arabs in the Near East, eventually including northwestern India, western Central Asia, Iran, North Africa, and Spain as well as Arabia; the Tibetan Empire in southeastern Central Eurasia; the T'ang Dynasty in China, which rapidly expanded into eastern Central Eurasia and other neighboring regions; the Khazar Kingdom and several other states founded by Turks in Central Eurasia, in addition to the still existing Türk Empire in the Eastern Steppe; and the old Eastern Roman Empire, which recreated itself as a new, more compact empire that was officially Greek in language. Central Eurasia and its flourishing economy became the focus of all major Eurasian states during the Second Regional Empire Period in Eurasia, which is generally known as the Early Middle Ages.

All of these states were focused on Central Eurasia, and all tried to conquer at least the parts of it nearest to their borders. The cultural flourishing of the Early Middle Ages (ca. AD 620–840) was thus accompanied by almost constant war in the region. Some new features of the warfare directly reflected the fact that the major empires of Eurasia had ended up bordering on each other: great inter-empire alliances were formed in opposition to other imperial alliances. The constant warfare escalated toward the middle of the eighth century during the Türgiš and Pamir wars in Central Asia, ending in victory for the Arab-Chinese alliance against the Central Eurasians. The recession that followed across much of Eurasia shows that the world had already become economically interconnected and dependent on the flourishing of the Central Eurasian economy, the Silk Road.

The Avar Empire in the Eastern Steppe

In the late fourth to early fifth century, the empire of the Avars or Jou-jan,[1] a people of unknown origin who had been subjects of the Hsien-pei, ruled the northern steppe from the northeast Tarim Basin to Korea. At the same time, the Hsien-pei Mongolic *Taghbač[2] ruled a great empire that included most of North China and the southern edge of the steppe zone. The two peoples were usually at war with each other until the early sixth century, when the *Taghbač, who were by then largely Sinicized, made peace with the kaghan or emperor of the Avars, Anagai. In 545, after the Wei Dynasty of the

---

[1] See endnote 18 for discussion of the equation of Avar and Jou-jan.
[2] See Beckwith (2005b) for this name.

*Taghbač divided into eastern and western halves, the Eastern Wei remained allied with Avars, but the Western Wei made an alliance with *Tumïn,[3] the *yabghu* or 'subordinate king' of the Türk, a vassal people of the Avars.

Around 546 *Tumïn heard that the T'ieh-le, a confederation living north of Mongolia, planned to attack the Avar realm. He led a preemptive attack against the T'ieh-le and defeated them. *Tumïn then asked the Avar kaghan Anagai for a royal princess in marriage. But Anagai insulted the Türk, calling them his "blacksmith slaves." *Tumïn angrily turned to China. In that year he asked for and received a royal marriage from the Western Wei. In 552 *Tumïn attacked the Avars and defeated them. Anagai committed suicide.[4] The Türk pursued the remnants of the Avars across the length and breadth of Eurasia, conquering as they went, until they had united under Turkic rule the entire Central Eurasian steppe and had come into direct contact with the Chinese, Persian, and Eastern Roman empires.[5]

The Avars were given refuge by the Eastern Roman Empire. Partly through clever alliances with other peoples they made their way into the Pannonian Plain, where they settled and continued to call their ruler the kaghan, to the great annoyance of the Türk.

The Türk Conquest

The center of Turkic power, at least in theory, was the Ötükän Yish, or 'Wooded Mountain of Ötükän', which was located somewhere in the Altai Mountains.[6] The Turkic ancestral cavern was located there, and every year a ritual or ceremony was carried out in the cave.[7] Whoever controlled the Ötükän held the dignity of supreme authority among all the Turks. In practice, it meant only that the ruler of the Eastern Steppe had the title of

---

[3] On the name *Tumïn, written T'u-men 土門, and the Old Turkic inscriptional form *Bumïn*, see endnotes 10 and 17.

[4] CS 50: 909.

[5] For discussion of apparently mythological elements that are presented as historical fact in the sources, see the Türk national foundation story in the prologue and the notes to it.

[6] Sinor (1990c: 295).

[7] It has been thought that this tradition, and the fact that the Türk really were skilled iron metallurgists—confirmed by both Chinese and Greek historical sources—indicate that the cave was actually an iron mine; cf. Sinor (1990c: 296). In view of the close mythological parallel with the Koguryo, in which the cave (also in the mountains in the eastern part of the realm) is the abode of the grain god, this might be questioned.

kaghan and theoretical primacy over the other Turkic peoples. The actual home encampment of the Türk was in the Orkhon River region (in what is now north-central Mongolia), the center of Eastern Steppe empires before and after them.

Classical Latin sources, which contain the first historical references to a Türk people, have them living in the forests north of the Sea of Azov.[8] The next reference to Turkic peoples is thought to be to members of the Hun confederation, based on their Turkic-sounding names. By the mid-sixth century at the latest, when they are recorded in Chinese sources, they had become pastoral nomads and had learned the skills of steppe warfare. They had also become skilled blacksmiths and continued to practice these skills. Their Avar titulature reveals that they must have learned how to establish and maintain a steppe empire from the Avars.

The religious beliefs of the Türk focused on a sky god, Tängri, and an earth goddess, Umay.[9] Some of the Turks—notably the Western Turks in Tokharistan—converted very early to Buddhism, and it played an important role among them. Other religions were also influential, particularly Christianity and Manichaeism, which were popular among the Sogdians, close allies of the Türk who were skilled in international trade. Although the Sogdians were a settled, urban people, they were like the Türk in that they also had a Central Eurasian warrior ethos with a pervasive comitatus tradition, and both peoples were intensely interested in trade.

Tumïn took the title kaghan and ruled over the eastern part of the realm, but died in the same year. He was succeeded by his son K'uo-lo, who ruled for a few months before he too died. Bukhan[10] (Mu-han, r. 553–572), another son of *Tumïn, then succeeded. *Tumïn's brother Ištemi (r. 552–576) ruled over the western part of the realm as subordinate kaghan—*yabghu* or *yabghu*

---

[8] In the mid-first century AD, *Turcae* 'Turks' are mentioned there by Pomponius Mela. They are also mentioned in the *Natural History* of Pliny the Elder (Sinor 1990c: 285), spelled *Tyrcae* 'Türks'. However, from the sixth century on there is a steady movement of Turks from east to west. See Czeglédy (1983); cf. Golden (1992).

[9] Their beliefs are similar to those of the Scythians and other early steppe peoples, as well as other later peoples. They seem to be important elements of the Central Eurasian Culture Complex and deserve the attention of historians of religion.

[10] Clearly the same name as the Turkic leader Βώχαν- Bôkhan, for Old Turkic *Buqan*, mentioned in Menander (Blockley 1985: 178–179, 277 n. 235). In standard "Middle Chinese," pace Pulleyblank (1991), *m*- before a vowel was regularly pronounced ᵐ*b*- (Beckwith 2002a, 2006b; cf. Pulleyblank 1984); there are many examples of this syllable onset used to transcribe Old Turkic words beginning with *b*.

kaghan—with a winter camp somewhere near Karashahr (Agni).[11] This gradually became the de facto independent realm of the Western Turks, while *Tumïn's successors reigned over the Türk, or Eastern Turks, and retained the full imperial dignity.[12]

In pursuing the Avars, Ištemi's forces reached the Aral Sea region by 555 and soon after the lower Volga. In 558 the first Turkic embassy reached Constantinople, seeking the remaining Avars who had not submitted, as well as a trade alliance with the Eastern Roman Empire.

In their expansion, the Turks encountered the Hephthalites, who by the early sixth century had conquered Sogdiana, eastward into the Tarim Basin, and up to the borders of the Avars and the *Taghbač (Wei Dynasty) in North China. The Hephthalites were thus major Central Asian rivals of the early Turks.

Soon after the Turks under Ištemi Kaghan arrived on the northern borders of the Persian Empire, Khosraw I (Anushirvan the Just, r. 531–579) made an alliance with them against the Hephthalites. Between 557 and 561, the Persians and Turks attacked the Hephthalites, destroyed their kingdom, and partitioned it between the two victors, setting the Oxus River as the border between them.[13]

At some time before 568, the Turks sent a trading mission of Sogdian merchants led by the Sogdian Maniakh to the Persian Empire to request permission to sell their silks in Persia. The Persians bought the silk but burned it publicly in front of the merchants. The offensive answer prompted the Turks to send another mission, consisting of Turks, but this time the Persians murdered them,[14] in violation of the time-honored law of international diplomatic immunity. A state of war existed from that point on between Turks and Persians.

The Turks, advised by the Sogdians, attempted to establish an alliance with the Eastern Roman Empire to go around the Persians. In 569 the Ro-

---

[11] The title *yabghu* (i.e., *yaβyu*) goes back to the title of the governors-general of the five constituent parts of the Tokharian realm in Bactria, one of whom eventually rose to power and founded the Kushan Empire (Enoki et al. 1994: 171).

[12] The ethnonym *Türk* is actually the same as the Anglicized *Turk*; the name was pronounced [tyrk], that is, Türk, and still is so pronounced in modern Turkish and most other Turkic languages today. The traditional scholarly convention of using the spelling Türk only for the people of the first two Turkic empires based in the Eastern Steppe is followed here. On the Chinese and other foreign transcriptions of the name, see Beckwith (2005, forthcoming-a).

[13] Frye (1983: 156), Sinor (1990c: 299–301).

[14] Sinor (1990c: 301–302).

mans sent a mission to the Turks. It returned the next year with a caravan load of silk. Although the Turks had thus secured their Roman flank by diplomacy, they could not capture the Persian fortifications. The two sides made peace in 571, though because the Persians continued to refuse to let the Turks trade freely with them, relations remained hostile between the two empires.

Between 567 and 571 the Western Turks took control of the North Caucasus Steppe, and in 576, the Western Steppe. Both regions apparently had already been populated at least partly by Turkic peoples, but now the Turks ruled over the entire Central Eurasian steppe zone. This was the second time in history that it had come under the control of a single ethnolinguistic group, though this time the unification was achieved by a single family or dynasty.[15] They were the political successors of the Avars, and before them the Hsiung-nu, but they far surpassed their predecessors.

The two halves of the empire became increasingly separate over time. In the Eastern Türk realm, based in the Eastern Steppe and western Manchuria, Bukhan Kaghan was succeeded by his younger brother Tatpar Kaghan[16] (r. 572–581). In the Western Turkic realm, Ištemi was succeeded by his son Tardu (r. ca. 576–603). By 583 Tardu was known as the Yabghu Kaghan of the Western Turks. His empire comprised the northern Tarim Basin, Jungharia,[17] Transoxiana, and Tokhâristân.[18]

The Western Turkic realm itself gradually became further divided: an eastern part consisting of the On Oq or 'Ten Arrows' of the Western Turks, based in Jungharia, the northern Tarim Basin, and eastern Transoxiana; the realm of the Yabghu of Tokhâristân in southern Central Asia; the Khazar Kaghanate, which developed by about 630, centering on the region from the lower Volga and North Caucasus Steppe to the Don; the Danubian Bulgar khanate west of the Khazars in the lower Danube region and lands to the west, founded in about 680 by Asparukh; and the kingdom of the

---

[15] The Scythians, or Northern Iranians, who were culturally and ethnolinguistically a single group at the beginning of their expansion, had earlier controlled the entire steppe zone. Like the later Turks, they gradually diverged over time.

[16] His name was formerly read Taspar. See Yoshida and Moriyasu (1999) and Beckwith (2005b).

[17] The name is an anachronism, but there is no other well-established geographical name for the region. It is also spelled Dzungaria, after the Khalkha dialect pronunciation. See the discussion of the name Junghar and its variants in Beckwith (forthcoming-b).

[18] Tokhâristân at this time was roughly equivalent to the territory of present-day Afghanistan and some adjacent areas.

Volga Bulgars, who moved north of the Khazars into the Volga-Kama area in the late seventh century.

There were only a few minor dialect differences among the different Turkic groups stemming from the imperial foundation in the Eastern Steppe, and it is generally believed that there were no major linguistic divisions in the early Old Turkic period. Nevertheless, the Bulgar and Khazar Turks soon spoke a Turkic dialect or language so distinct from the other Turkic dialects that it was difficult or impossible for other Turks to understand.

The Roman-Persian Wars and the Arab Conquest

By the end of the sixth century, the Sasanid Persians, who had been at war on and off with the Eastern Roman Empire for about three centuries, had gradually extended their power into the southern Arabian Peninsula. In around 598 they defeated the local ruler of the Himyarite Kingdom, making the conquered territory a province of the Sasanid Empire.[19] They thus controlled all international trade to and from India and further east by sea and dominated the trade routes by land as well.

In 602 the Eastern Roman emperor Maurice (582–602) was overthrown and killed along with his family. The leader of the insurrection, Phocas (r. 602–610), was proclaimed the new emperor. However, not only some Romans but also the Persian emperor Khusraw II considered Phocas to have usurped the throne. Khusraw's own throne had been recovered with Maurice's help, and he had made peace with the Romans partly at the cost of some Sasanid territory. The Persians lost no time in attacking the Romans, at first with only minor success, but in 607 they invaded Roman Mesopotamia and Armenia and captured most of the Armenian territory they had earlier lost to the Romans. In 608, while a plague ravaged Constantinople, the Persians marched deeper into Roman Mesopotamia and Armenia. In 609 they raided across Anatolia all the way to Chalcedon, across the Bosphorus from Constantinople itself.[20] The Roman exarch, or governor, of North Africa rebelled in Carthage against Phocas, and his forces succeeded in taking Egypt, which with the rest of North Africa constituted the main

---

[19] Frye (1983: 158).
[20] Treadgold (1997: 231–241).

source of grain for the capital. Heraclius (r. 610–641), the son of the exarch, then sailed to Constantinople with a fleet and troops from the provinces of Africa and Egypt. He executed Phocas and was crowned emperor in 610.

The Persians' advance continued, though, and before Heraclius could restore central authority, they had captured much of the empire outside the capital district, including Mesopotamia, Syria, Palestine, and part of Anatolia; in 614 they took Jerusalem and carried off the True Cross to Ctesiphon. At the same time, the Avars and Slavs marched on the empire from the north and captured most of Thrace and much other imperial territory there. By 615 the Eastern Roman Empire retained only the capital district, part of Anatolia, Egypt, and Africa. In 617 the Avars, evidently in alliance with the Persians, attacked the city from the north and put it under siege. In 618 the Persians invaded Egypt, taking Alexandria in 619 and cutting off the main grain supply to Constantinople. The Roman Empire was at its lowest point in history and seemed doomed to fall.[21]

Yet Heraclius did not give up. In 622 he made a truce with the Avars and reorganized the military forces still available to him, developing an earlier system of local support and stationing of soldiers into what became the "feudal" theme system.[22] He personally led the army east into Armenia, where he attacked and defeated the forces of the Persians. When news arrived that the Avars had broken the truce and invaded southern Thrace, he hurried back. Making another agreement with the Avars, he turned around and marched east again in 624. He took Armenia and pursued the Persians further east, defeating the main Persian forces sent against him in 625. Rather than returning home, he wintered with his army near Lake Van.

To counter the Roman advance, Khusraw made an alliance with the Avars to attack Constantinople. Nevertheless, with the help of superior intelligence agents, Heraclius foiled the attacks of the Persians and defeated them, and though the Avars did lay siege to the capital city, they too were

---

[21] Treadgold (1997: 239–241, 287–293).

[22] According to Treadgold (1997: 315 et seq.), the explicit reorganization of the empire into *themes*, or military governorships wherein the soldiers were settled on the land they defended, was the accomplishment of his grandson Constans II (r. 641–668), but the essentials of this reform seem to have been laid by Heraclius himself, on still earlier foundations; see the discussion by Ostrogorsky (1968: 96 et seq.). This "feudal" system had already spread far and wide across Eurasia and was also found among the Germanic, Arab, and Turkic peoples around the Byzantine Empire, including the Germanic Vandals who had settled in North Africa.

frustrated.[23] The turning point came in 627, when Heraclius made an alliance with the Khazars, a Turkic people who had established a powerful state in the North Caucasus Steppe and lower Volga;[24] the alliance was to prove of great importance to the empire throughout the Early Middle Ages. In autumn the allies advanced successfully across Azerbaijan. Though the Khazars withdrew for the winter, Heraclius went against tradition and remained on campaign. He invaded Mesopotamia and in December defeated a Persian army near Nineveh. He then moved on to the royal palace at Dastagird (now Daskara), east of Ctesiphon, and captured and plundered it in 628. Shortly thereafter, Khusraw was overthrown by his son, Kavad II (r. 628), and the two sides made peace. In 629 Heraclius negotiated return of the former Roman territories in Mesopotamia, Syria, and Palestine with the Persian general there, and in 630 he returned to Constantinople in triumph with the True Cross.[25]

Heraclius was not destined to enjoy his success against the Persians. During the long Persian-Roman war, the situation had become increasingly critical for the Arabs on the Arabian Peninsula. Many once prosperous towns had been deserted or turned into nomad encampments. The merchants of the western Arabian Peninsula, among whom were the Quraysh family of Mecca, had dominated a carefully maintained system of tribal alliances, involving security for pilgrimage and trade, running at least from the southwestern corner of the Arabian Peninsula northward to the Eastern Roman border region in Syria, and probably from there northeast to the Persian border region near the Lower Euphrates. Because of the Roman and Persian destabilization of the Arab frontier in the north, and the wars in which southern Arabia was devastated by Persians and Abyssinians, both internal and external trade[26] were much diminished, and the tribal alliance system was in trouble. The foreign penetration of Arabia seems to have been the final catalyst that brought about intensive internal ferment among the

[23] For detailed coverage of the Avars and their involvement in this war, see Pohl (1988).
[24] Much excellent research has been published on the Khazars, including Dunlop (1954), Golden (1980), and many papers by Golden and by Thomas Noonan; see http://www.getcited.org/mbrz/11063130 and http://www.getcited.org/mbrz/10075924.
[25] Treadgold (1997: 293–299), Frye (1983: 168–170).
[26] Crone (1987) carefully reevaluates earlier theories about this trade and the rise of Islam. Her contention that the Arabs were not involved in the high-value luxury goods trade is contradicted by the musk trade, which she does mention, but which the Arabs seem to have dominated from pre-Islamic times on. For this trade, and musk in general, see King (2007).

Arabs.[27] When the crisis became severe, a young scion of the Quraysh family, Muḥammad, proposed a radical solution: the unification of the people of Arabia and all of their many gods as one community, the *umma*, under one god, Allâh '*the* God'. Muḥammad's ideas were considered revolutionary and he was forced to flee for his life to Medina in 622. There he and his followers, the Muslims—'those who submit (to the will of Allâh)'—soon took command of the city and pressed forward with their plans to unify Arabia.[28]

The new Persian emperor Kavâd II died, apparently from the plague, after ruling for less than a year. He was succeeded by numerous relatives and generals who also reigned for less than a year. Finally, in 632, Yazdgerd III (r. 632–651), a grandson of Khusraw II, was crowned. But the Sasanid realm was disorganized and seriously weakened from the years of war and civil strife over the succession.[29]

In that same year Muḥammad died. The young Muslim community was unprepared for his succession. The Prophet had no male heir, and there was no other tradition to follow, so it was decided to choose his favorite and most respected follower, Abû Bakr (r. 632–634), as his *khalîfa* 'successor', or *caliph*. Under his chairman-like rule the rebellions that followed the death of Muḥammad were quickly put down. But by this time, after the wars of unification under Muḥammad and the wars of rebellion, trade across the peninsula had practically come to a standstill. In 633 the army of the most brilliant Muslim general, Khâlid ibn al-Walîd, who was largely responsible for the successful suppression of the rebellions, ended up on the borders of the Sasanid realm in the northeast, where the local Muslims were already raiding the Sasanids. Khâlid simply joined in, providing a solution to the economic crisis and also a means of rewarding the loyal Arabs in his army.[30]

In the following year, Abû Bakr sent an expedition against the Byzantines in southern Palestine. But the latter were relatively well organized and only suffered a minor defeat. The caliph then ordered Khâlid to join the expedition. He crossed the Syrian desert in five days, took command, and defeated the Byzantines in a major battle at Ajnâdayn, in Syria.

---

[27] Crone (1987: 246, 250).
[28] On the controversy over the role of trade in the early Islamic expansion, see endnote 62.
[29] Frye (1983: 170–171).
[30] On dubious views about Islam and the early Muslims in connection with the conquests, see endnote 63.

Under the second caliph, 'Umar ibn al-Khaṭṭâb (r. 634–644), the former rebels in Arabia were allowed to join the campaigns in the north. But the Sasanids crushed the Arabs with elephants in 634 at the Battle of the Bridge, while the Byzantines also strengthened their borders. The Arabs made an all-out effort, sending all their forces to the attack. In 637 they defeated the Persians decisively at the Battle of Qâdisiyya (near Kufa on the Euphrates), and the Arabs occupied Ctesiphon, capturing the Sasanid imperial regalia and other Persian treasures. The crown of Khusraw II was sent to the Kaaba (Ka'ba).[31]

In the same year, the Arabs also defeated a major counterattack by the Byzantines at the Battle of the Yarmûk, in Southern Syria, forcing them to withdraw from Syria. The Arabs followed their stunning first successes with victory after victory in the Near East. They captured Egypt in 640 and went on to conquer North Africa.[32] Within ten years of Muḥammad's death virtually all of the provinces of the Eastern Roman Empire except southeastern Europe, Anatolia, and Armenia had fallen to the Arabs.

Heraclius had reorganized the Eastern Roman Empire a few short years earlier in order to save it from the Persians and their allies and had increased the people's support for the government. Now he saw the empire's most productive territories once again taken away from him. Yet while the Persian Empire fell entirely to the Arabs,[33] his reorganization of his empire into *themes*, and his alliance with the Turkic kingdom of the Khazars, formed the basis for the long-term survival of the Byzantine Empire—the new nation-state he and his grandson Constans II (r. 641–668) created out of the remnants of the Eastern Roman Empire.[34]

Upon the decisive defeat and collapse of the Persian Empire in 637, Yazdgerd III fled northeast into Khurasan with his remaining forces. In 642 the

---

[31] On the popular but erroneous idea that the Arabs destroyed Persian and Greek libraries, see endnote 64.

[32] Shaban (1971: 24–34).

[33] The Iranocentric view that the lands of Central Asia where Iranian languages were spoken, including Margiana, Bactriana, and Transoxiana, were Persian territories, and their people Persians, is incorrect. See endnote 65.

[34] Latin was abandoned as an administrative language. In its place Greek was made the official language of the empire (Ostrogorsky 1968: 106), though the Byzantines always referred to themselves as Romans right down to the end of their "Roman Empire" in 1453. In view of the Arabicization of nearly all of the non-Iranian-speaking regions of the Near East and North Africa after the Arab conquest, Heraclius may well have saved the Greek nation and language from disappearance.

Arabs destroyed the last Sasanid army at the Battle of Nihâvand. In Central Asia Yazdgerd attempted to gather the support of the local nobility from his base in Marw, but as the Arabs approached, the *marzbân* of Marw and the Hephthalite prince of Bâdghîs attacked him and defeated his forces in 651. Though the emperor himself escaped, he was killed shortly thereafter in the vicinity of Marw.[35] The Arabs attacked and took Marw in the same year, followed by Nishapur.

In 652 the Arabs captured the cities of northern Tokhâristân, including Balkh, a great commercial city and the northwesternmost center of Buddhism, with its famous circular-plan monastery, Nawbahâr 'the New Vihâra',[36] where the Chinese traveler monk Hsüan Tsang (ca. 600–664) had stayed and studied for a month with the master Prajñâkara in 628 or 630.[37] The city dwellers of former Sasanid Khurâsân and the former Hephthalite principalities were forced to pay tribute, to accept Arab garrisons, and to make room for the Arabs in their houses. At about the same time, other Arab forces moved through Kirman into Sîstân (Sijistân, in what is now southwestern Afghanistan), capturing the westernmost part.[38] Marw, which was a great commercial city, became the Arabs' major base for military operations in Central Asia. Although they suffered a temporary setback during the civil war between the fourth caliph, 'Alî (r. 656–661), and Mu'âwiya, the governor of Syria, which ended with the death of 'Alî and establishment of Mu'âwiya as caliph and founder of the Umayyad Dynasty in 661,[39] the Arabs very quickly reestablished their authority and continued their expansion deep into Central Asia.

---

[35] Shaban (1970: 18–19). His son Pêrôz eventually fled to China. A *marzbân* was a 'warden of the march, markgrave', usually a district governor or military governor in the late Sasanid Empire and early Arab Caliphate (Kramers and Morony 1991). Yazdgerd is said to have been killed by the *marzbân* Mâhûî Sûrî in 31 AH/AD 634 (Yakubovskii and Bosworth 1991).

[36] It was known at the time that the complex had originally been built as a Sasanid provincial capital. For the design, and the plan of the City of Peace, the Abbasid capital at Baghdad, which was based on the underlying plan of both Nawbahâr and Ctesiphon, see Beckwith (1984b), where Ctesiphon is incorrectly ruled out.

[37] The usual date is 630; according to Ch'en (1992: 42–53), he was there in 628. On his studies there, see endnote 66.

[38] A general uprising broke out there in 653; though an army sent to subdue the rebellion was successful, the region again broke away immediately afterward. Upon Mu'âwiya's succession as caliph, he sent a great expedition to Sîstân. The Arabs recaptured Zarang and took Kabul. However, most of the conquered areas long remained de facto independent.

[39] Shaban (1971: 70–78). On the civil war, see endnote 67.

Chinese Reunification and Imperial Expansion

In 589 the period known variously as the Sixteen Dynasties or the Northern and Southern Dynasties came to an end with reunification by the Sui (581–617). Much like the Ch'in Dynasty 700 years earlier, the Sui reunification was a bloody affair accompanied by prodigious public works, in this case by the building of the Grand Canal, which for the first time provided a reliable means of transportation between southern and northern China and also tied the provinces along the eastern coast together. China was never to stay divided for long again.

Like the Ch'in, the Sui was also a short-lived dynasty. It was brought down by a number of factors, the most important of which were the disastrous campaigns of the second ruler Yang-ti (r. 604–617)[40] against the Koguryo Kingdom, which stretched from the Liao River east to the Sea of Japan and southward halfway down the Korean Peninsula. But again like the Ch'in, the Sui laid firm foundations for the stable, strong, long-lasting dynasty that followed.

The T'ang Dynasty (618–906) was founded in 618 by Kao-tsu (Li Yüan, r. 618–626), the Duke of T'ang, who was the Sui garrison commander of T'ai-yüan (in the northern part of what is now Shansi Province), six months after he led anti-Sui rebel forces into the Sui capital in 617.[41] The Li family was from the north and was related to the royal families of both the Northern Chou Dynasty (557–581) and the Sui Dynasty and had intermarried with members of the *Taghbač aristocracy of the Northern Wei Dynasty. They were acquainted with and intensely interested in things Central Eurasian. The very foundation of the T'ang Dynasty owed part of its success to an alliance Kao-tsu had made with the ruler of the Eastern Türk, Shih-pi Kaghan (r. 609–619), who provided horses and five hundred Türk warriors to assist the T'ang forces in defeating the Sui.[42]

The myth that the Türk were a threat to China at this time is based on their involvement with one or another rebel in the civil war that ended the Sui Dy-

---

[40] He was the son of the dynastic founder and Tu-ku Ch'ieh-lo, who was from a non-Chinese aristocratic family.

[41] Wechsler (1979a: 150–153).

[42] Wechsler (1979a: 159). This was hardly a "diplomatic offensive *against*" the Eastern Türk (Wechsler 1979a: 187; emphasis added).

nasty; in support of their allies, Türk forces entered the Sui frontier on several occasions. The idea that there was a "threat of an attack by the Eastern Turks and their allies"[43] and that their ruler *Hellig (*Ellig, Hsieh-li) Kaghan (r. 620–630) "made himself a thorough nuisance and a menace,"[44] necessitating the destruction of the Eastern Türk Empire, is not correct. It is true that the Türk still supported various rebels against the barely established dynasty throughout its first years, but again, they were invited in—they did not invade China. It took most of the reign of the first emperor to eliminate rebels throughout the Chinese domain in general, including areas very far from the northern frontier. The carefully crafted stories about supposed Türk invasions are ultimately disinformation intended to justify the subsequent massive aggression by the T'ang against the Türk and everyone else on the existing frontiers of China. The sources tell us little about the Türk except that they "raided the frontier" in such and such a place and time; no actual historical reasons are given other than the standard stereotypes that the Türk were greedy or violent. When more historical information is available, it is clear that they were not raids, and there was usually a good reason for the Türk actions.[45]

The T'ang, like earlier Chinese dynasties, intended to build the biggest empire in history. The Türk were no different in their desire to enlarge their empire, but the "Chinese" areas they tried to expand into were parts of the Central Eurasian steppe zone that had been occupied, garrisoned, fortified, and walled off by the Chinese, whose declared intention was to continue expanding in all directions to conquer "the peoples of the four directions" until they ruled all of Central Eurasia as well as China. In short, the idea that the T'ang experience with the Türk in their early years made the Chinese realize the danger of allowing a strong foreign nation to exist so close to their power base is almost the opposite of the truth. The T'ang were also keenly aware of the history of the great Classical period dynasty, the Han, and openly expressed their desire to emulate the Chinese conquests of the Classical period. According to the official histories, the Han Dynasty had succeeded in defeating the Hsiung-nu, conquering the cities of the Tarim Basin, and capturing Korea as well. Although none of this was completely true, the T'ang rulers saw themselves as the heirs of the Han and wanted not only to restore the Classical age but even to outdo the Han Dynasty.

[43] Wechsler (1979a: 157).
[44] Sinor (1990c: 308).
[45] See the epilogue for further discussion.

T'ai-tsung (Li Shih-min, r. 626–649), Kao-tsu's son, took power in a dynastic coup d'état. In the process, two of his brothers were killed—he personally decapitated the crown prince—and Kao-tsu was forced to hand over power.[46] T'ai-tsung immediately turned his attention to the Türk.

The traditional Chinese policy toward foreign peoples outside their territory was "divide, dominate, and destroy." To this end, the T'ang actively fomented unrest and internal division in both the Eastern and Western Türk empires. T'ai-tsung was given his casus belli by the attack of Liang Shih-tu, the last remaining rebel from the period of the fall of the Sui, whose base was in the northern Ordos. Liang called a large Türk force in to attack the fledgling T'ang Dynasty on his behalf. The Türk reached the Wei River only ten miles west of the capital, Ch'ang-an, in 626. T'ai-tsung had no choice but to pay *Hellig Kaghan to withdraw.

Fate was not kind to *Hellig after this, however. In 627 several Central Eurasian peoples subject to the Eastern Türk, including the Uighurs, Bayarku, and Hsüeh-yen-t'o, revolted, and late in the year the weather turned bad too—unusually deep snowfall caused the death of so many animals that there was a famine on the steppe. Deprived of Türk assistance, Liang Shih-tu was vulnerable, and T'ai-tsung jumped at the opportunity. Early in 628 the T'ang forces attacked his camp and Liang was killed by one of his own men. The T'ang also strongly supported a new kaghan chosen by the peoples who had revolted against the Türk. In 629 *Hellig Kaghan requested permission to submit to China. T'ai-tsung refused and instead sent an enormous army against him. They attacked his camp on the south side of the Gobi Desert and slaughtered great numbers of the Türk. *Hellig was taken alive in 630 and brought to Ch'ang-an. He died in captivity there in 634.

The Chinese Empire grew in all directions in the early T'ang, with few setbacks, reaching its greatest extent during the rule of Emperor Hsüantsung (685–756 [r. 712–756]).[47] In the first half of the eighth century, China—especially the western capital, Ch'ang-an—enjoyed the most cosmopolitan period in its entire history before the late twentieth century. The city was the largest, most populous, and wealthiest anywhere in the world at the time, with perhaps a million residents, including a large population of foreigners

---

[46] Wechsler (1979a: 185–186).
[47] Dillon (1998: 360).

either residing permanently or visiting in various capacities. Hsüan-tsung patronized Western music and the poetry influenced by it, as well as the new Western-influenced painting style that had been introduced from Khotan in the early T'ang period. This was the greatest age of Chinese poetry, when many major poets lived, including the two most brilliant Chinese poets,[48] Li Po and Tu Fu, who were famous in their own lifetimes. Li Po was born in Central Asia and may have been only partly Chinese. He was an outsider socially and "remained, in a profound way, a solitary and unique figure," probably due to his "foreign" behavior and to some extent to the rather un-Chinese image of himself he projected in his poetry,[49] which is characterized by a love of the exotic in general.

Yet the T'ang hunger for territorial expansion at all costs, especially under Hsüan-tsung, was such that the great Chinese historian Ssu-ma Kuang later accused the T'ang house of trying to "swallow the peoples of the four directions."[50] The internal devastation of northern China by unending conscription and ruthless taxation, remarked on by poets and historians, would have to be paid for.

The Tibetan Empire

The economic, cultural, diplomatic, and other motivations behind the appearance of a great new power, which are known in other historical cases, have not been identified in the case of the rise of the Tibetan Empire. The only known motivations are the sociopolitical features of a culture with the Central Eurasian Culture Complex.[51]

---

[48] They were not, however, supported by Hsüan-tsung. Considering his actions with respect to An Lu-shan even before his rebellion, as well as many similar examples, it can only be concluded that Hsüan-tsung was a poor judge of character in general.

[49] Owen (1981: 143). Li Po (701–ca. 763) was born in Central Asia and lived in Suyab (near what is now Tokmak in Kirghizstan). At some point in his youth his family moved to Szechuan, where he grew up. They may have been merchants, and it is suspected that he was only part Chinese. See Eide (1973: 388–389); cf. Owen (1981: 112). Though Li Po influenced other important poets of his day—most famously Tu Fu—he was ignored by most other poets during his lifetime.

[50] *TCTC* 216: 6889.

[51] In the Tibetan case, these elements include the ruler and his heroic companions, the comitatus, as the pinnacle of society; the burial of the ruler together with his comitatus, horses, and personal wealth in a great tumulus; and a strong interest in trade.

In the early seventh century a group of clan chiefs in southern Tibet swore an oath of fealty to the leading power among them, calling him *btsanpo* 'emperor'. Together they plotted to overthrow Zingporje, their oppressive alien overlord, who was apparently a vassal of the shadowy Zhangzhung realm that ruled much of the Tibetan Plateau at the time. The conspirators carried out their plan successfully and were rewarded by the emperor, whom they also refer to as Spurgyal.[52] The emperor rewarded them with fiefs, and young noblemen from each of the clans joined his comitatus to cement the clans' relationship to him. After having established themselves in their home territory, the new people defeated the lord of Rtsang and Bod, the areas—now Central Tibet—that lay directly to their north. They adopted the ancient name *Bod* for their country, but to the outside world it became known by the foreign name *Tibet*.[53]

The circumstances in which the Tibetans first[54] came into conflict with the Chinese are known. In 634 the T'ang sent a huge expeditionary force against the T'u-yü-hun Kingdom in the Kokonor region. The T'u-yü-hun, a Hsien-pei Mongolic people, had occupied the pasturelands around the Kokonor in the third century[55] and expanded via Kansu into the eastern part of East Turkistan so as to control the southern trade routes between China and Central Asia. The T'ang campaign was successful, but it brought the Chinese into conflict with the Tibetans, who considered the T'u-yü-hun to be their vassals. After being rebuffed politically by the Chinese, Khri Srong Rtsan ('Srong Btsan Sgampo', r. ca. 618–649), the first historically well-known Tibetan emperor, defeated a T'ang force sent against him in 638. When the T'ang inflicted a minor defeat on them in turn, the Tibetans requested a marriage treaty with the T'ang. T'ai-tsung agreed and made peace with the Tibetans with the marriage of a T'ang princess to the son or younger brother of the Tibetan emperor.[56] The T'ang did not succeed in gaining firm control over the T'u-yü-hun and effectively accepted the Ti-

[52] On the title Spurgyal and current ahistorical use of it by some scholars, see endnote 68.

[53] 'Tibet' is an exonym—a foreign name for the country. The name is related to the name of the Mongolic T'o-pa, or *Taghbač, and has nothing at all to do with the native name of the country, *Bod*. See the detailed discussion in Beckwith (2005b).

[54] Actually, the Tibetans had earlier met the Sui Dynasty Chinese in exactly the same unpleasant circumstances; their realm was then known to the Chinese as *Fu kuo* 'the kingdom of Fu' (Beckwith 1993: 17–19). The transcription *Fu* might reflect *Spu* or *Bod*, as many have suggested, but it would in either case be highly irregular.

[55] Molè (1970: xii).

[56] Beckwith (1993: 23). On the continuing misunderstanding of this marriage, see endnote 69.

betans' claims to their territory except for the Kansu corridor, which the T'ang needed in order for Chinese forces to be able to attack the cities of the Tarim Basin.

After thus securing his left flank, T'ai-tsung expanded westward into the Tarim Basin, conquering the city-states there one by one: Qocho or Kao-ch'ang (640), the chief city of the East Tokharians,[57] in the Turfan oasis; and Agni or Karashahr (648) and Kucha (648), the chief cities of the West Tokharians and centers both of commerce and of Sarvâstivâdin Buddhism. Kashgar, Yarkand, and Khotan,[58] the chief cities of the Sakas or Eastern Iranians in the western Tarim Basin, voluntarily submitted to Chinese overlordship between 632 and 635. Against the advice of his leading ministers, T'ai-tsung then established a colonial government over the region, the Protectorate General of the Pacified West,[59] known for short as An-hsi 'the Pacified West' and also as 'the Four Garrisons of An-hsi'. Its seat was moved from Qocho west to Kucha in 649. The T'ang now controlled most of eastern Central Eurasia.

The death of both Khri Srong Rtsan and T'ai-tsung in 649 was followed by a gradual chilling of relations between their empires.

In 657 the armies of T'ai-tsung's son and successor, Kao-tsung (r. 649–683), broke the power of the Western Turks. Ho-lu Kaghan was captured alive and taken to the Chinese capital. With the Chinese defeat of the Western Turks in the Tarim Basin and Jungharia, the area—which was already called Turkistan by other Central Eurasian peoples—theoretically then came under T'ang rule. But the Western Turks as a whole did not come under actual Chinese control.[60] Instead, with the removal of the ruling clan, a great power struggle ensued.

At the same time, the Tibetans expanded into the territory of the former Zhangzhung Kingdom in the western Tibetan Plateau and on into the Pamir region, which straddled the trade routes from the Tarim Basin in Eastern Central Asia to Tokhâristân in Western Central Asia. By 661 to 663 they had subdued the Pamir kingdoms of Balûr (or Bruźa) and Wakhân, and an area

---

[57] However, they seem to have spoken West Tokharian by about this time. The precise periodization (and localization) of the Tokharian languages of East Turkistan remains to be established.

[58] Khotan, unlike the northern cities, was a strong center of Mahâyâna Buddhism.

[59] Or Pacify-the-West Protectorate.

[60] The claim that they really did is repeated in virtually everything written on the subject, but it is based on taking the grand statements in the Chinese dynastic histories at face value.

around Kashgar. In 663 also, Mgar Stong Rtsan the Conqueror decisively defeated the T'u-yü-hun and incorporated their land and people into the Tibetan Empire. The T'u-yü-hun kaghan, his Chinese princess, and several thousand families of T'u-yü-hun fled to China. The Tibetans subdued Khotan as early as 665, and two years later, after fighting off constant Chinese attacks, the Western Turks nominally accepted Tibetan overlordship. This relationship developed into the Tibetan–Western Turk alliance, which lasted for almost a century, through several changes of regime on both sides.

In 668 the Tibetans constructed defensive fortifications on the Jima Khol (Ta fei ch'uan), a river in the former T'u-yü-hun realm, in anticipation of a Chinese attack. In the early spring of 670, with Khotanese troops, the Tibetans attacked and took Aksu. That left two of the Four Garrisons, Kucha and Karashahr, in Chinese hands. Instead of fighting back, the T'ang withdrew and apparently left East Turkistan to the Tibetans. Later that same spring, though, they responded. The T'ang sent a huge army to attack the Tibetans in the former T'u-yü-hun realm. In a great battle at the Jima Khol, the Chinese were defeated by Mgar Stong Rtsan's son Mgar Khri 'Bring. The T'ang moved their Protectorate General of the Pacified West back to Qocho. For the next twenty-two years East Turkistan was theoretically under Tibetan rule. In fact, though Khotan and the region to the west of it do seem to have been under direct Tibetan control, most of the Tarim Basin countries were at least semi-independent during this period.

The 680s were marked by unsettled internal conditions in the home territories of the Arab, Tibetan, and Chinese empires. The Central Asian areas remained much as they were, nominally under the rule of one or the other of these three states. A change began in the later part of the decade, when the Tibetans attacked Kucha and other areas to the north. Tibetan control increased, despite T'ang resistance, until the young Tibetan emperor Khri 'Dus Srong focused all his attention on an internal problem: wresting personal control of his government from the leaders of the Mgar clan, who had held the actual power while he was a child. At the same time, the T'ang—from 690 actually called the Chou Dynasty, under the usurping female ruler Emperor Wu Chao (r. 690–705)[61]—planned to retake the Four Garrisons. In 692 the

[61] Despite Wu Chao's de facto replacement of the T'ang and her ascension to the throne as China's first and last female emperor (the practice of calling her Empress Wu is incorrect), she did not eliminate the T'ang rulers she supplanted, namely Chung-tsung (r. 684, and again 705–710) and Jui-tsung (nominal reign 684–690, and again 710–712). Like Wang

Chinese governor of Kucha, which was again in Chinese hands, led an army of Chinese and Turks against the Tibetans and defeated them, reestablishing the Four Garrisons. Despite the Tibetans' attempts to hold onto the region with the help of their subordinate Western Turkic allies, they were decisively defeated by the T'ang in 694 at both of the Tibetans' strategic points of entrance into Central Asia.

Inside Tibet, Emperor Khri 'Dus Srong massacred the entire Mgar clan in cold blood.[62] He then led the army to the eastern frontier of the Tibetan Empire, where he was killed in 704 during a campaign against the Nan-chao Kingdom (located in what is now Szechuan and Yunnan). The de facto rule passed to his mother, Khrimalod, who governed Tibet at about the same time Wu Chao and her female successors ruled China. The Tibetan Empire recovered only slowly over the next decades and went increasingly on the defensive with respect to T'ang China.

Establishment of the Second Türk Empire

In the Eastern Steppe, the Türk were unhappy under Chinese overlordship. They rebelled unsuccessfully several times until Elteriš Kaghan (r. 682–691), a distant descendant of *Hellig Kaghan, working tirelessly out in the steppes, united the scattered, weakened peoples under his banner. In 682 the Türk again revolted, this time successfully. Elteriš reestablished an independent Türk Empire on the Eastern Steppe. His brother Kapghan Kaghan 'Buk Chor' (r. 691–716) succeeded him and further strengthened and expanded the realm. In the very beginning of the eighth century the lands of the Western Turks based in Jungharia and eastern Transoxiana had come under the control of a new confederation of peoples, known as the Türgiš. In 712 the Eastern Turks, under Köl Tigin (Kül Tigin), son of Elteriš, defeated the Türgiš kaghan, *Saqal. They reestablished the long-lost Eastern Türk dominion over the Western Turks, becoming by extension the overlords of Ferghana, Tashkent, and probably most of Sogdiana, in place of the Türgiš.

Mang, she has thus been categorized as a usurper. Both ruled China effectively, but neither achieved legitimacy, and when, in each case, the supplanted imperial house was restored, their historical fate was sealed.

[62] Some escaped to China, where they served in the T'ang military.

Arab Conquest of Western Central Asia

The rebels of Khurasan—Central Asia—were resubdued by the Arabs in 671–673. In 673 Mu'âwiya made Khurasan a separate governorship and appointed 'Ubayd Allâh ibn Ziyâd its first governor. The latter crossed the Oxus River in 674 and raided Baykand (Paykand), the commercial city of the Bukharan Kingdom, forcing Bukhara to pay tribute. When Mu'âwiya died in 681, the succession was troubled and turned into a civil war (684–692), during which most of Khurasan became de facto independent again. After revolts and other internal troubles, 'Abd al-Malik (r. 685–705) became caliph, and control over the nearer parts of Khurasan was eventually restored. In 695 he appointed a new governor over Iraq and the East, al-Ḥajjâj ibn Yûsuf, still retaining Khurasan, along with Sîstân, as a separate governorship. Due to disastrous rebellions and weak governors, though, 'Abd al-Malik added Sîstân and Khurasan to al-Ḥajjâj's governorship in 697. This gave al-Ḥajjâj control over half of the Arab Empire for the rest of 'Abd al-Malik's reign and all that of his son al-Walîd I (r. 705–715).

By the late seventh century, not only were the Arabs living in the cities of Khurasan; some of them had acquired land and were becoming assimilated to the local people. Some became so assimilated that they lost their status as tax-exempt Arabs. The relationship with the local people was stronger in Marw than elsewhere. The Arab government even borrowed money from the Sogdians in Marw for an expedition against Sogdiana itself in 696.[63] Two of the leaders of the merchant community in Marw at the turn of the century were Thâbit and Hurayth ibn Qutba, each of whom had acquired his own comitatus of *châkars*. Eventually they joined the Arab rebel Mûsâ ibn 'Abd Allâh ibn Khâzim in Tirmidh and rallied the princes of Transoxiana, Tokhâristân, and the Hephthalites of Bâdghîs in a rebellion against the Umayyads. The alliance broke up, both brothers were killed, and al-Ḥajjâj appointed another governor, al-Mufaḍḍal ibn al-Muḥallab, who finally crushed Mûsâ's rebellion in Tirmidh in 704. Al-Ḥajjâj then appointed Qutayba ibn Muslim al-Bâhilî governor of Khurasan (705–715).

---

[63] Shaban (1970: 48) suggests it was to reduce the taxes on their home principalities, which would be *dâr al-salâm* (pacified territory) rather than *dâr al-ḥarb* (enemy territory).

Qutayba was trained by al-Ḥajjâj himself, and reorganized Arab administration of the province when he arrived in Marw. He also resecured Arab control over Tokhâristân and in the next years captured Paykand, a center of the Chinese trade, and Bukhara, which was finally conquered in 709.[64] In 709–710 he took Kišš and Nasaf and also crushed the revolt of Tokhâristân and the Hephtalites, capturing the Yabghu of Tokhâristân, who was sent to the Arab capital of the time, Damascus.[65] In 712 Qutayba seized Khwârizm by trickery and settled an Arab colony there. In that year, he also besieged Samarkand. Its king appealed to Tashkent for help, so as overlords of Tashkent the Eastern Türk sent an army led by Köl Tigin into Sogdiana in his support. But Qutayba prevailed. The Türk were forced to withdraw, and the Arabs established a garrison in Samarkand.[66]

In 714 Qutayba invaded deep into Transoxiana, as far as Ferghana. By this time he had acquired a personal comitatus known as the Archers. Qutayba heard about his patron al-Ḥajjâj's death (in 714) when he was coming back from a campaign against Shâsh (Tashkent), but he was confirmed by al-Walîd as governor. In 715 Qutayba invaded the Jaxartes provinces again. This time he made an alliance with the Tibetans and a faction of the Ferghana royal family. Together they overthrew the ruler of Ferghana, Bâšak, and replaced him with Alutâr, a member of another royal family.

The same year, while Qutayba was still in Ferghana, al-Walîd died and Sulaymân (r. 715–717) succeeded as caliph. Knowing he would be recalled, Qutayba rebelled. But his army turned against him. Only his comitatus, the Archers, stood by him to the end. All were killed.

Meanwhile, Bâšak had fled to the Chinese in Kucha. The T'ang military governor there organized an expedition and, together with Bâšak, invaded Ferghana in December of the same year, deposed Alutâr, and restored Bâšak to the throne—now as a Chinese dependent.[67]

Kapghan Kaghan was killed on campaign in 716 shortly after withdrawing from the Türgiš territory. He was succeeded by his nephew, Elteriš's son Bilgä Kaghan, who was greatly aided by his brother Köl Tigin. *Suluk, the head of the Black Bone clan[68] of the Türgiš, became kaghan in the Western

---

[64] Shaban (1970: 66).
[65] Shaban (1970: 67).
[66] Shaban (1970: 67–75).
[67] Beckwith (1993).
[68] The previous rulers had belonged to the Yellow Bone clan.

133

Türk domains. He promptly restored Türgiš power and rapidly expanded their territory further than had his predecessors. The Türgiš asserted their claim to the former Western Turkic hegemony over the lands of Transoxiana and Tokhâristân. They thus became the supporters of the local peoples against the Arabs and Islam and also the close allies of the Tibetans.

The Chinese saw the Türgiš alliance with the Tibetans as the realization of a connection between north and south, feared from Han times, that would cut China off from the West.[69] As conscious imitators of the Han, the T'ang were bound to attempt to break the alliance. They and the Arabs made a secret alliance of their own and planned the downfall of the Türgiš and Tibetans.

The T'ang-Silla Conquest of Koguryo

The monumental Sui and early T'ang attempts to reestablish the Han Dynasty dominion over southern Manchuria and northern Korea had failed one after the other, defeated by the redoubtable forces of the Kingdom of Koguryo. But in 642 internal troubles struck Koguryo when the usurper *Ür Ghap Somun (Yŏn Kaesomun)[70] seized power. He murdered the king and some hundred aristocrats[71] and put a son of the dead king on the throne as his puppet. Nevertheless, under his regency Koguryo was able to repulse yet another massive Chinese invasion—this time led by the T'ang emperor T'ai-tsung himself—in 645.[72]

Under Kao-tsung (r. 649–683), the T'ang made an alliance with Silla, a kingdom in southeastern Korea that had been expanding in the southern

---

[69] This fear is explicitly discussed at some length in the dynastic histories for both the Han and the T'ang. Despite the frequently expressed claim (by the Chinese of the time and historians since then) that the Chinese did not need international trade and were uninterested in it, clearly they did need it and were intensely interested in it.

[70] The first two syllables of his full Old Koguryo name are *Ür and *Ghap (*fiaɨp ~ *yap); see Beckwith (2007a: 46, 62–63). The second syllable is not *kaj³ (Pul. 102), the Middle Chinese ancestor of the later reading Kai, Sino-Korean Kae; the reading seems to be a medieval error. His unknown personal name is conventionally transcribed in Sino-Korean form as Somun. Old Koguryo *fiaɨp 'great mountain', from Archaic Koguryo *fiapma 'great mountain', is cognate to Old Japanese *yama 'mountain' (Beckwith 2007a: 46, 121).

[71] These men were probably the king's comitatus, but the sources are extremely laconic and do not give enough information to allow more to be said about them.

[72] Wechsler (1979b: 232–233).

Korean Peninsula at the expense of the other kingdoms. Together the allies attacked Paekche, the most highly civilized and second strongest kingdom in Korea, by land and by sea. Despite troops sent by the Koguryo and a fleet sent by the Japanese, the T'ang and Silla defeated Paekche and its allies in 660 and completed their subjugation and occupation of the country in 663.

Then, in 666, *Ür Ghap Somun died. His son Namsaeng succeeded to the position of regent, but his two brothers contested the succession, and Namsaeng appealed to the Chinese for help against them. The T'ang strategists saw their chance. They and the Silla launched a massive offensive against Koguryo from two fronts. Despite a valiant resistance, the Koguryo were crushed in 668, and some 200,000 of them, with the Koguryo king, were taken captive to China. The remaining Koguryo people rebelled against the T'ang in 670, but the Chinese brutally repressed the rebellion four years later, executing the leaders and exiling the survivors deep inside central China. In 676 the T'ang colonial government was forced to withdraw from Pyongyang to Liaotung, and within a few years Silla supplanted T'ang rule in the former Paekche and Koguryo territories except for the northern part of Koguryo, which was incorporated into the new kingdom of Parhae.[73] The Koguryo language was still spoken by a few people in the mid-eighth century, but shortly thereafter the people and their language—the only well-attested continental relative of the Japanese-Ryukyuan languages—disappeared completely.[74]

The Franks

After the Great Wandering of Peoples finally ended in Western Europe, the people who dominated northern Gaul and western Germania were the Franks. They owed their success to the skill of several great leaders, most famously Clovis I (Hludovicus, r. 481–511), the son of Childeric I (d. 481) and grandson of Merovech (d. 456 or 457). Clovis established the capital of Francia in Paris in 508. He unified the Franks—mainly by killing the leaders of the other Frankish peoples—and established them as uncontested rulers of northern Gaul and environs. His sons completed the conquest of most of

---

[73] Twitchett and Wechsler (1979: 282–284), Beckwith (2007a: 46–49).

[74] On the Koguryo (or Puyo-Koguryo) language and its relationship to the Japanese-Ryukyuan languages, see Beckwith (2005a, 2006e, 2007a).

Gaul, Belgium, western Germania, and part of what is now Switzerland. Their control often slipped due to the perennial internecine succession struggles that plagued the Merovingian Dynasty, but Dagobert I (r. 629–639) inherited from his father, Chlothar II (Lothair, r. 584–629), a united kingdom. He and his successors were under the strong influence of the family of Pippin, Mayor of the Palace, whose members, from one branch or another, increasingly controlled the actual government of the Merovingian realm.[75] After Dagobert's death, the Merovingian rulers were puppets of the "pre-Carolingian" mayoral dynasty of the Pippinids and Arnulfings. By the early seventh century, the government had come completely under the family's control. Mayor of the Palace Carl (Charles Martel, r. 714–741) subdued rebels throughout the kingdom, including Eudo of Aquitaine, whom he defeated in 725. But the Arabs had invaded Spain in 711 from North Africa and conquered it, and Eudo (who was of Gascon or Basque origin) made an alliance with the neighboring Berber leader, Munnuza, whose stronghold was in the Pyrenees. Under ʿAbd al-Raḥman (r. 731–733/734), the new governor of Spain, the Arabs attacked Munnuza in the Pyrenees, defeated him, and continued on into southern Gaul, where they defeated Eudo north of the Garonne River. They plundered Bordeaux and Poitiers and then attacked Tours, where they were defeated by Carl in 733 or 734.[76] Carl and his brother Hildebrand (father of Nibelung) also subjugated Narbonne and Provence, which had similarly allied with the Arabs.[77] On his death, Carl was peacefully succeeded as Mayor of the Palace by his son, Pippin III (Pippin the Short, or Pepin, r. 741–768), who pursued his father's policies and extended the Frankish realm as far as Spain, the Mediterranean, and Italy in the south, Saxony in the north, and the Avars of Pannonia in the east.

The Silk Road and Early Medieval Political Ideology

One of the most remarkable and least appreciated facts about the historical sources on the Early Middle Ages in Eurasia as a whole is their overwhelming emphasis on Central Eurasia, especially Central Asia. The Chinese, Old Tibetan, and Arabic historical sources, in particular, are full of detail on

---

[75] Wood (1994: 146–147); Scherman (1987: 232–233).
[76] This is the traditional Battle of Poitiers, q.v. Wood (1994: 283).
[77] See Wood (1994: 273–274, 281–284) for details and problems.

Central Asia, while even the more parochial Greek and Latin sources emphasize the significance of Central Eurasia for their realms. The reason for all this attention is clearly not modern historians' imaginary threat of a nomad warrior invasion, which is virtually unmentioned in the sources. The reason for the attention seems rather to be the prosperous Silk Road economy and the existence of a shared political ideology across Eurasia that ensured nearly constant warfare.

This common ideology was one of the driving political-ideological forces behind all of the early medieval Eurasian state expansions, beginning with the Türk conquest.[78] Every empire had a distinctive term for its own ruler and never referred to any foreign ruler by that term in official documents.[79] Each nation believed its own emperor to be the sole rightful ruler of "all under Heaven," and everyone else should be his subjects, whether submitted and dutiful ones or not-yet-subjugated, rebellious "slaves." The punishment for rebelling or refusing to submit was war, but war was inevitable anyway throughout early medieval Eurasia as a whole, both because of the shared imperialistic political ideology of the time and because regular warfare had been a normal part of life since prehistoric times.

Each emperor thus proclaimed and attempted to actually establish his rule over the four directions, each of which was theoretically assigned to one of his subordinates. The clearest examples of the ideal Central Eurasian political structure, sometimes referred to aptly as the "khan and four bey system,"[80] are attested in the Puyo and Koguryo kingdoms;[81] the Türk Empire, about which the Byzantine ambassador Maniakh told the Roman emperor that they had four "military governorships"[82] plus the ruler,[83] who

---

[78] The ideology was maintained as late as the Mongols and is very clearly expressed in the Mongol rulers' letters to other rulers demanding their submission.

[79] Beckwith (1993: 14–15, 19–20). On the title emperor among the Franks and Avars, see endnote 70.

[80] See Schamiloglu (1984a), whose description largely refers to the Mongol Empire and post-Mongol period. This was an "ideal" political organization system in most of Central Eurasia, much noted in the sources from the earliest times. The extent to which it was put into actual practice in all regions "on the ground" should be examined carefully.

[81] The Chinese accounts of the early Puyo Kingdom list a sovereign plus four subdivisions; for Koguryo they name five directions or subdivisions, of which the center or Yellow subdivision was that of the royal clan (*SKC* 30: 843; *HHS* 85: 2813; Beckwith 2007a: 41–42). This is similar to the later-attested Khitan (Liao Dynasty) system.

[82] This would seem to be the intended meaning of Menander's term ἡγεμονια *hêgemonia*, translated as "principalities" by Blockley (1985: 114–115).

[83] Blockley (1985: 115). On the name of the Türk royal clan, *Aršilas, see endnote 71.

belonged to the *Aršilas[84] clan; the Tibetan Empire (the highly theoretical four-horn structure[85] seems to be best explained in this way); the T'ang Empire, which established not only a Protectorate of the Pacified West but one over each of the other three directions as well;[86] the Khitan Empire; and later in the Mongol Empire and its successor states.[87]

Partly because of this ideology, all early medieval empires attempted to expand in all directions. This was not unlike empires in other periods and places, but during the Early Middle Ages, for the first time in history, the great empires came into direct contact with each other and knew they were not alone. Each empire was forced to face the fact that it was actually one among equals. At first, none could accept this fact, so a diplomatic protocol developed in order to handle the practical necessity of dealing with foreign empires: the envoys of one empire to the other paid obeisance to the foreign ruler at his home court; the envoy's obeisance was recorded locally in terminology that expressed his home empire's subservience to the local empire; and when the envoy returned home, usually in the company of an envoy from the people visited, the latter similarly paid obeisance to the foreign envoy's emperor.[88]

When the cultures and nation-states of Eurasia collided in the early eighth century, each knew that the others coveted control of Central Eurasia as much as it did. Each eagerly sought products, knowledge, and people from the other empires. They all made political alliances and coordinated military action, down to details, and even modified their own practices and beliefs to agree with or differ from the others. Despite the

[84] For discussion of proposed etymologies of the name *Aršilas, see endnote 72.
[85] See Uray (1960).
[86] One of them, An-nan 'the Pacified South', survives in name to modern times as Annam, an old name for Vietnam. The capital Ch'ang-an 'Eternal Peace' would appear to have been conceptually in the middle, but it is an ancient name and seems not to be mentioned in connection with the four geographical units. The usual Chinese name of China itself, Chung-kuo, is thought to have meant, originally, 'the Central States' rather than 'the Middle Kingdom', which is a later reinterpretation of the name.
[87] Manz (1989: 4) notes, "Chinggis divided his steppe empire into four great territories, later known as the four uluses, which he assigned to his sons along with sections of his army." The Chinggisids are well known for their quadripartite state structure (Schamiloglu 1984a).
[88] The pretense was maintained at all official levels until the early ninth century, when the first true bilateral treaty in eastern Eurasia was signed between the Chinese and Tibetan empires (Beckwith 1993). However, the imperial ideology did not disappear entirely from Eurasia. The Mongols under Chinggis Khan still followed it in the thirteenth century, and the Chinese have continued to follow it down to modern times.

constant, unabashed warfare all across Eurasia in this period, the Silk Road economy prospered and grew mightily at least until the middle of the eighth century. The Eurasian world was connected together ever more closely politically, culturally, and especially economically, due mainly to the efforts of the Central Eurasians.[89]

[89] Cf. de la Vaissière (2005a: 186).

6

The Silk Road, Revolution, and Collapse

ཚ་ཚ་ཚ་ཚ་ཚ།
ཚ་ཚ་ཚ་ཚ་ཚ་ཚ་ཚ་ཚ་ཚ

> He has led you away
> and separated you from me
> He has made me partake of every suffering
> and taken away all my joy
> —From an anonymous Tokharian poem[1]

Mercantile Power, Monasticism, Art, and Science

Within a thirteen-year period in the mid-eighth century, every empire in Eurasia suffered a major rebellion, revolution, or dynastic change. The turmoil began in 742 with the overthrow of the Türk dynasty in the Eastern Steppe and establishment of the Sogdian-influenced Uighurs, and simultaneously a major rebellion in the Byzantine Empire. These were followed in short succession by the Abbasid revolution in the Arab Empire, organized by merchants in the Central Asian trading city of Marw; the Carolingian revolution in the Frankish kingdom; a major rebellion in the Tibetan Empire in 755; and beginning late in the same year, a great rebellion in the Chinese Empire organized and led by An Lu-shan, a Turco-Sogdian general in the T'ang army.

The reestablishment of peace was followed by the building of carefully planned, symbolic cultural centers by the younger imperial powers: the Arabs' circular-plan cosmological City of Peace palace-and-mosque complex at Baghdad, designed in accordance with Central Asian Iranian ideas and settled with Central Asians; the circular-plan Tibetan monastic complex of Samye at Bragmar; and the sixteen-sided[2] cathedral of the new Frankish capital at

---

[1] This is my slightly free translation of the last lines of the original, Nr. 496 = T III. MQ 17.39, q.v. Sieg et al. (1953: 307–308). Mallory (Mallory and Mair 2000: 273) gives the complete poem.
[2] Actually, the church has sixteen sides on the outside, but the number of sides is reduced by piers to eight in the interior, giving it the effect of being circular outside and octagonal inside.

Aachen. Each of these states, and the other young empires as well, declared their official support for a particular world religion or sect.

The most significant developments in the following century were the spread of national literacy across Eurasia; the further shift of the world's commercial, cultural, and scientific center to Western Central Asia; and the northward shift of trade routes—in the West, the routes between the caliphate and Europe shifted to a northern route running from Central Asia via the Volga River to Old Ladoga and the Baltic Sea, greatly stimulating economic development in Northern Europe, while in the East the routes between China and Central Asia shifted north to pass through Uighur territory. The capital of the Arab Empire under al-Ma'mûn was in Marw in Central Asia itself for a decade; when the caliph finally moved it back to Baghdad, he brought with him another influx of Central Asians and Central Asian culture. This brought about a brilliant fusion of intellectual-scientific culture in the Arab Empire. Some of the epoch's achievements, later transmitted to Europe via Islamic Spain, were fundamental to the Scientific Revolution.

The Revolutions and Rebellions of the Mid-Eighth Century

The causes of the great upheaval in Eurasia in the middle of the eighth century remain to be established. Given the interconnectedness of the Eurasian world by that time, it is perhaps conceivable that the changes that occurred in Central Asia and the Eastern Steppe between 737 and 742 set in motion a domino effect that spread across the continent. However, this does not seem to account for the Carolingian Revolution in 751 or the Tibetan Rebellion in 755. A few common elements are known. By far the most important of these is surely the fact that all of the better-known rebellions or revolutions, beginning with the very first one, in the Eastern Steppe, were led by merchants or people closely connected to merchants and international commerce.

THE TURKS IN CENTRAL ASIA AND THE EASTERN STEPPE

The Türgiš in the lands of the Western Turks were the overlords of the Central Asian trading cities, the heart of the Silk Road commercial system. Many explicit references in the Arabic and Chinese sources reveal that they were the protectors and patrons of commerce in Jungharia and most of the rest of Central Asia as well.[3] However, the relentless attacks of the Chinese and Arabs against them in the 730s eventually were successful and utterly destroyed the Türgiš Kaghanate between 737 and 740.[4] This created a power vacuum where clan raided clan, leaving the Chinese and Arabs free to tighten their grip on the Central Asian cities.

In the Eastern Steppe, the Türk Empire declined rapidly after the death of Köl Tigin in 731 and Bilgä Kaghan (r. 716–734) in 734. Although the two brothers had fought valiantly for two decades and achieved many victories, they were ultimately unable to maintain Türk power much beyond the Eastern Steppe. In 742 a Turkic coalition consisting of Uighurs, Basmïl, and Karluks overthrew the Türk. The three victors, of whom the Uighurs were by far the most numerous and powerful, then fought among themselves. The Basmïl were defeated first, then the Karluks, and in 744 the Uighur Kaghanate was established. In Jungharia and the eastern part of the Central Steppe in general, the place of the Türgiš was quickly filled by the Karluks, who had previously bordered on the Türgiš in the west. They absorbed the remnants of the Türgiš but did not attain the political-military power of their predecessors. In the Eastern Steppe, the Uighurs—like their Türk predecessors—were under very heavy Sogdian influence.

THE BYZANTINE EMPIRE

In 741 or 742 the newly crowned Byzantine emperor Constantine V (r. 741–775), an ardent iconoclast who was married to Princess Tzitzak,[5] daughter of the Khazar kaghan, was attacked and defeated by his brother-in-law, the Armenian general Artavasdos. The latter was crowned emperor in Constantinople and reigned there until Constantine V defeated and deposed him as a usurper in 743.

Because Artavasdos was Armenian and a supporter of icon veneration, he was accordingly supported by the iconodules (icon worshippers or anti-iconoclasts), and the sources and modern histories have paid attention to

---

[3] See Beckwith (1993); cf. above, the discussion of the Eastern Türk campaign against the Arabs in Samarkand.

[4] Beckwith (1993: 111–124).

[5] *Tzitzak* is the Greek spelling of Old Turkic *Čičäk* [ʧitʃɛk] 'flower'. She was baptized as a Christian and given the name *Eirênê* 'Irene'.

little else. His possible annoyance at Constantine's succession to the throne (instead of Artavasdos himself) does not explain his rebellion, the underlying causes of which seem to be unknown. Perhaps the devastating Arab invasion of Khazaria in 737 and other strife in the area near Armenia at that time may be connected to the rebellion.[6]

THE ARAB EMPIRE

The Abbasid Rebellion broke out in 747 in Marw, one of the greatest commercial cities in Eurasia at the time. It was led by merchants of Arab and Central Asian origin.[7] They overthrew the Umayyads in 750 and proclaimed the new Abbasid Dynasty, with its first caliph Abû al-'Abbâs (al-Saffâḥ, r. 749/750–754).

The strongly commercial, Central Asian character of the rebellion is hard to ignore. Although some would place the emphasis on Central Asianized Arabs[8] rather than on Arabicized Central Asians,[9] this disagreement does not change the unquestioned facts: the rebellion was largely organized in Central Asian cities by and for Central Asians, who were both Arab and non-Arab by origin; it was proclaimed openly in the Central Asian city of Marw, where there was a Sogdian Market and a Bukharan quarter, including a palace of the Bukhâr Khudâ, the king of Bukhara;[10] and the defeat of the Umayyads was undertaken and accomplished by a Central Asian army, the Khurâsâniyya.[11]

THE FRANKISH EMPIRE

In 751 Pippin III (r. 741/751–768), the Frankish Mayor of the Palace, overthrew the Merovingian Dynasty, which had existed only nominally for several decades. He established the Carolingian Dynasty, and had its legitimacy

---

[6] The one detailed study of the rebellion (Speck 1981) is concerned exclusively with religious issues. The causes of the rebellion should be investigated by Byzantinists familiar with the Arabic sources. On the Arab and Khazar wars, see Golden (2006).

[7] The Abbasid Revolution was organized and led by merchants and men pretending to be merchants.

[8] Shaban (1970).

[9] Daniel (1979).

[10] See de la Vaissière (2005a: 282).

[11] These well-known, uncontested points indicate that there was more to the revolution than the political propaganda that dominates the source material and which has therefore received by far the bulk of modern historians' attention.

proclaimed in much propaganda and in public works. The Frankish Empire[12] found stable rulers in the Carolingians. The background of their overthrow of the Merovingians is fairly well understood and appears to be wholly political and internal.

Other factors, however, may have been involved as well. Jewish merchants were extremely influential among the Carolingians, who protected and patronized them.[13] The Carolingians also did much to foster international trade between the Frankish Empire and the Islamic world by coining silver deniers modeled on Arab silver coins. They developed a good relationship with the Abbasids and expanded into the trade routes to Central Eurasia by conquering the Saxons, to their northeast, and the Avars in Pannonia, to their southeast.[14]

THE TIBETAN EMPIRE

In 755 a major rebellion shook the Tibetan Empire. The reigning emperor, Khri Lde Gtsug Brtsan ('Mes Ag-tshoms', r. 712–755) was assassinated, and the crown prince, Srong Lde Brtsan, could not be enthroned for a year.[15] When he was finally enthroned, as Khri Srong Lde Brtsan, he remained in a politically weak position for two decades.

To say that the reasons for the rebellion are unknown is an understatement. However, two things are clear. The rebellion had something to do with legitimacy. It also certainly had something to do with the T'ang military successes against the Tibetans, who had lost so much ground that the empire itself was in very grave danger. A Tibetan vassal in the northeastern part of the realm surrendered to the T'ang early in 755. The great ministers who led the rebellion were perhaps only trying to save the Tibetan Empire from disintegration and conquest by the Chinese.[16]

---

[12] The European historical terminology of kingdom versus empire, grounded in Roman and Byzantine practice, is irrelevant in the case of the Frankish kingdom, which was an empire according to modern terminology (cf. Scherman 1987: 258).

[13] Bachrach (1977).

[14] In view of the pan-Eurasian character of the mid-eighth century changes, it would seem worthwhile to investigate if any of these factors influenced or even impelled Pippin's decision to depose the last Merovingian king.

[15] Unfortunately, the major Old Tibetan historical source, the *Old Tibetan Annals*, is fragmentary just at this point and it is not possible to determine the exact cause and immediate outcome of the rebellion; see Beckwith (1983; 1993: 142).

[16] For some of the problems hinted at by the sources, see endnote 73.

THE CHINESE EMPIRE

In 750 a T'ang general of Koguryo origin, Ko Sŏnji (Kao Hsien-chih), campaigned against the Tibetans in the Pamirs and defeated them there. He followed this success with intervention in a war between the kings of Ferghana and Shâsh (Čâč, now Tashkent). He and the king of Ferghana captured Shâsh in 750. Nevertheless, though the king of Shâsh surrendered peacefully, Ko broke the agreement. He sent his army in to rape, murder, and plunder, and took the king to Ch'ang-an, where Emperor Hsüan-tsung had him executed. The crown prince of the city escaped to the Arabs in Samarkand and pleaded for help. The Abbasids dispatched an army, which met Ko Sŏnji's army in the Battle of Atlakh, near Talas, in July, 751. In the midst of the battle, the Karluk Turks, who had formed part of the T'ang forces, changed sides and joined the Central Asians and Arabs. The T'ang army was destroyed and the Arabs were victorious.[17]

Despite this setback, and increasingly severe problems at home caused by the constant T'ang military campaigns, Hsüan-tsung continued his policy of expansion. By 753 the T'ang had captured all of the Tibetans' Central Asian territories and kept pressing deeper into the Tibetan Plateau. The Tibetan realm was riven by a great revolt in 755; the empire seemed destined to be defeated by the T'ang.

Then, at the end of 755, An Lu-shan,[18] a T'ang general of Sogdian-Turkic merchant origin,[19] openly rebelled against his longtime patron, Hsüantsung, and almost brought down the T'ang Dynasty. He had the assistance of many other Sogdians and Turco-Sogdians, who were also warrior-

---

[17] Beckwith (1993: 139). It is popularly known as the Battle of Talas. One of the indirect results of the battle was the transmission of the technique of papermaking (a Chinese invention) to the Arabs in Samarkand by captive Chinese soldiers. One of the captives, Tu Huan, traveled on to the Arab capital. He eventually returned home and wrote the *Ching-hsing chi* 'Record of the Travels', a work that is unfortunately lost. Some of the book survives as quotations in the *T'ung tien* 'Comprehensive Treasury', an encyclopedia written by the T'ang scholar Tu Yu, one of Tu Huan's relatives.

[18] Lu-shan is a Chinese transcription of his personal name in Sogdian, *Roχšan* 'the luminous'. The same word is the root of the name given to the famous Central Asian woman married to Alexander the Great, Roxana (Roxane).

[19] His actual birth origin is uncertain; he was apparently adopted and raised by a Sogdian father and a Turkic mother (Beckwith 1993: 142 n. 212; Des Rotours 1962: 1–2; cf. de la Vaissière 2005a: 215–216; cf. Pulleyblank 1955).

merchants.[20] And like any great Sogdian or Turkic leader, he had a large personal comitatus, consisting of Khitans and other Central Eurasians.[21]

What is astonishing, though, is that An and his co-conspirators used the merchant network of North China and neighboring Central Eurasian territory to prepare for their rebellion over a period of eight or nine years—in other words, the Sogdians in the Chinese Empire were secretly involved in planning a rebellion against the T'ang Dynasty at the very same time as the Sogdians in the Arab Empire were planning a rebellion against the Umayyad Dynasty. The description of the activities of An Lu-shan and the other warrior-merchants[22] reads like a mirror image of what the Central Asian conspirators based in Marw did in their preparations for the Abbasid Rebellion against the Umayyad Dynasty. In these two instances, at least, it is probable that the conspirators knew each other and kept in touch via the international component of the Silk Road trade system, which was dominated by the Sogdians. The overwhelming influence of the Sogdians among the Uighurs, who overthrew the Türk Empire of the Eastern Steppe, is well known. It must therefore be wondered if the Tibetan Rebellion of 755 had anything to do with the Sogdian rebellions that covered much of Eurasia. Another question is whether there was any central organization that coordinated the rebellions or revolutions.

Only in 757, with the military help of the Uighurs, did the T'ang manage to recapture both capitals, Ch'ang-an and Lo-yang, and regain control over the central parts of North China. But most of northeastern China, especially Hopei, the center of the rebellion, became semi-independent, and the T'ang lost many of their most important foreign conquests, including the eastern frontiers of the Tibetan Empire and the Liao-hsi and Liao-tung regions near Korea in the Northeast. With the severe weakening of China's military and economic power after the rebellion, the T'ang also soon lost much of East Turkistan and the lands south of the Gobi to the Tibetans and the Uighurs.

---

[20] On the An Lu-shan Rebellion and the Sogdian warrior-merchants in China, see de la Vaissière (2005a: 217–220) and Moribe (2005); on the warrior and the merchant in Sogdian culture, see especially Grenet (2005).

[21] See endnote 25; cf. de la Vaissière (2005a: 219; 2005b: 142–143).

[22] See de la Vaissière (2005a: 217–220).

Religion and the State after the Revolution

With the Arabs' interest in and fostering of commerce, the Arab Empire under the Abbasids became increasingly prosperous. The second caliph, Abû Ja'far al-Manṣûr, built a new imperial capital near the ancient town of Baghdad on the Tigris near where the Tigris and Euphrates approach each other, not far upriver from the former Sasanid capital of Ctesiphon. The palace-city complex, the City of Peace, had a remarkable circular design based on the plan of several Sasanid imperial capitals, including that of the old capital of Ctesiphon and that of the Central Asian Buddhist monastery of Nawbahâr, the 'New Vihâra', which had originally been built as a Sasanid provincial capital complex at Balkh. The circular Sasanid plan had been adopted from the Parthians, the Central Asian Iranians who ruled Persia before them. The plan of the City of Peace was the work of Khâlid ibn Barmak, the sometime vizier and son of the last Buddhist abbot of the Nawbahâr.[23] In the center of the City of Peace was the palace of the caliph, which was topped by a great "heavenly" sky-green dome.[24] Around the capital structure, Abû Ja'far settled the Abbasid Dynasty's Central Asian army, the Khurâsâniyya.

The Tibetan Rebellion was quickly suppressed and the empire soon expanded back into many of its former conquests. After some two decades of military success—which included capture of the T'ang capital Ch'ang-an for a brief period in 763[25] and capture of the southern Ordos and the cities along the Great Wall there[26]—the new emperor, Khri Srong Lde Brtsan (r. 756–797), was politically secure enough to proclaim Buddhism as the state religion. He built a large circular monastery complex, Samye (Bsam-yas),

---

[23] See Beckwith (1984b), where the discussion of the source of the plan should be modified to accord with the view presented here (at the time I wrote the article I did not know that the plan of the early, Parthian city of Ctesiphon had originally been circular); cf. endnote 28. Khâlid is said to have earlier been a *châkar* of an Umayyad caliph: "Barmak was brought before Hishâm b. 'Abd al-Malik in a body of 500 *châkars*. Hishâm treated him with honour, increased his status and was favourably impressed with him. Barmak then became a Muslim" (de la Vaissière 2005b: 146–147, quoting Bosworth 1994: 274; Bosworth's translation "slaves" for Arabic *shâkirî*—an Arabicized loanword from Central Asian *châkar*—is corrected here).

[24] See Beckwith (1984b) for discussion and a translation of the account of the ritual in which the caliph laid out the city.

[25] Beckwith (1993: 146).

[26] Beckwith (1987b).

at Brag-mar, one of the imperial estates in south-central Tibet.[27] It symbol-
ized the Buddhist universe, the emperor's position as a righteous Buddhist
ruler, and the establishment of Buddhism as the state religion of the Tibetan
Empire. The particular form of Buddhism eventually settled on was Indian
Mahâyâna, with a Sarvâstivâdin institutional foundation. The teachers and
translators in Central Tibet came from practically all directions under Tibetan imperial rule, including parts of what are now Nepal, India, Kashmir,
Afghanistan, Central Asia, and China,[28] and from countries further away,
including Korea and Ceylon.

The Uighurs, who adopted Manichaeism and proclaimed it to be their
state religion in 763, built their capital, Khanbalïk (Karabalgasun), into a
large city. The political center of the realm was a fabulous golden tent, a
domed yurt wherein the kaghan "sat upon a golden throne."[29] The Kirghiz,
the chief enemies of the Uighurs, swore to capture the golden tent. The Uighurs partly settled in their capital city, but they remained a traditional
Central Eurasian steppe zone people with a strong interest in international
trade[30] down to the overthrow of their empire. The pacifistic nature of Manichaeism had little effect on their politics.

At the other end of Eurasia, the Franks under Charlemagne (Carolus
Magnus, 768–814) conquered most of continental Western Europe, including the Avar Kingdom. The capture of the kingdom's great fortified capital,

[27] Like Abû Ja'far al-Manṣûr at Baghdad, Khri Srong Lde Brtsan laid out the plan of his symbolic complex in a ritual, carefully described down to details (see the translation in Beckwith
1984b), which is practically identical with the description of the ritual foundation of the
original circular city of Rome by Romulus.
[28] On historiographical problems in the transmission of Buddhism to Tibet, see Walter (forthcoming) and endnote 74.
[29] Allsen (1997: 65). Similarly, the kaghan of the Khazars had a golden dome (Dunlop 1954: 98),
apparently a yurt like the one belonging to the Uighur kaghan. The Tibetan emperor had a
marvelous golden tent too, which held several hundred people (Demiéville 1952: 202–203; cf.
Beckwith 1993: 168 n. 160). The Abbasid caliph had the equivalent, the Heavenly Dome of the
Palace of Gold, under which was his throne, in the exact center of his circular-plan capital
(Beckwith 1984b), and so did Charlemagne, emperor of the Franks, whose throne still sits
under the great dome of his cathedral in Aachen. It seems that no one has ever done an
in-depth study of these domes and why they were so important at this particular point in
time across Eurasia. The Kereit khan's court had "a sumptuous gold palace-tent (ORDO) with
golden vessels and a special staff," which was captured by Chinggis after his defeat of the
Kereit (Atwood 2004: 296); cf. Dunlop (1954 n. 38). Allsen (1997: 13–15) describes in great
detail the later medieval Mongol khans' golden tents, which were lined with gold brocade
(nasij).
[30] See Beckwith (1991).

the Ring of the Avars, was followed by subjugation of Pannonia. This is said by his biographer to be one of Charlemagne's greatest accomplishments, the other being the conquest of Saxony. Both areas occupied the most strategic land trade routes to Central Eurasia. The Carolingians, unlike the Merovingians, claimed to be truly orthodox "Roman" Catholics. In his new capital at Aachen (Aix-la-Chapelle) Charlemagne built the sixteen-sided—essentially circular—church dedicated to the Virgin Mary, with its great dome[31] and centrally placed royal throne. The Carolingians also had a very close alliance with the Catholic popes, who blessed both Pippin the Short and Charlemagne as rightful rulers of the Frankish Empire and were rewarded with Frankish suppression of the popes' enemies. The popes also supported the Carolingians' attempts to rein in the Frankish church.

The Khazars, the close allies of the Byzantines, adopted Judaism as their official religion, apparently in 740,[32] three years after an invasion by the Arabs under Marwân ibn Muḥammad. Marwân had used treachery against a Khazar envoy to gain peaceful entrance to Khazar territory. He then declared his dishonorable intentions and pressed deep into Khazar territory, only subsequently releasing the envoy. The Arabs devastated the horse herds, seized many Khazars and others as captives, and forced much of the population to flee into the Ural Mountains. Marwân's terms were that the kaghan and his Khazars should convert to Islam. Having no choice, the kaghan agreed, and the Arabs returned home in triumph.[33] As soon as the Arabs were gone, the kaghan renounced Islam—with, one may assume, great vehemence. The Khazar Dynasty's conversion to Judaism is best explained by this specific historical background, together with the fact that the mid-eighth century was an age in which the major Eurasian states proclaimed their adherence to distinctive world religions. Adopting Judaism also was politically astute: it meant the Khazars avoided having to accept the overlordship (however theoretical) of the Arab caliph or the Byzantine emperor.[34]

The T'ang and Byzantine empires recovered from their rebellions with the restoration of their displaced dynasties. The T'ang was seriously weakened, however. Unlike the postrevolutionary leaders of the new Eurasian

---

[31] At the time, and for long afterward, it was the highest dome in Western Europe.

[32] On the controversial date of the Khazars' conversion to Judaism, see endnote 75.

[33] Dunlop (1954: 80–86).

[34] See endnote 75. Many Jews had long lived in Khazar territory near the Black Sea, and many more immigrated there as refugees from persecution by the Byzantines.

empires, the only legitimizing activity the Chinese and Byzantine rulers undertook was to harken back to the golden age of their glorious predecessors and continue their religious policies, which in both cases took an extremely brutal turn sooner or later.

In this respect, it is remarkable that the two older empires maintained idiosyncratic official religious policies throughout the Early Middle Ages, particularly insofar as they were otherwise rigidly orthodox throughout most of their history.

The T'ang Dynasty officially supported Taoism, which was not popular with rulers at any other time in Chinese history and was generally frowned on by the orthodox Confucians who ran the government. The T'ang treated all other religions, including even Buddhism, increasingly severely, despite the fact that a number of T'ang rulers were practicing Buddhists.

Similarly, the Byzantine Empire, which was otherwise rigidly orthodox throughout most of its history, officially supported one or another heterodox doctrine, most notably and longest Iconoclasm, for more or less the entire early medieval period. The government enforced its views with torture and murder, especially under the long reign of Constantine V in the eighth century.

The Late Central Eurasian Culture Complex

The ritual suicide or execution of the comitatus was inseparable from the ideas about the afterlife held by those who swore the oath of the core comitatus. They believed that death in battle fighting for their lord was "like returning home,"[35] and apparently that after death everything would be much as it was in life, at least with respect to the comitatus members' duty to fight for their lord, and the lord's duty to reward his men with riches. The lord had to be buried with great wealth in order to be rich in the afterlife, and the warriors needed their horses and weapons, which were buried with them.

When the dominant Central Eurasian peoples, all of whom practiced the comitatus at the beginning of the Early Middle Ages, adopted world reli-

[35] See the extensive discussion and quotations in the prologue.

gions in the eighth century, their ideas about the afterlife began to change. Suicide and murder are sins in the major world religions. In order to retain the comitatus, the usefulness of which was obvious to everyone, it was necessary eventually to eliminate the members' suicide or ritual execution.[36]

The main practical purpose of the comitatus was to serve as a lord's personal guard corps—one loyal to him personally, not to the state. The institution was too valuable to be abandoned, despite its cost, so it was retained in one form or another down to the end of Central Eurasian independence in early modern times. But the changes it did undergo are significant.

In the case of the Sogdians and other Western Central Asians, whose comitatus was most highly developed and tended to contain many members, little did actually change. The adoption of Islam resulted in conversion of the Central Asian comitatus to the *ghulâm* system, which was, in essence, simply a traditional comitatus without the members' ritual suicide or execution.[37]

In the Tibetan Empire, due to the paucity of source material it is difficult to say how long the comitatus was maintained as such after the adoption of Buddhism, but it seems clear that at least to a certain extent it was transmuted into a monastic form. The Tibetans' chosen form of Buddhism emphasized devotion to a spiritual teacher. This devotion was little different from that of the comitatus members to their lord.[38] When the Tibetan emperor was proclaimed to be a Buddhist ruler—a *dharmarâja* 'religious king' or *cakravartin* 'one who turns the wheel (of the Buddhist law)'—the monks were ultimately in his service. It is not surprising then to find that monks

---

[36] It certainly did not happen overnight, since "the already Judaized 10th century Khazar Qaghans were still buried with human sacrifices—as were also the Islamized early Ottoman rulers" (Peter Golden, per.comm., 2007).

[37] A great deal has been written in the past couple of decades on the topic of the guard corps in the Arab Empire. Unfortunately, some scholars have not paid attention to what the sources tell us, unusually clearly, but instead pursue arguments based on modern nationalistic or other agendas. It is shown in some detail already in Beckwith (1984a) that the Arabs in Central Asia itself had adopted the local comitatus "as is" more than a century before the Abbasid caliphs did. On the change from the comitatus to the *ghulâm* system, de la Vaissière argues that the transition between the directly adopted form, the *shâkiriyya* (or *châkar*) system, and the developed *ghulâm* system, may have taken some time. See de la Vaissière (2005b, 2007), and Golden (2001, 2004).

[38] Not long after the fall of the empire Tibetan spiritual leaders achieved political power and a kind of immortality through the system of recognized reincarnations, or *sprulsku* (typically spelled *tulku* as a loanword among English-speaking Buddhists).

fought in the army in the late imperial period.[39] By the end of the Early Middle Ages there was a large monastic establishment in the Tibetan Empire.

In the case of the Uighurs, who adopted Manichaeism, and the Khazars, who adopted Judaism, the outcome with respect to the comitatus is unknown, though it was certainly long maintained in one form or another after their adoption of world religions.[40] It continued unchanged to the north of the Khazars, principally among the Norse and Slavs who eventually destroyed them, and it also continued to the north and east of the Uighurs, particularly among the Khitan and Mongols who succeeded the Uighurs as rulers of the Eastern Steppe. These peoples are all known to have had a form of the comitatus centuries later. Because the Slavs were theoretically Christian by the time their comitatus, the *družina*, is mentioned in historical records and other literature, it is probable that it was becoming, or had already become, a guard corps without ritual death and burial together with the comitatus warriors' lord.

Central Asian Buddhist and Early Islamic Culture

The Arab capital had moved frequently throughout the first century of Islam. In the middle of the eighth century, the Abbasid Revolution brought a huge army of Central Asianized Arabs and Arabicized Central Asians, the *Khurâsâniyya* 'Khurasanis' or 'Easterners' into the heart of the Arab Empire, where they were finally settled by al-Manṣûr around Baghdad when he built his new capital there, the City of Peace. The capital stayed in Baghdad with the exception of the reign of the son of Hârûn al-Rashîd, al-Ma'mûn (r. 808/813–833), whose capital was in Central Asia itself, in Marw, for a decade until he left in 818 to move, slowly, back to Baghdad.[41] The Arab conquest of Tokhâristân and neighboring parts of Central Asia, which until then had been solidly Buddhist, had a powerful, formative influence on Islamic culture. Central Asian thinkers, many of whom at that time were non-Muslim

---

[39] See Beckwith (1993: 169–170 n. 174; 1983: 11 et seq.) and Uray (1961).

[40] See the discussion of the Khazar comitatus by Golden (2002: 141–144; 2006).

[41] Daniel (1979: 174–182), Shaban (1976: 47). He arrived there in 819.

by training, found themselves inside the increasingly cosmopolitan Arab Empire, where their knowledge and practical skills must have been highly valued.

Under the first Abbasid caliphs, the position of vizier was often held by one or another member of the Barmakid (Barmecide) family, beginning with Khâlid ibn Barmak (d. 781/782). The Barmakids cultivated Indian science and sent several expeditions to India to bring books and scholars to Baghdad. Some of the learning so acquired was translated into Arabic.[42] Islamic theology and metaphysics developed the theory of atomism, which "had become firmly established in theological circles by the middle of the ninth century" and owes its fundamental view not to Greek atomism but to "Indian influence" that has not yet been precisely identified but was undoubtedly transmitted directly to the Arabs via Central Asian Buddhism, in which atomic theories were prominent features.[43] The great Indian treatise on astronomy, the *Brāhmasphuṭa-Siddhānta* by the seventh-century author Brahmagupta was translated into Arabic by Muḥammad ibn Ibrâhîm al-Fâzârî (d. 806) and others as the *Sindhind*, which became one of the foundations of Islamic astronomy and mathematics.[44] The single most brilliant scientist of this period, Muḥammad ibn Mûsâ al-Khwârizmî (Algorithmus, fl. 807–847), wrote during the reign of al-Ma'mûn. He laid the foundations of modern mathematics with two of his works. In a book known in translation in medieval Europe as *The Book of Algorithmus*, he introduced Indian place-system numerals and "algorithmic" mathematical calculation; in a book that came to be known in the West as *The Algebra*, he reworked and systematized the algebraic calculation methods used in Indian astronomical works.[45] One of the world's earliest monuments of linguistic science, a careful description of Classical Arabic, was composed at this time by Sîbawayh (Sîbawayhi, *Sêbôe, fl. late eighth century), a non-Arab scholar who studied in Basra and was perhaps Persian in origin. The approach to phonology in the work appears to derive from the Indian linguistic tradition.[46]

---

[42] On the "Indian Half-Century of Islam" in modern scholarship, see endnote 76.

[43] Fakhry (1983: 33–34, 213 et seq.). On the transmission of Central Asian Buddhist ideas to early Islam, see endnote 77.

[44] Fakhry (1983: 7–8), Sezgin (1978: 116 et seq.).

[45] Vernet (1997: 1070). The word *algebra*, taken from part of the title, is Arabic *al-jabr* 'the restoration'.

[46] On the scholarly controversy about foreign sources for early Arab linguistics, see endnote 78.

Significantly, the text of the attested book, *al-Kitâb* ('The Book'), is known to be the work of Sîbawayh's main pupil, al-Mujâshiʿî (better known as al-Akhfash al-Ausaṭ), who was from Balkh in Central Asia and in his own day was accused of altering his teacher's views in significant ways.[47]

Central Asian scholars also developed an Islamic system of higher education modeled on the Central Asian system of the Buddhist *vihâra*, or monastic college. The *vihâra* was supported by a tax-exempt pious foundation that paid the expenses of the students and also of the teacher or teachers, who lived in the *vihâra* with the students. The primary method of teaching was oral lecture and debate, and the main subject of study was the Dharma, or Buddhist law and theology. These fundamental elements were taken over wholesale by the Arabs, who adopted even the distinctively Central Asian form of the *vihâra* architectural plan—a square structure with a large courtyard, each side of which contained chambers for the students and teachers plus four *îwân*s, large half-open halls in the form of gateways. The *vihâra* seems to have been Islamicized as the *madrasa* in Central Asia in the eighth and ninth centuries, though it is only noted in historical sources somewhat later.[48]

Under the caliph al-Maʾmûn, Greek scientific and philosophical literature began to be translated in earnest, first from Syriac translations, and then directly from Greek. The Greek tradition rapidly submerged the Indian tradition, but many areas of knowledge in classical Islamic culture, including astronomy, linguistics, mathematics, metaphysics, meditational mysticism, and to some extent medicine, nevertheless remained largely Indian in their fundamental inspiration, as did the education system and educational methods of the *madrasa*. The Arabs had learned the secret of papermaking from captive Chinese soldiers in Samarkand after the Battle of Atlakh (Battle of Talas) in 751, so the production of books became easier and cheaper, and libraries multiplied.

---

[47] Sezgin (1984: 43–54, 68).

[48] Barthold, cited by R. Hillenbrand in Pedersen et al. (1986: 1136); cf. Litvinsky and Zeimal (1971). The *madrasa* spread rapidly across the Islamic world after the tenth century. See Makdisi (1981) on the Islamic *madrasa* and its spread to Western Europe as the *college*. The thrust of Makdisi's argument appears to be correct, though much work is still needed on the details.

Spread of Literacy and Knowledge across Eurasia

The official support of distinctive organized world religions spread literacy and developed distinctive literature-based cultures that further redefined the imperial states, leading to the establishment of most of the ethnolinguistic regions of the premodern Old World. Before the Early Middle Ages most of Eurasia, including nearly all of Central Eurasia, was essentially a blank. The languages spoken in most of its subregions before that time are unknown, and in many places not even a foreign literary language was written, so there is no local history, literature, or other record of the cultures there. This is true to a great extent even in some large technically literate areas, including the Iranian world and India, for which most historical information must be gleaned from numismatics, accounts written by foreign travelers, or comments in histories written in neighboring countries. By the end of the Early Middle Ages there are local literatures in nearly all areas of Eurasia except for the most remote areas, the Arctic and sub-Arctic regions and the mountainous jungles of Southeast Asia. By no means was everyone educated and literate, but in most kingdoms and empires throughout Eurasia those who needed to be able to read and write could do so in one language or another.

The literate areas and cultures include Ireland, where texts were composed in Old Irish as well as Latin; England, with Old English and Latin; Wales, with Old Welsh and Latin; the Scandinavian countries, with Runic Old Norse; Spain, with Arabic and Latin; the lands of the Frankish Empire, with Latin, Old French, and Old High German; Kievan Rus, with Old Russian; the Byzantine Empire, with Greek; the Arab Empire, with Arabic; the Khazar Kaghanate, with Arabic and Hebrew;[49] Western Central Asia, with Arabic, Bactrian, Sogdian, and New Persian; Eastern Central Asia, with Sogdian, West Tokharian, East Tokharian, Old Khotanese, Old Tibetan, Old Turkic, and Chinese; Tibet, with Old Tibetan and other languages;[50] India,

---

[49] The Khazars, Bulgars, and other western Central Eurasians of the period also used runic scripts, which have not yet been fully deciphered. See Kyzlasov (1994) and Shcherbak (2001).

[50] There are several Tibeto-Burman languages recorded in Old Tibetan alphabetic script, some of them in lengthy texts, such as the one published by Thomas (1948). Though the texts are easily legible, and a few scholars have worked on them in recent years (e.g., Takeuchi 2002), so far none of the languages themselves have been deciphered or identified for certain.

with Sanskrit, Pali, various Prakrits, and Dravidian languages; Southeast Asia, with Pali, Pyu, Old Mon, Khmer, Cham, and Old Javanese; China, with Chinese; the Eastern Steppe, with Old Turkic and Sogdian; Korea, with Chinese; and Japan, with Old Japanese and Chinese.

This new literacy was in most cases the result of the conversion of these peoples to one or more of the great world religions, all of which are founded on literary texts. It was necessary to be able to read the holy texts in the original, to copy them to help spread the word throughout the people's territory, and, if the language was sufficiently different, to translate them into the local language. A great copying activity took place under the Carolingians in Western Europe, where Classical Latin texts and Latin translations of Greek texts were copied; the Islamic world, where Sanskrit, Syriac, Greek, and Middle Persian texts were translated into Arabic; the Tibetan Empire, where Sanskrit and Chinese texts were translated into Tibetan; Turkic Central Asia, where Tokharian and Prakrit texts were translated into Old Turkic; and Japan, where Chinese texts were copied. This transmission activity was of permanent importance. The texts copied or translated, and thus transmitted from one culture and age to another, established the basis not only for the intellectual blossoming of the High Middle Ages but for premodern Eurasian civilization as a whole.

With the tool of literacy at their disposal, and literary models from Antiquity and other neighboring cultures, the writers in these languages also developed art literature, which had previously been found only in the ancient civilizations. Japanese poetry, Chinese poetry, Arabic poetry, and English poetry, in particular, achieved levels of perfection rarely seen before or since. Along with the poetry went music, because poetry was always chanted or sung, not simply read.[51] Central Asian music spread to China, brought by whole orchestras that were sent or brought to Ch'ang-an. It soon completely replaced the earlier Chinese musical tradition and spread to Japan as well.[52] Because the literature was written, and writing was itself a highly developed art, calligraphy, the transmission of literature also involved the transmission of artistic styles and motifs. The Early Middle Ages

---

[51] On the collapse or destruction of traditional arts in modern times, see chapter 11.

[52] The "new" tradition, transmitted orally with little if any reference to the manuscript scores, survives to the present day as *gagaku*, Japanese classical orchestral court music, albeit changed in very many respects (most strikingly the tempos). See the important studies by Picken (1981, 1985–2000).

was thus one of the most creative periods in history for poetry, music, and graphic art.

Political Weakness and Economic Decline

The caliphate under the Abbasids started out slightly smaller than it had been under the Umayyads due to the loss of Spain, which remained Umayyad. But the caliphate soon became even larger than before. It expanded deeper into Central Asia and southeastward into India, in both of which directions the Arabs encountered the Tibetans.

In the late eighth century, the Tibetans reconquered all of their lost territories from the Chinese and expanded further, extending their influence into the west as far as Kabul, into the north as far as Jungharia, and into the northeast all the way across the Ordos. By 790 the Chinese had withdrawn from what was left of their Tarim Basin realm, leaving East Turkistan to the Tibetans and Uighurs, who fought increasingly bitterly over it, with several cities changing hands more than once. By the 820s the Tibetans were firmly in control of the southern Tarim, while the Uighurs controlled Jungharia and the cities of the northern Tarim.[53]

International commerce is generally thought to have been seriously hampered by the continuing warfare in Central Asia. This is unlikely. The Central Eurasian economy had thrived throughout the seventh and early eighth centuries despite constant warfare that was much more destructive. The cause of the depression that increasingly hurt the economies of the Chinese, Tibetan, and Uighur empires, as well as others further afield, has not yet been determined, but certainly international commerce involving China was not helped by the Chinese massacre of Sogdian men, women, and children, and of anyone who looked even remotely non-Chinese, after the suppression of the An Lu-shan Rebellion. Those who survived attempted to hide their origins and became Chinese.[54] This could hardly have been beneficial to maintaining the international trade system.

Although the T'ang Dynasty had been restored, at least in name, and participated in international trade via the Uighur Empire in the north[55] and

---

[53] Beckwith (1993, 1987b).
[54] De la Vaissière (2005a: 220 et seq.).
[55] Beckwith (1991).

via the maritime routes from Canton in the far southeast, the Chinese ruling class and the T'ang government itself fell deep in debt to Uighur moneylenders in Ch'ang-an. The economic situation worsened in the early ninth century. The Chinese economy—which had never been fully monetized—came to depend increasingly on barter. Officials were paid in kind, not with money. The economic troubles of China, whatever their cause, had severe repercussions for all of eastern Eurasia because of China's already immense population and the concomitant size of its total economy.

By the third decade of the ninth century, the war between the Tibetans on one side and the Uighurs and Chinese on the other had become unsupportable by all parties. The reason does not seem to be any sudden desire for peace, but rather the inability to continue to pay for war. The three nations made peace in 821–822. The Tibetans and Chinese erected bilingual treaty inscriptions, while the Uighurs reaffirmed their alliance with the Chinese via another dynastic marriage of a Chinese princess to the Uighur kaghan; they made a separate treaty with the Tibetans.[56] Peace finally reigned in most of Central Eurasia, but it came too late.

Collapse of the Early Medieval World Order

The worsening economic situation in most of Eurasia, aggravated or caused by climatic changes during the late 830s noted in Chinese sources,[57] continued to decline. In the West, too, there was a remarkable decline in commerce even within the caliphate. The reign of Hârûn al-Rashîd and the Central Asian period of the reign of al-Ma'mûn had been very prosperous, and large numbers of new silver dirham coins had been minted. But from 820 on there was a sharp drop in the number of new coins, and very few were minted for several decades.[58]

Late in the 830s, internal dissension within the Uighur ruling clan—undoubtedly aggravated by the economic situation—caused one of the contenders to flee to the Kirghiz, the Uighurs' sworn enemies. He led the Kir-

---

[56] Szerb (1983).

[57] Mackerras (1990: 342).

[58] Noonan (1981/1998: 55–56), who notes, "relatively few dirhams from 820–49 appear in the hoards from European Russia perhaps because few were struck in the Islamic world" (Noonan 1981/1998: 79). In 869 the rate at which new coins were being minted rose once again.

ghiz armies through the Uighur defenses to the capital, where the Uighurs were taken by surprise and totally crushed in 840. The survivors fled in all directions. The Kirghiz were unable or unwilling to take control of the Eastern Steppe, and they did not replace the Uighurs with a new Turkic dynasty.[59] Instead, the steppe became increasingly dominated by Mongolic-speaking peoples migrating in from the east.

Some of the Uighur survivors fled into the western part of their realm, where they continued as what became a small kingdom based in Qocho and Beshbalik.[60] The majority, though, many thousands of them, fled to the frontier just north of the Ordos bend of the Yellow River at the end of 840, seeking assistance from their Chinese allies. According to one Chinese border official, their yurts covered the horizon: "From east to west for 60 *li* I cannot see the end of them."[61]

Li Te-yü, the chief minister of Emperor Wu-tsung (r. 840–846), attempted to send the Uighurs back north, but that was an impossibility for them. He soon found out that they intended to stay where they were, hungry, demoralized, and dangerous. Moreover, they refused to submit to China, the normal procedure for refugees to be taken in. The refugees' kaghan maintained an increasingly independent, belligerent stance, presumably in hopes of winning further help and concessions from the T'ang. Instead, his refusal to submit only caused the T'ang court to worry about a possible attack on China. The T'ang did send food and clothing, attempting to stave off any Uighur attack while they strengthened their forces in the north. Finally, the Chinese decided on drastic measures: in early 843 they sent in an army to attack the Uighur camps and slaughtered most of them.[62]

With the full realization that the power of the Uighurs, their allies and rivals, had been destroyed, the Chinese became consumed with xenophobia. A month after the massacre of the Uighur refugees, the T'ang ruler suppressed Manichaeism in China. This entailed closing all Manichaean temples (which

---

[59] Drompp (2005: 200–201).

[60] Beshbalik was located near what is now Jimsar in northern East Turkistan. The Uighurs who fled into the northeastern part of the Tibetan Empire and settled there fared better. Their descendants remain there to this day as the Yugurs or 'Yellow Uighurs', the only direct survivors of the ancient Uighurs.

[61] Drompp (2005: 42).

[62] Dalby (1979: 664–665). See Drompp (2005) for details, including translations of the primary-source documents written by the chief minister Li Te-yü, who was in charge of the crisis and also of the suppression of foreign religions in China.

had been built at the behest of the Uighurs), confiscating their wealth, and executing Manichaean priests.[63] Finding that to be a profitable undertaking, similar measures increasingly began to be applied to Buddhism, which had already been suffering from persecution by the emperor and his adherents. The tragedy peaked in 845, when the T'ang confiscated the wealth of the Buddhist temples and closed most of the monasteries in China. The persecution was accompanied by much brutality, including massacres of monks and nuns.[64] This movement not only ended the power of Buddhism in China, it ended the T'ang as a distinctive, brilliant cultural period in Chinese history. Although the dynasty itself survived for more than a half century longer, with ever shrinking powers, it never recovered its lost prestige, power, wealth, or culture.

Charlemagne's son and successor, Louis the Pious (r. 814–840), though almost the antithesis of the great man his father had been, somehow managed to hold the Frankish Empire together. When he died in 840 his three sons fought over the succession. The civil war ended in 843 with the agreement known as the Oaths of Strasbourg, the text of which has been preserved in three languages, Old French, Old High German, and Latin. The nucleus of what became France was the realm of Charles the Bald, while Louis the German received territories that developed into Germany. Although Lothair is not mentioned, the part that fell to him, as the imperial heir, was the middle, which came to be called Lotharingia (now Lorraine). At the time it extended from northern Italy and southeastern France up to the North Sea and included the capital, Aachen.

The economic weakness in the Tibetan Empire forced the government to stop supporting the Buddhist monastic establishment, which had become large and very expensive. In 842 a tantric monk, Lhalung Dpalgyi Rdorje, assassinated the last emperor who ruled over a united Tibetan Empire, Khri U'i Dum Brtsan (Glang Darma, r. 838–842).[65] The imperial succession was

---

[63] Weinstein (1987: 121).

[64] Weinstein (1987: 121–128). The persecution is referred to as the Hui-ch'ang Suppression of Buddhism, after the Hui-ch'ang reign period (841–846) during which it took place. Wu-tsung's successor immediately ceased the persecution and punished the main living perpetrators of it. However, despite his attempt to restore Buddhism, the religion never recovered institutionally in China, although thenceforth it flourished intellectually and spiritually even more than it had previously.

[65] Although the kernel of the story rings true, and the name of the assassin appears to be historical, the tradition about the assassination of Glang Darma contains much that is symbolic and undoubtedly ahistorical. Nevertheless, extremely little is actually known about the po-

contested, and the Tibetan Empire broke up. Some Central Asian parts of the realm, particularly in the northeast, survived longer than Tibet itself before the last remnant of the empire fell in 866.

The Byzantine Empire was capably ruled by the energetic Theophilos II (r. 829–842) until his death, at which point his wife Theodora, a devoted iconodule, took effective power as regent for her then three-year-old son Michael III (the Drunkard, r. 842–867). She instituted a religious revolution that restored icon worship throughout the empire and suppressed iconoclasm ruthlessly and thoroughly. With the increasing weakness of the peoples around them, the Byzantines recovered economically and politically, and gradually extended their influence into parts of the former Eastern Roman Empire.

The Arab Empire under al-Ma'mûn gave up direct control over most of its western Central Asian dominions, one of the richest and most populous parts of the empire, when he appointed Ṭâhir ibn al-Ḥusayn, one of the leaders of the caliph's "second Abbasid revolution," to the governorship of Khurasan. Ṭâhir and his successors thus functioned as the legitimate governing authority of Khurasan—and eventually even of Iran and part of Iraq—on behalf of the caliphs. Under Ṭâhir's rule Arab Central Asia quickly became semi-independent; he minted coins with his own name on them, and his position became hereditary, developing into an autonomous Tahirid "dynasty." Nevertheless, Western Central Asia remained Muslim and continued to grow (after the recession that began in the 820s), partly because of its inclusion in the vast Islamic world, but mainly due to the strength of the Central Asian local economy—which was solidly based on local agriculture and internal trade[66]—as well as to the continuing transcontinental commerce.

The central government in Baghdad came increasingly under the influence of the Islamicized Central Asian comitatus—the *shâkiriyya*, or *châkars*.[67] The comitatus was passed on as a unit to the ruler's successor and

---

litical history of the late Tibetan Empire and even less about its aftermath. The whole period is in need of serious study. For the history of Buddhism in the empire and in the early post-imperial period, see Walter (forthcoming).

[66] Shaban (1976) notes that the Tahirids "were traditional rulers whose main concern was with the long established families in their regions. In other words, they contented themselves with enforcing the treaties of capitulation concluded at the time of the [Arab] conquest with the *dihqâns* there. As these *dihqâns* were by definition the big landowners it is possible to conclude that the economy was mostly based on agriculture."

[67] In most modern histories of the period they are usually referred to as Turks, but many were Sogdians or other Central Eurasians. See the prologue, Beckwith (1984a), and de la Vaissière (2007).

thus grew bigger, more powerful, more expensive, and more unreliable, until the caliphs fell into the hands of their guard corps and the increasingly hereditary government officials.[68] In 836 al-Muʻtaṣim (r. 833–842), the last caliph who ruled in more than name, moved the capital to Samarra (Sâmarrâ'),[69] about seventy-five miles north of Baghdad, purportedly to eliminate conflict between his comitatus and the people of Baghdad, but probably mainly in an attempt to remove himself from the murderous politics and social turmoil there. Upon his death he was succeeded by his son, al-Wâthiq (r. 842–847), who had little interest in governing and was not in much of a position to do it anyway. Although the government continued to exercise official sovereignty over much of the former Arab Empire, and indeed, the Abbasid Caliphate existed in name for centuries more, the death of al-Muʻtaṣim in 842 marks the effective end of the Arab Empire as an actual state.

[68] The early form of the comitatus would thus seem to have been better from the point of view of *Realpolitik*.

[69] It remained the official capital until 892 (Northedge 1995: 1039).

7

The Vikings and Cathay

Братие и дружино
Луче же бы потяту быти
  неже полонену быти
а въсядѣмъ братие
  на своѣ бързыѣ комонѣ
да позьримъ синего Дону
—Слово о пълку Игоревѣ[1]

Brothers and companions!
Better would it be to be killed
  than to be captives!
So let us mount, brothers,
  on our swift warhorses,
for a look at the dark blue Don!
—From *The Lay of Igor's Host*

The Age of Princes

After the collapse of the early medieval world order, new states appeared, but they were much smaller in size than the ones they followed. The only exception was the Byzantine Empire, which survived intact and even expanded a little, although it never recovered most of the territory it had lost to the Arabs. Perhaps because of the larger number of states, both within Central Eurasia and in the periphery, the world economy recovered and started growing again, eventually bringing cultural resurgence across Eurasia.

Unlike the Early Middle Ages, high culture in this period was primarily religious in orientation to begin with, and this determined the direction of further development. The burgeoning development of monastic institutions in all major Eurasian regions spread literacy further. At the same time, the growth of powerful monastic orders in much of Eurasia meant that the influence and control of rigid orthodoxies greatly increased too.

---

[1] Paragraphs 10 and 11 of the online edition (http://titus.uni-frankfurt.de/texte/etcs/slav/aruss/slovigor/slovi.htm), based on the 1964 edition by Roman Jakobson, prepared by Sigurdur H. Palsson (Vienna 1994), TITUS version by Jost Gippert, November 13, 2004.

The cultural brilliance of the Islamic world was in the ascendant in the period following the collapse of the Arab Empire, especially in Central Asia. Virtually all of the greatest philosophers and scientists of classical Islamic civilization were either from Central Asia or of Central Asian origin. But the still young Islamic intellectual tradition came under attack by fundamentalists, who rejected philosophy in favor of mysticism and eventually succeeded in replacing reason with doctrine across the Islamic world.

While the Central Steppe continued to be dominated by nomadic peoples, the appearance in both the Western Steppe and the Eastern Steppe of states that straddled the geographical boundary between the nomadic and the non-nomadic brought increasing agrarian influence over the steppe zone. While the Viking-Slavic kaghanate of Rus expanded European agrarian-urban culture into the Western Steppe, the Chinese, under the aegis of dynasties founded by Central Eurasians, spread their agrarian-urban tradition into the Eastern Steppe.

The Formation of Small Hegemonies

Following the breakup of the great early medieval empires, and in connection with the apparent climatic downturn at that time, the peoples at the northern edge of Central Eurasia began migrating southward in a smaller-scale repeat of the Great Wandering of Peoples.

THE WESTERN STEPPE

The Khazars were threatened in the 830s by someone, probably the Hungarians (Onogurs),[2] who had been their allies or subjects. They asked the Byzantines for help. Greek engineers helped the Khazars build a great fortress, Sarkel, on the lower Don in 840–841.[3] The Hungarians are known to have

---

[2] A mixed people with Turkic and Finno-Ugric elements, they are frequently called Turks in the sources, but the Magyars, a Finno-Ugric people, came to dominate the Turkic element at the time of their migration into Pannonia, and it is the Magyar language that has survived as the language of Hungary. The name Hungarian is generally believed to be in origin the Turkic name 'Onogur'.

[3] Zuckerman (1997). Dunlop (1954: 186–187) suggests the Rus as perhaps the enemy against which the fortress was built. Rus attacks against the Khazars are not mentioned in the sources for such an early period (which is hardly to say that they did not happen), but if they were the enemy, the lower Don location would be ideal for a fortress against them, because

been in the Western Steppe by 839, from which base they raided up the Danube into Pannonia in 862 and attacked the Slavs in 870–880.[4]

In 889[5] the Khazars and Ghuzz attacked the Pechenegs in their homeland between the Volga and Ural rivers, in the western part of the Central Steppe. The Pechenegs fled into the Western Steppe, defeated the Onogurs, and occupied their territory. From the Danube basin the Hungarians again moved north into Pannonia. In 892, under Árpád (fl. 895), they allied with Arnulf, the king of East Francia, against Svatopluk, king of Moravia, and in 894 again raided in Pannonia and Moravia. With their defeat by the Bulgarians in 895, and facing Pecheneg pressure on their steppe territory, the Hungarians under Árpád settled in Pannonia, following in the footsteps of the earlier Huns and Avars. From there they raided across Central and Western Europe, generally as mercenaries or allies of one or another European prince, reaching Italy in the spring of 899.[6] Their activities continued for several more decades. They eventually reached as far as Spain, in 942,[7] as they concluded alliances and extracted tribute from defeated rulers wherever they went—in other words, as they built an imperial state in traditional fashion. They were finally defeated at the Battle of Lechfeld, near Augsburg, on August 10, 955,[8] by their German rival Otto I (the Great, d. 973), who was in the process of building his own empire in the same way as the Hungarians. His victory over them ensured that he was to succeed at it. The Hungarians then settled down in Pannonia and established the Hungarian Kingdom. On Christmas Day of the year 1000, the Hungarian ruler Stephen was crowned king of Hungary and began the conversion of his people to Christianity.[9]

The Khazars were threatened from another direction as well. Although the Frankish successor states were increasingly Mediterranean in culture, the Scandinavian peoples still largely belonged to the Central Eurasian Culture Complex and constituted the northwesternmost outlier of it. Like other

---

the Rus were northwest of the Khazars, and being part Viking in origin, they were skilled sailors, usually trading and raiding by water.

[4] Sinor (1959: 17).

[5] Sinor (1959: 17).

[6] See Sinor (1959: 21–22), who remarks that Brother Heribaldus writes in the annals of the monastery of St. Gall south of Lake Constance (in what is now Switzerland) that he never had "a better time than during the Hungarians' stay in his monastery."

[7] Schamiloglu (1984b: 216).

[8] Sinor (1959: 27–28).

[9] Sinor (1959: 28–36).

peoples who belonged to that culture complex, the Vikings, despite their popular reputation as warriors, are now known to have been primarily trad-ers, and they moved into the more southerly, civilized states mainly to trade. Although they are famous, or infamous, for their military actions in the British Isles and Francia via the North Sea, and settled permanently in parts of those countries, their eastern movement ultimately had greater import. They sailed the Baltic eastward into the Finnic areas and southeastward down the rivers to the lands of the Slavs west of the Khazar Kaghanate.

In the early ninth century the Vikings had become intensely involved in commerce with the Islamic lands of the Near East via the Russian rivers. This trade route had first been developed by the Khazars, Jews, and Muslims and only then came under the domination of the Vikings.[10] Three Viking chiefs led by Rurik founded the Rus Kaghanate[11] in the area of Novgorod around 862, and around 882 Rurik's successor Oleg conquered Kiev and established the Rus Kaghanate as an imperial state stretching from the Bal-tic Sea to the Black Sea.[12] Sailing west on the Black Sea, the Rus reached the Byzantine commonwealth of Orthodox states, including the Slavicized kingdom of Bulgaria, and the imperial capital of Constantinople itself. The Byzantine emperors, who had earlier acquired a comitatus of Ferghanians and Khazars,[13] immediately saw the usefulness of the Vikings and hired them as mercenaries, thus constituting the famous Varangian Guard.

Via the Volga the Vikings reached the Caspian Sea and the Islamic lands across it, but they ran into conflict with the Khazars, who controlled the lower Volga basin. It was not long before war broke out between the Khazars and the Rus. Between 965 and 968/969 Sviatoslav, king of Kievan Rus, in-flicted a devastating defeat upon the Khazars, capturing Sarkel and destroy-ing the capital Atil (or Itil, on the lower Volga River) and other cities. Al-though the Rus returned to Kiev after their campaign and the Khazars survived as a people for a long time after their defeat,[14] the Khazar realm never recovered its former power. It gradually shrank and fell prey to other foes, and the Khazar nation eventually disappeared.

[10] Noonan (1981/1998: 53).
[11] See Golden (1982). For citations of the title *kaghan* used for the king of the Rus, see Dunlop (1954: 237).
[12] Christian (1998: 334).
[13] See the prologue.
[14] Dunlop (1954: 254 et seq.).

WESTERN AND SOUTHERN CENTRAL ASIA

As the Arab caliphate weakened and broke up, Western Central Asia became semi-independent under a succession of hereditary governorships that ruled the region in the name of the Abbasids: the Tahirids (821–873), Saffarids (873–900), and Samanids. All were of Iranian Central Asian origin. The Samanids, whose realm was founded by Ismâ'îl (r. 893-907),[15] were increasingly pressed over time by the Karakhanids, a people of Karluk Turkic stock who were based in a large territory from the Jaxartes to the T'ien Shan; they had converted to Islam in the tenth century.[16] The Samanids were overthrown in 999 and the last Samanid ruler, named Ismâ'îl like the first, was killed in 1005 in the Kara Kum Desert. The Karakhanids then took control of most of Transoxiana, not including Khwarizmia, which had remained largely independent even during the heyday of the caliphate.

While the Karakhanids were expanding into Western Central Asia, the eastern territories of Southern Central Asia had come under the control of a Samanid governor, the former *ghulâm* Alptigin (Alp Tegin 'Prince Alp'), who had established himself in Ghazne (Ghazna, in what is now southeastern Afghanistan) in or around 962 but still recognized the suzerainty of the Samanids. In 994 Sebüktigin (Sebük Tegin 'Prince Sebük', r. 994–997), who had formerly been Alptigin's *ghulâm* and seems to have been a Karluk in origin, subdued a rebellion of the Samanid provinces south of the Oxus and added their territories to what had become a de facto Ghaznavid Empire. His son Maḥmûd (Maḥmûd of Ghazne, r. 997–1030) declared his independence of the Samanids. He annexed their former territories in 998 and invaded Khwârizm in 1017, adding the entire region to his empire and thereby containing the Karakhanids from further expansion to the west and south. He also expanded into northwestern India and, at the end of his life, captured northern Iran.[17] After the death of Maḥmûd, the Ghaznavids rapidly lost much of their support, especially in the regions further from their home base.

---

[15] Christian (1998: 313–319).

[16] Their predecessors were apparently the Karluks, whose kaghan converted to Islam in the late eighth or early ninth century, according to al-Ya'qûbî (Beckwith 1993: 127 n. 114). For another view on the origins of the Karakhanids, see Kochnev (1996).

[17] Bosworth (1968: 6–8, 12), Christian (1998: 370).

At the end of the tenth century, a Turkmen (Türkmen)[18] people led by Seljuk (Saljuq) migrated into the Khwarizmian region around the Jaxartes delta. Seljuk's father had earlier served the king of the Khazars, and after his death Seljuk had been raised at his court. Seljuk's sons bore the Old Testament–sounding names of Mûsâ (Moses), Mikâ'îl (Michael), and Isrâ'îl (Israel), which testify to their Khazar background.[19] Not long after they arrived, they converted to Islam and raided the non-Muslim Turkmen and others in the region, often serving as mercenaries under one or another rival prince in Transoxiana. After being defeated by their rivals in the area in the third decade of the eleventh century they gradually began moving south into Sogdiana. Although the Seljuks were a new and largely unknown quantity in Central Asia proper, the corruption, greed, and rapid military-political decline of the Ghaznavids led city after city in Khurasan to voluntarily surrender to the Seljuks. When Sultan Mas'ûd finally decided to attack the Seljuks in force, he was decisively defeated by them in the desert west of Marw in 1040. Two years later, the Seljuks returned to Khwârizm. They overthrew their rivals and appointed a Seljuk governor over the region. The Ghaznavids retained power in their home territory around Ghazne and northwestern India, and even recovered enough strength to stave off further Seljuk expansion into their territory and temporarily pushed them back to the northwest. But under Alp Arslan (r. 1063–1072) and his son Malik Shâh (r. 1072–1092), the Seljuks secured their eastern frontier by an alliance with the western Karakhanids, whose empire had split in 1041/1042.[20] To the west, the Seljuks expanded across Iran, Iraq, Armenia, and deep into Anatolia. There Alp Arslan resoundingly defeated an army of the Byzantine emperor Romanus at the Battle of Mantzikert

---

[18] They belonged to the Oghuz branch of Turks. Some of them had been nomadizing near the North Caucasus Steppe in 921–922 when the Arab envoy Ibn Faḍlân passed through during his journey to Volga Bulgaria (Bosworth 1968: 16). There are several translations of his fascinating account, most recently by Frye (2005).

[19] Dunlop (1954: 260). Bosworth (1968: 18) argues that the king of the Turks mentioned in some sources was the Yabghu, a local Oghuz ruler in Khwarizmia, but this seems to be the result of confusion with the Khazar kaghan, because the Seljuks moved from Khazaria to the lower Jaxartes, which was under the rule of an Oghuz king who had the title Yabghu. A number of sources specifically mention Seljuk's father serving under the Khazars—who still existed in his day—and the names of his sons are so remarkable that there does not seem to be any reason to doubt that he had indeed been raised at the court of the Khazar ruler, as the sources say (cf. Dunlop 1954: 260–261).

[20] The eastern half was based first in Balâsâghûn, then in Kashgar, while the western half was based first in Uzkand (in eastern Ferghana) and later in Samarkand.

(Malâzgird) in 1071. From this time onward Anatolia became increasingly Turkicized by the immigration of Turkmen and other Oghuz peoples who were not under the control of the Seljuks. Although Turks had earlier raided Anatolia at one time or another, Byzantine control had been firm enough that the area remained largely Greek and Armenian speaking. Now the Turkish language began to take root.

TIBET

From the mid-tenth century on, after a century about which very little is known, a cultural resurgence in the form of the restoration of institutional Buddhism began in the former lands of the Tibetan Empire. Because the postimperial historical sources on Tibet are almost completely religious in interest and were written by monks,[21] little is known about the political entities that supported the Buddhist revival. It is generally accepted that monastic Buddhism has always spread widely only with state support, and indeed, the earliest movement to reinstitute Buddhism is known to have been undertaken by King Yeśes 'Od of Guge in western Tibet, who was captured during a military campaign against the Karluk Turks and died in captivity. It is thus clear that the religious restoration followed political expansion, just as it did in the rest of Eurasia.[22] The fact that the Guge royal dynasty claimed descent from the lineage of the Tibetan imperial family, whether justified or not, strongly supports the supposition that their primary goal was the restoration of the family's long-lost imperial power.

The Buddhist movement began in three areas outside of Central Tibet: the east (modern Khams Province), the northeast (modern Amdo Province), and the Guge Kingdom in the northwest (modern Mngáris Province). The variety of Buddhism that spread again in Tibet was perhaps a continuation of the form that had developed there during the Tibetan Empire and had been barely maintained by monks living in frontier regions. However, under the influence of the great Guge teacher Rin-chen Bzangpo (985–1055), who had studied in India, and especially after the arrival of Âtiśa (d. 1054)— an Indian teacher from the monastery of Vikramaśîlâ in Magadha, India,

---

[21] Also, the few modern scholars who have worked on them have been interested almost exclusively in religious matters.

[22] The story of his campaigns and death are presented in completely religious garb and have generally been taken at face value, but the sources do say that he was captured during a military campaign.

who had come to the kingdom in 1042 at the invitation of Byang-chub 'Od, brother of the new king 'Od-lde—a newer form of Buddhism spread at the expense of the older teachings. This form of esoteric Buddhism was based on the New Tantras translated by Rin-chen Bzangpo and Âtiśa, among others.[23] Âtiśa subsequently moved to Central Tibet and taught there until his death; it is probable that his move there was accompanied by the political movement of his Guge patrons in that direction as well.

The most important single political-religious development in Tibet at this time was, however, due to 'Brog-mi, a contemporary of Âtiśa, who had studied in Vikramaśîlâ for eight years before returning to Tibet. In 1043 he built a monastery in Gtsang Province in Central Tibet, brought a teacher from India, and took in students, including members of the powerful 'Khon clan. In 1073 he founded the monastery of Saskya, which was kept under the control of one or another branch of the 'Khon clan by having the usual succession of celibate abbots pass from uncle to nephew. The power of the 'Khon clan grew along with their Saskyapa sect until they were the leading Tibetan Buddhist sect, and perhaps the dominant political power, by the early thirteenth century.

The major sectarian division of Tibetan Buddhism developed at this time. The majority practitioners, who relied on texts translated from Sanskrit for their legitimacy, referred to Buddhism as *Chos*,[24] while the others referred to it as *Bon*.[25] Within the *Chos* tradition many sects developed.[26] Buddhism in its new forms quickly spread across Tibet and displaced earlier forms of the religion.

NORTH CHINA AND THE EASTERN STEPPE

After the Rebellion of Huang Ch'ao (d. 884), which grew from banditry to devastate much of the remaining T'ang realm—including even the far south-eastern port of Canton, where the rebel slaughtered an estimated 120,000

---

[23] Hoffmann (1961: 112–122).

[24] They thus narrowed the more general meaning of *chos*, which perhaps meant something like 'customary belief' already in Old Tibetan, during which period it also began to be equated with Sanskrit *dharma*. The original meaning of *chos* in Tibetan is disputed; it may be a derivative of a verb meaning 'to create, make'.

[25] On the problematic Tibetan word *bon* and the names Bon and Bonpo, see endnote 79.

[26] The main dichotomy that eventually developed within the Chos tradition was between those who followed mainly the Old Tantras (who eventually developed into the *Rñingmapa* sect) and those who followed mainly the New Tantras (all the other sects).

people, mainly Arab, Persian, and other foreign merchants—the power of the T'ang Dynasty effectively ended and Littoral zone commercial ports further south, outside China, supplanted Canton in importance.[27] The northern and western regions that had been under Chinese domination, including the southern part of the Eastern Steppe and the eastern edge of Central Asia, were dominated by Central Eurasian peoples in Chinese-style semi-independent states, many of which gradually became fully independent.[28] They ruled over territory that included both part of Central Eurasia and part of North China and competed with each other and with Chinese-ruled states to the south.

As the T'ang collapsed, a plethora of small local dynasties were created by former governors and generals in what had been T'ang territory. One of the earliest Sino-Central Eurasian states to form, and the first large one, was based in Ho-tung, the province east of the great bend of the Yellow River. It began as a semi-independent province ruled by the Sha-t'o Turkic general Li K'o-yung (r. 883–907), who defeated Huang Ch'ao in 883 and forced him to withdraw from North China. In 913 Li K'o-yung's son Li Ts'un-hsü (r. 907–926) defeated the ruler of Lu-lung, the long-independent northeastern province that had been An Lu-shan's power base. In 923 he overthrew the large realm of Later Liang (907–923), which had included the two former T'ang capitals and had been founded by the former ally of Huang Ch'ao who brought about the violent final end of the T'ang.[29] Li Ts'un-hsü then declared his establishment of the Later T'ang Dynasty (923–937). With the Sha-t'o unification of North China proper, plus most of the Sino-Central Eurasian frontier west of Manchuria (except for the Tangut-ruled area of the eastern Ordos along the Great Wall directly across the Yellow River to their west), the Sha-t'o, followed by the Chin (937–946) and Han (947–950) dynasties, had to face the growing power of their erstwhile ally—the Liao Dynasty founded by the Mongolic Khitan to their north and northeast—who repeatedly attacked them in the 940s.[30]

---

[27] The dynasty officially ended in 907, but it had ceased to exist in all but name outside the capital district not long after Huang Ch'ao's rebellion.

[28] For an up-to-date overview of the post-T'ang realms in the Eastern Steppe and North China, see Drompp (2005: 197 et seq.).

[29] Somers (1979: 760–765).

[30] Franke and Twitchett (1994: 6).

The Hsi-hsia ('Western Hsia') Dynasty, based in the Ordos, owed its founding to the descendants of Tibeto-Burman-speaking Tangut (Miñak) people there, most of whom had migrated from their homeland in northeastern Tibet under pressure from the growing Tibetan Empire. They had been settled in the eastern Ordos region in the early T'ang period. By the time of the An Lu-shan Rebellion, the Tanguts were the dominant local power in the region. Late in the T'ang, their chief T'o-pa Ssu-kung (r. 881–ca. 895), head of the traditional leading clan of the Tangut, drove the rebel Huang Ch'ao from the capital, Ch'ang-an and, as a reward, was appointed military governor of the three prefectures of Hsia, Sui, and Yin. Under his successors, the Tanguts slowly expanded to the southwest in the direction of their old homeland in northeastern Tibet and westward toward Central Asia. In 1002 they captured Ling-chou, to the west of their Hsia-chou home, and made it their first capital, renaming it Hsi-p'ing-fu the following year. They formally proclaimed their dynasty in 1038. As the Tanguts prospered and their state continued to grow, they built a new capital directly to the west across the Yellow River.[31] They gradually added half of Kansu and the former Tibetan Empire territories south of Hsi-ning as far as the Tibetan Ch'ing-t'ang Kingdom and established a prosperous, stable empire that lasted into the Mongol epoch, despite frequent wars with the Tibetans and others to their southwest and with the Chinese of the Sung Dynasty (Northern Sung 960–1125; Southern Sung 1125–1279)[32] on their southeastern border. The Tanguts came to dominate east-west trade from China to Central Asia—to some extent resuscitating the early T'u-yü-hun realm in this respect—but they also controlled some of the north-south trade between China and the Eastern Steppe because their empire also extended to the east across the Ordos, where it faced the Khitan to the north and east.

A number of small kingdoms founded by Chinese, Uighurs, and Tibetans arose in the Kansu and Kokonor area that had constituted the heart of the Mdosmad Province of the Tibetan Empire. The most important of these was Ch'ing-t'ang, in the Kokonor area. The kingdom prospered by serving as an alternative route for merchants passing between Eastern Central Asia

[31] Its Chinese name was Hsing-chou, then Hsing-ch'ing-fu (1033), and later Chung-hsing; it was known as Eriqaya (Erighaya) in Mongol (de Rachewiltz 2004: 552, 968; cf. Dunnell 1994: 178). This account of the Tanguts is derived largely from Dunnell (1994); cf. Dunnell (1996).
[32] Dillon (1998: 294).

and Sung China. It also occasionally assisted the Sung militarily in its strug-gle with the Tanguts, who expanded up to the borders of Ch'ing-t'ang and exerted a great deal of pressure on the kingdom.[33]

The Khitan, a Mongolic-speaking people whose ancestors had come out of the Hsien-pei confederation in late Antiquity,[34] had begun dominat-ing the area to the northeast of China in the early T'ang period.[35] After the T'ang Dynasty's collapse, under the leadership of A-pao-chi (r. 907/916–926, posthumously T'ai-tsu), founder of the Liao Dynasty (916–1125), they ex-panded into northeastern China, the Eastern Steppe (924),[36] and southern Manchuria.[37] The Khitan thus ruled the eastern area of the frontier that overlapped former North China and Central Eurasia, while the Tanguts ruled the western area of the frontier. Both realms included territory inhab-ited mainly by Chinese and territory inhabited mainly by Central Eurasians. Like some other Central Eurasian peoples in the northeast, the Khitan still practiced the traditional comitatus, at least during their formative years, and their state was clearly organized around the "khan and four bey" sys-tem, with a particularly interesting variant in which the Khitan had five capitals, or *ordu*, one for each of the four directions plus one for the center.[38] The Khitan maintained a strong presence in the Eastern Steppe partly be-cause of opposition to Sinicization by Khitan conservatives who wanted to preserve their nomadic life-style. Both steppe and settled Khitan were later of crucial importance to the Mongols' success in North China. The Khitan es-tablished a very close relationship with the Uighurs during the Liao Dynasty

---

[33] The best account of Ch'ing-t'ang commerce is in Shiba (1983), a groundbreaking article with much valuable information on trade in eastern Eurasia in general in this period. Cf. Petech (1983) for information on the kingdom's political history.

[34] On the linguistic relationships of Khitan, see endnote 80.

[35] An Lu-shan had campaigned frequently, and usually unsuccessfully, against them. On the name of his comitatus of Khitan and other warriors, more than 8,000 strong, whom he treated as his own sons (*TCTC* 216: 6905), see endnote 25.

[36] Biran (2005: 15).

[37] Twitchett and Tietze (1994: 60–62); Drompp (2005: 200–201, 202–205) shows that the Kirghiz did not form a steppe empire to replace that of the Uighurs.

[38] See the classic work of Wittfogel and Fêng (1949) on this topic and much else concerning the Khitan. The Khitan made the city of Yen-ching—now Peking (Beijing 'Northern Capital')—one of their five capitals and the administrative center for the agricultural regions of the empire. This was the beginning of the city's rise to prominence (Franke and Twitchett 1994: 16). Johannes Reckel (cited in Di Cosmo 1999: 10 n. 29) argues that the Khitan adopted their multiple capital system from the conquered state of Po-hai (in southeastern Manchuria and northern Korea), which was partly heir to the Koguryo heritage.

period.[39] Between 1120 and 1123 the Liao Dynasty was overthrown by the Tungusic Jurchen, who had long been enemies of the Khitan.

The Jurchen were in origin a Southern Tungusic–speaking forest people from far eastern Manchuria (the modern Russian area of Primor'e). They were not steppe nomads like the Mongolic Khitan and later Mongols. Nevertheless, they became acquainted with the steppe style of warfare and state formation during the long period in which the Jurchen were subjects of the Khitan. After soundly defeating the Khitan armies sent against them in Manchuria, in 1115 the Jurchen declared themselves an empire under the Chin ('gold') Dynasty. They pressed their advantage against the weakened Liao, capturing their remaining territory in southern Manchuria. In 1117 the Sung Dynasty attempted to reach an agreement with the Chin to cooperate in the defeat and partition of the Liao territory. The Sung hoped thereby to restore Chinese territorial control over much of the region once governed by the T'ang in the north. But the Jurchen had already become strong enough that they did not need the Sung, and the Sung attacks on the Liao failed. The Chin and Sung then signed a treaty in 1123 whereby the Chin would allow the Sung to retake a small part of the Liao territory in return for payment annually of 200,000 taels of silver and 300,000 bolts of silk as recompense for lost income from the territories in question. With the capture and deposition of the last Liao prince in 1125, the Jurchen replaced the Khitan as rulers of northeastern China and Manchuria. However, Sung relations with the Jurchen deteriorated, and in 1125 the Jurchen invaded Sung, capturing Shansi and Hopei and crossing the Yellow River to besiege the Sung capital at K'ai-feng, directly east of Loyang.

The Sung accepted the Chin peace terms, by which the Sung gave up the lost provinces and agreed to pay an annual indemnity of 300,000 taels of silver, 300,000 bolts of silk, and one million strings of bronze coins. In 1126 the king of Koryo (Korea) accepted Chin vassal status, as had the Tangut Hsi-hsia. When the Sung violated some terms of the treaty, the Chin again attacked, this time capturing and sacking K'ai-feng. The emperor and the retired emperor Hui-tsung (one of the greatest artists and calligraphers in Chinese history) and many other members of the imperial court were taken

---

[39] Even after the fall of the Liao, the Kara Khitai maintained that relationship down to the eve of the Mongol conquest.

captive. Hui-tsung abdicated, and the Sung enthroned another emperor, but the dynasty was essentially defeated. The Chin returned home in 1127, leaving a diminished Sung, which was forced to move the capital still further south to Hang-chou, in 1138. Nevertheless, the Sung proved stronger than the Jurchen had anticipated and recovered some of its lost territory. Another treaty was finally signed in 1142, in which the border was set as the Huai River and an annual tribute of 250,000 taels of silver and bolts of silk were to be paid to the Chin.[40]

When the Liao Dynasty fell to the Jurchen, a Khitan leader, Yeh-lü Ta-shih, proclaimed himself *wang* 'prince' and abandoned the inept last Khitan ruler in 1124.[41] He fled north into the steppe to the Khitan garrison at Kedun in the Orkhon River region to gather the forces that remained there. In 1130 he led his followers, including Khitans, Mongols, and Chinese, among others, northwestward out of Kedun. In 1131 or 1132,[42] during what became a careful move that turned increasingly westward, he took the innovative title Gür Khan 'universal ruler',[43] declared a Chinese-style dynastic reign-period title, and renewed the traditional Khitan overlordship over the Uighur Kingdom in the northern Tarim Basin.[44] In 1134 the Eastern Karakhanid ruler in Balâsâghûn, in the Chu River valley near the Issyk Kul, asked for Yeh-lü Ta-shih's help against the Karluk and Kangli tribesmen in his territory. Yeh-lü Ta-shih accepted. He marched into Balâsâghûn unopposed and promptly made the Karakhanid his vassal. Yeh-lü Ta-shih established his capital there in a new Khitan-style imperial encampment, Quz Ordo, and began sending his governors over all the territory of the former Eastern Karakhanids.[45] Failing in an attempt to overthrow the Jurchen in 1134, he abandoned any further attempts to reestablish the Khitan in their former eastern realm. Despite such setbacks, he continued to expand his new empire until he had established his authority in the east over Kashgar, Khotan, the Kirghiz, and Beshbalik. In the west he defeated the Western Karakhanid ruler at Khujand in May 1137 and cemented the victory

---

[40] This account of the Chin and their wars with the Liao and Sung is based on Franke (1994).
[41] Biran (2005: 25–26).
[42] Biran (2005: 36).
[43] For discussion of the title, see endnote 83; cf. Biran (2005: 39 n. 146).
[44] Biran (2005: 32–38).
[45] Biran (2005: 39).

by his subsequent defeat of Sultan Sanjar, ruler of the Seljuks, on September 9, 1141, in the Battle of Qaṭwân, near Samarkand. As a result, Yeh-lü Ta-shih added Transoxiana to his realm and extended his sway as far as Khwârizm, whose ruler he forced to pay tribute (from 1142).[46] The new empire came to be known as the Kara Khitai or 'Black Khitan' and also as a Chinese-style dynasty, the Western Liao. After the death of the Gür Khan Yeh-lü Ta-shih in 1143, the Kara Khitai focused their attention entirely on their new empire, which in the east encompassed East Turkistan and Jungharia, extending as far as western Mongolia, and in the west Transoxiana, extending as far as the growing realm of Khwarizmia.

In the Eastern Steppe, the political situation changed after the Jurchen overthrow of the Khitan. With their conquest of much more of China than the Khitan or Tanguts had, the Jurchen center of gravity was heavily Chinese. Although the Jurchen maintained some northern traditions, including the Khitan five-capital system, they became much more Sinified. They did not have more than a fleeting steppe presence even at the beginning and soon abandoned any serious attempt to control the Eastern Steppe, preferring to exert their influence indirectly. This created instability there, which the many peoples of the region, who belonged to different ethnolinguistic groups but were mostly Mongols or Turks, attempted to rectify. The most powerful single people, the Tatars, were supported by the Jurchen against the rising power of the Mongols. Although the Chin actually invaded the steppe in an attempt to subdue the Mongols, they failed and by 1146/1147 recognized them as a state. The Mongol leader, Khabul Khan, was proclaimed "Ancestral Originating Emperor." The Chin gave him a title that suggested vassal status, but also "very generous presents."[47] Although the Mongols had thus risen to power in the Eastern Steppe, the Tatars, with the support of the Jurchen, generally still dominated the political situation there.

Intellectual Growth in the High Middle Ages

The limitation in the size of states in the period between the Early Middle Ages and the Mongol Conquest limited the evil that governments and politi-

---

[46] Biran (2005).
[47] Franke (1994: 238).

cians could do to individuals. Especially in Western Europe, the Islamic world, Tibet, and East Asia, it became possible for philosophers, scientists, and other creative people to escape to another more amenable state when they were endangered in their homeland. The result was increased international movement, and with it continued intellectual growth.

At this time, the Islamic world attained its apogee in science and mathematics, philosophy and metaphysics. Most of the greatest minds in these subjects, including al-Farghânî (Alfraganus, fl. 833–861, from Ferghana), al-Fârâbî (Alfarabius or Avennasar, d. 950, from Fârâb [Utrâr]), Ibn Sînâ (Avicenna, 980–1037, from Afšana, near Bukhara), al-Birûnî (973–ca. 1050, from Kâth, in Khwarizmia), al-Ghazâlî (or al-Ghazzâlî, Algazel, 1058–1111, from Ṭûs, in Khurasan), and many others, were from Central Asia. The first historical Sufi mystic, Abû Yazîd al-Bisṭâmî (d. 875), was from Bisṭâm in western Khurasan. He introduced the Indian yogic practices and teachings he had learned from his guru, a non-Muslim, Abû ʿAlî al-Sindî.[48] Central Asia eventually became a stronghold of Sufism and home to many Sufi monastic orders.

The great cities of Central Asia were centers of culture, libraries, and education. The Samanids are famous for having supported Rûdakî and Daqîqî, the first poets to write great poetry in New Persian, while the Ghaznavids also patronized New Persian literature, most famously the *Shâhnâmeh* 'the Book of Kings', a literary epic poem composed by Firdausî (d. 1020) that was based partly on Iranian oral epics.[49] The great poet Niẓâmî (1141–1209/1213) lived at this time too. It is notable that this literary activity took place in Central Asia, under Central Asian rulers' patronage, not in Iran (Persia).

The guiding hand behind the Seljuks at their height, under Alp Arslan and Malik Shâh, was Niẓâm al-Mulk (1017/1019–1092). He was an astute

---

[48] The most balanced general treatment of early *mystical* Sufism (which must be sharply distinguished from other early types of Sufism, though it usually is not) is by Fakhry (1983: 241), but the long Western scholarly tradition of identifying the Indian elements with Hinduism is questionable. It is the result primarily of early European scholars' lack of knowledge about any form of Buddhism except South and Southeast Asian Theravâda Buddhism, which had become markedly different from other forms of Buddhism by the time of Muḥammad. It is long past time for an objective scholar expert in both Islamic and Buddhist studies to investigate this issue. The fact that the area of Central Asia near Bisṭâmî's homeland of Khurasan had been Buddhist for centuries before Islam, and only became Muslim rather slowly, suggests that it was no accident that he was influenced by "Indian" ideas. See also endnote 77.

[49] Maḥmûd shortchanged Firdausî and earned the poet's revenge, a blistering satirical poem.

politician and sometimes ruthless strategist. His most famous work is a 'mirror for princes', the *Siyâsat-nâmeh*, which attempts to teach the ruler how to be a more effective despot. He was also a great patron of learning and built and endowed many large standardized *madrasas*, known as Niẓâmi-yya, which spread the *madrasa* system of higher education across most of the Near East. Though his motives were in part political, these *madrasas* were influential in the cultural flourishing of the following two centuries there, and from those centers to the rest of the Islamic world. The scholastic method of dialectical disputation developed in Central Asia and spread across the Islamic world. It was brought to Spain by Abû ʿAbd Allâh al-Azdî of Cordoba (d. 969),[50] where it flourished and eventually produced the great philosopher Averroës (Ibn Rushd, d. 1198).

Although Central Asian Islamic cities together constituted the brilliant commercial and intellectual center of Eurasia in this period, an anti-intellectual reaction developed among religious conservatives. It was given strong support by the Central Asian philosopher and theologian al-Ghazâlî, who taught for awhile at the Baghdad Niẓâmiyya. He ultimately rejected philosophy per se in favor of a conservative form of Sufism and built a Sufi monastery (a *khânqâh*) for himself and his disciples in Nishapur, where he taught for some years at the end of his life. He and the other conservatives used the ideas and methods of the great Greek and Islamic thinkers against them with the express goal of suppressing freedom of thought outside of dogma. He devoted his most famous work, *Tahâfut al-falâsifa* 'The Incoherence of the Philosophers', completed in 1095,[51] to the suppression of philosophy, arguing at one point that those who stubbornly supported some of the philosophers' positions should be killed. Al-Ghazâlî's arguments were subsequently refuted by Averroës (Ibn Rushd) not long after in his book *Tahâfut al-tahâfut* 'The Incoherence of the Incoherence', but he wrote in Spain and it was already too late. Though Averroës had a powerful impact on European thought, he had none at all in the Islamic world, where his works were largely unknown until modern times,[52] and he saw the destruction of Islamic intellectual life by rabid religious conservatives in his own

---

[50] Makdisi (1981: 131).

[51] The title is also translated as 'The Destruction of the Philosophers' or 'The Collapse of the Philosophers'. See the extensive discussion in Fakhry (1983: especially 222 et seq.).

[52] Bergh (1954).

lifetime. The conservatives' suppression of scholastic dialectical disputation, in which ideas, including received texts, were open to logical analysis and debate, was central to their goal, the suppression of independent thought. Al-Ghazâlî and the conservatives won. Thinkers who questioned what became increasingly rigid doctrines were persecuted or went into hiding, and the possibility of thinking freely not only about philosophy but almost anything else, including science, gradually disappeared altogether in most of the Islamic world.[53]

Medieval Western European culture grew intellectually as a direct result of contact with Muslim Spain and Palestine. The translation into Latin of Arabic books introduced new, exciting, and often controversial ideas. The work of al-Khwârizmî[54] (Algorithmus) translated as the *Book of Algorithmus* introduced Arabic numerals, including the zero and "algorithmic" calculation along with them, while the *Algebra* introduced advanced algebraic mathematics. They were revolutionary to the scientifically oriented minds of Western Europe. The translation of previously unknown philosophical and logical works of Aristotle, along with the works of the great Islamic Aristotelian philosophers, also caused fundamental restructuring of Western European thought. The ideas accompanied at least one important institution. The first European *college*,[55] the Collège des Dix-huit or 'College of the Eighteen Scholars', was established in Paris in 1180 by Jocius of London (Jocius de Londiniis) after his return from the Holy Land.[56] It was the oldest of the colleges that formed the original University of Paris. The college retained most of the essential characteristics of its direct ancestors,

---

[53] Cf. Makdisi (1981: 136–139), who however ascribes the suppression to disputations becoming unruly and participants injured. The intellectual decline of the Islamic world was thus already underway even before the coming of the Mongols, not to speak of the Europeans. On recent antihistorical claims related to this issue, see endnote 81.

[54] See chapter 6.

[55] The *college*, an endowed pious foundation that paid the expenses of the resident students and master or masters, must be distinguished from the *university*, a self-governing corporation. The latter was a local European development.

[56] Makdisi (1981: 226, 228), who notes, "Though madrasas were not known to have existed in Jerusalem proper, by 1180 they were numerous in the neighboring areas." The original charter (*CUP* I: 49) specifically refers to Jocius of London as having returned from Jerusalem, but of course it was necessary for him to travel through the "neighboring areas" in order to reach that landlocked city. *Madrasas* were ubiquitous in the Islamic Near East, and it would have been difficult for Jocius to have traveled in the Holy Land without encountering at least one *madrasa* and learning what it was, perhaps by actually staying in it overnight.

the *madrasa* and *vihâra*, including the pious foundation that supported the student residents and a professor,[57] and perhaps the architectural form as well.[58] The transmission of Islamic knowledge, techniques, and institutions to the West thus fueled the intellectual revolution of the High Middle Ages.

Many small kingdoms formed in Tibet after the century it took to recover from the collapse of the Tibetan Empire. The kingdoms were mostly centered not on cities but on fortresses and on the great new fortified monasteries, in which medieval Tibetan Buddhist civilization developed. The doctrinal differences among the many new orders encouraged active debate, both oral and written, on points of Buddhist canon law, doctrine, and other topics. The habit of writing having become firmly ingrained, a relatively small number of Tibetans quickly produced a vast literature, mainly on metaphysical, mystical, and ritual topics, but also on history, medicine, and other subjects. The political history of this period is still little known. The states seem to have been closely connected to the monastic powers, but their relationship to them is uncertain.[59]

The Tanguts of the Hsi-hsia Dynasty developed a close relationship with Tibetan Buddhists, some of whom resided at the Tangut court. Despite the Tanguts' presumed familiarity with Tibetan (a related language) and the simple, clear Tibetan alphabet, they developed a complicated native writing system based on the Chinese character model. They translated Chinese classics and composed new works on many topics. Because they translated the well-known Chinese Buddhist canon into Tangut, it has been possible to read many of the surviving Tangut texts.[60] The Khitan too developed a writing system on the Chinese model, though it was little used. Finally, although Chinese was by far the most important written language in the Chin Empire, the Jurchen followed the Tangut and Khitan pattern and developed their

---

[57] The teacher is not mentioned in the laconic charter of the Collège des Dix-huit, but colleges in Paris are known to have consisted of "a body of students governed by a master" by the beginning of the following century (Rashdall, quoted in Makdisi 1981: 236), only a few years later, suggesting the exemplary first college was structured in this way too.

[58] This possibility is based on my own casual observation of the design of some of the old cloisters at Oxford. There may be many more with similar designs. The problem needs to be studied carefully and the idea either confirmed or refuted.

[59] Perhaps the most insightful study is still Wylie's (1964).

[60] On the Tangut writing system and its interpretation, see endnote 82.

own Chinese-style script to write their language,[61] which is the direct ancestor of Manchu.

Although much of China was united under the Sung Dynasty, the northern territories that overlapped with or extended into the Eastern Steppe or
Central Asia remained independent and under non-Chinese dynasties. The
fact that none of these states could dominate the other forced the Chinese to
develop means for dealing with international relations on a more or less
equal basis. The old xenophobia and superiority complex that had long
caused trouble for the Chinese people continued to dominate among politicians regardless of the kingdom they ruled, but the existence of several Chinese states lessened the degree of terror wielded by the rulers compared to
that wielded by rulers of dynasties that succeeded in unifying China.

The Sung Dynasty was not in direct contact with Central Asia or the
Steppe Zone, and thus not in contact with most of the rest of Eurasia. Perhaps as a result of this relative isolation, writers and other intellectuals
among the elite turned increasingly inward. Painters produced the greatest masterpieces of Chinese art. The most famous examples lack heroic,
imperial themes and instead emphasize nature and withdrawal from the
world.

It was at this time that Chinese perfected xylographic printing, and developed movable type as well.[62] Books and paper money began to be printed
in earnest. At the other end of the spectrum, the Chinese also invented
bombs, rockets, and precursors of guns during the Five Dynasties and
Sung period.[63]

Finally, perhaps partly due to the Sung political distance from Central
Eurasia, Chinese maritime commerce flourished in the opposite direction,
though this was not an officially supported movement. In fact, southern
regions and their peoples continued to be looked down on culturally, and

---

[61] Unlike the Tangut and Khitan scripts, the Jurchen script is much more systematic phonetically, and also unlike the other two languages Jurchen has a close relative that is attested in
early modern and modern times and very well recorded, Manchu. Accordingly, it has been
possible to reconstruct the language to a high degree of precision, q.v. Kiyose (1977).

[62] Gernet (1996: 335). Also known as wood block printing, xylography proved to be cheaper and
more efficient for printing Chinese, with its thousands of characters, so movable type did not
supplant it there until modern times.

[63] Gernet (1996: 311). Gunpowder itself was developed by alchemists in China during the T'ang
period.

most of the movement took place outside political China. It was thus not the Chinese elite but independent-minded merchants who spread Chinese culture in that direction when they established trading colonies in the littoral region from the South China Coast into Southeast Asia and the South Seas.

8

Chinggis Khan and the Mongol Conquests

In Xanadu did Kubla Khan
A stately pleasure dome decree:
Where Alph, the sacred river, ran
Through caverns measureless to man
Down to a sunless sea.
   —S. T. Coleridge, *Kubla Khan*

The Pax Mongolica

After the death of Khabul Khan, who had been recognized by the Jurchen as paramount ruler in the Eastern Steppe, the nascent Mongol realm broke up. Civil war raged until Temüjin, great-grandson of Khabul Khan, forged the Mongols into a new nation. As Chinggis Khan, he led the Mongols in a series of lightning campaigns that unified most of Central Eurasia and some of the periphery as well. His sons continued the conquests, until at its height the empire stretched from Eastern Europe to the East China Sea and from Siberia to the Persian Gulf. The Mongols reunified and reexpanded Central Eurasia by conquest of all of Central Eurasia and parts of the littoral, including the steppe zone, Russia, Persia, Central Asia, Tibet, and China. The Mongol Empire was the world's first land superpower.

Though the successors of Chinggis Khan soon began fighting among themselves, they succeeded in bringing much of Eurasia into one commercial zone that produced staggering amounts of wealth for the Mongols and others who participated in the commerce. But the spread of the Black Death across the continent in the fourteenth century devastated many areas, especially Western Europe, and conflicts among the Mongol successor states weakened them, bringing an end to the Pax Mongolica.

The weakness of the Mongols' Central Asian successor states was exploited in the late fourteenth century by a brilliant general of Mongol origin, Tamerlane, who conquered an empire from the Near East to India and from Russia to the Persian Gulf. Though the empire quickly fissioned into its constituent parts upon his death, its core, Western Central Asia, experienced a last blaze of cultural glory under Tamerlane and his successors, the Timurids.

The Mongol Conquests

The beginnings of the Mongol Empire are to be found in the intertribal politics and warfare on the Eastern Steppe following the overthrow of the Khitan by the Jurchen. The Tungusic-speaking Jurchen were not a steppe people like the Khitan and did not maintain a military presence in the steppe. Instead, they supported the strongest single people there, the Tatars. The peoples of the Eastern Steppe were divided, and none of them could establish dominance over the others in the face of the powerful Tatars. When Khabul Khan, head of the Borjigin lineage, managed to put together a Mongol confederation, and the Jurchen were unable to dislodge him by force, they recognized his position as paramount ruler of the Mongols (in 1146/1147), though they also officially considered him their vassal. After his death, his successor, his cousin Ambaghai, was captured by the Tatars and sent to the Chin court, where the Jurchen killed him. The Mongols then selected Khabul Khan's third son Khutula to succeed as Khan, giving rise to enmity against him and his descendants by the descendants of Ambaghai. Khutula attacked the Tatars, largely unsuccessfully, and his end is unknown. After him the early movement toward a unified Mongol realm disintegrated into internecine warfare, which dominated the Eastern Steppe when Khabul Khan's grandson Yesügei (d. 1175/1176), who had begun to reconstitute a Borjigin confederation, was murdered by the Tatars and his people and flocks were taken away by a pretender to the succession, leaving Yesügei's wife and children alone in the steppe.

The rise of the Mongols in the Eastern Steppe coincided with the decline of their Mongolic neighbors, the Kara Khitai, in the west. The last Gür Khan, Mânî (r. 1177/1178–1211),[1] was weak and unable to stop the growth of the Khwarizmian Empire, especially under its most aggressive ruler, Muḥammad Khwârizmshâh (r. 1200–1220), who though the vassal of the Kara Khitai captured Transoxiana from them in 1210–1212. With the loss of much of their wealth and power, other vassals fell away.

In the Eastern Steppe, Yesügei's eldest son Temüjin (ca. 1167–1227) and his brothers stayed in the wilderness with their mother, living off the land.[2]

---

[1] Biran (2005: 58).

[2] See the prologue for this and other "historical" accounts of Central Eurasian nation founders. However, the murder of Temüjin's father and other ancestors by the Tatars or their

Temüjin grew up wily, courageous, and strong. Slowly the scattered remnants of his clan reassembled under his banner. Eventually other clans joined him, and he acquired powerful allies. In 1196 he and the chief of the Kereit made an alliance with the Jurchen, who had earlier broken with the Tatars. Together they attacked and defeated the Tatars. As a reward, the Chin gave the Kereit chief the title Ong Khan,[3] while Temüjin received a lesser title. In 1202 Temüjin led his forces against the Tatars once again and this time crushed them, executing all adult males in revenge for their murder of his father and other ancestors.[4]

Temüjin defeated his last major rival, his intermittent friend and ally Jamukha, who in 1201 had been proclaimed *Gür Khan* 'Universal Ruler'. Having unified the peoples of the Eastern Steppe, Temüjin was given the title Chinggis Khan (Genghis Khan) 'Universal Ruler' in 1206 at a great meeting of the Mongol tribal leaders.[5] With the power and mandate bestowed upon him by Heaven, as he and his sons believed, he set out to subjugate the unsubmitted peoples of the four directions.

Rather than immediately attacking the Jurchen's large and powerful Chin Dynasty, most of which was in alien Chinese territory, in 1209 Chinggis led an army against the Tangut, who were the neighbors of the Chin on the south and southwest. Their Hsi-hsia Dynasty controlled not only the north-south trade routes from the western part of the Eastern Steppe to Central Asia and China but also the major east-west trade routes between China and Central Asia. Although the Mongol siege of the Tangut capital was unsuccessful, in 1210 the Hsi-hsia ruler agreed to acknowledge Chinggis as his lord and to supply troops for future Mongol military actions. The

---

patrons the Jurchen—to whom the Tatars delivered their enemies to be killed, cruelly (Atwood 2004: 529)—appears to be historical.

[3] *Ong* is the Mongol pronunciation of Chinese *Wang* 'prince'. Ong Khan had taken refuge in the Kara Khitai Empire in the early 1190s, but the latter realm was already unable to help him. He then returned to Mongolia and allied himself with Temüjin. According to the *Secret History*, Ong Khan also had, or took, the title Gür Khan (Biran 2005: 64–65).

[4] Although, like other empire builders everywhere (not only in the steppe), he destroyed his most implacable enemies, normally he accepted defeated peoples' submission to him as subjects within his realm and incorporated their warriors into his army.

[5] Allsen (1994: 331–343). The timing and title are certainly not accidents. The proclamation took place after the defeat of the Tatars had been completed, and specifically upon the capture and execution of Temüjin's chief rival Jamuqa. The latter's title *Gür Khan* (or *Gür Qa*) 'universal ruler', is defined by Juwayni and Juzjani as *khân-i khânân* 'khan of khans' (Bosworth 2007); it was the same title as that held by the Kara Khitai ruler. On Temüjin's new title Chinggis Khan, see endnote 83.

treaty was sealed with the marriage of a Tangut princess to Chinggis, and the Mongols withdrew.

The Kara Khitai Empire had been the main power to the west of the Tanguts during Chinggis's rise to power. While it had been severely weakened by the attacks of the Khwârizmshâh, nevertheless, it remained a force in its central domains east of Transoxiana. Küčlüg (Güčülük), a leader of the Naiman nation,[6] who had opposed Temüjin's rise to power down to the end, fled west to the Kara Khitai realm, where he was admitted in 1208. Having become an adviser to the ruler, Mânî, he used his position to carry out a coup and take control himself in 1211.[7]

In that year Chinggis received the voluntary submission of the Uighurs in the northern Tarim region,[8] and of the Karluks as well. Both had been vassals of the Kara Khitai,[9] and both sought the protection of the Mongols in the face of the internal turbulence and external attacks destroying their former overlords. The Mongols thus gained unhindered access to Eastern Central Asia, and indirect control over part of it.

In the same year, Chinggis finally attacked the Jurchen. But he encountered an unexpected problem. Though the Mongols easily defeated Chin armies in the field, they had little success against Chinese cities, which were fortified with enormous walls. Yet the Mongols soon found they had valuable allies within the Chin state—the Khitan who had settled in the region under the Liao Dynasty and still lived there under Jurchen rule.[10] With the help of the Khitan and the Chinese they had taken into their army, as well as the Uighurs, the Mongols learned how to use siege machinery to capture cities. When Chinggis discovered that the Jurchen had moved their administrative capital to K'ai-feng, he attacked the Central Capital (Peking), which he had already approached in his earlier attacks into Chin. On May 31, 1215, the city surrendered to the Mongols.[11]

---

[6] They were probably Turks ethnically, not Mongols, despite their Mongol name *Naiman* 'the Eight (clans or lineages)'; see Atwood (2004: 397).

[7] Biran (2005: 75–78).

[8] Their ruling house was forced to retreat eastward into Yüan territory in Kansu in ca. 1283 due to pressure from the Chaghatai Khanate (Allsen 1997: 41).

[9] Allsen (1994: 350).

[10] The Khitan also understood the Chinese administrative system and helped the Mongols to govern the conquered territories of North China, as well as the rapidly growing Mongol Empire as a whole. One of the most important councillors of Chinggis Khan and his son Ögedei was Yeh-lü Ch'u-tsai (1189–1243), a descendant of the Khitan imperial family (Biran 2005: 6).

[11] Franke (1994: 254).

In the twelfth and early thirteenth centuries, the rulers of Khwârizm had expanded their realm to an empire by means of campaigns across Central Asia and Iran into Iraq. The Khwârizmians stationed garrisons across this large territory to hold their new conquests. By 1215 the realm of the ruling Khwârizmshâh, 'Alâ' al-Dîn Muḥammad (r. 1200–1220),[12] included Iran and nearly all of Western and Southern Central Asia with the exception of the remnants of the former Kara Khitai Empire he had not been able to take from his overlords. In the process of expansion, he had moved his capital from Khwârizm to the more centrally located city of Samarkand. His army was large, strong, and battle-hardened. He had already become the most powerful single ruler in the Islamic world at the time, and his realm was still expanding. His eye was mainly fixed upon the politically revitalized caliphate based in Baghdad, the ruler of which was the direct successor of the early Abbasids and the bestower of legitimacy on Islamic rulers. At the same time, though, he was hungry for the weakening realm of the Kara Khitai. In 1215, having learned of the newly unified Eastern Steppe, he sent an embassy to the Mongols.

In 1216 Chinggis sent his general Jebe to the west after Küčlüg. Jebe defeated the Kara Khitai forces sent against him and took several cities. Because Küčlüg was a Buddhist convert and persecuted Muslims, the local people, most of whom were Muslim, hated him. When Jebe announced a reversal of Küčlüg's religious policy, the overjoyed Muslims went over to him, and Küčlüg fled for his life.[13] Jebe's forces chased Küčlüg into Badakhshan (northeastern Afghanistan), where he was killed in 1218.[14] The Mongols thus secured a strategic outpost in Western Central Asia.

In that year, Chinggis sent an embassy to the Khwarizmians to propose a peace treaty. It was agreed upon within a few days of their arrival. Not long afterward, a large Mongol trade mission consisting of some 450 Muslim merchants arrived in Utrâr. It was stopped by the Khwârizmshâh's governor, who accused the merchants of being Mongol spies, confiscated their property, and executed them. However, one of the men escaped back to the

---

[12] He reigned until December 1220 or January 1221 (Boyle 1968: 310).

[13] Boyle (1968:305). The name Küčlüg (or Güčülüg) is Turkic, *küčlüg* 'strong', a name or epithet "borne by members of the Naiman royal family" (de Rachewiltz 2004: 699). See the preceding note. The story of Jebe's success over Küčlüg sounds a little too simplistic to take at face value.

[14] Biran (2005: 74 et seq.). Most of the Kara Khitai, after fighting in vain to hold on to their former territory in Transoxiana, joined the Mongols (Biran 2005: 87).

Mongols. Chinggis sent an embassy to the Khwârizmshâh to demand wergild for the murdered men and punishment of the governor responsible for the outrage. Instead of responding as requested, or sending another embassy to negotiate the matter, the Khwârizmshâh insulted the Mongols and killed the envoys.

Chinggis then put aside his war with the Jurchen to deal with the Khwârizmshâh. In 1219 the Mongols invaded the Khwarizmian Empire with three huge armies. The Khwârizmshâh had posted his forces in garrisons around his newly conquered territory. Rather than gathering them to face the Mongols together, he kept them at their posts. The Mongols easily captured the garrisoned cities one by one and thus defeated the huge, seasoned Khwarizmian army, taking control of most of Western and Southern Central Asia by 1223. Though the Mongols pursued the Khwârizmshâh across his realm without catching him,[15] they subdued his empire, leaving on the throne those local rulers who submitted to them and stationing Mongol tax collectors there. When some cities subsequently rebelled and killed the Mongol representatives, the Mongols retook the cities and, following traditional Asian warfare practice, executed most of the inhabitants.[16]

Chinggis retired to Mongolia in 1223. He now turned his attention to the Tanguts, who had failed to send their warriors to join the campaign against the Khwarizmians in 1218, as they had promised to do as vassals of the Mongols. The Tanguts had also withdrawn their troops from the campaign against Chin in 1222,[17] and when Chinggis sent envoys to them warning them to mend their ways and keep to the terms of the treaty, they reviled him. Although Chinggis died before the completion of this campaign, the Tangut realm was conquered in 1227. It was fully incorporated into the Mongol Empire and became one of its most important appanages or fiefdoms. One reason it was important is the fact that the Tangut Empire had developed a culture that was as refined as China's and in some ways similar to it, but nevertheless distinctively non-Chinese (and also non-Jurchen Chin). Although the Mongols had of necessity to rely upon the Chinese for help in ruling Chinese territory under their control, they generally distrusted and disliked the Chinese and were much more inclined toward fel-

---

[15] He was killed by Kurdish bandits in 1231 (Allsen 1994: 357, 370).

[16] See the epilogue on the normal fate of rebellious cities from Antiquity through the Middle Ages in most of Eurasia.

[17] Allsen (1994: 359).

low Central Eurasians, especially in matters connected with religion and state organization.

Chinggis had four sons, three of whom survived him. His son Ögedei (r. 1229–1241) succeeded him as Great Khan. The Mongols continued their attacks on the Jurchen and in 1234 overthrew the Chin Dynasty. At the same time, Ögedei organized a great campaign into the west. Earlier, while campaigning against the Khwârizmshâh, the Mongols had passed through southern Russia. They now set out to completely subdue it as the inheritance of Batu, son of Chinggis's eldest son Jochi, who had died before his father in 1227.[18] Along with Batu as the nominal commander went Ögedei's son Güyük, Tolui's son Möngke, and Sübedei, the Mongols' most brilliant general. In 1236 the Mongols attacked the Finno-Ugric and Turkic peoples of the Volga-Kama region, then the Russians to their northwest, taking Vladimir (east of Moscow) in 1238 and Kiev in 1240, subjugating the region by 1241. Sübedei continued the campaign further west into Poland and eastern Germany, where he defeated the Polish and German forces of Duke Henry of Silesia at Liegnitz and, turning south, the Hungarians and Austrians, before returning to Hungary to spend the winter.[19] But Great Khan Ögedei died in December of that year, and the Mongols withdrew as soon as they learned about it.

Batu remained in the West with a large force. He made his capital at Saray on the lower Volga River and controlled all of western Central Eurasia from the Black Sea and northern Caucasus up to Muscovy and east through the Volga-Kama region. Many of his forces settled at Kazan, not far from the old city of Bulghâr, where they soon shifted to the language of the majority ethnic group in the army, Kipchak Turkic, which came to be known as Tatar. The realm of what was later to be called the Golden Horde soon became de facto independent, but Batu remained committed to his grandfather's vision of a Mongol world empire and participated fully in the governance of the empire and in imperial military campaigns.[20]

After the short reign of Ögedei's son Güyük (r. 1246–1248), a power struggle ended with the succession of Tolui's son Möngke (r. 1251–1259),

---

[18] Jochi was not actually fathered by Temüjin. This seems to have been the main reason for the enmity between him and his (half) brothers.

[19] King Béla IV (r. 1235–1270) fled the country, but returned after the Mongols left and continued ruling until his death.

[20] Allsen (1994).

who became the next Great Khan.[21] He organized a massive campaign to establish firm Mongol control over the lands of Central Asia and the Near East and generally to push the limits of the Mongol Empire toward the sunset. Möngke's brother Hülegü, commanding the imperial forces, set out in 1253. In 1256 they attacked and destroyed the Assassins, the Ismâ'îlî order that had long terrorized the Islamic world from their base in the Elburz Mountains of northern Iran. By 1257 the Mongols had taken Alamut, the Assassins' main fortress, and their leader, who was executed by order of Möngke himself. The Mongols then proceeded into Iraq and in 1258 attacked Baghdad. The caliph refused to surrender, despite the reasonable Mongol offer and explanation of what would happen if he resisted. The city was put under siege and eventually succumbed. An estimated 200,000 people were killed in the sack of the city, and the caliph too was put to death.[22]

The Mongols proceeded westward into Mamluk Syria and were making good progress until news reached them about Möngke's death and Hülegü withdrew with most of the imperial forces. The Mamluks attacked the remaining Mongols and crushed them in the Battle of 'Ayn Jalût, in Galilee, on September 6, 1260.[23] This was the first setback for the Mongols in Southwestern Asia.

Nevertheless, Hülegü soon returned, and the Mongols succeeded in establishing their power over most of the Near East. They eventually made their home encampment in northwestern Iran near Tabriz, where there were good pasturelands. Hülegü founded the Il-Khanate, which ruled over Iraq, Iran, and some of the neighboring territories; warred periodically with the northerly Golden Horde and with the Central Asian Chaghatai Horde, the successors of Chinggis's son Chaghatai; and extended his influence as far as Tibet.

---

[21] Like much of the account of the Mongols given here, this depends largely on Allsen (1994); cf. his excellent account (1987) of the reign of Möngke.

[22] Allsen (1994: 404). There are several accounts of the caliph's death, all interesting. The most appealing one is that told by Marco Polo, to the effect that the Mongols locked the caliph up in his treasury and told him he could eat his treasure. However, the most likely one is that they followed traditional Mongol practice—they wrapped him inside a carpet and suffocated him to avoid violating the Mongol taboo about shedding a ruler's blood on the earth.

[23] Rossabi (1988: 54–55).

Khubilai Khan, Tibet, and the Yüan Dynasty

Tolui's inheritance included the former Tangut realm. Under Ögedei, his second son Köden (Godan, d. 1253/1260), who was assigned Tangut as his appanage, was responsible for the nearly bloodless subjugation of Tibet. In 1240 Köden sent a small force into Tibet under Dorda Darkhan. The Tibetan monasteries evidently resisted it; two were attacked and damaged, and some monks are said to have been killed.[24] The Mongols eventually withdrew, having been told to contact the leading cleric in Tibet, Saskya Paṇḍita (d. 1251). Köden sent a letter to him in 1244 summoning him to the Mongol camp. In 1246 the elderly monk arrived in Liang-chou, having sent ahead his two nephews, 'Phagspa (Blogros Rgyal-mtshan, 1235–1280)[25] and Phyag-na-rdorje (d. 1267). In 1247 the Tibetans surrendered to the Mongols. Saskya Paṇḍita was appointed viceroy of Tibet under the Mongols and Phyag-na-rdorje was married to Köden's daughter to seal the treaty. After the death of Saskya Paṇḍita in 1251, the Mongols sent another expedition, under a certain Khoridai, who restored their control in Central Tibet in 1252–1253.[26] Köden, who because of his chronic illness—for which he had been treated by Saskya Paṇḍita—had been passed over for the throne in favor of his elder brother Güyük, seems to have been dead by this time.[27]

Khubilai (b. September 23, 1215, r. 1260/1272–February 18, 1284) was one of the sons of Tolui. He married Chabi, a fervent Buddhist. When their first son was born in 1240, they gave him the Tibetan Buddhist name Dorji (Tibetan *rdorje* 'vajra; thunderbolt'). Already by 1242 Khubilai had begun assembling Chinese and Tibetan Buddhist teachers at his appanage in Hsing-chou, in Hopei.[28] With the accession of his brother Möngke as Great Khan in 1251, Khubilai was in direct line to succeed to the throne. His brother appointed him to several other appanages in North China, greatly strengthening Khubilai's power and making him effectively the Mongol

---

[24] Atwood (2004: 320). Cf. Petech (1983: 181), who adds "five hundred men were butchered" at the Bkágdamspa monastery of Rgyal Lhakhang. However, this classic number of 500 individuals occurs time and again in Tibetan Buddhist accounts, many of which are pious fabrications. It is certainly not a historical number. Accordingly, the entire story is doubtful.

[25] The Tibetan epithet by which he is generally known is *'Phagspa blama* 'Exalted lama'.

[26] Atwood (2004: 539).

[27] Atwood (2004: 321, 539).

[28] Rossabi (1988: 14–17).

viceroy over this rich, populous region. In 1253 Khubilai called for 'Phagspa and his brother to be sent to him. They arrived and were well received by the Mongol prince. He left shortly afterward in command of an imperial campaign to conquer the Kingdom of Ta-li (in what is now Yunnan Province) as a preliminary flanking movement before invading the large and aggressive Sung Dynasty, which had been repeatedly attacking Mongol territory to its north.

After a year's preparation, Khubilai's forces, with Sübedei's son Uriyang-khadai as general in chief, set out late in 1253. Before attacking the Ta-li forces, he sent envoys to them with an ultimatum demanding their surrender and assuring their safety if they did. When they responded by executing the envoys, the Mongols attacked and defeated them, forcing them to retreat to their capital. The Mongols notified the people of the city that they would be spared if they surrendered. They did so, and Khubilai then took the city, establishing Mongol power over Ta-li with a minimum of bloodshed. General Uriyangkhadai continued the Mongol campaign in the southwest with considerable success, eventually marching southeast to Annam (the area of modern northern Vietnam) by 1257, where however the Mongols suffered from the heat and insects. When the ruler offered to send tribute to the Mongols, Uriyangkhadai withdrew.

In 1256 Khubilai, who had returned to his appanage after the victory in Ta-li, began work on a summer capital, K'ai-p'ing (renamed Shang-tu 'Xanadu' in 1263). It was about ten days' journey north of Chung-tu (Peking) in an area with both agricultural and pasture lands.[29] In 1258, after Khubilai answered accusations made against him by conspirators at court, his brother put him in command of one of the four wings of the army in his new campaign against the Sung. In 1258 the invasion was launched, with Möngke himself leading the campaign in Szechuan, while Khubilai attacked southward from his appanage in the east.

When Möngke died of fever outside Chungking (Chongqing) in Szechuan (August 11, 1259),[30] the campaign against the Sung came to a halt. Arik Böke, his youngest brother, who had been left in Karakorum to guard the homelands, began assembling his forces to contest the succession. Hülegü halted his campaign in Syria and hurried home to support Khubilai at the

---

[29] Its location is thirty-six miles west of Dolon Nor in what is now Inner Mongolia (Rossabi 1994: 418–419).
[30] Atwood (2004: 364).

great *khuriltai*, but Arik Böke too had substantial support and sent forces to attack Khubilai's appanage. When Khubilai finally reached his capital at K'ai-p'ing, a *khuriltai* was assembled in May 1260, and Khubilai was elected Great Khan. The decision was vehemently opposed by Arik Böke, who had powerful adherents—including Berke, the successor of Batu, and Alghu, ruler of the Chaghatai Khanate in Central Asia. They proclaimed him Great Khan in June 1260, and civil war broke out. Khubilai outmaneuvered Arik Böke at every turn, despite the latter's many supporters. Alghu broke with him in 1262, and in the following year Arik Böke surrendered to Khubilai.[31] The civil war was over. In 1266 Khubilai began building a new winter capital, Ta-tu 'great capital', slightly northeast of the old city of Chung-tu (the site of modern Peking),[32] moving the power base of the Great Khanate further into China and solidifying his control there.

After spending the next few years settling affairs within the Great Khanate, Khubilai returned to the Sung problem. First he sent an embassy to the Sung (May 1260) to propose a peaceful solution. But the chancellor of Sung detained the envoys and sent his forces to attack the Mongols (August 1260). After Khubilai retaliated in early 1261, the Sung invaded three times in 1262. The Chinese also refused to release Khubilai's envoys. Finally, the Mongols attacked the Sung in force, defeating them soundly in Szechuan early in 1265 and following with a full-scale invasion in 1268. The war with the Sung was not an easy matter. Mongol victory came only in 1276, when the Sung empress dowager surrendered and handed over the imperial seal and regalia. In 1279 the last resistance ended.

The new Chinese-style Yüan Dynasty officially began on Chinese New Year's Day, January 18, 1272.[33] Despite the orthodox procedures followed in the establishment of the dynasty, and in much of the structure of the administration, the new government was very clearly Mongol. Unlike their Jurchen predecessors in North China, the Mongols generally did not trust the Chinese. Khubilai himself did have many important Chinese advisers, but his successors put Mongols, Central Asian Muslims, Tibetans, Tanguts,

---

[31] Arik Böke died in captivity a few years later (Rossabi 1994: 424).

[32] In Turkic the city was called *Khanbalik* 'royal capital'. It is the same as Marco Polo's *Cambaluc*. Khubilai kept his summer capital north of the Great Wall of China at Shang-tu ('Upper Capital'), the *Xanadu* of Coleridge's famous poem.

[33] Mote (1994: 616), Langlois (1981: 3–4), q.v. for a full translation of the imperial edict proclaiming the establishment of the dynasty.

or other non-Chinese in all key administrative positions. The Great Khanate continued to exist, and included Mongolia and Tibet as major constituent parts that were recognized as not being Chinese. While in many respects Yüan China was integrated into the Mongol Empire, the Great Khanate continued to be the larger unit. The two were not equated with each other.

One of the most important events of Mongol history took place at this time. The early Mongols had already come under the influence of various world religions, and some of the nation's constituent peoples had converted, at least theoretically, to one of them—for example, the Naiman and Kereit had converted, at least nominally, to Nestorian Christianity, and the Mongols of Khubilai's generation were already becoming Buddhists under Uighur and, especially, Tibetan tutelage. But, on the whole, the Mongols had remained pagan and for long were suspicious of all organized religions. The early European travelers' accounts note how much the Mongols relied on their soothsayers in all things. But by the time of Marco Polo, the Mongols of the Great Khanate had unofficially, but enthusiastically, adopted Buddhism, mostly of the Tibetan variety.[34] With its idea of the *dharmarâja* or 'religious king', the religion provided legitimation for Khubilai's rule and also gave the Mongols access to a great body of learning and wisdom that was not Chinese.

When Khubilai decided he wanted to have a unified "Mongol" script for all the languages of the Mongol Empire, he appointed to the commission the Tibetan Buddhist leader 'Phagspa, who was his National Preceptor and the viceroy of Tibet.[35] The new script, based on the Tibetan alphabet (but written vertically like Chinese script and Uighur-Mongol script), was promulgated as the official writing system in 1269. Known today as 'Phagspa Script, it is in effect the world's first multilingual transcription system. Examples of it are preserved in several languages from around the Mongol Empire, including Chinese,[36] and it is thought that the script influenced the later creation of the Korean *Han'gul* writing system. 'Phagspa was also in charge of other intellectual projects, including the compilation of a great comparative

[34] See Beckwith (1987b).
[35] He was later appointed imperial preceptor—head of all the Buddhists in the entire empire. He learned the Mongol language and Mongol habits and had picked up some Tangut ideas at Köden's court, becoming much less "Tibetan" than his countrymen liked.
[36] See Coblin's (2006) dictionary of Chinese in 'Phagspa script.

catalogue of the Chinese and Tibetan Buddhist canons, the respective compendia of translations of sacred texts from Sanskrit.

The Black Death

In 1331 an epidemic broke out in part of North China, killing nine-tenths of the population.[37] This appears to mark the initial outbreak of the Black Death, the worst pandemic in recorded history. In Persia Abû Sa'îd, the last Il-Khan, contracted the plague and apparently died of it in 1335.[38] In 1338–1339 a Nestorian merchant community near the Issyk Kul in Central Asia was devastated by bubonic plague.[39] In 1346 plague struck a Mongol army besieging the Crimean port city of Caffa on the Black Sea. The epidemic spread to the city, and ships spread it from there like wildfire throughout the Mediterranean and into Europe. At least a third of Europe's population died from the previously unknown disease, which came to be known as the bubonic plague.[40]

The disease is now popularly believed to have been due to the Mongol conquests, the argument being that it was inadvertently carried west and south by them from the plains of central Manchuria and the Gobi Desert, where it is thought to have first arisen. However, the great discrepancy in time—nearly a century—between the end of the conquest period and the appearance of the plague in China makes it clear that the Mongol conquest itself could not have had anything to do with its spread.[41] It is possible, though, that the increase in direct communication between East, West, and South Asia via Central Eurasia under the Pax Mongolica provided a ready pathway for the rats and fleas who carried the disease to be transported to all parts of Eurasia, and beyond, from its home. In any case, the Black Death was disastrous for the Mongol successor states as much as for the other states of the time.

---

[37] Atwood (2004: 41, 610) has Honan; according to him, it spread to the coastal provinces (1345–1346). "Finally, in 1351 massive epidemics began to strike throughout China yearly up to 1362, causing catastrophic population decline" (Atwood 2004: 41). Cf. McNeill (1977: 143, 263).

[38] Boyle (1968: 412).

[39] Based on an actual modern archaeological and epidemiological examination (McNeill 1977: 145–146).

[40] McNeill (1977: 147 et seq.).

[41] McNeill (1977).

The Mongol Political Heritage

The fourteenth century was afflicted with plague, famine, floods, and other disasters without precedent in world history. Much of the world suffered so greatly it is not surprising that rebellions and dynastic collapses were endemic. Despite their efforts to cope with the natural disasters, the Mongol dynasties of the Il-khanate in Iran and the Yüan in China both collapsed, probably much earlier than they would have in better times.

In China, a rebellion broke out against the Mongols, who were denounced as evil alien rulers. In 1368 the Yüan capital at Ta-tu was captured by the forces of Chu Yüan-chang, founder of the Ming Dynasty (1368–1644). Toghon Temür (r. 1333–1368 in China and Mongolia), the last Great Khan who was also emperor of the Yüan Dynasty, escaped on horseback with much of his court to Mongolia, where he continued to rule over the shrunken Great Khanate in the Eastern Steppe until his death in 1370.[42]

In the Central and Western steppes, the Golden Horde maintained itself very well for another two centuries. By contrast, with the death of the last great Il-Khan, Abû Sa'îd, in 1335, the Il-Khanate was torn apart by tribal and sectarian violence.

In Central Asia, the Chaghatai Horde had very early fractured into several warring factions and suffered perennial instability. After the death of Tarmashirin Khan (r. 1318–1326), the Chaghatai Horde split into western and eastern halves: the western part centered in Transoxiana retained the Chaghatai name, while the eastern part, with a more heavily nomadic population, came to be known as Moghulistan 'Mongolia'. The western part also acquired some of the most important cities across the Oxus to the south, including Balkh and Herat, around this time.

Membership in the lineage of Chinggis Khan had become the legitimizing factor in a ruler's establishment in Central Asia, but the failure of a Chaghatayid to establish firm rule there led to the end of the direct line when Kazaghan (r. 1346/1347–1357/1358), emir of the Kara'unas people, killed the last Chaghatayid khan, Kazan, in 1346/1347. Although Kazaghan and his successors maintained the fiction that they ruled in the name of the

---

[42] Atwood (2004: 609).

Chaghatayids, and installed puppet khans to legitimize their reigns, they actually ruled in their own names.

Tamerlane and the Timurids

Tamerlane (Temür or Timur the Lame) was born in the 1320s or 1330s in Kišš (modern Shahr-i Sabz), a settled agricultural region of Western Central Asia near the great city of Samarkand.[43] He was a Barlas by birth, and the Barlas were in origin the Mongol Barulas. However, Tamerlane and the other Barlas spoke Central Asian Turkic and Persian, not Mongol, as did other Mongol peoples who had settled in Central Asia. He was also not a nomad and never attempted to conquer the steppe zone; like most of the other leaders and warriors of the region at that time he was perfectly at home in walled cities.[44]

By the time Emir Kazaghan was assassinated in 1357/1358 Tamerlane had a personal comitatus[45] and perhaps a small additional force of his own.[46]

---

[43] Manz (1989: 13) remarks, "In the Eurasian politics of Temür's time the Ulus Chaghatay held not a powerful but a central position. Both settled and nomadic populations were strongly entrenched within it, and its borders touched on both steppe and settled powers. There was almost no important Eurasian region with which the Ulus Chaghatay did not have some contact; on its eastern border it adjoined the eastern Chaghadayids and the cities of the Silk Route, on the North it bordered the Jochid powers and to the south the Iranian principalities."

[44] The idea that Tamerlane and the others with or against whom he fought during his rise to power were nomads, which is repeated by many, including Manz (1989), is incorrect. They did not nomadize with herds but lived in and around the agricultural-urban areas of Central Asia. Manz herself notes that "the Chaghatay nomads frequently took refuge within fortified cities. One should note moreover that when Temur gained control over the Ulus a year or two after this, he immediately built fortifications at Samarkand" (Manz 1989: 55).

[45] These were the "nontribal" men Manz (1989) usually refers to as his "personal following" or "companions"; she does not otherwise refer to the Islamicized comitatus, or *ghulâm* system.

[46] The Islamic histories—most of which are full of nothing but vitriol when it comes to Tamerlane—consider him to have been a common brigand. He is said to have begun his path to fame as leader of a band of warlike young men, one among many such bands in Central Asia at the time, whose exploits are mostly unknown. It is thus widely claimed that he acquired the lameness which gave him his sobriquet Tamerlane—*Timur-i leng* 'Timur the Lame'—from arrows shot at him while stealing sheep, a story related also by Clavijo. However, this story is fiction. Tamerlane is known to have received the wound in question on a campaign in Sîstân in 1364 (Manz 1989: 48). Perhaps the story ultimately reflects a lost mythological national origin story (as in those presented in the prologue) that was already circulating in Tamerlane's own time. Little is actually known about his youth.

When the Moghuls (or Mughals, i.e., Mongols) of Moghulistan invaded the Chaghatayid realm early in 1360, Tamerlane submitted to them and was rewarded with appointment over the Barlas and the territory of Kišš. The appointment was confirmed two years later by the Moghul khan, who appointed his son Ilyâs Khwâja (Khoja) to rule the Transoxiana part of the reunified Chaghatayid realm. But Tamerlane and many other local leaders considered the Moghuls to be tyrants and withdrew outside their territory.

The grandson of the assassinated Emir Kazaghan, Emir Ḥusayn, had an army larger than Tamerlane's, so Tamerlane made an alliance with Ḥusayn. In 1364 the two attacked and defeated the Moghuls. In spite of setbacks, they eventually succeeded in eliminating them from Chaghatayid Central Asia. Then, through good leadership and clever intrigue, Tamerlane united most of the leaders of the Chaghatai realm and defeated Ḥusayn. By April 9, 1370, Tamerlane was sole ruler. He spent the next dozen years cementing his actual control over the Chaghatai territory.

The eyewitness accounts of his day show Tamerlane to have been an intelligent, generous ruler, brave in battle, who was absolutely ruthless with rebels and anyone he thought was unworthy to rule, for whatever reason. He was also one of history's greatest generals, several times defeating forces much larger than his own. Having established his largely unopposed rule in Western and Southern Central Asia,[47] Tamerlane led his army on far-ranging conquests outside his home region of Transoxiana. They began in 1384/1385, when he took northern Iran and Mazandaran.

In 1385/1386, Tokhtamïsh, khan of the Golden Horde, who had won his throne with crucial help from Tamerlane, attacked the Timurid city of Tabriz, in Azerbaijan. In 1386 Tamerlane campaigned in Iran and the Caucasus. He established his power in central Iran, Azerbaijan, and Georgia. Other rulers in the area voluntarily submitted to him.

In 1387, with Tokhtamïsh on his way to attack the Caucasus again, Tamerlane sent an army and defeated him. Then Tokhtamïsh attacked Transoxiana, invading as far south as the Oxus, while Tamerlane was away campaigning to the south in Iran. Unaware of the threat to his home territory, Tamerlane campaigned against the Turkmen Kara-Koyunlu around Lake Van, then via Kurdistan down to Fars, where Isfahan and Shiraz submitted.

[47] Manz (1989: 58–62, 67).

When Isfahan rebelled, Tamerlane retook the city and ordered that the population be executed. Then he found out about Tokhtamïsh's invasion of Transoxiana.

In response, Tamerlane turned to the north, defeating and completely subjugating Khwârizm, which had joined with Tokhtamïsh. In 1388/1389 Tamerlane turned back Tokhtamïsh's attacks and in the late fall of 1390 prepared for a great expedition against him. In June 1391 he met Tokhtamïsh's forces and defeated them, took and sacked the Golden Horde capital, and chased Tokhtamïsh up the Volga.

In fall 1392 Tamerlane campaigned in Iran again. He and his sons subdued the country in 1392 and 1393, and in the summer of 1393 they took Baghdad. He also demanded that the Turkmen of western Iran and Anatolia submit to him.

At the end of 1394, he learned that Tokhtamïsh had again raided his territories in the Caucasus. He campaigned once more against the Golden Horde, defeating Tokhtamïsh and advancing as far as Moscow. He then returned, sacking the Golden Horde cities on the way. This was too much for the people of the Golden Horde, who overthrew Tokhtamïsh. The Golden Horde was now so seriously weakened it was no longer a threat to Tamerlane.

In 1398 Tamerlane invaded northwestern India, capturing and sacking Delhi in December 1398. There his troops apparently got out of control and inflicted great damage, killing thousands of people. He returned home in 1399. In that fall, he went to western Iran to suppress a rebel, retake Georgia, and retake Baghdad.

In the same year he also campaigned against the Mamluks in Syria, who had murdered his ambassadors and also had sheltered rebels against him and refused to hand them over.[48] In 1400/1401 he captured Aleppo, Homs, and Damascus, but did not establish any permanent administration in Syria. On July 20, 1402, his army met a larger Ottoman force in the Battle of Angora (ancient Ancyra, now Ankara), crushing them and taking Sultan Bâyazîd captive.[49] Tamerlane campaigned through Ottoman territories, collecting

---

[48] Manz (2000: 511).
[49] Manz (2000: 511). Bâyazîd actually was well treated by Tamerlane but died a few months after his capture.

tribute from its major cities, before withdrawing. As in Syria, he did not establish any permanent administration in Anatolia.[50]

Back in Samarkand in 1404, Tamerlane met foreign envoys, including Ruy Gonzáles de Clavijo, an envoy from King Enrique III (Henry III) of Castile and León, and then prepared for his biggest campaign of all, the conquest of China. He gathered an enormous army and set off in late fall 1404. He reached Utrâr, where he stopped to spend the winter, but he was already ill and died there on February 17 or 18, 1405.[51] His body was brought back to Samarkand, where he was buried in an ebony casket in the beautiful mausoleum now known as the Gur-e Emir 'Tomb of the Prince'.

On the whole, Tamerlane's campaigns were indistinguishable from those of a European, Persian, or Chinese dynastic founder. There were no lightning cavalry raids across vast distances nor, of course, any great naval campaigns. He had cavalry in his army and used it to great effect, but the vast majority of his forces were infantry, and his targets were exclusively cities, which he was an expert at capturing.

He was content with the submission of his enemies, especially if they submitted voluntarily, and he nearly always left rulers on their thrones as long as they paid taxes and did not rebel against him.[52] "He was interested in controlling and garrisoning the largest cities, in collecting and organizing taxes through the use of bureaucrats from his settled territory, and in using soldiers from these territories in further campaigns."[53]

Tamerlane's rule marks the first and only time that urban Central Asia was both the cultural and the political center of Eurasia. His attempt to reconquer the territories of the former Mongol Empire partly succeeded, but his failure to establish a stable imperial government structure in his empire, and his children's rejection of his succession plan, doomed his efforts to failure. In short, while Tamerlane was a brilliant general, he was a true product of his fractious Central Asian homeland and his urban and agrarian upbringing.

His heirs were not content with the shares of his empire he had allotted them. They fought for some fifteen years until only his youngest son, Shâh

---

[50] This was undoubtedly not because he did not want to annex them (*pace* Manz 1989), but because both regimes were strong and relatively distant from his home base.

[51] Manz (1989: 13). The above summary of Tamerlane's campaigns is based on Manz (1989: 70–73).

[52] Manz (1989: 16).

[53] Manz (1989: 12–13).

Rukh (1377/1405–1446), remained alive. By that time most of the empire outside of Transoxiana and neighboring regions had broken up into its constituent parts. The legacy of Tamerlane and the Timurids was to be in patronage of the arts.

The Apogee of Central Asia and the Silk Road

The Mongols established, or at least patronized, the first known large-scale international trade and taxation system, the *ortaq*.[54] It was essentially a merchant association or cartel, run mainly by Muslims, which lent money for caravans and other enterprises and included tax-farming services for the rulers. Partly due to a government interest subsidy, it was incredibly lucrative.[55] Depending on the administration in power, government policy toward the *ortaq* varied from eager participation and overindulgence (as under Ögedei) to strict control (as under Möngke).[56] The openness of the empire to commerce, and the unprecedented safety merchants and craftsmen could expect, drew businessmen from the four corners of Eurasia. Italian merchants such as the Polo family traveled to and from the Mongol capitals conducting their very profitable business.[57] They were impressed by the high level of culture and wealth they encountered in eastern Eurasia. Marco Polo (1254–1324) left for the Great Khanate in 1271 and remained there for two decades, only returning home to Venice in 1295. He eventually told his story to a romance writer, Rustichello of Pisa, who wrote it up and published it.[58] Rustichello's embroidered version of Marco Polo's account[59] fascinated the Europeans of his day and was ultimately responsible for stimulating European sailors to try and find a direct route to the Orient.

[54] Mongol *ortoy*. The Turkic word *ortaq* means 'partner'; the Mongols borrowed the word along with the institution (Allsen 1989: 112, 117; cf. Endicott-West 1989: 129 et seq.).
[55] Rossabi (1981: 275, 282–283; 1988: 122–123) Cf. Endicott-West (1989). This important, powerful institution deserves much further study.
[56] Allsen (1989) gives an overview of the Mongol rulers' changing policies vis-à-vis the *ortaq* merchants and discusses taxation of merchants.
[57] See also the western Silk Road merchant's guide by Pegolotti (fl. ca. 1340), *La pratica della mercatura* (Pegolotti 1936).
[58] There are several good translations, the most accurate being that by Moule and Pelliot (1938), the most readable and accessible Latham's (1958). The book is brilliantly annotated in great depth by Pelliot (1959–1963).
[59] On the historicity of Marco Polo's travels, see endnote 84.

As "pagans," the Mongols were also the target of every organized religion with which they came into contact. Missionaries were sent to convert them, and though the Mongols were uninterested in all religions and sects—except, eventually, Tibetan Buddhism—the missionaries kept trying. The most notable result of this effort was the production of first-person accounts of the Mongols and other peoples who were encountered by the missionaries.[60]

The Mongol conquest was a significant event in world history. However, the widely held view that it was a fundamental, formative event, a watershed dividing Eurasia before and afterward,[61] does not really accord with the historical evidence. Most significantly, the major ethnolinguistic divisions of Eurasia in post–Mongol Empire times and those in pre–Mongol Empire times were all in place and remained virtually unchanged down to the twentieth century. One of the undoubted side effects of the Mongol conquest was the transmission of some practical elements of Chinese culture and technology to Western Europe, most important of which were gunpowder and firearms.[62] Another was the stimulus to Western Europeans to find out more about the fabulous lands described by Marco Polo.

The Il-Khans were great patrons of the arts and sciences. They constructed numerous splendid mosques and other building projects, most of which have since fallen into ruin. Their most notable accomplishment was the creation of "Persian" miniature painting. It developed as a result of the Mongols having brought with them numerous Chinese scholar officials to help them run the Il-Khanate. The Chinese wrote with a brush, and painted with it too, and began painting pictures for the Mongols and each other. The Muslims learned from them how to paint in the Chinese style and, by imitating them, developed a new, hybrid style that mixed elements of Byzantine art, Arabic calligraphy, and traditional Near Eastern styles with the Chinese style, thus producing one of the great traditions of world art, Islamic miniature painting. The Yüan court, in turn, brought astronomers, physicians, materia medica, and other people and things from the Islamic world.[63]

Tamerlane made Samarkand his capital. He rebuilt its walls, which had been torn down by the Mongols, and beautified the city with palaces, gar-

---

[60] For readable translations of the major European accounts, see Dawson (1955).
[61] This is the dominant view (q.v. Di Cosmo 1999: 5). For a brief criticism of it, see endnote 85.
[62] The earliest known cannon, found in China's Heilongjiang Province, which was formerly Mongol territory, is dated 1282 (Atwood 2004: 354).
[63] See Allsen (1997: 9) for a brief discussion and further references.

dens, and religious buildings. He continued to improve Samarkand, making it a model city and an unusually beautiful one, partly by furnishing it with trophies taken from conquered cities during his campaigns and partly by patronizing the best artists and architects of his day. Many of the innovations that characterize the Timurid architectural style—the Central Asian ancestor of the Persian-Mughal style—appeared in buildings erected in his own day, most famously in what became his own mausoleum in Samarkand. To his reign and those of his immediate successors belong not only some of the world's greatest architecture and city plans but also the greatest Persian poet, Hafiz (Ḥâfiẓ, ca. 1320–1389/1390), who met Tamerlane and was honored by him.

9

Central Eurasians Ride to a European Sea

اگر آن ترک شیرازی بدست آرد دل ما را
بخال هندویش بخشم سمرقند و بخارا را
— حافظ

> If that Turk of Shiraz
>   would take my heart in her hand
> I'd trade for her beauty-mark[1]
> Bukhara and Samarkand.
> —Hafiz

The Third Regional Empire Period

Beginning in the mid-fifteenth century, large new empires were created by Central Eurasians. They comprised most of Eurasia, including Central Eurasia and nearly all of the periphery except Western Europe, Southeast Asia, and Japan. At the same time, the Portuguese discovered the direct sea route to Asia around Africa and, followed soon after by other Western Europeans, developed the old Littoral trade routes into a distinct economic sphere, the Littoral System. The premodern world thus consisted of "continental" Eurasian empires of Central Eurasian origin and "coastal" European empires that were essentially global and based on knowledge and control of the sea routes around the world.

The Second Central Eurasian Conquest of Eurasia[2] began when the continental Ottoman Turks conquered the Byzantine Empire and restored its traditional maritime sphere of influence. The Turkmen, led by the Safavids, founded a new Persian Empire on the Iranian Plateau in the traditional Persian home area from the Caucasus to the Persian Gulf, while the Mughals conquered northern India and spread Timurid-Persian culture into South Asia and the Indian Ocean. Between the mid-sixteenth and mid-seventeenth centuries, the continental Russians defeated the Golden Horde successor states

[1] Literally, a 'Hindu beauty-mark' (or *bindi*), applied to the forehead by Indian women.
[2] The first was that by the early Indo-Europeans, q.v. chapter 1.

and expanded across Siberia to the Pacific in the east, the Manchus conquered China, and the Junghars established a steppe empire in Central Eurasia itself. With the construction of St. Petersburg on the Baltic and the transfer there of the Russian imperial capital, Russia became a maritime power too, with even grander ambitions, including in Central Eurasia.[3]

In 1498 Vasco da Gama crossed the Indian Ocean to India. In the following half century the Portuguese established trading posts from the Persian Gulf, via the Bay of Bengal, Malacca, and South China, to Japan. The Portuguese, and the Spanish as well, were still essentially medieval in most respects and, as such, followed a Central Eurasian model of the commercial imperative practically identical to the model followed by the Scythians and other early Iranians in their establishment of the Silk Road economy. The only significant difference was that the Europeans used ships and cannons instead of horses and compound bows to force the opening of trade when negotiations failed. The Central Eurasian model drove the Portuguese voyages of discovery to reach the Orient; their sometimes forcible establishment of trading rights;[4] their building of "factories" (trading posts), which became fortresses and political outposts; and finally their eventual struggle with the great continental Asian powers and with other European competitors. Like the Central Eurasian nomads, the Portuguese depended heavily on local expertise—Asian pilots, cartographers, merchants, and others—throughout their expansion.[5] Sailing in the other direction, the Spanish established a direct east-west trade system via the Americas and the Philippines. The European discovery and conquest of the open-sea routes to the Orient and the Americas began Western European political, military, and cultural domination of the world. By the nineteenth century the British dominated most of the new, European-created Littoral System and the open-sea trade to India and China, although no one European power was ever able to entirely eliminate the others or the traditional local coastal shipping.

---

[3] The construction of the Orenburg Line of forts combining military and commercial activity across the northern steppe at this time was coupled with an aggressive stance vis-à-vis the trade with Asia, "especially with the Bukharan Khanate" (Levi 2007b: 105 et seq.).

[4] "In the majority of cases, establishment of 'factories' (trading stations) or building of forts was accomplished after discussion and negotiation with local potentates." One of the major exceptions was Gujarat. "Until the Portuguese succeeded in obtaining permission (1535) to build a fort at Diu, Gujarati-Portuguese relations were hostile" (Russell-Wood 1998: 21).

[5] Vasco da Gama depended on a Muslim pilot, Aḥmad ibn Majīd, to guide his ships across the Indian Ocean (Russell-Wood 1998: 18).

CHAPTER 9

The Second Central Eurasian Conquest of Eurasia

The late Renaissance conquests that established the great premodern Eurasian continental empires are not connected to the conquests of Tamerlane, which in most areas only interrupted or delayed their normal development. Upon Tamerlane's death in 1405, the Ottomans almost immediately restored their empire and resumed their long-term expansion,[6] eliminating the remnant Byzantine Empire in 1453. The relatively early chronology of the Ottoman Empire's reestablishment vis-à-vis the other empires mirrors the out-of-synch chronology of Byzantine periods of growth, which were usually during periods of weakness elsewhere in western Eurasia. This was evidently the result, in great part, of the region's coastal character—the Ottoman Turkish realm covered almost exactly the same eastern Mediterranean littoral territory as the old Eastern Roman Empire of a millennium earlier. The other early empires only began forming a century after Tamerlane, with the establishment of the Safavid Dynasty in Persia in 1501 by the Turkmen (who were Oghuz Turks and thus ethnolinguistically related to the Ottomans) and the simultaneous foundation of the Mughal (Moghul) Empire in Afghanistan and India by Babur and his Central Asian Turks.

While these states were in the process of being established, the focus of Eurasian power began to shift toward the sea in tandem with a great worldwide revolution that had its beginnings at the exact midpoint of the millennium: the establishment of European maritime domination over the Littoral and from there over the entire Eurasian continent. As one historian remarks, in the Ottoman and Mughal empires, "the dissolution of the core matched the emergence of the periphery."[7]

The shift took place even within Europe itself. The Spanish *reconquista*, in which the last remnant of Arab rule in Spain was crushed with the capture of the Muslim capital of Granada in 1492, can be seen as a microcosmic version of the great Central Eurasian movement. Granada is not only inland, it is surrounded by mountains. The Alhambra,[8] the palace and residence of the

---

[6] There is considerable debate about Ottoman origins. For the leading recent views, see Kafadar (1995), Lindner (2005), and Lowry (2003). The Ottomans seem to have started out as a Central Eurasian lord-and-comitatus group.

[7] Matthee (1999: 10).

[8] The name is Arabic al-ḥamrâ 'the red one'.

206

rulers, is a fortress perched on top of a high hill or plateau overlooking the great valley around it. The Spanish victory was one of the littoral over the continent: the Christians were not only successful warriors on land but skilled sailors as well. The subsequent history of European colonial exploration and empire building is marked by the success of the major Atlantic littoral states—Portugal, Spain, Holland, England, and France—to the exclusion of nearly all other contenders. There were to be no important Swedish colonies, German colonies, Austro-Hungarian colonies, Italian colonies, and so on.[9] Even though all these states were seafaring nations too,[10] their maritime tradition was almost exclusively local in nature. They were primarily continental powers, and remained continental, while the littoral powers expanded—first across the sea and later against their continental neighbors.

THE OTTOMAN RECOVERY

By 1413 the civil war following the Ottomans' devastating defeat by Tamerlane in 1402 was over. The victor, Mehmed I (r. 1403–1421), recaptured the territories that had been conquered by his great-grandfather Murad I, and also subjugated part of the Balkans.

Under his grandson Mehmed II (the Conqueror, r. 1451–1481) the Turks laid siege to Constantinople, the capital of what was left of the Byzantine Empire. By that time the once great city sheltered only about 20,000 people, and much of the territory inside its walls had been turned into agricultural fields. Its only defenses were its great walls, which had repeatedly defeated Byzantine enemies of old. But the days were long past when Byzantine engineers were more advanced than their enemies and the Byzantine navy ruled the Aegean and the Black Sea. This time the attackers had the advanced weapons. The Turks hired military engineers from Italy and other European countries to bombard the walls with cannons. In short order the defenses were breached, and on May 29, 1453, Mehmed entered the city. He declared it the capital of the Ottoman Empire and immediately began rebuilding and repopulating it.

---

[9] The existence of a few exceptions—such as the Danish colony of Tranquebar on the southeastern Indian coast, founded in the early seventeenth century, or various short-lived colonies in the Americas or Africa—prove the rule.

[10] In some cases—such as Sweden, home of the Rus Vikings—they had earlier been successful seafaring conquerors. The Swedes continued to dominate the Baltic Sea coast for several more centuries.

Though the fall of Constantinople, the capital of the Roman Empire, was a landmark event symbolically, it did not signify very much in practice. The Ottomans already had conquered all but a few small outliers of the shrunken Byzantine realm[11] and had begun to expand beyond it into lands that had not been ruled from the city for hundreds of years. Under Mehmed II the Ottomans took Greece and most of the rest of the Balkans, and completed the conquest of Anatolia by defeating the Kingdom of Trabizond in 1461 and incorporating it into the empire. Mehmed also defeated the troublesome Ak-Koyunlu in northwestern Persia in 1473 and conquered south to the borders of Mamluk Syria. Selim I (the Grim, r. 1512–1520), who finally defeated the Mamluks (in 1516–1517), took Kurdistan, northern Mesopotamia, Syria, and Egypt, extending Ottoman power down the Arabian coast as far as Medina and Mecca. His successor Suleyman the Magnificent (r. 1520–1566) conquered most of Hungary, laid siege to Vienna (unsuccessfully), and extended Ottoman political influence, if not direct rule, across most of North Africa and into the Red Sea. The Ottomans' advance into the western Mediterranean was finally stopped by a Christian European coalition at the Battle of Lepanto in 1571. Nevertheless, the Ottomans had to a large extent reconstituted the Eastern Roman Empire as it was under Heraclius before the Arab conquests.[12]

THE SAFAVID EMPIRE

In northern Iran, the collapse of the Timurid successors returned the Ak-Koyunlu Turkmen to power. The Ak-Koyunlu's persecution of the aggressive Sufi order of the Safavids (Ṣafawiyya)—a sect of extremist Shiites[13] also known as the Kïzïlbaš 'red-heads', which was predominantly Turkmen—galvanized the Safavids into a revolutionary movement. The Ottoman defeat of the Ak-Koyunlu in 1473 weakened the latter and paved the way for the Safavids, whose comitatus-like dedication to their leader,[14] de-

---

[11] One of the reasons for the Ottomans' success was their generosity toward the conquered peoples. In particular, their reputation for fair dealing and good government encouraged the subjects of the Byzantine Empire to open their gates to the Turks in order to be rid of the tyrannical Byzantine government.

[12] This section is largely derived from Bosworth et al. (1995).

[13] They are said to have openly declared their belief that the Safavid leader was God, and his son the son of God (Savory et al. 1995: 767).

[14] In his discussion of the three main elements of the Safavid forces, Savory et al. (1995: 767) remark that "the Ṣūfī disciples (murīds) of the Ṣafawīd order owed unquestioning obedience to their murshīd-i kāmil . . . , the head of the order, who was their spiritual director."

spite many setbacks, eventually ensured their success. In 1501 the forces of Ismâ'îl I (b. 1487, r. 1501–1524) defeated the Ak-Koyunlu and captured Tabriz. The Safavids declared their sect of Shiism to be the official religion of Persia.[15] During the first decade of his rule, Shâh Ismâ'îl conquered northern and southeastern Iran, Fars (south-central Iran), and eastern Iraq (1508). The Persians defeated the Uzbeks at Marw in 1510 and killed their leader, Shaybânî Khan, in battle, though the Uzbeks prevailed in Transoxiana and the Safavids never dislodged them there. In 1514 the Ottomans defeated the Safavid forces with guns and artillery and restored eastern Anatolia and northern Iraq to the Ottoman Empire, under whose rule those regions were to remain.

Shâh Ismâ'îl's son Shâh Tahmasp (r. 1524–1576), a strong ruler who campaigned against the Ottomans and Mughals, was followed by two weak, contentious rulers who lost much territory to the Ottomans and were unable to prevent the Uzbeks from raiding northeastern Iran. When Shâh 'Abbâs the Great (r. 1588–1629) took the throne he immediately set about recapturing territory his predecessors had lost to the Ottomans, Uzbeks, and Portuguese.

In 1515 the Portuguese had established a colonial trading post and naval base on the island of Hormuz (Hormoz) in the Persian Gulf, and the Persians had been unable to remove them. When, a century later, the British and Dutch had become increasingly dominant in the Persian Gulf and Indian Ocean in general, Shâh 'Abbâs acted. In line with his attempts to strengthen the Persian economy—and state control of it, especially of the silk trade[16]—he allowed the English East India Company, a quasi-governmental organization, to establish trading centers in Isfahan and Shiraz. In 1621 he gave the Dutch East India Company permission to build a trading center at the port city of Bandar 'Abbâs on the Persian Gulf. The following year, with the help of British ships, which ferried his troops to Hormuz, Shâh 'Abbâs defeated the Portuguese and ejected them from the island. The British were also given permission to open a trading center in the port

---

[15] This created a long-lasting problem because most Muslims in Persia, as in the rest of the Islamic world, were Sunnites.

[16] Matthee (1999: 7) notes, "the trade in Safavid silk invariably involved the state. . . . until its demise, the Safavid state continued to have a crucial role in the collection, sale, domestic manufacturing and distribution of silk." State control goes a long way toward explaining the steady economic decline of Persia down to modern times. Its cultural decline clearly had other causes.

town of Bandar 'Abbâs, which grew quickly and became an important commercial port, though not a very large one. The British were shortly afterward
defeated and largely replaced by the Dutch, who controlled the Persian Gulf
trade in the second half of the seventeenth century, though they were eventually evicted by the British.

Shâh 'Abbâs also built a beautiful new imperial capital at Isfahan in south-
central Iran and moved poets, artists, carpet makers, and other artisans to
the city, along with merchants to further enrich it. What he did not do well
was handle his succession. He killed or blinded all of his sons, whom he
suspected of plotting against him. He was succeeded by his weak grandson,
Shâh Ṣafî (r. 1629–1642) and then the more able 'Abbâs II (r. 1642–1666). The
Safavids became increasingly bigoted and parochial, and their power declined rapidly. Finally, a band of Afghans besieged and captured the capital
in 1722, ending the dynasty.[17]

THE MUGHAL EMPIRE

Although Tamerlane's youngest son, Shâh Rukh, survived the other contenders for the Timurid throne, by the time the war of succession ended
there was not much left of his father's vast conquests beyond Transoxiana
and Khurasan. Even in Central Asia itself, wars of secession continued to
break out, and the Timurid realm steadily shrank.

Babur (Bâbur, 1483/1484–1530), prince of Ferghana, was a scion of both
the Timurid imperial line and the Chinggisid imperial line of the Mughals
(Moghuls, Mongols). In 1504 he led an army southward into what is now Afghanistan, where he attacked and took Kabul, gained indirect control over
Ghazne, and in 1522 took Kandahar. Having become involved in the succession struggle for the throne of the Lodi Sultanate in Delhi, in 1526 Babur led
a small army of about 12,000 soldiers into India. He was met by a much larger
army of Indians, aided by Afghan cavalry. But with his Central Asian cavalry, and the considerable help of cannons and muskets—which his opponents did not have—he defeated the Delhi Sultanate in the Battle of Pânipât,
near Delhi, and occupied the city. He also captured Agra, which he made his
capital. By 1528 he had destroyed the power of the Rajputs and taken Rajasthan as well. At the time of his death in Kabul in 1530 he had created a Mughal
Empire that extended over much of Afghanistan and northwestern India.

[17] Savory et al. (1995).

Babur's son, Hûmayûn (r. 1530–1540, 1555–1556), was faced with opposition to Mughal rule from all directions, including his brother Kamran, who had received Afghanistan as his inheritance. Hûmayûn failed to secure his rule over his part of the new realm and was crushingly defeated in 1540 by the forces of the Afghan ruler of Bihar and Bengal, Sher Khan Sur (r. 1540–1545), who captured all of northern India and had himself crowned Shâh. Hûmayûn fled via Rajasthan and Sind to Safavid Persia, where Shâh Tahmasp gave him refuge.[18]

European Expansion around Eurasia by Sea

On May 20, 1498, the Portuguese explorer Vasco da Gama, having completed the first successful European sea voyage around Africa to Asia, landed near the port of Calicut (now Kozhikode, in Kerala state) on the Malabar coast of southwestern India. European discovery of the direct sea route to the Orient, and the opening of direct trade between Persia, India, Southeast Asia, and Europe, was revolutionary not only for Western Europe but for the development of the eventual Littoral System all around Eurasia, especially in South, Southeast, and East Asia.

Although he was robbed of most of the goods he had acquired in trade and barely escaped with his life, Vasco da Gama returned to Portugal from Calicut with Indian trade goods worth 3,000 times the investors' costs.[19] The next Portuguese expedition to arrive, led by Pedro Alvarez Cabral, who discovered Brazil on the way, resulted in a much more serious attack on the Portuguese by the Zamorin, the local Hindu prince of Calicut, who was in league with the Muslims who controlled the Indian Ocean trade with Calicut. Many Portuguese were killed in the attack. In retaliation Cabral destroyed the Muslim ships there and bombarded the city, causing much damage, but was unable to complete his mission satisfactorily and finally returned to Portugal, having lost six out of twelve ships on the voyage to India and back.[20]

---

[18] This section is largely dependent on Richards (1993).

[19] Diary of Vasco da Gama, http://www.fordham.edu/halsall/mod/1497degama.html.

[20] From the history of Fernão Lopes de Castanheda, volume 2, chapter 6, section 3, much of which consists of nearly verbatim quotations from the original Portuguese accounts of the explorers themselves (see http://www.columbia.edu/itc/mealac/pritchett/oogenerallinks/kerr/

In 1502 Vasco da Gama returned in force and attacked the Muslims in Calicut, bombarding the town with cannons and largely demolishing it. In 1510 the Portuguese under Afonso de Albuquerque took the port of Goa from its Muslim rulers and continued the lightning Portuguese advance around the Asian littoral, capturing the port of Malacca, on the Malay Peninsula, in 1511. In 1515 he took the Persian island of Hormuz, which he made into a trading center and naval base. The Portuguese built a fort at Colombo, in Ceylon, in 1518 and gained the port of Diu on the northwestern Indian coast in 1535 through a political alliance. The Chinese gave them permission to land and trade at Macao in 1535, and by 1577 they had built a colony and trading center there under the command of a Captain Major.[21] By 1543 the Portuguese reached Japan, and in 1550 Nagasaki, where by 1571 they began making regular annual visits, mostly carrying goods from Macao in China, but also from as far as Goa in India, and some items traveled all the way from Europe.[22] Having pioneered the routes and paved the way partly with guns, the Portuguese traders soon found themselves threatened not so much by the Asian rulers but by their own missionaries (whose aggressive political tactics in Japan eventually turned the Japanese rulers against the Portuguese) and by the other Europeans who followed them.

Even in their very first voyage to India, the Portuguese sometimes ended up using force to conduct trade and return safely home. This should not be surprising from the historical perspective of Central Eurasia. The earliest known Silk Road traders, the Scythians, and their cultural relatives the Hsiung-nu, were also fierce warriors. Considering the generally overlooked fierceness of their neighbors—the Greeks, Romans, Persians, Arabs, and Chinese, among others—Central Eurasians had to be fierce. While Central Eurasian peoples are more famous for war than for trade, and their empires were certainly mainly created by conquest, like all empires, the sources reveal unambiguously that the primary motivation behind the historically best-known Central Eurasian imperial expansions, those of the Türk, Rus, and Mongols, as well as the European maritime expansion

volo2chapo6secto3.html). Castanheda's work was published in Coimbra in 1552–1554 and first translated and published in English in 1582 (http://www.columbia.edu/itc/mealac/pritchett/oogenerallinks/kerr/volo2chap 06secto1.html).

[21] Wills (1998: 343).

[22] See below on the trade goods.

of the Age of Exploration, was commerce and taxation, not robbery and destruction.

Although the early Portuguese did use force rather consistently while first establishing their control of shipping in the Arabian Sea, on the whole they are actually remarkable for their restraint.[23] In Asia, the Europeans generally established their trading ports and built their fortresses by leave of a local ruler, who for one reason or another—usually a conflict his state was involved in with another neighboring state—allowed or even encouraged them to do so.[24] This too is strikingly similar to the way the Central Eurasians expanded.

Why then was it necessary to use so much force, exceptionally, in the Arabian Sea? Instances where there is sufficient source material, whether narrative histories or first-person accounts such as the diary of Vasco da Gama, show that the opposition to the traders came from the regional merchants already involved in international trade in the target area, and from the local ruler of whatever port city with which the Portuguese wanted to trade. Each local ruler had become accustomed to controlling his particular corner of the old point-to-point Littoral trade routes, but he was also dependent on the goodwill of the merchants. Although these local port regimes are usually supposed to have supported free trade before the Europeans appeared, in fact the local merchants and their political allies were fully willing to use force to oust any newcomers who would compete with their virtual monopoly, as Vasco da Gama found out on his very first trip to Calicut. In addition, in the Arabian Sea the trade was more or less exclusively controlled by Muslims; non-Muslims were unwelcome, and the Portuguese were outspoken about their Christianity.[25]

Nevertheless, because Vasco da Gama was the very *first* European to reach India by sea, the local Muslims and Hindus hardly had the excuse of being afraid of a European Christian taking over their trade or capturing

---

[23] Russell-Wood (1998: 21). The striking comparison really is between the Portuguese, Spanish, French, Dutch, British, and other Europeans' relative restraint toward Asians and the violence they habitually used *against each other* both in Asia and, especially, at home in Europe.

[24] Russell-Wood (1998: 21), Pearson (1987: 31 et seq.). The latter often portrays the Portuguese as trigger-happy conquerors, for example, "Another great port city, Diu, was conquered in 1535." But in the very next paragraph he notes that "Diu, Bassein and Daman were acquired by treaty" (Pearson 1987: 32). Note also that Diu was not a "great" city.

[25] One can perhaps imagine the havoc that would have broken out if an Indian ship had sailed into Lisbon harbor in 1498 to trade odds and ends with the Portuguese, and its crew openly proclaimed that they were Muslims searching for local Muslims.

their port. They simply did not want competition and were willing to cheat, steal, and murder to force any new competitors out. "Among the [Muslim] merchants competition was fierce, even cut-throat; a lone outsider would find it almost completely impossible to break in on one of the established quasi-monopolistic routes. There is evidence of some extortion in customs houses, and of arbitrary actions by local officials. As a further blemish, piracy was widespread in the Indian Ocean at the start of the [sixteenth] century, and land powers took few steps, and these mostly ineffective, to control it."[26] The newcomers, being Europeans, were more than ready to respond with military force if necessary.

Yet force generally was unnecessary. One clear sign of the overwhelmingly commercial character of the European move into Asia is the fact that, after the Portuguese, it was led almost exclusively by private trading companies.[27] They did have the backing of their governments, and the right and means to use force if necessary, but they were commercial enterprises above all. It is thus not surprising that, for the first two centuries of their domination of the maritime routes, Europeans had very little political or cultural impact on Asia.[28]

The contest between the rulers, merchants, and military leaders of the Portuguese and other European nations, on the one hand, and those of the Asian nations, on the other, did end up being decided militarily in the Arabian Sea. The main resistance to the Portuguese there came at first not from the rulers of the neighboring empires—the Safavid Dynasty of Persia, the Sultanate of Delhi, the Mughal Empire—but from the Muslim merchants and local rulers who controlled the trade by sea from Calicut, Diu, and other ports on the west Indian coast to the Persian, Arabian, and Egyptian ports to the west and northwest, as well as from the southeast Indian coast across the Bay of Bengal to Malacca in Malaya. These were profitable links in the middle of the old Littoral zone trade routes that extended from Japan via the Near Eastern land bridge and the Mediterranean to the south coast of Europe. The Portuguese discovery of a direct route to the Orient that bypassed the Near East was soon to be understood by the Muslim merchants—

[26] Pearson (1987: 29).
[27] Although the Portuguese royal government was involved, the Portuguese too were driven almost completely by trade.
[28] Matthee (1999: 9) remarks that the "claim that the European political and cultural impact on early modern Asia was minimal is as true for Safavid Iran as it is for China and Japan."

especially those operating between Europe and India—as a major threat to their prosperity. In their struggle with these competitors and their political patrons, the Portuguese deliberately used their control of the sea to cut the maritime routes from India to the Red Sea. The Mamluks and other Muslims, including the ruler of Calicut, supported by the Venetians, attempted to stop the Portuguese. In 1507 and 1509 the Mamluks sent large fleets against them, but in the Battle of Diu in 1509 the Portuguese inflicted a decisive defeat on them. When the Portuguese actually took possession of Diu itself in 1535, the contest over control of trade in the western Indian Ocean came to a head. By this time the Ottomans had taken a serious interest in the situation. In 1538 Suleyman the Magnificent sent a large Ottoman fleet to lay siege to Diu. But the Portuguese defeated the Muslims and further strengthened their presence on the western coast of India. Although in 1546 the Ottomans took Iraq and with it Basra, from which they besieged nearby Hormuz in 1551–1552, they could not dislodge the Portuguese, who controlled the seas and were still expanding. In view of the fact that Western Europeans had developed superior seagoing ships, maritime skills, and weapons, Portuguese victory was inevitable.[29]

By the mid-sixteenth century, a mere fifty years after their first appearance in the Indian Ocean, the Portuguese had secured their control over the maritime routes all the way from Western Europe to Japan and had established forts or trading posts at the major stopping points along the way, all without controlling the interior or seriously threatening the major powers, which they could not have done even if they had wanted to.[30]

It is certainly true that the competition—the Muslim merchants and their Italian commercial allies—did not rest. The Portuguese suffered setbacks

---

[29] On Pearson's (1987) argument that the Portuguese accomplishments were trivial historically, see endnote 86.

[30] Matthee (1999: 9–10 says that in the early premodern period in question, "Unlike India, where nature made the interior relatively accessible from the coast, Iran could only be approached from the southern ports of entry, which were separated from the capital and the country's most productive regions by 1,000 km of semi-desert and formidable mountain ranges. Unlike Ceylon and most of southeast Asia, including the Indonesian archipelago, where fragmented political power enabled Europeans to establish local footholds, Iran was a centralized state or at least a state with a central power structure." The Portuguese and their successors did get involved in the local political scene and, in many cases, took control, sooner or later, of the territory immediately adjoining their port cities. Nevertheless, the eventual European penetration of the interior of India was not accomplished until the decline of the Mughals more than two centuries after the Portuguese first established their trading centers on the Indian coast, and similarly for the interior of the other regions mentioned.

and did not profit as much as they could have if they had managed their new maritime empire better and if the business cycle had not taken a serious downturn later in their century of greatness.[31] But it is equally true that beginning with the Portuguese conquest of the sea routes between Europe and East Asia, European power in the Asian Littoral zone only increased over time. Despite a temporary revival of the old maritime trade via the Near East and Venice,[32] the eventual result of the European domination of the open-sea routes was decline of the old spice and silk trade system connecting the Near East and the Mediterranean to Southern Europe.

The European drive to discover the sea routes to the Orient was fueled completely by desire to trade with the producers of silks, spices, and other precious things. The prices of such goods in Europe were astronomical compared to their cost in Asia; they were the stuff all merchants' dreams are made of.[33] What economic historians have dismissed as "luxury goods"[34] were thus just as much of fundamental economic importance in the newly developing Littoral System as they were in the continental Silk Road.

Asian opposition to European participation in Littoral zone trade brought about the unhesitating deployment of European naval military force at sea and in the continental periphery—at first, exclusively in the Littoral zone. This has been condemned rather moralistically by many modern historians,[35] but the Europeans' motivations for the military activity in Asia *on land* were mostly not genuinely imperialistic in nature until the end of the nineteenth century.[36] Even then, it is very difficult to feel much sympathy for the governments that the European *merchants* had to deal with from Arabia to Japan.[37]

---

[31] This section is based largely on Pearson (1987: 30 et seq.).

[32] This was also probably connected with the business cycle and thus actually a sign of economic decline rather than revival, as it has been portrayed by Pearson (1987).

[33] Pearson (1987: 41) notes that, even accounting for "shrinkage, wastage, shipwrecks and freight" and also "the costs of the forts in the Malabar towns," the Portuguese profit in Lisbon was about 90 percent or "even higher" according to other estimates.

[34] For discussion of this widespread misconception (computers and cell phones are modern "luxuries"), see endnote 87.

[35] For example, Pearson (1987).

[36] At that time, the corruption and weakness of Asian peripheral governments made the intervention of the European merchants (see the following note) unavoidable, and this subsequently allowed the Europeans to misuse the power they had gained.

[37] This is not to say that European governments at the time were much better, though the rule of uncapricious law often seems conspicuous by its absence in Asia.

At first, due to the lack of interest in maritime trade by the imperial governments,[38] the problem the Europeans faced was mainly the opposition of local merchant groups and local potentates to competition by newcomers. The great empires were on the whole uninterested in maritime or other trade and almost totally ignored it. For example, "most of the extant documentation relevant to trade in Safavid Iran springs from the quills of the Western company agents and ... most Persian-language sources yield virtually no data on trade, indigenous and international alike."[39] This disinterest is probably to be explained in the case of Mughal India by the fact that maritime trade accounted for a tiny percentage—estimated (generously) at perhaps 5 percent—of its total revenues, nearly all of which were derived from control of land.[40] "The Mughals came from interior Asia. Babur (1526–30), the first of the dynasty, never saw the sea." Similarly, in none of the contemporaneous political struggles in southern India "did maritime matters play any role at all."[41]

After the establishment of European control of the sea, and of bases in and around the Littoral, the Europeans had increasingly to deal with the direct representatives of the great powers themselves—Safavid and Qajar Persia, Mughal India, the Manchu-Chinese Ch'ing Dynasty, and Tokugawa Japan. The detailed accounts left by early trader-explorers show that they sometimes found it necessary to force the Asian rulers to follow the rules of peaceful diplomatic and commercial relations. For example, much of the widespread piracy that struck at the heart of the Europeans' maritime interests was approved or even sponsored by the local rulers of the port towns, who were frequently just as piratical on land. Like Central Eurasians, European traders had the backing of their governments and generally did not need to acquiesce to the extreme forms of corruption and summary violence that were customary among the officials and military of the local governments of Asian ports.

---

[38] Pearson (1987: 26–27).

[39] Matthee (1999: 6).

[40] "At 1500 none of the major states of India played any important role in maritime affairs. In the north, the declining Lodi sultanate, and then the new and expanding Mughal empire, were entirely land based in terms of both resources and ethos. The vast bulk of the revenue of the Mughal state came from land revenue.... Only perhaps 5 percent came from customs revenue.... the revenue resources of the Mughal empire were overwhelmingly from the land" (Pearson 1987: 26–27).

[41] Pearson (1987: 26–27).

In short, in order to be able to participate in international trade, the Europeans needed to stabilize the trade routes and the port cities by establishing their political dominance over them, exactly as the Central Eurasians were forced to do over and over for the two millennia that the Central Eurasian economy flourished—the period of existence of the Silk Road. The result was European military defeat of the local Asian rulers, or pressure on them, and the growth of European political power in Asia. As long as the major Asian states were strong enough, and European technological superiority was only marginal, it was not possible for Europeans to gain more than footholds on land in the Littoral zone.[42] They established their right to maritime trade in the region, secured it with fortified trading posts, and took control of the open seas.[43] It was only when the great Asian peripheral empires lost most of their effective power in the nineteenth century that Europeans stepped in to fill the power vacuum. But the Europeans' primary goal, at first, was still not to build new empires but simply to stabilize the political situation to ensure the continuation of peaceful, profitable trade. Again, this was exactly what the Central Eurasians did time and again in their relations with the peripheral powers. Central Eurasians almost never attacked strong, unified urban-agrarian empires—and usually did not have a chance to do so, because the latter attacked them first in their expansive phase; even in their decline, the urban-agrarian empires were usually too strong to be attacked by the smaller, weaker Central Eurasian nations. It was only when the peripheral empires became feeble, or actually collapsed, that the Central Eurasians attempted to set up new governments or otherwise stepped in to attempt to stabilize things. This is just what the Europeans did in India and China in the nineteenth and early twentieth centuries. In both the Silk Road and the Littoral System cases, only gradually did the Central Eurasians and the Europeans, respectively, become involved in attempting to govern directly.

Another unanticipated result of the European Age of Exploration was the opening of direct trade routes from Spanish America to East Asia. The wealth

---

[42] Pearson (1987: 45 et seq.).

[43] This was essentially true of the Russian expansion by land also. Russia's experience includes a gradual shift from being a member of the Silk Road system in the early period (e.g., the Kievan Rus khanate), through the Cossack-led fur-trading, fort-building race across Siberia to the Pacific, to the Russian Empire's eventual emergence as a Littoral System European power.

of the Spanish Empire was based overwhelmingly on its New World colonies, which among other things produced silver. The Spanish, like other Europeans, desired the silks, spices, porcelains, gemstones, and other precious goods of the Orient. They sent their galleons across the Pacific to Manila and on to China, where they spent as much as 20 percent of their New World silver. This trade not only further enriched the Spanish and paid for their empire's European wars, it flooded China with immense quantities of silver.[44]

Finally, the Europeans brought with them their religion. They sought to impress the Asians they met with what they imagined to be the superiority of Christianity over the local religions. In the early years of the European expansion, the Jesuits made a powerful first impression on the Japanese and early Manchu-Chinese ruling classes. But the later missionaries, who were not as highly educated and disciplined as the Jesuits, had less success. Most Asians were not much impressed with Christianity because they already had adopted one or another world religion and generally looked down on all the others as much as European Christians did. In Islamic and Buddhist civilizations, in particular, where the educated people of the ruling class understood more than just the basic elements of belief, most of whatever success the missionaries had was among the poor and uneducated, who did not know their local religions well. Moreover, Asian rulers and religious leaders also rightly saw a connection between the spread of the European religious establishment and the spread of European political power.

THE NEW LITTORAL COMMERCE

The impact of the extremely rapid growth of international trade under the Portuguese and their successors has yet to be fully recognized. Europe was directly connected by sea to India, Southeast Asia, the East Indies, China, and Japan.[45]

From Europe the Portuguese brought cloth, wine glasses, crystal, lenses, prisms, and Flemish clocks and other mechanical devices to the Orient, along with firearms, swords, and other weapons. Some of these goods were sold as far as Japan.[46]

---

[44] Wakeman (1985, I: 2–6), who also notes that part of the reason for the influx of silver to China was its relatively high price there.

[45] At the same time, European ships obviously connected each of these regions to each of the others, but oddly with almost no effect among the Asians so connected until modern times.

[46] Russell-Wood (1998: 133).

Portuguese trade ships left their mother port of Goa (India) and sailed to Nagasaki via Malacca, Macau and other Far East ports, finally returning to Goa after about three years. Goods imported to Japan by the Portuguese ships included raw silk, silk fabric, cotton and woolen cloth, ivory, coral and sugar. Exports were comprised mainly of silver but also included iron, folding screens and other art works, and swords. There were also unusual items among the import cargo, such as tigers.[47]

Trading locally within Asia on their way, Portuguese ships reached Macao with European goods as well as Indian products, especially pepper. In Macao they acquired silk (fabrics, raw silk, and floss), porcelain wares, musk, and gold. They then sailed to Nagasaki (after 1571), sold their goods, and bought silver, lacquerware, cabinets and painted screens, kimonos, swords, gold, and other items. Upon their return to Macao they used the silver to buy more gold, copper, silk, musk, porcelain wares, ivory, and pearls and sailed with them for Goa.

The Portuguese were greatly helped in their expansion by the xenophobic Chinese. The Ming Dynasty's policy of the Great Withdrawal, which forbade Chinese merchants to trade with the Japanese, created a virtual monopoly on shipping for the Europeans, who carried Chinese goods such as silk, gold, musk, and porcelain wares to Nagasaki, where they traded them for silver and copper. "It has been estimated that the Portuguese were the carriers of between a third and a half of all silk that left China by sea. By the 1630s, silk imports into Japan were more important than gold."[48]

As well as producing great profits, the trade brought merchants from distant realms of Eurasia into close contact with both producers and consumers, increasing the availability of and familiarity with previously rare goods. And the once fabulous lands of the Orient had become real. Fascinated European travelers wrote extensive, detailed accounts of India, China, Japan, and points in between. They observed the different languages, studied them, and wrote descriptions of them. The already intense European curiosity about the world shifted into high gear. Soon, not only in physical

---

[47] http://www1.city.nagasaki.nagasaki.jp/dejima/en/history/contents/index001.html. Where did the Portuguese buy live tigers? What did the Japanese do with them?

[48] Russell-Wood (1998: 135).

sciences and technology but also in history, literature, linguistics, anthropology, and other fields of knowledge relating to Asia, European scholarship progressed until in many respects it surpassed even the best native Asian scholarship about the Asians' own traditions.[49]

THE MUGHAL RESTORATION

As a refugee in Persia and under Safavid pressure, Hûmayûn agreed to become a Shiite. Only then did the Safavid ruler agree to help his cause. It took eight years of war, but eventually the combined Persian-Mughal forces recaptured Kandahar and in 1553 Kabul, where Hûmayûn deposed and blinded his brother. Upon the death of Sher Shâh's son Islam Shâh Sur in 1553, North India was divided among the successors and weakened by drought. In late 1554 Hûmayûn descended into India. He met and crushed the forces of the Sur family's ruler in the Punjab, entered Delhi in the middle of 1555, and restored the Mughal Dynasty.[50]

Hûmayûn died from an accident a few months later, leaving the empire to his young son, Akbar (r. 1556–1605), the greatest of the Great Mughal rulers. He suppressed the remaining opposition by the Sur family of Afghans, his brother in Kabul, and Uzbek rebels and conquered the rest of northern India, including Gujarat, Kashmir, and the northern part of the Deccan, the southern Indian plateau. He promoted a cultural and, to some extent, religious fusion of Islam and Hinduism, and under him the Mughal Empire reached its height of prosperity and culture.

Akbar's son and successor Jahângîr (r. 1605–1627) was followed by Shâh Jahân (r. 1628–1657). Both rulers largely continued Mughal policies and furthered the arts, especially architecture. Aurangzeb (r. 1658–1707) took the throne during a war of succession that broke out when his father became ill in September 1657. Although Shâh Jahân recovered, by that time Aurangzeb had already defeated the imperial forces and those of his main competitor for the throne, in the process capturing Agra and his father Shâh Jahân, whom he imprisoned in Agra Fort for the last five years of his life. Aurangzeb was a bigot who rejected the laissez-faire attitude of his predecessors, persecuted the Hindus, and warred almost constantly with the kingdoms of southern India. He expanded the territory of the Mughal Empire to its

---

[49] On the vicissitudes of the adoption of Western sciences in Asia, and the Modernist anti-intellectual reaction against Western scholars studying Asia, see endnote 88.
[50] Richards (1993).

greatest extent, but he also alienated many of the people in his empire, rebellions became more frequent, and the Dutch and British East India Companies took control over India's international maritime trade. The British, who acquired the island and harbor of Bombay in 1661, came into brief conflict with Aurangzeb, which ended by the British negotiators paying reparations to the Mughals. Nevertheless, British Bombay was fortified and continued to grow rapidly into one of the major Indian ports, as did British-held Madras, and then even Aurangzeb was unable to dislodge them. When he died, half of the realm rose in rebellion due to his long oppression. The Mughal Empire never recovered, and the British became one of the major de facto powers on the subcontinent.[51]

THE RUSSIAN EMPIRE

When Tamerlane had invaded Russia, the dukes of Muscovy paid him off or otherwise miraculously, they believed, escaped destruction. The successor state of the lineage of Jochi—better known as the Golden Horde—was not so lucky. Due to the foolish attacks on him by Tokhtamïsh, Tamerlane devastated the Golden Horde lands from south to north. In the mid-fifteenth century[52] it broke into several smaller khanates, including the Kazan Khanate in the area of the Volga-Kama confluence, the Astrakhan Khanate on the Volga River mouth at the Caspian Sea, and the Noghay or Blue Horde of the Khanate of Sibir, whose people nomadized in the Central Steppe south of the Ural Mountains from the Volga east to the Irtysh in Siberia.

In 1547 the grand duke of Moscow, Ivan IV (the Terrible, r. 1533–1584), had himself crowned the first Russian *czar* ('caesar') or 'emperor', declaring Russians to be the Orthodox heirs of the Byzantines and the Russian realm, now the Russian Empire, to be the heir of the Eastern Roman Empire. Russia had already become involved in civil strife within Kazan. Although the Russians had arranged to move into the city peacefully, at the last minute there was yet another shift in the power balance in the city. Ivan then took command of the Russian forces besieging Kazan and captured the city in October 1552.[53] In 1556 the Russians took Astrakhan and added the territory of that khanate to their realm too.

---

[51] This survey of Mughal history depends largely on Richards (1993).
[52] Golden (1992: 317–330).
[53] Perdue (2005: 81).

Meanwhile, in 1563 Kuchum, khan of the Noghay Horde, had defeated and killed the khan of Sibir, a successor state of the Golden Horde located to the east of the Ural Mountains. The khan of Sibir had nominally been the vassal of Ivan IV. Kuchum promptly assumed his Siberian predecessor's position of Russian vassal and sent envoys to present tribute, so the Russian czar, who was busy with the Livonian War at the time, did not protest the takeover. Instead, he awarded to a private family, the Stroganovs, the right to establish settlements east of the Urals and to hire Cossacks to defend them. When the Stroganovs discovered silver and iron in western Siberia, they asked for and received permission to extend their land holdings. They then hired five or six hundred Cossacks under the command of Yermak (Ermak) Timofeyevich. On September 1, 1581, a Cossack force of 840 men[54] armed with guns attacked Khan Kuchum and crushed his forces. On October 25, 1583, Yermak captured the capital, Sibir.[55] Khan Kuchum retreated south to his original territory in the Noghay Horde to assemble an army to attack the Russians, while Yermak wrote to Ivan IV to request reinforcements. The emperor responded by sending money and a force of 500 soldiers. Kuchum marched north and met the Russians in battle. Though Yermak died during the conflict and the Russians had to retreat, they nevertheless retained the territory of the former Khanate of Sibir. In 1587 they constructed the towns of Tobolsk (near Sibir, which had been destroyed) and Tara on the Irtysh River, and in 1598 again defeated Kuchum, who was shortly thereafter killed by his own people. His khanate was annexed by Russia.[56]

With their main local enemies out of the way, there were few obstacles to Russian expansion eastward. What drove the expansion was primarily commerce—above all, the fur trade. Moreover, the Russians were a people of the forest and mixed forest-steppe zones. By expanding eastward through that zone in northern Central Eurasia, they avoided confronting the powerful steppe peoples on their own territory.[57] Using the many rivers and their tributaries as highways, they continued their march eastward. Following the Lena River into the northeast they established Yakutsk in 1632 and, turning

---

[54] Perdue (2005: 86).

[55] This is the traditional, historical name. It has been given various other names in recent times.

[56] This section depends largely on Hosking (2001), Perdue (2005), and Bergholz (1993).

[57] Bergholz (1993: 27).

east, reached the Pacific Ocean and established the first Russian settlement there, Okhotsk, in 1647.[58] The Russians also moved east of Lake Baikal to the Amur River basin. In 1651 they stormed a local town, Albazin, located on the upper Amur where the river turns south. They built and garrisoned a fort on the site and began settling colonists there. The Manchus, who had at that point barely established their authority in China, considered the territory to be theirs due to campaigns of conquest undertaken by Hung Taiji between 1641 and 1643.[59] They strenuously objected to the Russian actions. When diplomacy did not succeed, the Manchus finally attacked and captured Albazin in 1685. The Russians were forced to cede the territory to the Manchus in the Treaty of Nerchinsk in 1689,[60] but they gained trade concessions from the Manchus and continued to maintain themselves at Okhotsk on the Pacific coast.

In other directions, the Russian Empire expanded northwestward into the Finnic-speaking areas of the eastern Baltic. Peter the Great (1672–1725 [r. 1682/1696–1725])[61] defeated the Swedes there in 1703 and founded St. Petersburg, giving the Russians a western port, which he also made the capital of the empire. With this foothold on the Baltic, he immediately ordered construction of a large fleet. The Russians used it to defeat the powerful Swedish navy in 1714, securing and expanding Russian possession of the region.[62] After their defeat of the Ottoman Empire's forces by land and by sea in 1769–1770, the Russians finally incorporated the Crimea into their empire (in 1783). The Black Sea became Russia's southern border.[63] The Russians established a Black Sea fleet, with its home in their new port of Kherson, at the mouth of the Dnieper River.

---

[58] A cossack winter camp was established there in 1647; two years later a stockade was constructed (*GSE* 19: 116). For the founding of Okhotsk, others have 1647 (Perdue 2005: 95), 1648 (Hosking 2001: 143), 1649 (Perdue 2005: 87), or 1650 (Bergholz 1993: 27); I assume the *Great Soviet Encyclopedia* can be trusted on this one. According to Spence (2002: 151), Nerchinsk was founded in 1658 and Albazin in 1665.

[59] Bergholz (1993: 123–127).

[60] In the 1860 Sino-Russian Treaty, the Russians acquired the Ch'ing territory north of the Amur River and east of the Ussuri River, extending down to the northeastern border of Korea (Fletcher 1978: 347). The treaty thus effectively established the modern borders of Russia and China between Mongolia and the sea. The region east of Manchuria is known as Primorskiy Kray 'Maritime Province', or simply 'Primor'e', q.v. chapter 10.

[61] Millar (2003: 1168).

[62] Hosking (2001: 186–187).

[63] Hosking (2001: 231).

With four coasts—the Black, Baltic, Arctic, and Okhotsk seas—under their control the Russians then began expanding southward into the Caucasus and the steppe zone.

THE MANCHU-CHINESE EMPIRE OF THE CH'ING DYNASTY

In 1616 Nurhachi (Nurhači, 1559–1626), the leader of the Jurchen in southern Manchuria north of Liaotung, established a Chinese-style dynasty, the Later Chin, named after the Chin Dynasty of his Jurchen forebears. In 1618 he captured Liaotung from the Ming Chinese and in 1625 moved his capital south to Mukden (Shenyang). In 1636 his son and successor Hung Taiji (1592–1643) changed the dynasty's name to Ch'ing ('Clear') and in 1635 adopted a new ethnonym, Manju (Manǰu) 'Manchu', apparently after the name of the Bodhisattva of wisdom, Mañju-śrî 'Lord Mañju'.[64]

In that year a rebellion broke out against the crumbling Ming, and Peking was taken by the rebels. The Ming government invited the Manchu prince-regent Dorgon in to help quell the rebellion. He defeated the rebels and captured Peking in 1644, but found that the Ming had already collapsed in North China, so instead of returning to Manchuria, the Manchus began their conquest of China, which they completed in 1662.[65]

Like their Jurchen Chin ancestors, and unlike the Mongols, the Manchus were willing to adopt Chinese culture, at least in order to learn better how to rule China.[66] Although they generally did not allow ethnic Chinese to hold the highest administrative positions in the Manchu Empire, Chinese officials were allowed to rise to the level of a provincial governorship within China itself. Like the Mongols before them, the Manchus distinguished between "China" and "the whole Empire," but unlike the Mongols and the Yüan Dynasty, the Manchus and the Chinese considered the Ch'ing Dynasty to be that which ruled the entire empire. Nevertheless, the Manchus

---

[64] On the Manchu conversion to Buddhism and the controversy over their new national name, see endnote 89.

[65] See below. A contingent of Ming loyalists captured the island of Formosa (Taiwan) from the Dutch in 1622 and raided the coast for several decades. The island was finally taken in 1683 (Struve 1984: 256 n. 99). Several memorial steles in Manchu and Chinese were erected on the island and still stand in Tainan.

[66] The Jurchen and Manchu receptivity to Chinese culture—relative to the stronger opposition to it expressed by Mongolic peoples, Turks, and Tibetans—may perhaps be explained by the facts that the Jurchen were not steppe people, they lived at the eastern margin of Central Eurasian culture, and they depended much more on agriculture than the others.

also used dynastic marriages, personal oaths of vassalage, and religious connections to cement their relationships with Central Eurasians, whose territories were mostly not incorporated into the Ch'ing Dynasty system as
provinces, with the notable and very late exception of East Turkistan, which
was made a province, Sinkiang (Xinjiang 'New Territory') shortly before the
end of the dynasty. The fusion of Manchus and Chinese was rapid and
eventually total. The combination produced a powerful Manchu-Chinese[67]
state.

The Manchus were efficient, energetic rulers. Under Ch'ing rule, China
grew quickly in population, and due to the conquests in Central Eurasia, the
territory dominated by the dynasty grew greatly in extent. Like the Europeans who had reached China overland during the Mongol Empire period, the
first Europeans to arrive by sea in the late Ming and early Ch'ing periods
were astounded by the country's prosperity and high cultural level, which
they considered to be far ahead of Europe's. But by this time the Europeans
already had some technology that was ahead of anything known in China.
Recognizing this, the K'ang-hsi Emperor, perhaps the most intelligent of all
Manchu rulers, patronized some of the Europeans, particularly the Jesuits,
who introduced traditional European mathematical astronomy in the seventeenth century.[68] When Manchu-Chinese power eventually began to decline, and European power in Asia increased, the Ch'ing came to see the
Europeans as a military and political threat.

THE JUNGHAR EMPIRE

Following the defeat of the Noghay Horde by the Russians, the Western
Mongols or Oirats who had been part of its confederation were freed and
began expanding into its territory. In 1591 the Russians granted them the
right to trade duty-free in Tara and the other towns of Russian Siberia at
the Oirats' northern frontier, and some did reach Tara in 1606. In 1607–
1608, some of the western Oirat leaders submitted formally to the Russian
emperor, expecting him to defend them against their enemies the Kazakhs

---

[67] I have therefore used the term Manchu-Chinese in most cases as a sort of joint ethnonym for
the Ch'ing Dynasty ruling peoples, parallel to the similar Chinese expression *Man-ch'ing*
'Manchu-Ch'ing', or *Man-Han* 'Manchu-Chinese'.

[68] However, already under the Ming in the sixteenth century the Jesuits—most famously Matteo Ricci—had exerted significant influence on the sciences in China.

and the Eastern Mongols. However, the chief of the Junghars, Khara Khula Khan (d. 1634 or 1635)—a descendant of Esen Taiši (r. 1443–1454, Khan 1453–1454), who had united the Oirats briefly in the previous century[69]—gradually built his prestige and power within a new Oirat confederation, beginning in 1608–1609. Because Russia was undergoing a period of political instability known as the Time of Troubles, the Oirat leaders broke with Russia. When the Russians recovered a few years later (electing as the new emperor Michael Romanov, who founded the Romanov Dynasty), they sent Cossack forces to attack the Oirats and forced them to retreat south in 1612–1613. Following a disastrous winter and a major victory over them by the Eastern Mongols, the Oirats lost much territory and again submitted to the Russians for peace and protection. But the Russians did not produce the expected help against the Eastern Mongols, and by 1623 the Oirats abandoned the Russian agreement. In that year the unified Oirat forces under the command of their titular khan, Baibaghas, who was chief of the powerful Khoshuts, attacked the Eastern Mongols under Ombo Erdeni Khan (d. 1659)[70] and won an indecisive victory. At this time, some of the Oirats—particularly the Torgut—remained implacably opposed to the formation of a unified state; they migrated westward as far as the lower Volga and across it into the North Caucasus Steppe, where they entered into a tributary relationship with the Russian emperor. Another unified Oirat campaign against Ombo Erdeni in 1628–1629 led to victory, and Oirat territory in Jungharia and East Turkistan was once again returned to their control.[71]

In 1630 the Oirat khan, Baibaghas, died and was succeeded by the Khoshut leader Gushi Khan (d. 1655). He and Khara Khula Khan cemented a family alliance by the marriage of Gushi Khan's daughter to Khara Khula's son and heir Baatur Khungtaiji (r. 1635–1653). Khara Khula Khan took the title of Khan himself in 1634, but because he did not belong to the Chinggisid line, many Mongols opposed this move and killed him the following

[69] At its height, his realm "extended from Uriyanghai and the Jurchens in the east to Hami in the west" (Perdue 2005: 59).

[70] He was known to the Russian Cossacks as Altïn Khan and was a Chinggisid (Atwood 2004: 310).

[71] On the name Junghar and its variant spellings and etymology, and the historiographical treatment of the Junghars, see Beckwith (forthcoming-b).

year.[72] This seems not to have affected the family alliance at first. Gushi Khan,[73] and Khara Khula's son and successor Baatur campaigned together against the Kazakhs in 1634–1635.[74] But Gushi Khan, who was a Chinggisid, remained an obstacle to Baatur's goal of achieving a unified Junghar Empire. When Coghtu Taiji, a follower of Ligdan Khan (d. 1634), who had been attacking Dgelugspa monasteries in the Kokonor region, sent his son with an army against Lhasa, the Fifth Dalai Lama asked for help. Gushi Khan then led some 100,000 Khoshut on a campaign against Coghtu Taiji in 1636,[75] and early in 1637 crushed his forces. In the same year he sent a mission to the Manchu emperor in China,[76] and in 1642 was rewarded for his deeds by the Fifth Dalai Lama, who appointed him Khan of Tibet.[77]

Although the southern Mongols had been incorporated into the Manchu Empire by 1634, and in 1635 the Manchus had set up the Mongol Banners in what later became Inner Mongolia,[78] the Manchus themselves were still barely established in China. Until they caught and executed the last legitimate claimant to the Ming throne in 1662,[79] the Manchus remained focused on eliminating all opposition to them in China. Their policy toward Central Eurasia at that time was thus pacifist and noninterventionist toward nearly all factions.

The economy of Central Eurasia, including transcontinental trade, prospered once again under the Junghars.[80] In 1641 Baatur negotiated solutions to conflicts with the Russians and gained access to duty-free trade at Tobolsk, Tara, and Tomsk. These towns prospered from the trade and drew "Bukharan" merchants from Islamic Central Asia, who served as intermediaries.[81] He also built a small fortified capital city and Buddhist monastery at Kubak Zar between Lake Yamish and the Irtysh River, and several other

---

[72] His Junghar predecessor Esen, who also had no Chinggisid blood, had suffered the same fate when he similarly assumed the title.

[73] Ahmad (1970: 187).

[74] This section largely depends on Perdue (2005: 101–107).

[75] Perdue (2005: 105).

[76] Bergholz (1993: 48).

[77] Atwood (2004: 550, 633).

[78] Di Cosmo and Bao (2003: 14). The early banners were 300 men supported by land grants and imperial payments.

[79] Struve (1988: 710).

[80] Gommans (2007: 46–47), who points out that Torgut (Kalmyk) horses from the Volga were sold as far as Köke Khoto in what is now North China.

[81] Perdue (2005: 106), who notes that the Junggars traded "horses, cattle, sheepskins, and furs for handicrafts made of cloth, leather, silk, silver, walrus ivory, and metal."

towns, and brought peasants from Central Asia to cultivate agricultural fields around them. The Junghar capital grew into a major commercial center, where horses, Chinese products, slaves, metals, textiles, glass, and other goods changed hands. The settlement around Lake Yamish "became the largest trading center in Siberia until the designation of Kiakhta as the China trade center in 1689."[82] Baatur had accomplished much in his lifetime, but when he died in 1653, his son and heir Sengge and his other sons fought. The Junghar realm weakened due to the internal strife and Sengge's increasing hostility toward the Russians.[83] Finally Sengge was killed in 1670. His brother Galdan (b. 1644, r. 1671–April 4, 1697), who was a Buddhist monk and had long lived in a Tibetan monastery, renounced his vows and returned home. He executed the brothers who had killed Sengge. He also defeated and killed his father-in-law, the leader of the Khoshuts, in 1676 or 1677; suppressed the rebellion that followed, securing his control over power; and restored good relations with Russia.[84] The Oirats had finally succeeded in building the Junghar Empire, the first major steppe realm since the Mongols of Chinggis Khan.

A Eurasian Renaissance

The Renaissance occurred not only in Western Europe but throughout the Eurasian continent. In many respects it represents the artistic and intellectual apogee of Central Eurasia. While the European achievements in art, architecture, and music are well known, the achievements of the Islamic world, especially in Western Central Asia, Persia, and northern India, and of the Buddhist world, especially in Tibet, are much less well known.

In the Islamic world, the Renaissance had begun at the time of Tamerlane, when Persian poetry attained perfection in the works of Hâfiz. Islamic miniature painting reached its height with the greatest Islamic miniature painter, Bihzad (ca. 1450/1460–ca. 1535), and others of the Timurid school of Herat. In 1522 Shâh Ismâ'îl, who patronized the arts in general, especially miniature painting and architecture, brought Bihzad from Herat to Tabriz.

---

[82] Perdue (2005: 106–107).
[83] Bergholz (1993: 60–61).
[84] Perdue (2005: 108–109), Bergholz (1993: 66–67).

Bihzad introduced the Timurid school of miniature painting and trained a new generation of artists. Together they produced some of the greatest miniature paintings in the Islamic tradition. Shâh Tahmasp was also a patron of Islamic miniature painting, literature, and manuscript production. The most long-lasting accomplishment of Shâh 'Abbâs was the building of a new capital at Isfahan, located in south-central Iran. Its plan was based on the Timurid city plan, with a huge central public square or *maidân* surrounded by beautiful mosques, bazaars, and palaces.

The Persian variant of the Timurid architectural style was brought to perfection in the gemlike buildings of Isfahan. Similarly, the Ottomans blended Islamic and Byzantine architectural forms to produce grand mosques and other monuments in the Ottoman Empire. Throughout the Islamic world, monastic orders grew in numbers and influence, with the accompanying construction of monasteries or *khânqâ*, and other buildings. Mendicant orders and pilgrimage to saints' shrines also became widespread, necessitating the construction of caravanserais and the expansion and beautification of the shrines.

In the Mughal Empire, Akbar built in Delhi and other cities, but especially in Agra, where Babur had built the gardens of Arambagh. Agra was one of the four main capitals of Akbar's long reign and became the main Mughal capital. Artistic works created under his patronage and that of his immediate successors reflect his attempt at an Indian fusion of Islam and Hinduism. The height of the Mughal variant of the Timurid or "Persian-Mughal" architectural style was reached under his son Shâh Jahân, whose crowning achievement was the Taj Mahal (Tâj Mahâl 'Crown of Mahâl'), the mausoleum he built for his beloved wife Mumtaz Mahâl. It has been considered by many architectural historians to be the most perfect monumental building in the world. The Mughals sponsored a brilliant flowering of culture in general in northern India. Many of the great works of Mughal architecture, painting, literature, and music have survived them.

Among the Tibetan-, Mongolian-, Turkic-, and Manchu-speaking Buddhist populations of eastern Central Eurasia, a great intellectual revival took place following the solidification of rule by the Dgelugspa school of Tibetan Buddhism under the leadership of the incarnate Dalai Lama lineage. Buddhist scholars from Tibet, Mongolia, Tuva, China, and neighboring areas produced a vast literature, mostly written in Classical Tibetan, on

Buddhist philosophy and other topics. Tibetan became the "medieval Latin" of "High Asia." Tibetan painters developed uniquely Tibetan styles and produced some of the world's most sublime paintings,[85] while Tibetan architects reached for the skies in soaring buildings, the most famous of which is the Potala in Lhasa, one of the world's most stunning architectural monuments.

---

[85] These paintings (q.v. Combs 2006), however, are mostly ignored by Tibetologists, who are mainly interested not in aesthetics but in other things. The same applies to the study of Tibetan music and literature.

10

The Road Is Closed

Peripheral Conquest and Partition of Central Eurasia

The Junghar Empire, the last great Central Eurasian steppe realm, had barely been established when it was undermined by the 1689 Treaty of Nerchinsk, between the Russians and the Manchu-Chinese Ch'ing Dynasty, which effectively partitioned Central Eurasia between the two powers. The Ch'ing massacre of most of the Junghars in 1756–1757 eliminated them as a significant nation. In the eighteenth century the Ch'ing completed its subjugation of eastern Central Eurasia, including the Eastern Steppe, East Turkistan, and Tibet, and in the nineteenth century the Russians conquered the Caucasus and the last remaining Central Asian khanates. Mongolia and Tibet were not made into Ch'ing provinces and remained semi-independent, but in all of Central Eurasia only the kingdom of Afghanistan survived as a fully independent state—a buffer between the Russians, the Manchu-Chinese, and British India.

The British became the world's maritime superpower. Their empire included, among many other colonies around the globe, most of India, much of Africa and North America, and Australia and New Zealand. But because of the shifting network of alliances within Europe itself, not even the British were able to establish sole, uncontested domination of the high seas.

Under Western European management the volume and value of Asian Littoral zone commerce increased tremendously, attracting people, culture, and technology to the port cities. By the nineteenth century Eurasian commerce, wealth, and power had shifted completely to what had become the Littoral System, and the European-dominated port cities kept growing in size and in economic and political importance. This happened even in the Russian Empire; despite its conquest of a vast swath of Central Eurasia, its capital was on the Baltic Sea, and its strategically most important new city in the late nineteenth century was Vladivostok, on the Sea of Japan, a city that was for long supplied mainly by sea. Unlike Russia, the old peripheral empires founded by non-European Central Eurasians were unable to change quickly enough to avoid destruction, and fell one by one. Mughal India was incorporated into the British Empire; the Qajar Dynasty of Persia replaced the Safavids after a period of Afghan rule, but the country was largely partitioned into Russian and British sectors; and Ch'ing Dynasty China was divided up into European spheres of influence. The Eurasian economy had changed from one focused on the continental-based Silk Road system, with an auxiliary sea-based system in the Eurasian littoral, to a coastal Littoral System alone. Central Eurasia disappeared.

The Manchu Conquests in Central Eurasia

The Manchus knew they had to neutralize or, even better, subjugate the Mongols in order to achieve their dream of reestablishing the empire of their Jurchen ancestors, the Chin Dynasty, without succumbing to the Chin fate, which was to be conquered by the Mongols—though the Manchus apparently did not appreciate the quite different circumstances and background under which that conquest had happened. The Manchus' carefully crafted strategy entailed incorporating the Mongols into their state as participants rather than ordinary subjects. The Mongols, as recent converts to Buddhism, were fervent believers and strongly devoted to the Dalai Lama. The Manchus adopted the same school of Tibetan Buddhism, partly via Mongol teachers, and chose the same patron Bodhisattva and the same fierce Protector as the Mongols, Mañju-śrî and Mahâkâla, respectively. As mentioned above, they even chose Manju (English 'Manchu') as their new national name.[1] Mongol attempts to stave the Manchus off were defeated by the Mongols' constant internecine warfare, the vast resources of the newly established Manchu Empire's Ch'ing Dynasty in China, and the Ch'ing-Russian alliance.

By October 1679 Galdan had completed the Junghars' conquest of East Turkistan as far east as the Kokonor region (which remained in the hands of the Khoshut) and sent a message to the Ch'ing saying of the latter region, "I want it back."[2] He also notified the Manchu emperor that the Fifth Dalai Lama had awarded him the title Boshughtu Khan, 'The Khan with the Heavenly Mandate'. To the Manchu-Chinese, this meant that the Junghar ruler had declared himself to be the equal of the Ch'ing ruler,[3] though they did not yet consider the Junghars to be a threat.

In the 1680s the Manchu-Chinese came close to war with the Russians over the Amur dispute and even attacked the Russian fortress of Albazin on the Amur in 1684 and 1686. They also wanted to maintain and expand their control over the Mongols in the Eastern Steppe. Despite their strong military position in the Amur region, the Manchu-Chinese knew that the Junghars were on friendly terms with the Russians.

In 1687, in connection with the long-running civil war among the Mongols in the Eastern Steppe, Galdan Khan's younger brother was killed by Tüsiyetü Khan, the preeminent leader among the Khalkhas. In revenge, Galdan led the Junghars deep into Mongolia, where they smashed the Khalkha forces. They also captured and plundered Erdeni Zuu (located at Karakorum), the greatest monastic establishment in Mongolia, ostensibly because its abbot, the Jebtsundamba Khutukhtu—the younger brother of Tüsiyetü—had claimed to be of equal rank with the Dalai Lama (the former superior of Galdan, who had long lived as a monk in Tibet). The Khalkhas were shattered and fled in all directions, into Ch'ing, Russian, and Junghar territory.[4] The defeat of the Eastern Mongols by Galdan, ruler of the Junghar Empire, therefore threatened Ch'ing power in Mongolia.

[1] See endnote 89. Their conscious choice of a new ethnonym with Buddhist significance is strikingly similar to the *Taghbač (T'o-pa) experience (q.v. Beckwith 2005b).
[2] Perdue (2005: 140).
[3] Perdue (2005: 140–141).
[4] Perdue (2005: 148–149), Bergholz (1993: 260–261, 267–269).

After Galdan's initial victory in Mongolia in 1687, and another victory over Tüsiyetü Khan in 1688,[5] the only way the Ch'ing could prevent the Junghars from conquering Mongolia and establishing a truly powerful steppe empire—essentially restoring the steppe realm of Chinggis Khan—was to reach a firm peace agreement with the Russians. The Russians too desired peace, partly because of their weakness in the Far East and partly because of Russian losses against the Crimean Tatars much closer to home. The Ch'ing and the Russians both had so much to gain and so little to lose that they quickly reached an agreement and signed the Treaty of Nerchinsk on August 29, 1689, setting the frontier between the two empires and establishing strict rules for international trade.[6] The treaty was to remain the basis for Ch'ing-Russian relations down to the mid-nineteenth century.

Freed from the necessity of fighting the Russians and the possibility that the Junghars would forge an alliance with them, the Manchu-Chinese turned to their Mongol problem. With Tüsiyetü Khan and most of the broken Eastern Mongols already having submitted to the Manchus, who had begun incorporating them into the Manchu banner system,[7] the K'ang-hsi Emperor (r. 1662–1722) formally requested the Dalai Lama to negotiate a peace settlement between the Junghars and the Khalkhas. This had no effect because, unknown to practically everyone, the Fifth Dalai Lama had died in 1682. The regent (*sdesrid*), Sangs-rgyas Rgyamtsho (d. 1705), who had kept the death of the Dalai Lama a secret,[8] was the actual ruler. The regent supported the Junghars in opposition to the Khalkhas in Mongolia and the Khoshuts in the Kokonor region.

By this time, Galdan's nephew Tsewang Rabtan (son of Galdan's assassinated brother Sengge) had grown up and had begun threatening Galdan's power. Galdan's efforts to eliminate him in 1688 failed, and when the khan was away in Mongolia campaigning against the Khalkhas, Tsewang Rabtan attacked Hami. This forced Galdan to return west, where he remained in 1689–1690, attempting to restore his control there. Finally, on June 9, 1690, Galdan led his forces east to again attack Tüsiyetü Khan and his allies,[9]

---

[5] Perdue (2005: 150).

[6] Perdue (2005: 138, 161–171).

[7] Perdue (2005: 151). "The original Ch'ing banners had been composed of companies of 300 men supported by imperial stipends and grants of land" (Liu and Smith 1980: 202).

[8] He announced that the Dalai Lama was in deep meditation.

[9] Perdue (2005: 151).

leaving Tsewang Rabtan as de facto ruler in Jungharia and vicinity from 1690 on. Despite Galdan's apparent strength, he was now in a weaker position, and the Russians, reminded to stick to their treaty by the Manchu-Chinese, refused the Junghar ruler's request for additional troops.

Although Galdan appears to have had no intention of threatening China, and continued to behave as a peaceful neighbor, when he moved eastward along the Kerülen River and then southeast toward Jehol, he is said to have been positioned to attack Peking.[10] However, he was actually so far away, and so much inhabited and fortified Manchu and Chinese territory intervened, that it is hardly conceivable he could have had any such intentions. Quite to the contrary, his location was conveniently close for Ch'ing forces to attack him, and indeed, the Ch'ing intelligence agents eagerly pounced on the fact, arguing that Galdan was weak and vulnerable. Opportunity, not fear, was certainly the motivation for the Manchu-Chinese decision to attack the Junghars. The K'ang-hsi Emperor promptly announced the organization of a great three-pronged military campaign against the Junghars in Mongolia and personally led the armies northward. Nevertheless, the expedition was unsuccessful. A defeat by the Junghars in August was followed by another inconclusive battle in September, by which time the emperor had returned to Peking, evidently due to illness. But with considerable Manchu-Chinese forces still facing Galdan, and more on the way, the Junghar ruler publicly swore an oath that he would move away from the Ch'ing borders. The oath was reported to the emperor, who publicly accepted it but privately hoped he could still catch Galdan. Yet by that time Galdan had indeed moved far from his enemies' reach, and the emperor finally ordered the overextended, undersupplied Ch'ing forces to withdraw.

The subsequent decade of peace seems to have been merely a truce, at least from the Manchu-Chinese perspective: a truce that gave them time to recover their strength to attack the Junghars once more.[11] In 1696 the Ch'ing government was ready for an all-out campaign against Galdan. Again led by the emperor himself, the armies marched north. One wing met Galdan's forces in the Battle of Jao Modo, near Urga (now Ulaanbaatar), on June 12, 1696. The Ch'ing crushed the Junghars, and Galdan's wife was killed. Galdan

---

[10] Spence (2002: 154).

[11] Perdue (2005: 152–159) says that both sides worked on outmaneuvering each other in this period, but it does not seem that the Junghars did anything in particular to this effect.

himself escaped with a small remnant of his forces.[12] The Ch'ing army continued westward after him, pursuing the Junghars without rest. The pressure continued until finally Galdan, reduced to a small, rebellious following, was murdered on April 4, 1697.[13]

Despite the Manchu-Chinese defeat of Galdan, the Junghars remained a great power in Central Eurasia. Tsewang Rabtan (r. 1697–1727), Galdan's nephew, succeeded him and continued to control the central Junghar lands, including Jungharia and East Turkistan.

In Tibet, however, things took a turn for the worse. In connection with the campaigns against Galdan, the K'ang-hsi Emperor learned in 1693[14] or 1696[15] that the Fifth Dalai Lama had actually died in 1682, and that Tibet had been governed since then by his son, the regent Sangs-rgyas Rgyamtsho, a strong partisan of Galdan. The emperor was outraged, though he could do nothing yet. Eventually, under pressure from all sides, the regent installed the Sixth Dalai Lama, Tshangs-dbyangs Rgyamtsho (1683–1706), who had been duly discovered and educated in secret. But the young man was a libertine or a freethinking tantric mystic[16]—to outside appearances there was little difference—who had a talent for composing popular love songs.[17] Opposition to him mounted among religious conservatives, and in 1705 Lhazang Khan of the Khoshuts, with the support of the Manchus, invaded Lhasa. The young Sixth Dalai Lama was taken in captivity to the Kokonor region, where he died on the way under mysterious circumstances in 1706. The Khoshuts installed their own pretender on the throne, with the support of the Ch'ing, but the Tibetans rejected him. When a boy was born in Lithang, eastern Tibet, in 1706 and identified as the Dalai Lama's reincarnation, he was seized by the Manchu-Chinese, who kept him captive in Hsining.

Meanwhile the Tibetans, protesting against the Khoshut actions, requested help from the Junghars. Tsewang Rabtan sent his cousin Tseren (Tsering) Dondub, who led ten thousand Junghars over the forbidding Kunlun

---

[12] Spence (2002: 155). His son was captured by the local ruler of Hami and turned over to the Manchus.

[13] Perdue (2005: 202). He appears to have been poisoned (Perdue 2005: 202–203). According to Ahmad (1970: 322), he committed suicide on June 3, 1697, but this date must be a mistake for the arrival of the news of Galdan's death at the Manchu-Chinese imperial camp (Perdue 2005: 202).

[14] Perdue (2005: 178).

[15] Perdue (2005: 192).

[16] Hoffmann (1961).

[17] There are numerous translations of the love songs of the Sixth Dalai Lama.

Mountains to invade Tibet from the northwest in 1717. They defeated the Khoshut and killed Lhazang Khan in battle.

It is clear that the Junghars saw themselves as the protectors of the Dalai Lama,[18] but they were overly zealous devotees of his Dgelugspa sect, and when they occupied Tibet, Tsewang Rabtan's chief monk oppressed the other sects, causing widespread unrest. To make matters worse, on November 30, 1717, Tseren Dondub, who had previously been a monk in the rival city of Shigatse, ordered Lhasa and its monasteries to be sacked. A relief army sent by the Ch'ing from Hsining was destroyed by the Junghars in September 1718 before it could even get close.[19]

In spring of 1720 a new Ch'ing army marched to Tibet, followed shortly afterward by the young Dalai Lama. The Junghars abandoned Tibet to the Manchu-Chinese, who entered Lhasa unopposed on September 24, 1720 and formally enthroned the Seventh Dalai Lama, Bskal-bzang Rgyamtsho (1708–1757).[20] Their establishment shortly thereafter of a protectorate in Tibet[21] cemented Manchu-Chinese control over all of eastern Central Eurasia except the Junghar dominions in East Turkistan and Jungharia.

Upon the death of Tsewang Rabtan in 1727, his son Galdan Tseren (r. 1727–1745) succeeded as ruler of the Junghars. He reorganized the empire and attempted to push the Manchu-Chinese out of the Khalkha Mongol lands in 1730 and 1731, but he was defeated both times and finally made peace with the Ch'ing in 1739. He then attacked the Kazakhs, who separated the Junghars from their Torgut (Kalmyk) relatives far to the west on the lower Volga. The Junghars established their domination deep into Western Central Asia.

At the same time, the agreement with the Manchu-Chinese included allowance for trade, and the Junghars took full advantage of it. Although of-

---

[18] Certainly Galdan Khan had felt that way and responded angrily to what the Junghars felt was insubordination by the chief Eastern Mongol incarnate lama, the Jebtsundamba Khutukhtu, and the latter's disrespect for the Dalai Lama.

[19] Perdue (2005: 234–235).

[20] Perdue (2005: 234–235), Hoffmann (1961: 178–181).

[21] However, Tibet proper was never incorporated into the Manchu-Chinese Empire or the Ch'ing Dynasty realm, unlike the Kokonor region. Tibet remained a "protectorate" right down to the fall of the Ch'ing Dynasty in 1911. It was an independent country with a resident *Manchu* protector (and his personal guard, consisting of a few Manchu-Chinese troops), who exercised the oversight of a suzerain but no formal sovereignty or de facto control over the Tibetans' administration of their country. The casual opinions of contemporaries are irrelevant.

ficial Junghar trade missions were allowed only every other year, the Manchu-Chinese government representatives of border towns were ordered to be lenient, so the Junghars actually traded at the frontier every year. A very high percentage of the Junghar traders were not Mongol ethnically or nomads by occupation, but Turkic Muslims from the cities of East Turkistan or further west. The caravans "were dominated by experienced Central Asian merchants who moved bulk goods and currency along the ancient Silk Roads. In 1748, for example, of a total of 136 men, 46 were Mongols and 90 were Turkic Muslims (Chantou Hui). Three of the four headmen of the caravan were Turkic."[22] To give an idea of the amount of trade involved in one of these official trade missions, in 1750 the Junghars "brought goods worth 186,000 taels, the largest amount ever, which they exchanged for 167,300 taels' worth of cloth and tea, with the balance in silver."[23] The Junghars certainly profited from the trade, as did the urban peoples and merchants involved.

Like all Central Eurasian nomad rulers, the Junghars were intensely interested in fostering trade and, to that end, minted their own coins to unify the diverse currencies of the different petty states in their territory of East Turkistan.[24] The prosperity of Central Eurasia increased markedly under the Junghars at least into the mid-eighteenth century,[25] even after the death of Galdan Tseren in 1745 and that of his successor in 1750, despite the subsequent contested succession and civil war in the Junghar Empire.

The Junghars, however, were devastated not only by civil war but by natural disasters that included a smallpox epidemic. Finally, when Amursana, the leader of one Junghar faction, went to the Ch'ing leaders, offering to submit if they would appoint him head of the Junghar nation, the Manchu-Chinese saw their chance. By the time the two Ch'ing armies arrived, the Junghars had fragmented and lost the support of allies and subjects such as the Kazakhs. The Ch'ing forces quickly defeated the Junghars and occupied Jungharia in 1755.[26] Subsequently, the Junghars made an attempt to regain their independence under Amursana. He led the remaining independent-

---

[22] Perdue (2005: 263–264).

[23] Perdue (2005: 265). A tael or Chinese ounce was equivalent to slightly less than forty grams, or a little more than a troy ounce.

[24] Perdue (2005: 392–393).

[25] Cf. Millward (2007: 92–94).

[26] Perdue (2005: 256–265), Millward (2007: 94–95).

minded Junghars in a "rebellion" against the Manchu-Chinese, who after two years of concerted efforts could not catch him. The Ch'ien-lung Emperor went nearly mad with fury and frustration. In the winter of 1756–1757 he ordered that the Junghars be exterminated. His armies massacred nearly half of the Junghar people, including men, women, and children; the majority of the remainder died of smallpox or starvation; only about 10 percent of the Junghars, mainly women and children, survived. They and other Junghars who had previously surrendered to the Ch'ing were moved away from Jungharia and settled among other peoples who were considered more loyal. Amursana, who had received insufficient support from the exhausted and weakened Junghar people, died of smallpox on September 21, 1757, while in Tobolsk seeking support from the Russians.[27] The massacre of the Junghars and the subjugation of the Torgut (Kalmyks)—those on the Volga by the Russians and those who later returned east to Jungharia (to escape the Russians) by the Manchu-Chinese—destroyed the power of the Western Mongols, the last free steppe people.

The leaders of East Turkistan, deprived of their Junghar protectors, now found themselves under direct Ch'ing pressure. But despite their valiant attempt to emulate the Junghars and repel the Manchu-Chinese, they were defeated in 1759. Ch'ing power was thus established throughout Eastern Central Asia,[28] which came to be called in Chinese Sinkiang (Xinjiang) 'New Territory' during the Manchu campaigns there.[29] The Manchu-Chinese replaced the Junghar imperial coinage of East Turkistan with Manchu-Chinese coins they began minting in Yarkand in 1759. But the once robust economy of East Turkistan, the plum over which eastern Eurasian empires fought for almost two millennia, had already begun to decline. After the Ch'ing conquest, not only East Turkistan (Xinjiang) but even Kansu (Gansu) and other largely Chinese regions that bordered on Central Eurasia actually had to be subsidized with taxes drawn from the wealthier central provinces of China.[30] The economic and cultural destruction of Central Eurasia had begun.

[27] Perdue (2005: 275–288).
[28] Perdue (2005: 291).
[29] Perdue (2005: 32), Millward (2007: 97).
[30] Perdue (2005: 392–393), Millward (2007: 103, 116).

European Domination of Eurasia from the Littoral

In the century following the Manchu-Chinese conquests in eastern Central Eurasia, the Russians conquered and colonized Western Central Asia, while the British displaced the Mughals as rulers of most of the Indian subcontinent. All three powers established tightly controlled borders around their empires. This effectively closed Central Eurasia.[31] Though the fall of the Junghar steppe empire had been a blow to the Central Eurasian Silk Road economy, it was in itself not the fatal blow. The death stroke was delivered by the Russian and Manchu-Chinese politicians who crafted the Treaty of Nerchinsk of 1689 and the Treaty of Kiakhta in 1727, establishing strict, exclusive controls over international trade.

After 1689, refugees, deserters, and tribespeople had to be fixed as subjects of either Russia or China. Maps, surveyors, border guards, and ethnographers began to determine their identities and their movements. The treaties served both empires internally and externally by stabilizing movements across borders and enabling the suppression of groups who did not fit into imperial definitions of space.[32]

In fact, the closing of the borders, severe restriction of international trade, and elimination of all significant Central Eurasian polities destroyed the economy of Central Eurasia. Both the internal component of the Silk Road economy and its long-distance component were thus largely put out of business.[33] The direct result was the severe impoverishment of Central

---

[31] Although the British in India still wanted to trade with Central Eurasia, they had insufficient patience with Asian politicians. In 1904 the British invaded Tibet, defeated the Tibetan forces opposing them, and imposed their own terms.

[32] Perdue (2005: 161).

[33] Certainly it did not entirely disappear. Virtually nothing ever *entirely* disappears, and caravans of one sort or another have continued down to our own day. But that does not mean the Silk Road economy continued its former importance right down to modern times, as has been claimed by some—for example, Millward (2007: 76–77), who, however, actually provides many explicit examples that demonstrate the exact opposite: trade in Central Eurasia actually declined precipitously after the destruction of the Junghar Empire. It is difficult not to see that Central Eurasia, including Central Asia, the heart of the Silk Road economy, became impoverished and strikingly backward technologically (as well as intellectually and artistically) long before the twentieth century.

Eurasia—especially its center, Central Asia—and its rapid plunge backward into darkness in technology and every other aspect of culture.

Because the peripheral empires were partly dependent upon international trade, and traditionally by far the most important part of it had been conducted by land with Central Eurasia, they harmed themselves too. But by this time they had an alternative to the Silk Road: the new, fast growing Littoral System. Despite their lack of interest in getting involved seriously in maritime trade themselves, the Manchu-Chinese already profited from the silver trade with the Spanish. While the Russians had reached Central Asia in the west, from which they could obtain Oriental goods directly, their treaty with China allowed them to obtain East Asian products directly as well, and their possession of ports on the seas around them gave them access to the developing Littoral System.

It is not surprising that the great peripheral powers of continental Asia did not have as highly developed naval and navigational technology as the Europeans and therefore could not fight the latter at sea. This may be explained by their Central Eurasian origins and traditional continental orientation. Yet the continental powers also seem not to have made any attempt to acquire the technology or at least to hire mercenary Europeans to help them take control of their own coastal trade. It is clear not only that they paid little attention to the Littoral route commerce[34] but also that they did not understand it and did not take advantage of their political power on land to attempt to control it or profit by it.[35] Accordingly, the Western European littoral countries Portugal, Spain, Holland, Great Britain, and France acquired or opened trading ports and naval bases almost at will all around eastern Eurasia from Persia to Japan. The development of these ports into the dominant great metropolises of Asia as a whole, coupled with the Italian and Ottoman Empire control of most of the Mediterranean, established the Littoral System as the only functioning international economy in Eurasia by the nineteenth century.

---

[34] Pearson (1987: 26–27).

[35] Millward (2007) notes that although some Manchu-Chinese officials advocated turning to the littoral instead of the interior, tradition and strategic worries kept the Ch'ing government focused on Central Eurasia. It seems likely that the strategic worries expressed in the sources were not real, contemporary threats but traditional ones.

Japan and the Completion of Littoral Domination of Eurasia

For some two millennia local Littoral zone trade had extended around the coast of Eurasia from northwestern Europe to northeastern Asia, where its terminus was the Japanese Archipelago. Japan was founded by migrants who had traveled there by sea and colonized the islands sometime in the first millennium BC. They continued to trade with the neighboring areas of northeastern Asia, especially the Korean Peninsula, and eventually developed the skill to be able to sail against the current to China and beyond.

By the time Europeans reached the country—the first were two or three Portuguese merchants who arrived aboard a Chinese ship in 1543[36]—Japan was a highly civilized, populous land that produced silks, swords, and other products the Europeans coveted and wanted to purchase. The Europeans brought firearms and other products unknown in Japan, though the bulk of their trade items came from nearby China. The Japanese were part of the old pre-European, local Littoral zone trade route system, so they were accustomed to international commerce and were willing to trade. But the Europeans brought something else new that was not as welcome: Christianity.

The bigotry of the Portuguese Jesuits, who had introduced Christianity to Japan shortly after they first arrived, and the attraction to Christianity of separatist political groups, eventually provoked an extreme reaction. The civil war that racked Japan during the sixteenth century ended with the reunification of much of Japan by General (*shôgun*) Toyotomi Hideyoshi in the 1590s.[37] He decreed the suppression of Christianity in 1597 and ordered the Jesuit missionaries to leave, though he did not actually enforce his edict.[38] However, the persistence of the missionaries, especially some newly arrived Spanish Franciscans, who were preaching in the imperial capital Kyoto itself, and the revelation of apparent designs on Japan by the Spanish government, led Hideyoshi to drastic measures. Twenty-six Christians, including Franciscans, Jesuits, and Japanese converts, were executed, and on February 5, 1597,

---

[36] Elisonas (1991: 302).

[37] Hall (1991: 4). This was the Momoyama Period, in which the *shôgun*'s capital was still in the Kansai region, at Hideyoshi's castle in Osaka.

[38] Elisonas (1991: 360–363).

Hideyoshi issued an edict proscribing Christianity in Japan.[39] Upon his sudden death in 1598 during the Japanese-Korean-Chinese War (1592–1598),[40] a succession struggle broke out that was finally won by Tokugawa Ieyasu (1542–1616) at the Battle of Sekigahara in 1600. The continuing separatist movement, which had come to have a strong Christian element, finally led the Tokugawa to expel the Portuguese in 1639 and cut relations with all Catholic countries. After 1635, travel abroad by Japanese was punishable by death. Japan was effectively closed.[41]

Although Japan was then almost completely inaccessible to Europeans, one trading post operated by the Dutch, who were Protestants, was allowed to remain at Nagasaki—on an artificial island, Dejima, specially constructed for the purpose. Through this office some of the advances of European science and technology, and glimpses of the knowledge about the rest of the world that had been acquired by Europeans, slowly filtered into Japan.

The more than two-century-long isolation of Japan was broken when the Americans, exasperated by Japanese refusal to negotiate the return of American sailors shipwrecked in Japan, or even of Japanese sailors shipwrecked in America, sent a naval expedition under Commodore Matthew C. Perry, who reached Edo Bay in 1853. The Japanese were forced to sign a treaty in 1854 that effectively opened the country to American ships. Later in 1854 the British negotiated a similar treaty, and in 1855 so did the Russians.[42] The resulting sudden introduction of European and American people, ideas, and technology triggered a revolutionary movement. A coup d'état in January 1868 overthrew the Shogunate and restored the imperial family to power. Edo, where the Tokugawa Shogunate had been based, became the imperial capital, renamed Tokyo.[43] Under Emperor Meiji's[44] enlightened rule (r. 1866 [1868]–1912), Japan adopted European and American ways. In the incredibly short space of less than four decades, the Japanese modernized their industry and created a European-style army and navy, with which they as-

[39] Elisonas (1991: 363–364).
[40] Asao (1991: 70–73).
[41] Elisonas (1991: 369).
[42] Beasley (1989: 270–271).
[43] *Tôkyô* 'Eastern Capital' was thus contrasted with the old imperial capital *Kyôto* 'the Capital'.
[44] Actually, Meiji is the name of his reign period, so he should properly be called "the Meiji emperor," along the lines now traditional for Manchu-Chinese emperors of China.

tonished the Russians and the world by winning the Russo-Japanese War in 1905.[45]

There are some important reasons why Japan "modernized" or "Westernized" so quickly and became the lone Asian power among the otherwise exclusively European and American group of nations ruling most of the world in the late nineteenth and early twentieth centuries. As an island country, Japan was a Littoral zone culture familiar with ships, the sea, and maritime trade. Compared to the peoples of the continental Asian empires founded by Central Eurasians, there was not as much of a conceptual or practical gap for the Japanese to bridge in order to catch up with the European maritime powers. Japan also had an unusually high literacy rate, partly due to the "temple school" system. And finally, the country had not in reality been completely closed but had slowly assimilated some of the most important developments of European science via the "Dutch learning," translations of books acquired through the Dutch trading post in Nagasaki harbor.

The Great Urban Shift to the Littoral

The European establishment of shipping routes directly to South Asia, Southeast Asia, and East Asia eventually bypassed Southwest Asia completely. At first, Persia and the rest of the Near East, which had profited from international trade for some two millennia, did not lose much, and under the early Safavids Persia was still fairly strong. Trade flourished for a time at the British and Dutch trading posts authorized by Shah 'Abbâs at Bandar 'Abbâs, the small Persian Gulf town that replaced Hormuz as the dominant Persian port after the British and Persians ousted the Portuguese there in 1622.[46]

For a number of reasons,[47] however, the Persian trade was relatively unprofitable for the Europeans. The British, under pressure from the Dutch, moved their trading post to the deepwater port of Basra, located at the head

---

[45] They had earlier won the Sino-Japanese War of 1894–1895. The most significant Japanese territorial gains from the latter were Korea and Taiwan.

[46] Savory (1995: 772), Matthee (1999: 105–106).

[47] Partly, Safavid government control over commerce and industry; see above.

of the Persian Gulf. Basra, founded by the Arabs in the seventh century, had been one of the most important western termini for the shipping of the old local Littoral route before the European discovery of the sea route around Africa. In the second half of the seventeenth century, the Dutch attacked and destroyed the British post in Basra and completely dominated the Persian Gulf, but their shipping to Persia subsequently decreased along with the decline of the Safavid Empire and growth of piracy in the region during the early eighteenth century.[48]

The Ottoman Empire and the Middle East in general had already been undergoing a long, slow cultural, political, and economic decline. The southern ports of the region were or became backwaters, local centers for the continuing traditional regional point-to-point trade between India, Persia, Arabia, Ethiopia, and Egypt. The great new high-volume international commerce of the Littoral System increasingly bypassed the shrinking economy of the Middle East. By the late eighteenth century, Persia was in very poor economic condition: the British East India Company reported that "the comparison between the past and present state of Persia, in every respect, will be found truly deplorable."[49] Despite the continued regional importance of Basra, it never grew into a great Littoral city. Bandar 'Abbâs once again became a sleepy little town, and no new Persian port ever rose up to take its place. Despite its long coastline, Persia remained a continental country completely oriented to the interior and determinedly reactionary in almost every respect.[50]

The contrast between the history of the Middle East and that of the Asian littoral to the east of Persia is striking. None of the eventual great port cities of Asia east of the Persian Gulf existed as such in the sixteenth century; those that existed at all were fishing villages or small towns. Even the major ports of the old Littoral trade route were quite small, and their rulers so unimportant that they were largely left to themselves by the imperial powers; Calicut and many others were all but independent. That changed completely over the course of the three centuries after the Portuguese con-

---

[48] Savory (1995: 772–773).

[49] Savory (1995: 774), quoting Issawi (1971: 86).

[50] It is remarkable that even the opening of the Suez Canal—a European project from start to finish—did not succeed in resuscitating commerce in the Middle East itself, not to speak of intellectual and artistic life. Since the decline of the Safavids, the only significant (though short-lived) exception to this turn into darkness in Persia was the Pahlavi Dynasty in the mid-twentieth century. The fate of that regime sums up the problem of the Middle East to this day.

quest of the sea routes to the East. In virtually all instances, the great cities that developed along the Asian coast by the end of the nineteenth century were founded by Europeans or grew under their influence from villages into cities because of the rapid growth of maritime trade. While the inland cities focused increasingly on the past and became centers of conservative or reactionary movements, the new coastal cities were points of transfer for culture and technology and became the dominant political and economic centers in Asia.

INDIA

Delhi, the inland capital of the late Mughal Dynasty in North India, became a neglected, old-fashioned town, surpassed by Bombay, the early British East India Company capital, and by the later British colonial capital at Calcutta. Delhi began to recover only when the British moved their capital to the city in 1911.

The deepwater harbor of Bombay (now Mumbai), one of the few on the western coast of India, was largely unknown before the Portuguese acquired it from the sultan of Gujerat in 1534, along with most of the northwestern coast from Bombay to Diu. After the British received Bombay as part of the dowry of Charles II's Portuguese bride Caterina according to the Anglo-Portuguese Treaty of 1661,[51] the new owners greatly encouraged commerce there and the city grew rapidly[52] until it achieved unrivaled importance in the western Indian Ocean.

Calcutta (now Kolkata), located in the delta of the Ganges River, was founded by the British East India Company in 1690 and secured by the building of Fort William a decade later. Calcutta became the center of British commercial interests in eastern India. During the following centuries, the British gradually established their power over the entire Indian subcontinent. Calcutta was made the capital of the British colonies in India in 1772 and grew until it became the greatest city of India.

BURMA

The capitals of Burma before the British conquest, including Pagán (on the Irrawaddy River about ninety miles southwest of Mandalay, Ava (a few miles

---

[51] Newitt (2005: 258, 245).
[52] Conlon (1985).

south of Mandalay, and Mandalay, were all located in the north, far away from the coast and its port towns. Rangoon, an old Mon settlement at the mouths of the Irrawaddy River, was occupied by the British during and after the First Anglo-Burmese War (1824–1826).[53] When the British won the Third Anglo-Burmese War in 1885, they moved the capital of the country to Rangoon.[54] Though it began as a small colonial city, Rangoon soon became the commercial and political center of Burma and an important metropolis.

THAILAND

Thailand was the only Southeast Asian country to escape colonization or political domination by Europeans, perhaps because the Thais recognized their danger in time and responded to the change in economic and political conditions. Ayutthaya (Ayodhya), about 100 kilometers from the sea (though actually accessible by river for small ships), was the Thai capital up to the Burmese invasion and destruction of the city in 1767.[55] During the subsequent reconquest of the kingdom, the Thai king Taksin moved the capital to a port town on the Chao Phraya River, "Thonburi, which being only twenty kilometers from the sea was better suited for seaborne commerce."[56] Taksin was succeeded by Rama I (r. 1782–1809), who moved the capital across the river to Bangkok. It is possible that by moving the capital to the Littoral early enough, more than anything else, Taksin and Rama effectively saved Thailand from European colonization.[57] Bangkok grew in population and wealth, while Ayutthaya became a rural town with the crumbling ruins of former Thai royal splendor.

MALAYA

Singapore was founded by the British agent Sir Thomas Raffles in 1819 on the site of a sleepy local port town that then had a population of about a thousand people.[58] It is an ideal harbor, strategically situated at the southern

---

[53] Thant Myint-U (2001: 18–20).

[54] Bečka (1995: 217).

[55] Wyatt (2003: 122). "When the Portuguese captured Malacca in 1511, they immediately sent a mission to Ayutthaya . . . [;] in 1518 a third mission confirmed the peace pact concluded in 1511. . . . Siamese international commerce must have kept up with the steady growth in seaborne trade that followed, *doubling* between about 1500 and 1560" (Wyatt 2003: 74, emphasis added).

[56] Wyatt (2003: 124).

[57] On early European commercial and political relations with Ayutthaya, see Wyatt (2003: 95–104).

[58] Joo-Jock (1991: 6).

tip of the Malayan Peninsula and the southern edge of the South China Sea, at the entrance to the Straits of Malacca, the main shipping channel leading to the Indian Ocean in the west.[59] As it was located midway between China and India on the busy European-dominated shipping routes, it soon eclipsed all other cities between India and China in commercial importance.

CHINA

By the late nineteenth century the position of the Ch'ing Dynasty capital at Peking (Beijing) as the leading cultural and commercial city of China had been lost to the burgeoning European trading ports along the coast. The adherents of a growing Chinese popular uprising against foreigners and the Manchu-Chinese government, the Boxer Rebellion, were brought to Peking and given imperial troops by the Empress Dowager. They attacked the foreign legations there, and many foreigners and Christian converts were killed. An international force consisting mainly of Russians, British, French, Americans, Italians, and Japanese defeated the Boxers and government forces in August 1900, destroying parts of Peking and other cities in the process.[60] The international alliance imposed staggering indemnities on the Ch'ing Dynasty and also took further control of the country. The international port cities continued to grow, but Peking sank under the weight of bureaucratic corruption, inertia, and xenophobia. It still looked to the past and its roots in continental Central Eurasia.

By the end of the nineteenth century, the entire China coast was not only dominated by Europeans and Japanese, but was effectively ruled by one or another European power. In 1841 the British took possession of the island of Hong Kong,[61] across the Pearl River estuary from Portuguese Macao. By the end of the century, dozens of cities on the China coast were open to foreigners, but by far the most important of them was the port of Shanghai, which had been opened to European colonists in 1843 and grew from "a small country town" to become "the metropolis of China" because of its location in the Yangtze delta on the China coast midway between Canton in the south and Tientsin and Japan in the north.[62] It was divided into politically separate foreign "concessions," which were outposts of the home countries'

---

[59] Joo-Jock (1991: 12).
[60] Hsu (1980: 118–125).
[61] Wakeman (1978: 199–201).
[62] Fairbank (1978: 224, 237 et seq.).

cultures. With the decline of the Ch'ing Dynasty, Shanghai grew rapidly in size and influence, soon becoming the commercial and financial center of China and one of the largest cities in the world. The modern view held by Chinese and Sinologists alike that the shift of power to the Littoral was due to the Europeans is correct. Its cause, however, was not imperialistic colonization but international commerce, as some Chinese officials understood but were unable to convince their government to do anything about; the regime's continental fixation was unshakable.[63]

JAPAN

The age-old imperial capital of Kyoto is surrounded by mountains deep inside the Kansai region of western Japan. Most Japanese capitals were in that region until after the Portuguese had been trading with Japan for half a century. The capital of the Tokugawa Shogunate was then established in the port town of Edo, in the Kanto region of Eastern Japan. During the following period of self-imposed isolation, Japan's imperial capital remained at Kyoto, while the de facto capital remained at Edo, which grew into a great metropolis. In 1868, shortly after the Americans forcibly reopened Japan to the world, the Tokugawa Shogunate was overthrown and in the following year Edo was made the official capital, renamed Tokyo. The former Tokugawa castle there became the imperial palace.[64] Kyoto, which remained a secondary capital, did not change much. It continued to be an important, though much smaller, city, noted for its monuments, cultural conservatism, and political liberalism.

RUSSIA

The city of St. Petersburg was founded by Peter the Great in 1703 on territory he had just captured from the Swedes that year. He moved the Russian imperial capital there in 1712.[65] After his victory over Sweden, Russia became a minor naval power in Europe. The eastern extremity of the Russian Empire ended at the Sea of Okhotsk, named after the small port town of Okhotsk, which, though blocked by ice for much of the year, was the main Russian port in the Pacific until the mid-nineteenth century.[66] In 1858 the territory of Primor'e (or

---

[63] Millward (2007: 126–127). He notes quite rightly that to a great degree the fixation continues down to the present day.

[64] Frédéric (2002: 624); cf. Jansen (1989).

[65] *GSE* (14: 380). St. Petersburg was the imperial capital from 1712 to 1728 and from 1732 to 1918.

[66] *GSE* (19: 116).

Primorskiy Kray, 'the Maritime Province'), which had been assigned to the Manchus under the Treaty of Nerchinsk in 1689, came under Russian control. In 1860 the Russians founded Vladivostok, on the Sea of Japan at the southern tip of Primor'e, near Korea and China.[67] It grew very rapidly, becoming a city in 1880. After the completion of the Trans-Siberian Railway in 1903, Vladivostok became a large, prosperous city and Russia's major Pacific port.[68]

The Silk Road System and the Littoral System

The development of a continental, land-based international trade system dates to prehistoric times. Although international trade by sea also began very early, it appears to have been strictly local until the Bronze Age, when ship-borne trade expanded to cover the Mediterranean and even extended via the Atlantic as far as Britain. In the east, the sea routes were less protected and perhaps for that reason long continued to be more local, but no later than Classical Antiquity local maritime trade flourished all around the Asian littoral and indirect maritime trade connected East Asia with the Near East. That is, ships traveled along the coast back and forth between one port and the next; the same ship did not sail directly even between East Asia and India, though individual merchants did begin traveling the entire route no later than mid-T'ang times in China, when a large population of Arab and Persian merchants resided in Canton (Guangzhou). This local, "internal" point-to-point trade was however not distinct from the "internal" continental trade of the Silk Road.

Throughout history up until early modern times, there was no sharp line or distinction drawn between international trade conducted overland, by rivers, or by sea. But the partition of Central Eurasia effectively eliminated that world area as a significant link in the Eurasian economy as a whole, and a distinction between the two did appear. The Silk Road system—though, practically speaking, it no longer existed—then truly became a counterpart of the seaborne commerce of Eurasia, which is thenceforth properly known as the Littoral System. Before this time, although it might be thought ideal to ascribe equal importance to the Silk Road trade routes and the Littoral

---

[67] The Russians sold Alaska to the Americans shortly afterward, in 1867, ending their direct participation in the European conquest of the Americas.

[68] *GSE* (5: 539).

zone trade routes, they were not equal. Even the most superficial perusal of, for example, the major historical sources in Chinese, Arabic, and Persian for the medieval period, and right up to the closing of the Silk Road, reveals that, except for the internal politics of the authors' home regions, the sources are focused above all on Central Eurasia, to which they give an amazing amount of detailed attention. By contrast, the Littoral zone is barely mentioned and it is difficult to find out much about it except in foreign (mainly European) sources.[69] This remarkable difference deserves some attention.

While the great peripheral states of Eurasia were deeply interested in Central Eurasia—especially Central Asia—from the time of the Scythians down to the end of the Junghar Empire, and spent a great amount of time, money, and energy on policies directed toward that area, none of the states on the Eurasian coast were noticeably invested in the Littoral trade route. Even the Byzantine Empire, which would seem to be a littoral state par excellence, was not founded on or sustained by international maritime trade—though the Byzantines certainly did profit by it—but rather by taxes and tribute imposed on subject peoples in lands conquered by the Romans and retained or reconquered by the Byzantines. Similarly, the Mughals received the overwhelming majority of their income internally, despite the active international trade conducted (mostly overland) by fellow Muslims between India and the Near East. And although China was involved in Littoral route maritime trade already in Han times via Canton, it must be stressed that even in the T'ang period Canton was a distant, uncouth frontier town, small in size compared to the great cities of the north, and of note (if at all) only because of its heavily non-Chinese population.

The same was true of all the known ports of the old Littoral route from England to Egypt (via the Mediterranean) and from Arabia to Japan. The great capital cities and metropolises were never seaports themselves, though they were typically located on major rivers and were often close to ports. In Europe, Constantinople comes to mind as the outstanding exception, and London[70] is accessible by navigable river, making it a port, but even today most West and East European capitals are continental. Paris is inland. Ber-

---

[69] This is true even for Antiquity.

[70] However, in the Early Middle Ages the capital of the leading Anglo-Saxon kingdom, Mercia, was solidly inland.

lin is inland. Rome is inland. Athens is inland. Madrid is inland.[71] The major capital cities of the Near East—Cairo, Jerusalem, Damascus, Mecca, and Baghdad, as well as the historical capitals of Persia (Susa, Persepolis, Ctesiphon, Isfahan, Tehran, and others)—are all inland. Further east, Delhi in India; Pagán, Toungoo (Taungoo), Ava, and Mandalay in Burma; Ayudhya (Ayutthaya) in Thailand; Ch'ang-an (now Xi'an), Loyang (Luoyang), and Peking (Beijing) in China; Pyongyang and Seoul in Korea; and Nara and Kyoto in Japan, are all inland. If Littoral route commerce had been the lifeblood of any of these countries, this distribution would not make any sense, and the movement in the last centuries of the second millennium AD also would not make sense. Even in the case of Athens, a commercially oriented city-state, Thucydides notes that the city's location nine miles inland was chosen out of fear of piracy, as in the case of the other old Greek cities.[72] Before the Littoral System came to dominate the world, fear of the sea and its denizens prevented most states from having much to do with it.

That would seem to account for the fact that trade along the coast had existed for time out of mind, mostly "under the radar": no one ever paid much attention to it until very late in history. While it was certainly profitable for the merchants involved in it, as testified to by actual historical and geographical accounts, as well as by the Sindbad stories of the *Thousand and One Nights* and other romantic tales, it seems to have been overlooked that states of all shapes and sizes that had coastline along the Eurasian continent did not build their great cities there. The people in these states, including the rulers, were on the whole interested in trade, even if they rarely mentioned it publicly—Chinese and Romans, in particular, looked down on merchants and commerce, and rarely discussed it in their literature—but the fact

---

[71] Oddly, all Scandinavian countries have ports as their capital cities, but none of these countries were prominent during the Age of Exploration and in the establishment of the Littoral System. On the other hand, Lisbon, the capital and leading city of Portugal, though not historically a great metropolis, was and is a port and figured prominently in the pioneering explorations and conquests of the Portuguese, who are ultimately responsible for the establishment of European power in the Asian Littoral.

[72] Lattimore (1998: 6) translates: "As for cities, those built later in a time of increased seafaring and with more abundant wealth were fortified establishments right on the coast and occupied the isthmuses for trade as well as defense against their neighbors. The old cities, however, on account of the long survival of piracy, were usually built away from the sea, whether on the islands or the mainland (for the pirates raided both one another and the nonseafaring populations of the coast), and are inland settlements to this day."

remains that not a single politically significant Asian city[73] was actually located on the coast at the beginning of the European Age of Exploration, and some states (most notably the Mughal Empire) did not even bother to establish direct control over much of their own coastal territory; they let it be ruled by local potentates who had submitted nominally to them. By contrast, though Mecca, Damascus, Baghdad, Delhi, Ch'ang-an, and other capitals were inland, they were merchant cities as well as centers of political power, as were all the cities of Central Eurasia.

The focus of traditional states everywhere in Eurasia was control of land. To accomplish that goal it was necessary to hold the territory with walled fortified cities, the terms for which are often translated incorrectly as 'forts' or 'fortresses'. In early medieval terminology all across Eurasia, there is usually only one unitary word for the two English concepts—Arabic *madîna*, Persian *shahristân*, Old Tibetan *mkhar*, Chinese *ch'eng* (城), Archaic Koguryo *kuru*, and so on—because it was in fact one thing: an urbanized area surrounded by fortified walls. In order to maximize the control effected by each of these 'fortified cities', and to better protect them from capture by enemies or defection to them, or to hold firmly onto them and prevent them from trying to become independent, they were best located well inside a country's territory. The frontiers of each state were thus by definition the furthest places from the controlling political power. Merchants, then as always, relished the freedom to trade with as little interference or taxation as possible. At the frontiers they could do business without attracting much attention to themselves.

The simple physical geographical facts about Western Europe, Arabia, Southeast Asia, and Northeast Asia discouraged the creation and maintenance of large empires there. This created more frontiers and simultaneously encouraged local international trade by sea. Although the Japanese and Koreans are known to have traded intensively with each other from the earliest records on, and while they also traded somewhat with China, they did not sail further. Far to the south, from Canton to Southeast Asia and from thence to India, there was again considerable regional trade by sea.

---

[73] Tokugawa Ieyasu moved to Edo, in the Kanto region, as part of a trade made with his then ally Tokugawa Hideyoshi. The town became the de facto capital when he became sole ruler of Japan in 1600. Edo, the future Tokyo, was at the time still just a local port, though it was famous for horses, an important resource for the army. Even today several prominent locales in central Tokyo have names connected to horse rearing.

The trade passed from Bengal down to Ceylon and ports in southern India, and from there on to ports on the western Indian coast, Persia, Arabia, and Egypt, always keeping close to land. Commerce was very important indeed in the kingdoms of southern Southeast Asia, especially in the long-lived kingdom of Srivijaya, centered on Sumatra and the southern Malay Peninsula, but the power of the realms in that region seems nevertheless to have rested primarily on agriculture, much of their wealth on natural resources (particularly gold), and their military strength mainly on armies, as in the rest of Asia. In Europe, there was a good deal of commerce in the Baltic Sea and North Sea, and from the Early Middle Ages onward there were a number of important trading towns—not quite cities until rather late—yet rarely did ships sail south into the Mediterranean, a distant and dangerous voyage.

Moreover, there were no large thalassocracies—maritime-based empires—anywhere in the Littoral zone.[74] Some of the realms built by the ancient Greeks (who coined the term *thalassocracy*) may have been exceptions, but they were not very large, and in any case do not seem to have been *based* on commerce, though they fostered it and prospered from it.[75] The greatest merchants of the Early Iron Age, the Phoenicians, who traded as far as Spain, seem not to have established an actual empire to support their trade.[76] Nor, later on, did the far-ranging Vikings, or the Muslim merchants in the Indian Ocean. In each case, when a political entity evolved out of a trading center, it was a strictly local affair—for example, the regime of the Vikings in Normandy was originally unconnected to the Viking realms established in Britain, Ireland, Russia, and so on.

In short, although the Littoral routes had existed for some two millennia before the Europeans set out across the open ocean to Africa, Asia, and the Americas, they were *politically* and *culturally* unimportant, and therefore barely noticed. It was only when the Europeans established trading posts and began reaping huge profits from international trade that the Littoral zone became truly significant. When the port cities, some of them completely new foundations, began to grow large and prosperous, international

---

[74] Some of the larger Southeast Asian realms, notably Srivijaya, have been said to be thalassocracies, but not perhaps in the sense intended here.

[75] The closest to a genuine thalassocracy seems to have been the ancient Athenian "empire."

[76] Some of their descendants—notably the Carthaginians—did, but this was a long time after the heyday of the Phoenicians proper.

maritime trade around Eurasia was reborn as the new Littoral System, which finally became so important economically that the political capitals of some of the smaller peripheral states of Asia actually moved there.

Much like the low-profile old Littoral route trade, transcontinental trade had begun in prehistoric times. It went on not directly but indirectly from its beginnings, and continued largely unnoticed until the time of the first great Central Eurasian empires formed by steppe nomads, those of the Scythians and Hsiung-nu, who became noticeably rich on this trade. From that time on, the flourishing of the Central Eurasian steppe nomads and the Central Eurasian cities is inseparable from the flourishing of their internal economy, which included its international commerce component, altogether constituting the Silk Road economic system.

Unlike the ports of the old Littoral route, the commercial emporia in Central Eurasia had continental locations. The fortified cities of the Silk Road were therefore often large and politically important. Yet like the Littoral route trade, much of which consisted of local shipping from one Asian country to another nearby one—even after the European conquest of the Littoral zone, when European ships largely replaced the local Asian ships—the vast bulk of the commerce in Central Eurasia was conducted by small merchants in a small way, locally.[77] Accordingly, much like the nonexistence of thalassocracies in the Littoral System, no one has ever heard of a Sogdian Empire or a Jewish Empire in Central Eurasia, because they never existed either. One of the notable characteristics of the history of Sogdiana is its disunity. Throughout its history it was only unified by conquest, and then only for a very short time. However, it was almost always under the suzerainty of an imperial power, such as the Achaemenid Persians, or the Hsiung-nu, or the Kushans, or the Türk, or the Arabs, who served to keep the trade flowing between the de facto independent city-states of the region. Tamerlane, though he came from a town near Samarkand in the heart of former Sogdiana, was neither an Iranian nor a merchant. Perhaps that is the reason he was able to conquer a huge empire from his capital in

[77] It is sometimes thought that most of the truly international trade was conducted by Sogdians, Jews, and other "third party" merchant nations because they could cross borders, and it was in these merchants' best interests to maintain distinctive neutral national identities that were easily recognizable and known not to be overtly connected to any political entity, but this appears not to be accurate, at least with respect to the Sogdians, the Turks, and the Vikings. See de la Vaissière (2005a) and the papers in de la Vaissière and Trombert (2005).

Samarkand. But all the same, his empire did break up immediately after his death.

The remarkable political fact about the great cities along the Silk Road (in Antiquity and the Early Middle Ages, at least) is that they were all essentially city-states. Rarely did any of the little kingdoms consist of more than one important city. Left to their own devices, therefore, the politics and commerce of the Central Eurasian towns were as unconnected and unimportant as they were in the towns of the Littoral. That is why the cities shrank physically and in every other way, and the Central Asians passed out of historical consciousness, several times in premodern history. The cause of this loss of connectedness, and resulting economic decline, is evidently that there was no steppe-empire suzerain. Without the steppe peoples' infrastructure and careful tending and nurturing, the Silk Road tended to wilt.[78]

In every recorded case when the traditional Graeco-Roman, Persian, or Chinese empires of the periphery became too powerful and conquered or brought chaos to the Central Eurasian nomadic states, the result for Central Asia, at least, was economic recession.[79] The Han Dynasty destruction of the Hsiung-nu resulted in chaos in much of Central Eurasia. Though the Hsienpei replaced the Hsiung-nu on the Eastern Steppe, it was several centuries before the Türk, the next nomadic people who understood the Silk Road, could restore the system. There is no denying the fact that the T'ang Chinese succeeded in building a large, prosperous empire that included huge Central Asian colonial territories, but the prosperity of Central Asia itself suffered. When the Chinese and Arab alliance against the Tibetans and the Western Turkic empire of the Türgish succeeded and the Türgish were utterly destroyed, the result was chaos in that part of Central Eurasia, bringing with it a severe recession, followed by rebellions and revolutions led by Sogdians and other merchant peoples that affected most of the continent. Finally,

---

[78] This is suggested, usually backhandedly, by many, for example, Millward (2007: 93–94): "Thus the Zunghars provide a good and well documented example of the importance of the caravan trade to the nomadic states of Inner Asia."

[79] It may be objected that the Arab conquest did not result in an economic recession in Central Asia. That is apparently true, but there seem to be good reasons for it. Arabia belonged to the old Littoral zone economy, the Arabs were strongly pro-commercial throughout their history, and there was an important nomadic element in Arabia. The Arab conquests during the time of their empire (up to the collapse of direct caliphal authority in the early ninth century) also paralleled the steppe nomadic conquests in many respects.

when the Manchu-Chinese and Russians partitioned Central Eurasia and the Ch'ing Dynasty destroyed the Junghar Empire—the last great Central Eurasian nomad-ruled state—the economic devastation they wrought within Central Eurasia itself was so total that even at the turn of the millennium in AD 2000 the area had not recovered. The only reason Eurasia as a whole did not collapse economically along with it is that the Littoral route had developed, under European management, into the full-blown Littoral System, which completely replaced the Silk Road in several respects.

Trade was not merely critical to the existence of the nomadic states, which were critical to the existence of the Silk Road. The nomadic peoples and the settled urban peoples were *mutually inseparable components* of any successful Central Eurasian empire.[80] Every such empire had to include pastoral nomads, agriculturalists, and cities. The nomads therefore participated in trade, they encouraged it, and they coddled it, just as the agriculturalists and urbanites in their empires did. The fact that the rulers were usually steppe nomads does not change the fact that they went to war above all to force peripheral empires to allow trade.[81] The Central Eurasian steppe peoples were in this respect the exact mirror images of the West European maritime peoples who built and maintained the Littoral System. The result of the steppe peoples' efforts was the flourishing of the Silk Road, the internal and external economy of Central Eurasia. It grew to the point that the peripheral empires—who never actually understood it, despite all the posturing and preposterous assertions made by their politicians, advisers, and historians—saw it as the proverbial goose that lays the golden egg. They attempted many times to capture it and eliminate its owners, the nomads. As long as they did not succeed, the Central Eurasian economy (the Silk Road) continued to flourish. When they did finally succeed, they killed it.[82]

But by that time, the Western European nations developing the open-sea routes to Asia had done exactly the same thing that the nomads had earlier

[80] This might be thought to suggest an explanation for the collapse of the Tibetan Empire and the failure of later Tibetans to once again form a large state. But it is a historical fact that Tibet was subjugated by the Mongols (or, to be precise, surrendered to them) and was thus incorporated into the larger Mongol Empire. With the partial exception of brief interregnum periods, Tibet continued to be largely unified under the rule of one or another Mongol state down to the defeat of the Junghars by the Manchu-Chinese—under whose protectorate Tibet remained a largely unified state. Tibet is therefore no exception to the rule. A state-based national history of Tibet remains to be written.

[81] See the epilogue.

[82] On recent arguments that the Silk Road did not really decline, see the discussion in endnote 90.

done by land. The Europeans too were passionately interested in trade, so they encouraged, protected, and participated in it. Their interest was in profit, the same as with the nomads. In neither case did the political patrons go to all that trouble out of altruism, but it was not the "greed of the barbarians," as traditional historians of East and West have termed the activities of both the Central Eurasian nomads and the European maritime merchants. It was something more like the "virtue of selfishness." It was in the European rulers' own interests to take care of the merchants and their suppliers. When such economic interests eventually became vital to the European states that dominated the Littoral System, their navies covered the open seas in the same way that the nomads and their hordes once covered the steppe lands of Central Eurasia. The Littoral System then came into its own, eventually including most of Europe plus port cities and hinterlands along the coast of India, most of Southeast Asia, and China, and even a trading post in Japan, controlled or dominated by Europeans.

The impact of international maritime trade had long remained much less than that of the continental trade, despite the volume and value of the maritime trade. One of the main reasons is that until the European conquest, Littoral zone trade was not a distinct, fundamental element of the local economies connected by the merchants involved. It also never constituted a distinct economic zone *separate* from the Central Eurasian continental economic zone but was fully integrated into the continental system, which had Central Eurasia, or the Silk Road economy, as its center.[83]

The old maritime trade routes and the continental trade routes thus did not conflict, though the possibility of obtaining goods by more than one route may have exerted some competitive downward pressure on prices. The two existed throughout history, but purely as different subsystems of transportation and distribution within one Eurasian continental trade system, the center of which remained the Silk Road, the Central Eurasian economy. The region where the two routes met and interacted most intensely was Southwest Asia, primarily meaning Iran, Iraq, Egypt, Syria, and Anatolia. To some extent the political power of Persia throughout history is inseparable from its strategic position between East, South, and West by land and by

---

[83] This is not what David Christian (1998) means by his newly coined terms "Outer Eurasia" versus "Inner Eurasia." I cannot agree with this usage, especially in view of the existing terminological confusion in Central Eurasian studies. He later refers to the "Afro-Eurasian region" (Christian 2000: 2).

sea. The same is true of Anatolia and Greece, which supported the Eastern Roman Empire, the Byzantine Empire, and the Ottoman Empire.[84]

At the height of the new European-run Littoral System, the international trade of Eurasia was conducted largely by sea. By that time, what trade did go by land did not go very far. Other than a tiny trickle of local low-value trade and the rare caravan, the Silk Road commerce no longer existed. The reason is that the conquest and occupation of the steppe zone and most of the native Central Eurasian states by peripheral powers eliminated local Central Eurasian governments, which were replaced by the colonial officials of the peripheral empires. The loss of their independence and the total suppression of independent-minded leaders in Central Eurasia eliminated the lords, their courts, their guard corps (the late form of the comitatus), and much else. That eliminated most of the internal Central Eurasian economic demand for silks and other high-value international trade goods. The Russians and Manchu-Chinese established official border trading posts, but they were designed specifically to control a strictly binational "official" trade between Russia and China, and to exclude Central Eurasians from participating in it. With the destruction not only of the basis for Central Eurasia's internal economy but even of the possibility of continuing the already shrunken caravan trade, by the mid-nineteenth century the Silk Road dwindled into insignificance, and Central Eurasia sank into poverty.

This process affected every major region of Central Eurasia, including—to use their modern names—Mongolia, Tibet, Afghanistan, Western Central Asia (or West Turkistan), and East Turkistan (or Xinjiang). East Turkistan, which has recently received considerable scholarly attention, may be taken as an example.

The expansion of the Junghar Empire happened at the same time as that of the Manchu-Chinese, Russian, and British Indian empires. But the peripheral powers "effectively hemmed in Xinjiang and the rest of Central Eurasia, marking the end of the nomadic steppe empire." Though the Junghars themselves had brought Central Eurasia into "unprecedented contact with a wider world,"[85] introducing goods and technology from the peripheral states, with the destruction of the Junghars and conquest and subjugation of Central Eurasia by the Manchu-Chinese and Russians the opposite happened: the

---

[84] One can probably include the Trojan realm as well as that of the Hittites, though the latter was based in Central Anatolia.

[85] Millward (2007: 79–80).

local economies suffered increasingly, to the point that by the mid-nineteenth century what highly regulated international commerce did exist consisted of goods such as Chinese "brick tea and some cloth" and Russian "livestock, hides, furs, and manufactured goods."[86] From the Ch'ing conquest on, as early as the Ch'ien-lung emperor's reign in the eighteenth century, "Xinjiang could not generate sufficient revenue to fully support the military forces required to hold it, and millions of ounces of silver had to be shipped annually from China to Xinjiang to pay military salaries."[87] The "last trickle of trade" in mid-nineteenth century East Turkistan consisted of "re-exporting Chinese tea, silver, and other items."[88] In the early twentieth century, "Russian liquor, metal goods, fabrics, lamps, ceramics, watches, cigarettes and so forth were all much cheaper than their Chinese counterparts on Xinjiang markets."[89] These are all inexpensive goods with low unit value. The conspicuous absence of high-value luxury goods among them is in sharp contrast to the situation from Antiquity to the end of the Middle Ages, and even as late as at the height of the Junghar Empire. Their absence is direct evidence for the disastrous economic decline suffered by Central Eurasia.

The East Turkistanis finally rebelled against the intolerable conditions in 1864 and came under the rule of Yaqub Beg (r. 1865–1877), whose diplomatic astuteness brought the region international attention. Unfortunately, the Ch'ing Dynasty was not willing to let go. The Manchu-Chinese reconquest, completed in 1878, was followed by the annexation of the entire territory as a province, Sinkiang (Xinjiang), in 1884.[90] By the late nineteenth century, the little commerce of any significance that still existed was in the hands of Russian and Chinese merchants. The stagnation and backwardness of culture in East Turkistan was remarked on by the few foreign travelers who braved the opposition of the peripheral imperial rulers, as well as local

---

[86] Millward (2007: 156).

[87] Millward (2007: 102–103).

[88] Millward (2007: 121).

[89] Millward (2007: 158).

[90] Millward (2007: 130–137). Despite his argument that China (what is traditionally often referred to as "China proper") and the other parts of the Ch'ing Empire except for Tibet all had essentially the same political status, this was not really the case. The status of Mongolia was different from that of East Turkistan, and both were different from that of Tibet. The official change of Sinkiang (Xinjiang) into a full-fledged province was a deliberate political move. Though it might not at first have had much significance for the ordinary people living there, its impact over time has been enormous. Cf. the comments of East Turkistanis mentioned by him (Millward 2007: 158), and see the following note.

dangers, to enter the region and describe it.[91] All the wars and the long Ch'ing mismanagement had ruined the economy, infrastructure, practically everything.[92]

With access to Central Eurasia so tightly controlled from all directions, it became culturally isolated and ceased to keep up with technological and other changes that were affecting most of the rest of the world at that time. In particular, the industrial-commercial revolution and the cultural changes that went along with it completely bypassed Central Eurasia, which increasingly became a primitive, poverty-stricken colonial backwater more like Central Africa or the Amazon jungle than the center of world culture it once had been.

The bad conditions in Central Eurasia hardly made it attractive or interesting to most Russians and Manchu-Chinese, who increasingly paid these colonial territories little attention, though they did manage to make it almost impossible for Europeans or Americans to go there. Indeed, because travel to Central Eurasia—including Afghanistan, West and East Turkistan, Mongolia, and Tibet—was mostly forbidden outright, information about the region became almost nonexistent anywhere outside it. Even inside it, the isolation and poverty of Central Eurasian peoples lowered their level of education, resulting in widespread ignorance about their own territories, histories, and cultures.

The mysterious disappearance of the Silk Road coincided with the appearance of the new Littoral System, so it was natural for historians to attempt to find a causal connection between the rise and fall of what seemed to be two distinct commercial systems. In reality, deprived of its independence and its commercially minded local rulers, Central Eurasia suffered from the most severe, long-lasting economic depression in world history. It declined into oblivion, while the coastal regions of Eurasia, nurtured by the commercially minded European navies, prospered as they never had before.

---

[91] Millward (2007: 159). He considers the Westerners' observations to be "the smug racism of imperialists." It should be added that the smug racism of those Westerners' contemporaries, the Chinese imperialists, was noticed by the Westerners of that period, who complained loudly about it, but it remains unnoted in China and most of the rest of the world. It continues down to the present day, and under its aegis the innocent people of East Turkistan are right now being oppressed without a squeak of protest from a single powerful foreign government.

[92] Even today, "Xinjiang . . . still requires large central governmental subsidies" (Millward 2007: 103). The same was true in the Soviet Union, to the extent that no effort was made by the bankrupt Russians to hold onto the impoverished federal republics in Central Asia when those countries declared their independence, in contrast to the effort made to hold onto the Baltic states. Economically, Central Asia was a bottomless pit as far as the Russians were concerned.

11

Eurasia without a Center

April is the cruelest month,
Breeding lilacs out of the dead land.
  —T. S. Eliot, *The Waste Land*[1]

Modernism, War, and Cultural Decline

The twentieth century represents the culmination of the revolutionary movement of Modernism, with its fight against tradition, natural law, and nature itself in all areas, levels, and aspects of culture. It was especially calamitous in Eurasia, where Modernist revolutions of different kinds instituted populist, totalitarian, and fundamentalist tyrannies and brought devastating wars and mass murder at unprecedented levels. Disastrous Modern economic policies helped to produce the worst global recession in recent history, the Great Depression, which lasted from 1929 to the Second World War in many countries. Culturally, the ruthless application of radical "revolutionary" programs resulted in the cultural devastation of Central Eurasia: destruction of thousands of monasteries, shrines, mosques, churches, synagogues, and educational institutions affiliated with Buddhism, Islam, Christianity, and Judaism, as well as destruction of books and torture or execution of clerics. Central Eurasia suffered more than any other region of the world from the ravages of Modernism.

Mongolia and Tibet regained independence upon the fall of the Ch'ing Dynasty in 1911, and parts of East Turkistan followed, briefly, a few decades later. But shortly after the Second World War the communists won the civil war in China and the Chinese quickly seized Inner Mongolia, East Turkistan, and finally Tibet (in 1951). The three countries were put under military occupation and were flooded with Chinese settlers.

---

[1] Eliot's work in many ways best characterizes twentieth-century Modernism and the triumph of populism. Rossa (2006) notes, "The poem had great impact from the moment of its publication; the critic Lawrence Rainey has said, 'the publication of The Waste Land marked the crucial moment in *the transition of modernism from a minority culture to one supported by an important institutional and financial apparatus*'." Quoted from http://www.lib.udel.edu/ud/spec/exhibits/pound/wasteland.htm; emphasis added.

After the Second World War and the Chinese invasion, Central Eurasia was even more isolated than before. The eastern and western extremes of Eurasia were dominated by the United States of America, a non-Eurasian state, and the planet was divided into communist and capitalist camps. Their protracted struggle, known as the Cold War because the two camps rarely used open military force against each other directly, focused above all on control of Eurasia.[2] The anticommercial "socialist" systems of the large communist empires—the Union of Soviet Socialist Republics (the Soviet Union) and the People's Republic of China (Communist China) brought poverty and isolation to both of those states as a whole and, in particular, to Central Eurasia, most of which they occupied militarily.

The Littoral System and the Silk Road

In the Modern period, Eurasia continued to be dominated by the Littoral System, which ultimately grew out of the much earlier Littoral zone commerce. That earlier commerce should certainly not be overlooked, nor can it be doubted that it was significant; however, it has been argued that the maritime commerce of Asia was not merely as significant as the continental Silk Road commerce, it was much more important. This argument misses the point of what the Silk Road was, even according to most traditional treatments of it, and obscures what happened to it.

The Silk Road was actually unparalleled by anything in the Littoral zone. Before the Portuguese discovery of the direct sea route from Europe, and their domination and cultivation of it, the Littoral zone maritime trade system was in essence only that: a commercial transportation network or, perhaps more accurately, an interconnected system of regional transportation networks. By contrast, the Silk Road was not in essence a commercial transportation network at all. It was the entire Central Eurasian economy, or socio-economic-political-cultural system, the great flourishing of which impressed itself upon the people of Antiquity and the Middle Ages, and the records and remains of which impress even the people of today.

---

[2] When the Soviet and Chinese communists turned against each other, the resulting Sino-Soviet cold war turned hot, briefly, in the Ussuri River Incident of 1969.

Until the destruction of the last steppe empire and the partition of the region by peripheral states in modern times, the society, economy, political systems, and culture of Central Eurasia as a whole (including the herding, agricultural, and urban peoples, and the warriors, artists, intellectuals, and others) were the equal of the other contemporaneous major world regions of Eurasia: East and Southeast Asia, South Asia, Southwest Asia, and Europe. During the early Modern period, as shown in chapter 10, Central Eurasia became an impoverished backwater. In the Modern period it remained so, but sank even lower, becoming one of the most deeply depressed and poverty-stricken regions in the entire world, far beyond what might have been expected from political conquest alone, with few monuments or other physical reminders of what had once been great cultures. The question of why that happened must be answered.

The reason adduced here is the conquest and partition of Central Eurasia by the early modern European and Asian peripheral powers. Because Central Eurasia thus no longer existed as an independent entity or group of entities during the Modern period, its nations became "frontier problems" for the colonial powers.[3] The entire region was thus largely ignored during the twentieth century, and its participation in Modern history was limited almost completely to being the victim of one or another Modern horror. Accordingly the history of Central Eurasia in the twentieth century is to a large extent subordinate to the history of the Eurasian periphery, particularly Western Europe, Russia, and China.[4] This chapter outlines that history, with an eye out for its effects on Central Eurasia and the eventual beginnings of a new imperial order at the end of the century.

The Radical Modernist Revolutions

Before the First World War, the ideals of monarchy and aristocratic cultural tradition prevailed nominally in most of the European-dominated world, despite the challenge of populist forces emanating from those countries that

---

[3] Study of Central Eurasia was even referred to as "border studies" by some scholars who had no knowledge of Central Eurasian languages and took their views almost entirely from writers of the peripheral states in which they specialized, particularly China and Russia.

[4] On sources used for the present treatment of the Modern period, see endnote 91.

had adopted a republican form of government. After the disastrous First World War, most of the remaining monarchies of Europe were overthrown, or the monarchs were stripped of any remaining actual power.[5] They were replaced with overt Modernist "democracies," all of which were republics, at least theoretically. The institution of compulsory national education in all modern republics brought with it the indoctrination of children in the ideology of "democracy" so they would not oppose the programs of those who held actual political power but would instead unwittingly support them.

THE FIRST MODERNIST REVOLUTION IN CHINA

The first significant Modernist revolution of the century began in China. It was led by Sun Yat-sen (1866–1925), a Cantonese intellectual who emigrated to Hawaii in 1897 and subsequently lived in Hong Kong, Japan, Britain, and the United States.[6] The revolutionaries stated as their goal the overthrow of what they called the "alien" Manchus—who were by then actually indistinguishable from ethnic Chinese in culture, language, and national identity—and the establishment of a "democratic" government. Both of their then radical goals derived from European and, specifically, American influences. They finally succeeded in overthrowing the Ch'ing Dynasty in 1911. The Central Eurasian protectorates of Mongolia and Tibet immediately pointed out that, as their political relationship had been with the "alien" non-Chinese Manchus specifically, not the Chinese, they were fully independent again. In East Turkistan, the imperial occupation forces were taken over by the new republican leadership. They retained control there partly because of the country's multiethnic composition and consequent lack of national political unity.[7]

The new Chinese republic was weak, and warlords took over much of the country. Upon the capture by General Chiang Kai-shek (1887–1975 [r. 1926–1949 in China, 1949–1975 in Taiwan]) of the then capital, Peking,[8] and his establishment as leader of the Nationalist Party,[9] the capital was

---

[5] Part of the reason for this was populist politicians' need for a scapegoat; the monarchs, and monarchy itself, were unjustly blamed for the war.

[6] Dillon (1998: 302).

[7] Millward (2004: 4).

[8] After Peking (Beijing 'Northern Capital') was captured by Chiang Kai-shek's armies (on June 8, 1928), its name was changed to Peiping (Beiping 'Northern Peace') to signify its demotion from capital status and its replacement by the new capital, Nanking (Nanjing 'Southern Capital').

[9] Dillon (1998: 160). The Chinese Nationalist government was declared in Nanking on April 18, 1927 (Eastman 1986: 116).

moved south to Nanking (Nanjing). The new capital was located on the navigable Yangtze River only 140 miles west of Shanghai, which was a great internationally dominated port and already the largest, most prosperous city in China.

The First World War

The mutual distrust lingering from the previous century among the major European powers, coupled with a genuine desire for war, built up tension and armaments to the bursting point. When an excuse for war took place in the Balkans, the multinational alliances went into effect and the First World War (1914–1918) began. The combatants belonged to two groups. The Allied Powers were Britain, France, Serbia, Russia, and Japan, which were joined during the war by Italy (1915), Portugal and Romania (1916), and Greece and the United States (1917). The Central Powers were Germany, Austria-Hungary, and the Ottoman Empire, which were joined during the war by Bulgaria (1915).[10] The war was especially devastating in northwestern Europe, where most of the major battles and other destruction took place. In a few weeks of battle about one million young men perished.

The nations openly at war were more or less exclusively in Europe, though due to the extensive alliances the warfare did extend into the Ottoman Empire in the southeast, where it had far-reaching effects and led to the fall of that regime. It was thus not quite a "world" war but was called one because the major participants considered Europe and its immediate neighbors in the Near East to be all the world that mattered.[11]

The United States entered the war in 1917, and the entry of American troops into combat in spring 1918 turned the tide in favor of Britain and the other Allied Powers. The First World War ended that year with the defeat of Germany and the other Central Powers. The victors blamed the entire war on the Central Powers and punished them mercilessly. Both the German Empire and the Austro-Hungarian Empire were broken up in accordance with the provisions of the Treaty of Versailles (1919). An international organization, the League of Nations, was founded in an attempt to prevent an-

---

[10] Teed (1992: 506).

[11] On World War I and the largely unchanged Eurocentric view of world history, see endnote 92.

other great war, but the United States refused to join—Congress was as usual controlled by the most aggressively ignorant and self-serving among the populists. This seriously weakened the new organization's effectiveness.

The treaty ending the First World War was a disaster for Europe and a primary cause of the Second World War. The importance of Germany to the European economy as a whole was not then sufficiently appreciated. The physical damage wrought by World War I, together with the crushing war debts incurred by the major European powers and especially their ill-advised economic policies, are partly responsible for the Great Depression, while the war indemnities, treaty restrictions, and humiliation imposed on the defeated Central Powers, Germany and Austria, made it politically certain that the latter would rearm at the first opportunity. As the First World War was ending, radical socialist or communist revolutions broke out in several of the major combatant nations, including, most significantly, Russia and Germany.

Radical Modernist Revolutions after the First World War

THE RUSSIAN REVOLUTION

The long festering internal socioeconomic problems in Russia were compounded by the unpopular First World War. The democratic revolution of March 1917 overthrew the Romanov Dynasty,[12] but the new government still did not pull out of the war. The weakness of the new regime and the continuing losses from the war lent popular support to a more radical revolution. On November 7, 1917 (October 25, 1917, according to the Julian calendar), the Marxist revolutionary Lenin (Vladimir Iljič Uljanov, 1870–1924 [r. 1917–1924]) announced the fall of the Provisional Government and the next day proclaimed a new socialist "Soviet" regime.[13] Lenin did not, however, pull Russia out of the war right away, and after further losses upon the resumption of the German offensive in February 1918, the capital

---

[12] The last emperor, Nicholas II, abdicated in February 1917. He and all members of his family in Russia, including distant relatives, were murdered by the Bolsheviks on July 17, 1918 (Millar 2004: 1298).

[13] Because the Julian calendar was then still in use in Russia, the event has traditionally been called the October Revolution.

was moved from St. Petersburg back to the continental city of Moscow, the old capital.

Almost immediately after the declaration of the new socialist government, a civil war (1917–1920) broke out among different factions of revolutionaries, as well as between the socialists, or Reds, and the antisocialists, or Whites. Lenin and his supporters used terror and mass executions to hold onto power while drafting soldiers into a new army to fight against both Russian opponents and the European and American powers who supported the White faction against the Reds and sent substantial military forces into the country at various points. But the socialists, with the full force of extreme Modernism behind them, prevailed.

The Soviet regime was responsible for radical change throughout the huge empire, some of it positive. Literacy and education was extended to all nationalities, even the smallest tribal peoples. Though the primary initial reason was to indoctrinate everyone in the new "socialist" ideology, it also spread advanced European science and technology throughout Northern Eurasia, Soviet Central Asia, and the Soviet client state of Mongolia.

Lenin died in 1924 and was succeeded by Josef Stalin (Iosif Vissarionovič Džugašvili, 1879–1953 [r. ca. 1929–1953]), a Georgian whose faction was victorious over his rivals by 1927. By 1929 he had taken all power and become absolute dictator. He is responsible for the death of many millions of people—especially intellectuals, who were executed, and farmers, an estimated ten million of whom were starved to death—in a reign of terror and mass-murder unprecedented in world history.[14]

THE GERMAN REVOLUTIONS

As the First World War was ending late in 1918, populist revolutionary movements with strong socialist leanings broke out in Germany. Kaiser Wilhelm II (1859–1941 [r. 1888–1918]) abdicated, ending the reign of the Hohenzollern Dynasty. The socialist and communist elements were defeated by the moderate and nationalist elements, and the "Weimar" republic of Germany was established in 1919. But the new government was weak, the economy remained a shambles, and the continuing treatment of Germany as a second-class nation

---

[14] Stearns (2002), Florinsky (1961). There is a considerable literature on Stalin's terror (the Purges) and the Great Famine; see, inter alia, Conquest (1968, 1986, 1990).

by some of the other European governments encouraged the growth of extreme nationalism.

When Germany was struck severely by the Great Depression, Adolf Hitler (1889–1945 [r. 1933–1945]), the Austrian-born leader of the radical National Socialist Party, or Nazis, who had been imprisoned briefly after a failed revolutionary coup attempt a decade earlier, saw his chance. He promised to save Germany from its woes and restore the country to its former greatness. In several successive elections his party won an increasingly higher percentage of the vote. Finally, in 1933, after winning the second largest number of votes, he was duly appointed chancellor of the German Republic. The Nazis rapidly took full power and began putting their revolutionary proposals into action.

Some of the new government's programs were admirable. A new, inexpensive, but technically advanced automobile, the Volkswagen or 'people's car', was designed to allow all Germans to be able to own one,[15] and construction was put fully underway on a system of superhighways intended to crisscross the country for citizens to tour on. Other changes were understandable. Hitler began secretly rebuilding the German military, in violation of the Treaty of Versailles. When he felt confident of his power, he stopped all payment of war indemnities. German industry joined with German science, which was then the most advanced in the world, to build the country into a military and economic power.

But Hitler went much further. He cultivated his personal power through huge rallies in which he used his electrifying oratorical skills and incendiary rhetoric to whip the people into a frenzy on whatever topic he chose. He and his followers, like many other people in Europe and America at that time, blamed their country's woes on minority groups. Immediately after taking power, Hitler ordered the government to begin a program of methodical elimination of the Jews, beginning with extreme racism and economic oppression to the point that many people were no longer able to support themselves and their families. A flood of refugees left Germany seeking safety elsewhere.[16] As the Nazis extended their program to the territories that came under German control during the Second World War, it became an organized genocidal campaign, which eventually was respon-

---

[15] However, it did not actually go into production before the Second World War began.

[16] Albert Einstein and a number of other leading scientists who escaped put their knowledge and talents to work in the Second World War to help the Allied Powers defeat Germany and its Axis allies Italy and Japan.

sible for the murder of an estimated six million people, including most of the remaining German and Polish Jewish populations, among other people targeted for destruction.[17]

In the First World War, because the Ottoman Empire had been allied with Germany and the Austro-Hungarian Empire, the British in Egypt fought directly against the Ottomans and also indirectly via the Arabians and other rebellious subjects of the Ottomans who allied themselves with the British throughout the Near East.

The Ottomans' defeat and loss of most of their colonial empire paved the way for the "Young Turk" revolutionaries led by the charismatic nationalist leader Kemal Atatürk (Mustafa Kemal, 1881–1938 [r. 1922–1938]). In 1922 the Ottoman Dynasty was abolished and replaced by the secular, "democratic," European-oriented Turkish Republic. In 1923 Atatürk moved the capital from Constantinople (which he renamed Istanbul)[18] to the continental Anatolian city of Angora (ancient Ancyra), which he renamed Ankara.

The Allies' vengeance against the Ottomans did not win long-term colonial power in the region for the British, as they had hoped. The British did dominate Palestine, Jordan, and Iraq, as well as Egypt, until shortly after the Second World War, but the great diminution of British power after that war forced them to abandon most of their colonies. As they withdrew from Palestine in 1947, a civil war broke out and a radical Jewish nationalist ("Zionist") state formed. The results were incendiary.[19]

The British-led breakup of the Ottoman Empire after the First World War, and the Turks' establishment in self-defense of the nationalistic, inward-looking Turkish Republic, had serious, long-term consequences for Southwestern Asia.[20] Persia also continued to be weak, and thus the age-old division of Southwestern Asia between two large powers, one centered in Greece

---

[17] Weiss (2000). The Nazis also targeted members of other ethnolinguistic groups they especially disliked, notably the Romani (Gypsies), as well as homosexuals, crippled or otherwise disabled people, and others.

[18] On the etymology of the name Istanbul, see endnote 93.

[19] The British foreign minister Jack Straw has publicly admitted his government made "quite serious mistakes" in Palestine and in India, among many other countries of Southwest and South Asia (http://news.bbc.co.uk/2/hi/europe/2481371.stm).

[20] "The most far-reaching consequence of European intervention [in the Middle East] was *the destruction of the Ottoman Empire* after World War I. In lands that had formerly been unified, the Europeans laid the foundation for an entirely *novel system of states* that, in spite of its

or Constantinople and another in Persia, could not be reestablished. The fragmentation and animosity in the Middle East worsened and led to ever increasing instability during the latter part of the twentieth century.

Modern Central Eurasia before the Second World War

In Turkic-speaking Central Eurasia, the liberalizing movement known as Jadidism (*uṣûl-i jadîd'*, literally, 'the new methods')[21] spread from its birth-place in Kazan, Tatarstan,[22] around 1880 to other leading Islamic cities. East Turkistani intellectuals introduced modern Western-style schools and curricula, journals and other modern media, and along with them modern nationalistic ideas. With the spread of the revolution to Central Asia, some Jadidists became involved in the Bolshevik movement in the early years of the revolution, believing that it would help free their homeland from the op-pressive rule of the conservative Muslim leadership and the local rulers of the old regime.[23]

One indirect result of the First World War was the 1921 communist revo-lution in Mongolia, which then came under increasingly powerful Russian influence over the course of the century.

In East Turkistan, the Soviets crushed a local civil war that broke out in the 1930s and installed a Chinese warlord in Ürümchi. The first, ephemeral, East Turkistan Republic (November 1933 to February 1934), based in Kash-gar, was quickly suppressed.[24] However, the influence of the Soviet Union spread there as well.

Tibet enjoyed nearly a half century of restored full independence, despite the periodic ravages of one or another Chinese warlord in its eastern prov-inces.

---

artificiality, persisted into the late 20th century with few modifications" (Stearns 2002: 751; emphasis in the original). "Novel" and "artificial" hardly seem sufficient here.

[21] Despite its name, which could also be translated as 'modernism', and what could be called its "modernizing" aims, this movement had almost nothing to do with the twentieth-century Western movement described here as Modernism. Jadidism is essentially another name for Westernization or Europeanization in a liberal Islamic context.

[22] Kazan, the capital of modern Tatarstan, was one of the leading intellectual centers of Russia and Europe in general in the late nineteenth century. Some of the great minds of the age taught in its university.

[23] Khalid (2007).

[24] Millward (2004: 4–5).

The Soviet Union and the Great Depression

The weak postwar economy in Europe was aggravated by the end of Lenin's liberalized New Economic Policy in the former Russian Empire and substitution of the disastrous socialist economic policies of Josef Stalin, marked by the institution of the first centrally directed Five-Year Plan in 1929 and in the following year the beginning of the forced "collectivization" of agriculture.[25] Foreign trade was also severely limited, and not only was the currency made nonconvertible (from 1926–1928 on), but it became a crime to convert it. As a result, the Soviet economy shrank drastically, and the Soviet Union—including Russia and nearly all of Central Eurasia—was almost completely cut off from "capitalist" world commerce.[26]

In light of the damage to the European economy inflicted by the First World War and the postwar economic punishment of Germany and Austria and, it appears, by the closing of the Soviet Union (including Russia and most of Central Eurasia) to world commerce, it is not surprising that the Great Depression, a worldwide economic recession worse than any previously known, struck at the end of 1929.[27] Millions of people lost their savings, their jobs, and their homes, and were on the edge of starvation. Unlike earlier recessions, the Depression lasted for many years in the countries hit hardest by it. As a direct outcome of both the Depression and the continuing effects of the sanctions imposed after the First World War, in Germany a new government was elected, completely "democratically." The new chancellor, Adolf Hitler, leader of the National Socialist (or Nazi) Party, turned his adopted country and Europe as a whole toward war once again. Yet he was not alone in his mania.

In the early twentieth century, intellectuals and artists in the West thought it was worth fighting for or against various solutions to political, intellectual, and artistic issues. For different reasons, many of them rejected the sociopolitical order of the world of their day and preferred instead a

---

[25] Although the exact sequence of events has not yet been clarified, it is certain that many millions died during the severe famine of 1932–1933, which was aggravated, if not actually caused, by government policies.

[26] Florinsky (1961).

[27] The Great Depression also affected North America and Australia unusually severely, for unknown reasons. The causes of the Great Depression are still hotly debated in general.

totalitarian system. Their number included several of the most prominent English-language writers of the early to mid-twentieth century.[28] Of them, Ezra Pound very publicly supported Fascism and Nazism through the Second World War and until his trial afterward.[29] Pound's close friend T. S. Eliot was very strongly influenced by French fascist ideas, and both of them, and D. H. Lawrence as well, were openly anti-Semitic.[30] Even W. B. Yeats was attracted to the idea of violently overthrowing the sociopolitical order of Western Europe in the 1920s and 1930s, which, like many other leading intellectuals of the day, he considered to be completely corrupt and beyond salvation short of total war. These writers shared the view that great art could not be produced under the conditions of the world in their time and drastic measures were necessary to produce conditions that, they thought, would be amenable to art. The next great war was inevitable, and as before many actually welcomed it.

The Second World War in the Eurasian Periphery

Although once again Eurasia—especially Europe and East and Southeast Asia—was the central locus of the war, this time it was more nearly a global conflict. It not only devastated Northeast Asia, East Asia, Southeast Asia, and Oceania (1937–1945) in addition to most of Europe and North Africa (1939–1945), but it also extended into the colonial territories of the Americas and Australia and included combatants from all corners of the globe.

In East Asia, the war was presaged in 1931–1932 by the Japanese conquest of Manchuria, which had earlier been the easternmost region of Central Eurasia, but by that time had been largely Sinified by Chinese colonists. They established the puppet Manchurian kingdom of Manchukuo in 1932 and placed P'u-i, the deposed last ruler of the Manchu-Chinese Ch'ing Dynasty, on the throne. The local Japanese military leaders in the colonies of

---

[28] Harrison (1966).

[29] Unlike Pound, Wyndham Lewis stopped supporting fascism before the war because "he saw the mass-hysteria which fascism aroused," and he realized that the Nazi Regime, in particular, "had certain characteristics in common with what he called democracy" (Harrison 1966: 93–94, 103).

[30] Their rhetoric on this issue can politely be described as nauseating.

Korea and eastern Manchuria were responsible for beginning the Second World War there. They and other pro-militarists increasingly took control over the Japanese government, bringing the country under de facto military rule. A minor military incident at Marco Polo Bridge in Peking (July 7, 1937) provided the excuse for full-scale war. By 1939 the Japanese occupied the Chinese coast and northeast China, as well as the rest of Manchuria.

In August 1939 the Soviet Union and Germany concluded a nonaggression treaty, the Molotov-Ribbentrop Pact, which involved the partition of Poland between them. When the two countries invaded Poland in September, Britain and France, Poland's allies, declared war on Germany. The Second World War thus broke out in Europe. In the summer of 1940 the Germans began the aerial bombardment of Britain in preparation for a planned invasion. Following radical changes in Hitler's relations with the Soviet Union, he launched an invasion of the country on June 22, 1941. By the end of 1941 the Nazis occupied nearly all of continental Western Europe, extending eastward as far as the Western Steppe zone region of the Don River and the Black Sea coast, and excepting only neutral Sweden, Switzerland, and Spain, as well as the Axis states of Italy and southern France. The Axis powers also held much of North Africa.

In June 1941 the Japanese completed their military occupation of French Indochina. That summer the Western nations, including the United States (which was then still officially neutral),[31] froze Japanese assets abroad and declared a trade embargo, ostensibly in an attempt to force the Japanese to leave China. The Japanese military, which was by that time running both the war and the government, depended completely on imported oil; the only option open to them was to go to war with the United States, Britain, and the Netherlands, who controlled the oil supplies in Asia.[32] On December 7, 1941, the Japanese bombed the naval base of Pearl Harbor in the American colony of Hawaii,[33] killing more than two thousand sailors and

---

[31] The United States was already aiding the Nationalist Chinese government against the Japanese and had sent a clandestine air squadron and planes to Asia to fight the Japanese under the Nationalist Chinese flag. Though these units did not actually enter combat in China until after the bombing of Pearl Harbor, the Japanese were hardly unaware of much, if not all, of this activity.

[32] Dunnigan and Nofi (1998: 164–165).

[33] An American coup d'état overthrew Queen Liliuokalani on January 17, 1893. On July 4, 1894, the American leader in Hawaii declared a "republic," and in 1898 the U.S. "annexed" Hawaii (Brune 2003).

other personnel and destroying part of the Pacific Fleet. This act finally brought the United States to declare war on the Axis powers.[34]

It must be stressed that the Pearl Harbor attack was not isolated or poorly planned, or haphazard in any way, as it is sometimes represented. Precisely simultaneously with the bombing of Pearl Harbor, the Japanese also attacked the British colonies of Hong Kong and Malaya and invaded the Philippines, which was then still an American colony.[35] By May they had defeated the Americans and taken the Philippines.[36] In fifty-five days the Japanese marched south through the Malay Peninsula, defeating all resistance, and captured the strategic port city of Singapore.[37] Moreover, only a month after Pearl Harbor, in January 1942 they invaded the British colony of Burma. By March they occupied Rangoon, and by April they took Central Burma, cutting the Burma Road, the sole remaining Allied land link with China. By May the Japanese had driven the remaining Allied forces from Burma.[38]

All of these countries were at the time colonies of the Europeans and Americans. China too had been partially colonized. It was essentially the colonized Chinese coast, and China's colony of Manchuria, that the Japanese captured during the war. Thailand was at the time the only independent, uncolonized country in South and Southeast Asia. Rather than taking Thailand by force, the Japanese signed an alliance (December 21, 1941) with the country. The entire war in the East was thus fought over the countries of Southeast Asia and the Pacific that had been colonized or had come under European domination at the end of the period of commercial expansion begun by the Portuguese four centuries earlier.

After the Americans joined the war effort, the Allies slowly began pushing the Axis back. On the western front, the Americans and British attained naval and air superiority over the Germans in each theater of operations. In November 1942 Anglo-American forces landed in French

---

[34] On the Pearl Harbor conspiracy theory, the known background of the attack (or *an* attack), and whether or not it could have been a surprise to the American leadership, see endnote 94.

[35] Although the invasion began on December 8 Philippine time, it was December 7 Hawaiian time. The Philippines had been ceded to the United States in 1898 by Spain, the former colonial ruler of the islands, following the American victory in the Spanish-American War (Brune 2003).

[36] Whitman (2001).

[37] Dunnigan and Nofi (1998: 387–388).

[38] Dunnigan and Nofi (1998: 120–121).

Morocco and French Algeria. The Axis forces capitulated in French Tunisia in May 1943. From North Africa, the Allied forces invaded Italy in July 1943, but though they had achieved air superiority the campaign there was slow and difficult and did not measurably contribute to the eventual Allied victory over Germany.

The tide of the war on the western front turned decisively when on June 6, 1944, the Allies landed a major invasion force on the beaches of Normandy.[39] Their troops included Americans, British, French, and others from occupied European countries, especially Poland, and soldiers from colonies or former colonies of the Allied countries in the Americas, Africa, and Australasia. They advanced rapidly. On August 15, 1944, U.S. and French forces landed on the southern French coast between Nice and Marseilles and continued their offensive northward up the Rhone River valley. The Allies coming from Normandy captured Paris on August 25, Belgium on September 4, and Luxembourg on September 11.[40]

While the Western Allies invaded the Axis realms from the west and south, on the eastern front the Soviets stopped the German armies in several long, bloody siege battles, the most crucial of which took place at Stalingrad (before Stalin, Tsaritsyn; now Volgograd) from August 1942 to February 1943. More Soviet victories followed.[41] With the assistance of military, industrial, and other supplies sent by the Americans and British, the Soviets pressed westward toward Germany.

The Allies were much aided in the war by two technical developments unknown to the Axis: they broke the top-secret communications codes of both the Germans and the Japanese[42] and by 1940 had developed a functioning radar defense system. These were essential elements in the rapid Allied victory. By the end of January 1945, the Allies had completed recovering the territory they had lost in the strong German counteroffensive attack known as the Battle of the Bulge (December 16–26, 1944). They quickly broke the remaining German resistance and marched into Germany from both east and west. On April 28, 1945, Benito Mussolini, the Fascist leader of Italy, was captured and shot to death by Italian anti-Fascists near Lake

[39] Dear and Foot (1995).
[40] Brune (2003).
[41] However, it must be recognized that the Soviet Union suffered more than any other country. An estimated twenty million Soviet citizens died in the war.
[42] Layton (1999: 1193).

Como. Two days later, on April 30, 1945, Adolf Hitler committed suicide in Berlin.[43]

In East Asia the Second World War ended the Japanese colonial empire. American forces captured Shanghai and other Chinese coastal cities, and sent troops to Peiping (Beijing) and Tientsin (Tianjin). After the Americans dropped the atomic bomb on the southwestern Japanese cities of Hiroshima (August 6, 1945) and Nagasaki (August 9, 1945), the Japanese surrendered unconditionally on August 14, 1945 (formally signed on September 2, 1945), and the American military occupied Japan. On September 8, 1945, American forces occupied the southern part of Korea, which country was divided into an American-administered zone in the south and a Soviet-administered zone in the north.[44] The foundations for many more decades of misery in Korea had been laid by the Western and Soviet victors over the former Japanese colonial rulers there.

The Second World War in Central Eurasia

In eastern Central Eurasia, the Battle of Nomonhan (Khalkhyn Gol) developed out of skirmishes along the unfixed border between Inner Mongolia—then under Japanese rule—and the Mongolian People's Republic, which was allied with the USSR and had allowed the entry of some 30,000 Soviet troops into Mongolia. Hostilities began in spring 1939 and by July had become full-scale war. The Soviets crushed the Japanese forces by the end of August. A cease-fire was signed on September 16, and a nonaggression treaty was signed in May, 1941.[45] It was observed by the two nations until the last months of the war.

Western Central Eurasia did not escape the war. German forces had invaded deep into Ukraine and the south Russian steppe, reaching as far east as the Volga and as far southeast as the Caucasus. When in late 1942 the Germans entered the Kalmyk Republic, some Kalmyks encouraged cooperation with them as a way to achieve national liberation from the brutal Stalinist regime. A small number of them became attached to the German army and

---

[43] Brune (2003).
[44] Stearns (2002: 781).
[45] Atwood (2004: 302).

served as a rear guard during the German retreat. When the Soviets returned, the Kalmyk Autonomous Soviet Socialist Republic was abolished (December 27, 1943), the Kalmyk nation was accused of disloyalty, and the entire Kalmyk Mongol population was exiled to "special settlements"—essentially concentration camps—in Siberia, Central Asia, and Sakhalin Island.[46] Similarly, immediately after the Soviets recaptured the Crimea from the Germans, in May 17–18, 1944, they shipped the entire Crimean Tatar population to Central Asia in cattle cars. It is believed that as many as 200,000 perished in the process. Tatars who had been in the Soviet army during the war were sent to join their countrymen in the Central Asian "special settlements." The government aimed to erase the Crimean Tatars' history, culture, language, and identity.[47]

In East Turkistan, a second, "socialist" East Turkistan Republic was established in the summer of 1945 in the northern part of the region. It was strongly influenced and supported by the Soviet Union.[48] Schools were further modernized, and young East Turkistanis learned Russian as their second language.[49]

Tibet, caught between two enemies—the Chinese and the British, both of whom were fighting the Japanese—stayed neutral during the war.

The Post–World War II Revolutions

THE INDIAN REVOLUTION

The shock sent around the world by the First World War had had a great impact on British India, where the Indians, who saw their rulers weakened by the war, pressed very strongly for independence. In 1919 the British had

---

[46] Atwood (2004: 291–292). The inmates were prohibited from going more than five kilometers from their *spetsposelenie* 'special settlement'.

[47] On the brutal Soviet treatment of the Tatars, see Lazzerini (1996). Other nationalities, especially the Volga Germans, were also treated savagely (Hyman 1996). On American internment of Japanese Americans in concentration camps during the Second World War, and the subsequent application of similar Modern racist "solutions" to the American Indians, modeled in part directly on the Japanese American "solution," see Drinnon (1987). Other studies suggest American business and government involvement in foreign racist programs; careful study by historians is needed.

[48] Millward (2004: 5).

[49] Shih, per. comm., Taipei, 1974.

granted limited home rule to the Indians, with a British-style parliamentary "democracy" under the colonial government in Delhi.

During the Second World War, the Japanese captured most of Southeast Asia except Thailand, including the British colonies of Malaya and Burma, and threatened India. The British relied on their Indian forces to prevent the Japanese from joining up with the Germans in North Africa. They thus granted further autonomy to the Indians.

In 1946 the British finally agreed to grant full independence to India, and on August 15, 1947, India proper was divided into two nations, India and Pakistan. Burma and Ceylon became independent the following year. For the first time in history, India was not just a geographical and cultural region, or a small part of the subcontinent; it was a country, at least in name. Unfortunately, the politicians had created a political monster. Indian Muslims wanted their own state, so the British divided the subcontinent into two overtly religious states. This was an incredibly shortsighted move. Worst of all, the state created for the Indian Muslims, Pakistan, was itself divided into two parts separated from each other by some 800 miles of Indian territory. These and other poorly conceived decisions by British and Indian politicians were the cause of regular wars, internal bloodshed, and other needless suffering from 1947 onward.

THE SECOND CHINESE REVOLUTION

The Chinese civil war that had broken out between the nationalists and the communists in 1927 resumed as soon as World War II ended in Asia with the surrender of Japan in 1945. The communist Chinese, led by Mao Tse-tung (Mao Zedong), received many of the modern weapons of the surrendered Japanese army in northern China and the modern American weapons of nationalist soldiers who surrendered to the communists and joined them. After initial nationalist successes, the communists eventually defeated the nationalists militarily and declared the People's Republic of China on October 1, 1949, in Peking.[50] Mao and his followers were radical Modernists. They rejected all European-American influence except for Modern "scientific" communism. They moved the capital from coastal Nanking back to conti-

---

[50] Buck (2002), Buell (2002).

nental Peking and turned China's attention from the Littoral and the outside world to the continent and Central Eurasia.

Mongolian and Chinese communist revolutionaries had already taken
control of Inner Mongolia by 1949. On December 3, 1949, Mao declared the
country to be a part of the People's Republic of China.

The East Turkistan Republic survived until late 1949, when the communist Chinese army marched in and occupied the country. It was incorporated back into the colony of Sinkiang (Xinjiang).

The Tibetans became increasingly nervous about the growing power of
the Chinese communists, who openly threatened to invade their country.
Internal politics and the youth of the new Dalai Lama prevented any effective measures being taken until it was too late.

In 1950–1951 the Chinese invaded Tibet with an enormous modern
army.[51] The Tibetans, outmanned and outgunned, were forced to surrender.
But the Tibetans could not in any case have withstood the Chinese communists, who by the time of their victory over the Nationalists in 1949 had one
of the largest, most modern, battle-hardened armies in the world.

The Chinese incorporated these countries into their new communist empire as nominal "autonomous regions," superficially modeled on the Soviet
system, but in fact they soon pursued an overt policy of Sinification and
forced Modernization throughout them—meaning the imposition of Marxist dogma, including atheism, which amounted to the nearly total destruction of Central Eurasian cultures.

The people of Inner Mongolia who did not want to become Chinese qui-
etly fled across the open steppe and desert to Mongolia, where the presence
of the Soviet Army kept the Chinese out. Inner Mongolia rapidly became
Chinese in population, language, and culture.

Similarly, East Turkistan was soon flooded with millions of Chinese.
They took over the country from the Uighurs and other peoples, who had
nowhere to flee to and no sympathy from major world powers such as the
United States or from the United Nations or other world organizations. The
Uighurs periodically attempted to fight back, but the Chinese outnumbered
them and freely used their overpowering military force against them.

---

[51] The number of soldiers in the invading army is estimated to have equaled or surpassed that of
the entire adult male population of Tibet.

When the Chinese began implementing the same policies in eastern and northeastern Tibet, the Tibetans there rebelled. In 1959 open rebellion broke out in the capital, Lhasa, and the life of the political and spiritual leader of Tibet, the young Fourteenth Dalai Lama, was threatened by the Chinese. At the last moment he was secretly ferreted out of Lhasa and escaped with a small guard over the Himalayas to India. The Chinese government crushed the rebellion brutally and instituted an even more repressive regime in the country. Of 2,700 monasteries in Tibet, 80 percent were destroyed by 1965, according to figures given by the Chinese government of Tibet.[52] The terror imposed on the innocent, peaceful people of Tibet by the Chinese was unprecedented in the modern history of Central Eurasia.

Before the Chinese succeeded in suppressing the rebellion and closing the borders again, about 100,000 Tibetans fled over the Himalaya Mountains to India, Nepal, and other neighboring countries, some carrying nothing more than books in an effort to save their culture from destruction by the Chinese. From exile in India, the Dalai Lama and his followers attracted the attention of sympathetic people around the world, who in turn pressured their politicians to do something. In 1959 the International Commission of Jurists, an organization affiliated with the United Nations, investigated the Chinese actions in Tibet and declared that "acts of genocide had been committed in Tibet." Subsequently, the United Nations General Assembly issued resolutions in 1959, 1961, and 1965 calling for an end to the violations of the human rights of the Tibetan people.[53]

In the face of overwhelming Chinese immigration into their homeland, and the famine caused by the Great Leap Forward (1958–1961), some 60,000 Kazakhs, Uighurs, and others fled over the border from East Turkistan into Kazakhstan in the Soviet Union.[54] But the military occupation and oppression of the Uighurs continued unabated.

The extreme Modernist terror of the Cultural Revolution (ca. 1966–1976) in China devastated especially Tibet, East Turkistan, and Inner Mongolia. The slogan on one propaganda poster from 1967 summarizes what was preached and what was done: "Smash to pieces the old world! Establish the new world!" The picture shows a man in a communist Chinese uniform standing

---

[52] Shakya (1999: 512 n. 24).
[53] Van Walt van Praag (1987: 169, 195–196).
[54] Millward (2004: 6).

on a pile of artifacts including a crucifix, a statue of Buddha, and traditional Chinese books, about to strike them with a sledgehammer.[55] Of the remaining 20 percent of the thousands of Tibetan monasteries, all but thirteen of those in the Tibetan Autonomous Region were destroyed during the Cultural Revolution. The campaign against the Four Olds was ruthlessly pursued in Tibet. All identifiably Tibetan cultural practices, artifacts, and beliefs were officially proscribed, and those who did not comply were punished.[56]

The award of the Nobel Peace Prize to the Dalai Lama in 1989 served to maintain world pressure on the Chinese government to cease its military occupation and oppression of Tibet, but little changed.

THE IRANIAN REVOLUTIONS

The Qajar Dynasty (ca. 1779–1921),[57] which had become corrupt and weak, was overthrown in 1921 by Rezâ Shâh (r. 1925–1941), who founded the Pahlavi Dynasty. In 1941, during the Second World War, Rezâ Shâh was forced to abdicate in favor of his son Mohammed Rezâ Shâh. After the war, the young shâh gradually began a wide-ranging liberalization and modernization of Iran. By the early 1970s the country had far surpassed all the nations around it in prosperity, stability, and the speed of its growth. The shâh made a firm alliance with the American and West European powers and soon Iran itself became the dominant economic, political, and military power in the region.

But liberalization, economic growth, and secularization displaced the hyperconservative Shiite Muslim clerics who had formerly wielded nearly total power in the countryside over the largely illiterate masses. Under the leadership of the radical fundamentalist Ayatollah Khomeini (1899–1989 [r. 1979–1989]), who was living in exile in Iraq, Iranians began to agitate for the overthrow of the shâh and establishment of a Modern "democracy" in Iran. The ailing Shâh was deprived of any support from his erstwhile "democratic" Western allies, who openly supported the "democratic" movement. He was finally forced to flee the country. Khomeini returned to Iran

---

[55] Anonymous. http://buddhism.2be.net/Image:Destroy_old_world.jpg.

[56] Shakya (1999: 320–323). See the widely published photograph (e.g. in Shakya 1999: plate 15) of the ruins of most of Ganden Monastery, once one of the largest in Tibet, after the Cultural Revolution.

[57] Hambly (1991: 114 et seq.).

on February 1, 1979. He and his followers immediately seized power. On November 15, a constitution was proclaimed for the new Islamic Republic of Iran. Not surprisingly, the "republic" was actually a tyrannical dictatorship controlled absolutely by the Ayatollah Khomeini and his followers. After his death, the president of the "republic" was appointed *Walî-i Faqîh*, the supreme leader. The religious fundamentalists ruthlessly eliminated all those who opposed their rule, clamped down on the merchant class that had foolishly supported them,[58] and isolated Iran from the civilized world.[59]

THE COLD WAR

In Europe, the victorious Allies divided Germany into American, British, French, and Soviet sectors.[60] Berlin, which ended up inside the Soviet sector, was itself also divided up into four sectors. But the other Allies split with the Soviets almost immediately because the latter sponsored Socialist "revolutions" throughout Soviet-occupied Central and Eastern Europe and then established puppet governments (known to Western nations as "satellites") throughout the region. The relationship between the "capitalist" Western Europeans, Americans, Japanese, and many other nations on the one hand and the "socialist" Soviets, Chinese, and their satellites worsened over time. The great struggle that developed between the two major socioeconomic systems of Eurasia after the Second World War did not break out into full-scale open warfare. The reason is generally believed to be because of the development of nuclear weapons, which have such destructive power that they can destroy life on the planet as a whole. The threat of nuclear war hanging over the world thus paradoxically prevented the outbreak of an actual war. This struggle came to be known as the Cold War. It ultimately pitted Russian-led "communists" against American-led anticommunists or "capitalists."

During the Cold War, the most tense border between the two sides was in Germany, especially between the Soviet and non-Soviet sectors in Berlin,

---

[58] For example, Zamzam, the company that before the revolution had bottled Pepsi, an American soft drink, soon came under the control of "the Foundation of the Dispossessed, a powerful bonyad, one of many religious charities Ayatollah Ruhollah Khomeini used to quasi-nationalize Iran's economy.... the bonyads have become gold mines for the powerful. In the case of Zamzam, it answers to Iran's Supreme Leader, Ayatollah Ali Khamenei" (Ellis 2007).

[59] Calmard (1993: 300).

[60] Austria was similarly divided but regained full independence in 1955.

which were cut off from the rest of western Germany by part of the Soviet sector of Germany. After the Western powers agreed (June 1, 1948) to unite the non-Soviet sectors into a Federal Republic of Germany (West Germany), the Soviets reacted by closing all land and water communications to West Berlin. However, this move only further unified the Western nations, who imposed severe sanctions on the Soviet bloc.

The Americans and other Western European powers overcame the eleven-month Soviet blockade (June 24, 1948 to May 11, 1949) by airlifting supplies into the city. On May 8, 1949, amid negotiations with the USSR aimed at ending the blockade, the Federal Republic of Germany (West Germany) was formed, with its capital the small city of Bonn, near Cologne, in the former British sector. Three days later Stalin lifted the blockade,[61] but the Soviets countered later in the same year by creating the communist German Democratic Republic, or East Germany, with its capital in East Berlin.

With the support of other European countries and the United States, West Germany recovered from the war and eventually became the strongest country in Western Europe economically. East Germany and the other Eastern European countries, which lingered in a long postwar recession, fell far behind Western Europe. Their periodic attempts to free themselves politically, or even just economically, were repeatedly crushed by the Soviet army. The addition of West Germany to the American-supported North Atlantic Treaty Organization (NATO) in 1955 was immediately countered by Soviet creation of the Warsaw Pact. Europe thus remained divided into American and Soviet spheres of influence, with American military bases in the West and Soviet military bases in the East.

In the Soviet Union the Kalmyks and others who had been exiled to Central Asia or Siberia were eventually pardoned, partially, after Stalin's death (March 5, 1953). On January 7, 1957, the Kalmyk Autonomous Soviet Socialist Republic was restored largely within its old boundaries and the Kalmyks were allowed to return to their old homeland west of the Volga delta.[62] The Crimean Tatars and Volga Germans were never fully pardoned, their homelands were not restored, and pressure on them continued down to and after the end of the Soviet Union.[63]

---

[61] Brune (2003).

[62] Atwood (2004: 291–292).

[63] The Crimea was transferred to Ukrainian territory by Khrushchev, who took power after the death of Stalin, thus making the Tatars' political status in their homeland even more difficult.

Despite sporadic, belated Russian attempts to help their colonies in Central Eurasia after the war, the region remained isolated and continued to slide deeper into poverty. At the same time, the spread of the Russian education system introduced modern science and knowledge of the world to the Central Eurasian peoples, some of whose leaders were able to rise to high positions in the multinational Soviet Union.

China's form of communism, Maoism, was largely ignored by the Americans, who attempted to keep the country isolated. But the Maoist system was not just bad for the Chinese; it also devastated the Central Eurasians living under Chinese military occupation. Other nations and cultures living near the Peoples' Republic of China also fell under the spell of this new, highly toxic form of populist Modernism.[64] Southeast Asia descended into terror. Transmitted to Cambodia, the Asian form of communism took on an even more virulent form that caused the mass murder of between one and two million Cambodians by the Khmer Rouge revolutionaries of Cambodia under Pol Pot (Saloth Sar [r. 1975–1979]), the genocidal campaigns against non-Burmese nations of Burma under the repressive nationalist military rulers (from 1958 on), and other tragedies that continued into the next century.

Other twentieth-century wars caused further death and destruction in Eurasia, notably the Spanish Civil War (1936–1939), the Korean War (1950–1953), the Vietnamese Civil War (1956–1975), the Iran-Iraq War (1980–1988), the Balkan wars attendant upon the breakup of the former Yugoslavia (1991–1995), and in Central Eurasia, the Afghan Civil War (from about 1978 on). Most of these were, or are considered to have been, civil wars, but all included extensive foreign military involvement.

The international and civil wars that ravaged Europe and much of Eurasia in the twentieth century had the effect of spreading the power of the Eurasian-derived American client-culture around the world wherever European powers had previously ruled. Along with much else, Americans brought with them their own Modernist ideology, according to which only what they

---

Many Crimean Tatars have since returned anyway, braving official and unofficial opposition and severe deprivation (Lazzerini 1996). Since the collapse of the Soviet Union, the Volga Germans have mostly given up in despair and migrated to Germany (Hyman 1996). Neither people's autonomous republic has been restored.

[64] The successive French and American attempts to keep communism out of Vietnam were followed by its victory there.

called "democracy"[65] (a version of the republican form of government) was good, while all other forms of government were bad. They actively strove to overthrow legitimate governments around the world and replace them with Anglo-American-style Modern republics. By the end of the century, the republican form of government dominated the entire world, and even the few remaining monarchies, such as Nepal,[66] and the one remaining major communist power, China, had become heavily influenced by the Anglo-American model.

Radical Modernism in Central Eurasia

From the Manchu-Chinese and Russian conquests until the very end of the twentieth century, Central Eurasia did not exist as an independent political subregion of Eurasia. It was ruled as private property by its conquerors, who violently suppressed any objections the Central Eurasian people made to the rulers' imposition of whatever they wanted to impose. When radical socialism (communism) swept across Eurasia like a new Black Death, it infected all the cultures it touched. Central Eurasians were forced to give up their traditional life-styles, dress, culture, everything. Some changes were good—the spread of hygiene, education in the sciences, secular government, and so on, is surely to be applauded. But too much was destroyed. The communist Chinese crushed Tibetans and their culture after their failed attempt to eject the tyrannical invaders. Sympathetic Westerners clamored for justice—proclamations and denouncements were made, rightly accusing the Chinese of cultural genocide—but nothing could stop the rape of Central Eurasia.

---

[65] As a form of government, this was not and is not the "democratic" form properly speaking, but rather the "republican" form. The fact that these two terms are also the names of the two major political parties in the United States is a coincidence; they are names only. The United States is nominally a republic, but the practical policies of the two parties have little to do with actual democratic or republican ideas about government. The Americans' attempts to force their Modern system onto the rest of the world were (and are) eerily similar to the communists' attempts to do the same thing with their own system.

[66] The Nepalese monarchy lost a power struggle in 2006 due to a combination of factors, by far the most important of which was the blatant, undisguised spread of populist "democratic" propaganda by the international mass media on the scene in Kathmandu, who were so obviously brainwashed by Modernism they probably had no idea what they were doing. Monarchy is bad, Modern "democracy" is good.

Central Eurasian culture suffered the most of any region of the world from the devastation of Modernism in the twentieth century, even though the region was mostly not directly involved in the two world wars. But why? The reasons lie outside Central Eurasia, in the rulers' home cultures, so in order to answer this question it is necessary to understand the wrenching changes that took place during the twentieth century in Eurasia as a whole.

It began in the concatenation of economic, demographic, political, and intellectual changes that took place in Europe and the European-dominated Littoral System with the spread of industrialization and urbanization. The extreme commercialization and intense industrialization of the great cities of the Eurasian Littoral zone—whose raison d'être was after all commerce and industry from the very beginning—was accompanied by explosive demographic growth. By the early twentieth century, the largest, most industrialized, richest, and most influential cities in the world were the great cities of Europe, the Eurasian Littoral, and European colonies around the world. In those turbulent concentrations of humanity, consciousness of the great changes that were happening at an ever faster pace in science and technology encouraged those who sided with "the moderns" against "the ancients" in intellectual and artistic life. The leaders of the mass urban culture also favored populism, an idea developed by Enlightenment thinkers and revolutionaries. Joined together with other ideas and trends, they developed into the essential driving force behind the political, social, and cultural changes that so greatly affected the entire continent: Modernism.[67]

The core idea of Modernism is simple, and seems harmless enough by itself: what is modern—new and fashionable—is *better* than what it replaces. As long as it was just a general feeling about fashion, or technical progress, and as long as classicism (or the idea that what is old is better than what is new) still acted as a counterweight, premodern modernism had little effect on the world. But the classical and aristocratic became identified with each other in opposition to the modern and nonaristocratic, along with the spread of industrialization and urbanization, when nonaristocratic people doing modern industrial, urban things came to dominate Europe, North America, and eventually much of the rest of Eurasia. There

---

[67] On Modernism in contemporary historiography, see endnote 95.

was no longer any room for the classical and the nonurban aristocratic at all. But Modernism was not merely a finite sequence in which something new (the industrial and urban) replaced something old (the aristocratic and rural) and that was that. If *only* what is new is good, it is by definition necessary to continually create or do new things. Full-blown Modernism meant, and still means, *permanent revolution*: continuous rejection of the traditional or immediately preceding political, social, artistic, and intellectual order.

Permanent revolution meant that what went before, including any previous revolution (and its products), was bad and had to be rejected. Even Reason—free inquiry, independent thinking, logic, questioning—was identified as one of the old ideas and practices of old aristocratic intellectuals. It was relentlessly attacked by "conservative" religious leaders, politicians, and journalists. Such "conservatives" often were the most fanatic Modernists. The sociopolitical results—the tyrannies of fascism, communism, and political-religious fundamentalism, each of which required the unquestioning belief of the masses in the radical ideas preached by their leaders—were quintessentially Modern. It is not surprising that Modernism achieved its greatest successes with the horrific world wars and mass murder of the twentieth century.[68]

With the Modernist identification of monarchy as an old form of government, populists[69] succeeded in instituting Modern nonmonarchist forms of government in one form or another—ranging from totalitarian fascist or communist dictatorship to "democratic" republic—in nearly all countries in Eurasia by 1951.[70] Everything was done in the name of "the people," "the

---

[68] Even after the worst of the terror was over, Modernism in the arts continued to spread across Central Eurasia, especially via architecture, because the foreign rulers tore down traditional Central Eurasian–style buildings and replaced them with Modern buildings. The physical appearance of Central Eurasian cities changed drastically, and the cultural heritage of the region was impoverished accordingly.

[69] The term populism has been used in different senses. My usage of it should be clear from the discussion here. The spread into the Middle East and some other regions of religious-political fundamentalism, a particularly pernicious form of Modern populism, does not bode well for the future.

[70] By the end of the twentieth century, the populists had completely replaced all other forms of government. Except for a few countries, most of them small and isolated, every country in the world now claims to be a Modern democracy. In fact, none of them are true democracies, and most are not even true republics, but dictatorships or, at best, oligarchies.

masses," regardless of the titular political system. Most stereotypically, "mass culture" was the only kind acceptable under "scientific communism."

Revolutionary social, political, intellectual (or rather, anti-intellectual), and artistic (actually anti-artistic) Modernism began in the European-run Littoral System, at home in Europe. The proximal source of political Modernism, the driving force behind political life and death in recent times, is to be found in the Enlightenment. Its most influential thinker was Jean Jacques Rousseau (1712–1778), who proposed revolutionary ideas—many of them very good ideas—in nearly all spheres of life. But they turned out to be incendiary ideas. The French Revolution (1789–ca. 1799), which unleashed a reign of unspeakable cruelty and mass murder presided over by demagogues glibly preaching the virtues of "democracy," "liberty," and other ideas of the Enlightenment philosophers (who certainly never imagined the terror that others would perpetrate in their names), can be deemed the first major blow actually struck by Modernism in Europe. It was a harbinger of even worse things. The terrible wars of the nineteenth century, with their new technology that increasingly made it easier than ever to kill large numbers of people, were accompanied by the full onslaught of the Industrial Revolution and accompanying rapid urbanization in Western Europe, North America, and Japan. All three developments—military, industrial, and urban—shifted power to men who did not represent the traditional nonurban aristocracy and their high cultural ideals. Modernism had largely won by the late nineteenth century, and in the twentieth it reached its full development.

The Littoral powers—England, France, and their allies in Europe and America, and Japan in Asia—defeated and punished the continental powers in the First World War. The result, not surprisingly, was one radical revolution after the other in continental Eurasia, including Germany, Russia, and China (where the early communist revolution was largely suppressed by massacre in 1927). Throughout the twentieth century, earlier scientific theories, technologies, and ideologies were constantly replaced by new ones. The total victory of the populist "democratic" form of government concentrated unprecedented power in the hands of unscrupulous rulers who eagerly took advantage of the new possibilities. The result was the consciously directed mass murder of tens of millions of innocent people in Eurasia and the spread of the most vicious, destructive form of cultural Modernism across Central Eurasia.

Modernism and the Destruction of the Arts

Modernism arose in the great industrialized cities of Europe and the European-dominated Littoral zone. Because it was in part a reaction of urban, commercial, industrialized Littoral zone people against elite, aristocratic, land-based continental people, it inevitably had a powerful effect on Central Eurasia, which was at the mercy of its colonial rulers.

During the reign of unbridled Marxist socialism in the Soviet Union, especially in the 1930s under Stalin, and again later in the People's Republic of China, especially between 1966 and 1976 under Mao, radical Modernism savaged Central Eurasia.[71] Thousands of monasteries, temples, churches, mosques, madrasas, shrines, and synagogues, which contained the artistic and architectural heritage of Central Eurasian peoples, were closed or destroyed. For example, by the end of the 1930s in the Soviet Union, "visible religious life had been virtually destroyed. Out of the 50,000 Orthodox churches in the Russian Empire on the eve of the Revolution only a few hundred remained open."[72] Of the many synagogues in the Russian Empire, by 1966 the number remaining in the entire USSR was thought to be "only sixty-two."[73] Whereas in 1917 there were 26,279 mosques in the empire, in the USSR at the end of the Brezhnev (r. 1964–1982) era there were about 200. In Azerbaijan alone, there were approximately 2,000 mosques in 1917 but only 55 in 1990.[74] Of the approximately 2,700 monasteries in the Tibetan Autonomous Region (covering about half the total area of Tibet; the rest of the country has been divided up among neighboring Chinese provinces), 80 percent were destroyed by 1965, according to Chinese government figures; only *thirteen* were left after the Cultural Revolution.[75] The

---

[71] It also destroyed very much in China itself.

[72] Walters (1993: 16). Many were converted to other uses, such as barns and warehouses.

[73] Rothenberg (1978: 190). According to a government source, "between 1917 and 1927, 23 percent of synagogues (366 out of 1,400) and churches had been closed, but these figures are much too low. Some cities had over one hundred synagogues and the total number as well as the confiscations were greater." The figure of 1,400 evidently referred only to Ukraine, where the number of synagogues was "reduced to 1,034 by 1927" (Levin 1988: 82). By 1980, despite de-Stalinization, there were only 92 synagogues in the entire Soviet Union (Levin 1988: 774).

[74] Ramet (1993: 40).

[75] Shakya (1999: 512). "In China, monasteries in Inner Mongolia were generally closed down in the Great Leap Forward, 1958–1960. I would guess that by 1960 there were no surviving functioning monasteries" (Christopher Atwood, per. comm., 2007). In the Soviet Union, "In

CHAPTER 11

same happened in Mongolia during the Stalinist period.[76] The men who staffed those institutions, who embodied the wisdom of the ages, were forcibly removed and secularized, and often imprisoned or sent to labor camps, if not killed outright,[77] and many of their books and art objects were destroyed. The Modern schools and universities that were eventually built in Central Eurasia by the Soviet and Chinese communists could not—and still cannot—compete with even the smallest colleges in Europe or America in their level of education, not to speak of making new contributions to scholarship and science.[78] The representatives of the old elite secular culture, whether aristocrats, petty "bourgeois," or intellectuals, were generally treated even worse—they were imprisoned or executed outright. Culturally, Modernism thus devastated Central Eurasia much more than any other part of the world.

In art, as in politics, the beginnings of Modernism can be discerned as far back as the eighteenth-century Enlightenment. But before the twentieth century, although the greatest artists nearly all achieved their success by striving against tradition and sometimes breaking the rules, there was a balance between the two forces: the goal of the upward-aiming aristocratic system was to achieve success by creating artworks that were as near to perfection as possible within the parameters of the traditional rules based on the natural order. The goal of the downward-aiming modern tendency was to achieve success by creating art works that effectively changed the traditional or previously followed rules. Because these two forces were in balance, the great artists of the past did not destroy the existing rules, they stretched them or otherwise modified them. But when the entire political and cultural system of the West shifted to Modernism by the early twentieth century, not only monarchy was rejected: thrown out along with it were the palaces and princesses and all other elements of the old culture, especially traditional intellectual and artistic ideals. The substitution of

Buriatia, the move to eliminate Buddhism began around 1932 and by around 1937 there were no functioning monasteries. Ivolga Datsang was reopened after the Second World War. In Kalmykia the chronology was similar, but no monasteries were ever reopened until the late 1980s" (Christopher Atwood, per. comm., 2007).
[76] "In Mongolia, the government had to retreat in 1932 due to armed insurrection, but in 1936 pressure began again and by 1939, the last functioning monasteries were closed down. Gandan-Tegchenling was reopened in 1944" (Christopher Atwood, per. comm., 2007).
[77] On forced laicization in Mongolia and neighboring regions, see endnote 96.
[78] Unfortunately, they still cannot compete, though foreign nongovernmental organizations are trying to improve things.

populist ideals for aristocratic ones necessarily eliminated the idea of cultural paragons—the great men who, as Yeats put it, "walk in a cloth of
gold, and display their passionate hearts, that the groundlings may feel
their souls wax the greater."[79] In all spheres of society there was no longer
any higher model to aspire to. Money and power, which were attainable by
anyone clever or ruthless enough, made the newly rich "robber barons" of
the late nineteenth and early twentieth centuries into a rough apparent
substitute for the old aristocracy, but they and the new populist political
leaders were mostly inspired by ordinary greed. They also did not have the
aristocrats' tradition of responsibility toward their subjects, which was one
of the last, faded cultural memories of the courtly culture derived from
feudalism and, in turn, from the comitatus relationship of the Central
Eurasian Culture Complex. The aristocratic idea of the enlightened patron
or cultural paragon was cast down like everything else that belonged to
the old order, including the idea that there was, or should be, an accepted
set of rules, based on the natural order, for determining the creation of
works of art.[80]

The sociopolitical stripping of the elite aristocracy's hierarchical position
above ordinary "commoners" and the institution of populism was thus mir-
rored in intellectual and artistic life by the elimination of the dichotomy
between the elite, which strived for perfection, and the ordinary, which
strived for the commonplace. Modern poets stripped poetry of its elite status in relation to prose: free verse, a thinly disguised form of prose that
anyone could write and was therefore accessible to anyone, replaced poetry.
Painting called for little training or aesthetic taste (and, indeed, Modernism
explicitly demanded its suppression); it required only the ability to splash
paint on a canvas. In painting, poetry, and music, among other high arts,
traditional forms were rejected and there was unrelenting pressure to abandon any new forms that arose to replace the old ones.[81] The result was literally

---

[79] Harrison (1966: 47).

[80] It is not that artists were unaware of the need for rules. The serial, dodecaphonic, or
twelve-tone method of composition developed mainly by the Austrian composer Arnold
Schoenberg (Schönberg, 1874–1951) prescribes formal rules to be followed in serial compositions. These rules do not, however, derive from the traditional rules, which are ultimately
based on nature's overtone system; they are an explicit rebellion against them and the natural harmony they produce.

[81] The much-hyped "Postmodernism" or "Post-Modernism" by no means replaced Modernism.
"In the years following World War II the term 'Post-Modern' became current, but no coherent 'Post-Modern' aesthetic ever emerged" (Teed 1992: 309). Indeed, although in some fields

the loss of the meaning of Art and even Beauty,[82] and the mass rejection of contemporary arts by many of the elite, who turned instead to the preservation and cultivation of the art forms of earlier centuries. A new form of popular music, rock and roll, with simple melodies, simple harmonies, and simple rhythms that practically anyone could play or sing, replaced the music of the elite.[83] Modernism spread through all the arts, leaving no survivors except in museums and universities, which entombed them and the dead elite culture.

Painters and other graphic artists, most of whom depended on the direct sale of the originals of their works, found that the easiest way to attract attention—in order to gain customers and thus succeed in the artistic marketplace—was to be more offensive in some way than other artists. In the beginning, this was accomplished most easily, and often quite unintentionally, by the artist's abandonment of one or another pre-Modern artistic practice or convention. Soon it became necessary to be more offensive than previously, until shock value produced name recognition and, eventually, market value. It is not that representational art is good, and it is bad that painters rejected it. Representation per se has nothing whatever to do with the problem, which is that artists explicitly rejected the idea of Beauty conceived of as perfection (in some way, abstract or not) of the visual order of Nature.[84] As the Modern aesthetician Adorno perceptively says, "Natural beauty . . . is now scarcely even a topic of [aesthetic] theory." Yet, natural beauty and art beauty are bound together; "reflection on natural beauty is irrevocably requisite to the theory of art," and even more so to its practice.[85]

Because Modernism, as permanent revolution, was "a phenomenon of reaction,"[86] it was necessary for artists to change by rejecting what had al-

---

(particularly literature) Postmodernism has taken on other meanings, the rejection of a coherent aesthetic is one of its characteristics in general. It is in large part simply another twist of the mutating virus of Modernism, in that it is ultimately the result of an attempt by some to establish themselves as the new avant-garde in distinction to the "old" avant-garde Modernists.

[82] See the extensive discussion of various aspects of this issue by Adorno (1997).

[83] The success of rock music throughout society as a whole was paralelled by the revival of Baroque music among the young elite, most of whom also listened to rock and folk music. The strong rhythms and clear melodic lines of Baroque music were often compared to rock. See also endnote 101.

[84] Adorno (1997) comments at great length on the shifting focus of graphic art and the relative dominance of the idea of the Ugly—an indispensible prerequisite for the idea of Beauty.

[85] Adorno (1997: 61, 62, 65).

[86] Botstein (1998: 255).

ready been done. Pablo Picasso (1881–1973), generally considered to be the greatest Modern painter of the century, changed styles several times for the same reasons that Igor Stravinsky did in music: it was *necessary* for them to change, to be different from others, even from their earlier selves, in order to *remain* Modern and thus sell their output. The unforeseen effect of this process was the devaluing of older works of Modern art *as art* by comparison with works of pre-Modern periods. Picasso's middle period works had great shock effect at the time, but by the end of the century perhaps the only ones that retained much *artistic* value, as against commercial[87] or primarily historical value (such as *Guernica*, his most famous painting),[88] were his earliest works, which though representational and essentially traditional did not make any overt attempt to succeed via shock value—an essentially nonartistic or anti-artistic approach. Only the domination of academics and museums over Modern artistic life have maintained awareness of works, famous in their time for their shock value, which would otherwise have been forgotten decades ago.

Modernism in the arts thus developed during the twentieth century into the establishment of a kind of superficial permanent revolution parallel to the superficial permanent revolution of the republican form of government (theoretically achieved through the election system). In both cases the result was, and remains, permanent mediocrity.[89] In the arts, the Modernists did not really react to the ideas or practices of their predecessors;[90] they simply overthrew them and replaced them with entirely new ones—they wanted to clean the slate and start over again. The inevitable result of thus constantly expelling "the preestablished" was "complete impoverishment: the scream of the destitute, powerless gesture."[91] Once the

[87] The de facto Modern view is that the artistic works with the highest price in the marketplace are the "greatest" works. Accordingly, the incredibly high prices fetched by some artworks continue to mislead people into thinking they are great works of art.

[88] My view of most of Picasso's opus is undoubtedly unpopular, as many do consider it to retain some aesthetic value; but I believe that whatever such value it may retain, it is a fundamentally historical or academic aesthetic. *Guernica* is a canonical painting—it is perhaps *the* Modern artwork of the academic art canon, and thus certainly important for art history—but that does not mean it is (or was) a great work of art, *as art*. Speaking purely of art per se rather than artists, the works of the American abstract painter Jackson Pollack (1912–1956) are perhaps more quintessentially Modern than those of Picasso, but the latter was much more successful in developing a cult of personality that identified him as *the* great Modern artist.

[89] Cf. Adorno (1997: 29–30).

[90] Reaction might have resulted in refinement and improvement of what had gone before.

[91] Adorno (1997: 30).

slate was cleaned and traditional practices in the arts were gone, the only practice left that was identifiable as artistic was the dunce's job of cleaning the slate. As a result, artists necessarily rejected other artists' previous work, as well as their own previous creations, and attempted to replace them with totally different fashions. The logical extreme to which many artists succumbed was to break the slate and throw it away: they rejected Art itself under any known or imaginable definitions. The result of the loss of the meaning of Art could only be the meaninglessness of the artifacts produced by "artists."[92]

Poets abandoned the traditional elements that defined literature as poetry and embraced free verse, poetry lacking the defining characteristics of what had been poetry (as distinct from prose) throughout history in most of the world: regular rhythms based on meter or stress patterns, various types of rhyme (in some languages mainly consonance and assonance), and other musical elements. This shift was facilitated and encouraged in European cultures by the earlier loss of the tradition of chanting or singing poetry, so that, even before Modernism struck, it was read, like prose. Most Modern poets in the West had never heard poetry sung or chanted in the traditional fashion; they grew up with little or no understanding of the fact that poetry—both lyric and epic—had once been *defined* as language written to be sung or chanted. Free verse was different from prose only in the odd punctuation, vocabulary, and grammar used by Modern poets to mark their productions as "poetic." Poets recited their works aloud in an odd form of diction peculiar to them.[93] It is thus not surprising that Modern poets found it difficult to write poetry that was not, by all known definitions, essentially prose. The American-British writer generally considered to be the greatest English-language Modern poet of the century, T. S. Eliot (1888–1965), was unable to produce his masterpiece *The Waste Land* (1922) without radical editorial help from another Modern poet, his friend Ezra Pound (1885–1972); nevertheless, it remains seriously flawed at best as art.[94] Eliot's work in general is surpassed by the work of twentieth-century poets writing in other

---

[92] On the loss of art itself through Modern radicalism, see endnote 97.

[93] On the loss of the connection between poetry and music in European and other Modernized traditions, see endnote 98.

[94] While many perceptive readers noticed the flaws even before the discovery and publication of Ezra Pound's radical reworking of Eliot's manuscript, some critics had already noted that "even *The Waste Land* is marred" (Dyson 1968: 627).

languages, and even by a few writing in English, such as the Irish poet W. B. Yeats (1865–1939) and the Welsh poet Dylan Thomas (1914–1953), yet Eliot received more attention than any other twentieth-century English poet.[95] This was not because his work is better as Art but because in the beginning, when he made his reputation, it was more shocking and offensive, and thus more Modern,[96] and was canonized very early in the Modern movement.

Although Modern composers' "atonal" compositions often had a compelling extramusical intellectual component—typically mathematical, graphical, textual, or philosophical in essence rather than auditory[97]—the "music" they produced was devoid of precisely those elements that defined music in virtually every world culture: rhythm, melody (especially a full tune), and natural harmony.[98] In particular, musicians rebelled against the dominance of the harmonies and melodic lines built on the overtone system—which is based on nature's own acoustics, including the acoustics of human language—and also rejected natural rhythms. It is not surprising that Modern composers killed off the audience for new Western art music along with the classical tradition itself: because of the structure of the human auditory faculty, sounds of any kind that conflict too extremely with the natural overtone system are physically painful. In an age when it was necessary for an artist to acquire a popular following in order to survive, Modern musicians'

[95] In view of the massive number of practicing English-language poets, surely the constraints of Modernism explain why none of them have produced great poetry. The same applies to the incredible number of composers.

[96] This is true also of his first major work, *The Lovesong of J. Alfred Prufrock* (1915), which is superior to *The Waste Land* in many respects *as poetry*, but perhaps even more repulsive aesthetically.

[97] The same may be said even of harmonically conservative music, such as the tone poems of Richard Strauss (1864–1949). But Strauss was otherwise different. After having composed much avant-garde art music, culminating in his opera *Elektra*, he decided that European art music was taking a wrong turn; he rejected the Modernist doctrine of "progress" in musical structure, which was already leading to anti-musical Modern academicism, and continued to write great music until his death; cf. endnote 99.

[98] This was taken to its logical extreme in the latter half of the century by the avant-garde composer John Cage, whose most famous work is *4'33"* (Four Minutes and Thirty-three Seconds), which consists only of silence. (This is comparable in painting to Kazimir Malevich's paintings *White on White*, *Black Square*, and others from the mid-teens of the twentieth century.) Of other Modern approaches, the most successful was Minimalism, typified by the works of musicians such as Philip Glass, who rebelled against Serialism and composed works consisting of a small number of pitches or simple musical phrases drawn out and repeated over and over with minimal change. Note that by "natural harmony" I do not mean traditional European, Asian, or any other particular harmonic system, but simply any harmony based on the natural overtone system.

compositions sent audiences, including other Modern composers, running from the concert halls.[99] Their compositions represented the opposite of the unintellectual or even openly anti-intellectual "popular music," which was appropriately so called in contradistinction to the extremely *un*popular Modern art music. By the First World War, popular music had begun to acquire a following even among classes of people who would never have admitted listening to it in the nineteenth century. It soon became more Modern and sophisticated to listen to jazz—and it certainly was more enjoyable than putting up with the boredom and aural torture of the "arcane surface" of most Modern composers' works.[100]

The man widely considered to be the greatest Modern composer of the century, the Russian Igor Stravinsky (1882–1971), several times during his long life adopted new styles that had been innovated by other Modern composers. His repeated attempts to achieve the shock effect he had attained with his early ballet *The Rite of Spring*,[101] which caused a riot at its premiere in Paris in 1913, eventually succeeded in alienating practically everyone except other Modern composers, for most of whom Stravinsky could do no wrong. By the end of the twentieth century, the works of Stravinsky that had become by far the most widely accepted in the repertoire were his early ballets, including *The Rite of Spring*,[102] which are still essentially tonal in the broad sense. The eventual, very long-lived fashion among professional composers for Serialism, which explicitly rejected harmony based on the natural overtone system, resulted in the loss of the traditional concert audience for new art music.

---

[99] Some scholars consider music to be an exception to the rule, but this does not seem to be accurate; see endnote 100.

[100] Modern music "implicitly encouraged, as a result of its arcane surface, renewed enthusiasm for popular and commercial music among late twentieth-century intellectuals and artists as worthy of high status and critical attention" (Botstein 1998: 259). Botstein's "arcane surface" is a euphemistic expression designed to draw attention away from the plain-language fact: "music" that violates the natural harmonic system of the overtones will sound harsh or even painful to most people anywhere in the world, for purely natural physical reasons, not because of theory, education, or taste.

[101] The audience at the premiere of *The Rite of Spring* was outraged by the crude sexuality of the dancing as well as by the music. Both had been consciously, deliberately designed to shock the audience. On possible influences on Stravinsky's music, see endnote 101.

[102] Stravinsky adopted Serialism for awhile after the death of Schoenberg, its pioneer, though the latter had openly satirized Stravinsky, calling him Modernsky in his *Drei Satiren für gemischten Chor*, opus 28 (http://www.schoenberg.at/6_archiv/music/works/op/compositions_op28_texts_e.htm#Seitenanfang).

The vapidity and deliberate anti-aestheticism of Modern art was a direct result of the intellectual barrenness of the entire age. Because man must be a natural creature, the doomed rebellion of Man against Nature, with the accompanying worship of human products (particularly machines), was guaranteed to result in contradiction and destruction. Although Modernism began in the Enlightenment, a period characterized by the ideal of Reason, as Modernism increasingly merged with populism, the rule of the intellect and rationality—not something characteristic of the common man—became identified with the traditional order. Because that was in turn equated with the aristocratic elite, the ideal of Reason was rejected along with that of the traditional artistic ideals of order and beauty. Perhaps this is the source of the Postmodern mutation of Modernism in scholarship.

Although it proved to be impossible to create new styles wholly uninfluenced by the natural order, or by older works that had been based on it, Modernism forced artists to overtly deny any such relationship with their own works. As a result, they were unable to establish what exactly it was they did that was "artistic," what it is artists were supposed to do, and why. They were utterly incapable of defining the meaning of the words *art, music,* and *poetry.*

> It is the mark of the present period in the history of art that the concept of art implies no internal constraint on what works of art are, so that one no longer can tell if something is a work of art or not. Worse, something can be a work of art but something quite like it not be one, since nothing that meets the eye reveals the difference. This does not mean that it is arbitrary whether something is a work of art, but only that traditional criteria no longer apply.[103]

When popular artists first began to fill the void created by Modern anti-artists, they were mostly not recognized as artists at all. It was only when the equation of market value with art value became firmly established that popular artists—mainly musicians and dancers—began using the term

---

[103] Danto (2003: 17). Cf. Adorno (1997: 1), "It is self-evident that nothing concerning art is self-evident any more, not its inner life, not its relation to the world, not even its right to exist."

artist.[104] Yet, however one may judge their actual works, they at least thought of themselves as artists in the full original sense of the word—someone devoted to making beautiful things—unlike most Modern "artists," who rejected all definitions of the words *art*, *beauty*, and even *artist*.

Life undoubtedly has always been difficult for creative people, but it used to be that there was a fairly fixed socioeconomic slot for artists and artisans, because the aristocrats needed them. The aristocrats, bad as they sometimes might have been in reality or in practice, represented an ideal, not only something people could look up to but something the aristocrats expected of themselves, too. Looking upward, they demanded perfection, or as close to it as they could get, so they hired the best artists and artisans to produce it, and those working for them tried their best to achieve it. If artists were not looking up and doing their best to serve God, they were doing their best to serve men they *thought* were "better"; it had nothing to do with whether the church or the aristocrats really were somehow better. Trying to upend things, to set the basest type of man above the others, cannot actually replace the old order—no one can look up to someone who is by definition as low as can be—so the result is the elimination of order itself. Today, the artist/artisan socioeconomic slot no longer really exists (one need only ask a young artist), and nothing has really replaced it. But the entire purpose or goal of art is largely gone anyway. The total victory of Modernism meant the conscious rejection of the traditional values of Reason, artistic order, and Beauty.

Because Modernism was not so much a philosophy or movement as a total world-view, it was applied to all aspects of life. The victory of radical political Modernism—specifically, Marxist-Leninist socialism—in Russia (from 1917) and China (from 1949) led to implementation of its totalitarian agenda all across Central Eurasia. The destruction of almost all aspects of tradi-

---

[104] The market value of the works of some popular artists—notably musicians—is far greater than the most valuable works of any kind by contemporary Modern school artists, who have become increasingly academic. It is also greater than that of most works of pre-Modern art. Some popular musicians, dancers, and others are truly dedicated to their art, and deserve the name "artists". Unfortunately, the lack of elite elements (such as elegance, beauty, and striving for perfection) in most of their work continues to prevent it from rising to the level of "high" Art and finally replacing Modern art, most of which belongs in museums of curiosities.

tional culture, including material artifacts, by the despotic Russian and Chinese communist rulers, though resisted by Central Eurasian peoples, was ultimately successful.

The difference between the history of Modernism in Central Eurasia and in Western Europe is striking. In Europe, despite the Second World War and the occasional Modern building, Paris is still characterized by its beautiful old traditional architecture, and the libraries and museums are full. Modernism mainly prevented the creation of new works of art. Very little of the inherited cultural tradition was destroyed. In Central Eurasia, by contrast, only a few famous monuments were *not* destroyed, and only a tiny percentage of the once vast number of old books was preserved. By the end of the twentieth century, the evil done in the name of Modernism and "progress" left Central Eurasians bereft of much of their past.

Central Eurasia Reborn

ي, اش ئىدۇق ئۆزۈن سەپەرگە ئاتلىنىپ ماڭغاندا بىز،
ئەمدى ئاتقا مىنگەندەك بوپ قالدى ئەنە نەۋرىمىز.
ئاز ئىدۇق مۈشكۈل سەپەرگە ئاتلىنىپ چىققاندا بىز،
ئەمدى چوڭ كارۋان ئاتالدۇق، قالدۇرۇپ چۆللەردە ئىز.
قالدى ئىز چۆللەر ئارا، گايى داۋانلاردا يەنە،
قالدى نى - نى ئارسلانلار دەشت- چۆلدە قەۋرىسىز.
قەۋرىسىز قالدى دىمەڭ يۇلغۇن قىزارغان دالدا،
گۈل- چىچەككە پۈركىنۇر تاڭنا باھاردا قەۋرىمىز.
قالدى ئىز، قالدى مەنزىل، قالدى ئۇزاقتا ھەممىسى،
چىقسا بوران، كۆچسە قۇملار ھەم كۆمۈلمەس ئىزىمىز.
توختىماس كارۋان يولىدىن گەرچە ئاتلار بەك ئورۇق،
تاپقۇسى ھىچبولمىسا، بۇ ئىزنى بىر كۈن نەۋرىمىز،
يا ئەۋرىمىز.

-- ئابدۇرېھىم ئۆتكۈر، " ئىز"

We were young when we rode out on the long journey;
Now it seems those grandchildren of ours are riding horses.
We were few when we rode forth on that hard journey;
Now we're called a Great Caravan that left tracks in the wastelands.
The tracks remain out in the wastes, in the valleys and mountain
     passes, and
There are very many heroes left graveless in the desert.
Do not say graveless: In the tamarisk-reddened wilderness, at
Dawn, in the spring, our graves are covered with
     rose-blossoms.
Our tracks remain, our dreams remain, everything remains,
     far away, yet
Even if the wind blows, or the sands shift, they will never be
     covered, our tracks.
And the caravan will never stop along the way, though our
     horses are very thin;
One way or another these tracks will be found someday, by our
     grandchildren;
               Or, our great-grandchildren.
                    —Abdurehim Ötkur, *Tracks*[1]

The Fourth Regional Empire Period

Toward the end of the twentieth century, capitalism spread in China and India and the economies of those imperial states grew very rapidly, though politically very little changed in either one. When the Soviet Union collapsed in 1991, the tensions of the Cold War appeared to have eased. The former Russian Soviet Socialist Republic was reorganized as an independent Russian national-imperial state. The other former federal republics also regained their independence, including those in Western Central Asia, the Caucasus, and the former western Pontic Steppe. Suddenly and unexpectedly, much of Central Eurasia was once again independent.

One of the most striking developments of this period was the growth of the European Union in size, unity, and economic strength. By 2007 it included nearly all European states west of Russia, Belarus (Belarus'), and Ukraina (Ukraine, the Ukraine). Though often hampered by the selfish, shortsighted policies of populist politicians, the European Union and the new or reformed imperial states developed politically along with the economic growth in the Eurasian periphery, producing a new imperial world order there. All of the large polities surrounding Central Eurasia—China, India, the European Union, and Russia—grew very fast.

However, Central Eurasia itself was not so fortunate. Although more than half of the major Central Eurasian nations were once again independent, with the continued lack of a unifying Central Eurasian polity, whether a government or an economic-political bloc such as the European Union, weakness, poverty, backwardness, and foreign domination continued. Persian-speaking southern Central Asia (Afghanistan) and Southwestern Asia (Iran and Kurdistan), as well as the Near East and Pakistan, remained dominated by religious and nationalistic tyrannies. The weakness of the entire region contributed greatly to the economic and political weakness of neighboring Western Central Asia—former Soviet Central Asia.

The Russians also unfortunately did not free the remaining Central Eurasian countries under their control—including the Kalmyks, Tuvins, Altaians,

---

[1] The text is taken from the beginning of Ötkur's novel, *Iz* (1985/1986), where the poem was originally published; it differs slightly from the later popular version reproduced in Rudelson (1997: 174). Ötkur (1923–1995) was one of the greatest Uighur writers, as the original of this poem well demonstrates.

Sakha, and Evenkis,[2] and the Chechens in the North Caucasus region. With the recovery of the Russian economy, a new populist autocracy began to develop that once again threatened internal and external critics with violence. At the same time, the Chinese continued their military occupation of the nations of East Turkistan, Inner Mongolia, and Tibet, enforced with the indiscriminate use of terror and violence. Both the Russians and the Chinese contributed directly to the failure of Central Eurasia as a whole to recover economically in this period.[3]

Culturally, too, Central Eurasia had been devastated by the long, oppressive rule of the peripheral states, especially those regions which had been, or continued to be, under the rule of the communist empires. The onslaught of radical Modernism had destroyed most of the traditional arts and sciences of the region and failed to provide effective replacements. With the coming of independence or capitalism, the long official suppression of full European Modernism in the arts was ended in much of Central Eurasia. Artistic Modernism thus spread, with almost no traditional cultural establishment to resist it. On the other hand, religious communities rejoiced, and many old churches, mosques, synagogues, and other religious buildings that still existed were repaired and reopened, while in other cases new ones began to be built.

The Beginnings of Eurasian Recovery

The worldwide Cold War between the communist and capitalist camps was won by the capitalists when the Soviet Union finally[4] collapsed. The collapse was due partly to internal structural failure and partly to the crushing burden of supporting the increasingly impoverished countries of Central Eur-

---

[2] The Evenkis are very often mistakenly called "Evenks" in English, even in linguistic works (whose authors should know better), due to the popular Russian misanalysis of their name as a Russian plural.

[3] See chapter 10.

[4] The collapse of the Soviet Union was predicted by the courageous Soviet writer Andrei Amalrik (1938–1980), who in 1969 published his essay, *Will the Soviet Union Survive until 1984?* Nevertheless, most Western Sovietologists ignored Amalrik and his prediction and even insisted, right down to the actual declaration of its dissolution, that the Soviet Union was doing well economically. This stubbornness is incredible in the face of the economic barrenness that was obvious to any visitor (certainly in 1972, when I was there). Amalrik was imprisoned and then forced into exile in 1976. He died before his negative prediction came true only seven years after the ironic date in his book's title.

asia while maintaining an enormous military and developing new military technology in order to keep up with the capitalists. When the Soviet Union's federal republics, led by the tiny Baltic states, began declaring their independence, one by one, in 1990, the federal government attempted to clamp down on them. But after a failed coup in August 1991, still more of the federal republics declared their independence. Finally President Mikhail Gorbachev (b. 1931 [r. 1985–1991]) declared the dissolution of the Union of Soviet Socialist Republics on December 21, 1991.[5]

The constituent federal republics, including those in the Caucasus and Western Central Asia, thus suddenly and quite unexpectedly[6] became independent. The Russians also withdrew their military forces from Mongolia and the countries of Central and Eastern Europe that had been under Soviet occupation since the Second World War. However, unfortunately none of the "second-rank" autonomous Soviet republics or other autonomous regions were freed. Despite the collapse of the Soviet Union, many Russians were determined to hold onto these conquests of their imperial czarist and socialist forebears, whatever the consequences. The Russian decision to accept capitalism was at first more theoretical than practical, considering that the government continued to consist almost entirely of former communists who only slowly allowed actual independent businesses to operate legally. With the reopening of China to international trade and investment, however, most of Eurasia had converted to capitalism as an economic system—if not true capitalism—by the end of the century.

The success of Modernism in twentieth-century politics was phenomenal. By 1951 populists[7] had succeeded in instituting Modern nonmonarchist governments of one kind or another—ranging from totalitarian fascist or communist dictatorships to liberal "democratic" republics—in nearly all countries in Eurasia. By the end of the twentieth century, populism had completely replaced all other forms of government. Every country in the world (except for a few small, isolated countries) claimed to be a Modern democracy. In fact, none of them were actual democracies, and most were not even republics; they were dictatorships or oligarchies at best. The victory of Modernism was complete.

---

[5] He resigned as president on December 25, 1991.

[6] See note 4 above.

[7] See note 69 in chapter 11 on the term populism.

ECONOMIC RECOVERY OF CHINA

In 1978, only two years after the death of Mao Tse-tung, the Chinese leaders began slowly shifting their desperately poor country back to capitalism. They first allowed a small amount of capitalist investment, mostly by foreign companies using China as a cheap labor farm for manufacturing. The move was successful, in that it was extremely profitable for the foreign investors, as well as for the communist leaders, who suddenly became rich as well as powerful. The Chinese developed a kind of "state capitalism," which quickly grew into state-supervised full-blown capitalism. The extremely rapid growth of the Chinese economy, as well as Chinese science and technology, allowed the country to move from the ranks of the poor, undeveloped states to one of the world's leading economies, with a strong space program, within a mere three decades. The future for Chinese economic development looked bright. Unlike the Russians, however, the Chinese did not free any of the Central Eurasian nations they occupied. Instead, they oppressed them more grievously, especially East Turkistan.[8] Even worse was the fact that while many Chinese seemed strongly desirous of joining the civilized world, the government leaders were at the same time threatening the independent nations around them, who, they claimed, "belonged" to China. This was the same language used for the countries that the Chinese had already occupied militarily. At the turn of the millennium the failure of the Chinese people to recognize, resist, and overcome their government's brainwashing did not bode well for the rest of the world.

ECONOMIC RECOVERY OF INDIA

Though little noted, by the end of the twentieth century India was growing economically at almost as rapid a rate as China, at about the same time, and demographically it grew even faster. India's economic and political presence in the world increasingly became an accepted fact. Unfortunately, the spread of Hindu fundamentalism threatened political stability and the possibility of cultural growth beyond the relatively primitive stage in which much of the countryside still languished. In addition, the growth of Maoist communism in Hindu-dominated Nepal, on the southern Himalayan frontier of Tibetan Central Eurasia, further threatened stability in the region. Nevertheless, In-

[8] See especially Bovingdon (2004).

dia's rapid economic growth and technical progress ensured that the country would have a major role to play in the world in the new century.

RECOVERY OF RUSSIA

In dissolving the Soviet Union, the Russians divested themselves of their peripheral liabilities but retained the most valuable conquests from czarist imperial times. The most important of these had been Russianized, including the port cities of St. Petersburg[9] and adjacent territory on the Baltic Sea; the port of Sochi and the northeast coast of the Black Sea and the north coast of the landlocked Caspian Sea; the Russian Far East, with the port of Vladivostok on the Japan Sea of the Pacific Ocean; and Murmansk on the Barents Sea of the Arctic Ocean.

With the end of the Soviet Union, Russians turned their attention to their devastated economy. The country officially adopted a noncommunist "democratic" political system and with great difficulty, due to the opposition of the mostly communist politicians, very slowly allowed some legal capitalistic economic activity. The promising early beginnings of recovery were crushed when members of the government of President Boris Yeltsin (1931–2007 [r. 1991–1999]) embezzled billions of dollars of foreign aid intended to help stabilize Russia's currency and fledgling banking system. The result was collapse of the banks, severe inflation of the currency, and inability of the government to pay either its officials or the tens of millions of people still paid by government-owned enterprises. For several years in some areas, especially parts of Siberia and the Far East, many people starved or froze to death in the winter, making the Russian population decrease at the fastest rate in the world.

The country was saved by the continued existence of the unofficial parallel economy, essentially the same as a black market, which as a natural economy had already developed the essentials of capitalism during the communist period. At the beginning of the twenty-first century, the new Russian economy was booming, despite persecution of businessmen by the government, damage from widespread organized crime (which was not clearly distinguishable from the government), the spread of ultranationalism (including an increase in racist attacks on Russian Jews, non-Russians, or anyone who did

---

[9] On June 12, 1991, the people of Leningrad voted to restore the city's name to St. Petersburg. It had been renamed in honor of Lenin in 1924.

not look sufficiently "Russian"), and the restoration of many Soviet-era political policies and military programs.

REEMERGENCE OF MUCH OF CENTRAL EURASIA

When the non-Russian federal republics became independent, the Caucasus countries of Georgia, Armenia, and Azerbaijan became independent along with much of the rest of Soviet Central Eurasia. In what was once the western Pontic Steppe, Ukraina[10] became fully independent, but the eastern part of the Pontic Steppe down to the Sea of Azov in the Black Sea, as well as the North Caucasus Steppe down to the Caspian Sea at Astrakhan, remained part of Russia. Some of these regions had by then been largely Russified, but many areas, especially those in the North Caucasus region, including the Mongol-speaking Kalmyk Republic in the North Caucasus Steppe between the lower Volga and the Caucasus, remained culturally non-Russian.

In Central Asia, Kazakhstan, a vast country with a large Russian population, along with Turkmenistan, Uzbekistan, Tajikistan, and Kirghizstan[11] all became independent. These countries were barely able to stay afloat economically, and mostly fell prey to rapacious politicians who kept them poor, weak, and in desperate need of help in every way. Nevertheless, independence gave them hope, and access to the wider world.

The peoples of many non-Russian "autonomous republics" and "autonomous regions" also clamored for independence. The most successful were the Tatars of the former Tatar Autonomous Soviet Socialist Republic and the Sakha of the former Yakut Autonomous Soviet Socialist Republic, whose status had already been close to that of the federal republics because they were large and endowed with natural resources, which gave them a strong bargaining edge with the Russians. They acquired a semi-independent status that would have been better for them than full independence, because they did not have to bear the heavy burden of developing a military and some other expensive attributes of a fully independent country and could thus devote their energies to development. However, along with the recovery of Russia's economy went the restoration of Russian nationalism and

---

[10] Also Ukraine. Traditionally in English it was called *the* Ukraine. Here I use the native name, *Ukraina*, to refer specifically to the newly independent country.

[11] This is the traditional English form of the name. It is now usually transliterated Russian-style from Kirghiz Cyrillic script (Кыргызстан) as 'Kyrgyzstan'.

political-military imperialism, threatening the Tatar and Sakha peoples' control over their own resources and endangering their existence as distinctive peoples and cultures.

Others, such as the Chechens of Chechnya, had much less success. The former Chechen-Ingush Autonomous Soviet Socialist Republic had been abolished, and the entire native population exiled, in 1944; they had been "reinstated" only in 1956–1957. When their neighbors in the Caucasus became independent, the Chechens sought full independence too. After an initial conflict with Russia, the Chechens signed a treaty that promised them independence after five years. Instead, the Russians invaded the little country, initiating a long, bloody, highly destructive war that killed many Chechens and destroyed much of Chechnya, while Chechens killed many Russian soldiers and civilians.[12]

Although Mongolia was already formally independent, as a Soviet ally and satellite the country had long been occupied by Soviet troops. Its continued poverty and backwardness, as well as the danger posed by China—which continued to threaten Mongolia—kept its relationship with Russia very close.

THE EUROPEAN UNION

One of the most remarkable developments of this period is the formation and rapid growth of the European Union.[13] When Soviet power collapsed, the countries that had been occupied by the Soviet military became fully independent again. East Germany was rejoined to West Germany, one of the founding European Union members, on October 3, 1990.[14] Poland, the Czech Republic, Slovakia, Slovenia, Hungary, Estonia, Latvia, Lithuania, Cyprus, and Malta were admitted in 2004,[15] followed in 2007 by Romania and Bulgaria. The European Union thus included nearly all European states west of Russia, Belarus, and Ukraine. Even without a true central government the European Union became a major political power in the world. Despite setbacks caused mainly by the demagoguery or greed of populist politicians, the European Union continued to grow in influence and prosperity.

---

[12] Nichols (2004).
[13] Formerly the European Community (from 1967), in 1994 its name was changed to the European Union.
[14] Berlin was made the capital of reunited Germany in 1991.
[15] McGeveran (2006).

THE CONTINUED WEAKNESS OF CENTRAL EURASIA

While many Central Eurasian countries had regained their political independence, and set out to restore their cultural independence as well, the extreme poverty in the entire region, coupled with the long Soviet legacy, conspired to establish repressive dictatorships—all of which claimed to be democratic republics—throughout the area. Only slowly did some of these states overcome this political legacy and become less repressive and more open.

East Turkistan and Tibet, especially, suffered from repression, since they remained under Chinese military occupation. The nationalists in both countries were crushed whenever and wherever they were discovered by the Chinese. The rapid growth and prosperity seen in much of China was largely missing in East Turkistan and Tibet except among the aggressive, nationalistic Chinese colonists there.

Despite the appearance around the world of secularly oriented commercial trading blocs, no such union developed in Central Eurasia. In 2007 it still did not seem likely that one would develop soon, due to the continuing instability of Afghanistan caused by fanatic fundamentalists (primarily the Taliban and their allies), the establishment of repressive pseudo-capitalist or crypto-communist regimes in Russia and the other former Soviet states, and the continuing Chinese military occupation of East Turkistan and Tibet. Consequently, Central Eurasia as a whole remained characterized by continued weakness, poverty, lack of economic and cultural development, and political repression.

On September 11, 2001, several thousand people in the United States were killed by terrorist attacks on civilians and military organized by the Al-Qaeda (al-Qâ'ida) terrorist group, which was based in Afghanistan and was openly supported by the Taliban government of that country. In response, the American government declared a "war on terrorism" and lent full American military support to the Tajiks and others in the northeastern province of Badakhshan, the lone remaining enclave in the country not under Taliban control. After a short civil war, the Taliban regime was overthrown in November 2001 and a democratic system led by Hamid Qarzai (elected president, 2002) was installed. The Al-Qaeda terrorists were largely suppressed or driven out. Unfortunately, Afghanistan was still torn by violent separatists, and the Taliban fundamentalists soon recovered. The Taliban increasingly adopted the terrorist tactics of Al-Qaeda in their attempt to destroy their country once again.[16]

Amid the beginnings of a new Regional Empire Period on the continent, the distinction between the old Littoral states and the peripheral states remained. Korea remained divided and separate both from Japan and from the continent; Southeast Asia continued to be divided into a small number of relatively compact states; most of the Arabian coast was divided among small commercially oriented principalities; the Levant remained divided into a small number of states; and England, though formally a member of the European Union, remained uncooperative and in general very much apart from the other European nations in many ways. On the whole, by the beginning of the new period the Littoral System states continued to be relatively prosperous and politically influential for their size.

The major peripheral powers around Central Eurasia—India, China, Russia, and the European Union—also were strong and rapidly growing. Only Southwest Asia was missing a major power or powers, due to the destruction and repression brought on the region by local and foreign fundamentalisms.

The restoration of much of Central Eurasia partially reestablished the world order of Eurasia before the destruction of the Junghars and the subjugation of the other major Central Eurasian nations. The newly independent Central Eurasian states—essentially, Western Central Asia and the Central Steppe (former Soviet Central Asia), Southern Central Asia (Afghanistan), and the Eastern Steppe (Mongolia)—were politically at odds with each other, poor, and vulnerable to outside pressure. They could be compared to the Littoral System, but the comparison would not be apt in view of Central Eurasia's lack of its former commercial prosperity and the political strength produced by commercial strength.

Economic and Political Prospects

Most of the governments of the newly independent Central Eurasian states are modern "democracies": pseudo-republics ruled by greedy tyrants or

---

[16] McGeveran (2006).

demagogues. The danger of the spread there of religious-political fundamentalism, the most pernicious and destructive form of Modernist populism, remains very great. The opinion in the region has been that the only way to prevent a fundamentalist takeover is soviet-style political and religious repression. Prospects for Central Eurasian recovery therefore look dim.

The Central Eurasian Culture Complex will obviously not be revived in order to restore the old Silk Road internal economy. The newly independent states of Western Central Asia depend overwhelmingly on the production of commodities such as oil and gas, cotton, and (in Afghanistan) illicit drugs. The last-named are pure luxury goods according to economic theory, but the political pressure against this trade will undoubtedly prevent it from taking the place of the old Silk Road internal and external trade in luxury goods. Mongolia, the only nation of eastern Central Eurasia to be fully independent again, is also poverty-stricken and run by self-serving old politicians who have no idea how to modernize the country's economy. East Turkistan and Tibet continue to be occupied by the Chinese army, and China continues to repress those countries.[17] Will they succeed in regaining independence in time to save their cultures and languages?

In short, can Central Eurasia recover as a world area, or will it continue to be poverty-stricken, prey to fundamentalism, and home to terrorists that could affect the rest of Eurasia?

A positive answer to these questions depends to a great extent on whether China will free most of Tibet and most of East Turkistan so those peoples can peacefully join with the already freed states to form a new Central Eurasian confederation. As Central Eurasia is surrounded on three sides by the fast-growing economies of Russia, China, and India, the result would surely be strong economic growth, cultural recovery, and the stabilization of that potentially explosive region. But Central Eurasia proper will only recover if and when a relatively coherent unifying political system develops there: not a monolithic sovereignty that would crush the lo-

[17] The Chinese communist regime has been spreading a new myth of China's historical domination of Central Eurasia as justification for its domination of the foreign territories occupied by its armies. The opposite view, that because the Mongols once conquered China they can claim that Chinese territory should "belong to" Mongolia (and the same for other peoples who once ruled part of what is now China), seems not to have been remarked in China. The government line is obviously propaganda, but its absolute control of the compulsory Modern education system ensures that few Chinese citizens, secure in their indoctrination, will think about or question those policies, let alone oppose them. Cf. Bovingdon and Tursun (2004).

cal states in a federal union, but a generous suzerainty like the benevolent influence once exercised by the nomadic empires, one that would help everyone to work together to improve the economy and the political situation of Central Eurasia. If independent Central Eurasians eventually come to understand this and manage to create an enlightened, liberal confederation like the European Union, perhaps they can then work with the Chinese toward the liberation of the East Turkistanian and Tibetan ethnolinguistic regions.

Similarly, the Middle East—essentially, Iran and the Near East—will only begin to recover and grow if Middle Eastern peoples can agree to cooperate to build a peaceful, prosperous, safe, multicultural confederation such as the European Union. The chances of Middle Eastern countries doing so look very slim. Although stability, economic growth, and liberalism—or at least de facto separation of church and state—are now evident in several of the far outlying states of the Arabic-speaking world, proving that it is possible, much of the Middle East remains dominated by hatred and the fanatic rhetoric of Modern fundamentalist populism, including various Islamic, Jewish, and Christian forms.

Modernism and the Arts in Contemporary Central Eurasia

In Central Eurasian cities today, it is not difficult to find evidence that Modernism is the ruling force in the arts. In fact, it is increasingly difficult to find evidence of anything that has survived its onslaught there. The architecture of the major cities, such as Tashkent[18] or Urumchi, is overwhelmingly Modern, as is the "art" that adorns it. In Lhasa, which once contained many of the loveliest gems of Tibetan domestic architecture, the Potala (preserved as a museum and tourist attraction) looks down over a Modern concrete Chinese city.[19] In Central Eurasia, old monuments of the traditional local culture are rare, and the size and aggressive style of the Modern buildings makes the traditional buildings look out of place. Young artists study in

---

[18] Much of the city's old architecture was destroyed in a powerful earthquake in 1966. When the city was rebuilt, most of the damaged old buildings were replaced by Modern ones built according to the severe anti-artistic dictates of Modern architecture.

[19] See the photograph dated 1996 in Shakya (1999: plate 17); since the photograph was taken, the situation has become even worse.

universities and art institutes, where they are taught Modernism, which as always is presented as new and therefore better than anything old.

Because Central Eurasia was so thoroughly depressed economically, and isolated politically and culturally from the rest of the world, Modernism has not yet completely won there. For decades, the most extreme forms of Modern art were forbidden in the communist empires, where the only acceptable art was "socialist realism," which blended some Modern ideas with elements of the pre-Modern elite culture of Western Europe. For that reason, Modernism in the arts is still new in Central Eurasia. That is the stage at which the virus is most deadly, but interest in the traditional arts remains relatively high, especially among religious adherents. There is still time to save the arts, if Central Eurasians learn to value their own traditions, in which Art and Beauty retain their historical meanings, and especially if they can understand and recognize Modernism for what it really is.

The source of Modernism in the arts is Europe and its cultural offshoots in the Littoral and around the world. The fact that it is necessary still to talk about Modernism at all—it is, after all, a century-old "revolutionary" movement—brings up many other questions that seem not to be raised, particularly:

> Why have Modern artists failed to produce much real art after an entire century of revolution and experimentation?
> Why does the rule of Modernism remain unchanged and, evidently, a mystery to all?

For a century every new generation of Modern artists has openly asserted that the art of the preceding generation—Modern art—is a failure as art. Most styles or movements of Modernism thus succeeded at most to be fashionable for a short time (i.e., they were considered to be art, or good art) before they were made unfashionable (i.e., non-art, or bad art) by the next Modern avant-garde movement created to displace them. So far there is no indication that this vicious cycle in the arts—Modernism—is going to end.

The phenomenon of Modernism and the destruction of art has been addressed already by a radical writer and painter of the early twentieth century, who in 1954 notes that after *forty years* of "extremism" and endless rejection of what has preceded, young artists knowingly or unknowingly only repeat what has been done before, thinking it new and provocatively original. The artist has become "a slave of the great god Progress, who is a very jealous god indeed."[20] Since then, *another fifty-three years* have passed at the time of writing, with no change.

Why have the arts not recovered? Why have they remained in a state of permanent revolution ever since the early twentieth century, with no sign of any tendency to recover stability to match the contemporary world's relative sociopolitical stability? Clearly, while the artists' expression of their feelings about society and politics is reflected in their art, and artists depend on society to feed them and appreciate their art, the two spheres of endeavor are otherwise unrelated. The art world, having adopted Modernism whole-heartedly, is now a prisoner of the demon of permanent revolution—the necessity of rejecting anything that went immediately before—in order to remain Modern, up-to-date, avant-garde. For the artist, "*nothing* is permitted"[21] other than this vicious cycle of rejection, which has by now become nearly total—that is, there is probably nothing that has not been tried by "experimental" avant-garde artists, and practically nothing left of the essence of Art. "The rational limit has already been overstepped—there is nothing more to be anticipated. Indeed, what has been reached is hardening into a canon."[22] Only cosmetic labeling remains, as most clearly seen in graphic art, where nothing more is required than a signature (the only indispensible element), frame (sometimes omitted), and label (optional). An artistic poem is a piece of literature written with obscure diction, a title (often omitted), and unjustified margins. Art music is deliberately produced sound in which the harmony, the melody (sometimes omitted), and the rhythm are at extreme variance with anything found in nature, not to speak of anything "popular." The social niche or behavioral template for "artists" remains (though not the economic niche), but what they produce is literally no longer art, poetry, or music, because the very definition of those things, and the ability to redefine them, has been lost: graphic artists cannot define art, poets cannot define poetry, composers cannot define music—nor can the army of critics who feed off the status quo. In other words, the professionals

---

[20] Lewis (1954: 40). His book, aptly titled *The Demon of Progress in the Arts*, has had absolutely no impact on the arts, which remain firmly under the control of the demon more than half a century later. Despite all the change dictated by Modernism, nothing at all has changed.

[21] Lewis (1954: 40).

[22] Lewis (1954: 37).

cannot explain what art, music, or poetry is to or for them.[23] They cannot explain what it is because they do not know what it is. Modernism's rejection not only of all previous artistic forms but even of artistic Reason—the acceptance of the ordering principles of Nature, or at least the idea that such principles exist—has inevitably led to the destruction of the traditional arts as methods for producing genuine art.

The achievement of stability and prosperity, and even some support for artists—commercially successful ones—has resulted in making artistic Modernism institutionalized: truly permanent revolution. This is disastrous. "For quite a time it has been so unwelcome to point out the realities of the present period that a sort of conspiracy of silence has developed. Everyone pretends, including the horde of impoverished artists, the professional pundits, the picture-dealers and so on, everyone pretends that we enjoy normal conditions, and even that art is flourishing."[24] But in fact, we now have a world without genuine new art: permanent revolution actually means stasis.

The critical literature on Modernism only confirms that above all else what needs to be done is to *create* true art—graphic art, music, poetry, and the other arts. True high art has not been created for a very long time, and is still not being created. Until artists, musicians, and poets realize this and decide to focus their minds on the creation of a new high art tradition, the world will continue to depend on the artists of the past, including now the recent past of Modernism, sanctified by academics, preserved in the formaldehyde of museums, concert halls, and libraries, studied and intellectualized and made the point of departure for still more intellectualized, dead, academic anti-art.[25]

It has been argued that Modernism was a necessary stage in the development of the arts, a "cleaning of the slate" to allow something new to develop. Whether necessary or not, it succeeded. The explicit rejection of the ideal of Beauty, of natural order, and other principles that underlie all great art, and their substitution over the period of an entire century with the ideal of the plain and the ugly, has finally eliminated any legitimacy—*among profes-*

---

[23] What it "really" is should perhaps be of no major concern to anyone except philosophers, but it could hardly hurt anything at this point if artists were to at least begin asking some questions along these lines.

[24] Lewis (1954: 27).

[25] The overintellectualization of art by academics and academy-trained artists is obvious on nearly every page of Adorno's classic Modern work on aesthetics, but my perception of this is clearly different from Adorno's own; see endnote 102.

sional artists—for the pre-Modern arts, which have become museum arti-facts, connoisseurs' treasures, and financial investments.

Nevertheless, while the self-destruction of the arts by professional artists under the spell of Modernism (including its political message, which often was more important than the art for many) did indeed clean the slate, no new or-der was ever created by the Modern avant-garde. They could not stop cleaning the slate, but have kept on doing it over and over down to the present day.[26]

Modernism, which has eliminated all hierarchies and replaced them with the idea of "equality," has given birth to an age of "unartists" with the inability to understand the concept of Beauty and the inability to judge between Art and trash. This pernicious movement thus continues to afflict the arts in most of the world, and continues to make most "art" not worth experiencing. Until art-ists and others realize that their lives have been dominated by Modernists who have been dedicated, literally and explicitly, to depriving the world of beauty, there will be no more new beauty except by chance. That is a sad prospect.[27]

However, the absence of satisfying new elite art has had a perhaps unex-pected result. New art forms have arisen to replace the old ones. In addition to wholly new art forms introduced as a result of technical innovations, such as photography and the cinema, new forms of old arts have appeared, most re-markably in the realm of music, where a unique new form of popular music, rock and roll, made its sudden, explosive appearance in the United States half a century ago. Within a single decade it took most of the world by storm.

By the end of the century, in Mongolia, Tibet, and other Central Eurasian countries, as in the rest of the world, local rock or "pop rock" bands were

---

[26] Because Modernism was openly proclaimed to be new and a replacement for what preceded, because it succeeded in its efforts to replace the old, and because it lasted so long, Modernism itself inevitably became old in turn. Although Modernism had not yet ended, artists and art historians began to look on Modern *styles* as old-fashioned and in need of replacement. Some of them accordingly proclaimed that they rejected Modern style, and announced Post-Modernism. But this hyper-Modernism is of course simply another mutation of Modernism. It has been most successful as a fashion in architecture and fields ancillary to the arts such as literary criticism and intellectual history, not in the fine arts proper. Professionally trained artists today are educated in universities or university-like institutes, where Modernism (and Post-Modernism) has been canonized and drummed into their heads uncritically.

[27] The extension of Modernist theories to art history, and the consequent projection of their spurious ideas onto the art of the past, has forced art historians to turn to the discussion of the sociology of the artists' world, psychology, mathematics, whatever—*anything except art per se*, which remains unexamined and unexaminable from the Modernist viewpoint, while Modernism itself, as a phenomenon, also remains largely unexamined. For discussion of the scholarly tension between Modernists and anti-Modernists in recent times, see endnote 103.

performing essentially the same music. It has strongly influenced folk music and to a large extent supplanted it in everyday life in the cities of Central Eurasia. Although it is not yet possible to call it "high" art, at least it really is music; perhaps one day it will develop into an elite art.[28]

The hope for the arts now lies in the largely untutored popular new arts developed in the absence of guidance from the professionally trained, academicized, avant-garde elite, who have continued to be mesmerized by Modernism and its mutations. It is necessary to recognize and understand the still primitive new arts and begin to develop them from the inside, to create new art with them without destroying the Art in them. It may be that trained artists will themselves adopt the new arts and pioneer a new fine arts themselves. But it must be stressed that the word "new" here is an adjective. It should not obscure the primacy of the noun "arts." That is, the new arts cannot follow totally new rules constructed ex nihilo by academic "artists," with no regard to the natural world or existing traditions. Great artists produce art, but they need some basis for it. No one can create art out of a vacuum. The slate has already been scraped clean. It is not necessary to scrape it anymore.

It is time for artists to reject the death grip of Modernism and again embrace the art forms that they love and strive to achieve greatness with art itself. Will it happen in Central Eurasia, amid a new flourishing of culture there, as it flourished once before? That would be a true revolution. If it happens, maybe the world will enjoy a flourishing, satisfying artistic life once more.

The earliest of the great civilizations known from archaeology—the Nile, Mesopotamian, Indus, and Yellow River valley cultures—were born in the fertile, agricultural periphery of Eurasia. But modern world culture does

---

[28] In fact, people all around the world from all walks of life, including artists and intellectuals as well as businessmen and laborers, listen to this music every day. However, until musicians realize what has happened to music, decide to be artists rather than anti-artists, and take the new world language of popular music that has grown out of rock music and develop it—gradually and carefully—into art, there will be no new, genuine art music in the world, but only new varieties of primitive popular sounds substituting for it. On attempts by some musicians to do this, and on the Renaissance model of *how* to do it, see endnote 104.

not derive from them. It comes from the challenging marginal lands of Central Eurasia.

The dynamic, restless Proto-Indo-Europeans whose culture was born there migrated across and "discovered" the Old World, mixing with the local peoples and founding the Classical civilizations of the Greeks and Romans, Iranians, Indians, and Chinese. In the Middle Ages and Renaissance their descendants and other Central Eurasian peoples conquered, discovered, investigated, and explored some more, creating new world systems, the high arts, and the advanced sciences. Central Eurasians—not the Egyptians, Sumerians, and so on—are our ancestors. Central Eurasia is our homeland, the place where our civilization started.

At the start of the twenty-first century, and the third millennium, Eurasia is poised at the beginning of what could be a great new era of prosperity and intellectual and artistic growth. There are many grave problems, but also a few bright lights, the most promising politically being the European Union, and technologically the Internet, which has had a powerful enlightening influence.

Will the peoples of Central Eurasia—and of Europe, Russia, the Middle East, India, and China—learn from the past, or will they continue to repeat its mistakes? Can they recover from the disasters wrought by Modernism, fundamentalism, and nationalist racism without destroying themselves and the rest of the world? And will the Europeans, Russians, Iranians, and Chinese who now dominate Central Eurasia, our common heartland, finally allow that font of creativity the freedom to flourish once again?

It depends on whether they can restore the rule of Reason, reject the Modernist legacy of populist demagoguery, and make a firm commitment to join the rest of the world not as fanatics or tyrants but as partners.

EPILOGUE

—

The Barbarians

Και τώρα τι θα γένουμε χωρίς βαρβάρους.
Οι άνθρωποι αυτοί ήσαν μιά κάποια λύσις
—Κ. Π. Καβάφης,
  Περιμένοντας τους Βαρβάρους

> And now what will become of us, without any barbarians?
> Those people were some kind of a solution.
> —C. P. Cavafy, *Waiting for the Barbarians*

The origins of modern civilization go back to the Indo-European migrations that began four thousand years ago in the center of Eurasia. The Proto-Indo-Europeans lived in a marginal region where they developed an innovative quickness unparalleled by any of the other Eurasian peoples of the periphery, none of whom adapted in time to prevent the Indo-Europeans from dominating their territory. The Indo-Europeans possessed a powerful dynamism that was generally passed on to other peoples directly, in many cases by outright conquest. Through their servitude, the subjugated peoples within Central Eurasia (and even in the periphery, if only temporarily) learned the First Story and adopted the Central Eurasian Culture Complex, as described in the prologue. In doing this, the Indo-Europeans mixed with local peoples wherever they migrated and developed distinctive local creoles, the daughter languages or ancestors of the branches of the Indo-European family, with cultures characterized by the dynamism of the Proto-Indo-Europeans and their early Central Eurasian daughter peoples.

Among the essential features of the Central Eurasian Culture Complex was the political necessity of supporting the comitatus warriors of the ruler and the lords subject to him and providing them with luxurious gifts. This created a powerful economic need that could only be satisfied by trade. With the establishment of the nomad-ruled empires, a trade-oriented Central Eurasian economy combining the efforts and products of the pastoral nomadic peoples, the agricultural peoples, and the urban peoples of Central Asia came into being. Although the popular term "Silk Road" is misleading, it can still be used to refer to the foreign trade component of this economy, as long as it is understood that what drove the economic engine of the Silk Road was first of all internal Central Eurasian trade, based on internal demand not only for the products of their own peoples but for those of neighboring Central Eurasian states and the peripheral states. Trade with the peripheral states created a demand there for the products of the Central Eurasian states or products acquired through them. The connection of these economies by interregional trade produced a healthy international commerce. At the center of the Silk Road system was the Central Eurasian aristocracy of the native states, in which most of the rulers were of steppe nomadic origin.

The destruction of the Silk Road is, or should be, no mystery. It is even precisely documented. In the late seventeenth century the Russians and Manchu-Chinese partitioned Central Eurasia between themselves. The Ch'ing then destroyed the last pastoral nomadic empire, that of the Junghars, seized their territory, and massacred most of the Junghar people. The Russians conquered and colonized most of the rest of Central Eurasia, through the middle of which closed borders were established. It is hardly surprising that the Silk Road economy—the economy of the Eurasian heartland—collapsed, and the peoples of Central Eurasia, including the once-great high civilizations of Central Asia and Tibet, sank into poverty and backwardness.

The nations who once dominated Central Eurasian history—the Scythians and Hsiung-nu, the Huns, Turks, Tibetans, Mongols, Junghars, Manchus, and others—and their descendants disappeared from world historical consciousness for a very long time. Now some of them have reappeared, sometimes under different names, in modern European-style nation-states, and in nearly all cases bereft of any real power. One is entitled to at least ask, "What happened to the old Central Eurasians?" Or to put it wrongly, "What happened to all the *barbarians*?"[1]

The Idea of the Barbarian

History writing about Central Eurasia, from Herodotus down to the present day, has been dominated by stereotypes, *topoi*, and powerful biases. The

[1] For the background of the discussion of Chinese terminology in this chapter, see endnote 105.

problem ultimately goes back to the fully developed idea of the *barbarian* and its division of the world into good and bad peoples and cultures. Merely stating this is, of course, not enough, so this chapter is devoted to analyzing the rhetoric and the main arguments that tend to come up in any discussion of Central Eurasia—especially of the empires formed and ruled by people practicing the pastoral-nomadic way of life.

The essential difference between the pastoral nomad-dominated Central Eurasian states and the peripheral states not dominated by pastoral nomads was that the Central Eurasian pastoral nomads lived in the steppe zone, which was the home of the horse and the best pastureland for horses in Eurasia. They grew up with horses and on them; they were mobile and could easily traverse great distances in a short time. They also learned how to use the compound bow to protect their flocks and to hunt, so they already had some skills useful in war. All this is well known, and undoubtedly true. However, it has been taken much further in the theory of the natural warrior, which is based on ancient and medieval ideas that "associated physical and psychological traits with characteristics of the environment," so that, because of their harsh steppe climate, the Central Eurasians were not only skilled at riding and shooting, they were tough, courageous, ruthless, and warlike, much "superior to the aristocratic and peasant armies of the sedentary states."[2] While ancient and medieval theories of the climates and humors and so forth are no longer taken seriously, casting doubt on this stereotype, there is a more serious problem here: this seemingly innocent characterization is simply a cleaned-up, pejorative-free, modernized version of the two and a half millennium old idea of the *barbarian*.

Central Eurasians are regularly castigated for their supposed aggression, ruthless cruelty, and love of violence in general—that is, after all, the core of the idea of the *barbarian*. It is noted throughout most writing on Central Eurasia that the rulers came to power only after brutal massacres, wanton murder, and so forth. Steppe empires were formed by "vicious and prolonged struggle amidst nomadic tribal formations,"[3] what has been called "bloody tanistry."[4] It cannot be denied that Central Eurasian rulers were responsible for the deaths of many people in these and many other

---

[2] Di Cosmo (2002b: 4). The received view of Central Eurasians remains extremely pervasive. Practically all specialists and nonspecialists have expressed such views.

[3] Di Cosmo (2002b: 7); see the preceding note.

[4] Joseph Fletcher, quoted in Di Cosmo (2002a: 185).

instances. But this too must be viewed in perspective. All historical Chinese, Persian, and Graeco-Roman empires or dynasties were founded in exactly the same way—after a long, bloody, treacherous civil war. And after the empire's foundation, the "greatest" rulers of both kinds of empires were nearly always conquering heroes first—they killed their rivals and enemies, sometimes personally—and good administrators second. The most famous European empire builders, the Romans, were "morally speaking no better than, or even worse than, the barbarians" in "terms of their political ruthlessness, or of their frequent inhumanity to foreign peoples and their own slaves."[5] All "great" realms were and are built on the same principles that "advanced" primate societies in general are built on, the alpha male hierarchy. There is thus no reason to single out Central Eurasians in this respect.

Yet, while the bloody victories of Attila, Chinggis, or Tamerlane are still deplored, the equally bloody victories of the Graeco-Roman, Persian, and Chinese emperors are related with enthusiasm by historians past and present. Non–Central Eurasian historians from Antiquity to the present have been blind to the savagery and unrelenting aggression of their own ancestors. The most famous, or infamous examples, the Romans, are chastised not because they were so cruel to their slaves and tortured and killed so many people for public entertainment in such vicious ways, but because some of those they tortured and killed were Christians.[6] Ancient and medieval sources reveal the extent of the aggression, treachery, and institutionalized brutality of ancient "civilized" cultures, but modern historians continue to praise those peoples for the successes they achieved against Central Eurasians, whom they accuse instead of being violent and cruel. Certainly there are plenty of instances of Central Eurasians' inhumanity to each other or to peripheral peoples, but they cannot begin to be compared, for sheer cruelty and relentless aggression, to the Romans, the Persians, the Chinese, and their successors right down to modern times.

A reviewer of two recent archaeological monographs on the Scythians, after commenting on the well-known beauty of the golden artifacts found in Scythian burial mounds says:

---

[5] James (2001: 19).

[6] The pro-Roman bias is not necessarily true of all historians (e.g., Gibbon). Nevertheless, most classicists of recent times have tended to be anti-Christian (in that respect including Gibbon), but pro-Roman, at least in the sense of pro-Cicero.

It was not the well organised production of cheese and wool that gave the elite its buying power. *This was a society that valorised violence and made it pay.* It may be that the true nature of the Scythian phenomenon is hidden from us by a surfeit of textual and archaeological riches. The striking congruencies between the Greek written sources (especially Herodotus and Hippocrates)[7] and aspects of the archaeological record might suggest that *there exist no great problems to be solved.*[8]

This statement repeats the traditional view that the Scythians and other nomadic peoples acquired most of their wealth through their unusually expert use of violence and claims that there is little wrong with our understanding of them. Yet it is known even from ancient Greek sources that the Scythians acquired most of their wealth by trade and taxation, not war. About four centuries after Herodotus, Strabo discusses the agricultural exports of the nomads at some length and then remarks on their avoidance of war:

> Now although the Nomads are warriors rather than brigands, yet they go to war only for the sake of the tributes due them; for they turn over their land to any people who wish to till it, and are satisfied if they receive in return for the land the tribute they have assessed, which is a moderate one . . . ; but if the tenants do not pay, the Nomads go to war with them . . . [;] if the tributes were paid regularly, they would never resort to war.[9]

The misperception of the Scythians and other steppe zone peoples today is generally based on the widely held theory of the "needy nomads," according to which steppe-zone Central Eurasians did not themselves produce enough of the necessities of life and depended on the agricultural products, textiles, and other goods of their peripheral neighbors, whose wealth they coveted.[10] When the Central Eurasians could not obtain what they needed or desired by trading their animals and other goods with the "advanced" peripheral empires—who did not need or want the nomads' pitiful, barbaric products—the Central Eurasians invaded to take them by force. This

---

[7] On the pseudo-Hippocrates text, see the justly critical comments of Rolle (1989).

[8] Taylor (2003), emphasis added.

[9] Jones (1924: 242–245).

[10] For criticism of Khazanov's (1984) widely accepted view, see endnote 106.

theory has rightly been criticized at length by Nicola Di Cosmo, who points out that neither the historical sources nor the archaeological findings support it. It is now well established that Central Eurasians practiced agriculture themselves and either taxed or traded peacefully with peoples who provided what they needed or wanted but did not themselves produce. When the nomads did attack a peripheral area, for whatever reason, they invariably carried off livestock and people, not agricultural products.[11] It needs to be emphasized here that the Central Eurasians, especially the nomadic peoples, actually produced more than enough food for their needs. As a result, they generally were bigger and healthier than the peripheral agricultural peoples.

They also produced their own everyday clothes, jewelry, tools, wagons, housing, horse gear, and weapons and were skilled metalsmiths. The problem here is the mistaken equation of a mode of production (e.g., agriculture, metalsmithing, commerce, or nomadic herding) with a state, that is, the equation of the primary means of subsistence of one group of people in a society with the nation or state as a whole. According to this approach, state formation would actually be impossible anywhere, including societies where many people are agriculturalists, because the rulers must of necessity spend all of their time ruling, not farming, and those who produce weapons, for example, must not spend their valuable time doing something they are not specialized in either. The mistake, in short, is that states based in the Central Eurasian steppe zone must have consisted only of "pure" nomads and were thus "simple." If that were true, the theory would be correct, because no known actual mode of production is sufficient to produce everything needed by a fully functioning society. But it is not true. *All nomadic pastoralist-dominated states that we know anything about, from the Scythians to the Junghars, were complex.* The text of Herodotus alone, which discusses in some detail the different kinds of Scythians who lived in Scythia, is sufficient to demonstrate the impossibility of the "non-autarkic" or "needy nomad" theory and its more pernicious offshoots. The Scythians practiced not only very many different modes of production but the very same modes the

---

[11] Di Cosmo (2002a: 168–171). He notes, "While it is true that much of the history of the relations between nomads and agriculturalists along the frontier is a history of raids and wars, both sides tended to incorporate parts of the other's people, economic resources (such as land and livestock), or territory." The region between the two was "neither purely nomadic nor purely sedentary but a combination of both." Cf. similarly Psarras (1994: 5).

peripheral peoples practiced, because the states of both regions regularly expanded by force into each other's territories and peoples who practiced agriculture and herding were found in both kinds of state.

Central Eurasian states also were multiethnic, and it is perhaps their multiethnic, multicultural nature that has caused much of the trouble, because it is so different from the ideal modern nation-state dominated by one ethnolinguistic group, which has developed out of the relatively compact (not empire-sized) premodern, typically multiethnic European state.[12] With the imposition of this state type throughout Central Eurasia by the peripheral powers, Central Eurasia has been changed beyond all recognition compared to its status throughout premodern history. But projecting modern situations and ideas into the past is hardly the way for historians to proceed.

Central Eurasians, including pastoral nomads, did desire exotic, luxurious products from neighboring countries, but there is no evidence that their desires for exotic luxuries were any different from those of the peripheral peoples,[13] except perhaps that the Central Eurasians were willing and eager to trade their own surplus goods, or goods they had obtained in trade elsewhere, in order to obtain what they wanted, even in time of war.[14]

The medieval Arab geographers took great interest in the products produced, bought, and sold in the places they describe. The lists of trade goods of the great Central Asian emporiums include all kinds of raw materials as well as processed and manufactured goods produced locally or imported from near and far. All of the lists include much that was produced by the steppe peoples. For example, a description of the goods exported from Central Asia in the tenth century includes:

[12] Cf. Tilly (1975, 1990) and Hui (2005).

[13] Di Cosmo (2002a: 170) rightly notes that the existence of centers "of agricultural production and of other economic activities, including handicraft and trade" in nomadic Central Eurasian states themselves calls "into question the historical validity of theories based on the premise that Inner Asian empires were created by nomads for the purpose of forcing agriculturalists, by the sheer power of military force (or the threat of it), to surrender products the nomads needed or desired, namely, cereals and luxury products." Di Cosmo's arguments effectively disprove the theory.

[14] Allsen (1989: 92) notes, "Li Chih-ch'ang 李志常, the chronicler of the travels of the Taoist master Ch'ang-ch'un 長春, records... that when his party encountered coral merchants in the Hindukush, the Mongolian officers in his escort purchased their wares in a straight business transaction. No attempt was made to exact them by force."

from Khorezmia, sables, miniver, ermines, and the fur of steppe foxes, martens, foxes, beavers, spotted hares, and goats; also wax, arrows, birch bark, high fur caps, fish glue, fish teeth, castoreum, amber, prepared horse hides, honey, hazel nuts, falcons, swords, armour, khalanj wood, Slavonic slaves,[15] sheep, and cattle. All these came from Bulghār, but Khorezmia exported also grapes, many raisins, almond pastry, sesame, fabrics of striped cloth, carpets, blanket cloth, satin for royal gifts, coverings of mulḥam fabric, locks, Āranj fabrics, bows which only the strongest could bend, rakhbīn (a kind of cheese), yeast, fish, boats (the latter also exported from Tirmidh). From Samarqand is exported silver-coloured fabrics (sīmgūn) and Samarqandī stuffs, large copper vessels, artistic goblets, tents, stirrups, bridle-heads, and straps; from Dīzak, fine kinds of wool and woollen clothes; from Banākath, Turkistān fabrics; from Shāsh [Tashkent], high saddles of horse hide, quivers, tents, hides (imported from the Turks and tanned), cloaks, praying carpets, leather capes, linseed, fine bows, needles of poor quality, cotton for export to the Turks, and scissors; from Samarqand again, satin which is exported to the Turks, and red fabrics known by the name of mumarjal, Sīnīzī cloth, many silks and silken fabrics, hazel and other nuts; from Farghāna and Isfijāb, Turkish slaves,[16] white fabrics, arms, swords, copper, iron; from Ṭarāz (Talas) goatskins; from Shalji, silver; from Turkistān, horses and mules are driven to these places, and also from Khuttal.[17]

Barthold notes, "The greatest advantage from the trade with the nomads was derived by the Khorezmians, whose prosperity, according to Iṣṭakhrī, was founded exclusively on their trade relations with the Turks."[18] The

[15] Maqdisī's text (de Goeje 1877/1967: 325, line 3) has *al-raqīq* 'slave(s)'. This particular word implies 'chattel slaves' and is not used to refer to comitatus warriors, who would not be considered slaves in the English sense. A study of medieval Arabic terminology for unfree categories of people is a great desideratum; the many Arabic words for them (all of which are usually translated with the one English word 'slave') had different meanings in the context of medieval Islamic society.

[16] Maqdisī's text (de Goeje 1877/1967: 325, line 15) has *al-raqīq*.

[17] From Barthold's (1977: 235–236) translation of Maqdisī (de Goeje 1967: 323–326); cf. Christian (1998: 320–321). Barthold notes that the fish teeth are evidently walrus tusks.

[18] Barthold (1977: 237), citing Iṣṭakhrī (de Goeje 1870/1967: 305).

remarkable extent to which the trade goods in the above list were related to the steppe peoples (the Turks of the account) is a direct reflection of the fact that Central Eurasian peoples—who in theory lived in three different ecological-cultural zones and practiced three distinct modes of life—not only traded with each other but were tightly interconnected in *a single economy*. The traditional Silk Road conception notes only the international component that reached the peripheral states and assumes that—there being nothing of worth in Central Eurasia except poor nomads and a few "oasis" cities—the valuable goods that appeared at one or the other extreme of the Silk Road must have passed through by long-distance caravan, as if in a pipeline.[19] Even those who have a much more balanced view of Central Eurasia see it as essentially a trade route or collection of routes. For example, Christian defines "the Silk Roads as the long- and middle-distance land routes by which goods, ideas, and people were exchanged between major regions of Afro-Eurasia," and despite some qualification continues to refer to the "Silk Roads" as "a system of exchanges," noting, "The plural form is important because the Silk Roads consisted of a constantly shifting network of pathways for many different types of exchange."[20] This characterization, while perhaps an improvement over many previous ones, is still in need of emendation. The Silk Road was *not* a network of trade routes, or even a system of cultural exchange. It was the entire local political-economic-cultural system of Central Eurasia, in which commerce, whether internal or external, was very highly valued and energetically pursued—in that sense, the "Silk Road" and "Central Eurasia" are essentially two terms for the same thing. In its more restricted economic sense, the Silk Road was the Central Eurasian economy.

Chinese, Greek, and Arabic historical sources agree that the steppe peoples were above all interested in trade. The careful manner in which Central Eurasians generally undertook their conquests is revealing. They attempted to avoid conflict and tried to get cities to submit peacefully. Only when they

---

[19] For further comments in this vein by Allsen, see endnote 107.

[20] Christian (2000: 2–3). The term Silk Road is already misleading enough. The plural form should be avoided even more because it emphasizes the misconception of Central Eurasia only being a system of trade routes. Similarly, Franck and Brownstone (1986: 7–9) talk about trade and other exchange between the steppe zone peoples and peoples in and along the "Silk Roads" and related "routes," remarking that "the transverse routes were not just tacked onto the arterial routes. They were older than the arterial routes, and were always integral to the functioning of the Silk Roads."

resisted, or rebelled, was retribution necessary according to the code of the time, a code known from ancient Europe as well,[21] but even in such cases Central Eurasians normally did not kill everyone: they spared merchants, artisans, and any other especially productive men, and enslaved the women and children. This reveals very clearly that the sources were right in at least this respect: the Central Eurasians' conquests were designed to acquire trade routes or trading cities. But the reason for the acquisition was to secure occupied territory that could be taxed in order to pay for the rulers' sociopolitical infrastructure. If all this sounds exactly like what sedentary peripheral states were doing, that is because it was indeed the same thing.[22]

The old predatory, parasitic nomad model continues to be supported by some scholars, the most widely quoted being Barfield, who claims, for example,

> The rise of the Turks, like that of the Hsiung-nu, was due to their military might. As soon as they had established themselves, the Turks began to extort subsidies from the two rival courts in north China, Chou and Ch'i. The Turks did not need to invade China to impress them. Both courts had been terrified by the earlier destruction of the Jou-jan [Avars] and the conquests on the steppe. The Turks received lavish gifts from each court.... Trade flourished, with the Turks exchanging horses for silk. In 553 the Turks brought 50,000 horses to the frontier. During Mukan's reign (553–72) the Chou court made an annual gift of 100,000 rolls of silk to the kaghan and was forced to lavishly maintain a host of Turkish visitors in the capital as a goodwill gesture. Ch'i was not far behind in making its bribes.... The eastern Turks extracted the silk from China and the western Turks traded it to Iran and Byzantium.[23]

The stereotype-filled view in this sample is based on distortion of the most tendentious of the Chinese sources. It does not take into account the

---

[21] Alexander the Great's army, for example, methodically executed all surviving men when they captured a city that had resisted them.

[22] Di Cosmo (2002a: 170) rightly notes that there were "no large demarcations between nomads and sedentary peoples" in internal economy or political organization.

[23] Barfield (1989: 133). The quoted passage was chosen purely at random. For another, see endnote 108.

biases and internal contradictions of those sources, or the problem that this view is explicitly contradicted by other, more reliable accounts in the very same sources. It has been well criticized by specialists in Central Eurasian history.[24]

But, one might protest, if the nomads were not really powerful aggressive *barbarians*, and if they only really wanted to trade with the peace-loving "sedentary" peoples, why were the latter forced to build walls and other fortifications to defend themselves against the Central Eurasians?

It is true that many frontier walls were built by peripheral area states in Antiquity. In China during the Warring States period, the different polities of the time, most but not all of which were "Chinese," built a good number of such walls. They were primarily designed to hold territory conquered from neighboring states and to prevent loss of population to them (more or less exactly like the Modern-period Berlin Wall). The consolidation and extension of the northern walls into one Great Wall, the accomplishment of the First Emperor of the Ch'in Dynasty, not surprisingly had the same purpose: it was intended to hold the vast territory conquered from the Hsiung-nu[25] and to prevent the loss of Chinese population to them. The frequent "raids" of the Hsiung-nu into Chinese territory after Emperor Wu's "abandonment" of the peace treaty should hardly be surprising: the emperor's unilateral breaking of the treaty was a declaration of war against the Hsiung-nu.[26] The raids were thus not random acts by violently inclined Hsiung-nu but desperate military actions against the war declared on them by a much stronger, violently inclined expansionistic people, the Chinese.

Psarras[27] notes that breaches of the treaties occurred on both sides, typically for internal political reasons. However, it is not possible to be certain about this on the Hsiung-nu side because we have no Hsiung-nu sources and must attempt to read between the lines and reinterpret the Chinese sources. As noted elsewhere, when the Chinese sources are extensive enough, they

---

[24] See the studies of Psarras (2003), Di Cosmo (2002a), and Noonan (1997). For a detailed examination of the economics of the trade in Turkic horses and Chinese silk in the early medieval period, see Beckwith (1991).

[25] Located in the area of Inner Mongolia, which has been almost completely Sinified under Chinese communist rule.

[26] Psarras (2003: 141 et seq.).

[27] Psarras (2003: 141).

virtually always suffice to inform us that the Hsiung-nu actions were defensive or in reaction to an aggressive political move by China.[28]

Certainly the Hsiung-nu, like other Central Eurasians who formed great states (and also like the Chinese and other peripheral peoples who formed them), were aggressive toward their neighbors during their state-formation phase, and one should expect the aggression to include attacks on the peripheral states. Nevertheless, later cases that are historically much better known, such as that of the Junghars, make it manifestly clear that the steppe zone peoples fought almost exclusively among themselves, and mostly went out of their way to avoid conflict with the dangerous peripheral states.[29] The Junghars seem never to have invaded Chinese territory, though the reverse is certainly true. Amid all the self-righteous proclamations of indignation and anger by the Manchu-Chinese, and accusations of all kinds of crimes supposedly committed by the Junghars, as well as by selected Tibetans and Uighurs,[30] one fact stands out: at no time during the Manchu-Chinese Dynasty did any Junghar army invade China, nor did any Tibetan army, nor any East Turkistani army. The only offense these peoples committed against the Manchu-Chinese was their steadfast insistence on not "submitting" and on remaining the independent rulers of their own Central Eurasian lands. Nevertheless, the Manchu-Chinese continue to be portrayed as righteous, enlightened, civilized people who were the innocent victims of Central Eurasian *barbarians*.

In the West, it seems evident that the Huns' invasion of the Eastern Roman Empire was ultimately the result of the Goths' empire-forming wars. The Goths apparently attacked the Huns but were defeated. The Huns chased those Goths who did not surrender to them into the Roman Empire, where they came into conflict with the Romans, who wanted to keep the Goths to use as mercenaries. The Romans' own historians tell us how the Romans

---

[28] The reasons for Chinese aggression are manifold, but fairly consistent throughout Chinese history. "I have found that the Xiongnu merit the attention paid them since the Han, not because of any threat they posed to China, but because they were China's equal. It is this equality which constituted the supposed menace to China" (Psarras 2003: 60).

[29] The theory of Central Eurasian military superiority is followed by nearly everyone, including specialists (e.g., Drompp 2005: 11–12).

[30] This is the modern name for the modern urban-agricultural Turkic Muslims of East Turkistan. Their language, Uighur (pronounced with an initial vowel *u*—[uy.ɣur]—not *w*, as in "[wi.ɡɚ]" or the like), and Uzbek are dialects of each other. In premodern times Uighur refers to a different Turkic language.

mistreated the Goths and, subsequently, the Huns, and brought reprisals by the victims against the Romans.

It is often argued that Central Eurasians' attacks against peripheral peoples were motivated by poverty and greed.[31] Yet Psarras[32] remarks that Barfield, "despite his contention that the *heqin*[33] was invented by the Xiongnu as a means of blackmailing the Han, nonetheless demonstrates that the actual costs to the Han were low compared to the maintenance of border guards, for instance. This being the case, one cannot but wonder why Barfield would imagine the Xiongnu engaging in 'blackmail' for so little return." The same is true of the laughably petty amounts of tribute the Huns forced the Romans to pay them: they were symbolic, not substantial, and were in general fully justified. If the Central Eurasians had been desperately poor and needed money, food, and so forth, they would have asked for it.

Moreover, if life on the steppe was so hard, and the people there were so poor, why should peasants from peripheral states want to defect to them? The reason is that most nomads might have been poor, but most peasants were much poorer[34] and worked incalculably harder just to avoid starving to death. That much is clear not only from logic but from explicit statements in Chinese historical texts (paralleled by exactly the same kind of statements in sources on the Roman Empire). What some may find surprising is the identity of some of those defecting:

> In the early years of the Han dynasty, Chinese defectors to the Hsiung-nu included such important men as Liu Hsin (king of Han), Lu Wan (king of Yen), Ch'en Hsi (chancellor of Tai). . . . It is also important to point out that some of the Han frontier generals had previously been merchants, and therefore probably maintained trading relations with the Hsiung-nu.[35]

[31] Barfield (1989), following Khazanov (1984), focuses on the idea that the Central Eurasian mode of life was based on "extortion" from the peripheral agricultural peoples. For more on this claim, see endnote 109.

[32] Psarras (2003: 300), citing Barfield (1989: 46–47).

[33] That is, *ho-ch'in*, the usual peace treaty sealed by dynastic marriage.

[34] Most Americans are actually poor, or at least not wealthy, but that does not stop even poorer people from wanting to emigrate to the United States in *hope* of a better life.

[35] Yü (1986: 385). Some generals also undoubtedly fled to the Hsiung-nu to avoid execution by the Han government for losing battles, or for being on the losing side in court politics.

The early Chinese accounts of the Hsiung-nu, like later Greek accounts of the Huns, reveal that some of the peripheral peoples—especially those living in frontier areas—were fully aware of the fact that life in the nomad-ruled states was easier and freer than life in the peripheral agricultural states, where peasants were treated little better than slaves.[36] Tacitus remarks on the relative freedom enjoyed by the Germans, and the desperateness of the agricultural population is well known to historians of the ancient West.

> Totila [king of the Ostrogoths (r. 541–552)] not only accepted slaves and *coloni* into the Gothic army—and apparently in large numbers—but even turned them against their senatorial masters by promising them freedom and ownership of land. In so doing he permitted and provided an excuse for something that Roman lower classes had been willing to do since the third century: "to become Goths" out of despair over their economic situation.[37]

The Chinese dynastic histories are full of the same kind of comments. It is undoubtedly true that some historians from both realms intended to mask their own criticism of their imperial governments by putting it into the mouths of foreigners, but the fact that they consistently say the same kind of thing, and that the early texts which do exist in Central Eurasian languages—such as the Old Turkic inscriptions—also say the same thing, indicates the criticism was truthful. In short, the border defense theory is not supported by the sources.

The border garrisons were intended to support these goals and also to prevent Chinese from attacking innocent Hsiung-nu, to keep Chinese border officials from mistreating the local non-Chinese people in Chinese employ within the borders, and for other similar purposes. The only way to avoid losing population, power, and wealth to Central Eurasia was to build walls, limit trading at frontier cities, and attack the steppe peoples as often

---

[36] This would seem to supply the motive behind Chinese and Graeco-Roman officials' proclamations about the superiority of their cultures to those of the non-Chinese and non-Graeco-Romans of Central Eurasia. The historical picture has been muddied because in China the government was run by Confucians who wrote the official accounts that are often our only historical sources. The Confucians maintained that they and other Chinese were superior beings who did not need to stoop to unsavory activities such as commerce. The Roman elite had exactly the same view of commerce. A merchant could not be a senator.

[37] Wolfram (1988: 8).

as necessary to destroy them or keep them away. Only thus could the conquered territory be held and the conquered people assimilated. Defense from Hsiung-nu raids was actually the least of the Chinese worries, as is detailed explicitly in an official Han Dynasty document discussing the northern frontier fortresses.[38] The sources even note that the walls and frontier fortresses were of little or no use for that purpose when an actual attack did take place—that is, if their purpose had been to prevent Central Eurasian incursions, they failed whenever they did attack. If the Central Eurasians had really been as aggressive and dangerous as claimed, they would have constantly been invading and conquering. There would have been no Chinese Empire, no Persian Empire, no Roman Empire, but only Central Eurasian empires that included China, Persia, and Rome as constituent parts.

There is one additional piece of evidence. The Koguryo Kingdom of southern Manchuria and northern Korea built walls to try and keep the Chinese out. They did not work for the Koguryo for that purpose. The Chinese were not deterred by the walls. Only the all-out effort of the Koguryo army and its inspired generals managed to repulse the repeated invasions—all of them unprovoked and unjustified—by massive Sui and T'ang Chinese armies. The Chinese eventually succeeded in destroying the Koguryo Kingdom and obliterating the Koguryo people only because of internal political dissension and treachery within that kingdom. The uselessness of walls for defense and the explicit statements about their true purposes by the peoples who built them[39] demolish yet another cornerstone of the Central Eurasian myth.

There is a pervasive belief that the Central Eurasian steppe peoples were a genuine military danger to the Chinese, Persian, or Roman empires—that is, by definition, to unified states. This myth is repeated over and over again in the official Chinese dynastic histories and, accordingly, in modern histo-

---

[38] *HS* 94b: 3803–3804. The very same concerns existed in the T'ang period, and certainly in less well-known periods as well. They have existed throughout the entire history of Chinese–Central Eurasian relations down to modern times.

[39] The chief intention most of the builders had for constructing such walls was clearly to fortify and hold conquered territory and the subjects acquired along with it, as well as to keep the conquerors' military, colonists, and other subjects within the borders (cf. Di Cosmo 2002a). They were thus primarily offensive, not defensive. In addition to those already mentioned, the Byzantines, Sasanid Persians, and Rus' also built walls.

ries as well.[40] Nevertheless, it is untrue. No Central Eurasian people ever actually invaded and conquered any of these massive, highly populous, advanced states except in periods of division or civil war, and rarely even then. In the Chinese case, the Central Eurasians were generally invited in by one or another Chinese faction in such periods, as Chinese histories themselves relate in some detail; the same is true of the best-known Roman case, that of the Goths and Huns. This is clearest in the most recent instances because there are more extensive sources, some of them in Central Eurasian languages, but it is also evident as one moves back in time.

For example, the Manchus were invited into China by the feeble, corrupt Ming Dynasty to quell a rebellion. They did as requested and took Peking from the rebels, but—so the histories claim—they were chosen as the new rulers by the local people. The latter detail may or may not be a fabrication, but it is certainly true that the Manchus had long been enemies of the Ming, and both sides had attacks, defeats, and massacres to their credit. Having been invited in and done what they had promised to do, the Manchus stayed in China, where they established a new, strong dynasty to replace the Ming.

Several centuries earlier the Mongols, under the brilliant leadership of Chinggis Khan, became famous for lightning-swift campaigns of conquest in the West. But Chinggis Khan was mainly interested in the Jurchen of the Chin Dynasty of North China, who had supported the Mongols' enemies in Mongolia and had kept Chinggis and his people subservient to them. The Jurchen and their steppe allies were the real danger to the Mongols. Yet despite the Mongols' famed speed, it took many years for them to subdue the Jurchen in Northern China and Manchuria. It was only much later, decades after the death of Chinggis, that the Mongols finally established firm control over the former Jurchen territory and decided to subdue the Sung Dynasty— which, incredibly, had continued attacking the Mongols and mistreating their envoys.

Still earlier, the Uighur Turks entered China proper (i.e., areas that had been Chinese for hundreds of years) in 757 only after they had been invited in to quell the An Lu-shan Rebellion. Their destruction there—notably the

---

[40] For example, Sinor (1990a), Barfield (1989), Drompp (2005). The received view is presented succinctly by Di Cosmo (2002b: 7): "Their raids were fairly serious threats to the security of the frontier, to trade and to settlement in peripheral areas—and could swell to critical proportions in the case of mass migrations."

repeated sack of the eastern capital, Loyang—was specifically authorized by the financially strapped T'ang court as a reward or payment to the Uighurs for their services.[41] All other recorded incidents of Uighur destruction within China appear to be in repayment for treaty breaking, deception, diplomatic affronts, and insults by the T'ang.[42]

The sources for the T'ang period, and modern histories as well, repeat that the nomads were dangerous and China needed to keep them at bay.[43] It has been argued that T'ang China's aggression against its neighbors was justified because they were dangerous, and the institutional changes that aided in Chinese expansion and retention of conquered territory were therefore defensive in nature:

> Following the major set-backs suffered in the final decades of the seventh and the beginning of the eighth centuries, a new institutional framework was developed for the maintenance of an expanded empire which now stretched from southern Manchuria to the Pamirs and from Inner Mongolia to Vietnam. These changes . . . came about in response to increased foreign military pressure, principally from the renascent Eastern Turks, the Khitan and the Tibetans. In the face of recurrent conflicts with these powerful and well-organized neighbours, the T'ang regime was gradually forced to erect a permanent, large-scale defence system. The fact that this system in time acquired significant offensive capabilities has tended to obscure its defensive beginnings. . . . But critics have frequently overlooked the basic strate-

[41] Before the battle in which the T'ang and their Uighur allies retook the western capital of Ch'ang-an, the T'ang gave the Uighurs "the right of plunder should the capital be retaken" (Mackerras 1972: 18–20). Because Loyang, the eastern capital, was still in rebel hands, the Chinese asked the Uighurs to postpone their reward until that city was retaken. The same reward obtained later when Loyang, which had been lost to the rebels once more, was again recaptured with Uighur help in 762. Mackerras's sympathy for the Chinese and antipathy for the Uighurs reflects the emotions of the Chinese sources, but it is unjustifiable on the basis of the actual events, which we know about from those very same sources.

[42] This is all remarkably clear in the summary of events provided in Mackerras's (1972: 14 et seq.) introduction to his valuable translation of the T'ang official accounts on the Uighurs, despite the fact that it repeats the strong pro-Chinese and anti-Uighur sentiments found in the sources even when those sentiments are actually intended to be critical of Chinese behavior and attitudes (some are almost openly sympathetic to the Uighurs). A critical analysis of Mackerras's text would provide excellent examples of virtually all the points discussed in this epilogue.

[43] Peterson (1979: 467). These misconceptions, which are shared by most other historians of China, have been questioned very little, or not at all, in the literature.

gic considerations which impelled the extension of Chinese military power well beyond the limits of possible Chinese settlement. It was only in this way that highly mobile nomadic neighbors could be prevented from making rapid, destructive penetrations into the interior.[44]

In fact, the newly created "institutional framework" referred to—a military governorship system that was strikingly similar to the Byzantine *theme* system—was (in the T'ang case) designed to hold conquered foreign territory and use it as a base for further invasions into neighboring lands. It was from the outset *strictly offensive* in nature, and the appointment mainly of submitted Central Eurasians as military governors was due not only to their skill at war and Chinese fear of them but also to their relative loyalty compared to ethnic Chinese.[45]

The truth is that T'ang China was the dangerous "loose cannon." Chinese sources revel in proclaiming the devastation inflicted upon the Central Eurasians by T'ang heroes and their armies. The early T'ang invaded, defeated, and subjugated all of the peoples around them at one time or another except for the Tibetans, who only barely managed to repel the T'ang at its height. The dynasty's armies expanded even more deeply into Central Eurasia than the Ch'in and Han dynasties had, with greater negative consequences. The Romans, the Persians, and the Chinese could and frequently did invade and defeat the Central Eurasian states, even when they were strong and united, and incorporated the lands and peoples they conquered into their empires.[46] It took the unified Mongols, at the height of their military power, nineteen years (1215–1234) to conquer the Chin Dynasty. It was an additional *forty-five years* before the Sung Dynasty was finally overthrown in 1279 by Khubilai Khan. This is hardly what one would call a lightning invasion and conquest. The complex conditions before, during, and after the wars that resulted in the eventual Mongol victory cannot be ignored. The sources unambiguously record that the Mongols repeatedly sought to secure peaceful relations and trade without any war at all. The wrong idea that "the Mongols' goal was to defeat any nation or fortified city foolish enough to resist

[44] Peterson (1979: 464–465).

[45] This judgment by the T'ang Chinese is practically the same as that made by the Arabs from the early ninth century on with respect to Central Eurasians versus Arabs.

[46] The aggression of the peripheral states against the Central Eurasians has been noted by others; cf. Golden (1987–1991, 1991).

them, but not to occupy and govern it" presents the Mongols, once again, as wild barbarian raiders.[47] The picture is unsustainable in the face of the sources, which emphasize the Mongols' overriding interest in trade and taxation—peacefully, if possible—from the beginning to the end of their period of domination.

The territory of Central Eurasia continued to shrink throughout history from the middle of the first millennium BC down to its almost complete disappearance in the early modern period. Even strong Central Eurasian states could be, and were, defeated by strong peripheral states, as is clear from the history of the Ch'in and Han dynasties, and again the early T'ang Dynasty; even relatively weak peripheral states, such as the post–Han period Chin Dynasty and the late Western Roman Empire, were often able to defeat powerful Central Eurasian states. By contrast, despite the occasional successful Central Eurasian raid or capture of part of the periphery, a unified, strong Central Eurasian state never conquered a unified, strong peripheral state.

The idea of the Central Eurasian pastoral nomads as natural warriors, hard, tough, fearless, and virtually unconquerable, requires the existence—which is present by implication in all histories of Central Eurasia—of soft, weak, fearful peripheral-state peasant soldiers. Yet surely no historian of the Romans would argue that the Roman peasant, who was also the Roman soldier, was weak and unable to bear hardship. The Chinese soldiers of Ch'in Shih Huang-ti and Wu-ti, who conquered enormous empires for their rulers, were no weaklings either. Roman and Chinese peasants formed the rank-and-file troops that fought the successful battles of those huge empires, including the many battles in which the peripheral armies were victorious over Central Eurasian armies. The peasants of traditional agricultural societies in Eurasia worked like slaves and had to survive on very little, as already noted. As a result, they were strong indeed and inured to hardship, despite their smaller size and shorter lives. An armed, fully trained soldier of one of the peripheral empires of Eurasia was to be feared as much or more than a Central Eurasian steppe nomad. Certainly the nomads were tough in war, and learned skills useful in steppe warfare (mainly archery and riding) early in life. They celebrated their martial prowess, praised their war heroes,

[47] Mote (1994: 622), whose treatment of Mongol history in China is, however, in general relatively balanced and sensitive to the sources.

and attempted to frighten peripheral peoples with reports of their ferocity. But the descriptions written by travelers who personally met Central Eurasian people, from Herodotus on, over and over emphasize the ordinariness and unwarlikeness of actual Central Eurasians compared to their scary reputations. The facts, and especially the long-term history, do not match the stories: the Central Eurasians won some battles but eventually lost the war. On the whole, the peripheral peoples were actually much more powerful, dangerous, ruthless, and cruel than the Central Eurasians ever dreamed of being.

By comparison with the peripheral agricultural empires, Central Eurasian states ruled by pastoral nomads had several critical weaknesses.[48] There were few nomads spread out over a vast area, and they could not store up the products of their animal husbandry for a bad year when the animals died, so they lived at the mercy of the weather even more than peasants did. The cities under nomad-state control were not located within the steppe zone itself, with a few rare exceptions, and in any case the pastoral nomads could not have kept vast herds of animals inside city walls when attacked.[49] That left the nomads extremely vulnerable to attack by any determined peripheral zone foe—who, when victorious, typically took hundreds of thousands of sheep and cattle as booty, leaving the Central Eurasian owners who escaped on horseback to face death by starvation.

Steppe zone Central Eurasians also had to be very careful not to fight many full-scale battles on their own (i.e., without infantry auxiliaries), because if they suffered a major defeat they did not have enough men to fill the ranks again. It was necessary for them to frighten their foes into submission and to use force only when necessary. This is known from historical accounts as early as those on the Scythians and Hsiung-nu and on down through the Mongol period. The suddenness of a nomadic army attack was designed for shock effect and was primarily psychological. Because such armies could not capture fortified cities, and large cities—which were always fortified—were the prize, how did they manage to capture the cities that resisted? They used infantry and siege engines, exactly as the peripheral

---

[48] For discussion of similar problems, see Di Cosmo (2002b: 5–7).

[49] Although most cities in the nomad states were located outside the steppe zone proper, some did exist in the steppe zone itself—more in some areas and periods than in others—and some of them have been examined archaeologically. The best known of the latter is one of the Scythian cities, on which see Rolle (1989). See also note 58.

peoples did. The problem was that as nomads they did not have such engines. That meant they could capture cities by force only in an all-out war in which they were able to mobilize their non-nomadic subjects to march on foot to the target city and attack it for them. Gone thereby was the possibility of genuine surprise. The "raid and destroy" construct is a myth. Moreover, it is well known in military history that infantry armies have always been stronger than mounted armies (whether of the nomadic type or not), when other factors were approximately equal. The guerrilla tactics of feinting and skirmishing are the classic means of resistance by a weaker people faced with a more powerful enemy within their territory.[50] They were the nomads' only defense against invading infantry armies, which they could not afford to attack head on.

Central Eurasians had good reason to fear the peripheral peoples, who time and again invaded and defeated them and seized substantial portions of their territory.[51] As the Old Turkic inscriptions from the Eastern Steppe poignantly recall of the fate of the Türk people after the conquest of the First Türk Empire by the T'ang Dynasty of China, "Their lordly sons became slaves of the Chinese people, and their ladylike daughters became concubines."[52]

The history of the Roman conquest of Gaul is a case in point. The Celtic Gauls were crushed, their territory was colonized by the Romans, and the surviving Celts eventually became Romans.[53] This was simply Roman expansion into Gaulish territory. It was from a military or political point of view no different from the Romans' expansion into the many other countries very far from Rome into which they expanded with their armies in the course of establishing their vast empire. But in one respect it was different: Gaul, which had formerly been typically Central Eurasian in culture, became Mediterraneanized and removed from the Central Eurasian culture zone, unlike most of Germania, which successfully resisted the Romans and

---

[50] See the account of the Persian invasion of Scythia in chapter 2. Cf. Arreguín-Toft (2005).

[51] This began very early in China. "The gradual encroachment of central states [i.e., Chinese] on the northern region, and their subjugation and incorporation of Di [Ti] and other frontier peoples, eventually brought China into direct contact with the nomads, primarily in the Ordos region" (Di Cosmo 1999: 950–951).

[52] Köl Tigin (Kül Tigin) inscription, east face, line 7 (Tekin 1968: 233; for his translation, see 264).

[53] The process is exactly paralleled by the Anglo-American conquest of North America and the seizing of Indian lands, q.v. Drinnon (1987).

did not become Mediterraneanized (or Europeanized) until the Middle Ages.

No part of the civilized periphery of Eurasia has ever been added permanently to the Central Eurasian cultural-economic zone. By contrast, the resistance by Central Eurasians against the attacks by the peripheral peoples took many forms over the centuries, but the end result was the same: the Central Eurasians lost.

As often in history, the true picture is in the middle somewhere between the two extremes. In this case, the extremes are the stereotypes of the violent, poor, half-starved, primitive Central Eurasians versus the gentle, rich, well-fed, enlightened Chinese, Persians, and Graeco-Romans. The stereotypes are based on many misconceptions, some of which have been noted above. One of the most important of them has been recognized to some extent by specialists in Central Eurasian history, but only partially, and its ramifications have not been understood. This is the idea that Central Eurasians were nomadic steppe warriors whose enemies were sedentary agriculturalists and urban peoples.

It has become well known among specialists that archaeology and historical research both show there were actually quite a few towns, and even a few cities, located in the steppe zone.[54] The culture of the people in them, as well as the culture of the agriculturalists there, is not significantly different from that of the pastoralists. Therefore, it has been quite rightly concluded that the steppe zone empire builders had their own urban and agricultural resources and did not need to rob the people of the peripheral empires for food[55] and other necessities, and indeed, there is no evidence that they did so.[56] Though this is certainly a corrective to the usual received view, it still omits too much from a full description of known steppe nomad-ruled empires.

Central Eurasians were pastoralists, agriculturalists, and urbanites, and their empires included vast tracts of territory that were not pastoral land.

[54] Di Cosmo (2002a), Nagrodzka-Majchrzyk (1978).

[55] Central Eurasian peoples were, however, quite interested in foreign foodstuffs and were willing to trade for them, as noted below. One of the main ways they used grain was for pasta, which they seem to have acquired a taste for through contact with Chinese. See Golden (1995).

[56] Di Cosmo (2002a: 169–170) says, "Historical sources repeatedly indicate that nomadic raiding parties, sometimes as large as armies, carried away animals and people, not agricultural products." On nomad "raids," see endnote 110.

Certainly the pastoralist component moved around a great deal to avoid exhausting the pastures. But the structure of all known Central Eurasian empires included all three socioeconomic elements. Because pastoral nomads are essentially just farmers of "crops on the hoof,"[57] the socioeconomic structure of Central Eurasian empires was not significantly different from that of peripheral cultures, which had three main components: urban, rural-suburban (the farmers living in close proximity to cities or large towns, serving their needs to a large extent, and often partly engaged in nonagricultural economic pursuits as well), and rural (the farmers living somewhat further from cities or large towns). The one significant difference in Central Eurasia is that the ethnolinguistic identity of the urbanites and proximal farmers (the settled agriculturalists) was usually different from that of the distal farmers (who were pastoral nomads).[58] The pastoralists were also naturally more mobile than the others, exactly the opposite of the distal agriculturalists of the periphery, who were the least mobile members of their society. Otherwise, the contrast between the sophisticated urban culture of the Central Eurasian cities (the urbanites) and the simpler rural culture (the agriculturalists and pastoralists) is identical to that between the sophisticated urban culture of the peripheral cities and the simpler rural culture of the peripheral agriculturalists (both proximal and distal). In other words, there was no fundamental distinction between the economic and political structure of the empires ruled by people belonging to pastoral nomadic ethnic groups on the one hand and empires ruled by people belonging to agricultural ethnic groups on the other.[59]

---

[57] Note the well-chosen title of the anthropologist Robert Ekvall's (1968) book on Tibetan nomads, *Fields on the Hoof.*

[58] See the careful analysis of the Khazar economy by Noonan (1997), and note Tamîm ibn Baḥr's description of the extensive agriculture in the steppe zone itself (and not just around the capital city) in the Uighur Empire (Minorsky 1942), a typical natural feature of Central Eurasian cities in or near the steppe zone, *pace* Barfield (1989: 157 et seq.). The studies of Noonan on the Khazar economy and to some degree those of Pletneva (1958, 1967) point to rather complex mixed economies, with agricultural elements, some clearly stemming from ex-nomads or semi-nomads.

[59] This was pointed out very early by Bosworth (1968: 4–5), who notes that the traditionally supposed existence of "two naturally antipathetic groups," the "pastoral nomads" and "the rural peasantry and even the town populations of Transoxiana," is belied by "the economic facts, well brought out by the Arab geographers," who "say that the economy of the pastoralist Turks from the steppe was complementary to and interdependent with the economy of the agricultural oases and towns of the Iranian Tājiks." He goes on to say, somewhat less accurately, "The settled regions supplied the nomads with cereals, manufactured goods, and arms, and the nomads reared stock animals and brought dairy products, hides, and furs to

Historians have divorced the pastoralists from the other components in their states, creating the mythical "pure" nomad and at the same time the unexplained presence of cities and agriculturalists, as well as the completely mysterious existence of the Silk Road, which is generally treated as if it were a pipeline that passed from China to Rome without having anything to do with the intervening lands through which it passed—except that merchants are believed to have been robbed on a regular basis by the nomads. The three components of Central Eurasian states are actually noted as early as Herodotus (who, however, clearly did not understand what he described in this respect). The fact that the people living in the cities were usually not the same ethnolinguistically as the pastoral nomads does not change anything. What is important is that the steppe-nomad-ruled empires *always* included control—exercised as a light kind of suzerainty—over many cities. The Scythians had this kind of control over the cities on the Black Sea coast and other areas, most of the inhabitants of which were Greeks and Thracians. The Hsiung-nu had the same kind of suzerainty over the cities of the Silk Road and maintained it even in the presence of Han Dynasty armies and governors. And so on, through the Turkic, Mongol, and Junghar empires. Just as distal peripheral farmers living deep in the countryside—that is, far from cities—did not have or build cities by definition, it was rare that pastoral nomads built or personally occupied cities of their own. In the nomads' case it is difficult to imagine how they would have managed to both live in cities and move their herds around in the steppe pasturelands. This accounts for why the nomads had so few cities *in the steppe zone.* But it was necessary for their empires to include cities, and they always did. In short, the urban component was inseparable from the rural component (or components) in Central Eurasian empires, exactly as the two were inseparable in the peripheral empires.

It seems to have been widely overlooked that the act of unilateral establishment of a border (invariably far beyond the previously established border), construction of fortifications to hold the new border (the unilaterally proclaimed "national territory" of the aggressor), and closing the border

---

the farmers." This list of items produced and exchanged is not completely correct on either side. For example, the steppe peoples produced arms and other metal goods, they were involved extensively in commerce beyond that necessary for their own needs, and they are rarely known to have been very interested in eating grain foods. Nevertheless, the essential point is well made.

and cutting off trade relations with those outside it, are overt acts of war.[60] It is impossible to understand them as anything else. Not only did Central Eurasians understand this, and act accordingly, but the peripheral states that were the aggressors understood it as well. Although their historical accounts rarely point this out openly, occasionally they do so, or the words of a dissident voice are preserved (usually in order to condemn him as a rebel, enemy sympathizer, or other bad person).

Central Eurasians were acutely aware of the danger to them from the peripheral states and instantly understood the latter's belligerent intentions when walls were built in Central Eurasian territory, armies were moved to the frontier, trade relations were cut, and so forth—all acts of war. Whenever the peripheral states were not thus at war with the Central Eurasians, peace and prosperity ensued. But peace and prosperity were not the goals of empire builders. Their goals were uncontested, absolute power and the expansion of the territory and people under their rule to the maximum extent possible. When a Central Eurasian founded an empire, he too had the same goals, but they were temporary. A Central Eurasian empire was designed not only to establish secure boundaries and a stable internal political system—in other words, peace—but also to support and expand the local and international economy, by means of which prosperity was increased for everyone.

Central Eurasians' insistence on trade relations with the peripheral-empire cities that were nearby, as well as their clear, careful policy toward cities anywhere even in wartime, shows how important cities and trade relations were to them. It also explains one of the main reasons for conflict along the frontier. The nomadic peoples needed to be able to trade directly, themselves, where they happened to be, exactly as the agriculturalists in the peripheral states needed to have access to market towns. Moreover, the normal state of affairs on the Chinese and Roman frontiers with Central Eurasia from at least the pre-Classical period onward was that the nomadic peoples traded with the Chinese or Romans in the market towns there. When peripheral states officially closed the frontier cities to the nomads, or made trading there practically impossible, and abused the nomads when they attempted to negotiate, the Central Eurasians saw these acts as intended to provoke war. They had little choice but to attack the perpetrators. Examples

[60] Chinese expansion into Central Eurasia in this way was paralleled by Russian expansion through the steppe zone into Central Asia.

of this kind of deliberately created conflict occurred right down to the partition of Central Eurasia in the seventeenth and eighteenth centuries.[61]

Central Eurasians' regular insistence on free trade at border markets, through the millennia, across the length and breadth of Central Eurasia, regardless of ethnolinguistic identity, is remarkable. The peripheral-state sources that tell us this are also full of anti–Central Eurasian xenophobia and strong anticommercial prejudice—not surprisingly, because their authors were almost exclusively from the landed aristocracy, not the merchant class—and at the same time they blame the Central Eurasians for the disruption of commerce and use that as an excuse for invading Central Eurasian territory. Modern historians have preferred the negative views about Central Eurasia in the peripheral-state sources.

Speaking about the conflict between the Ming Dynasty and the Mongols in the early sixteenth century, Perdue says, "Hard-liners regarded trade or negotiation with the irredeemably violent Mongols as impossible."[62] But a page later he notes, "In 1551 the [Ming] emperor prohibited all trade with the Mongols on pain of death,"[63] and adds:

> Altan Khan (1507–1582), the grandson of Batu, had risen to power in the mid-sixteenth century as the next great Mongol raider of the Chinese empire. He never unified the Mongols, but he led the twelve Tümed (ten thousand-man units) under his control north of Shaanxi and Shanxi in continuous attacks along the frontier, followed by requests for permission to conduct tribute trade—requests which the Chinese nearly always rejected. This repeated cycle of "request, refusal, raid" continued for forty years until 1570.[64]

At that point, much debate ensued at the Ming court about the relative merits of trade versus war with the Mongols. "Only under the next emperor's

---

[61] My analysis disagrees with the "trade or raid" theory—summarized, critically, by Di Cosmo (1999b: 11 n. 32)—according to which "periodic conflicts between China and the nomads are to be attributed to China's unwillingness to allow trade or to subsidize nomadic economy with tribute, which forced the nomads to organize themselves into raiding parties and make use of their military superiority to fulfill the economic function of trade. While addressing some of the reasons that allegedly led to a cyclical alternation of peace and war, this theory does not explain the rise of nomadic empires, instead dismissing them as anomalies."

[62] Perdue (2005: 63).

[63] Perdue (2005: 64).

[64] Perdue (2005: 64).

reign (Longqing, 1567–1572) could the Ming, in a brilliant stroke of frontier diplomacy, bring itself to negotiate peace on the frontier."[65] This genius insight was the realization that, after all those decades in which the Mongols repeatedly told the Chinese they needed to open their markets to them, "Altan Khan wanted peaceful trade relations; he raided only if tribute was refused."[66] After it was finally decided to allow trade once more, "Merchants flocked to the frontier to sell silk, fur, grain, and cooking pots to the Mongols; the government collected taxes on the trade and used the income to buy poor horses at high prices from the nomads."[67] The last disparaging comment is hardly to be believed, whatever its source; Perdue notes shortly before it, "The Ming had reinforced its walls and mainly needed horses from the Mongols for the mobility of the garrisons."[68]

This can all be summed up as follows. The Chinese occupied large tracts of territory in Central Eurasia and attempted to impoverish the Central Eurasians by denying them access to their market towns. Coupled with the belligerent, aggressive stance of the Chinese toward the Central Eurasians, the result, not surprisingly, was war, which included Central Eurasian attacks on the Chinese. But the Central Eurasians did not want war, they wanted trade, and repeatedly sought peaceful trade relations with China. After the Chinese grew tired of the expense and suffering of war, they reopened trade relations with the Central Eurasians. Peace and prosperity resulted on both sides of the frontier.

It is thus no secret that the source of the conflict between the Mongols and the Ming Chinese was the deliberate Chinese prohibition of trade. It was openly discussed at the Chinese court, and after Chinese attempts at a military solution (destruction of the Mongols) failed, the prohibition was lifted and peace ensued.[69]

Similarly, the only real problem between the Junghars and the Ch'ing Dynasty *should* have been the latter's periodic restriction or even prohibition of trade, because as soon as these constraints were removed peace was the result.[70] While much good research has been done in recent years on

---

[65] Perdue (2005: 65).

[66] Perdue (2005: 65). Here "tribute" is the literal English translation of the loaded Chinese term for officially sanctioned trade.

[67] Perdue (2005: 66).

[68] Perdue (2005: 65). This need probably explains the policy change.

[69] Perdue (2005: 63–66).

[70] Perdue (2005: 256–265).

Manchu-Chinese history, nearly everything that has been written about the broader picture of the Junghar-Ch'ing conflict and its supposed sources is misleading. The real source of the conflict was the Manchu-Chinese desire to expand further into Central Eurasia. Because the ruling Central Eurasians of the day, the Junghars, attempted to prevent the Manchu-Chinese from achieving that goal, the Ch'ing did everything they could to destroy them. Whenever they failed in their attempts at a military solution, they made peace with the Junghars and allowed trade. As soon as the Ch'ing had a chance to destroy the Junghars militarily, they immediately set out to do so, and the conflict resumed. The final result was Manchu-Chinese success, their massacre of most of the Junghars, and Ch'ing conquest of much of Central Eurasia, which had been protected by the Junghars. Despite all the historical detail, therefore, most of which concerns personal conflicts and masks the course of events and their causes, it was purely Manchu-Chinese expansionism that drove the destruction of the Junghars. There were no Junghar attacks against the Ch'ing, and no "greedy barbarian" traders were involved. Certainly the Junghars were not angels and fault can sometimes be found with them, but on the whole it is impossible to understand this crucial episode of Eurasian history in any other way.[71]

A peripheral state's closure of its frontier cities to the steppe peoples was the exact equivalent of the closure of its interior market towns to its own agriculturalists: a deliberate attempt to ruin the economy in the region. The ability to do this gave the peripheral states the power to use trade in the frontier cities as a political-economic weapon, to force the Central Eurasians to negotiate for their air and water. As Yu notes, perhaps unintentionally (because in the same article he refers to the extensive commercial relationships among the frontier Chinese and the Hsiung-nu), "Although private trade between the Chinese and the Hsiung-nu probably had been going on along the border for a very long time, a large-scale *government-sponsored* market system did not come into existence until Wen-ti's reign [180–157 BC]."[72] It must not be forgotten that the frontier areas of both empires were located deep within Central Eurasia, so the idea that Central Eurasians were invading when they wanted to trade there makes no sense unless one adopts

---

[71] It is thus hard to sympathize with Sinologists who lament China's weakness when faced with the Europeans. The latter ran up against the same policy and prejudices on the part of the Manchu-Chinese.

[72] Yü (1986: 388), emphasis added.

347

a pro-Chinese bias. Further, the idea that the nomadic peoples unjustly attacked the border markets for no reason other than a love of violence, or the desire for booty, is not only unsupported by the sources, it is contradicted by them. Despite the anti-Hun prejudice of Thompson (like most other writers on the Huns), and his fundamental misunderstanding of Hun economy, society, and political motivations, he rightly notes that a primary concern of the Hun leaders was to ensure that the Roman market towns "open to the Huns . . . should continue to be so, that the terms prevailing there should be fair, and that access to these markets should be attended with no danger to the Huns."[73]

In this connection it has been noted with some puzzlement that the Scythians, who are said by Herodotus to be fearsome warriors, are otherwise quite nice in the rest of his description. Similarly, the Mongols in the period after the First World War—who lived "under conditions of life that probably did not differ substantially from those of their ancestors of the thirteenth century"—were regarded by an American spy in Mongolia as an "unwarlike people." In both cases, the scholars who have noted these discrepancies have drawn what might appear to be logical conclusions, *if* the received view of Central Eurasians were correct—namely, that the Scythians must have been a different people entirely,[74] while the Mongols must have changed over time because of protracted peace, or possibly due to the influence of Buddhism or Chinese rule.[75] The same is routinely said about the Tibetans after the period of the Tibetan Empire, among other peoples.

---

[73] Thompson (1996: 195). He also remarks perceptively in this connection, "It is difficult to resist the impression that the continued existence of the Hun empire must have been recognized by many Roman subjects as essential to their prosperity" (Thompson 1996: 194).

[74] According to Drews (2004: 122), Herodotus says that "the natives of the Pontic-Caspian steppe called themselves *Skolotoi*, and that only the Greeks called them 'Skythians.' . . . There was, however, one very important difference between the nomadic *Skolotoi* north of the Black Sea and the Skythians of western Iran: the *Skolotoi* appear to have been pastoralists and not raiders. That the hospitable and congenial 'Skythians' north of the Black Sea were the same people as the real Skythians, who had terrorized much of the Near East for a generation, is most unlikely." This conclusion is odd; even the usual misconceived idea of a Central Eurasian nomadic people equates "pastoral nomads" with "terrorizing raiders." The only thing that is unlikely in Herodotus here is the idea that the Scythians terrorized anyone without good reason (as explicitly noted by Strabo); in fact, most of the time we simply do not know what the reasons for their campaigns were. At any rate, it is known for certain that the two names are merely different pronunciations of the same name and do actually refer to the same people (Szemérenyi 1980); cf. appendix B.

[75] Di Cosmo (2002b: 9), who, however, also indicates some doubt about the correctness of the natural warrior theory.

Yet these descriptions of what are thought to be exceptional (peaceful) Central Eurasians are strikingly similar to the actual first-person accounts of two of the most fearsome warriors in Central Eurasian history, Attila the Hun and Tamerlane. Both are described in the accounts as intelligent, modest, sober, generous, just rulers.

A related topos about Central Eurasians is the supposed "moral and physical decline of the once-hardy nomads" when seduced by the luxuries and easy life of peripheral cultures' cities, because of their having forsaken "the hard life of the steppe, thus weakening their martial spirit, and leading to their being overthrown either by the local populace or by some other un-diluted nomadic force."[76] Luxury-loving, lazy, dissolute Central Eurasians do not fit the received view of "real" Central Eurasians; something must have changed. Anthropologists and other scholars who have visited and studied Central Eurasian pastoral nomads in recent times have revealed that indeed, nomads did have a fairly easy life and were generally rather lazy. They also ate and dressed better than the peasants of the neighboring agricultural states. This is not really news. In premodern accounts of peripheral-state envoys who met with Central Eurasian pastoral nomads, it is remarked that the Central Eurasians would not dismount but preferred to sit comfortably on their horses to negotiate. Tacitus remarks about the ancient Germans, "When not engaged in warfare they spend a certain amount of time in hunting, but much more in idleness, thinking of nothing else but sleeping and eating." They thus "show a strange inconsistency—at one and the same time loving indolence and hating peace."[77] Similarly, visitors in recent times comment on Central Eurasian nomads' preference for riding even the short distance between two yurts in the same settlement, rather than walking. However, there is also no reason to go to the other extreme and regard the pastoral nomadic peoples of Central Eurasia at any time as especially weak, despite their socioeconomic vulnerabilities, or lazier and more indolent than humans in any other society, if given the chance.

Traditional historical accounts of Central Eurasians focus to a great extent on the personalities of the leaders and other characters in the stories related about them. They are full of the often emotional-sounding decisions of one or another leader—whether of a Central Eurasian state or a peripheral

---

[76] Di Cosmo (2002b: 8–9).
[77] Mattingly (1970: 114).

state is immaterial—to wage war against a neighbor. In our eyes, sufficient justification is often lacking. Because we know so much less about Central Eurasia than we do about the periphery, and most of what we do know is written by peripheral historians, the Central Eurasians are almost universally portrayed as acting without justification, impulsively, violently, greedily,[78] and so forth, avoiding the balanced, careful, considered decisions made by the peripheral leaders to do, often, exactly the same thing. In general we simply do not know enough about the history and psychology of the Central Eurasians concerned or the background conditions that might have influenced them to be able to judge the rightness or wrongness of their actions. But when we do know enough, their actions usually are understandable, and justifiable as well. This is not to say they are always excusable, but only that there is no difference between Central Eurasian and peripheral states in this respect. The decision to go to war was often made by an individual leader, often for personal reasons, or simply in error.[79] Though playing favorites is probably unavoidable—historians are human too—it should not distort the final picture to the extent that it no longer is a fair approximation of the truth. Yet this is what has happened in Central Eurasian history, where Central Eurasians are demonized regardless of whether they are aggressors or victims. When they appear very clearly not to be aggressive *barbarians*, the conclusion is drawn that they are therefore necessarily not Central Eurasians at all but some other people.

In connection with these misconceptions, there is also a pervasive myth that Central Eurasian peoples such as the Huns and Mongols attacked the innocent cultured peoples of the periphery unexpectedly and without provocation or reason. There are several problems here. The main fallacy is that Central Eurasians were unique in trying to expand their realms at the expense of their neighbors, who are treated as innocent, peace-loving victims. The unprovoked aggression of the Chinese, Persian, and Graeco-Roman conquerors, among others, is conveniently forgotten, and the Central Eurasians alone are guilty of following the natural human impetus to form states, which necessarily entailed the attempt to subjugate their neighbors. Historians' obsession with state formation in Central Eurasia should not blind everyone to the fact that peripheral peoples formed states too, begin-

---

[78] On the historical topos of "the greed of the barbarians," see Sinor (1978).

[79] It still is, as witness many armed conflicts in the contemporary period.

ning in prehistoric times; state formation there also entailed subjugating the neighbors. There is no evidence that any empire was ever formed without violent conquest of the founding people's neighbors, and plenty of evidence that dynastic founders everywhere eliminated their rivals at home in particularly unpleasant ways, so one wonders why the history of this sort of thing in Central Eurasia is the subject of so much puzzlement by scholars. Moreover, as noted above, there are extremely few, if any, verifiable accounts of completely unprovoked Central Eurasian attacks on *peripheral* powers.

Central Eurasians are also blamed for specific conflicts when they had already formed an empire and relations had already become hostile between them and a neighboring peripheral state. In such cases, the absence of source material on the cause of the conflict, and the usual bias of whatever historical sources do exist, rarely allow one to confidently establish the reasons for it. In most instances there simply are no sources at all relating to the early history of the Central Eurasian peoples in question and their contacts with the peripheral peoples, encouraging the continued belief in this myth. Yet where historical sources do preserve detailed records of such conflicts, even though they are written by non–Central Eurasians, they usually show that the Central Eurasians were defending themselves or retaliating for perfidy committed by their enemies, generally an earlier attack or outright invasion by the peripheral people. The Romans' own historical sources recount over and over how the wars with the Central Eurasians (including the Germanic peoples) were caused by the Romans themselves, who hired Central Eurasians to attack the Romans' enemies and then cheated them or otherwise mistreated them so grievously that they had no choice but to rebel. It is not that the Central Eurasians were never guilty of perfidy. The point is that it is impossible to establish historically that the Central Eurasians were uniquely or even usually guilty of such evils, nor perhaps were the peripheral peoples. Both sides were guilty of wanting to expand their domains.

None of this is intended to excuse either Central Eurasians or peripheral peoples from all the killing. Nevertheless, while both sides were responsible, it is impossible to simply accept the usual pro-peripheral viewpoint. There are no Hun sources that tell us the Hun side of the story, but the Romans' own best witness, Priscus, plainly describes, in language that cannot be misunderstood, the repeated betrayals, attempted murder, and other Roman offenses against the Huns in the very short time covered by his first-person account of an official Roman diplomatic mission to the Hun royal court. The same is true for the history of most other Central Eurasian peoples right down to the partition and conquest of Central Eurasia by peripheral powers in early modern times. The reason for doubt about the usual pro-periphery view presented in the available historical sources is that when detailed source material is available—usually in the very same peripheral sources—it invariably reveals, often inadvertently, that the causes of the conflicts were complex, but that the peripheral empires were ultimately to blame due to their attempted military expansion into the steppe zone and the city-state region, and that the Central Eurasians were defending themselves or attempting to retake territory that had earlier been seized from them by the peripheral power in question.

The historical accounts of the northern Chinese frontier in the late T'ang period are full of the raids, attacks, predations, and so on of one or another group of people against the others, the victims usually being portrayed as innocent Chinese. But amid all their suffering, some details escape to reveal the other side of the picture.

Numerous incidents reveal that the increasing tribal wealth in livestock attracted the greed of Chinese frontier officials, who exploited them by means of unfair market practices or outright seizure of their animals. In revenge, the Tanguts, often with Tibetan help, raided border prefectures in the Hsia-Yen area. The T'ang's communication lines to Ling-chou grew ever more precarious just at the same time as control over livestock production and horse supplies, so vital to the Chinese and their armies, passed into Tangut hands.[80]

It cannot be denied that Central Eurasian peoples often attacked each other, as well as the peripheral peoples, though as noted, the reasons are generally not those given. So too did the peripheral peoples often attack each other and the Central Eurasians. The Romans boasted about their victory over the Goths around Marcianopolis:[81]

[80] Dunnell (1994: 161).
[81] Marcianopolis was the capital of the Roman province of Lower Moesia, which extended eastward along the right (south) bank of the lower Danube to the Black Sea (Vallhé 1910); it is modern Devnya, not far from Varna in Bulgaria.

Many kings were captured, noble women of divers tribes taken prisoner, and the Roman provinces filled with barbarian slaves and Scythian husbandmen. The Goth was made the tiller of the barbarian frontier, nor was there a single district which did not have Gothic slaves in triumphant servitude. How many cattle taken from the barbarians did our forefathers see? How many sheep? How many Celtic mares, which fame has rendered renowned?[82]

Both sides were human, and until very recent times war was an accepted, normal part of life. Peace happened too, locally, but on a continent-wide scale it was extremely rare, if it ever existed at all.[83] For Central Eurasians from Proto-Indo-European times on, attacking neighbors who had unjustly stolen one's cattle—whether recently or at any time in the past—was heroic, and as the preceding quotation and many others like it from both East and West show, the peripheral peoples thought it was heroic too.

Successful warlike behavior is what defines a hero throughout history in every Eurasian society, with very rare exceptions. If a Greek is a hero because he killed his enemies, why should a Central Eurasian not be a hero for the very same reason? Or, rather, why should either of them be heroes? Moreover, the existence of vendetta in most Eurasian cultures ensured that there was never any shortage of enemies who could be raided without any moral twinges. Because most of the long history of mutual raiding between Central Eurasian peoples and peripheral peoples actually took place in former Central Eurasian territory which had been seized by the latter from the former, it is hard not to see the Central Eurasians' point of view. The peripheral peoples' anger at the Central Eurasians for fighting back when attacked is also understandable, as is their use of terms of opprobrium for them—in the Graeco-Roman-speaking world, βάρβαροι or *barbari* 'barbarians',[84] and

---

[82] Burns (1984: 17–18), quoting the *Scriptores Historiae Augustae*.

[83] Bryce (2002: 98) remarks that "since the beginning of recorded history scarcely more than three hundred years have been free of major wars. To put this another way, if we were to take at random any period of a hundred years in the last five thousand, we could expect ninety-four of them on average to be occupied with large-scale conflicts in one or more parts of the globe."

[84] The word βάρβαρος 'barbarian' was not originally pejorative in meaning. It only meant someone who could not speak Greek. Herodotus, despite his sensationalistic stories, was not prejudiced against the Scythians, and does not use the word in a pejorative sense. The negative connotations leading to its modern sense derive largely from the Greeks' later feelings about the Persians (whom they also called βάρβαροι 'barbarians') after the Graeco-Persian wars (Liddell et al. 1968: 306). Aristotle, for example, remarks in his *Nicomachean Ethics* vii,

in the Chinese-speaking world 虜 *lǔ* 'captives' or other generic pejorative words that were used for Chinese as well as for foreigners.[85] But none of this should mislead us today.

It is also undoubtedly true that the Scythians and other Central Eurasians were as fierce as possible in war and encouraged the peripheral peoples' fear of them, as did the ancient Germanic and Hunnic peoples and the medieval Mongols. Tacitus remarks about one of the Suebi peoples in the northeast:

> As for the Harii, not only are they superior in strength to the other peoples I have just mentioned, but they minister to their savage instincts by trickery and clever timing. They black their shields and dye their bodies, and choose pitch dark nights for their battles. The shadowy, awe-inspiring appearance of such a ghoulish army inspires mortal panic; for no enemy can endure a sight so strange and hellish. Defeat in battle always starts with the eyes.[86]

One is, however, forced to ask why it seems to have been overlooked that the peripheral peoples, principally the Greeks and Romans, the Persians, and the Chinese, were also fierce and, indeed, much more cruel and barbaric to each other and to foreign peoples than were the foreigners they called *barbarians*, as even a cursory glance at the incredibly gruesome history of the Roman Empire, for example, not to forget the gruesome histories of the Persians and Chinese right down to the present day, quickly reveals. Moreover, the peripheral empires were usually much more successful at warfare than the Central Eurasians, despite occasional spectacular Central Eurasian successes, and the peripheral peoples certainly made their Central Eurasian enemies fear them, despite all the bravado on both sides. The pretense of fierceness put on by Central Eurasians is not really borne out by their actual history. It is difficult to imagine the Chinese allowing a known Hsiung-nu spy to live in China, marry, and have children and not kill him outright; yet the Hsiung-nu twice allowed a known Chinese spy, Chang Ch'ien, to enter

---

that "a bestial character is rare among human beings; it is found most frequently among barbarians (ἐν τοῖς βαρβάροις)" (Rackham 1934: 376–377). The idea that barbarians have culture, though an "uncouth" one—that is, they are not savages or wild men—apparently also derives from the Persian connection.

[85] There was and is no word or expression in Chinese equivalent to the Western term and concept of the *barbarian*, as explained below.

[86] In *Germania* xliii (Mattingly 1970: 137).

Hsiung-nu territory and stay there in precisely this way. With few exceptions Central Eurasians were truly fierce only when a polity that had submitted rebelled and murdered its new overlords' representatives, or a city that was besieged in time of war refused to surrender peacefully.[87]

Yet Roman conquests are still celebrated, while Hun conquests are condemned. Roman victories over the Huns were good, but Hun victories over the Romans were bad. In the case of the Huns, as with other Central Eurasians, from the time we have detailed historical accounts of them rather than vague, stereotype-filled references to little-known distant aliens, virtually all of the attacks against the Romans, east or west, are explicitly known to have been in retaliation for Roman incursions, treaty violations, or other offenses. When the Huns were victorious, the Romans were sometimes forced to sue for peace and pay indemnities. Exactly the same thing happened between the Hsiung-nu and the Chinese in eastern Eurasia. But this should not induce anyone today into believing that the Romans or Persians or Chinese, of all people, were simply innocent victims of *barbarians*.

The idea that Central Eurasians, as people, were naturally powerful, or unusually violent, or specially skilled at war—characteristics of *barbarians*—is unsupported by history, archaeology, or anthropology. Central Eurasians were urban and rural, strong and weak, fierce and gentle, abstainers and drinkers, lovers and haters, good, bad, and everything in between,[88] exactly as all other known people on earth.

The Nonexistence of Barbarians in Eastern Eurasia

It is clear that the ancient and medieval European idea that certain peoples were *barbarians* and Central Eurasia was the home of *barbarians* continues to be accepted by modern historians, whether explicitly or not, though there

[87] The practice of slaughtering most of the defendants in such cases is attested among virtually every Eurasian people down to premodern times. The comments of Bryce (2002: 98 et seq.) on this practice, and on the constancy of warfare and rarity of peace and the acceptance of warfare as a normal part of life and death, applies not only to Antiquity but to most of history. This is not to excuse anyone's butchery of their fellow man but only to insist that no nationality seems to have been uniquely virtuous.

[88] Similarly, Allsen (1997: 4–5) remarks that "all premodern empires, including that of the Mongols, were possessed of 'multiple personalities,'" and that "they were, by turn, destructive and constructive, brutal and paternal, exploitative and beneficent, coercive and attractive, conservative and innovative." I would delete only the word "premodern" from this characterization.

has been a slight shift in the meaning of the word *barbarian* in modern times. It has also come to be the most widespread mistranslation for a large number of terms for foreigners in Classical Chinese, none of which have anything to do with the idea of the *barbarian*. It is remarkable that this relic of the ancient Greeks' encounter with foreign nations—especially the Persians (whom they admired and copied, despite the many wars with them)[89]—continues to dominate historians' views of Central Eurasians down to the present day.

Some contemporary historians, embarrassed by the obviously offensive semantics of the word and its relatives, put the term in quotes. But this does not fix the error. Use of the term by ancient, medieval, or modern writers tells us only about those who use it, and it does not tell us anything good. The situation would therefore seem to be bad enough already, but in reality it is even worse. East Asianists, in particular, have become attached to the use of "barbarian"—now regularly in quote marks—and very many are loath to abandon it.

It must be understood that neither the name *barbarian* nor the idea behind it is applicable to the peoples to whom it has been applied either historically or in modern times. The entire construct is, appropriately enough, best summed up by popular European and American fiction and film treatments such as *Conan the Barbarian*. In actual fact, no nation has ever been known to have viewed its own people as barbarians. This includes even the kingdoms of Western Europe in the period after the fall of the Western Roman Empire. Those new states are still commonly referred to by modern historians as "the barbarian kingdoms," but though the writers of those times refer sometimes to members of *other* ethnic groups as *barbarians*, they never use the term in reference to themselves. This point alone ought to be decisive. Nevertheless, although it has become generally recognized that *barbarian* is a pejorative term and should not be used, most specialists in East Asian history continue to use it. This is a much more serious problem than it appears at first sight and calls for a closer look.

No one would deny that premodern Chinese apparently disliked foreigners in general and looked down on them as having an inferior culture. It is thus not surprising that the Chinese often used characters with negative meaning to write the names of some of the many foreign peoples and categories of foreign-

---

[89] Miller (1999).

ers they knew—though it must be emphasized that, as far as we know, all of the names are actually phonetic transcriptions of foreign names in origin. None of this is problematic. The problems are as follows.

There are *many* words used by the Chinese to refer to *many* foreign peoples and categories of peoples—perhaps two dozen in common use over the course of Chinese history. None of them are completely generic. Although one can etymologize some of the characters, the original meaning of most of the names is actually, "transcription of the foreign name X of foreigner Y," pure and simple (as evidenced in part by the variant transcriptions seen of some "foreigner" words). The fact that the Chinese did not *like* foreigner Y and occasionally picked a transcriptional character with negative meaning (in Chinese) to write the sound of his ethnonym, is irrelevant.[90] Moreover, as noted above, most Central Eurasians, or at least those about whom we know enough to say what they thought, intensely disliked the Chinese and looked down on their culture. That is, the Hsiung-nu, the Turks, the Mongols, and so on generally despised the Chinese right back. This is well attested in the historical literature.

The English form of the European culture word under discussion is *barbarian*. It has the adjective form *barbaric*, among other derived forms. It is true that the original meaning of the original Greek word βάρβαρος *bárbaros* in early Greek is believed to be simply someone who could not speak Greek (or could not speak it correctly),[91] from which we get the derived word *barbarism*. But about two and a half millennia ago the Greeks became involved in wars with the Persians and the meaning of the word βάρβαρος changed. The Greeks considered not only that those particular foreigners— the Persians—could not speak Greek but that they were strong and militarily skilled, they were fierce and sometimes cruel to their enemies, and they had a culture of their own, though in the eyes of the Greeks it was not as refined as Greek culture. This particular complex of ideas eventually became fused to this one particular linguistic form, the root *barbar-*, such that in order to express that same idea every European language has had to

---

[90] Many people in many countries are prejudiced about people of particular nationalities and hate even the mention of their names. But does this mean the *names themselves* are pejorative—that is, the *words*, not the letters or characters used to transcribe them? This would only be possible if the people of the foreign nations despised themselves, or thought they were less virtuous or less cultured than the people who despised them, and accordingly gave themselves names expressing such feelings. This is hardly conceivable.

[91] Liddell et al. (1968: 306).

borrow the word itself and nativize it. The spread of the word and concept began with the Romans, who applied it to people who did not speak Greek or Latin, who were militarily adept, who were fierce or cruel to their enemies, and who had a non-Graeco-Roman culture. The spread of the complex has continued down to modern times.

The Chinese, however, have still not yet borrowed Greek *barbar-*. There is also no single native Chinese word for 'foreigner', no matter how pejorative, which includes the complex of the notions 'inability to speak Chinese', 'militarily skilled', 'fierce/cruel to enemies', and 'non-Chinese in culture'. There is nothing remotely close to it in Chinese even today. Until the Chinese borrow the word *barbarian* or one of its relatives, or make up a new word that explicitly includes the same basic ideas, they cannot express the idea of the 'barbarian' in Chinese. The usual modern Mandarin Chinese translation of the word is 野蠻人 *yěmánrén*, which actually means 'wild man, savage'.[92] That is very definitely not the same thing as 'barbarian'. The English words 'wild man', 'savage', and 'barbarian' all have very different meanings. In short, it is impossible to translate the word *barbarian* into Chinese because the concept does not exist in Chinese. It should also be noted that, from at least the Romans onward, foreigners referred to as *barbarians* have often been glorified in the West, especially those foreigners who were defeated heroes. This aspect of glorification continues in the meaning of the word today, as in the uses of it in fiction and cinema. The fictional character Conan the Barbarian actually comes quite close to summing up the idea of what a *barbarian* is. Until very recently, at least, this idea too was completely missing in Chinese.

To look at it from the other direction produces much the same results. If one looks up in a Chinese-English dictionary the two dozen or so partly generic words used for various foreign peoples throughout Chinese history, one will find most of them defined in English as, in effect, 'a kind of barbarian'. Even the works of well-known lexicographers such as Karlgren do this. This is much like looking up the many words for specific plants and birds and get-

---

[92] Etymologically, it literally means 'wild *Mán* person', where *Mán* alone (often combined with the word *nán* 'south' to make *Nán-Mán* 'southern *Mán*') is the name normally used for foreigners living to the south of the Chinese heartland. Northern Chinese traditionally looked down on southerners in general, not only foreigners. Note that the Chinese word *mán* (*Mán*) is unrelated to the English word *man*. It seems to have been pronounced *mal or *bal or the like in Old Chinese.

ting the definition 'a kind of grass' or 'a kind of bird'. Those words do not actually mean 'a kind of grass' or 'grass' in general; they mean a particular variety or species of grass, such as 'wild rye', or they refer to some specific aspect of grass, such as 'dry grass (straw)', and the dictionary maker either could not find out what it was or was too lazy to define it accurately. Only the Chinese generic word 草 *cǎo* can be equated well with the English generic word *grass* (and *cǎo* is not 'a kind of grass'). This is comparable to the situation with *barbarian*, but is more difficult because Chinese has no generic word equivalent to *barbarian*, or indeed any one word that is even close to it, while English has no words for the many foreign peoples referred to by one or another Classical Chinese word, such as 胡 *hú*, 夷 *yí*, 蠻 *mán*, and so on.[93]

It can further be demonstrated that the Chinese did not have the *barbarian* ensemble of ideas about foreigners purely conceptually. Classical Chinese writers sometimes express admiration for the people of foreign cultures, usually those who lived in cities, had written literature, and so on: that is, people who were, technically speaking, civilized. The texts say they are "most like the Chinese" among the other "foreigners"—here using one of the generic terms frequently used for the foreigners of that region in general, *including those who lived in cities, nomads, and any others*. The Chinese writers compare particular aspects of the foreign culture to the corresponding ones in Chinese culture. Why would they do that if those cultures were *barbaric*? They certainly were *not* barbaric in the eyes of the Chinese who wrote the reports. But the Chinese word used for the admired foreign people and their culture is the same one used for Central Eurasians such as the Hsiung-nu and many other peoples the Chinese usually did not admire, for example 胡 *hú*, which is used for both the urban civilized peoples of the west and for the Hsiung-nu and other nomads in the same region and further to the north. The word cannot possibly be translated correctly as 'barbarian'.

In the T'ang period there is a true generic word for 'foreigner' and 'foreign country', 番 *fân*.[94] Unlike the modern dictionary definition 'foreign, barbarous', however, 番 *fân* itself has no negative connotations in T'ang texts, as is evident from the copious Chinese sources that exist on the T'ang period. In T'ang texts the term is often used like one would say today

---

[93] Cf. the careful discussion of these and other terms by Michael Drompp (2005: 172–175).
[94] Also written 蕃 *fân*.

'abroad', without naming any particular place. It is also used—instead of other sometimes pejorative words—in bilingual diplomatic documents such as the T'ang-Tibetan treaty of 821–822, where the language of the inscription erected in Lhasa in 823 is extremely polite and sensitive to that sort of thing. In other words, this particular generic term for foreigners, perhaps the only true generic at any time in Chinese literature, was practically the opposite of the word *barbarian*. It meant simply 'foreign, foreigner' without any pejorative meaning.

T'ang writers had reason to hate the Uighurs after their repeated sack of Loyang, despite the Uighurs' help in restoring T'ang Dynasty rule in China, and despite the little-noted fact[95] that the sacking had been authorized by the T'ang government as a means of repaying the Uighurs for their services. This hatred does indeed come through, in many explicit and implicit ways, from that time until the destruction of the Uighur Empire, but they still call them 番 *fân* much of the time. The usual angry word for Uighurs or other foreigners giving the Chinese trouble was 虜 *lŭ* 'prisoner, slave, captive',[96] which is used even when the foreigners in question clearly never were slaves or captives of anyone. The idea one gets from the texts is 'those miscreants who should be locked up' or something to that effect. In case anyone might think that this is the missing Chinese word for 'barbarian', it must be pointed out that the same texts more often than not use the word to refer to internal *Chinese* bandits, rebels, or simply, 'miscreants who should be locked up'.[97] The word does not even mean 'foreigner' at all, let alone 'barbarian'.

In sum, the word *barbarian* embodies a complex *European* cultural construct, a generic pejorative term for a 'powerful foreigner with uncouth, uncivilized, nonurban culture who was militarily skilled and somewhat heroic, but inclined to violence and cruelty'—yet not a 'savage' or a 'wild man'. The idea of the *barbarian* was simply nonexistent in China, and there was and is no Chinese equivalent of the word. Reading Chinese historical texts

---

[95] Recorded in the same Chinese historical works that express animosity toward the Uighurs.

[96] This is usually translated absurdly as 'caitiff', an archaic English word that etymologically means 'captive' but in current literary usage is defined as 'cowardly' or 'despicable', which is certainly not the meaning of the Chinese word.

[97] Many modern Sinologists are still strongly attached to the use of the word *barbarian* as a translation of the two-dozen or so commonly used Chinese words for foreigners, none of which can be shown to mean anything like 'barbarian'. This cannot be loyalty to the Chinese, who never had the word *barbarian*, or the idea of 'the barbarian', and still do not have it. Surely it is better to represent Chinese or Sinitic cultures, as well as the cultures of the peoples near them, as accurately as possible.

reveals that among the many Chinese words for foreigners, those which refer to Central Eurasians include civilized, urban people (whom the Chinese
sometimes admired), nomads, fishermen (in Manchuria, in the South China
Sea, etc.), agrarian people living in villages, and so on. None of the words for
them encode the ideas of military prowess, nonurban nonagrarian life-style,
and uncouth culture, three of the primary meanings of the European word
barbarian, which therefore cannot possibly be equated with a single one of
the many ancient and medieval Chinese terms for foreigners, including
Central Eurasians.

Many, perhaps all scholars who have written on Central Eurasians in
Chinese sources, have at one time used the English word *barbarian* in connection with them, so no one needs to be blamed for such sins of the past.[98]
Now the problems with it have been pointed out in print. The present explanation of why the term is not usable for histories based on Chinese sources
is specific to that part of Eurasia, but the principle is the same for the rest of
the world. James remarks, "Many historians in the last two centuries, oddly
enough, have rather admired the clothed and uniformed Romans, whose
idea of warfare emphasized discipline and ruthlessness, rather than the individual heroism of the Celtic warriors. It is more difficult in a post-colonial
world with a post-fascist consciousness."[99] Yet scholarly books continue to
appear on *barbarians*, East and West.

The meaning and implications of the word *barbarian* are clear. Using
it—even in scare quotes—to translate Chinese language words, more or less
all of which are ultimately phonetic transcriptions of foreign names and not
demonstrably pejorative in themselves, superimposes a powerful, uniquely
European concept on the Chinese sources, giving the false impression that the
Chinese had the same ideas about Central Eurasians as the Europeans did.

---

[98] I am guilty of having translated 虜 NMan *lǔ* as "barbarians" in some instances in my first
book (Beckwith 1987a/1993: 153) and perhaps elsewhere. My enlightenment on this issue
(Beckwith 1987c) seems to have come after that book was already in press (by 1986). I did not
notice the error when the paperback edition was being prepared. On the application of *lǔ* and
other pejorative terms equally as much to Chinese (especially rebels) as to foreigners, and the
semantic neutrality of most words for foreigners, see now Drompp (2005: 172–175).

[99] James (2001: 19). Note also that in the purely European context the word *barbarian* does not
usually have significant "racist" meaning (though it does in some older works focusing on
Central Eurasia). However, in the European-language literature on the premodern and early
modern East Asian context—that is, in the overwhelming majority of all literature about East
Asia—the European word *barbarian* is frequently used explicitly and more or less exclusively
as a pejorative term for Caucasian-race Europeans. That makes it literally a racist term.

Except for literal translations of Western texts that use the term or its etymological relatives, or direct quotations of European language sources or earlier scholars who use the word, it should no longer be used as a term by any writer.

The Fate of the Central Eurasians

What, then, happened to the peoples so many would call *barbarians*? They have in many cases not disappeared at all. A few of them have managed to preserve much of their traditional culture and life-style against the onslaught of the peripheral peoples and their cultures. Some have once again become independent and are energetically trying to rebuild their devastated countries. But many others are still ruled by oppressive foreign regimes and are slowly being driven to extinction. Their languages and cultures, and in some cases the people themselves, are seriously endangered.

The most prominent cases are the Tibetans of Tibet (and the many "autonomous" districts into which the Chinese have divided that country) and the Uighurs of East Turkistan. Both are labeled "minorities" by the Chinese, even though they are living in their own countries, where they suffer severe Chinese political, military, economic, demographic, linguistic, and cultural repression. Other peoples, smaller in population and less well known, are threatened even more immediately. The Turkic Tuvins of the Altai region and the Mongolic Kalmyks of the North Caucasus Steppe, among others such as the Evenkis of Siberia who remain under Russian rule, are so reduced in size and population, and so bereft of any real influence over their political destinies, that their cultures are seriously endangered as well.

The disastrous Manchu-Chinese and Russian conquest and partition of Central Eurasia has thus not been completely reversed, while Southern Central Asia (most of which is now in Afghanistan) has been ravaged for three decades by almost constant civil war connected to fundamentalism, the extreme form of Modernism that has taken hold in parts of the country.

It is quite possible that Central Eurasia will continue to be impoverished, and could become increasingly disenchanted and dangerous, unless the peripheral powers allow it to once again assume its rightful, historical place as the heartland of Eurasia.

APPENDIX A

—⁂—

The Proto-Indo-Europeans and Their Diaspora

There is a huge literature devoted to the Indo-European migrations and development of the Indo-European daughter languages, all of which is based ultimately on the reconstruction of the ancestral language, Proto-Indo-European.[1] Because the traditional reconstruction of the Proto-Indo-European phonological system embodies a fundamental mistake—first recognized implicitly in a brilliant article by Hermann Grassmann published in 1863—scholars attempting to draw conclusions about the nature of the protolanguage and the course of its development into the attested daughter languages (i.e., the daughter families, such as Germanic, Italic, Slavic, Indic, and so on), all of which work depends on historical phonology above all, have in many cases drawn wrong conclusions. Despite Grassmann's contribution,[2] he was not able to solve the fundamental problem with the reconstruction of Indo-European, mainly because he wrote before the discovery or invention of the phoneme.[3]

The problem, as now acknowledged by all Indo-Europeanists, is that the traditional reconstruction of the Proto-Indo-European stop consonants

---

[1] For an excellent, readable survey, see Mallory (1989). On the competing theories, see Mallory and Adams (1997, 2006).

[2] One of Grassmann's (1863) contributions was to show that the phenomena he discusses, those described by Grassmann's Law in the strict sense (one of the most important single discoveries in Indo-European linguistics), apply only to Greek and Sanskrit. They cannot be reconstructed back to Proto-Indo-European. He thus demonstrated formally that convergent phenomena affected nongenetic subgroups of Indo-European after the primary divergence had taken place. My formulation of three groups or "waves" of Indo-European divergence (Beckwith 2007c) depends ultimately on Grassmann's work.

[3] A *phoneme* is a meaningful unit of linguistic sound, defined by the opposition of contrasting phonemes. For example, the English words *pat*, *bat*, and *fat* are distinguished by their initial consonants; there is thus said to be a phonemic distinction in English between /p/ (an unvoiced labial stop), /b/ (a voiced labial stop), and /f/ (an unvoiced labiodental fricative), which are all phonemes in the language. *Allophones* represent recognized subphonemic distinctions, for example, the sounds written with the letter *p* in *pot* and *spot* are not the same phonetically. The *p* in *pot* is aspirated [pʰ], whereas the *p* in *spot* is unaspirated [p]; the difference between these two allophones, however, is not meaningful (or *phonemic*) in English, so only one letter is needed to write the phoneme /p/.

—⁂—

has an unvoiced unaspirated series (e.g., *p, *t, *k), a voiced unaspirated series ([*b,] *d, *g), and a voiced aspirated series (*bh, *dh, *gh). When it became generally recognized that this is a typologically unlikely, if not impossible, phonological system that has other significant problems—most importantly, initial *b cannot be reconstructed in this theory of Proto-Indo-European—it was agreed that correction of the reconstruction was necessary. Several attempts have been made to solve the problem, and in fact they are a major topic of Indo-European linguistics—for example, in addition to Szemerényi's attempt, Gamkrelidze and Ivanov published a monumental work on the glottalic theory.[4] None of the proposals have worked, however, and none have achieved general acceptance, because they do not actually solve the problem. Although some prominent linguists have accepted Gamkrelidze and Ivanov's proposal, it not only does not solve the problem at hand, it actually makes it worse.

The solution to the problem[5] is that the traditional three-way opposition of stops is an incorrect reconstruction from the point of view of the phonemic status of the phones involved. It has been known for most of a century, if not longer,[6] that the putative phonemes in question do not occur freely in all positions. Analysis of the accepted constraints shows that the two voiced series ([*b]: *bh, *d : *dh, *g : *gh) occur in complementary distribution and are thus allophones of a unitary voiced phoneme series (*b, *d, *g). They reflect the history of a temporary allophonic distinction that later became phonemic in some of the daughter languages, though in all attested languages that unnatural system has been changed to a natural two-way or four-way opposition of stops. The distinctions therefore can be reconstructed only for a temporary, convergent group consisting of languages that share the characteristic of having a reconstructible three-way opposition in the stops. A three-way system thus cannot be reconstructed to Proto-Indo-European, which had only a two-way phonemic opposition of stops—that is, *p : *b, *t : *d, *k : *g—and no missing *b. Because the other Indo-European daughter languages have either a two-way series in the stops, or a one-way series system (i.e., phonemic *p, *t, *k only) with residual evidence of an earlier

---

[4] Szemerényi (1996), Gamkrelidze and Ivanov (1995).

[5] This appendix is a brief, highly simplified summary of the argument and data presented in Beckwith (2007c), q.v. for details.

[6] Szemerényi (1996).

two-way system, Proto-Indo-European could only have had a two-way phonemic opposition in its stops.

It is a fairly simple matter to show that, as a result, all known Indo-European languages belong to one of three *Sprachbund*-like groups, membership in which is determined by the number of categories in the attested or internally reconstructed phonemic stop systems of each daughter language family. Group A, the first-wave languages (with only unvoiced stop phonemes, though there is evidence of the former existence of both unvoiced and voiced stops), consists of Anatolian and Tokharian. Group B, the second-wave languages (with unvoiced, voiced, and voiced aspirate phonemes), consists of Germanic, Italic, Greek, Indic, and Armenian. Group C, the third-wave languages (with unvoiced and voiced stop phonemes), consists of Celtic, Slavic, Baltic, Albanian, and Iranian.[7]

It is true that "Anatolian distinguishes inherited voiceless and voiced stops, though admittedly not word initially,"[8] and these distinctions in Anatolian may be reconstructible as such back to the proto language, but the remark "not word initially" is a key point. Tokharian, the other member of Group A along with Anatolian, also has some reflexes that suggest a two-way opposition of stops, but like Anatolian, no word-initial voiced stops. In other words, the two languages, *as attested* synchronically, do not have a phonemic distinction between voiced and unvoiced stops; the historical distinctions that are preserved word-internally are allophonic. The two daughter families thus belong in the same group from the point of view of both the fundamentally important linguistic phenomenon on which it is based, namely the distribution of the stops, as well as archaeology (on the basis of which both daughter languages appear to have migrated away from the Indo-European homeland around 2000 BC). The distinctions preserved in Anatolian and Tokharian do, however, support the two-way opposition of stops better known from Group C, and thus the reconstruction of the same bipolar system for Proto-Indo-European.

Avestan and Vedic: Aspects of a Problem

It is frequently noted that Avestan, which is believed to be the "earliest-attested" form of Iranian, is astonishingly close to Vedic Sanskrit, the

---

[7] With the exception of Avestan; but see below on the putative Avestan evidence for Iranian having belonged to Group B. Poorly attested languages are not included.

[8] This comment was made by an anonymous reviewer of the manuscript of this book.

"earliest-attested" form of Indic, in phonology, morphology, syntax, and lexicon. In addition to these linguistic features, the contents and religious purposes of the texts in these languages are so remarkably similar in several respects, though of course radically different in overt doctrinal religious content, that based on their evidence it has been possible to reconstruct not only a Proto-Indo-Iranian language but a culture as well. More specifically, it is believed that the Avestan and Vedic texts preserve languages very close to what is thought to be an earlier Proto-Indo-Iranian language representing a stage midway between Proto-Indo-European and the Proto-Indic and Proto-Iranian daughter languages. The Avestan and Vedic texts are thus thought to faithfully preserve the languages, and to a great extent the cultures, of the late Proto-Iranian and late Proto-Indic peoples respectively, if not the putative Proto-Indo-Iranians themselves. The texts themselves are now generally believed to have been transmitted orally, with extremely few later intrusions, from about three and a half millennia ago.[9]

However, there are several problems with these views. First, the Avestan texts and the Vedic texts are actually attested from less than one thousand years ago.[10] The idea of dating them—as texts—to three or four millennia ago is romantic but hardly supported by much evidence. The usual practice of referring to the Avestan and Vedic texts as the earliest-attested forms of their respective languages is thus a gross distortion. The earliest-attested Avestan manuscripts are actually dated to the thirteenth century AD and are based on an archetype dated to only about three centuries before that.[11] By contrast, the Old Persian language is recorded from the middle of the first millennium BC. Yet, because of the Indo-Iranian theory, above all, Avestan is thought to be a much older form of Iranian, chronologically, than the Old

---

[9] The opinions of individual scholars have varied greatly over the past century, some having argued for dates as much as a millennium younger than that, and others for dates several millennia earlier. For a discussion of such views, including those influenced by Indian nationalism, see Bryant (2001).

[10] *EIEC* 306–307. Both also have been shown to contain some "late" intrusive elements. Bryant cites T. Y. Elizarenkova's demonstration that some Middle Indo-Aryan features are "present in Vedic, but absent in Sanskrit" (Bryant 2001: 138), indicating contamination of the oral tradition by later dialect forms during its transmission. Unfortunately, the intrusive elements do not provide a sure means to date the composition of the texts or the earliest date at which they could have been memorized or otherwise recorded.

[11] *EIEC* 307. Even Middle Persian and other Middle Iranian languages are attested much earlier than Avestan, many of them in extensive literary texts. On the mythical lost libraries of Avestan and Middle Persian texts, see endnote 111.

Persian texts.[12] Because the Avesta are the holy texts of the Zoroastrian religion, they are also believed to preserve references to the putative common Indo-Iranian pantheon and other common Proto-Indo-Iranian beliefs and cultural practices. However, the earliest-attested data on Iranian religious beliefs—including the early Old Persian inscriptions—contain no reflections of Zoroastrianism per se. The belief system found in the early Avestan texts is not attested until Late Antiquity.

Second, the earliest truly attested forms of Iranian are the North (or "East") Iranian and South (or "West") Iranian words and phrases in Assyrian and Greek texts; the first actual texts written in an Iranian language are the Old Persian texts (inscriptions, clay tablets, and seals) of the sixth and fifth centuries BC. These Iranian languages are very different from Avestan.

Third, Avestan is said to be an East Iranian language, but it has been shown that the now-usual arguments for placing it—and the home of Zoroaster—in Central Asia are chimerical. The apparent "East Iranian" features of Avestan are due to the influence of an East Iranian language during the transmission of the text.[13] The language cannot be placed firmly anywhere in the known Iranian-speaking world, or for that matter any*when*, until the Avestan texts were transcribed into Middle Persian script.

Fourth, it is extremely curious that except for Avestan, phonologically Iranian as a whole—in Old Persian and other early forms, in the Middle Iranian languages, and in the modern Iranian languages—is solidly, unquestionably, a Group C third-wave language, with a clear two-way phonemic opposition in the stops. Only Avestan contains occasional reflexes of a three-way stop system parallel to the system reconstructed on the basis of Vedic Sanskrit, which belongs to the Group B *Sprachbund*.

Finally, a major problem with Avestan that has so far apparently been overlooked would seem to vitiate, or at least call into serious question, both the traditional view of its linguistic relationship and the theories derived from it. As noted above, it has been remarked, "The Avestan speech is very closely related to Sanskrit," so astonishingly close, in fact, that "we are able

---

[12] If the Indo-Iranian theory is accepted, Avestan is certainly a more "archaic" form of Iranian than Old Persian, but Avestan could have been spoken in an isolated area for a very long time—and thus preserved much of the ancient "Proto-Indo-Iranian" structure—before Zoroastrianism was adopted by the Persians and the Avestan texts became known in the general Iranian-speaking world. However, it is uncertain if Avestan really is an Iranian language to begin with.

[13] Schmitt (1989: 28); cf. the perceptive remarks of Kellens (1989) in the same volume.

to transpose any word from one language into the other by the application of special phonetic laws."[14] Avestan's extensive case system and verbal conjugation system is not just similar to that of Vedic Sanskrit; it is almost *identical* to it. That is extremely odd. To demonstrate the similarity of the two languages, Indo-Iranian specialists have translated Avestan passages into Vedic Sanskrit, or "Old Indic"—for example, the following Avestan sentence (from Yašt 10.6):[15]

Avestan	*təm amanvantəm yazatəm*
Old Indic	*tám ámanvantam yajatám*
Proto-Indo-Iranian	**tám ámanvantam yaǰatám*
English gloss	This powerful deity,

Avestan	*sūrəm dāmōhu səvištəm*
Old Indic	*śúram dhā́masu śáviṣṭham*
Proto-Indo-Iranian	**ćúram dhā́masu ćávištham*
English gloss	strong, among the living the strongest,

Avestan	*miθrəm yazāi zaoθrābyō*
Old Indic	*mitrám yajāi hótrābhyaḥ*
Proto-Indo-Iranian	**mitrám yǎǰāi jhǎutrābhyas*
English gloss	Mithra, I honor with libations.

Due to this incredible, unprecedented closeness, Indo-Europeanists believe, "The Indo-Iranian languages clearly derive from an ancestor intermediate between Proto-Indo-European and the earliest individual Iranian and Indo-Aryan languages, i.e., one can reconstruct a Proto-Indo-Iranian language."[16]

However, the astounding closeness of Avestan and Vedic Sanskrit, together with the other points noted above, allows—or perhaps, demands—a very different conclusion. Avestan looks less like an Iranian language than like a phonologically Iranized Indic language.[17] The many inexplicable problems of Avestan and the culture thought to be represented in the text of

---

[14] Noted as early as Remy (1907) and repeated very widely; cf. Bryant (2001: 131).

[15] *EIEC* 304; cf. Mallory (1989: 35); cf. the comments of Schmitt (1989: 26–27).

[16] *EIEC* 303–304.

[17] The early Indo-Europeanists considered Avestan to be an Old Indic dialect; see the discussion in chapter 1 and notes thereto. Avestan could perhaps be an Iranized creole of the Old Indic dialect, that is, an actual language that was once spoken, but this seems much less likely. Still another possibility, that it is an Indicized Iranian language, is ruled out by the dif-

the *Avesta* can be accounted for as an artifact of Iranians having adopted an oral religious text—clearly a heterodox one by comparison with the Vedas—from an Old Indic dialect. As required of Indic religious practitioners, they memorized it exactly, but in the process, or afterward, it underwent specifically Iranian sound shifts in the mouths of the Iranian-speaking oral reciters. As noted above, Avestan is known exclusively as a literary language of the Zoroastrian religion—it is not known where it was spoken or even if it was ever spoken at all (which seems unlikely)—and it is only attested quite recently.[18] Simple phonological change due to Iranian speakers attempting to preserve an Old Indic dialect text orally over a long period of time would thus explain virtually everything about Avestan. If nevertheless Avestan can still be shown without question to be a genuine Iranian language (which seems unlikely), it would have to constitute an independent sub-branch of its own. If not, and the language is removed entirely from the Iranian family tree, Iranian would then make internal linguistic sense as an Indo-European daughter family. The theory of a Proto-Indo-Iranian language—a striking exception to the otherwise exclusively radial, non-nodal *Stammbaum* of the Indo-European daughter families (despite the many attempts to construct other models)—would then have to be abandoned, along with much else based on the Indo-Iranian theory. In particular, theories about the culture of the putative Proto-Indo-Iranians and chronological theories concerning the movements of the Proto-Indic and Proto-Iranian peoples would need to be thoroughly revised, but so too would almost everything else in early Indic and Iranian studies.

The Indo-European Creoles

Each of the Indo-European daughter languages—the ancestors of the modern Indo-European languages—retains the bulk of the Indo-European basic lexicon and a significant amount of Indo-European morphology, but it has some local loanwords and, in particular, distinctive phonology. This distribution of features is characteristic of creoles. It must be understood that the

---

ficulty of explaining the many elements not found in any other Iranian language but typical of Old Indic.

[18] In the text I have followed the view that the hostility thought to be shown in the *Avesta* toward Vedic religious elements suggests ethnolinguistic animosity between the early Indians and Iranians, but it has been argued that the apparent demonization of the Vedic elements is not consistent. Resolution of this point also depends on the results of the reconsideration of the *Avesta* and Avestan.

term "creole" is not precisely delimited by specific features. It is used for everything from languages containing loanwords—and all known languages contain loanwords—to languages that have undergone major structural changes due to convergence with other languages.

In this book, "creole" is used to refer to languages that have undergone significant changes due to convergence with other languages, but not the kind of radical simplification of structure that is stereotypically said to characterize creoles, the usual (if not the only) example being Haitian Creole, a form of French. As many have noted, modern Indian English—the native speakers[19] of which have full English grammar and lexicon, with a very small number of Indian loanwords—has a phonological structure more akin to Indian languages than to English or other Germanic languages. Although some have claimed that this is a unique artifact of British colonial policies,[20] one must wonder why the same (actually, worse) policies in North America did not produce another creole there. Leaving aside the political aspects involved in such judgments, it is clear that in the former case the English speakers succeeded in imposing their language to some extent but not in eliminating the ruled people, unlike in the latter case. The result of the former was and is a creole. Much the same can be said of other modern Englishes spoken around the world in areas where English is an intrusive language, some with more "creolization" than others.

It is known from observed and recorded modern contact situations that creoles are produced in a very short period of time, not centuries or millennia. Languages are not spoken unchanged over millennia, nor do they take millennia to undergo major changes. That is, the daughter families of Indo-European could not have developed by glacially slow changes over millennia, as the old idea of Indo-European has it, and as most Indo-Europeanists still believe. Modern evidence, as well as modern research on languages undergoing change, shows that the traditional theory is typologically unpre-

---

[19] Many Indian speakers of Indian English have acquired it as a second language and thus speak it much less well.

[20] Cf. the comments and references in Hock (1999b: 149). It should also be noted that comparisons of the Indo-Aryanization of northern India and the Anglicization of India under the British generally include ahistorical preconceptions. The British may have come from far away to India, but they did not "conquer" India, at least not in the usual sense, and certainly not suddenly. It took them centuries to gradually end up in a position of dominance there before they finally took over.

cedented and therefore, essentially, impossible. Languages do undergo some internal changes, very slowly, over time, but because these changes can never be isolated from external influences, it cannot even be shown that slow chronological change actually takes place purely on its own without external stimuli.[21] Nevertheless, leaving aside the probable fact of the latter type of change, it is unquestionably the case that major language shifts take place as a result of contact. The Indo-European daughter languages, or branches, are thus to a greater or lesser extent creoles, including even the very earliest recorded Indo-European languages: Hittite, Old Indic, and Mycenaean Greek. This is certainly not unusual. It has been said that "all mature languages are creoles."[22]

What is unusual is the idea that Indo-European, uniquely among the languages of the world, should have preserved its ancestral form (Proto-Indo-European) for thousands of years, then broke up purely via internal chronological change over more thousands of years, and finally developed into the attested daughter languages, all without any creolization. Creolization is explicitly rejected as a factor in the development of the Indo-European daughter languages[23] despite the fact that the daughter languages are mostly attested first in areas quite distant from the areas where the other daughter languages are first attested, and none of them are attested in the Proto-Indo-European homeland region until after they are attested elsewhere. That means the Indo-European speakers must first have settled in areas where other peoples already lived and mixed with them, producing different creoles of the inherited language, before their languages are first attested.

In addition, the astonishing fact (for the traditional theory) that none of the Indo-European daughter languages were spoken outside the world area where they are first attested cannot be overlooked, as it has been. Early Italic is unknown outside the region of Italy, Greek outside the region of Greece, Tokharian outside the Tokharian region of East Turkistan, and so

---

[21] For further discussion and references, see Beckwith (2006a).

[22] Haiman (1994: 1636).

[23] Arguments about the chronology of Indo-European are more or less all still based on the slow chronological change theory, as are the highly charged disputes over the dating of the daughter languages and their speakers. Leaving aside nonscholarly motivations, much of the Indo-Aryan migration debate is founded upon linguistic naiveté (e.g., Bryant 1999, 2001).

forth.[24] Moreover, the spatial arrangement of the daughter languages according to isogloss information corresponds to their spatial arrangement geographically—that is, their attested earliest locations.[25] The traditional theory is typologically unprecedented anywhere in the world and does not accord with the evidence.

Each Indo-European daughter language—the protolanguage in turn of an Indo-European daughter family—is thus a creole, the result of immigrant speakers mixing with local people who spoke different languages. The immigrants' Indo-European language was spoken by their local wives and children with a local accent and some grammatical changes, producing a dialect or creole which was simply an altered local version of the dominant Indo-European language.

The reconstructibility of Proto-Indo-European morphology has been seen as evidence of the incredible conservatism of Indo-European languages by comparison with other languages. But there is considerable evidence against this idea of Indo-European's incredible—or more accurately, unbelievable—conservatism and slow phonological change over thousands of years: Hittite and the other Anatolian languages. The oft-repeated theory that the Anatolian languages were spoken in Anatolia for thousands of years before they were first recorded is based on the old idea of slow chronological change. Yet Anatolian languages and cultures are so full of local, non-Indo-European elements that it has been difficult to find any vestiges of Indo-European religious beliefs and sociopolitical practices among them. How could they have adopted so much from non-Indo-Europeans, but somehow magically preserved a highly archaic "pure" Indo-European language, or an "Indo-Hittite" or "Pre-Proto-Indo-European" language, as some would have it? Because some of the complex morphophonological features reconstructed to Proto-Indo-European have been shown to be restricted to the Group B languages,[26] or should be so restricted—Proto-Indo-European is based largely on the early forms of those very languages (Greek, Latin, Germanic languages, and Sanskrit)—the absence of those features in Anatolian is not surprising. The putative conservativeness of Proto-Indo-European

---

[24] As noted above, Old Indic is first attested in the area of upper Mesopotamia and the Levant, and only later in India, but this is clearly due to the migrating Indic speakers being separated by the migrating Iranian speakers.

[25] Hock (1999a: 13–16).

[26] Grassmann (1863), Beckwith (2007c).

morphophonology is actually evidence for the recentness of the daughter languages' separation. They may have diverged after the departure of the Proto-Anatolian speakers, but the appearance of the latter in Anatolia still cannot be dated much earlier than the nineteenth century BC. Significant phonological and lexical changes happened at the point in time (within one generation, or at most two generations) of the intrusion of an Indo-European group into areas where the local language was different, or when an Indo-European group was linguistically heavily influenced by a non–Indo-European group, as happened with the formation of Group B. The major structural changes distinguishing each daughter language from each other and from Proto-Indo-European thus did not take centuries to develop. Certainly some changes, once initiated, did take centuries to work themselves out, but that is a different matter. Observation of the way the phonology of daughter languages develop in modern times—Indian English being one of many well-known examples—indicates that creolization, as in the scenario presented here, is the main driving force.[27] The complexity of the changes in Indo-European would seem to be explained by the stages of the migrations, of which there were at least two for most, perhaps all, of what became the Indo-European daughter languages: first from the common homeland to some intermediate place or places (this is clearest in the case of Group B), and then again to the final destinations where the languages are first attested.

The Indo-Europeans, particularly the warrior segment of the population, had an extremely patriarchal, male-dominated society. In many cases, they and their mixed descendants were heavily outnumbered by the original inhabitants and eventually disappeared, leaving only some linguistic residue such as the names of their kings and gods and some other cultural words (as happened in the Mitanni kingdom and elsewhere in the ancient Near East), or even a few short inscriptions (as happened with many languages once spoken in Southern Europe). In other cases the Indo-Europeans imposed their language and maintained it long enough that it could be relatively well recorded. Both scenarios were played out time and again. The most important of these two processes for linguistic history is the second, because it provides sufficient material for careful reconstruction.[28]

[27] Cf. Lefebvre et al. (2006).
[28] It is also possible to observe the same process in action today, because Indo-European languages, especially English, Spanish, and Russian, continue to spread at the expense of native

The relevance for Central Eurasian history is clear. The Indo-Europeans spread from their homeland in Central Eurasia to other parts of Central Eurasia as well as to parts of the Eurasian periphery. They accepted elements of the local cultures with which they mixed and also spread crucial aspects of their own culture. In so doing, they spread the earliest form of the Central Eurasian Culture Complex extensively enough that it survived and became the dominant culture of Central Eurasian peoples in protohistorical and early historic times, as described in the prologue and elsewhere in this book.

---

languages in large parts of the world. Indo-European languages are dominant territorially today in every continent except Africa; demographically, the main exceptions are East and Southeast Asia.

APPENDIX B

---·······---

Ancient Central Eurasian Ethnonyms

The reading or interpretation of the names of many ancient Central Eurasian peoples is controversial, and as a result the identification of the peoples themselves is often disputed. The problem affects both little-known nations and some of the most famous empires. This appendix is devoted to the discussion of some of these problematic names.

Ch'iang ~ *Klānk- 'The Charioteers'

The name of the Ch'iang 羌 NMan *qiâng*, the main foreign enemies of the Shang Chinese, has been said to be either a transcription of a foreign name or a native Chinese word meaning 'shepherd'. The latter explanation[1] does not accord with Chinese usage because the word *ch'iang* is never used as a common noun meaning 'shepherd'; it always refers to a more or less specific foreign people. It seems likely, therefore, based on the very early date of their intrusion—as well as their skill with war chariots, and the fact that Tibeto-Burman words for 'horse' are mostly late borrowings from Chinese[2]—that the early Ch'iang were Indo-European speakers, not Tibeto-Burmans as generally believed.[3] Their name, Ch'iang 羌 NMan *qiâng* from MChi *kʰɨaŋ (Pul. 251) from OChi *klaŋ,[4] may also have an Indo-European etymology: the word *klānk-* in Tokharian means 'to ride, go by wagon',[5] as in 'to ride off to hunt from a chariot', so Ch'iang could actually mean 'charioteer'.

---

[1] For example, Beckwith (1993: 5).

[2] See Beckwith (2002a: 129–133; 2007a: 145–146).

[3] The belief is based on Han Dynasty and later Chinese usage in which the word does refer to early Tibeto-Burman peoples in the area of what is now Kansu and Amdo (northeastern Tibet). However, this does not tell us anything certain about Early Old Chinese usage because the Chinese, like many other ancient peoples, often applied earlier names for people living in one location to later peoples living in approximately the same location, regardless of any actual relationship or lack thereof.

[4] The source of the aspirated-unaspirated distinction in the stop and affricate phonemes in Middle Chinese, not only in this but in many other words, remains unexplained. In at least some cases it is due to a prefixed *s(V)- (q.v. Sagart 1999) added to some roots in the post-Shang period (Beckwith 2006c).

[5] Adams (1999: 220).

The Chiang 姜 NMan *jiāng* (from OChi *klaŋ) are generally believed to be related to or the same as the Ch'iang 羌 originally. The latter name may have been tabooed in the Chou period, or else written 姜 Chiang (with the 'woman' radical), because the people so named were the original maternal clan of the Chou Dynasty.[6]

Wu-Sun ~ *Aśvin 'The Cavaliers'

Wu-sun is the modern Mandarin Chinese pronunciation of 烏孫, which according to the usual current Old Chinese reconstruction is from Middle Chinese *ɔswən (Pul. 325, 297) from Old Chinese *âswin. However, Old Chinese syllable-initial *s- seems to have become Middle Chinese *χ- (Beckwith 2006c). If the reconstruction is correct, the *s* here should have become Middle Chinese *χ- too. What then could be the source of the *s* in the modern reading Wu-sun? In cases where a good number of Chinese words are derived from the same root—such as 三 NMan *sân* 'three', from Middle Chinese *sam (Pul. 271) and the many words for things that come in threes (or that are written with characters intended to suggest that the underlying word rhymes with a 'three' word)—as Sagart (1999: 150) remarks, "It seems impossible to suppose a root initial s- here." In the case of 三 NMan *sân*, the Early Old Chinese ancestor began with something other than *s, most likely the cluster *tr- or an affricate (Sagart 1999: 148–152). The *s* in Wu-sun should have come from something like *s but somehow different. Because it is necessary to take into consideration many other factors, the possibilities in the present instance may be narrowed down to a few, of which *ś [ç] is the most likely. This would make the underlying name *Aświn, a perfect transcription of Old Indic *aśvin* 'the horsemen', the name of twin equestrian gods. The Wu-sun people were markedly Europoid in appearance[7] and could well have been Old Indic speakers.

The name K'un-mu ~ K'un-mo 昆莫 NMan *kûnmù* ~ *kûnmò* from MChi *kwənmɔ or *kwənmak (Pul. 179, 220, 218) is certainly the word or title for the *Aśvin king, not a personal name, as is clear from the *Han shu* account of the Wu-sun kingdom,[8] where it is also written K'un-mi 昆彌 NMan *kûnmí*,

---

[6] For a well-attested precedent, see the discussion of Fu Hao ~ Fu Tzu in endnote 44.

[7] *HS* (96b: 3901).

[8] *HS* (96b: 3901–3910).

from Middle Chinese *kwənmji (Pul. 179, 212). Despite the traditional reading 'K'un-mo', with the second syllable taken as NMan *mò* from MChi *mak, the second reading obviously accords better with the alternative form 昆彌 NMan *kûnmí* and is therefore to be preferred. The first syllable should have been *kʷin (or perhaps *kʷil ~ *kʷir or *kʷēr etc.) in Han period Old Chinese, possibly transcribing a foreign *kin/*kēn (perhaps *kil/*kēl ~ *kir/*kēr) or *kon (perhaps *kol ~ *kor). As for the second syllable, 莫 NMan *mù* ~ *mò* from MChi *mɔ or *mak (Pul. 220), the phonetic is 日 *rì* 'sun', which may be reconstructed as dialectal Late Old Chinese *ñ(r)ēk ~ *mīk (Central dialect *ñīč, becoming *ñīt) from Early Old Chinese *mē(r)(e)k. According to the current reconstruction the Middle Chinese reading *mɔ must be from a Late Old Chinese *mâh or *meh, from *meks. The alternate form, 彌 NMan *mí*, from Middle Chinese *mjiǎ/mji (Pul. 212), reflects Late Old Chinese *mē. In Han times, however, theoretical Early Middle Chinese *m- often had the value *ᵐb- and is used to transcribe foreign *b-, as is the case in attested ("Late") Middle Chinese as well. The Chinese transcriptions thus represent a foreign syllable *mē ~ *bē or possibly *meh ~ *beh. In view of the Old Indic etymology of the ethnonym *Aśvin, an Old Indic etymology for the title of the king would seem to be indicated too.

Sai ~ *Sak* ~ Saka ~ Śaka ~ Sogdians ~ Scythians 'The Archers'

The name Σκύθας (later Σκύθης) 'Scyth(ian)' must be reconstructed as North Iranian *Skuδa, from Proto-Indo-Iranian *Skuda, from Proto-Indo-European *skud-o from *skeud-o- 'shooter, archer', as shown by Szemerényi.[9] In Herodotus's account of the Scythians' legendary origins (for which see the prologue) the text has two variants for the name of the third son, the ancestor of the later Scythians. One is Κολάξαϊς *Coláxaïs*, a textual error for *Σκολάξαϊς *Skoláxaïs, as noted by Abicht (who, however, corrects the text differently).[10] Legrand,[11] who does not cite Abicht, is puzzled by the text in this version of the myth, because the Scythians are said to call themselves Σκολόται 'Scoloti' after their king's name—the previously mentioned

[9] Szemerényi (1980: 16–21). The name is glossed in Greek via the name of the Scythian police force of Athens, oἱ Τοξόται 'the Archers', which is interchangeable with 'the Scythians' (Szemerényi (1980: 19).

[10] Abicht (1886: 8); cf. Macan (1895: 4–5 n. 6).

[11] Legrand (1949: 50–51 n. 5).

Κολάξαϊς *Coláxaïs* (i.e., *Σκολάξαϊς *Skoláxaïs*). Scoloti is simply a later form of the name Σκύθης Scythês, earlier transcribed by Hesiod (ca. 700 BC) as Σκύθας Scythas.[12] This is, as demonstrated by Szemerényi, the same name as *swyδa* ~ *sywδa* 'Sugda ~ Sguda' (with epenthesis in Old Persian as *Suguda), the name of Sogdiana and the Sogdians. In addition, Herodotus says that the Persians call the Scythians *Saka,* a fact confirmed by the Old Persian inscriptions. The name of the best-known Northern Iranian people in Chinese sources, the Sai 塞 NMan *sâi* from MChi *sək from *sak 'Saka', shows the usual dropping of the final short -a vowel in Indo-Iranian names. It typically lacks the -*l*- from -δ- found in the other names. But the same name also appears in other forms in early transcriptions, including the name of the Saka city So-chü 莎車 NMan *suôjû* *Saylâ 'Yarkand'[13] and So-li 索離 *Saklai, the name of the ancestral northern nation from which the Puyo-Koguryoic people stemmed, according to their origin myth,[14] both evidently from *Sakla. This name is clearly related to *Skula, the form of the name 'Scythian' attested in Herodotus and shown by Szemerényi to be one of the regular later phonetic developments of the name within Northern Iranian.[15] Like *Skula, the velar in Sakla is unvoiced and the *d has become *l*,[16] but in this case, like *Sugda 'Sogd', an epenthetic vowel has been inserted between the consonants of the original initial cluster *sk. Unlike *Sugda 'Sogd', another regular development of the same name (but one in which the velar has been voiced and the dental has not yet shifted to *l*), the epenthetic vowel in this case was obviously *a*, not *u*. The consonantism of *Sakla is thus the same as that of the name of the Scythian ruler Σκύλης *Skulēs*, the root of which, *Skula, is in turn identical to the root *Skula of the name Σκολόται *Scolótai*, given by Herodotus as the Scythians' own name for themselves.[17] The Persian form *Skudra* discussed by Szemerényi[18] is yet another form of

---

[12] Szemerényi (1980: 16 et seq.).

[13] See Hill (forthcoming).

[14] See endnote 13 on the textual problem involving So 索 NMan *suǒ* < MChi *sak. The Turks are also said to be descended from the So 索 'Sakas'; see endnote 53.

[15] Szemerényi (1980).

[16] The *d* shifted later in Sogdian as well. Cf. the name Su-i 粟弋 NMan *sùyì* from MChi *suawk-jik (Pul. 295, 369) from OChi *soklik ~ *soglik 'Sogdiana'.

[17] Szemerényi (1980: 22 n. 47), who notes "it is unimportant whether -*ta* in Skolotai is a plural morpheme or not."

[18] Szemerényi (1980: 23 et seq.).

the same name *Skuδa. Unfortunately, he follows the old idea (probably a folk etymology) that Saka is a Persian name for the Scythians derived from the Persian verb sak- 'to go, flow, run', and therefore supposedly could mean 'roamer, wanderer, vagrant nomad'.[19] However, his conclusion regarding the name Skudra states that it is "a derivative of Skuδa, name of the Scythians."[20] This means that because Old Persian actually preserves the earlier form *Skuδa in this local name, the usual Persian name of the Scythians changed at some point from *Skuδa- to Saka. Rather than being a completely new word, as Szemerényi argues, in view of the form *Sayla ~ *Saklai it seems clear that the name Saka, which as the sources say is the "Persian" name for all Scythians,[21] is a form of the very same ethnonym, *Skuδa, via the known intermediate form *Skula. The change evidently took place via insertion of the epenthetic vowel a to break up the initial cluster sk, as in other cases. The foreign (non-Persian) name *Sakula thus became Saka in Persian, probably via an intermediary *Sakla, or perhaps *Sak(u)δa ~ *Sak(u)ra.[22] It is significant that the Saka people are equated explicitly with the Scythians (who are equated explicitly with the *Skula) by all sources. While the existence of the verb sak- 'to go, roam' might well have aided or even motivated the development of the name Saka within Persian, it clearly cannot be in origin a Persian descriptive word referring to the habits of the people in question. The name is a specific ethnonym, not a generic term, in both Greek and Persian sources, and is of course the name of a foreign people, not a Persian people. The preservation of the earlier form *Sakla in the extreme eastern dialects supports the historicity of the conquest of the entire steppe zone by the Northern Iranians—literally, by the 'Scythians'—in the Late Bronze Age or Early Iron Age, as shown by archaeology and discussed in chapter 2, where various peoples, several of them historical, named Saka (usually transcribed *Sak) are attested in Chinese sources from Antiquity through the Early Middle Ages in the northern part of the entire Eastern Steppe zone as well as more to the south in Jungharia and the Tarim Basin. As Szemerényi remarks, "at first all North Iranian tribes of the steppe region had one common

---

[19] Szemerényi (1980: 45).

[20] Szemerényi (1980: 46).

[21] Szemerényi (1980: 23).

[22] The evident deletion of the *-l-, or *-ul-, needs to be addressed by Iranian specialists.

indigenous name, i.e. *Skuδa* 'archer'."[23] The Chinese transcriptions appear to reflect the period after the shift of OChi *s to MChi *χ and the restoration of *s by the shift of OChi *ś [ɕ] to MChi *s.[24]

Yüeh-chih ~ *Tok^war / *Tog^war 'The Tokharians'

The name Tokharian (or Tocharian) current in English and other European languages has been much discussed. Among philologists specializing in early Central Eurasia and China a consensus on the main issues was reached long ago, despite some unresolved problems. However, due to the nature of the sources—mainly Chinese historical and geographical texts, in which the names must be interpreted via Chinese historical phonology, an extremely arcane field—research on the topic remains a highly contentious subject that is largely opaque to scholars unfamiliar with Chinese philology and phonology. As a result, there is more confusion about the name or names of the Tokharians than about any other name in premodern Central Eurasian history.

The identity of the Tokharoi and Yüeh-chih *people* is quite certain, and has been clear for at least half a century, though this has not become widely known outside the tiny number of philologists who work on early Central Eurasian and early Chinese history and linguistics.[25] It is known that the Tokharoi and the Tokharians were the same people because the Tokharoi-Tokhwar-Yüeh-chih-Tukhâr- of Bactria and the Tukhâr-Toχar-/Toγar-Yüeh-chih of the Tarim Basin are identified as one and the same people in every source that mentions them. The principle facts may be summarized as follows:[26]

• In several languages of East Turkistan and neighboring regions the expression 'The Land of the Four Toghar ~ Tokhar (*Toγar ~ Toχar*, written

---

[23] Szemerényi (1980: 46).

[24] While these sound changes are fairly clear, they still need much work in order to be established more firmly.

[25] For example, an important Indo-Europeanist work claims that the "evidence for the identification of the Tokharoi with the 'Tocharians' is meager though not wanting altogether but the identification is more usually than not rejected. However, in the absence of any better name, the designation has stuck" (*EIEC* 590).

[26] This appendix is a brief summary of some of the main aspects of the problem; it is treated in greater detail in a study that I hope to finish in the near future. For extensive discussion and quotation of the earlier literature, see Hill (forthcoming).

twyr)'[27] occurs in Manichaean texts as the name of the region "from Ku-cha and Karashahr to Kocho and Beshbalik."[28] This is the exact region where the language now called Tokharian was still spoken in early medieval times. The Uighurs, who translated many Buddhist texts from the language, call it *twyry tyly* 'the language of the Toχari ~ Toγari'. This was read as *'Toχrï tili'* by F.W.K. Müller, who translated it as "Tocharisch," that is, 'Tokharian'.[29] Although it should be read in Old Turkic as *Toχarï tili* or *Toγarï tili*,[30] Müller's identification is impeccable philologically. Yet it has been questioned by some because of the existence of the name Tokhâristân 'the land of the Tokhâr' (Bactria), its connection with the Tόχαροι, and the fact that the people attested somewhat later as living in Tokhâristân wrote in an Iranian language now called Bactrian. However, this objection is vitiated by the well-known fact that all other linguistically identified early conquerors of Bactria, including the Greeks, the Turks, and the Arabs, shifted to the local Iranian language of the region, Bactrian, shortly after their invasion. In view of this fact, and of the small number of Tokharians (only one of three nations) in the confederation that conquered Bactria, it is extremely unlikely that they maintained their language; they may already have shifted to an Iranian language even before they entered the region.

- The apparent unrelatableness of the name *Toχ^war ~ Toχâr* 'Tokhar(ian)' and its variants with *yüeh* 月 NMan *yuè* 'moon' from Middle Chinese

---

[27] The usual reading of this name, from Müller on, has been 'Toχrï' or occasionally 'Toγrï'. However, very many words in the Sogdian or Sogdian-derived scripts in the region (such as Uighur) omit one or more vowels, as is well known. The letter used for the dorsal phone in the Sogdian-derived scripts of East Turkistan is ambiguous (it can be read as either γ or χ). Although in Early Old Chinese or Proto-Chinese the pronunciation of 月 (at least in the meaning 'night') had *-k- (Beckwith 2006b), it later became *-g- ~ *-ŋ- in some etyma; the Old Chinese transcription of the name thus may reflect an underlying *g ~ *γ, not *k ~ *χ, suggesting that the early medieval East Turkistan form of the name might have had -γ-.

[28] Clark (2000). The same cities are referred to as the *Tört Küsän* 'Four Kuchas' or 'Four Kushans'; the local form of the name *Kucha* was *Küsän*, a form of the name *Kushan*, on the variants of which there is a huge literature in scholarly journals from the early twentieth century.

[29] Müller (1907). In English-language scholarly works there are two spellings of this name, Tokharian and Tocharian. The general preference for the German-style spelling Tocharian in English works is mystifying. The 'kh' or 'ch' of the underlying name is the sound χ[x], normally represented in German by 'ch' but in English by 'kh'.

[30] Modern scholars, following Müller, usually read it *Toχrï tili*.

ñgwar [ᵑgʷar] (Tak. 372–373; Pul. 388 *ŋuat), the first part of the Chinese name Yüeh-chih 月氏 (or 月支) NMan *yuèzhî*, has been one of the main obstacles to acceptance of the specialists' solution.[31] The phonetic value of the unique Oracle Bone Inscription character for two homonyms that came to be distinguished in the Middle Old Chinese period as 月 NMan *yuè* 'moon' and 夕 NMan *xî ~ xì* 'night', has been independently reconstructed as Early Old Chinese *nokwet.[32] However, Early Old Chinese initial *n subsequently underwent an exceptionless sound-change, becoming *d, *t, or *l by the end of the middle period of Old Chinese; by Early Middle Chinese times at the latest in the Central dialects, reconstructed Old Chinese final *t had become *r, but in the Northwestern dialects (which were spoken near the ancient Yüeh-chih homeland), final *t had apparently merged with (or had become a sub-phonemic variant of) final *r and *n[33] by that time in Old Chinese dialects; and intervocalically *k eventually became *g (and then *ŋ) in the word 月 'moon'. Accordingly, in one of the highly archaic border dialects of Old Chinese[34] in Antiquity the word 月 'moon' would have been pronounced *tokwar or *togwar. The identity of this ancient form (i.e., the first part of the name 月氏, which is now read Yüeh-chih) with the Bactrian name Τοχοαρ (Toχwar ~ Tuχwar) and the medieval name *Toχar ~ Toχâr* (see below) cannot be a coincidence. As for the second character of the transcription, 氏 or 支, it is regularly reconstructed as Old Chinese *ke (Sta. 567). The same suffix or final compounding element in the name Yüeh-chih, with the same aberrant reading *chih* 氏 NMan *zhî* < OChi *ke,[35] occurs in the

---

[31] For the second syllable many seemingly plausible solutions have been suggested, so it has not been seen as problematic.

[32] Beckwith (2006b). I say "independently" because when I wrote the article it never occurred to me to consider the word's use in the transcription of the name of the Tokharians.

[33] The contemporaneous early transcriptions of the name Arsak 'Arsacid' and the name Alexandria, both using the same final in Chinese (Middle Chinese and Mandarin -*n*) to transcribe a foreign -*r* and a foreign -*n*, show clearly that these final coronals (at least) had merged (cf. Beckwith 2005b). There are many other instances—for example, the names *Tumen and Mo-tun (*Baytur)—where the "same" Old Chinese final (i.e., the same in Middle Chinese and Mandarin pronunciation) was used to transcribe different foreign coronals.

[34] There is a good example of the archaic nature of the northern dialect in the Chinese name of a Hsiung-nu defector, which includes the character 日 'sun', normally read NMan *rì* from MChi *ñit (Pul. 266), but in this case read NMan *mì* from MChi *mεjk (Pul. 213), corresponding to a traditionally reconstructable Old Chinese form 日 *mīk 'sun' (Beckwith 2002a: 142–143), evidently from early OChi *mērk ~ *wērk ~ *bērk.

[35] This corresponds exactly to the attested medieval West Tokharian 'ethnic' ('-ian, -ish, etc.) suffix -*ke*, as in *Kaṣake* "Kashgarian' (Adams 1999: 148), but this occurs mainly, if not exclu-

names of Hsiung-nu royalty. The Hsiung-nu overthrew the Yüeh-chih, their former overlords,[36] so it makes sense that the Hsiung-nu used the "royal" suffix or compounding element *ke for their overlords the Yüeh-chih or *Tokʷar-ke, and after overthrowing the Yüeh-chih used it for their own royalty. In any case, it is clearly not part of the ethnonym, which is *Tokʷar alone, as is very well known from the non-Chinese transcriptions.

• Chinese sources explicitly and consistently identify the *name* Hsiao Yüeh-chih 小月氏 'Lesser Yüeh-chih'—in connection with the lands of the Hsiao Yüeh-chih in southeastern East Turkistan and the homeland of the Yüeh-chih in the same region—with Sanskrit *Tukhâra*, the Indic name for 'Tokharian' and 'Tokhâristân'. The identifications include one by Kumârajîva (344–413), a famous scholar and traveler to India and China who, as a native of Kucha and son of a Kuchean princess, was certainly a native speaker of West Tokharian (Tokharian B) and knew what he was talking about.

• The identification of Tokharian elements in the Kroraina Prakrit texts[37]—for example, Krorainian (Tokharian C) *kilme* 'district' corresponding to East Tokharian (Tokharian A) *kälyme* 'direction'—is secured by the additional fact that they share Tokharian morphology.[38] This establishes the homeland of the Yüeh-chih, which included Kroraina, as the homeland of the Tokharians and their language in eastern Eurasia.

In conclusion, it is clear that the name now read Yüeh-chih is a transcription of *Tokʷarke, the name of the people from the northern and southeastern Tarim region who spoke a distinctive Indo-European language, *Tokharian*, as shown a century ago by Müller. The modern name *Tocharisch* 'Tokharian' he gave to the language does therefore represent the local name of the Tokharian people and language, though its meaning is unknown and it is unknown whether the name is an exonym or not.

---

sively, in Indo-Iranian loanwords; cf. the West Tokharian *nomen agentis* suffix *-ike* Adams (1999: 141), which also seems unlikely here.
[36] They did this exactly in accordance with the First Story, as outlined in the prologue, q.v.
[37] Burrow (1935, 1937).
[38] Mallory and Mair (2000: 278–279).

ENDNOTES

1. Although it is customary among specialists in Antiquity and the Middle Ages to speak of major near-contemporaneous historical works as "primary" sources, they are in fact almost all secondary works, compilations or literary compositions written by ancient or medieval authors and thus already shaped by the writers' perceptions and agendas; they are primary only in the sense that they are the earliest (sometimes the only) sources available on the subject. This is true even of the Chinese *shih-lu* or 'veritable records', the Old Turkic inscriptions, and so on. The same applies to modern histories of the Modern period, of course, though in this case historians do have massive amounts of primary source material at hand. In order to write this book, it has been necessary for me to rely in large part on secondary works, regardless of the period in question. This may seem more obvious to Modernists than to others, but there is in fact no chronological difference in my approach to the sources, which has been dictated by the large scale of the work. I have however gone into some questions in detail—for example, ancient ethnonyms and modern art—and in such cases have referred to primary materials to the extent necessary or possible, for example, inscriptions, manuscripts, or studies citing them in the former case, and works of art and art theoretical writings in the latter case.

2. I do not suggest that anyone repeat the received view, but a history of Central Eurasia written in the editorial-bibliographic approach, provided with citations of every significant relevant article and book, would be a great contribution to the field. An example of such a work, though of more limited geographical, chronological, ethnolinguistic, and topical scope, is Sinor (1963). I strongly encourage anyone interested in writing such a work to do so. It would of course have to be a series of encyclopedic volumes that would probably require many years, or decades, to finish. The Unesco volumes, *History of Civilizations of Central Asia* (Dani et al. 1992–2005), should have constituted such a work, but unfortunately the articles in them are uneven in quality and objectivity, there is no concept of Central Eurasia (their "Central Asia"), and their bibliographic coverage is generally minimal.

3. The numerous conflicting definitions and usages of "Central Eurasia", "Inner Asia," "Central Asia," and other terms used for the region as a whole or various subdivisions of it, have been treated by many writers; a full academic discussion would take a good-sized book. Here it is important to note that Central Eurasia *includes* Central Asia. In contemporary terminology, which is a relic of the Soviet period, Kazakhstan is considered a Central Asian state, but in fact it is not, even now, *culturally* or *ecologically* Central Asian, and neither is much of Turkmenistan and most of Kirghizstan. (Nevertheless, in chapters 11 and 12

I have followed current usage in order to avoid confusion.) Along with Mongolia and some countries retained by Russia after the dissolution of the Soviet Union—notably the Kalmyk and Tuvin republics—these regions constitute the modern continuation of the premodern nomadic steppe zone. While pastoralism is still practiced there, traditional nomadism seems largely to have disappeared.

4. It has earlier been claimed that Hittite myths are completely non-Indo-European in nature (i.e., they were borrowed, not inherited). However, Mazoyer (2003) has shown that the Hittites, who adopted the name and cult of the Hatti god Telipinu, adapted him to their own Central Eurasian storm god myth, adding his nation-founding character. According to Mazoyer (2003: 27), H. Gonnet (1990) "a eu la mérite pour la première fois d'attirer l'attention sur la fonction de fondateur de Télipinu." Telipinu fled from his temple in his home city (which was not Hattuša) because of the neglect of his cult by the last rulers of the Hatti, the non-Indo-European people whose kingdom was taken over by the Hittites (Mazoyer 2003: 27, 111–120, 149–150, 193–196). His career as a nation founder is similar to the foundation stories of Apollo, Cadmus, and Romulus (Mazoyer 2003: 156–158). It is also close to the story of Hou Chi 'Lord Millet', god of grain and founder of the Chou Dynasty in China, and the story of *Tümen, god of the ripe ear of grain and founder of the Puyo, Koguryo, and Paekche kingdoms in southern Manchuria and Korea.

5. The founding hero often seems to be an agricultural fertility god too (cf. the Puyo-Koguryo story). The combination of hero and fertility god in the person of the founder is widely thought to reflect the historical melding of two distinct peoples, but it is notable that the "sacral" Frankish kings embodied the same combination, which is in that connection thought to be a retention from antiquity.

6. The story given here is a conflation of the origin myths given by Herodotus (Godley 1972: 202–213). In one version this is Heracles, the son of Zeus. In the other version the father is named Targitáus, the son of Zeus and a daughter of the Dnieper River. In the version involving the horse theft, the hero is Hercules, and he sleeps with a creature who lives in a cave and is half woman (above) and half snake (below). The female ancestor would seem necessarily to be Hestia—in Scythian *Tabiti*—their main goddess. In the reply of the Scythian ruler to Darius during the Persian invasion of Scythia, the Scythian says, "for my masters, I hold them to be Zeus my forefather and Hestia queen of the Scythians, and none other" (Godley 1972: 328–329; cf. Rawlinson 1992: 347). Elsewhere Herodotus remarks, "The only gods whom they propitiate by worship are these: Hestia in especial, and secondly Zeus and Earth, whom they deem to be the wife of Zeus; after these, Apollo, and the Heavenly Aphrodite, and Heracles, and Ares. All the Scythians worship these as gods; the Scythians called Royal sacrifice also to Poseidon. In the Scythian tongue Hestia is called Tabiti: Zeus (in my judgment most rightly so called) Papaeus ['the all-father'

(Godley 1972: 257 n. 3)]; Earth is Api, Apollo Goetosyrus, the Heavenly Aphrodite Argimpasa, and Poseidon Thagimasadas" (Godley 1972: 256–259; cf. Legrand 1949: 82); Rawlinson (1992: 347) has "Thamimasadas" evidently after Abicht (1886: 54 n. 5), ". . . Denn im Zend ist Teme = mare, mazdâo = deus."

7. His Hsiung-nu title is written in Chinese 單于, traditionally read NMan *shànyú* or *chányú* (Pul. 48). Neither modern reading has much to do with the Old Chinese pronunciation of the characters, which must have been something like *Dar-ɣa (earlier) or *Dan-ɣa (later). The former suggests the well-known medieval Turkic and Mongolic title Daruɣači, for a high-ranking official with various functions. It might well go back to the Hsiung-nu, though the latter could of course have borrowed the title themselves.

8. The name Mo-tun 冒頓 NMan *mòdùn* is in MChi *mək (Pul. 217–218) -*twən³ (Pul. 84). It has not been identified, but as some have suggested, the Old Chinese pronunciation appears to represent a foreign *baɣtur, a relative of the later-attested Central Eurasian culture word *bayatur* 'hero'. The etymology of the word is unknown, though the first syllable is very likely the Iranian word *baɣ 'god, lord', an element in many later Central Eurasian titles. Mo-tun is presented as the founder hero in the story given in the Chinese sources, but he was actually the son of the founder (*Tumen). He was skilled with horses and the bow, the king (*Tumen) and his favored son attempted to use a stratagem to have him murdered, the prince was warned in time and miraculously escaped, he acquired a personal bodyguard of courageous warriors, and finally he attacked and killed the evil king and established a righteous and prosperous kingdom.

9. The version in the *Shih chi* (Watson 1961, II: 161; cf. Di Cosmo 2002a: 176, no Chinese source cited), according to which he was sent to the Wu-sun, is quite unlikely, because the sources generally say the enemies of the Hsiung-nu in that direction were the Yüeh-chih, and it was due to the Hsiung-nu defeat of the Yüeh-chih that the latter moved west of the Wu-sun, whose ruler later attacked them in revenge for the attack by them that killed his father, as related in the next story.

10. Old Turkic *tümen* 'ten thousand; myriarchy (a unit of ten thousand men)' has sometimes been identified with the name *Tumen (q.v. note 21). Both the name of the Old Turkic empire's founder, *Tumïn, and the word *tümen* are certainly borrowings from another language, because by form they cannot be inherited native Turkic words. The Old Turkic numeral *tümen* is certainly the same word as West Tokharian *t(u)māne* 'ten thousand, a myriad', East Tokharian *tmāṃ* 'id.', and the unknown source of Modern Persian *tumân* 'ten thousand' (Adams 1999: 301). Generally overlooked is Chinese 萬 NMan *wàn* 'ten thousand' from MChi *man (Pul. 318 *muan³), attested as *fiban* (Tak. 370–371), from *man. The origin of all these words and the directions in which they were loaned remain uncertain. The Chinese word is attested in Chou Dynasty inscriptions, but it is not necessarily the ultimate source. Its character 萬 (a rebus; graphically it

represents an insect) is the phonetic not only in the character 邁 NMan *mài* 'step, march', supposedly from OChi *mrāć (Sta. 574) ~ *mrats (Bax. 775), and 蠆 NMan *chài* 'scorpion' from putative OChi *srhāć (Sta. 574) ~ *hrjats (Bax. 749), but also 勵 NMan *lì* 'severe' from OChi *rać (Sta. 573) ~ *C-rjats (Bax. 773). The reconstruction of the syllable coda for the latter three series is particularly questionable, and the reconstructions of the onsets are not much better.

11. Di Cosmo (2002a: 176, 176 n. 50) notes that Mo-tun had created "an absolutely loyal bodyguard" and concludes, "Despite the legendary and romanticized elements in the account reported by Ssu-ma Ch'ien, to the extent that we accept the historical existence of Modun, we cannot exclude that his rise to power was achieved through the creation of an efficient bodyguard and the slaying of his own father." To this may be added the *Shih chi* comment on the burial of the Shan-yü: "When a ruler dies, the ministers and concubines who were favored by him and who are obliged to follow him in death often number in the hundreds or even thousands" (Watson 1961, II: 164). Either this account mixes up the comitatus burial with the burial of others (wives, slaves, etc.)—not surprisingly, because the Chinese observers were undoubtedly unfamiliar with the comitatus at the time—or the Hsiung-nu did in fact mix the two together in their royal burials. For a note on Mo-tun and the training of his comitatus as psychological conditioning, see Krueger (1961b).

12. In the Roman story the bird is a woodpecker, but the bird in the Wu-sun story is specifically said to be a crow. This could be a Chinese invention designed to explain the ethnonym Wu-sun, the transcription of which in Chinese characters literally means 'crow grandson'; it is certainly a phonetic transcription in origin. On the other hand, the woodpecker in the Romulus and Remus story is significant because it is sacred to the god of war, Mars, who is the boys' father in Plutarch's version of the story. It would seem to be a less likely bird than the crow, which often seems to have heavenly connections. At any rate, the essential motif is certainly a bird; whether it can be narrowed down more than that is unclear.

13. *Saklai 索離 NMan *suǒlí* from Late OChi *saklai, a later form of the original name of the Scythians, Sogdians, and Sakas, q.v. appendix B. In Beckwith (2004a: 31–32) I unfortunately followed other scholars' erroneous emendation of the texts. The initial character found in most texts, 索 NMan *suǒ* (MChi *sak)—or in some cases 橐 NMan *tuó* (MChi *tak)—is a phonetic transcription unconnected to the putatively "correct" *Ko (in Sino-Korean reading), which gives *Koryŏ, and nonsense, for both the Koguryŏ (= Koryŏ) and the Puyŏ myths. Although it is my fault for having trusted the "editions" I used, unfortunately there are no true critical editions (with critical apparatus, etc.) of those texts, or indeed of any Chinese texts, with a single exception (Thompson 1979), as far as I know. Critical editions of texts in Greek and Latin, as well as in Arabic and other medieval Western languages, have been produced since

the nineteenth century, but as pointed out by Thompson (1979: xvii), Sinologists, whether Chinese or non-Chinese, mostly do not even know what a critical edition is, and those who think they do know are adamantly opposed to them. Until this sorry state of affairs changes, Chinese texts will continue to be unreliable, and Sinology will remain in this respect a backward field.

14. In some versions the prince is born as a human child. In others he is born as an egg, and the king tries unsuccessfully to destroy the egg, but gives up. The prince subsequently hatches from the egg. I previously stated my belief that the egg version is earlier (Beckwith 2004a: 29), but I now think that two stories have been blended together. The basic story is in any case Central Eurasian in origin—the prince is a warrior hero descended from the sky god. The story is very close to several other versions, and particularly to the Chinese myth of Hou Chi 'Lord Millet', who is born as a human child. The egg birth detail seems to be an intrusive East Asian or Northeast Asian motif. It is reflected in the Japanese folktale of the hero Momotarô 'Peach Boy', who hatches from a large peach floating in a river; it is in many respects close to the Tümen story. In later medieval Korean versions of the story, which are evidently based on oral tradition, the bad king is a frog surnamed Kim 'gold'. Though this detail is not found in the brief ancient versions, it seems likely to be genuine. It could be that the birth story represents not only the results of a conflation of two different stories, one of which is more "southern," but the mixture of two different peoples, of which one people's story had a frog ancestor with a hero son born as an egg. However, there is no mention of a frog in any of the early versions.

15. The texts say that the name means 'shoots well' in Koguryo. The correctness of the gloss for the second syllable ('good, excellent') is confirmed by other Koguryo data, indicating its correctness for the other syllable, but in view of the repeated occurrence of the same name for the same historical function it is clear that at least two of the peoples who have this name in their national origin stories borrowed it from someone else. The gloss here suggests it could be a folk etymology designed to explain a problematic name, so it is possible that the *name* *Tümen is not Puyo-Koguryoic in origin. On the other hand, the now generally accepted etymology of the name Scythian as a development from Northern Iranian *Skuδa 'shooter, archer', and the attested form of the name of the original home of the Puyo-Koguryo people "in the north," *Saklai, a form of the name of the Scythians (see appendix B), suggests that the name 'Good Archer' may be a Puyo-Koguryo translation of the name *Sakla- 'Archer'. This problem deserves further attention.

16. Today *Alligator sinensis* is a rare, extremely endangered animal, found only in the lower Yangtze River area of Anhui Province, but in Antiquity it was found in the Yellow River basin (Ho 1999). Tomb 10 from the neolithic Dawenkou (Ta-wen-k'ou) Culture (ca. 4300–2500 BC) in Shantung contained eighty-four alligator bones, the vast majority of bones in the tomb; the other bones consisted of two deer teeth, two pig heads, and fifteen pig bones (http://depts.

washington.edu/chinaciv/archae/2dwkmain.htm). A bronze in the shape of an alligator was found in Shilou, Shanxi in 1959. It is 41.5 centimeters long and dates to the late Shang period (Gyllensvärd 1974: 48–49).

17. T'u-men 土門 NMan *tümén* < MChi *ʰthumən (Pul. 312, 211 *ʰtʰɔ²-mən¹) is written *Bumïn* in the Old Turkic inscriptions from the Orkhon. Modern scholars nearly all believe this to be the correct form. For example, Rybatzki (2000: 206–208, 218) argues that *Bumïn* is a loan from Indo-Iranian (Old Persian *bûmî* 'earth, land' Sogdian *βwm* 'world', Old Indic *bhûmi* 'earth, ground, soil, land'). This would mean the Chinese form would have to be a semi-calque translation, but this is unlikely in the extreme. Klyashtornyi and Livshits (1972) claim to have read the name *Bumïn* in the Sogdian inscription from Bugut (ca. 582, making it the earliest dated source on imperial Türk history), but this is contradicted by the recent study of the inscription by Yoshida and Moriyasu (1999), who see no such name. My own examination of the inscription concurs with Yoshida and Moriyasu's on this point. The chronological precedence of the Chinese form and the simple, clear, everyday characters used to transcribe the name in Chinese; the improbability of the Chinese form transcribing a Turkic taboo form (i.e., Tumïn as an avoidance form of an original Bumïn); the extreme unlikelihood of a Central Eurasian empire founder having a name that meant 'earth, world' or the like (as well as, for Turkic, the oddity of supplying a missing final *-n*); and, especially, the recurrence of the same name for the empire founder in the foundation stories of the Hsiung-nu and Koguryo, who also share other cultural elements with the Turks, most notably the ancestral cave, all indicate that the Old Turkic name was Tumïn, not *Bumïn. The reason for the erroneous form "Bumïn" in the Old Turkic inscriptions is unknown. It could have been a taboo avoidance of the founder's name or perhaps a scribal mistake that was repeated from one inscription to another, a real possibility because the texts consist in large part of verbatim repetitions of each other. See further Beckwith (2005b).

18. The Avars' Chinese name, variously written Jou-jan, Ju-ju, Juan-juan (or Rouran, etc.), has not yet been identified with an otherwise known ethnonym, and their language has also not been identified. As for the controversy over the identification of the Jou-jan with the Avars, the Byzantine Greeks called the new arrivals from the east Ἄβαροι 'Avars' from their first contact with them, and the Türk knew them as their former overlords—they were annoyed with the Avars for retaining the title *kaghan* 'emperor' even after the Türk victory. In his discussion of the "pseudo-Avar" problem, Pohl (1988: 34) rightly notes that the Avars certainly contained peoples belonging to several different ethnolinguistic groups, so that attempts to identify them with one or another specific eastern people are misguided. However, a key point, the significance of which seems not to have been fully appreciated, is that the Avars bore the title *kaghan*. The title is not known to have been used outside of the Eastern Steppe and North China before the Türk defeat of the Avars

and pursuit of them across Eurasia, so the Avar ruling clan must be equatable with the Jou-jan ruling clan or one or more legitimate heirs of it. As they are the leaders of the people who settled in Pannonia and became famous in Western sources as Avars, I have referred to them as Avars throughout. On the controversy, see Dobrovits (2004). Careful study of the Jou-jan names in the Chinese sources could shed light on the ethnolinguistic affinities of the Jou-jan; until that is done, speculation on the subject is premature.

19. The Sasanid comitatus and its members are referred to under several names, the most important of which are *gyânawspâr* (New Persian *jânsipâr*) 'those who sacrifice their lives' and *adiyârân* (or *adyâwarân* or *yârân*; New Persian *ayyârân*) 'friends, helpers, assistants'. They were an elite corps of fierce mounted warriors, highly skilled archers and swordsmen who were distinguished by their closeness to their ruler and by golden articles of adornment—bracelets, belts, and earrings are especially mentioned—that marked their rank. These strong, valorous, warlike men were the friends of their lord who sat near him in the royal hall during banquets and audiences. The Persian comitatus was "a community of free warriors who, through a ceremonial oath, voluntarily took upon themselves to remain faithful to a lord and constitute his subordinates and followers. To belong to this group was an advantage and brought with it prestige and dignity; on the other hand the increase in numbers would in-crease the prestige of the lord. The necessary condition for the formation of such a group was the fame of the lord as a successful warrior, probably also his noble descent, and a rich material base. The lord and his men formed a well-equipped, ever war-ready elite-group among the mass of free warriors capable of bearing arms" (Zakeri 1995: 87). This description is practically the definition of the classical comitatus. However, de la Vaissière (2005a: 143–144) states categorically that the Sasanids did not have *châkar*s or *ghulâm*s. Literally speaking, he is right—the references cited by Zakeri in support of their exis-tence *under those names* in Sasanid times are anachronistic, and Zakeri's dis-cussion sometimes leaves much to be desired. Nevertheless, the evidence from contemporaneous sources on the Sasanids, and before them the Achaemenids, is certainly there, and it is quite clear: the Persians most certainly did have the comitatus. That means they did have the warriors who were members of this elite guard corps, so the relevant source references, despite their unreliability in some respects, are correct in referring to the existence of comitatus *members* in the Sasanid realm, even if they incorrectly use the later non-Persian terms *châkar* or *ghulâm* for them instead of *gyânawspâr*, *adiyâr*, and so on.

20. The comitatus of the early Khitan, a Mongolic people, is known from the ac-counts of An Lu-shan's Rebellion. For a detailed treatment of the later Liao Dynasty of the Khitan, including discussion of its imperial guard corps, see the outstanding early study by Wittfogel and Fêng (1949). "Each [Khitan Liao] emperor had a separate *ordo*, or camp, with a 'heart and belly guard' of 10,000 to 20,000 households. . . . The members of this guard, particularly the non-Khitans,

were the emperor's private slaves, but their proximity to him gave them high status. After the emperor's death they guarded his mausoleum while his successor recruited a new *ordo* and guard" (Atwood 2004: 297). The Liao state, with its five capitals (*ordo*), seems to have been organized, theoretically, around the ideal of the "khan and four-bey" system. The khan of the Kereit, who were rivals of Temüjin during his rise to power, "had crack forces of *ba'aturs*, 'heroes', and a 1,000-man day guard, institutions Chinggis Khan would later imitate" (Atwood 2004: 296), along with the golden tent (*ordo*) connected to them.

21. The text says that the men who are sacrificed are killed "so that it may not be known in which of the [twenty burial] chambers is his tomb." A similar remark is made by the Roman who witnessed the burial of Attila. The accounts that claim those executed were killed so as to hide the location of the tomb are hardly to be believed—if even foreigners witnessed the burial (they describe it in great detail), the location of the tomb was no secret. It is certain from solid historical accounts that Central Eurasians bound by the comitatus oath did in fact commit suicide (they were even eager to do so) or were ritually executed, in order to be buried with their lord (Beckwith 1984a).

22. The Byzantine imperial comitatus, created circa 840, was called the *Hetaireia* and "consisted of three subgroupings, one of which was largely composed of Khazar and Farghânian (Φαργάνοι) mercenaries" (Golden 2004: 283–284). Cf. Constantin Zuckerman, cited by de la Vaissière (2005a: 285 n. 82) and Dunlop (1954: 219). The T'ang emperor T'ai-tsung, who had defeated the Eastern Türk and adopted the title Tängri Kaghan, took many Turkic warriors into the imperial guards. That these were not simply ordinary Chinese-style guards, at least in the minds of the men themselves, is clear from the fact that when he died, his two leading Turkic generals requested permission to commit suicide to be buried with him (Beckwith 1984a: 33–34).

23. In references "to Činggis Qan's own residence, especially in his ordinances concerning the Guard (*kešik*) duties, [the term *ordo ger* 'ordo-tents'] is rendered as 'Palace tent'. . . . [The] word *ordo* [is] an important term in Turkic from which it passed into Kitan, Mongolian, etc. In origin, *ordo* designated the camp of the elite cavalry guard [i.e., the comitatus] of the *qan* in the middle of which stood the *qan*'s tent or yurt" (de Rachewiltz 2004: 453–454).

24. Compare the Kievan Rus *družinniki* 'friends' (cf. Christian 1998: 390) of the *družina*, or Slavic comitatus, the word for which is in turn cognate to Common Germanic *druhtiz* 'comitatus', from (traditional) PIE *dhereugh (Lindow 1976: 17–18), that is, PIE *dereug. Old English *gedryht*, the usual word in *Beowulf* for the comitatus (which is also widely referred to as *weored ~ weorod ~ werod*) develops the general meaning 'army' and then simply 'group of men, band' in later Old English (Lindow 1975: 24–26).

25. This comitatus, which survived him (*TCTC* 220: 7047), was called *i-luo-ho* 曳落河 NMan *yì-luò-hé*, which in "the language of the Hu" means "the strong

warriors (壯士)" (*TCTC* 216: 6905). This term represents *yerlak χa in the archaic northern dialect pronunciation of Middle Chinese, corresponding to Mongol *erlik qaghan* 'ruler of the underworld', a loan from Turkic; cf. Old Turkic *ärklig khan*, literally 'mighty lord', an epithet for the ruler of the underworld (Clauson 1967: 224). In view of the transcription 河 *χa (q.v. Takata 1988: 304) for *qa (i.e., Kha) 'Khan', this would seem to be a Khitan (Mongolic) form; cf. the well attested Middle Mongol form *qa* 'Khan' (de Rachewiltz 2004: 457, 521, and his references). Although in T'ang contexts the word 胡 Hu is most frequently used for 'Indo-Europeans'—not merely 'Iranians from Central Asia', as usually believed (e.g., Pulleyblank 1991: 126–127), but even Indians in India—it also refers to Uighurs, Mongols, and others on the northern frontier (and in earlier times to the Hsiung-nu and their neighbors as far east as Manchuria); the expression 'the language of the Hu' can thus refer to Khitan, Old Turkic, Sogdian, or another language spoken in the area at that time. Moribe appears to have missed the earlier citation (see above in this note) and thus in his otherwise valuable discussion of *châkar*s in China during the An Lu-shan Rebellion he mistakes *i-luo-ho* 曳落河 for an ethnic name (Moribe 2005: 244). An's rebel troops are also referred to as *zhejie* (*che-chieh*)—*châkar*s—according to de la Vaissière (2003). Cf. his article on Sogdian *châkar*s in China (de la Vaissière 2005c). It is argued at length by de la Vaissière (2007) that the attested examples of the comitatus among Central Eurasians other than Sogdians are references either to Sogdians or to systems unrelated to the *châkar* institution found among the Sogdians. While it is undoubtedly the case that whatever the Sogdians were doing was not *identical* to whatever the Turks, or the Germanic peoples, or the Tibetans, etc., were doing at the same time, and for the same purposes, one does not need or expect to find total identity in cultural elements even within one ethnolinguistic group. It is understood that the Franks, the Tibetans, the Mongols, and so on had systems different from the Sogdians' *châkar* system, but they were all merely local variant forms of the comitatus, one of the central elements of the Central Eurasian Culture Complex. Unfortunately, the present book had already gone into production before I learned from him that his previously forthcoming monograph had actually appeared, so I was unable to do more than skim quickly through it and add this and one other brief comment. I hope I have not misconstrued his position.

26. The official Chinese histories claim that during the golden age of Emperor Hsüan-tsung (sometimes called Ming Huang, the 'Brilliant Emperor') the price of a horse was only one piece of silk. This has been taken at face value both by Chinese historians of the time and by scholars ever since. The official histories seem to have been purged of data on actual commercial transactions that would contradict this particular claim; that is, they suppress the actual prices involved in order to give Hsüan-tsung credit for impossibly cheap horses and to maintain the official pretense that after his time the Turks' horses were weak and emaciated, the nomads forced the Chinese to

buy horses from them, and the Chinese overpaid the Turks in excellent Chinese silks. Nevertheless, some data survived; see Beckwith (1991). By contrast, much (though certainly not all) of the silks with which the Chinese paid the Turks appear to have been of low quality—and the Chinese did have a monopoly over the production of many kinds of silk.

27. The cases Allsen (1997) and others cite of the capture of artisans and of valuable treasure as booty are good examples of what happened in warfare practically throughout Eurasia in Antiquity and the Middle Ages, not only warfare as practiced by Central Eurasians. While there does not seem to have been any significant coercion applied in the actual trading process at border markets, the obtaining of the *right* to trade was often a matter of diplomacy and involved the threat of war, just as it does today. Furthermore, all states, whether nomad-ruled or otherwise, used force or the threat of force or imprisonment to ensure payment of taxes and tribute from their subjects, just as they do today.

28. De la Vaissière (2005a: 283 n. 73) correctly remarks that the possibility of specifically *Buddhist* architectural influence on the plan of the palace is not supportable. It is known from Arabic, Persian, and Chinese sources that the Nawbahâr was originally built as an Iranian royal palace-city, as I point out in a paragraph at the very end of my article (Beckwith 1984b: 150–151); the possibility of Buddhist influence on the plan of Nawbahâr directly (and thus indirectly on the City of Peace), suggested in parentheses in my article, was not taken out because the journal was already in production when I ran across the *Ḥudûd al-'Âlam* passage, which I had overlooked, and by that time the interior of the article body could not be changed (except for the parentheses, which the editors kindly added). With respect to the Buddhist details of the Nawbahâr, my earlier interpretation (Beckwith 1984b: 148) of the name of the high, domed central building of the complex in the manuscripts of Ibn al-Faqîh, *al-Ašbat*, is erroneous and should be corrected. The name is certainly a transcription of the local form of the word *stûpa*, as suggested already by Herzfeld in 1921 (Beckwith 1984b: 159 n. 64); it should therefore be pointed so as to read *al-Istub* ('the stupa') or the like. Although some stupas were very large and had Buddhist statues in them, as in this instance, it may well be that the great stupa, like the rest of the complex, was also originally an Iranian imperial construction having nothing at all to do with Buddhism.

29. Virtually every account of successful Chinese campaigns into Central Eurasia includes information on the booty acquired, but it is generally ignored by modern historians, who, regardless of where their sympathies may lie, generally list only the number of "plundering raids" by Central Eurasians against the Chinese, for example, the "Chronological Table of Plunder by the Hsiung-nu" of Hayashi (1984: 86–92), who also argues that the Hsiung-nu raids were the major source of agricultural manpower in the steppe empire. The source material presented in his article, and to some extent his own arguments, show that the

Chinese in question were refugees from China who had escaped either on their own or in tandem with one of the Hsiung-nu raids in question. Cf. Di Cosmo (2002a: 202, 204).

30. It is important to realize that before the advent of telecommunications a unitary language could *only* be maintained by continuous, direct intercommunication among its speakers. Some have proposed that the various Indo-European daughter languages were simply the autochthonous, primordial languages of the areas in which they are first attested. For example, Van de Mieroop (2004: 112–113) says:

> Under the influence of an outdated nineteenth-century idea that there was an Indo-European homeland somewhere north of India, much attention has been devoted to finding out when and where the Indo-Europeans entered Anatolia and to finding evidence for an invasion. This search is futile, however. There is no reason to assume that speakers of Indo-European languages were not always present in Anatolia, nor can we say that they would have been a clearly identifiable group by the second millennium.

This claim makes no sense either linguistically or historically.

31. The scenario presented in the text accepts the traditional view of Indo-Iranian, which is based on the understanding of Avestan as the most archaic form of Iranian. However, this view now seems to me to be incorrect. It is interesting to note that some early Indo-Europeanists did not consider Avestan to be an Iranian language. "The similarities between the two languages were so great that some thought that the Avestan language was merely a dialect of Sanskrit" (Mallory and Adams 2006: 6–7). If Avestan's traditional linguistic status is indeed an error, it will not be possible to support the highly exceptional Indo-Iranian family, the early date of Zoroaster, the putatively shared early Indo-Iranian religious beliefs and practices, and much else. If current theory is wrong, all of the latter belong to Indic alone. However, because the phonological problem has just been discovered, and criticism of the traditional view will certainly be controversial until linguists investigate the problem in detail, I have refrained from modifying the text. See appendix A for further discussion.

32. The current consensus is that the Proto-Indo-European homeland was somewhere between the southern Urals and central Volga in the north and the North Caucasus and Black Sea in the south. However, the distribution of *mori 'lake, sea' in the daughter languages (Mallory and Adams 1997: 503–504; 2006: 127) suggests that this word was acquired during the Proto-Indo-Europeans' initial expansion, as posited here, meaning they would have earlier been nearer the Urals and middle Volga, which region is now considered by many to have been the homeland.

33. In the literature it is generally known as the Bactria-Margiana Archaeological Complex, or BMAC. See Witzel (2003), who discusses the "body of loan words preserved independently from each other in the oldest Indian and Iranian texts that reflects the pre-Indo-Iranian language(s) spoken in the areas bordering N. Iran and N. Afghanistan, i.e. the Bactria-Margiana Archaeological Complex. These loans include words from agriculture, village and town life, flora and fauna, ritual and religion." As noted above, the scenario presented here depends to a great extent on the received views of Indo-Iranian, and especially of the Avesta and the date of Zoroastrianism. In particular, the conclusions based on the once accepted idea of the Zoroastrian demonization of much that is thought to have been Indic now appear to be highly questionable. If the received view is incorrect, this scenario must be revised.

34. The lack of domestic horse bones from earlier sites in the pre-Chinese area, and the exclusion of wild eastern Eurasian horses (Przewalski's horse) from having contributed to the genetic makeup of domestic horses indicates that, as now accepted, domesticated horses were introduced to the western pre-Chinese area by the Indo-Europeans. As noted below, it is probable that the Proto-Tokharians brought the horses with them, though they seem to have kept them primarily for food. Second-wave Indo-Europeans would appear to be responsible for introducing chariot horses along with the chariot itself and a number of other cultural innovations.

35. Records in ancient Near Eastern languages, which go back centuries earlier than these references, are totally silent on Indo-Europeans anywhere and do not contain any Indo-European words until this very point in time. Considering that the bodies of people who must have spoken the Proto-Tokharian dialect of Indo-European were buried in the eastern Tarim Basin region beginning around 2000 BC, as noted above, and that the Proto-Anatolian dialect belonged, like Proto-Tokharian, to the Group A languages of Indo-European, the two groups would seem to have migrated at about the same time. They were the speakers of the first wave whose languages survived long enough to be recorded. It must be emphasized that membership in one or another of the three groups does not imply any genetic subgrouping. For example, Indic (Group B) and Iranian (Group C) are traditionally believed to belong to the same genetic subgroup, Indo-Iranian; however, see appendix A.

36. The earliest name by which the Hittites are known is Nesili (written *Nešili*), by which they refer to themselves in Hittite, but this name is derived from the name of the Assyrian colonial town of Kanesh (*Kaneš* or *Kaneš*) and means simply 'man of (Ka)nesh'. Melchert rightly notes that "Hittite is an unmistakeably Indo-European language in all respects." However, he also says, "Earlier claims about heavy non-Indo-European 'substrate' or 'adstrate' effects on Hittite ... were grossly exaggerated" (Melchert 1995: 2152). The problem with this is that the Proto-Indo-European language itself is not attested, and *all* of the daughter languages (or branches) are significantly different not only

from Proto-Indo-European but also from each other. The great differences among these languages can be explained best, if not solely, by assuming they were formed by individual creolizations of an original more or less unitary language. This explanation accords with what is known about language change in historical records from Antiquity to modern times. See Garrett (1999, 2006) and Beckwith (2006a), and appendix A.

37. The Old Indic chariot warriors of Mitanni—the *maryannu* (written *ma-ri-ia-an-nu*), from Old Indic *márya* 'young warrior' (plus the Hurrian plural *-nnu*)— and the Old Indic *marut* 'chariot warrior' are both connected specifically with horses and chariots (*EIEC* 277). The word for these warriors has a cognate in Old Persian *marīka* (from Proto-Indo-Iranian **mariyaka*) 'member of a retinue' (*EIEC* 630), that is, a band of warriors attached to a lord. "The OInd *márya* 'young man' (cf. Av[estan] *mairyō* 'villain, scoundrel') is employed to describe the wildly aggressive war-band [the Maruts—CIB] assembled around the leadership of Indra or Rudra in the Vedas. Although the Indo-Iranian form is usually derived from an *e*-grade **merio*- with cognates in other Indo-European stocks (e.g., Mayrhofer 1986–2000: 329–330), McCone suggests that the underlying form may well be an *o*-grade (**morios*) with a precise cognate in OIr[ish] *muire* 'leader, chief' " (*EIEC* 31). The correspondence of these forms suggests that the 'young warrior' words—from the Proto-Indo-European zero-grade root **mr̥*- and the *o*-grade root **mor* of words for 'to die, death, mortal, youth', and so on (*EIEC* 150; Pok. 735: **mer*-, **moro-s*; Wat. 42: **mer*)—are related to the derived word **marko* (with the highly productive suffix **-ko*) 'horse' (*EIEC* 274 **márkos*; Pok. 700 **marko*-; Wat. 38 **marko*-), the ancestor of English *mare*, attested only in Celtic and Germanic **marko* 'horse', which thus originally meant 'chariot warrior's horse'.

38. In the continuing absence of any clear archaeological dating of the appearance of the first Old Indic peoples in that region the question remains, were the Old Indic chariot warriors involved in the collapse of the Indus Valley civilization after all, as some believe the Rig Vedas say they were? Barbieri-Low (2000: 7) remarks, "Attendant on the collapse of Harappan civilization around 1500 B.C., was an influx of people from the north known as the Aryans. This Indo-European speaking group immortalized their ritual and culture in an epic known as the Rig Veda. In the Rig Veda, the Aryans use wheeled vehicles of several types, but the one they prize most is the horse-drawn chariot." If this is not correct—and so far no consensus seems to exist on the date of or reason for the collapse of the Indus Valley civilization—what other Indian non-Indo-European urban civilization was located in northwestern India whose towns could have been overthrown by non-urban Old Indic chariot warriors in the middle of the second millennium BC, as the Vedas would seem to describe? The problem cannot be brushed aside, as it now generally is. On the controversy— much of it politically motivated—over this and many other problems involved with the Old Indic entrance into India, see Bryant (2001), Bryant and Patton

(2005), and especially Hock (1999a, 1999b); in addition, recent general works on Indo-European (Mallory 1989; Gamkrelidze and Ivanov 1995; Mallory and Adams 1997, 2006) contain important material relevant to the controversy.

39. The design in a seal ring from Mycenae (Drews 1988: 161) shows a hunting scene with an archer on the chariot. Most Mycenaean portrayals, which are a couple of centuries or more later than the Shaft Graves, show a warrior holding a spear rather than an archer. There is much other material on Mycenaean chariots. M. A. Littauer, J. H. Crouwel, and Peter Raulwing, in many publications over several decades (e.g., Littauer and Crouwel 2002; Raulwing 2000), have argued strenuously against the idea that the Mycenaeans were Indo-European-speaking invaders who brought the chariot with them and used it in warfare. The remarkably intrusive culture of the Shaft Graves is not, for them, evidence of any new people, but only of "the rise of vigorous local chieftains" who mysteriously developed for reasons that are "not fully understood" (Littauer and Crouwel 2002: 70). They also argue that the chariot was mainly used for "conspicuous display" and "as an adjunct of the greater military," not as a key weapon in the armies of the day, the way it was certainly used in Anatolia and neighboring areas of the Near East, according to both textual and pictorial evidence. In addition, they argue that although the chariot "was not introduced to Mycenae by conquerors," it could have been brought in later—they suggest "gifts" from foreign royalty in the ancient Near East, where the first wheeled vehicles were developed and, they argue, predecessors of the chariot are first attested. They also contend—in face of direct evidence, such as the above seal ring from Mycenae showing a chariot with driver and archer—that, "In Greece, there is no evidence for the association between the military chariot and the bow so well documented in the Near East and in Egypt. Instead, chariots here functioned as a means of transport for warriors who fought not from the vehicle but on the ground with close-range weapons" (Littauer and Crouwel 2002: 70–71). Hunting from a chariot was the same as using it for war. They also ignore the evidence of the "disc-shaped bridle cheek-pieces which are attested in Mycenae from c 1600 BC and are found somewhat earlier in the steppe region" (*EIEC* 245), which agree with other correlations between the Shaft Grave burials and the North Caucasus Steppe burials. Littauer, Crouwel, and Raulwing's arguments do not make sense historically. They do not accord with the data that they and others present, according to which chariots are first attested archaeologically from the Volga-Ural area in about the twentieth century BC, and pictorially in the Near East at Kanesh (Littauer and Crouwel 2002: 45–46, figure 1), in the Kanesh Karum II site dated to ca. 1950–1850 BC (*EIEC* 245). This is the same site where the first linguistically attested evidence of an Indo-European language—Hittite—has been found, and the Hittites are also the first people known to have used chariots in warfare, in the seventeenth century BC. The Mycenaean Greeks

probably did not invent the chariot, nor did they ride in chariots from the steppe to Greece, but the area from which the Mycenaeans undoubtedly did come, or in any case through which they passed, namely the Caucasus region, had known chariots long enough for the Mycenaeans to acquire them if they did not already have them. Littauer and Crouwel's idea that the distinctive Mycenaean culture arose spontaneously out of nothing is disproved by the archaeology. As Drews (1988: 176) points out, the Mycenaean Shaft Graves simply have no antecedents in Greece, and "to explain the shaft graves as the result of the growth of an indigenous ruling class is circular: the only evidence for the growth of such a class [is] the shaft graves." See also Drews (2004) for corrections of some of his earlier arguments on the way the chariot was used in warfare. Most of the Near East–centered arguments about the origin, diffusion, and use of the horse and war chariot do not accord with the evidence and must be rejected.

40. It is often stated that 'China' is an anachronism when referring to any polity of East Asia before the unification of the country by the Ch'in Dynasty (whence our name *China*) under Ch'in-shih huang-ti in 221 BC. Other cultures that later were subsumed by the expanding Chinese people retained distinctive languages into the first millennium BC, at least, and it has been argued that it is not even certain if the Shang or Chou ruling strata spoke Chinese. However, though it is true that the *name* China is not earlier than the Ch'in kingdom—as is the idea of a unified country consisting of ethnolinguistically related parts that had earlier not been unified—it is not true that there was no earlier unitary state in the area of the Chinese homeland, the Yellow River region of the North China Plain. The ancestors of the Ch'in and Han empires were the Shang and Chou dynastic states centered in that same region. It is also incorrect to claim that the language of the Shang and Chou people was not Chinese. The Chou Dynasty, founded in 1046 or 1045 BC, as well as the preceding Shang Dynasty it replaced, were both unitary states in which Chinese was the only written language. It is true that it is unknown whether the native *spoken* language of the Shang and Chou conquerors who created their respective states was different from the local language of the region they conquered, but Ockham's razor tells us it must have been. What is significant linguistically is that in the Shang and Chou inscriptions essentially one language is recorded—though slightly different in some respects due perhaps to dialect and period changes— and that language is ancestral to the modern Chinese languages. Therefore, 'China' may be used without further quibbles to refer to the area that at any particular time in history was occupied by people who spoke a form of Chinese as their native language, from the Shang period to the contemporary era (bearing in mind the very small territory covered by the Shang realm). But the source of that language, which is clearly intrusive typologically in its "homeland," remains at present unknown, though it was undoubtedly a result, at least in part, of the Indo-European intrusion into the area. That is, it is still uncertain

whether Chinese is ultimately a minimally maintained Indo-European language or a local language influenced by Indo-European. This so far largely neglected problem deserves careful attention. For attempts to deal with it, see Beckwith (2002a, 2004b, 2006a).

41. The current consensus is challenged by Barbieri-Low (2000: 8–9 et seq.), who claims "no society could accept and adapt such a sophisticated package of machinery as the horse-drawn chariot so smoothly without extensive previous experience with wheeled vehicles." However, no earlier wheeled vehicles of any kind have ever been found in China proper. "In fact, no actual remains of vehicles other than chariots have been excavated at Anyang" (Barbieri-Low 2000: 48). Moreover, the modern history of the automobile and airplane indicates that, in order to introduce an advanced technology in a society without any related precursors, it is only necessary for an intrusive people to bring the technology in, use it, and allow the local people to learn how to use it. This is without question the way in which chariot technology and culture was transmitted in the second millennium BC in every location where chariots have been found or remarked outside Central Eurasia, including China. The dubious nature of the archaeological and other evidence he cites (Barbieri-Low 2000: 14–17) only further weakens this theory. Barbieri-Low (2000: 37) himself agrees that the fully formed chariot was introduced into China from outside rather suddenly in the Shang period, "around the reign of Wu Ding of the Shang Dynasty, that is around 1200 B.C." Elsewhere he suggests the more likely date of about a century earlier to account for the already localized technical and artistic treatment of chariot parts (Barbieri-Low 2000: 19 n. 40) and the fact that the Shang were fighting foreign people who had chariots. One Early Old Chinese inscription records the capture of "two chariots from an enemy group along with other weapons and prisoners" (Barbieri-Low 2000: 47). Piggott (1992: 65) says, "Chinese chariotry was a Chinese 'package' created on the Yellow River from the basic horse-and-chariot technological prerequisite, acquired incidentally without any linguistic affiliations, Semitic or Indo-European." This remarkable declaration ignores the impossibility noted by everyone, even Piggott (1992: 45–48) himself, of doing any such thing without extensive, long-term training by people who necessarily spoke one or another language—in this case certainly a Western one. As Piggott (1992: 45–47) also says, acquiring chariots "involved the acquisition of a techno-complex, a package-deal . . . involving not only things but people."

42. Among the weapons, notably including numerous bronze-tipped arrows (thus belying the usual argument that the chariots were somehow used with spears or halberds, a virtual impossibility), is a type of "semilunar-shaped knife which is topped by a ring or a fully-sculpted animal figure. In comparison to the motifs of mainstream Shang bronze-vessel decoration, these knives look very foreign. Their animal-style art is very common, however, in the Northern Zone which stretches to the north and west of Anyang. Pointing to the issue of tech-

nology, the shape and texture of some of these knives suggest that they were cast using a lost-wax casting method. Shang vessels were usually cast using the piece-mold casting method. Thus, these knives also seem to be part of an assemblage of items used by the Shang charioteer which trace their origin to the steppe zones and not to the Central Plain [i.e., ancient China proper—CIB]" (Barbieri-Low 2000: 42–43). In fact, the knives were ubiquitous and typical throughout the steppe zone north of China and farther west and have been much noted and discussed as a well-known intrusive northern element in China (Bagley 1999: 222–226; cf. Di Cosmo 1999a: 893–894).

43. It is remarkable that the characters of the Oracle Bone Inscriptions, the earliest form of Chinese writing, are structured exactly like the most typical forms of writing in the ancient Near East at that time—they consist mostly of derived pictographic (or "zodiographic") forms, rebuses, combinations of phonetic and semantic elements, and so on, rather than simple pictographs. For more precise terminology and analysis, see Boltz (1994). One might imagine that a totally unrelated writing system would be totally unrelated in structure, but this is not the case with the Oracle Bone writing system, as shown by Boltz, who however argues that the Chinese themselves invented this writing system de novo without any outside influence: "There is no tangible evidence known at present to suggest that . . . Chinese writing is the result of any kind of stimulus-diffusion, however indirect, from points outside China" (Boltz 1994: 34). Yet the Chinese writing system appears, fully formed, only in the thirteenth century BC, some two millennia after writing had been invented in the West, and it appears at the same time as the fully formed chariot, which was also invented long beforehand in the West. Humans are typically imitative more than inventive. The Chinese did not have wheeled vehicles before this period. They adopted the chariot from the foreigners who brought the fully formed artifact with them from the northwest. It is thus much more likely that the idea behind the Chinese writing system—though perhaps not the system itself—ultimately comes from the same direction. Boltz (1994: 35 et seq.) himself essentially debunks the theory that various marks found on Neolithic pottery are precursors of the Chinese writing system.

44. In Shang and early Chou practice, words referring to women often were written with the addition of the character for 'woman', sometimes instead of, or in addition to, the character for 'man, human'. For a good example and discussion, see the paper by Elizabeth Childs-Johnson (2003) on Fu Tzu 婦子 or 婦好 (whose name is usually read 'Fu Hao'). In the present case, the word Chiang 姜 (NMan jiâng) has the 'woman' significant instead of the 'man' significant in Ch'iang 羌 (NMan qiâng). In this case it is probable that Chiang 姜 is simply a taboo form. That is, the actual clan name, Ch'iang 羌, could not be written during the Chou Dynasty itself because the maternal line of the Chou was from this clan. Because the anomaly appears to exist solely for the Chou Dynasty period, the actual identity of the two ethnonyms (Chiang 姜 and Ch'iang 羌)

seems clear. The words are sometimes thought to be Chinese, meaning 'shep-herd (man ~ woman)'; however, this does not seem likely, because they are never used in the sense 'shepherd', but only as ethnonyms. For a possible Indo-European etymology of the name, see appendix B.

45. There are two attested Old Chinese dialect forms of the word 馬 'horse' Old Chinese *mraɣ from earlier *mraga, ancestor of New Mandarin *mǎ*, and Old Chinese *mraŋ from earlier *mraŋa, ancestor of the loanforms in Old Burmese *mraŋ*, Old Tibetan *rmaŋ* from *mraŋ, and Proto-Japanese-Ryukyuan *ᵐmaŋ from *mraŋ (Beckwith 2007a: 145–146). The latter dialect pronunciation is evi-dently also attested within Chinese via the phonetic of the character 馮 NMan *píng* 'tread on, rely on', from Middle Chinese *biŋ (Pul. 240) from Old Chinese dial. *ᵐbrəŋ (Sta. 589: *brəŋ), from *mraŋ. Both dialect forms derive regularly from earlier *mraga, from Early Old Chinese or Proto-Chinese *marka, as shown in Beckwith (2002a). Note that the final vowel is unknown, but it could not have been a high vowel; it was probably *a. On the dialectal shift of nasal onsets to prenasalized oral onsets in Old Chinese and Middle Chinese, see Beckwith (2002a: 121–127; 2006c: 186–188).

46. The word for 'wheel, chariot' in Chinese is written 車, which was originally a pictograph. It has two readings in Middle Chinese, *tʃa and *kü, the second of which can be reconstructed for Old Chinese as either *klâ or *krâ, from theo-retical Early Old Chinese *kelé ~ *kolé ~ *karé ~ *kore ~ etc. Because assumed Early Old Chinese *o and *we ~ *wa merged later within Chinese, the form *kolé is not distinguishable from *kwelé, which is itself clearly a form of the Indo-European word for 'wheel'. The wheel was introduced to China as a part of the chariot—in Early Old Chinese the one word has both meanings—so *kolé ~ *kwelé appears to be the correct form. However, the Old Tibetan word for 'wheel, circle', *fikorlo*, derives regularly from *kwerlwe ~ *kewrlew ~ *kwerlo ~ *korlew (etc.) in pre-Old Tibetan, which language has the same problem of the indistinguishability of earlier *o and *we ~ *wa. Of these forms, the Proto-Tibetan form *kwerlo corresponds perfectly to Proto-Indo-European *kweklo 'wheel' with the exception that Tibetan has *r* instead of the second PIE *k. This interesting anomaly may be due to an Old Chinese intermediary—syllable-final *ɣ was evidently phonetically close to [ʁ] (the standard French and German pronunciation of /r/) at some point in Old Chinese, because it was perceived as /r/ by Common Japanese-Koguryoic speakers, who borrowed OChi 鳥 'fowl, bird' as *tewr (Beckwith 2007a: 138, where *tawr should be corrected to *tewr), among other examples. The Old Tibetan form thus presupposes an Old Chi-nese donor form *kweʁlo, from *kweɣlo, from Early Old Chinese *kweklo 'wheel, chariot'. The fact that both Chinese readings of 車 have level tone, not rising tone (the normal reflex of Old Chinese syllable-final *ɣ) shows that within Central Old Chinese both syllables continued to be analyzed as open syl-lables, so *ɣ was still perceived as the onset of the second syllable (*ɣlo), not as the coda of the first syllable (i.e., not as *kweɣ), but in the donor dialect, *ɣ was

perceived as the coda of the first syllable (*kweɣ) and thus shifted to *kweʁ and was heard as *kwer by the Proto-Tibetans. It is also possible that the Tibetans borrowed the word directly from early Indo-European speakers and remodeled the first syllable on the basis of the Tibetan verbal root √kor 'to turn; revolve' (and its causative √skor 'to turn, encircle'), which could correspond to an o-ablaut form of PIE *(s)ker 'to turn, bend' (Wat. 78). In any event, the Proto-Chinese word for 'wheel, chariot' is certainly an Indo-European loanword and appears to be reconstructible as *kweɣlwe ~ *kweɣlo, from PIE *kweklo. Nevertheless, much more work is needed on this topic.

47. According to the current received view among Sinological linguists (as distinguished from archaeologists, who are no longer so parochial), Chinese culture developed essentially as an island surrounded by wasteland inhabited by wild animals and *barbarians*. The only foreign influences admitted are from the south: much discussion focuses on the putative contributions of the Hmong and Proto-Miao-Yao to the early Chinese. But Chinese culture was certainly by far the most advanced in the East Asian region at that time, regardless of its language or languages. The consequent unbelievability of such speculations—particularly the proposed direction of some of the loaning (from the Miao-Yao, etc., to the Chinese)—seems not to have been noticed. With the exception of E. G. Pulleyblank, contemporary Sinological linguists accept the existence of only a single Indo-European word (a loanword) in Old Chinese: the Tokharian word for 'honey'. Their refusal to look at the now undisputed archaeological evidence, or to attempt to relate it to the linguistic evidence, is baffling.

48. The *Mischsprache*, or 'mixed language', is supposedly a language that is so mixed its genetic ancestry is unclear, unlike a creole, the ancestry of which is clear. The *Mischsprache* theory has once again been disproved (Beckwith 2007a: 195–213; Mous 1996). In a book on the world's only putative example, Ma'a (or Mbugu), argued by Thomason and Kaufman (1988) to be a mixed language, Mous (2003) now waffles on the issue, claiming that Mbugu speakers do not simply use the Ma'a "language" as a code—exactly like English Romani, who speak English and also, for the sake of secrecy and ethnic solidarity, a register of English with a heavy admixture of Romani, as shown very clearly by Thomason and Kaufman (1988)—they actually speak two languages, Mbugu and Ma'a, which share one grammar. This is a step backward. The clear statement of Mous's (1996) article remains the simple, unvarnished truth about Mbugu and about Ma'a, which must be seen not as a language but as a register of Mbugu.

49. It has been argued that because the Sintashta-Petrovka chariot seems to be a ritual model and would probably be unstable if actually driven, it is therefore a Central Eurasian "imitation" of Near Eastern chariots, thus proving that the horse-drawn war chariot was invented in the ancient Near East, not Central Eurasia. But this argument depends on two highly questionable points: it is

argued, first, that the early chariot developed and spread in this way because of its "prestige value" rather than because of its practical military use and, second, that unrecognizably crude Ancient Near East portrayals of indeterminate beasts hitched to two-wheeled vehicles represent chariots (Littauer and Crouwel 2002: 45–52). For the Sintashta-Petrovka chariot one would assume the opposite to be more likely: ritualized objects used in burials would seem to be based on practical things long used in a culture, whether or not of local origin, whereas uncomprehended foreign objects, when placed in burials, would presumably tend to be the actual practical things (such as the chariots buried at Anyang), not ritualized versions of them. This problem should, however, be addressed by archaeologists.

50. Herodotus says that "the nomad Scythians inhabiting Asia, being hard-pressed in war by the Massagetae, fled away across the river Araxes to the Cimmerian country (for the country which the Scythians now inhabit is said to have belonged of old to the Cimmerians).... And to this day there are in Scythia Cimmerian walls, and a Cimmerian ferry, and there is a country Cimmeria and a strait named Cimmerian. Moreover, it is clearly seen that the Cimmerians in their flight from the Scythians into Asia did also make a colony on the peninsula where now the Greek city of Sinope has been founded; and it is manifest that the Scythians pursued after them and invaded Media, missing their way; for the Cimmerians ever fled by way of the coast, and the Scythians pursued with the Caucasus on their right till they came into the Median land, turning inland on their way" (Godley 1972: 210–213; cf. Rawlinson 1992: 299–300). Godley (1972: 213, n. 1) comments on Cimmeria: "The name survives in 'Crimea'"; his "strait named Cimmerian" is (literally) the 'Cimmerian Bosphoros'". Although some of this account appears to be due to late Persian stories, the archaeological record largely supports Herodotus.

51. The view presented here was written before I knew about and read the article of de la Vaissière (2005d), who emphatically rejects the consensus among Central Eurasianists that the Huns were unconnected to the Hsiung-nu. The case has been made for the Hsiung-nu having been Iranians (Bailey 1985: 25 et seq.), Kets (Pulleyblank 2000; Vovin 2000), or others. Certainly they were at least strongly influenced culturally by the Sakas, the eastern branch of the Northern Iranians, and it is quite possible that the name Hsiung-nu is actually a transcription of a form of the old North Iranian ethnonym *skuδa 'archer', but further work on Old Chinese reconstruction is required in order to either confirm or disprove this hypothesis. Although de la Vaissière makes the strongest, most convincing case so far in favor of the connection, there unfortunately remain many problems that he does not resolve. Most significantly, he does not discuss the phonology of the Chinese transcription. But that is after all the key issue. The evidence in that regard indicates that the Old Chinese form of the name began with an initial cluster, among other major differences from the Middle Chinese form. However, because de la Vaissière introduces some data

not previously utilized in the arguments back and forth, his argument calls for examination in depth. See also endnote 52.

52. It is accepted that at least some syllables with *sC(C)- onset clusters became reduced to the simple onset *χ- by Early Middle Chinese times at the latest. It is probable that all such onset clusters became so reduced in the Central Dialect, and quite possibly even the simple onset *s- also became *χ- (it certainly did so in some cases). The change was complete in the Central dialects by Middle Chinese times, but *s still existed in some positions in the early centuries AD because it shows up in Chinese transcriptions of Indic terms, as has been shown by Pulleyblank (1984) and others. It is thus probable that Old Chinese *s was still preserved in the early Western Han period. In view of the phonology of the name Hsiung-nu, it is unlikely that the onset did not begin with *s; the beginning of the first syllable thus had the shape *sV- or *sCV-; because the capital of the Western Han was in Ch'ang-an, it is probable that the official dialect of Chinese at the time had oralized nasals (e.g., Mo-tun represents *Baγtur, not *Maγtur). Accordingly, the transcription now read as Hsiung-nu may have been pronounced *Soγdâ, *Soγlâ, *Sak(a)dâ, or even *Skla(C)da, etc. See appendix B.

53. The best-known transcription of the name Saka in Chinese is Sai 塞 MChi *sǝk (Pul. 271). In view of the occurrence elsewhere of this word's phonetic (overlooked or ignored by Karlgren), the word might perhaps be reconstructed with initial *ś-, according with the expected Prakrit form of the name, Śak, from Śâka ~ Saka. The name of the Sakas ~ Scythians is also preserved in the old name of Yarkand, So-chü ~ Sha-ch'e 莎車 *Saklâ ~ *Śaklâ. However, due to the later date it may be that the transcription represents an underlying *s- rather than *ś-. The *s- vs. *ś- problem needs further investigation. For references on the early names of Yarkand, see Hill (forthcoming). With regard to the possible Hsiung-nu connection with the Saka, note that in the *Chou shu* account of the origins of the Turks, one of the two versions given says they are in origin a nation of the Hsiung-nu; the other says they came from the 'kingdom of the *Saka*' (So kuo 索國 NMan *suǒ* < MChi *sak; Pul. 1990: 298) to the *north* of the Hsiung-nu (*CS* 50: 907–908; cf. Sinor 1990a: 287–288). Although some rather fanciful semantic interpretations of the name So in So kuo have been proposed, it is most certainly a phonetic transcription of the name Saka. The same remark is made in Greek by Menander (Blockley 1985: 116–117): "The Turks, who had formerly been called the Sacae . . ." (i.e., the Sakas). As these are completely independent sources, this information is significant.

54. Dacia, the land of the Daci or Getae, a Thracian or Phrygian people, was a strong regional state in the area of what is now Romania and Moldova in the early first century BC. The Dacians extended their power eastward into the Pontic Steppe down to the Black Sea, and Julius Caesar (d. 44 BC) intended to attack them, supposedly because they were considered to have been a threat to Rome, but more likely because of their gold mines (in what is now Transylvania).

Periodic conflict between the Romans and Dacians continued until finally Trajan (r. AD 98–117) subjugated the country between AD 101 and 107 and incorporated it into the Roman Empire, moving large numbers of Romans into the region. Modern Romanian is the direct descendant of the Latin language spoken by the Roman colonists. The province was later abandoned to the Goths. Cf. Tacitus, *Germania*, x, xliii, xlvi (Mattingly 1970: 101, 136–137, 140).

55. This half line is what the manuscript has, not what is proposed as an emendation by Dobbie (1953), q.v. for other proposed emendations. The quoted passage, lines 81b through 90a in his edition, is translated according to the interpretation given in Beckwith (2003), where other solutions are discussed and it is shown that the usual emendation and interpretation of this half line cannot be correct. The translation of it given here is intended to represent my guess at what the text may originally have said at this point. How the Old English might be reconstructed is another matter.

56. Historians sometimes equate the Huns of the Western Steppe and Eastern Europe with the Hephthalites or 'White Huns' of Central Asia, who defeated the Sasanids in the fifth century and occupied a large area in Bactria and Transoxiana. The Hephthalites were apparently not Huns, and the application of the latter name to them seems to be either a misnomer or a generic usage. The recently discovered Bactrian documents from the Hephthalite period mention Hephthalites (ηβοδαλο), but not Huns (de la Vaissière 2005d: 19). The Chionites, a little-known people active on the eastern border of the Sasanid Empire in the reign of Shâpûr II (r. 309–379), who campaigned against them in 356–357, are sometimes said to be Huns, or to be connected to them (e.g., Frye 1983: 137; Bivar 1983: 211–212), but this too is apparently erroneous. It has been argued that the Chionites were Iranians, based on the derivation of their name in Pahlevi, *Hyon*, from Avestan *Hyaona* (Felix 1992: 485 and others), but this has been convincingly disproved (de la Vaissière 2005d: 5–10), leaving their ethnolinguistic identity unknown.

57. The trading market or markets are mentioned elsewhere by Priscus (Blockley 1983 II: 230, 243). In one account, the Huns attacked the Romans at a market. When the Romans sent an embassy to complain, the Huns explained that their attack was a reprisal for a serious offense against them: the Roman bishop of Margus (now Požarevac in Serbia) had crossed over into Hun territory and robbed their royal tombs. Although Priscus, and after him most commentators, dismiss the Hun claim, the fact that the bishop later surrendered to the Huns to save his skin suggests (perhaps counterintuitively) that the Huns really had been the victims in this case. This conclusion is supported by the pattern of behavior of border magnates toward Central Eurasians in the Roman Empire and indeed all along the frontier of Central Eurasia from West to East.

58. The Avars were not part of the Hsien-pei confederation—all of the linguistically identifiable peoples of which, including the *Taghbač, spoke Mongolic languages—but are connected to them, as subordinates, in the origin

story given in the Chinese sources. While the story is prejudiced against the Avars and bears every sign of having been related by one of their enemies, it strongly suggests that the Avars were a distinct ethnos and spoke a different language. Although some Avar names and titles do "sound" Mongolic, names and titles are often borrowed (as a well-known example, many of the Huns had Gothic names, and many of the early Turks had Iranian or Indic names). The name of the last Avar kaghan, A-na-kuei 阿那瓌 or *Anagai (CS 50: 908), is attested in Menander (Blockley 1985: 172–173, 178–179) far to the west as Ἀνάγαιος or Anagai, the name of the ruler of the presumably Turkic Utigurs (cf. Chavannes 1903: 240). Most Avar names and titles seem distinctly non-Mongolic in their phonology. The main problem with the Avars at the moment is not so much the relative paucity of source material as the extreme paucity of scholarly research on them; the topic has been neglected for far too long. Note that the medial *w of Middle Chinese reconstructions of foreign names (such as A-na-kuei) often does not correspond to anything in the actual foreign "original" forms of the same names.

59. The controversy over the ethnolinguistic history of early Korea and Japan is due partly to modern politics, including Korean nationalism (on which see Pai 2000); partly to Korean, Japanese, and foreign scholars' neglect of the major sources and studies of them; and partly to the widespread, deep misunderstanding or outright rejection of scientific historical linguistic and philological methods in the field of East Asian studies in general. The relevant materials and issues are examined in Beckwith (2005a, 2006e, 2007a; cf. Kiyose and Beckwith 2006).

60. The period is identified with the beginning of "Japanese" culture in Japan and is generally considered to begin in the fourth to third centuries BC. Recently some scholars, relying on carbon dating, have argued for a much earlier date. The problem is that carbon dating is well known to be unreliable for precisely this period in history. Until a careful dendrochronological sequence has been established for Korea and Japan for the first millennium BC and the first half of the first millennium AD it will continue to be impossible to date the Yayoi period precisely. See Kiyose and Beckwith (2008).

61. World histories pay a great deal of attention to the superficial effects of this movement on the peripheral cultures of Eurasia, particularly the Western Roman Empire, and much less attention to the causes. While some mention is usually made of possible causes, the underlying explanation that is given remains the same: the Central Eurasians were hungry, poor, and cold, but they were also aggressive, energetic, and naturally ready for war. They took advantage of the opportunity to plunder the weak agrarian peoples to the south and had unexpected success, such that they were able to establish their own states in the region. This characterization of the history of the period is misleading at best. It is based more or less completely on the mistaken belief that the Central Eurasians (excluding refugees from war, of course) were indeed hungry, poor,

and so on in their homelands and imputes to them motives for which there is no evidence. (See the discussion in the epilogue.) Being human, the Central Eurasians undoubtedly did attack their enemies—as much as their neighbors attacked them. But the simple fact is that we do not know why the Great Wandering of Peoples took place. Nevertheless, enough is known about the events themselves in the peripheral cultures, so the reason seems perhaps to be potentially discoverable.

62. The history of Arabian internal and foreign trade, Muḥammad, and the early Islamic expansion is an extremely contentious field. See the differing treatments of Shaban (1970, 1971, 1976), Crone (1987), and Peters (1994). The present treatment largely follows Shaban and, in part, Crone, particularly her conclusion on the primary driving force behind the expansion out of Arabia. She argues, via a process of elimination, that the putative natural belligerency of the Arabs (q.v. endnote 63) cannot explain the unique history of the foundation of Islam and the subsequent conquests, leaving as the only explanation the "foreign penetration" of Arabia (Crone 1987: 245–250): "Muḥammad's Arabia had thus been subjected to foreign rule on a scale unparalleled even in modern times" (Crone 1987: 246). On the early conquests, see also Donner (1981).

63. Crone (1987: 243–245) and others claim that the Arabs were greedy, rapacious conquerors: "Tribal states must conquer to survive, and the predatory tribesmen who make up their members are in general more inclined to fight than to abstain" (Crone 1987: 243). So too, in her view, were the Muslims: "Muḥammad had to conquer, his followers liked to conquer, and his deity told him to conquer: do we need more?" (Crone 1987: 244). These statements do not seem to have scientific justification. Their remarkable similarity to the received ideas about Central Eurasians discussed in the epilogue is not accidental; see the discussion of similar views on the Islamic comitatus in Beckwith (1984a).

64. It is often stated that there are so few books in Middle Persian or in any Persian literary language before New Persian because the Arabs destroyed the "great library of Ctesiphon." In fact, so few books in early Persian have survived because the Persians simply wrote few books, at least in Persian, before they adopted Islam and got the habit of writing from the Arabs. When the Arab Empire began dissolving in the early ninth century, a highly Arabicized literary language, New Persian, developed. The Persians thenceforth wrote copiously, like the Arabs. The story seems to have arisen to explain the paucity of books in Middle Persian by contrast with the great number in Arabic and, eventually, New Persian. This myth belongs on the dustheap of history along with the one that claims the Arabs destroyed the great library of Alexandria, which actually had disappeared centuries before the Arab conquest.

65. The Western and Southern subregions of Central Asia were conquered by Persian empires several times in recorded history, but those regions were never ruled directly by them for long. The local peoples were not Persians by culture or language. In fact, they spoke entirely different languages (Bactrian, Sogdian,

and so on). Although those languages are related to Persian in the Iranian family of languages, they belong to a different branch of the family. Much of the confusion is due to the name *Iranian*, which, however, has nothing specifically to do with modern Iran (formerly Persia); it is a scholarly term for the language family and the peoples who spoke the languages. Like the Persians, the Arabs quickly overran Western and Southern Central Asia, but they too never controlled it firmly, and they lost what control they did have rather early. The Chinese similarly had trouble establishing firm control over the Eastern subregion of Central Asia.

66. Hsüan Tsang spent his month at the Nawbahâr of Balkh studying the *Mahāvibhāṣaśāstra*, an important Sarvastivadin text (*TSFC* 2: 33) that is "an encyclopedia of Buddhist philosophy; in it opinions of several ancient and contemporary philosophies of different schools are carefully registered and discussed" (Ch'en 1992: 95 n. 9). Fortunately, he brought a copy back to China and translated it; subsequently it was lost in all other languages. Some good work has recently been done on the text and others related to it (Takeda and Cox forthcoming; Willemen et al. 1998).

67. The civil war broke out after the murder of the third caliph of the new Arab Empire, 'Uthmân (r. 644–656). Although the Prophet Muḥammad's cousin 'Alî (r. 656–661) succeeded, continuing discontent over the policies of 'Uthmân and the desire for revenge by Mu'âwiya, the governor of Syria, who was 'Uthmân's cousin, led the realm into civil war. 'Alî's eldest son, al-Ḥasan, succeeded, but quickly abdicated in favor of Mu'âwiya. The uprisings in Khurasan actually broke out shortly after the first Arab conquests there, and despite several expeditions to put them down, the Arabs had little success there until after the civil war (Shaban 1970: 26–27).

68. The title Spurgyal has usually been understood to mean 'king of Spu' (Beckwith 1993). Yet it is probably a mistranslation, and in truth we do not know what it means, though it does seem to be *possible* that Spu was the early dynastic name of Tibet, and the title does occur in imperial period texts. Recently some Tibetans and Tibetologists have begun using the title 'Spurgyal' to mean 'Tibetan Empire'. This seems to be ahistorical, and is actually contradicted by bilingual (Old Tibetan and Chinese) sources, which refer to the country as *Bod chen* 'Great Tibet', precisely parallel to (and undoubtedly modeled on) Chinese usage, for example, *Ta T'ang* 'Great T'ang'. The problem calls for scholarly attention.

69. It continues to be stated, based on postimperial Tibetan accounts, that the princess, Wen-ch'eng kung-chu (written *Mun caŋ koŋco* in the *Old Tibetan Annals*), was to be married to Emperor Khri Srong Rtsan (Khri Srong Brtsan, alias Srong Btsan Sgampo) himself. This is disproved by the account at the beginning of the *Old Tibetan Annals* as well as by the history of the other marriage treaty concluded with China in the eighth century. There are two possibilities. The princess was married to Gung Srong Gung Brtsan, the crown prince, who

became emperor and reigned for six years, but then died. Khri Srong Rtsan then assumed the throne again and, following the Central Eurasian custom of levirate, took the Chinese princess as one of his consorts before he himself passed away in 649–650. This view is supported by the fragmentary beginning of the *Old Tibetan Annals,* which explicitly says that Khri Srong Rtsan "cohabited with her for three years" before he died. However, the same text refers twice to the emperor as the *btsanpo gcen* 'the emperor, the elder brother', alongside his *gcung* '[imperial] younger brother', Btsan Srong. Although it is possible that Gung Srong Gung Brtsan was mentioned in the now lost portion, on the basis of what remains it seems more likely that he was not. That would leave the younger brother Btsan Srong as the probable groom. The *Old Tibetan Chronicle* refers to the same kind of dual rulership under Khri Srong Rtsan's father, and the same situation appears to have obtained again later in the early eighth century, when the T'ang treaty princess Chin-ch'eng kung-chu was evidently intended for the ruler now known only as *btsanpo gcen lha* 'the emperor, the elder brother Lha'; but, in any case, she was clearly not intended for Khri Lde Gtsug Brtsan ('Mes Ag-tshoms'), because negotiations for her had begun long before he was a possible candidate; see Beckwith (1993: 69–70). In view of the widespread practice of dual kingship elsewhere in Central Eurasia, this topic deserves further investigation.

70. The adoption of the Latin title *imperator* 'emperor' by the Franks on Christmas Day in 800 would seem to be the real source of their annoyance with the pope that comes through in Frankish historical sources. The Franks already had two distinctive terms of their own for their empire's supreme ruler, Latin *rex* and the Frankish equivalent of English *king.* Both were clearly distinguished from the neighboring Byzantine and Arab imperial titles, while by Charlemagne's time the title *imperator* was no longer exclusively "imperial." The ruler of the smaller realm of the Avars retained the title *kaghan* 'emperor' from their earlier history in the Eastern Steppe, but their state was conquered by Charlemagne's armies in 791.

71. The Türk royal clan is named Ἀρσίλας Arsilas in Menander (Blockley 1985: 172–173). In Chinese sources the name is given as 阿史那, read A-shih-na in Mandarin, from a Middle Chinese dialect pronunciation *Aṣinas evidently representing a foreign *Aršinas ~ *Aršilas. The final *s, which became the "departing tone" in standard Middle Chinese, is known from other early transcriptions to have existed into the early Middle Chinese period (Pulleyblank 1984); the *n* of the modern Chinese pronunciation was pronounced as *n, l,* or *d* in the same period. Greek script does not have these particular ambiguities, but is instead ambiguous about *s* and *ś,* which are distinguished by the Chinese transcription. The Chinese transcription and Menander's Greek transcription thus agree very well; the underlying form was *Aršilas. Though the etymology of the name remains unknown, it cannot be connected, as some would wish (see endnote 72), with the Old Turkic epithet *kök* 'sky-blue'

in the inscriptions, which surely refers to the blue sky: Heaven, abode of the god of Heaven, Tängri, from whom the Türk rulers claimed to be descended. The inscriptions say (translation by Sinor 1990a: 297), "When high above the blue sky and down below the brown earth had been created, betwixt the two were created the sons of men." The sky god, Tängri, and the earth goddess, Umay, are clearly what the writers had in mind. It is thus probable that *Kök Türk* means 'the Heavenly Blue Turks', as has long been believed by scholars. Although de la Vaissière (2007: 199–200) claims "on sait que le nom du clan royal turc est transcript en sogdien *'šn's* . . . c'est-a-dire très exactement Ashinās," no such form actually occurs in the two inscriptions in which it has been said to occur, as shown in Beckwith (2005b). He ignores the Greek transcription and most of my discussion of the name of the royal clan of the Turks in an appendix entitled "On the Royal Clan of the Turks" (Beckwith 1987a/1993: 206–208), saying only, "Ce n'est pas un titre—*pace* Beckwith—mais un nom de clan," the latter evidently a reference to a Tokharian title I give there, suggesting it is "perhaps the source" of the Turkic clan name.

72. Klyashtornyi (1994: 445–448) and others have argued that the name is Khotanese *āṣṣeiṇa* 'blue' (cf. Rastorgueva and Èdel'man 2000, I: 285) or Tokharian *âśna*, and corresponds to Old Turkic *kök* 'blue', which has traditionally been thought to be used as an epithet in the name *Kök Türk* 'the Blue Türk' in the Old Turkic imperial inscriptions from the Orkhon. Although the idea of Klyashtornyi et al. has gained some acceptance among Turkologists, there are insuperable problems with it. Identifying *kök* with A-shih-na ignores the fact that *kök*, as an adjective, must modify *türk* (those who say there is no adjective class in Turkic ignore syntax rules, but they cannot be ignored), whereas the name of the imperial clan certainly must be a noun. Using *kök* 'blue' *as a noun* would require *Kök Türk* to mean 'The Blue(s) and the Türk(s)' or the like, which makes no sense in the context of the inscriptions or Turkic history. The idea of equating A-shih-na and *kök* is based ultimately on the modern Mandarin reading A-shih-na and ignores the fact that the name was transcribed a millennium and a half ago in the Middle Chinese period, when it was pronounced quite differently. It also requires ignoring the very clear Greek transcription, which agrees with the Middle Chinese transcription; the resulting form Aršilas cannot be reconciled with the Khotanese word for 'blue'. The idea additionally ignores the name of the collateral aristocratic clan of Toñukuk, A-shih-te, though any etymology must explain both names. Claims to have found the name A-shih-na in Old Turkic or Sogdian texts are completely unfounded, as shown in Beckwith (2005b). Finally, attempts to identify Aršilas with phonetically similar names noted in Turkic, Arabic, or other sources should also be viewed with great skepticism. The name is phonologically very alien to Turkic, as are most other early Turkic names. "Of the fifty odd names given to Türk rulers in Chinese sources, only a handful have Turkic equivalents and even fewer are genuinely Turkic" (Sinor 1990a: 290). The

trouble the Turks must have had pronouncing the name Aršilas very likely accounts for the development of the numerous names similar to it attested in later Turkic history, many of which also seem to have been influenced by convergence with various foreign words and names; see Beckwith (1993: 206–208).

73. The sources relating to the rebellion of 755 in the Tibetan Empire are mostly late and full of misunderstandings of Tibetan imperial history, but they reflect something that seems to lie under the surface in the official *Old Tibetan Annals*. The consorts of the assassinated emperor had included the Chinese princess of Chin-ch'eng, who was long dead by the time of the rebellion. Among his grandfather's imperial consorts was a Western Turkic princess of *Aršilas blood known only by her Old Turkic title *khatun* (i.e., *qatun*) 'queen'. The emperor had succeeded to the throne as a child with the help of Khrimalod, who was probably responsible for the overthrow of the emperor known only as the "elder brother" *btsanpo* Lha. For more on the rebellion, see Beckwith (1983).

74. It is often remarked that this or that teacher or translator went to Tibet from one or another foreign country. Though this certainly did happen, in most cases the individuals in question seem to have been living at the time within the boundaries of the Tibetan Empire, which had expanded to include their homes. The famous teacher Padmasambhava, who is largely (if not wholly) legendary, would thus have gone to Central Tibet from Udyâna, which was then a tributary state of the Tibetan Empire. On the putative transmission of Central Asian or *Tazig* ('Arab') Buddhism to the former Zhangzhung area of western Tibet, where it later acquired the name *Bon* (a possible scenario that seems to be ahistorical), see Beckwith (forthcoming-c). If the latter event was not merely possible but actually historical, it would surely have happened in the same way—that is, while the Tibetans were a power in the area of eastern Tokhâristân (the area of modern eastern Afghanistan, southern Uzbekistan, and Tajikistan), which was a thoroughly Buddhist country at the time.

75. The year 740 is the explicit date in the Hebrew work of Jehuda Halevi (who wrote in Muslim Spain in 1140). However, the date remains much disputed. It could alternately have been later in the same century—al-Mas'ûdî (in his *Murûj al-dhahab*) has the Khazars converting to Judaism in the reign of Hârûn al-Rashîd (786–809)—or even in the following century, based on the "Moses coins," which are dated to 837–838, though the appearance of the Moses coins some three decades after the death of Hârûn al-Rashîd hardly confirms the latter's reign as the period in which the Khazars converted, because they could have converted at any time *before* 837/838 (Kovalev 2005). Moreover, the Khazar conversion was a remarkable event, for which a remarkable cause would seem to be needed. This cause was surely the physical devastation, religious oppression, and humiliation suffered by the Khazars under the Arabs in the 730s, as others have argued (Dunlop 1954: 86). And as noted previously, the major Eurasian states, for reasons that are still unclear, adopted one or another

world religion in the mid-eighth century. It was thus the right time for it. For detailed, informed discussion of the sources and arguments, see Golden (2007), who favors the early ninth century for the conversion.

76. The expression "the Indian Half-Century of Islam" was coined by an earlier scholar of Islamic cultural history. Unfortunately, I cannot remember who this unusually perceptive scholar is, and despite much searching have been unable to discover the work in which he writes on this topic. (I have also asked *many* prominent specialists in early Islamic studies I know or have met, but no one has recognized the reference.) As far as I know this scholar is the only one to have made a special point of treating the first half century of the Abbasids—in many ways the formative period of Islamic intellectual culture—as having come under heavy Indian influence. The fact that his work has evidently been completely overlooked, or forgotten, together with the strong opposition among Islamicists to any suggestion of significant Central Asian or Indian influence on Islamic civilization during the formative period, may be taken as confirmation that he was on the right track. Compare the similar reactions of Ancient Near East specialists and Sinologists with regard to outside influence on their respective areas of specialization, as noted earlier.

77. Fakhry (1983: 34) says, "The two Buddhist sects of Vaibhashika and Sautran-tika, the two Brahmin sects of Nyaya and Vaishashika, as well as the Jaina sect, had evolved by the fifth century an atomic theory, apparently independent of the Greek, in which the atomic character of matter, time, and space was set forth and the perishable nature of the world resulting from their composition was emphasized." Though Fakhry rightly includes the Buddhist sects in his discussion, scholarship on these topics in general continues to focus on Hinduism, ignoring the fact that the Arabs invaded and subjugated much of Central Asia by the late seventh century AD and thus came into intense, close contact with the region's high Buddhist culture, which is described in detail by the Chinese monk Hsüan Tsang, who passed through on his way to India a mere two decades earlier. The same remark would seem to apply to the development of the distinctive, high mystical, but "non-Islamic component of *Ṣūfism*" by Abû Yazîd al-Bisṭâmî (d. 875), a Central Asian from western Khurasan. His guru was Abû ʿAlî al-Sindî, a non-Muslim whose name indicates he or his family was originally from Sindh (Fakhry 1983: 241, 243–244).

78. Scholars disagree on the extent of Indian influence on early Arab grammarians. The most prominent specialist, M. G. Carter, in numerous publications (e.g., Carter 1997), argues for Syriac influence alone. However, this view seems to be based largely on the adoption from Syriac of vowel pointing in Arabic, which is not to be doubted but is orthographical and would not seem to have anything to do with the Indian-style treatment of phonology per se in *al-Kitâb*. The absence of Syrians among the early grammarians is notable; those scholars whose origin is known were nearly all non-Arabs, and, as noted, the actual author of the text was from Balkh, the Central Asian center of Buddhist learning.

This question calls for reexamination by scholars familiar with both the Indian and the Arab grammatical traditions.

79. The word *bon* is used in Bonpo texts as the exact equivalent of *chos* 'dharma, the Dharma'. In this sense it is apparently not etymologizable within Tibetan. Its source has not yet been identified. It should also be noted that despite continuing popular belief in the existence of a non-Buddhist religion known as Bon during the Tibetan Empire period, there is not a shred of evidence to support the idea. The first actual textual evidence for the existence of Bon—and of its followers, Bonpos—is in the postimperial period. Although different in some respects from the other sects, it was already very definitely a form of Buddhism. See Beckwith (forthcoming-c).

80. Twitchett and Tietze (1994: 45–46) express uncertainty about the linguistic affiliation of Khitan, but it has long been firmly established that they spoke a Mongolic language. This has been further confirmed by the progress being made in the decipherment of their script. The recent introduction of the non-linguistic term "Para-Mongolic" (Janhunen 2003: 391–402) for Khitan and other early Mongolic languages, and of similar terms for other languages in the vicinity, reveals unclarity about the nature of linguistic relationships, a problem that dominates the linguistics of eastern Eurasia in general. It has been demonstrated once again that there is no such thing as a *Mischsprache* or 'mixed language' (Beckwith 2007a: 195–213), so either Khitan was Mongolic or it was not Mongolic.

81. The claim has recently been made that the golden age of Islamic civilization, including philosophical thought, never ended or declined, but continued right down to the present. Note the defensive statements in Nasr (2006) regarding the suppression of *falsafa* 'philosophy' in the Islamic world, alongside his presentation of evidence of the suppression that directly contradicts his arguments. He stresses throughout that some aspects of philosophy were partially preserved in Shiite schools, among theologians (who were devoted to the explication of dogma), and in other bastions of religious conservatism—only confirming all the more strongly the nearly total loss of freedom of thought in the Islamic world down to modern times, when Western influences (his "modern thought") have restored some freedom, which he criticizes (Nasr 2006: 259 et seq.).

82. It is odd that the Tanguts, despite the relationship of their language to Tibetan, did not adopt or adapt the simple Tibetan alphabetic writing system, though they or others did use it occasionally to transcribe Tangut phonetically. Perhaps they chose to develop a completely new, Chinese-type system for political reasons, but it is notable that they also translated the Buddhist canon from Chinese, not from Tibetan. In any case, the phonology of the Tangut language remains a problematic subject as a result. Most of the scholarship on the topic, from Nevsky (1926) on, has rejected the evidence of the Tibetan interlinear transcriptions in favor of highly debatable interpretations of the complex

rhyme-book system the Tanguts created on the Chinese model, and pronouncements continue to be made about the superiority of the Tangut and Chinese rhyme-book traditions over segmental transcriptions and normal linguistics.

83. The title *Chinggis Khan* (traditionally, 'Genghis Khan', 'Jenghiz Khan', etc.) is believed to mean 'Oceanic [universal] Ruler'. This follows Ramstedt and Pelliot (cited by de Rachewiltz 2004: 460), who take Chinggis [čiŋgis] to be a loanword from Turkic *teŋiz* (Middle Mongol *teŋgis* 'sea' in the *Secret History*) 'sea, ocean' or a dialect form of it. The vowel of the first syllable reflects a Mongol dialect in which Turkic -*e*- shifted to -*i*- as it did in the borrowing of Turkic *tegin* 'prince' as *tigin, which became Middle Mongol *čigin*, or alternately, the form *čiŋgis* derives from a Turkic dialect that already had -*i*- in the first syllable. The title must have been carefully chosen with a view to other rival rulers past and present. Recently it has been proposed that *čiŋgis* here is an adjective meaning 'fierce, hard, tough', and Temüjin's title means 'Fierce Ruler'. This idea has been adopted by several prominent scholars; see the discussion and references in de Rachewiltz (2004: 460). Nevertheless, I find it difficult to accept. Traditional Central Eurasian titles make reference to celestial origins, heavenly mandates, universal rulership, and so forth; Chinggis and his heirs are famous for their explicit belief in these ideas. As noted previously, the title given Temüjin's rival Jamuqa, Gür Khan, means 'Universal Ruler', and the same title was taken by Temüjin's rival Küchlüg when he seized power in the Central Asian realm of the Kara Khitai (q.v. Biran 2005), where it had been the title of the rulers since its foundation. It is highly unlikely that Temüjin, who was or intended to be a much greater Central Eurasian ruler than Jamuqa or Küchlüg had ever been, could have taken a less magnificent title. The equation of 'oceanic' with 'universal' would seem to be supported by the Mongols' later bestowal of the title Dalai Lama 'Ocean Lama', that is, 'Universal Lama', on the head of the Dgelugspa sect of Tibetan Buddhism, to which they had just converted. Moreover, the legend of the Mongols' wolf and doe progenitors crossing the *Teŋgis* 'ocean' or 'sea' to reach the safe new land where they gave birth to the first Mongols was surely known to all. The name Chinggis Khan thus identified Temüjin with the very beginnings of the Mongol nation.

84. The efforts of generations of scholars to prove that Marco Polo was never in China or elsewhere in eastern Eurasia are based on the absolutely false assumption that the published account of his travels represents the true and correct statements of Marco himself. He did not actually write the book *Il Milione*, and he very likely had no say at all in what was finally published as his account. It is also well established that the man who did write the book, Rustichello of Pisa, was a popular romance writer. As such, it may be assumed that he was interested in selling as many copies of his work as possible; it has been demonstrated in great detail that much in the book is his own work, including "whole passages of narrative" taken from a fiction work written by him (Latham 1958: 17);

in general there is no way for us to know today what is Marco's and what is Rustichello's, or in many cases, what the sources of erroneous information are. Moreover, everyone knows, or should know from personal experience, that little if anything related orally to anyone is likely to be reported accurately and, in fact, is more than likely to be distorted out of shape. In view of these problems, the fact that so much accurate material has survived Rustichello's hand not only is astonishing, it shows beyond any reasonable doubt that Marco Polo's own account (which we do not have) was essentially true and accurate. The detail about China, and the Orient in general, that is found in *Il Milione* was and remains unprecedented in depth and accuracy for the period in which it was written: there were no Western written sources from which Marco or Rustichello could have gleaned their detailed information about China and about particular historical individuals and places named there until long after the book was published, and it was not to be superseded for several centuries after its publication. The work of Cleaves (1976), followed by that of Yang Chih-chiu in his 1985 *Yüan shih san lun* (Rossabi 1994: 463 n. 83), has shown conclusively that Marco Polo was in the Great Khanate during the reign of Khubilai.

85. The presence of distinct periods in world history, which many recognize (though few agree on their boundaries), suggests that there were watersheds or divides between the periods, but because historical change is primarily an accretional process, it does not occur at an even rate. There are short periods in which many important connected sequences of events take place. One of the best examples is the mid-eighth century, which was marked by rebellions, revolutions, and so forth across Eurasia. Such periods may be considered watersheds, but they are of course periods themselves. Some periods of history are thus shorter and more densely packed with significant change than others. The Mongol conquest was an important period in itself, worthy of study in its own right, but it did not bring about fundamental change of one kind or another in Eurasia, with the significant exception of the transfer of knowledge from East to West, and to a lesser degree from West to East.

86. Pearson (1987: 14) argues,

> One cannot see the Portuguese as the necessary precursors to the European dominance which in the eighteenth century became world dominance, thanks to the industrial revolution and related scientific and technological developments. The point surely is again that these developments must have produced western European dominance, at least for a time. The fact that the Portuguese rounded the Cape of Good Hope some two and a half centuries previous to this then had no bearing on the outcome. Portuguese navigational triumphs in the fifteenth century must be seen as strictly a *tour de force*.

This is not correct. Europeans dominated the globe before the eighteenth-century "industrial revolution" *because* the Portuguese, Spanish, and others sailed around the world and established trading posts and colonies wherever they could. They succeeded in large part because they already had technically superior weapons and ships, a practically oriented scientific tradition that allowed them to take advantage of opportunities when they presented themselves, and insatiable curiosity about the world. The spread of European power across the globe began with the voyages of Columbus, da Gama, and the other explorers. The question should perhaps be, would the eighteenth-century European "industrial revolution" ever have happened if the explorers had never sailed? Between 1405 and 1433, the Ming Dynasty sent out their Muslim official Cheng Ho on maritime expeditions that reached as far as the east coast of Africa, but after his death in 1434 they sent no more. The Ming declined and fell to the Manchus two centuries later. Despite the advanced cultural and technical level of China, no "industrial revolution" took place there until the twentieth century, and then only under very heavy Western influence.

87. Luxury goods are considered to be items of relatively high cost per unit or amount. Trade in them is contrasted with trade in massive quantities of commodities such as grain, timber, or plain cotton cloth, which have relatively low cost per unit or amount (e.g., Pearson 1987: 24–25). The overt basis of the "luxury goods" characterization of the former type of trade items is the idea that they are not necessary for everyday life and are therefore not an indication of the existence of "real commerce." The covert basis for the characterization is that they are somehow immoral. The fact that even today luxury goods such as computers, cell phones, automobiles, jet planes, and so forth dominate international trade and finance does not stop economic historians from repeating the old moralistically based ideas, which seem to go back to Antiquity. In the case of the trade in "coarse cloth" discussed by Pearson (1987: 25), he says, "It was these cloths which paid for many of the spices of southeast Asia. Indeed, in the sixteenth century in some agreements between the Portuguese and the suppliers, the price of the spices was fixed in cloths, not money." It seems likely that much of this cloth, perhaps most of it, was actually a standardized commodity used as a kind of money, as had long been customary in China (Beckwith 1991).

88. The introduction of Western astronomy and mathematics into China in the seventeenth century was only the beginning. It took Asians a long time to recognize that they had fallen behind Europe in technology, but in fact by the late nineteenth century they had fallen behind in nearly every field of learning, not only technology. Even today many do not realize that in humanistic scholarship Asia is still very far behind in many respects. This seems to be truer the further east one goes from Europe. In the Middle East and in Middle Eastern studies in the West, the concept of scientific critical edition of premodern texts not only is known and accepted among specialists in such literature, it is expected. In India and among foreign Indologists, the idea of critical edition is known and accepted, but in an earlier, much less developed form. In

East Asia and among foreign East Asianists, scientific critical edition is essentially unknown. (See also endnote 13.) In the late twentieth century some Asian writers, led by the journalist Edward Said (1978), accused Western scholars of having "stolen" Asian peoples' cultures *by studying them*. This extreme anti-intellectualism has been well criticized (Lewis 1982). Unfortunately, many Orientalists have unknowingly accepted Said's views and have abandoned the old word *Orientalist* as being somehow, vaguely, bad. From this standpoint all genuine scholars are bad, because they seek the truth and help to enlighten the world.

89. By the time of Nurhachi's son, Hung Taiji ('Abahai', r. 1627–1643, first as khan or 'emperor' of the Latter Chin Dynasty, then from 1636 as emperor of the Manchu-Ch'ing Dynasty), the Manchus had been converted to Tibetan Buddhism, mainly through the efforts of the Mongols and Uighurs, who had themselves converted to Tibetan Buddhism in the Mongol Empire period. The Manchus belonged to the "reformed" Dgelugspa ('virtuous school') sect headed by the Dalai Lama, who had become a politically important reincarnation lineage with the help of the Mongols, including both Eastern and Western Mongols. The dynastic name Ch'ing 'clear' is evidently connected to the name of the holy mountain Ch'ing-liang Shan ('Mount Clear and Cool') in Shansi (Shanxi), where Manchu, Mongol, Uighur, Tibetan, and Chinese Buddhists believed Mañjuśrī resided. The legitimacy of being declared a Buddhist *cakravartin* ruler, or *dharmarâja,* would give the Manchu ruler powerful support from these non-Chinese peoples. See Grupper (1980) and Farquhar (1978). There are other well-argued theories about the etymology of the name *Manju* (e.g., Stary 1990), and it is quite possible that the Manchus deliberately fostered different interpretations among the different peoples who made up their empire, but for the Manchus themselves it is difficult to imagine most of them, as fervent new converts to Buddhism, seeing the name as anything other than *Mañju,* the name of the Bodhisattva of wisdom.

90. Recently some scholars have argued that the Silk Road did not really decline. They have pointed out that the trade routes never completely shut down—which is not surprising, because major phenomena of this sort rarely completely disappear—and that reorientation is what occurred; see, for example, Levi (2002, 2007c). This important new body of scholarship focuses on the growth of trade routes and the movement of traders from India to Central Asia and Russia between the sixteenth and the nineteenth centuries and opens a new dimension in the history of Eurasia that deserves attention. Nevertheless, the trade routes per se, and the attendant traders, are not really the crucial point, as is argued in this book. Moreover, the contention that Central Asia did not decline after the Timurid period, which is not supported by the Central Asian specialists cited by the new view's proponents (e.g., Levi 2007a: 3–4; Markovits 2007: 124–125), is disproved by the attested shrinkage of cities and populations (Levi 2007b: 110; though as Levi points out, population fluctuations did occur

and a few cities simply moved to nearby locations); the cessation of innovations in science, technology, art, literature, and philosophy (which had already been replaced by bigotry; see above in the text); and the failure of Central Asia to keep up with the rest of the world in technology and practically all other fields of human endeavor. Certainly the Central Asian khanates put up a good fight against the expansion of the Russian Empire in the nineteenth century, but they were outclassed militarily and in every other way because of the already marked backwardness and poverty of the region. The final, complete Russian conquest of Western Central Asia and the Manchu-Chinese conquest and colonization of Eastern Central Asia were absolutely disastrous for the economy and culture of Central Asia and the rest of Central Eurasia, which thenceforth fell precipitously into "severe decline" (Markovits 2007: 144), leading to the disastrous situation well known from the late nineteenth century through the late twentieth century. Some space has also been devoted to arguing against the traditional view that the continental trade declined due to the opening of the direct maritime routes between Europe and Asia by Western Europeans (e.g., Levi 2007a; Gommans 2007); on this issue, see the discussion in the text.

91. As already noted, the present book is an attempt to correct the received view of the history of Central Eurasia and of relevant contiguous regions of Eurasia. Chapter 11 is focused on what I see as the main *issues* of the modern period. The inclusion of a small amount of factual detail (compared to the mind-numbing quantity available) is intended to bring the book's sketchy historical narrative more or less down to the present and to provide specific evidence for some of the arguments made; but that is as far as it goes. The modern period tends to dominate all history writing, partly because there is so much detailed information available on modern history (at least, in the eyes of this premodern specialist, who is accustomed to having a relatively small number of explicit, largely unquestioned facts). In order to avoid being drowned in the detail of modern historical works and, even more so, the sources for them, I have mostly relied on a number of standard reference works to get facts straight— for example, for World War II I have relied primarily on Sandler (2001), Dear and Foot (1995), Dunnigan and Nofi (1998), Goralski (1981), and Mowat (1968)— but I have not explicitly cited such sources except in cases where I give a verbatim quotation or depend on them for a substantial part of my argument. When necessary (mostly to find facts which no one else seems to mention, or at least to index) I have used the general works by Stearns (2002), Alexander et al. (1998), and Cook and Stevenson (1998), in addition to specialized works cited in the bibliography. On postmodernists' rejection of facts and abandonment of critical thought, see the preface.

92. Nearly all world history writers, from whatever country in the world, are fixated on Europe, perhaps because the idea of writing a unified "world history" began in Europe and was focused on Europe—the great Ilkhanid scholar and vizier Rashîd al-Dîn's *Jâmi' al-tawârîkh* is, as its name indicates, a 'Collection

of Histories', not a world history. But regardless of the skewed vision of many history writers, no one should be misled into believing that the First World War, however devastating, was in fact a world war, despite the usual name given to it today. It was a European war (Vyvyan 1968: 140; Teed 1992: 506) that bled over into the neighboring Ottoman Near East and to European colonial territories. It would thus be more accurate, and perhaps clearer, to call it the Great War, as was once normal practice, or better, the Great European War. Then the Second World War could be called the World War. For clarity's sake, I follow current practice.

93. The Greek name *Constantinopolis* was shortened and distorted in everyday speech over the centuries, producing a variety of different colloquial pronunciations derived from it, including several similar to 'Istanbul'. The popular theory argued by some scholars that the name Istanbul derives from an unrelated expression in Greek meaning 'into the city' (İnalcik 1997: 224) is incorrect. The Greek expression is clearly a folk etymology intended to explain the colloquial pronunciation of the name.

94. As for the conspiracy theory, and the "significant circumstantial evidence" (Heidenreich 2003: 579–582) that the U.S. leadership knew about the attack on Pearl Harbor beforehand, it is countered not by the misinterpretation of that evidence, or the existence of evidence that contradicts it, but by the impossibility of believing that any U.S. administration was clever enough to plan and execute the rather complex sequence of events required. It is far simpler, and more consistent with American history, to believe that the disastrous mistakes made on that day were due mainly to the stupidity, ignorance, and arrogance of the U.S. leadership, both civilian and military, locally and nationally, whereas the lucky escapes were due to the genuine heroism of the officers and fighting men on the ground, aboard the ships, and in the air. What seems to be widely overlooked is the fact that the covert allies of the United States were already at war with the Axis in Europe. When these allies declared a trade embargo against Japan, inclusive of oil—a critical mineral for a modern country (Japan had no oil of its own)—that was tantamount to a declaration of war. (Note that the first Gulf War in 1990–1991 was caused specifically by the Iraqi seizure of Kuwait and its oil fields.) While the Japanese attack on Pearl Harbor is not excusable, it should be seen in that light. It was only a matter of time, and could hardly have been a surprise to the U.S. political leaders, who indeed seem not to have been really surprised.

95. Although Modernism may be one of the least understood phenomena in world history, it is impossible to understand the Modern period *as history* without understanding it. This section is an essay that attempts to explain what happened in the twentieth century, and why it is still happening. My goal is to stimulate thought on what I see as a historical problem that continues up to the present, so it can be addressed and, maybe, solutions can be found for it. Modernism is on the whole treated very generously by historians, who emphasize

mankind's technical triumphs in the conquest of nature, a generally positive view of scientific progress, and so on. But this has little to do with Modernism as a force—a largely negative force—in modern history. Belief in progress, philosophical positivism, and so on, were certainly prominent elements at times, as usually noted by intellectual historians, but the overtly negative nature of Modernism can hardly be reconciled with the largely approving stance taken by most intellectual historians toward it. Scott (1988: 4–5) gives an excellent, often insightful survey of the usual idea of modernism, which he calls "high-modernist ideology": "It is best conceived as a strong, one might even say muscle-bound, version of the self-confidence about scientific and technical progress, the expansion of production, the growing satisfaction of human needs, the mastery of nature (including human nature), and, above all, the rational design of social order commensurate with the scientific understanding of natural laws. It originated, of course, in the West, as a by-product of unprecedented progress in science and industry." He connects this ideology to political power, insofar as it was necessary for the Modernists to get the backing of the state to carry out their programs, notably "huge dams, centralized communication and transportation hubs, large factories and farms, and grid cities," which "fit snugly into a high-modernist view and also answered their political interests as state officials." The central figures in this "high-modernism" are "planners, engineers, architects, scientists, and technicians whose skills and status it celebrated as the designers of the new order. High-modernist faith was no respecter of traditional political boundaries; it could be found across the political spectrum from left to right but particularly among those who wanted to use state power to bring about huge, utopian changes in people's work habits, living patterns, moral conduct, and worldview." Finally, he notes, "Nor was this utopian vision dangerous in and of itself. Where it animated plans in liberal parliamentary societies and where the planners therefore had to negotiate with organized citizens, it could spur reform." If an authoritarian state adopted the "high-modernist" ideology and was "willing and able to use the full weight of its coercive power to bring these high-modernist designs into being," however, then would "the combination become potentially lethal."

96. In eastern Central Eurasia, "forced laicization was the fate of most lamas, but mass executions have been documented (through the exhumation of mass graves, records, etc.) in Mongolia. This was probably the case also in Buriatia and Kalmykia, but I'm not as familiar with them. The physical infrastructure was heavily damaged in the 1930s (due to the significant resistance), but was mostly eliminated only in the succeeding decades" (Christopher Atwood, per. comm., 2007).

97. Adorno (1997: 29) says "radicalism itself must pay the price that it is no longer radical. . . . The more art expels the preestablished, the more it is thrown back on what purports to get by, as it were, without borrowing from what has become distant and foreign." But it is not the loss of fashionableness that matters,

or the danger of relying on the validity of earlier art traditions. There is no reason great artists cannot make great art in any tradition, whether abstractionism, expressionism, or whatever. But with the elimination of *Art itself*, no artists can make art, no matter what their style or fashion.

98. The vast majority of contemporary non-European poets writing in Europeanized traditions have abandoned the traditional connection between poetry and music that still exists in their own cultures. For example, it is now normal to hear Modern verse in Chinese read like prose—a truly unaesthetic experience. The genuine Chinese poetry of the past was chanted, and still is by a few traditionalists. The same goes for Persian and Japanese poetry, but although in those cultures the chanting tradition is still very much alive for *classical* poetry, modern verse is read and typically sounds just as pitiful as it usually does in English. It is quite logical and appropriate to read most *Modern* verse as prose—that is really what most of it is—but this then entirely vacates the world of genuine poetry for our own time. The practice of reading poetry has been extended to pre-Modern verse as well, thus destroying even the traditional art in those cultures where it still exists. If some poets prefer to write prose disguised as poetry, that is fine, but one would hope that some other poets would notice and begin writing, and even chanting, genuine poetry once again to fill the gap. The fact that some Modern writers, such as Ezra Pound and Carl Sandburg, advocated singing or chanting poetry, or actually went so far as to attempt such performances, with embarrassing results, is irrelevant. Modern poetry had already become completely divorced from an accepted musical tradition and neither they nor anyone else could reconnect the two.

99. After Strauss backed away from further movement toward atonality, he produced his greatest opera, *Der Rosenkavalier*. Szegedy-Maszák (2001: 250) rightly remarks, "Subversiveness or conservatism is a matter of perspective. The composer of *Elektra* was an avant-garde musician; that of *Vier letzte Lieder* was a conservative artist." Yet from the point of view of the "big picture," it does not really matter that *Elektra* was progressive, while *Der Rosenkavalier* was conservative; after all, both operas are marked by considerable musical innovation and Strauss's unique, brilliant sound. What is significant is that he recognized and rejected Modernism per se, the movement that culminated in the destruction of the Western art-music tradition during his own lifetime. That is why Strauss is one of the few composers who succeeded in writing great art music in the twentieth century.

100. "The failure of modernism in music vis-à-vis the public is perhaps unique with respect to twentieth-century modernism in general. Unlike modernism in architecture, painting, and literature, musical modernism did not experience any form of generalization or imitation in mass culture owing to its failure to win the allegiance of any of the traditional audiences of high culture" (Botstein 1998: 259). Botstein's statement is not really true for domestic architecture, where the public frequently can exercise some choice over its visual environ-

ment. In general domestic architecture has seen only a simplification of style and the increasingly vapid imitation of old forms. Also, with respect to the success of Modernism in painting and literature, the "generalization or imitation" mentioned by Botstein was rather superficial, with the exception of a few early works that were canonized soon after their production, such as T. S. Eliot's *The Waste Land*.

101. It is notable that in its music and program *The Rite of Spring* appears to be in part imitative of a then forgotten ballet by the Baroque composer Jean-Féry Rebel (1666–1747), *The Elements*, which begins with a scene, "Chaos," dominated by highly dissonant polychords. The ballet had been performed in Russia in Rebel's day. Stravinsky was deeply interested in Baroque music literature and very likely knew the composition. Ironically, one of the most remarkable developments in art music in the latter half of the twentieth century was the great popularity of Baroque music.

102. Though Adorno's book includes many brilliant flashes of insight, it also includes statements such as the claim that "modern art that laid claim to dignity would be pitilessly ideological. To act dignified it would have to put on airs, strike a pose, claim to be other than what it can be. It is precisely its seriousness that compels modern art to lay aside pretensions long since hopelessly compromised by the Wagnerian art religion. A solemn tone would condemn artworks to ridiculousness, just as would the gestures of grandeur and might. . . . Radical art today is synonymous with dark art; its primary color is black. Much contemporary production is irrelevant because it takes no note of this and childishly delights in color. . . . The injustice committed by all cheerful art, especially by entertainment, is probably an injustice to the dead; to accumulated, speechless pain" (Adorno 1997: 39–40). Adorno's intent—to make an aesthetics of art from the inside out—is as remarkable as his passion for art, but it really has nothing to do with the production of art itself. The basic problem is Modernism, which remains in place unchanged.

103. The only examination of Modernism so far is from the inside—that is, there are Modernist or crypto-Modernist analyses of Modernism, which hardly make much sense, but no others. So-called Postmodernist criticism and theory, which is in fact simply hyper-Modernism, is even less examined. The points raised here are to be distinguished from the traditional conflict between the Ancients and the Moderns, as in many works of literature and criticism going back many centuries. "William Ockham's work was, of course, only one factor in the crisis of medieval thought and culture, manifested on the intellectual side in the widespread triumph of the *via moderna* over Thomists, Scotists, and others, whose doctrines were lumped together under the label of the *via antiqua*" (Fairweather 1970: 372). Similarly, "Swift compared the Ancients to bees and the Moderns to spiders, using the opposition between productive and parasitic beings to suggest a distinction between creative originality and derivativeness, and went as far as emphasizing that 'the Moderns were much

the more ancient of the two,' in a work published in 1704 and entitled 'A Full and True Account of the Battel Fought last Friday, Between the Ancient and the Modern Books in St. James's Library'" (Szegedy-Maszák 2001: 61). The tension between the two tendencies referred to in the above quotations was on the whole beneficial in the creation of art. Artists agreed on the goal—Art—and on the ideal of Beauty (however defined); they only disagreed on how the two were to be achieved.

104. Some rock musicians have made laudable attempts to raise the artistic level of their music, but resurrecting old pre-Modern models or attempting to turn the negative Modern model into a positive one has not worked. Frank Zappa is perhaps the best-known artist who introduced Modern elements into his music. Many trained musicians have a high appreciation for his work, but despite the humor and intellect in Zappa's work, his Modern harmonies and melodic lines actually alienated many listeners. If he had gone a little further in that direction he would have lost more or less all of them, just as Modern art composers have, for the same reasons. It is necessary to accept the new music and work at improving it from within; trying to make it into something else will cause it to lose its essence, just as classical art music did. The object of artists' creative attentions must be treated gently, nurtured, and raised with careful regard to the cultivation of refinement and taste. It is necessary to raise the artistic level of rock or popular music while still following, essentially, its own rules and traditions. Renaissance musicians did just that, taking popular dance and song tunes and playing them more artistically, applying Renaissance polyphony to them, and so on, taking what was good and making it a little better, until classical music was born.

105. The section on Chinese terminology in the epilogue largely repeats an argument presented in a conference paper, "The Concept of the 'Barbarian' in Chinese Historiography and Western Sinology: Rhetoric and the Creation of Fourth World Nations in Inner Asia," which was given in a symposium at the Association for Asian Studies in Boston, 1987. The long-promised symposium volume never materialized, and by the time that fact became official I was interested in other topics. Unfortunately, the paper was written on a Bronze Age computer and at the time of writing I no longer have my own copy, though others evidently do. (It has circulated in samizdat ever since, and despite the exhortation emblazoned on it not to cite it without permission of the author, it has been cited nevertheless.) I have written the argument completely anew here.

106. The theory of Khazanov (1984) has been accepted by many, including specialists (e.g., Drompp 2005: 10–12; Di Cosmo 1999a), and taken to its logical extreme by nonspecialists, particularly Barfield (1989). Allsen (1989: 83) follows Khazanov's theory "that the nomads' economy is 'non-autarkic', that is, so specialized in pastoral production that many essentials are lacking." More specifically, he claims that "pastoral nomads do not and cannot supply all their needs

from domestic resources. . . . They regularly acquire necessary economic resources from the sedentary world and appropriate various aspects of sedentary
culture" (Allsen 1997: 101). Khazanov, in choosing one mode of production
(pastoral nomadism), insists that specialists in it should also be specialists in
another mode of production or else they are "non-autarkic." By this standard
nearly everyone in every society is non-autarkic, including the Roman or Chinese agriculturalists, urbanites, and so on. It is surely doubtful that any people
anywhere at any time, other than hunter-gatherers (and perhaps not even
them) have ever been truly "autarkic." Barfield goes much further, arguing that
"the primary purpose of the Hsiung-nu central government was to extract resources from China in the form of booty and tribute or to compel trade on ad-
vantageous terms" (Barfield 1989: 83).

107. Allsen (1997: 106) comments rightly, "The peoples of the steppe were not a premodern equivalent of United Parcel Service, disinterestedly conveying wares
hither and yon between the centers of civilization. Their history and their pri-
orities must be brought more fully into the discussion if we are to understand
these important contacts between East and West." His book concludes, "many
of the commodities and ideas that successfully made the long journey across
Eurasia from antiquity to early modern times did so because the intermediaries, 'those who lived in felt-walled tents,' and who in the best of times dressed
in gold brocade, found them meaningful in the context of their own cultural
traditions."

108. In another randomly chosen example of Barfield's approach, he notes that Li
Shih-min (T'ang T'ai-tsung), the son of the T'ang Dynasty's founder, "himself
had murdered two of his brothers and they had tried to poison him. He forced
his own father from the throne" (Barfield 1989: 142). This sounds promising,
but on further reading it transpires that Barfield is *not* arguing that the Chinese were just as bloody as the Turks could be, if not bloodier, but quite the
contrary. He concludes, "The palace culture for which T'ang was justly famous
in later times should not hide the fact that the early T'ang elite in the northwest
was close enough to the frontier Turks in so many ways that Li Shih-min could
become their kaghan without stepping out of character." See the text for the
underlying misconceptions here.

109. "Nomadic imperial confederacies came into existence only in periods when it
was possible to link themselves to the Chinese economy. The nomads employed
a strategy of extortion to gain trade rights and subsidies from China. They
raided the frontier and then negotiated a peace treaty with the Chinese court.
Native dynasties in China were willing to pay the nomads off because this was
cheaper than going to war with people who could avoid retaliation by moving
out of range" (Barfield 1989: 9). Sinor (1978, 1990b: 4 et seq.) focuses on greed.
Cf. Biran (2005: 14), Drompp (2005: 10 et seq.), and many others. Barfield (1989:
11), noting that the Mongols were an exception, makes the interesting distinction between "the nomads of Mongolia who established steppe empires that

ruled the frontier successfully in tandem with China for centuries, and the nomads from Manchuria who established dynasties within China but never created powerful empires on the steppe." The "Manchurians," however, were mostly not nomads.

110. In most, if not all, instances where sufficient sources exist to reveal the motivation for the attack (i.e., other than the bare fact that a "raid" on such and such a locality supposedly took place), they actually *were* armies. Di Cosmo's (1999b: 23 et seq.) earlier view, according to which the nomadic empires, despite severely limited resources, had significant military power that the nomads used to extort wealth from peripheral states by raids and forced tribute, apparently derives from Khazanov (1984). People captured by Central Eurasians or by peripheral peoples in war generally ended up on the slave market far from their homelands, though some were kept locally as domestic slaves. The history of slavery in Central Eurasia is not yet well understood.

111. It is remarkable that, like so much else in Iranian lore, thousands of volumes, or millions of verses, of Zoroastrian texts, supposedly in Avestan, are said to have once existed, but due to the evil deeds of one or another invading foreign nation the great libraries of the Persian kings were destroyed and all the books were lost. The dating of the texts is a highly contentious topic, but, textually speaking, any date that is earlier than the physically attested texts or their internal evidence, or specific external evidence such as quotations in dated texts, is hypothetical.

BIBLIOGRAPHY

Abicht, Karl Ernst 1886. *Herodotos, für den Schulgebrauch*. Zweiter Band. Zweites Heft: Buch IV. Dritte verbesserte Auflage. Leipzig: Teubner.

Adams, Douglas Q. 1999. *A Dictionary of Tocharian B*. Amsterdam: Rodopi.

Adorno, Theodor, et al., 1997. *Aesthetic Theory*. Trans. Robert Hullot-Kentor. Minneapolis: University of Minnesota Press.

Ahmad, Zahiruddin 1970. *Sino-Tibetan Relations in the Seventeenth Century*. Rome: Istituto Italiano per il Medio ed Estremo Oriente.

Alexander, Fran, et al., eds. 1998. *Encyclopedia of World History*. Oxford: Oxford University Press.

Allsen, Thomas T. 1987. *Mongol Imperialism: The Policies of the Grand Qan Möngke in China, Russia, and the Islamic Lands, 1251–1259*. Berkeley: University of California Press.

———— 1989. Mongolian Princes and Their Merchant Partners, 1200–1260. *Asia Major*, 3rd ser., 2.2: 83–126.

———— 1994. The Rise of the Mongolian Empire and Mongolian Rule in North China. In Herbert Franke and Denis Twitchett, eds., *The Cambridge History of China*, vol. 6: *Alien Regimes and Border States, 907–1368*, 321–413. Cambridge: Cambridge University Press.

———— 1997. *Commodity and Exchange in the Mongol Empire: A Cultural History of Islamic Textiles*. Cambridge: Cambridge University Press.

———— 2006. *The Royal Hunt in Eurasian History*. Philadelphia: University of Pennsylvania Press.

Anderson, Graham 2004. *King Arthur in Antiquity*. London: Routledge.

Anonymous 1990. Җаңһр: хальмг баатрлг эпос (=Джангар: калмыцкий героический эпос). Moscow: Glavnaja redakcija vostočnoj literatury.

Arkenberg, J. S., ed. 1998. *The* Karnamik-i-Ardashir, *or* The Records of Ardashir. Fordham University. http://www.fordham.edu/halsall/ancient/ardashir.html.

Arreguín-Toft, Ivan 2005. *How the Weak Win Wars: A Theory of Asymmetric Conflict*. New York: Cambridge University Press.

Asao, Naohiro 1991. The Sixteenth-Century Unification. Trans. Bernard Susser. In John W. Hall, ed., *The Cambridge History of Japan*, vol. 4: *Early Modern Japan*, 40–95. Cambridge: Cambridge University Press.

Atwood, Christopher P. 2004. *Encyclopedia of Mongolia and the Mongol Empire*. New York: Facts on File.

Audi, Robert, ed. 1999. *The Cambridge Dictionary of Philosophy*. 2nd ed. Cambridge: Cambridge University Press.

Babcock, Michael A. 2005. *The Night Attila Died: Solving the Murder of Attila the Hun*. New York: Berkley Books.

Bachrach, Bernard S. 1973. *A History of the Alans in the West: From Their First Appearance in the Sources of Classical Antiquity through the Early Middle Ages.* Minneapolis: University of Minnesota Press.

—— 1977. *Early Medieval Jewish Policy in Western Europe.* Minneapolis: University of Minnesota Press.

Bagley, Robert 1999. Shang Archaeology. In Michael Loewe and Edward L. Shaughnessy, eds., *The Cambridge History of Ancient China: From the Origins of Civilization to 221 B.C.,* 124–231. Cambridge: Cambridge University Press.

Bailey, H. W. 1985. *Indo-Scythian Studies, Being Khotanese Texts, VII.* Cambridge: Cambridge University Press.

Barber, Elizabeth Wayland 1999. *The Mummies of Ürümchi.* New York: W. W. Norton.

Barbieri-Low, Anthony J. 2000. *Wheeled Vehicles in the Chinese Bronze Age (c. 2000–741 B.C.).* Sino-Platonic Papers No. 99. Philadelphia: Department of Asian and Middle Eastern Studies, University of Pennsylvania.

Barfield, Thomas J. 1989. *The Perilous Frontier: Nomadic Empires and China.* Cambridge, Mass.: Basil Blackwell.

Barthold, W. W. 1977. *Turkestan down to the Mongol Invasion.* Trans. T. Minorsky. 4th ed. London: E.J.W. Gibb Memorial Trust.

Baxter, William H. 1992. *A Handbook of Old Chinese Phonology.* Berlin: Mouton de Gruyter.

Beasley, W. G. 1989. The Foreign Threat and the Opening of the Ports. In Marius B. Jansen, ed., *The Cambridge History of Japan,* vol. 5: *The Nineteenth Century,* 259–307. Cambridge: Cambridge University Press.

Bečka, Jan 1995. *Historical Dictionary of Myanmar.* London: Scarecrow Press.

Beckwith, Christopher I. 1983. The Revolt of 755 in Tibet. *Wiener Studien zur Tibetologie und Buddhismuskunde* 10: 1–16.

—— 1984a. Aspects of the Early History of the Central Asian Guard Corps in Islam. *Archivum Eurasiae Medii Aevi* 4: 29–43.

—— 1984b. The Plan of the City of Peace: Central Asian Iranian Factors in Early 'Abbâsid Design. *Acta Orientalia Academiae Scientiarum Hungaricae* 38: 143–164.

—— 1987a. *The Tibetan Empire in Central Asia: A History of the Struggle for Great Power among Tibetans, Turks, Arabs, and Chinese during the Early Middle Ages.* Princeton: Princeton University Press (= Beckwith 1987a/1993).

—— 1987b. The Tibetans in the Ordos and North China: Considerations on the Role of the Tibetan Empire in World History. In C. I. Beckwith, ed., *Silver on Lapis,* 3–11. Bloomington: Tibet Society.

—— 1987c. The Concept of the 'Barbarian' in Chinese Historiography and Western Sinology: Rhetoric and the Creation of Fourth World Nations in Inner Asia. Paper presented at the Association for Asian Studies annual meeting, Boston.

——, ed. 1987d. *Silver on Lapis.* Bloomington: Tibet Society.

—— 1989. The Location and Population of Tibet According to Early Islamic Sources. *Acta Orientalia Academiae Scientiarum Hungaricae* 43: 163–170.

—— 1991. The Impact of the Horse and Silk Trade on the Economies of T'ang China and the Uighur Empire: On the Importance of International Commerce in the Early Middle Ages. *Journal of the Economic and Social History of the Orient* 34: 183–198.

—— 1993. *The Tibetan Empire in Central Asia: A History of the Struggle for Great Power among Tibetans, Turks, Arabs, and Chinese during the Early Middle Ages*. Paperback edition, slightly revised, with a new afterword. Princeton: Princeton University Press (= Beckwith 1987a/1993).

—— 1996. The Morphological Argument for the Existence of Sino-Tibetan. *Pan-Asiatic Linguistics*, vol. 3, 812–826. Proceedings of the Fourth International Symposium on Languages and Linguistics, January 8–10. Bangkok: Mahidol University at Salaya.

—— 2002a. The Sino-Tibetan Problem. In C. I. Beckwith, ed., *Medieval Tibeto-Burman Languages*, 113–157. Leiden: Brill.

——, ed. 2002b. *Medieval Tibeto-Burman Languages*. Leiden: Brill.

—— 2003. Introducing Grendel. In R. Aczel and P. Nemes, eds., *The Finer Grain: Essays in Honor of Mihály Szegedy-Maszák*, 301–311. Uralic and Altaic Series, vol. 169. Bloomington: Indiana University.

—— 2004a. *Koguryo, the Language of Japan's Continental Relatives: An Introduction to the Historical-Comparative Study of the Japanese-Koguryoic Languages, with a Preliminary Description of Archaic Northeastern Middle Chinese*. Leiden: Brill. (2nd ed., Leiden: Brill, 2007.)

—— 2004b. Old Chinese. In Philipp Strazny, ed., *Encyclopedia of Linguistics*, vol. 2, 771–774. New York: Fitzroy Dearborn.

—— 2005a. The Ethnolinguistic History of the Early Korean Peninsula Region: Japanese-Koguryoic and Other Languages in the Koguryo, Paekche, and Silla Kingdoms. *Journal of Inner and East Asian Studies* 2.2: 34–64.

—— 2005b. On the Chinese Names for Tibet, Tabghatch, and the Turks. *Archivum Eurasiae Medii Aevi* 14: 7–22.

—— 2006a. Introduction: Toward a Tibeto-Burman Theory. In C. I. Beckwith, ed., *Medieval Tibeto-Burman Languages II*, 1–38. Leiden: Brill, 2006.

—— 2006b. The Sonority Sequencing Principle and Old Tibetan Syllable Margins. In C. I. Beckwith, ed., *Medieval Tibeto-Burman Languages II*, 45–55. Leiden: Brill, 2006.

—— 2006c. Old Tibetan and the Dialects and Periodization of Old Chinese. In C. I. Beckwith, ed., *Medieval Tibeto-Burman Languages II*, 179–200. Leiden: Brill, 2006.

—— 2006d. Comparative Morphology and Japanese-Koguryoic History: Toward an Ethnolinguistic Solution of the Altaic Problem. In Motoki Nakajima, ed., *Arutaigo kenkyû—Altaistic Studies*, 121–137. Tokyo: Daito Bunka University.

—— 2006e. Methodological Observations on Some Recent Studies of the Early Ethnolinguistic History of Korea and Vicinity. *Altai Hakpo* 16: 199–234.

——, ed. 2006f. *Medieval Tibeto-Burman Languages II*. Leiden: Brill.

—— 2007a. *Koguryo, the Language of Japan's Continental Relatives: An Introduction to the Historical-Comparative Study of the Japanese-Koguryoic Languages, with a Preliminary Description of Archaic Northeastern Middle Chinese.* 2nd ed. Leiden: Brill. (1st edition, Leiden: Brill, 2004.)

—— 2007b. *Phoronyms: Classifiers, Class Nouns, and the Pseudopartitive Construction.* New York: Peter Lang.

—— 2007c. On the Proto-Indo-European Obstruent System. *Historische Sprachforschung* 120: 1–19.

—— forthcoming-a. The Frankish Name of the King of the Turks. *Archivum Eurasiae Medii Aevi.*

—— forthcoming-b. A Note on the Name and Identity of the Junghars. *Mongolian Studies.*

—— forthcoming-c. On Zhangzhung and Bon. In Henk Blezer, ed., *Emerging Bon.* Halle: IITBS GmbH.

Benedict, Paul 1972. *Sino-Tibetan: A Conspectus.* Cambridge: Cambridge University Press.

Benjamin, Craig 2003. The Yuezhi Migration and Sogdia. In Matteo Compareti, Paola Raffetta, and Gianroberto Scarcia, eds., *Erān ud Anērān: Studies Presented to Boris Ilich Marshak on the Occasion of His 70th Birthday.* http://www.trans-oxiana.org/Eran/ (=*Erān ud Anērān. Studies Presented to Boris Il'ic Marsak on the Occasion of His 70th Birthday.* Venice: Libreria Editrice Cafoscarina, 2006).

Bergh, Simon van den, trans. 1954. Averroës, *Tahâfut al-Tahâfut (The Incoherence of the Incoherence).* London: Luzac. http://www.muslimphilosophy.com/ir/tt/index.html.

Bergholz, Fred W. 1993. *The Partition of the Steppe: The Struggle of the Russians, Manchus, and the Zunghar Mongols for Empire in Central Asia, 1619–1758.* New York: Peter Lang.

Bilimoria, Purushottama 1998. Kauṭilya (*fl. c.* 321–*c.* 296 BC). In Edward Craig, ed., *Routledge Encyclopedia of Philosophy,* 220–222. London: Routledge.

Biran, Michal 2005. *The Empire of the Qara Khitai in Eurasian History: Between China and the Islamic World.* Cambridge: Cambridge University Press.

Bivar, A.D.H. 1983a. The Political History of Iran under the Arsacids. In Ehsan Yarshater, ed., *Cambridge History of Iran,* vol. 3: *The Seleucid, Parthian and Sasanian Periods, Part 1,* 21–99. Cambridge: Cambridge University Press.

—— 1983b. The History of Eastern Iran. In Ehsan Yarshater, ed., *Cambridge History of Iran,* vol. 3: *The Seleucid, Parthian and Sasanian Periods, Part 1,* 181–231. Cambridge: Cambridge University Press.

Blair, Peter Hunter 2003. *An Introduction to Anglo-Saxon England.* 3rd ed. Cambridge: Cambridge University Press.

Blockley, R. C., trans. 1983. *The Fragmentary Classicising Historians of the Later Roman Empire: Eunapius, Olympiodorus, Priscus and Malchus*. 2 vols. Liverpool: Cairns.

——, ed. and transl. 1985. *The History of Menander the Guardsman*. Liverpool: Francis Cairns.

Boltz, William G. 1994. *The Origin and Early Development of the Chinese Writing System*. New Haven: American Oriental Society.

Bosworth, C. E. 1968. The Political and Dynastic History of the Iranian World (A.D. 1000–1217). In John A. Boyle, ed., *Cambridge History of Iran*, vol. 5: *The Saljuq and Mongol Periods*, 1–202. Cambridge: Cambridge University Press.

—— 1994. Abū Ḥafṣ 'Umar al-Kirmānī and the Rise of the Barmakids. *Bulletin of the School of Oriental and African Studies* 57.2: 262–282.

—— 1997. Khʷārazm. *E.I.*₂ IV: 1060–1065.

—— 2007. Ḳarā Khiṭāy. In P. Bearman, Th. Bianquis, C. E. Bosworth, E. van Donzel, and W. P. Heinrichs, eds., *Encyclopaedia of Islam*. Online edition. Leiden: Brill.

Bosworth, Clifford Edmund, et al. 1995. 'Othmānli. *The Encyclopaedia of Islam, New Edition*, vol. 8, 120–231. Leiden: Brill.

Botstein, Leon 1998. Modern Music. In Michael Kelly, ed., *Encyclopedia of Aesthetics*, vol. 3, 254–259. New York: Oxford University Press.

Bovingdon, Gardner 2004. *Autonomy in Xinjiang: Han Nationalist Imperatives and Uyghur Discontent*. Washington, D.C.: East-West Center Washington.

Bovingdon, Gardner, and Nebijan Tursun 2004. Contested Histories. In S. F. Starr, ed., *Xinjiang: China's Muslim Frontier*, 353–374. Armonk: M. E. Sharpe.

Boyle, John Andrew 1968. Dynastic and Political History of the Il-Khans. In John Andrew Boyle, ed., *The Cambridge History of Iran*, vol. 5: *The Saljuq and Mongol periods*, 303–421. Cambridge: Cambridge University Press.

Brooks, E. Bruce 1999. *Alexandrian Motifs in Chinese Texts*. Sino-Platonic Papers, No. 96. Philadelphia: University of Pennsylvania.

Brulet, Raymond 1997. La tombe de Childéric et la topographie funéraire de Tournai à la fin du Vᵉ siècle. In Michel Rouche, ed., *Clovis: histoire & mémoire*, 59–78. Paris: Presses de l'Université de Paris-Sorbonne.

Brune, Lester H. 2003. *Chronological History of U.S. Foreign Relations*. New York: Routledge.

Bryant, Edwin F. 1999. Linguistic Substrata and the Indigenous Aryan Debate. In Johannes Bronkhorst and Madhav M. Deshpande, eds., *Aryan and Non-Aryan in South Asia: Evidence, Interpretation and Ideology*, 59–83. Proceedings of the International Seminar on Aryan and Non-Aryan in South Asia, University of Michigan, Ann Arbor, 25–27 October 1996. Cambridge, Mass.: Harvard University Department of Sanskrit and Indian Studies.

—— 2001. *The Quest for the Origins of Vedic Culture: The Indo-Aryan Migration Debate*. Oxford: Oxford University Press.

Bryant, Edwin F., and Laurie L. Patton 2005. *The Indo-Aryan Controversy: Evidence and Inference in Indian History*. London: Routledge.

Bryce, Trevor 2002. *Life and Society in the Hittite World*. Oxford: Oxford University Press.

—— 2005. *The Kingdom of the Hittites*. New ed. Oxford: Oxford University Press.

Buck, David D. 2002. Chinese Civil War of 1945–1949. In David Levinson and Karen Christensen, eds., *Encyclopedia of Modern Asia*, 29–31. New York: Charles Scribner's Sons.

Buell, Paul 2002. Chinese Communist Party. In David Levinson and Karen Christensen, eds., *Encyclopedia of Modern Asia*, 31–32. New York: Charles Scribner's Sons.

Burney, Charles 2004. *Historical Dictionary of the Hittites*. Lanham, Md.: Scarecrow Press.

Burrow, Thomas 1935. Tokharian Elements in the Kharosthi Documents from Chinese Turkestan. *Journal of the Royal Asiatic Society* 1935: 665–675.

—— 1937. *The Language of the Kharoṣṭhī Documents from Chinese Turkestan*. Cambridge: Cambridge University Press.

Burns, Thomas S. 1980. *The Ostrogoths: Kingship and Society*. Wiesbaden: F. Steiner.

Byington, Mark E. 2003. A History of the Puyo State, Its People, and Its Legacy. Ph.D. dissertation, Harvard University.

Calmard, J. 1993. Mudjtahid. $E.I._2$ VII: 295–304.

Cancik, Hubert, and Helmuth Schneider, eds. 1996. *Der Neue Pauly: Enzyklopädie der Antike. Altertum. Band I*. Stuttgart: Metzler.

Carter, M.G. 1997. Sībawayhi. $E.I._2$ IX: 524–531.

Chadwick, John 1958. *The Decipherment of Linear B*. Cambridge: Cambridge University Press.

Chavannes, Édouard 1903. *Documents sur les Tou-kiue (Turcs) occidentaux*. St. Petersburg: Commissionnaires de l'Académie impériale des sciences; repr. Taipei: Ch'eng-wen, 1969.

Ch'en, Mei-Chin 1992. The Eminent Chinese Monk Hsuan-Tsang: His Contributions to Buddhist Scripture Translation and to the Propagation of Buddhism in China. Ph.D. dissertation, University of Wisconsin, Madison.

Childs-Johnson, Elizabeth 2003. Fu zi 婦子 (好) the Shang 商 Woman Warrior. Paper presented at the Fourth International Conference on Chinese Paleography, Chinese University of Hong Kong, October 15–17.

Christian, David 1998. *A History of Russia, Central Asia and Mongolia*, vol. 1: *Inner Eurasia from Prehistory to the Mongol Empire*. Oxford: Blackwell.

—— 2000. Silk Roads or Steppe Roads? The Silk Roads in World History. *Journal of World History* 2.1: 1–26.

Clark, Larry V. 1998a. Chuvash. In Lars Johanson and Éva Á. Csató, eds., *The Turkic Languages*, 434–452. London: Routledge.

—— 1998b. *Turkmen Reference Grammar*. Wiesbaden: Harrassowitz.

—— 2000. The Conversion of Bügü Khan to Manichaeism. In Ronald E. Emmerick, Werner Sundermann, and Peter Zieme, eds., *Studia Manichaica. IV. Inter-*

nationaler Kongress zum Manichäismus, Berlin, 14.–18. Juli 1997, 83–123. Berlin: Akademie Verlag.

Clauson, Gerard 1967. *An Etymological Dictionary of Pre-Thirteenth Century Turkish*. Oxford: Clarendon Press.

Cleaves, Francis Woodman 1976. A Chinese Source Bearing on Marco Polo's Departure from China and His Arrival in Persia. *Harvard Journal of Asiatic Studies* 36: 181–203.

Coblin, W. South 2006. *A Handbook of 'Phags-pa Chinese*. Honolulu: University of Hawai'i Press.

Colarusso, John 2002. *Nart Sagas from the Caucasus: Myths and Legends from the Circassians, Abazas, Abkhaz, and Ubykhs*. Princeton: Princeton University Press.

Combs, Kristie 2006. A Study of Merit and Power in Tibetan Thangka Painting. M.A. thesis, Indiana University, Bloomington.

Conlon, Frank F. 1985. Caste, Community and Colonialism: Elements of Population Recruitment and Rule in British Bombay, 1665–1830. *Journal of Urban History* 11: 181–208.

Conquest, Robert 1968. *The Great Terror: Stalin's Purge of the Thirties*. New York: Macmillan.

—— 1986. *The Harvest of Sorrow: Soviet Collectivization and the Terror-Famine*. New York: Oxford University Press.

—— 1990. *The Great Terror: A Reassessment*. New York: Oxford University Press.

Cook, Chris, and John Stevenson 1998. *The Longman Handbook of Modern European History, 1763–1997*. 3rd ed. London: Longman.

Coward, Harold G., and K. Kunjunni Raja 1990. *Encyclopedia of Indian Philosophies: The Philosophy of the Grammarians*. Delhi: Motilal Banarsidass.

Crone, Patricia 1987. *Meccan Trade and the Rise of Islam*. Princeton: Princeton University Press.

Čunakovskij, O. M., ed. and trans. 1987. Книга деяний Ардашира сына Папака. Moscow: Nauka.

Czeglédy, K. 1983. From East to West: The Age of Nomadic Migrations in Eurasia. Trans. P. Golden. *Archivum Eurasiae Medii Aevi* 3: 25–125.

Dalby, Michael T. 1979. Court Politics in Late T'ang Times. In Denis Twitchett, ed., *The Cambridge History of China*, vol. 3: *Sui and T'ang China, 589–906, Part 1*, 561–681. Cambridge: Cambridge University Press.

Dani, Ahmad Hasan, et al., eds. 1992–2005. *History of Civilizations of Central Asia*. Paris: Unesco.

Daniel, Elton L. 1979. *The Political and Social History of Khurasan under Abbasid Rule, 747–820*. Minneapolis: Bibliotheca Islamica.

Danto, Arthur C. 2003. *The Abuse of Beauty: Aesthetics and the Concept of Art*. Chicago: Open Court.

Dawson, Christopher, ed. 1955. *The Mongol Mission: Narratives and Letters of the Franciscan Missionaries in Mongolia and China in the Thirteenth and Fourteenth Centuries*. London: Sheed and Ward.

Dear, I.C.B., and M.R.D. Foot, eds. 1995. *The Oxford Companion to World War II*. Oxford: Oxford University Press.

de Goeje, M. J. ed. 1870. Abû Ishâq al-Fârisî al Istakhrî, كتاب مسالك الممالك (*Kitâb masâlik al-mamâlik*). Repr., Leiden: Brill, 1967.

—— 1877. Muhammad b. Ahmad al-Maqdisî, كتاب احسن التقاسيم فى معرفة الاقاليم (*Kitâb 'ahsan al-taqâsîm, fî ma'rifat al-'aqâlîm*). Repr., Leiden: Brill, 1967.

de la Vaissière, Étienne 2003. Sogdians in China: A Short History and Some New Discoveries. *The Silk Road Foundation Newsletter* 1.2. http://www.silk-road.com/newsletter/december/new_discoveries.htm.

—— 2005a. *Sogdian Traders: A History*. Trans. James Ward. Leiden: Brill.

—— 2005b. Châkars d'Asie centrale: à propos d'ouvrages récents. *Studia Iranica* 34: 139–149.

—— 2005c. Čākar sogdiens en Chine. In Étienne de la Vaissière and Éric Trombert, eds., *Les Sogdiens en Chine*, 255–256. Paris: École française d'Extrême-Orient.

—— 2005d. Huns et Xiongnu. *Central Asiatic Journal* 49.1: 3–26.

—— 2007. *Samarcande et Samarra: Élites d'Asie centrale dans l'empire abbasside*. Paris: Association pour l'avancement des études iraniennes.

de la Vaissière, Étienne, and Éric Trombert, eds. 2005. *Les Sogdiens en Chine*. Paris: École française d'Extrême-Orient.

Demiéville, Paul 1952. *Le concile de Lhasa: une controverse sur le quiétisme entre bouddhistes de l'Inde et de la Chine au VIIIe siècle de l'ère chrétienne*. Bibliothèque de l'Institut des Hautes études Chinoises, vol. 7. Paris: Imprimerie nationale de France.

Denifle, Henricus 1899. *Chartularium Universitatis' Parisiensis*. Paris; repr., Brussels: Culture et Civilisation, 1964.

de Rachewiltz, Igor 2004. *The Secret History of the Mongols: A Mongolian Epic Chronicle of the Thirteenth Century, Translated with a Historical and Philological Commentary*. Leiden: Brill.

Des Rotours, Robert 1962. *Histoire de Ngan Lou-chan (Ngan Lou-chan che tsi)*. Paris: Presses Universitaires de France.

Dewing, H. B., ed. and trans. 1954. *Procopius: History of the Wars*. Cambridge, Mass.: Harvard University Press.

Di Cosmo, Nicola 1999. The Northern Frontier in Pre-imperial China. In Michael Loewe and Edward L. Shaughnessy, eds., *The Cambridge History of Ancient China: From the Origins of Civilization to 221 B.C.*, 885–966. Cambridge: Cambridge University Press.

—— 1999b. State Formation and Periodization in Inner Asian History. *Journal of World History* 10.1:1–40.

———— 2002a. *Ancient China and Its Enemies: The Rise of Nomadic Power in East Asian History.* Cambridge: Cambridge University Press.

———— ed. 2002b. *Warfare in Inner Asian History (500–1800).* Leiden: Brill.

Di Cosmo, Nicola, and Dalizhabu Bao 2003. *Manchu-Mongol Relations on the Eve of the Qing Conquest: A Documentary History.* Leiden: Brill.

Dillon, Michael, ed. 1998. *China: A Historical and Cultural Dictionary.* Richmond, Surrey: Curzon.

Dobbie, Elliot van Kirk, ed. 1953. *Beowulf and Judith.* New York: Columbia University Press.

Dobrovits, Mihály 2004. "They called themselves Avar"—Considering the Pseudo-Avar Question in the Work of Theophylaktos. In Matteo Compareti, Paola Raffetta, Gianroberto Scarcia, eds., *Ērān ud Anērān: Webfestschrift Marshak 2003. Studies Presented to Boris Ilich Marshak on the Occasion of His 70th Birthday.* http://www.transoxiana.org/Eran/Articles/dobrovits.html (= *Ērān ud Anērān. Studies Presented to Boris Il'ic Marsak on the Occasion of His 70th Birthday.* Venice: Libreria Editrice Cafoscarina, 2006).

Donner, F. 1981. *The Early Islamic Conquests.* Princeton: Princeton University Press.

Drabble, Margaret, ed. 2006. *The Oxford Companion to English Literature.* 6th ed., rev. Oxford: Oxford University Press.

Drews, Robert 1988. *The Coming of the Greeks: Indo-European Conquests in the Aegean and the Ancient Near East.* Princeton: Princeton University Press.

———— 1993. *The End of the Bronze Age: Changes in Warfare and the Catastrophe, ca. 1200 B.C.* Princeton: Princeton University Press.

———— 2004. *Early Riders: The Beginnings of Mounted Warfare in Asia and Europe.* London: Routledge.

Drinnon, Richard 1987. *Keeper of Concentration Camps: Dillon S. Myer and American Racism.* Berkeley: University of California Press.

Drompp, Michael R. 2005. *Tang China and the Collapse of the Uighur Empire: A Documentary History.* Leiden: Brill.

Dunlop, D. M. 1954. *The History of the Jewish Khazars.* Princeton: Princeton University Press.

Dunnell, Ruth 1994. The Hsi Hsia. In Herbert Franke and Denis Twitchett, eds., *Cambridge History of China,* vol. 6: *Alien Regimes and Border States, 907–1368,* 154–214. Cambridge: Cambridge University Press.

———— 1996. *The Great State of White and High: Buddhism and State Formation in Eleventh-Century Xia.* Honolulu: University of Hawai'i Press.

Dunnigan, James F., and Albert A. Nofi 1998. *The Pacific War Encyclopedia.* New York: Facts on File.

Dyson, A. E. 1968. Literature, 1895–1939. In C. L. Mowat, ed., *The New Cambridge Modern History,* vol. XII: *The Shifting Balance of World Forces, 1898–1945;* 2nd ed., vol. XII: *The Era of Violence,* 613–643. Cambridge: Cambridge University Press.

Eastman, Lloyd E. 1986. Nationalist China during the Nanking Decade, 1927–1937. In John K. Fairbank and Albert Feuerwerker, eds., *Cambridge History of China*, vol. 13: *Republican China, 1912–1942, Part 2*, 116–167. Cambridge: Cambridge University Press.

Ebrey, Patricia Buckley 2001. *A Visual Sourcebook of Chinese Civilization*. http://depts.washington.edu/chinaciv/tindex.htm.

Edwards, I.E.S., C. J. Gadd, and N.G.L. Hammond, eds. 1971. *The Cambridge Ancient History*, vol. I, part 2: *Early History of the Middle East*. 3rd ed. Cambridge: Cambridge University Press.

Edwards, I.E.S., C. J. Gadd, N.G.L. Hammond, and E. Sollberger, eds. 1973. *The Cambridge Ancient History*, vol. II, part 1: *History of the Middle East and the Aegean Region, c. 1800–1380 B.C.* 3rd ed. Cambridge: Cambridge University Press.

Egami, Namio 1964. The Formation of the People and the Origin of the State in Japan. *Memoirs of the Research Department of the Toyo Bunko* 23: 35–70.

Ekvall, Robert B. 1968. *Fields on the Hoof: Nexus of Tibetan Nomadic Pastoralism*. New York: Holt, Rinehart and Winston.

Elisonas, Jurgis 1991. Christianity and the Daimyo. In John Whitney Hall, ed., *The Cambridge History of Japan*, vol. 4: *Early Modern Japan*, 301–372. Cambridge: Cambridge University Press.

Ellis, Eric 2007. Iran's Cola War. *Fortune*, February 6, 2007. http://money.cnn.com/magazines/fortune/fortune_archive/2007/02/19/8400167/index.htm.

Endicott-West, Elizabeth 1989. Merchant Associations in Yüan China: The *Ortoy*. *Asia Major*, 3rd ser., 2.2: 127–154.

Enoki, K., G. A. Koshelenko, and Z. Haidary 1994. The Yüeh-chih and Their Migrations. In János Harmatta, ed., *History of Civilizations of Central Asia*, vol. II: *The Development of Sedentary and Nomadic Civilizations, 700 B.C. to A.D. 250*, 171–189. Paris: Unesco.

Ewig, Eugen 1997. Le myth troyen et l'histoire des Francs. In Michel Rouche, ed., *Clovis: histoire & mémoire*, 817–847. Paris: Presses de l'Université de Paris-Sorbonne.

Fairbank, John K. 1978. The Creation of the Treaty System. In John K. Fairbank, ed., *The Cambridge History of China*, vol. 10: *Late Ch'ing, 1800–1911, Part 1*, 213–263. Cambridge: Cambridge University Press.

Fairweather, Eugene R. 1970. *A Scholastic Miscellany: Anselm to Ockham*. New York: Macmillan.

Fakhry, Majid 1983. *A History of Islamic Philosophy*. 2nd ed. New York: Columbia University Press.

Fan Yeh 1965. 後漢書 (*Hou Han shu*). Peking: Chung-hua shu-chü.

Farquhar, David 1978. Emperor as Bodhisattva in the Governance of the Ch'ing Empire. *Harvard Journal of Asiatic Studies* 38.1: 5–34.

Farris, William Wayne 1995. *Heavenly Warriors: The Evolution of Japan's Military, 500–1300*. Cambridge, Mass.: Harvard University, Council on East Asian Studies.

Felix, Wolfgang 1992. Chionites. In Ehsan Yarshater, ed., *Encyclopaedia Iranica, 5*. Costa Mesa: Mazda Publishers.

Fletcher, Joseph 1978. Sino-Russian Relations, 1800–62. In John K. Fairbank, ed., *Cambridge History of China*, vol. 10: *Late Ch'ing, 1800–1911, Part 1*, 318–350. Cambridge: Cambridge University Press.

Florinsky, Michael T., ed. 1961. *The McGraw-Hill Encyclopedia of Russia and the Soviet Union*. New York: McGraw-Hill.

Foster, B. O., trans. 1988. *Livy. Vol. 1: Books I and II*. Cambridge, Mass.: Harvard University Press.

Fowler, H. W. and F. G. Fowler 1905. *The Works of Lucian of Samosata*. Oxford: Clarendon Press.

Franck, I. M., and D. M. Brownstone 1986. *The Silk Road: A History*. New York: Facts on File.

Franke, Herbert 1994. The Chin Dynasty. In Herbert Franke and Denis Twitchett, eds., *Cambridge History of China*, vol. 6: *Alien Regimes and Border States, 907–1368*, 215–320. Cambridge: Cambridge University Press.

Franke, Herbert, and Denis Twitchett 1994. Introduction. In Herbert Franke and Denis Twitchett, eds., *Cambridge History of China*, vol. 6: *Alien Regimes and Border States, 907–1368*, 1–42. Cambridge: Cambridge University Press.

Frédéric, Louis 2002. *Japan Encyclopedia*. Trans. Käthe Roth. Cambridge: Cambridge University Press.

Frendo, Joseph D. 1975. *Agathias: The Histories*. Berlin: Walter de Gruyter.

Freu, Jacques 2003. *Histoire du Mitanni*. Paris: L'Harmattan.

Frye, R. N. 1983. *The Political History of Iran under the Sasanians*. In Ehsan Yarshater, ed., *The Cambridge History of Iran*, vol. 3: *The Seleucid, Parthian and Sasanian Periods, Part 1*, 116–180. Cambridge: Cambridge University Press.

———— 2005. *Ibn Fadlan's Journey to Russia*. Princeton: Markus Wiener.

Gamkrelidze, Thomas V., and Vjaceslav V. Ivanov 1995. *Indo-European and the Indo-Europeans: A Reconstruction and Historical Analysis of a Proto-Language and a Proto-Culture*. Trans. Johanna Nichols. Berlin: Mouton de Gruyter.

Garrett, Andrew 1999. A New Model of Indo-European Subgrouping and Dispersal. In Steve S. Chang, Lily Liaw, and Josef Ruppenhofer, eds., *Proceedings of the Twenty-Fifth Annual Meeting of the Berkeley Linguistics Society, February 12–15, 1999*, 146–156 (=http://socrates.berkeley.edu/~garrett/BLS1999.pdf).

———— 2006. Convergence in the Formation of Indo-European Subgroups: Phylogeny and Chronology. In Peter Forster and Colin Renfrew, eds., *Phylogenetic Methods and the Prehistory of Languages*, 139–151. Cambridge: McDonald Institute for Archaeological Research.

Gerberding, Richard A. 1987. *The Rise of the Carolingians and the Liber Historiae Francorum*. Oxford: Clarendon.

Gernet, Jacques 1996. *A History of Chinese Civilization*. Trans. J. R. Foster and Charles Hartman. 2nd ed. Cambridge: Cambridge University Press.

Gershevitch, Ilya, ed. 1985. *The Cambridge History of Iran,* vol. 2: *The Median and Achaemenian Periods.* Cambridge: Cambridge University Press.

Gibb, H.A.R., et al., eds. 1960–2002. *The Encyclopaedia of Islam.* New ed. Leiden: Brill.

Godley, A. D., trans. 1972. *Herodotus.* Cambridge, Mass.: Harvard University Press.

Golden, Peter 1980. *Khazar Studies.* Budapest: Akadémiai Kiadó.

—— 1982. The Question of the Rus' Qağanate. *Archivum Eurasiae Medii Aevi* 2: 77–97.

—— 1987–1991. Nomads and Their Sedentary Neighbors in Pre-Činggisid Eurasia. *Archivum Eurasiae Medii Aevi* 7: 41–81.

—— 1991. Aspects of the Nomadic Factor in the Economic Development of Kievan Rus. In I. S. Koropeckyj, ed., *Ukrainian Economic History: Interpretative Essays,* 58–101. Cambridge, Mass. Harvard Ukrainian Research Institute.

—— 1992. *An Introduction to the History of the Turkic Peoples: Ethnogenesis and State-Formation in Medieval and Early Modern Eurasia and the Middle East.* Wiesbaden: Harrassowitz.

—— 1995. Chopsticks and Pasta in Medieval Turkic Cuisine. *Rocznik Orientalistyczny* 49.2: 73–82.

—— 2001. Some Notes on the Comitatus in Medieval Eurasia with Special Reference to the Khazars. *Russian History/Histoire Russe* 28.1–4: 153–170.

—— 2002. War and Warfare in the Pre-Chinggisid Western Steppes of Eurasia. In Nicola di Cosmo, ed., *Warfare in Inner Asian History (500–1800),* 105–172. Leiden: Brill.

—— 2002–2003. Khazar Turkic ghulâms in Caliphal Service: Onomastic Notes. *Archivum Eurasiae Medii Aevi* 12: 15–27.

—— 2004. Khazar Turkic ghulâms in Caliphal Service. *Journal Asiatique* 292.1–2: 279–309.

—— 2006. Some Thoughts on the Origins of the Turks and the Shaping of the Turkic Peoples. In Victor H Mair, ed., *Contact and Exchange in the Ancient World,* 136–157. Honolulu: University of Hawai'i Press.

—— 2007. The Conversion of the Khazars to Judaism. In Peter B. Golden, H. Ben-Shammai, and A. Róna-Tas, eds., *The World of the Khazars: New Perspectives,* 123–162. Leiden: Brill.

Gommans, Jos 2007. Mughal India and Central Asia in the Eighteenth Century: An Introduction to a Wider Perspective. In Scott C. Levi, ed., *India and Central Asia. Commerce and Culture, 1500–1800,* 39–63. New Delhi: Oxford University Press.

Gonnet, H. 1990. Telibinu et l'organisation de l'espace chez les Hittites. In *Tracés de fondation, Bib. EPHE* XCIII: 51–57. (Cited in Mazoyer 2003: 27.)

Goralski, Robert 1981. *World War II Almanac: 1931–1945; A Political and Military Record.* New York: G. P. Putnam's Sons.

Gowing, Lawrence, ed. 1983. *A Biographical Dictionary of Artists*. New York: Facts on File.

Grant, Edward, ed. 1974. *A Source Book in Medieval Science*. Cambridge, Mass.: Harvard University Press.

Grassmann, Hermann 1863. Ueber die Aspiraten und ihr gleichzeitiges Vorhandensein im An- und Auslaute der Wurzeln. *Zeitschrift für vergleichende Sprachforschung auf dem Gebiete des Deutschen, Griechischen und Lateinischen* 12.2: 81–138. (Partial translation, "Concerning the Aspirates and Their Simultaneous Presence in the Initial and Final of Roots," in Lehmann 1967: 109–131.)

Grenet, Frantz 2003. *La geste d'Ardashir fils de Pâbag*. Die: Editions A Die.

——— 2005. The Self-Image of the Sogdians. In Étienne de la Vaissière and Éric Trombert, eds., *Les Sogdiens en Chine*, 123–140. Paris: École française d'Extrême-Orient.

Grupper, Samuel M. 1980. The Manchu Imperial Cult of the Early Ch'ing Dynasty: Texts and Studies on the Tantric Sanctuary of Mahākāla at Mukden. Ph.D. dissertation, Indiana University, Bloomington.

Guterbock, Hans G., and Theo P. J. van den Hout 1991. *The Hittite Instruction for the Royal Bodyguard*. Assyriological Studies No. 24. Chicago: Oriental Institute of the University of Chicago.

Gyllensvärd, Bo, ed. 1974. *Arkeologiska Fynd från Folkrepubliken Kina*. Katalog 19. Stockholm: Östasiatiska Museet.

Haiman, J. 1994. Iconicity and Syntactic Change. In R. E. Asher, ed., *The Encyclopedia of Language and Linguistics*, 1633–1637. Oxford: Pergamon.

Hall, John Whitney 1991. Introduction. In John Whitney Hall, ed., *The Cambridge History of Japan*, vol. 4: *Early Modern Japan*, 1–39. Cambridge: Cambridge University Press, 1991.

Hambly, Gavin R. G. 1991. Āghā Muḥammad Khān and the Establishment of the Qājār Dynasty. In Peter Avery et al., eds., *The Cambridge History of Iran*, vol. 7: *From Nadir Shah to the Islamic Republic*, 104–143. Cambridge: Cambridge University Press.

Harrison, John R. 1966. *The Reactionaries: A Study of the Anti-democratic Intelligentsia*. New York: Schocken.

Hayashi, Toshio 1984. Agriculture and Settlements in the Hsiung-nu. *Bulletin of the Ancient Orient Museum* 6: 51–92.

Heidenreich, Donald E., Jr. 2003. Pearl Harbor. In Peter Knight, ed., *Conspiracy Theories in American History*, 579–582. Santa Barbara: ABC-CLIO.

Hicks, Robert Drew, trans. 1980. *Diogenes Laertius: Lives of Eminent Philosophers*. Cambridge, Mass.: Harvard University Press.

Hildinger, Erik 2001. *Warriors of the Steppe: A Military History of Central Asia, 500 B.C. to 1700 A.D*. Cambridge, Mass.: Da Capo.

Hill, John E. 2003. The Western Regions according to the *Hou Hanshu*: The *Xiyu juan* "Chapter on the Western Regions" from *Hou Hanshu* 88, 2nd ed. http://depts.washington.edu/uwch/silkroad/texts/hhshu/hou_han_shu.html#sec8.

————— forthcoming. *Through the Jade Gate to Rome: A Study of the Silk Routes during the Later Han Dynasty, 1st to 2nd Centuries* CE. *An Annotated Translation of The Chapter on the "Western Regions" from the* Hou Hanshu.

Ho, Yeh-huan 1999. 揚子鱷在黄河中下游的地理分布及其南移的原因 (Yang-tzu o tsai Huang Ho chung-hsia you-te ti-li fen-pu chi ch'i nan-i-te yüan-yin). *Li-shih ti-li* 15: 125–131.

Hock, Hans Heinrich 1999a. Out of India? The Linguistic Evidence. In Johannes Bronkhorst and Madhav M. Deshpande, eds., *Aryan and Non-Aryan in South Asia: Evidence, Interpretation and Ideology*, 1–18. Proceedings of the International Seminar on Aryan and Non-Aryan in South Asia, University of Michigan, Ann Arbor, 25–27 October 1996. Cambridge, Mass.: Harvard University Department of Sanskrit and Indian Studies.

————— 1999b. Through a Glass Darkly: Modern "Racial" Interpretations vs. Textual and General Prehistoric Evidence on *ārya* and *dāsa/dasyu* in Vedic Society. In Johannes Bronkhorst and Madhav M. Deshpande, eds., *Aryan and Non-Aryan in South Asia: Evidence, Interpretation and Ideology*, 145–174. Proceedings of the International Seminar on Aryan and Non-Aryan in South Asia, University of Michigan, Ann Arbor, 25–27 October 1996. Cambridge, Mass.: Harvard University Department of Sanskrit and Indian Studies.

Hoffmann, Helmut 1961. *The Religions of Tibet.* New York: Macmillan.

Holmes, Richard, ed. 2001. *The Oxford Companion to Military History.* Oxford: Oxford University Press.

Hornblower, Simon, and Antony Spawforth, eds. 2003. *The Oxford Classical Dictionary.* 3rd ed., rev. Oxford: Oxford University Press.

Horne, Charles F., ed. 1917. *The Sacred Books and Early Literature of the East,* vol. VII: *Ancient Persia.* New York: Parke, Austin, & Lipscomb.

Hosking, Geoffrey 2001. *Russia and the Russians: A History.* Cambridge, Mass.: Belknap Press of Harvard University Press.

Howarth, Patrick 1994. *Attila, King of the Huns: Man and Myth.* London: Constable.

Hsu, Immanuel C. Y. 1980. Late Ch'ing Foreign Relations, 1866–1905. In John K. Fairbank and Kwang-ching Liu, eds., *Cambridge History of China,* vol. 11: *Late Ch'ing, 1800–1911, Part 2,* 70–141. Cambridge: Cambridge University Press.

Hudson, Mark J. 1999. *Ruins of Identity: Ethnogenesis in the Japanese Islands.* Honolulu: University of Hawai'i Press.

Hui Li 2000. 大慈恩寺三藏法師傳 (*Ta tz'u en ssu San Tsang fa shih chuan*). Ed. Sun Yü-t'ang and Hsieh Fang. Peking: Chung-hua shu-chü.

Hui, Victoria Tin-bor 2005. *War and State Formation in Ancient China and Early Modern Europe.* New York: Cambridge University Press.

Hutton, M. 1970. Tacitus. In M. Hutton et al., *Tacitus: Agricola, Germania, Dialogus,* 127–215. Cambridge, Mass.: Harvard University Press.

Hyman, Anthony 1996. Volga Germans. In Graham Smith, ed., *The Nationalities Question in the Post-Soviet States*, 462–476. London: Longman.

İnalcik, H. 1997. Istanbul. *E.I.*₂ IV: 224–248.

Issawi, Charles Philip 1971. *The Economic History of Iran, 1800–1914*. Chicago: University of Chicago Press.

Jagchid, Sechin, and Van Jay Symons 1989. *Peace, War, and Trade along the Great Wall: Nomadic-Chinese Interaction through Two Millennia*. Bloomington: Indiana University Press.

James, Edward 2001. *Britain in the First Millennium*. New York: Oxford University Press.

Janhunen, Juha, ed. 2003. *The Mongolic Languages*. London: Routledge.

Jansen, Marius B. 1989. The Meiji Restoration. In Marius B. Jansen, ed., *The Cambridge History of Japan*, vol 5: *The Nineteenth Century*, 308–366. Cambridge: Cambridge University Press.

Jansen, Thomas, Peter Forster, Marsha A. Levine, Hardy Oelke, Matthew Hurles, Colin Renfrew, Jurgen Weber, and Klaus Olek 2002. Mitochondrial DNA and the Origins of the Domestic Horse. *Proceedings of the National Academy of Sciences* 99.16: 10905–10910.

Johanson, Lars, and Éva Á. Csató, eds. 1998. *The Turkic Languages*. London: Routledge.

Jones, Horace Leonard 1924. *The Geography of Strabo*. Vol. 3. London: William Heinemann.

Joo-Jock, Arthur Lim 1991. Geographical Setting. In Ernest C. T. Chew and Edwin Lee, eds. *A History of Singapore*, 3–14. Oxford: Oxford University Press.

Kafadar, Cemal 1995. *Between Two Worlds: The Construction of the Ottoman State*. Berkeley: University of California Press.

Kazanski, Michel 2000. L'or des princes barbares. *Archéologia*, No. 371 (October): 20–31.

Keightley, David N. 1999. The Shang: China's First Historical Dynasty. In Michael Loewe and Edward L. Shaughnessy, eds., *The Cambridge History of Ancient China: From the Origins of Civilization to 221 B.C.*, 232–291. Cambridge: Cambridge University Press.

Kellens, Jean 1989. Avestique. In Rüdiger Schmitt, ed., *Compendium Linguarum Iranicarum*, 32–55. Wiesbaden: Dr. Ludwig Reichert Verlag.

Keydell, Rudolf, ed. 1967. *Agathiae Myrinaei historiarum libri quinque*. Corpus fontium historiae Byzantinae, vol. II. Berlin: Walter de Gruyter.

Khalid, Adeeb 2007. *Islam after Communism: Religion and Politics in Central Asia*. Berkeley: University of California Press.

Khazanov, Anatoly M. 1984. *Nomads and the Outside World*. Cambridge: Cambridge University Press.

King, Anya H. 2007. The Musk Trade and the Near East in the Early Medieval Period. Ph.D. dissertation. Indiana University, Bloomington.

Kiyose, Gisaburo N. 1977. *A Study of the Jurchen Language and Script: Reconstruction and Decipherment.* Kyoto: Horitsubunka-sha.

Kiyose, Gisaburo N., and Christopher I. Beckwith 2006. The Silla Word for 'Walled City' and the Ancestor of Modern Korean. *Arutaigo kenkyû—Altaistic Studies* 1: 1–10.

—— 2008. The Origin of the Old Japanese Twelve Animal Cycle. *Arutaigo kenkyû—Altaistic Studies* 2: 1–18.

Klyashtornyi, S.G. 1994. The Royal Clan of the Turks and the Problem of Early Turkic-Iranian Contacts. *Acta Orientalia Academiae Scientiarum Hungaricae* 47.3: 445–448.

Klyashtornyi, S. G., and B. A. Livshits 1972. The Sogdian Inscription of Bugut Revised. *Acta Orientalia Academiae Scientiarum Hungaricae* 26: 69–102.

Kochnev, B. D. 1996. The Origins of the Karakhanids: A Reconsideration. *Der Islam* 73: 352–357.

Kohl, Philip L. 1995. Central Asia and the Caucasus in the Bronze Age. In Jack M. Sasson, ed., *Civilizations of the Ancient Near East,* 2: 1051–1065. New York: Charles Scribner's Sons.

Kovalev, R. K. 2005. Creating Khazar Identity through Coins: The Special Issue Dirhams of 837/8. In F. Curta, ed., *East Central Europe in the Early Middle Ages,* 220–253. Ann Arbor: University of Michigan Press.

Kramers, J. H., and M. Morony 1991. Marzpān. *E.I.$_2$* VI: 633–634.

Krause, Wolfgang, and Werner Thomas 1960–1964. *Tocharisches Elementarbuch.* Heidelberg: C. Winter.

Krueger, John R. 1961a. *Chuvash Manual.* Uralic and Altaic Series, vol. 7. Bloomington: Indiana University.

—— 1961b. An Early Instance of Conditioning from the Chinese Dynastic Histories. *Psychological Reports* 9: 117.

Kyzlasov, I. L. 1994. Рунические письменности евразийских степей. Moscow: Vostočnaja literatura.

Labov, William 1982. *The Social Stratification of English in New York City.* Washington, D.C.: Center for Applied Linguistics.

Langlois, John D., Jr. 1981. Introduction. In John D. Langlois Jr., ed., *China under Mongol Rule.* Princeton: Princeton University Press.

Latham, Ronald, trans. 1958. *The Travels of Marco Polo.* Harmondsworth: Penguin.

Lattimore, Steven, trans. 1998. *Thucydides: The Peloponnesian War.* Indianapolis: Hackett.

Layton, Ronald V., Jr. 1999. Cryptography. In David T. Zabecki et al., eds., *World War II in Europe: An Encyclopedia,* 1192–1194. New York: Garland.

Lazzerini, Edward J. 1996. Crimean Tatars. In Graham Smith, ed., *The Nationalities Question in the Post-Soviet States,* 412–435. London: Longman.

Ledyard, Gari 1975. Galloping Along with the Horseriders: Looking for the Founders of Japan. *Journal of Japanese Studies* 1.2: 217–254.

Lefebvre, Claire, Lydia White, and Christine Jourdan, eds. 2006. *L2 Acquisition and Creole Genesis: Dialogues*. Amsterdam: Benjamins.

Legge, James, ed. and trans. 1935. *The Chinese Classics, with a Translation, Critical and Exegetical Notes, Prolegomena, and Copious Indexes*, vol. IV: *The She King*. Second edition with minor text corrections and a table of concordances. Shanghai; repr., Taipei: Wen-hsing shu-tien, 1966.

Legrand, Ph.-E., ed. and trans. 1949. *Hérodote: histoires, livre IV, Melpomène*. Paris: Société d'édition "les belles lettres".

Lehmann, Clayton M. 2006. Dacia. http://www.usd.edu/~clehmann/pir/dacia.htm.

Lehmann, Winfred P., ed. 1967. *A Reader in Nineteenth Century Historical Indo-European Linguistics*. Bloomington: Indiana University Press.

——— 1973. *Historical Linguistics: An Introduction*. 2nd ed. New York: Holt, Rinehart and Winston.

——— 1993. *Theoretical Bases of Indo-European Linguistics*. London: Routledge.

Levi, Scott C. 2002. *The Indian Diaspora in Central Asia and Its Trade, 1550–1900*. Leiden: Brill.

———, ed. 2007a. Introduction. In Scott C. Levi, ed., *India and Central Asia: Commerce and Culture, 1500–1800*, 1–36. New Delhi: Oxford University Press.

———, ed. 2007b. India, Russia, and the Eighteenth-Century Transformation of the Central Asian Caravan Trade. In Scott C. Levi, ed., *India and Central Asia: Commerce and Culture, 1500–1800*, 93–122. New Delhi: Oxford University Press.

———, ed. 2007c. *India and Central Asia: Commerce and Culture, 1500–1800*. New Delhi: Oxford University Press.

Levin, Nora 1988. *The Jews in the Soviet Union since 1917: Paradox of Survival*. New York: New York University Press.

Lewis, Bernard 1982. The Question of Orientalism. *New York Review of Books* 29.11 (June 24): 49–56.

Lewis, Wyndham 1954. *The Demon of Progress in the Arts*. London: Methuen.

Li, Rongxi, trans. 1995. *A Biography of the Tripiṭaka Master of the Great Ci'en Monastery of the Great Tang Dynasty*. Berkeley: Numata Center for Buddhist Translation and Research.

Liddell, Henry George, Robert Scott, and Henry Stuart Jones 1968. *A Greek-English Lexicon*. Oxford: Clarendon Press.

Lincoln, Bruce 1991. *Death, War, and Sacrifice: Studies in Ideology and Practice*. Chicago: University of Chicago Press.

Lindner, Rudi Paul 1981. Nomadism, Horses and Huns. *Past and Present* 92: 3–19.

——— 1982. What Was a Nomadic Tribe? *Comparative Studies in Society and History* 24.4: 689–711.

——— 2005. *Explorations in Ottoman Prehistory*. Ann Arbor: University of Michigan Press.

Lindow, John 1976. *Comitatus, Individual and Honor: Studies in North Germanic Institutional Vocabulary*. Berkeley: University of California Press.

Ling-hu Te-fen 1971. 周書 (*Chou shu*). Peking: Chung-hua shu-chü.

Littauer, Mary Aiken, and Joost H. Crouwel 2002. *Selected Writings on Chariots and Other Early Vehicles, Riding and Harness.* Ed. Peter Raulwing. Leiden: Brill.

Littleton, C. Scott, and Linda A. Malcor 1994. *From Scythia to Camelot: A Radical Reassessment of the Legends of King Arthur, the Knights of the Round Table, and the Holy Grail.* New York: Garland.

Litvinsky, Boris A., and Tamara I. Zeimal 1971. Аджина-Тепа. Moscow: Iskusstvo.

Liu Hsü et al. 1975. 舊唐書 (*Chiu T'ang shu*). Peking: Chung-hua shu-chü.

Liu Kwang-ching and Richard J. Smith 1980. The Military Challenge: The North-west and the Coast. In John K. Fairbank and Kwang-ching Liu, eds., *The Cambridge History of China*, vol. 11: *Late Ch'ing, 1800–1911, Part 2*, 202–273. Cambridge: Cambridge University Press.

Liu Yingsheng 1989. Zur Urheimat und Umsiedlung der Toba. *Central Asiatic Journal* 33.1–2: 86–107.

Loewe, Michael 1986. The Former Han Dynasty. In Denis Crispin Twitchett and Michael Loewe, eds., *The Cambridge History of China*, vol. 1: *The Ch'in and Han Empires, 221 B.C.–A.D. 220*, 103–222. Cambridge: Cambridge University Press.

Lowry, Heath W. 2003. *The Nature of the Early Ottoman State.* Albany: State University of New York Press.

Lyon, Bryce D. 1972. *The Origins of the Middle Ages: Pirenne's Challenge to Gibbon.* New York: Norton.

Macan, Reginald Walter 1895. *Herodotus. The Fourth, Fifth, and Sixth Books.* Vol. I, *Introduction, Text with Notes.* London: Macmillan.

Mackerras, Colin 1972. *The Uighur Empire According to the T'ang Dynastic Histories: A Study in Sino-Uighur Relations, 744–840.* Columbia: University of South Carolina Press.

——— 1990. The Uighurs. In Denis Sinor, ed., *The Cambridge History of Early Inner Asia*, 317–342. Cambridge: Cambridge University Press.

Mair, Victor, ed. 1998. *The Bronze Age and Early Iron Age Peoples of Eastern Central Asia.* Philadelphia: Institute for the Study of Man.

Makdisi, George 1981. *The Rise of Colleges: Institutions of Learning in Islam and the West.* Edinburgh: Edinburgh University Press.

Mallory, J. P. 1989. *In Search of the Indo-Europeans: Language, Archaeology and Myth.* London: Thames & Hudson.

Mallory, J. P., and D. Q. Adams, eds. 1997. *Encyclopedia of Indo-European Culture.* London: Fitzroy Dearborn.

——— 2006. *The Oxford Introduction to Proto-Indo-European and the Proto-Indo-European World.* Oxford: Oxford University Press.

Mallory, J. P., and Victor Mair 2000. *The Tarim Mummies: Ancient China and the Mystery of the Earliest Peoples from the West.* New York: Thames & Hudson.

Manz, Beatrice Forbes 1989. *The Rise and Rule of Tamerlane.* Cambridge: Cambridge University Press.

—— 2000. Tīmūr Lang. *E.I.*₂ X: 510–513.

Markovits, Claude 2007. Indian Merchants in Central Asia: The Debate. In Scott C. Levi, ed., *India and Central Asia: Commerce and Culture, 1500–1800*, 123–151. New Delhi: Oxford University Press.

Mathews, R. H. 1943. *Mathews' Chinese-English Dictionary*. Rev. American ed. Cambridge, Mass.: Harvard University Press.

Matthee, Rudoloph P. 1999. *The Politics of Trade in Safavid Iran: Silk for Silver, 1600–1730*. Cambridge: Cambridge University Press.

Mattingly, H., trans. 1970. *Tacitus: The Agricola and the Germania*. Rev. S. A. Handford. Harmondsworth: Penguin.

Mayrhofer, M. 1986–2000. *Etymologisches Wörterbuch des Altindoarischen*. Heidelberg: Carl Winter.

Mazoyer, Michel 2003. *Télipinu, le dieu au marécage: Essai sur les mythes fondateurs du royaume hittite*. Paris: L'Harmattan, Association Kubaba.

McGeveran, William A., Jr. 2006. *The World Almanac and Book of Facts, 2006*. New York: World Almanac Books.

McNeill, William H. 1977. *Plagues and Peoples*. New York: Anchor Books.

Melchert, H. Craig 1995. Indo-European Languages of Anatolia. In Jack M. Sasson, ed., *Civilizations of the Ancient Near East*, 4: 2151–2159. New York: Charles Scribner's Sons.

Melyukova, A.I. 1990. The Scythians and Sarmatians. In Denis Sinor, ed., *The Cambridge History of Early Inner Asia*, 97–117. Cambridge: Cambridge University Press.

Millar, James R., ed. 2003. *Encyclopedia of Russian History*. Indianapolis: Macmillan USA.

Miller, Margaret C. 1999. *Athens and Persia in the Fifth Century BC: A Study in Cultural Receptivity*. Cambridge: Cambridge University Press.

Millward, James A. 2004. *Violent Separatism in Xinjiang: A Critical Assessment*. Washington, D.C.: East-West Center Washington.

—— 2007. *Eurasian Crossroads: A History of Xinjiang*. New York: Columbia University Press.

Minorsky, Vladimir 1942. *Sharaf al-Zamān Ṭāhir Marvazī on China, the Turks and India: Arabic Text (circa A.D. 1120)*. London: Royal Asiatic Society.

—— 1948. Tamīm ibn Baḥr's Journey to the Uyghurs. *Bulletin of the School of Oriental and African Studies, University of London* 12.2: 275–305.

Molè, Gabriella 1970. *The T'u-yü-hun from the Northern Wei to the Time of the Five Dynasties*. Serie Orientale Roma, vol. 41. Rome: Istituto Italiano per il Medio ed Estremo Oriente.

Moribe, Yutaka 2005. Military Officers of Sogdian Origin from the Late T'ang Dynasty to the Period of the Five Dynasties. In Étienne de la Vaissière and Éric Trombert, eds., *Les Sogdiens en Chine*, 243–254. Paris: École française d'Extrême-Orient.

Mote, Frederick W. 1994. Chinese Society under Mongol Rule, 1215–1388. In Herbert Franke and Denis Twitchett, eds., *The Cambridge History of China*, vol. 6: *Alien*

Regimes and Border States, 907–1368, 616–664. Cambridge: Cambridge University Press.

Moule, A. C., and Paul Pelliot 1938. *Marco Polo: The Description of the World*. London: Routledge.

Mous, Maarten 1996. Was There Ever a Southern Cushitic Language (Pre-) Ma'a? In Catherine Griefenow-Mewis and Rainer M. Voigt, eds., *Cushitic and Omotic Languages*, 201–211. Proceedings of the Third International Symposium. Berlin, March 17–19, 1994. Cologne: Rüdiger Köppe.

—— 2003. *The Making of a Mixed Language: The Case of Ma'a/Mbugu*. Amsterdam: Benjamins.

Mowat, C. L., ed. 1968. *The New Cambridge Modern History*, vol. XII: *The Shifting Balance of World Forces, 1898–1945; 2nd ed.*, vol. XII: *The Era of Violence*. Cambridge: Cambridge University Press.

Müller, F. Max 1891. *Vedic Hymns*. Vol. 1. Oxford: Clarendon Press.

Müller, F.W.K. 1907. Beitrag zur genaueren Bestimmung der unbekannten Sprachen Mittelasiens. *Sitzunsberichte der Preussischen Akademie der Wissenschaften, philosophisch-historische Klasse* 19: 958–960.

Nagrodzka-Majchrzyk, Teresa. 1978. *Geneza miast u dawnych ludów tureckich (VII–XII w.)*. Wrocław: Zakład Narodowy im. Ossolinskich.

Nasr, Seyyed Hossein 2006. *Islamic Philosophy from Its Origin to the Present: Philosophy in the Land of Prophecy*. Albany: State University of New York Press.

Nevsky, Nicolas 1926. *A Brief Manual of the Si-hia Characters with Tibetan Transcriptions*. Osaka: Osaka Oriental Society.

Newitt, M. D. D. 2005. *A History of Portuguese Overseas Expansion, 1400–1668*. London: Routledge.

Nichols, Johanna 1997a. The Epicentre of the Indo-European Linguistic Spread. In Roger Blench and Matthew Spriggs, eds., *Archaeology and Language I: Theoretical and Methodological Orientations*, 122–148. London: Routledge.

—— 1997b. Modeling Ancient Population Structures and Movement in Linguistics. *Annual Review of Anthropology* 26: 359–384.

—— 2004. Chechnya and Chechens. In James R. Millar, ed., *Encyclopedia of Russian History*, 232–235. New York: Macmillan Reference.

Noonan, Thomas S. 1981. Ninth-Century Dirham Hoards from European Russia: A Preliminary Analysis. In M. A. S. Blackburn and D. M. Metcalf, eds., *Viking Age Coinage in the Northern Lands*, 47–117. The Sixth Oxford Symposium on Coinage and Monetary History. British Archaeological Reports, International Series 122. Oxford: B.A.R. (Reprinted in Noonan 1998.)

—— 1997. The Khazar Economy. *Archivum Eurasiae Medii Aevi* 9: 253–318.

—— 1998. *The Islamic World, Russia and the Vikings, 750–900*. Aldershot, Hampshire: Ashgate Variorum.

Northedge, A. 1995. Sāmarrā'. *E.I.*$_2$ VIII: 1039–1041.

Oren, Eliezer D., ed. 2000. *The Sea Peoples and Their World: A Reassessment*. Philadelphia: University Museum, University of Pennsylvania.

Ötkur, Abdurehim 1985. لز (Iz). Ürümchi: Shinjang Khälq Näshriyati. (3rd printing, 1986.)

Ou-yang Hsiu and Sung Ch'i 1975. 新唐書 (Hsin T'ang shu). Peking: Chung-hua shu-chü.

Owen, Stephen 1981. The Great Age of Chinese Poetry: The High T'ang. New Haven: Yale University Press.

Pai, Hyung Il 2000. Constructing "Korean" Origins. A Critical Review of Archaeology, Historiography, and Racial Myth in Korean State-Formation Theories. Cambridge, Mass.: Harvard University Asia Center.

Pan Ku et al. 1962. 漢書 (Han shu). Peking: Chung-hua shu-chü.

Pearson, M. N. 1987. The New Cambridge History of India, I, 1: The Portuguese in India. Cambridge: Cambridge University Press.

Pedersen, J., George Makdisi, Munibur Rahman, and R. Hillenbrand 1986. Madrasa. E.I._2 V: 1123–1154.

Pegolotti, Francesco Balducci 1936. La pratica della mercatura. Ed. Allan Evans. Cambridge: Medieval Academy of America.

Pelliot, Paul 1961. Histoire ancienne du Tibet. Paris: Maisonneuve.

——— 1959–1963. Notes on Marco Polo. Paris: Maisonneuve.

Perdue, Peter C. 2005. China Marches West: The Qing Conquest of Central Eurasia. Cambridge, Mass.: Belknap Press of Harvard University Press.

Perrin, Bernadotte, trans. 1998. Plutarch's Lives. Vol.1. Cambridge, Mass.: Harvard University Press.

Petech, Luciano 1952. I missionari italiani nel Tibet e nel Nepal. Parte II. Rome: Libreria dello Stato.

——— 1954. I missionari italiani nel Tibet e nel Nepal. Parte V. Rome: Libreria dello Stato.

——— 1955. I missionari italiani nel Tibet e nel Nepal. Parte VI. Rome: Libreria dello Stato.

——— 1983. Tibetan Relations with Sung China and with the Mongols. In Morris Rossabi, ed., China among Equals: The Middle Kingdom and its Neighbors, 10th–14th Centuries, 173–203. Berkeley: University of California Press.

Peters, F. E. 1994. Muhammad and the Origins of Islam. Albany: State University of New York Press.

Peterson, C. A. 1979. Court and Province in Mid- and Late T'ang. In Denis Twitchett, ed., The Cambridge History of China, vol. 3: Sui and T'ang China, 589–906, Part 1, 464–560. Cambridge: Cambridge University Press.

Picken, Laurence, et al. 1981. Music from the Tang Court. Vol. 1. London: Oxford University Press.

——— 1985–2000. Music from the T'ang Court. Vols. 2–7. Cambridge: Cambridge University Press.

Piggott, Stuart 1992. Wagon, Chariot and Carriage: Symbol and Status in the History of Transport. London: Thames and Hudson.

Pirenne, Henri 1939. Mohammed and Charlemagne. London: Allen & Unwin.

Pletneva, S.A. 1958. Печенеги, Торки и Половцы в южнорусских степях. *Trudy Volgo-Donskoi Arkheologicheskoi Ekspeditsii, Materialy i issledovaniia po arkheologii SSSR* 62: 151–226.

———— 1967. От кочевии к городам; салтово-маяцкая культура. Moscow: Nauka.

Pohl, Walter 1988. *Die Awaren: Ein Steppenvolk im Mitteleuropa, 567–822 n. Chr.* Munich: Beck.

Pokorny, Julius 1959. *Indogermanisches etymologisches Wörterbuch.* I. Band. Bern: Francke Verlag.

Psarras, Sophia-Karin 1994. Exploring the North: Non-Chinese Cultures of the Late Warring States and Han. *Monumenta Serica* 42: 1–125.

———— 2003. Han and Xiongnu: A Reexamination of Cultural and Political Relations (I). *Monumenta Serica* 51: 55–236.

———— 2004. Han and Xiongnu: A Reexamination of Cultural and Political Relations (II). *Monumenta Serica* 52: 95–112.

Pulleyblank, Edwin G. 1955. *The Background of the Rebellion of An Lu-shan.* Oxford: Oxford University Press.

———— 1984. *Middle Chinese: A Study in Historical Phonology.* Vancouver: University of British Columbia Press.

———— 1991. *Lexicon of Reconstructed Pronunciation in Early Middle Chinese, Late Middle Chinese, and Early Mandarin.* Vancouver: UBC Press.

———— 1995. The Historical and Prehistorical Relationships of Chinese. In William S. Y. Wang, ed., *Languages and Dialects of China,* 145–194. Journal of Chinese Linguistics Monograph Series, No. 8.

———— 1996. Early Contacts between Indo-Europeans and Chinese. *International Review of Chinese Linguistics* 1.1: 1–25.

———— 2000. The Hsiung-nu. In Hans Robert Roemer, ed., *Philologiae et Historiae Turcicae Fundamenta,* vol. 3, 52–75. Berlin: Klaus Schwartz Verlag.

Rackham, H., ed. and trans. 1934. *Aristotle: The Nicomachean Ethics.* Cambridge, Mass.: Harvard University Press.

Ramet, Sabrina Petra 1993. Religious Policy in the Era of Gorbachev. In Sabrina P. Ramet, ed., *Religious Policy in the Soviet Union,* 31–52. Cambridge: Cambridge University Press.

Rastorgueva, V. S., and D. I. Édel'man 2000. Этимологический словарь иранских языков, I–II. Moscow: Vostočnaja literatura.

Raulwing, Peter 2000. *Horses, Chariots, and Indo-Europeans: Foundations and Methods of Chariotry Research from the Viewpoint of Comparative Indo-European Linguistics.* Budapest: Archaeolingua.

Rawlinson, George, trans. 1992. *Herodotus: The Histories.* London: J. M. Dent & Sons.

Remy, Arthur F. J. 1907. The Avesta. *The Catholic Encylopedia,* vol. II. New York: Robert Appleton. Online edition, http://www.newadvent.org/cathen/02151b.htm.

Richards, John F. 1993. *The New Cambridge History of India*, I, 5: *The Mughal Empire*. Cambridge: Cambridge University Press.

Rolle, Renate 1989. *The World of the Scythians*. Trans. F. G. Walls. Berkeley: University of California Press.

Róna-Tas, András, and S. Fodor 1973. *Epigraphica Bulgarica*. Szeged: Studia Uralo-Altaica.

Rossa, Jesse 2006. *Ezra Pound in His Time and Beyond: The Influence of Ezra Pound on Twentieth-Century Poetry*. Newark: University of Delaware Library.

Rossabi, Morris 1981. The Muslims in the Early Yüan Dynasty. In John D. Langlois Jr., ed., *China under Mongol Rule*, 257–295. Princeton: Princeton University Press.

—— ed. 1983. *China among Equals: The Middle Kingdom and Its Neighbors, 10th–14th Centuries*. Berkeley: University of California Press.

—— 1988. *Khubilai Khan: His Life and Times*. Berkeley: University of California Press.

—— 1994. The Reign of Khubilai Khan. In Herbert Franke and Denis Twitchett, eds., *Cambridge History of China*, vol. 6: *Alien Regimes and Border States, 907–1368*, 414–489. Cambridge: Cambridge University Press.

Rothenberg, Joshua 1978. Jewish Religion in the Soviet Union. In Lionel Kochan, ed., *The Jews in Soviet Russia since 1917*, 168–196. Oxford: Oxford University Press.

Rudelson, Justin J. 1997. *Oasis Identities: Uyghur Nationalism along China's Silk Road*. New York: Columbia University Press.

Russell-Wood, A.J.R. 1998. *The Portuguese Empire, 1415–1808: A World on the Move*. Baltimore: Johns Hopkins Press.

Rybatzki, Volker 2000. Titles of Türk and Uigur Rulers in the Old Turkic Inscriptions. *Central Asiatic Journal* 44.2: 205–292.

Sadie, Stanley, and John Tyrell, eds. 2001. *The New Grove Dictionary of Music and Musicians*. 2nd ed. London: Macmillan.

Sagart, Laurent 1999. *The Roots of Old Chinese*. Amsterdam: John Benjamins.

Said, Edward 1978. *Orientalism*. New York: Pantheon Books.

Sandler, Stanley, ed. 2001. *World War II in the Pacific: An Encyclopedia*. New York: Garland.

Sasson, Jack M., ed. 1995. *Civilizations of the Ancient Near East*. New York: Charles Scribner's Sons.

Savory, R. M., et al. 1995. Ṣafawids. *E.I.$_2$* VIII: 765–793.

Schamiloglu, Uli 1984a. The *Qaraçi* Beys of the Later Golden Horde: Notes on the Organization of the Mongol World Empire. *Archivum Eurasiae Medii Aevi* 4: 283–297.

—— 1984b. The Name of the Pechenegs in Ibn Ḥayyân's *Al-Muqtabas*. *Journal of Turkish Studies* 8: 215–222.

—— 1991. The End of Volga Bulgarian. In *Varia Eurasiatica: Festschrift für Professor András Róna-Tas*, 157–163. Szeged: Department of Altaic Studies.

Scherman, Katharine 1987. *The Birth of France: Warriors, Bishops, and Long-Haired Kings*. New York: Random House.

Schmitt, Rüdiger 1989. *Altiranische Sprachen im Überblick*. In Rüdiger Schmitt, ed., *Compendium Linguarum Iranicarum*, 25–31. Wiesbaden: Dr. Ludwig Reichert Verlag.

Shcherbak, A. M. 2001. Тюркская руника. St. Petersburg: Nauka.

Scott, James C. 1998. *Seeing Like a State: How Certain Schemes to Improve the Human Condition Have Failed*. New Haven: Yale University Press.

Sezgin, Fuat 1978. *Geschichte des Arabischen Schrifttums, Band VI. Astronomie, bis ca. 430 H.* Leiden: Brill.

—— 1984. *Geschichte des Arabischen Schrifttums, Band IX. Grammatik, bis ca. 430 H.* Leiden: Brill.

Shaban, M. A. 1970. *The 'Abbāsid Revolution*. Cambridge: Cambridge University Press.

—— 1971. *Islamic History: A New Interpretation, I.* Cambridge: Cambridge University Press.

—— 1976. *Islamic History: A New Interpretation, II.* Cambridge: Cambridge University Press.

Shaked, Shaul 2004. *Le satrape de Bactriane et son gouverneur: documents araméens du IVᵉ s. avant notre ère provenant de Bactriane*. Paris: De Boccard.

Shakya, Tsering 1999. *The Dragon in the Land of Snows: A History of Modern Tibet since 1947*. New York: Columbia University Press.

Shaughnessy, Edward L. 1988. Historical Perspectives on the Introduction of the Chariot into China. *Harvard Journal of Asiatic Studies* 48.1: 189–237.

Shiba, Yoshinobu 1983. Sung Foreign Trade: Its Scope and Organization. In Morris Rossabi, ed., *China among Equals: The Middle Kingdom and Its Neighbors, 10th–14th Centuries*, 89–115. Berkeley: University of California Press.

Sieg, Emil, Wilhelm Siegling, and Werner Thomas 1953. *Tocharische Sprachreste, Sprache B. Heft 2: Fragmente Nr. 71-633*. Göttingen: Vandenhoeck & Ruprecht.

Sinor, Denis 1959. *History of Hungary*. New York: Praeger.

—— 1963. *Introduction à l'étude de l'Eurasie centrale*. Wiesbaden: Harrassowitz.

—— 1978. The Greed of the Northern Barbarians. In Larry V. Clark and Paul A. Draghi, eds., *Aspects of Altaic Civilizations II*, 171–182. Bloomington: Indiana University.

—— 1982. The Legendary Origin of the Turks. In E. V. Žygas and P. Voorheis, eds., *Folklorica: Festschrift for Felix J. Oinas*, 223–257. Uralic and Altaic Series, vol. 141. Bloomington: Indiana University.

—— 1990a. The Establishment and Dissolution of the Türk Empire. In Denis Sinor, ed., *The Cambridge History of Early Inner Asia*, 285–316. Cambridge: Cambridge University Press.

—— 1990b. Introduction: The Concept of Inner Asia. In Denis Sinor, ed., *The Cambridge History of Early Inner Asia*, 1–18. Cambridge: Cambridge University Press.

———, ed. 1990c. *The Cambridge History of Early Inner Asia.* Cambridge: Cambridge University Press.

Somers, Robert M. 1979. The End of the T'ang. In Denis Crispin Twitchett, ed., *The Cambridge History of China,* vol. 3: *Sui and T'ang China, 589–906, Part 1,* 682–789. Cambridge: Cambridge University Press.

Speck, Paul 1981. *Artabasdos, der rechtgläubige Vorkämpfer der göttlichen Lehren: Untersuchungen zur Revolte des Artabasdos und ihrer Darstellung in der byzantinischen Historiographie.* Bonn: Habelt.

Spence, Jonathan 2002. The K'ang-hsi Reign. In Willard J. Peterson, ed., *The Cambridge History of China,* vol. 9: *The Ch'ing Empire to 1800, Part 1,* 120–182. Cambridge: Cambridge University Press.

Ssu-ma Kuang 1956. 資治通鑑 (*Tzu chih t'ung chien*). Hong Kong: Chung-hua shu-chü.

Starostin, Sergei A. 1989. Реконструкция древнекитайской фонологической системы. Moscow: Nauka.

Stary, Giovanni 1990. The Meaning of the Word 'Manchu': A New Solution to an Old Problem. *Central Asiatic Journal* 34.1–2: 109–119.

Stearns, Peter N., ed. 2002. *The Encyclopedia of World History: Ancient, Medieval, and Modern, Chronologically Arranged.* Sixth ed. A completely revised and updated edition of the classic reference work originally compiled and edited by William L. Langer. Boston: Houghton Mifflin.

Struve, Lynn A. 1984. *The Southern Ming, 1644–1662.* New Haven: Yale University Press.

———1988. The Southern Ming, 1644–1662. In Frederick W. Mote and Denis Twitchett, eds., *The Cambridge History of China,* vol. 7: *The Ming Dynasty, 1368–1644, Part 1,* 641–725. Cambridge: Cambridge University Press.

Sullivan, Alan, and Timothy Murphy, trans. 2004. *Beowulf.* New York: Pearson/Longman.

Szádeczky-Kardoss, Samuel 1990. The Avars. In Denis Sinor, ed., *The Cambridge History of Early Inner Asia,* 206–228. Cambridge: Cambridge University Press.

Szegedy-Maszák, Mihály 2001. *Literary Canons: National and International.* Budapest: Akadémiai Kiado.

Szerb, János 1983. A Note on the Tibetan-Uighur Treaty of 822/823 A.D.. In Ernst Steinkellner and Helmut Tauscher, eds., *Proceedings of the Csoma de Kőrös Memorial Symposium Held at Velm-Vienna, Austria, 13–19 September 1981,* vol. 1, 375–387. Vienna: Arbeitskreis für Tibetische und Buddhistische Studien, Universität Wien.

Szemerényi, Oswald J.L. 1980. *Four Old Iranian Ethnic Names: Scythian—Skudra—Sogdian—Saka.* Österreichischen Akademie der Wissenschaften, Philosophisch-Historische Klasse, Sitzungsberichte, 371 Band. Vienna: Verlag der Österreichischen Akademie der Wissenschaften.

—— 1996. *Introduction to Indo-European Linguistics*. Oxford: Oxford University Press.

Syme, Ronald 1939. *The Roman Revolution*. Oxford: Oxford University Press.

Ṭabarî: Abû Jaʿfar Muḥammad b. Jarîr al-Ṭabarî 1879–1901. تاريخ الرسل و اللوك (*Taʾrîkh al-rusul wa al-mulûk*). Ed. M. J. de Goeje et al. Repr., Leiden: E. J. Brill, 1964–1965.

Takakusu Junjirô, Ono Genmyô, ed. 1932–1934. 大正新修大藏經 (*Taishô shinshû daizôkyô*). Tokyo: Daizô Shuppan.

Takata, Tokio 1988. 敦煌資料による中國語史の研究 ： 九・十世紀の河西方言, (*A Historical Study of the Chinese Language Based on Dunhuang Materials*). Tokyo: Sôbunsha.

Takeda, Hiromichi, and Collett Cox, trans. forthcoming. Existence in the Three Time Periods *Abhidharmamahāvibhāṣāśāstra* (T.1545 pp. 393a9–396b23).

Takeuchi, Tsuguhito 2002. The Old Zhangzhung Manuscript Stein Or 8212/ 188. In C. I. Beckwith, ed., *Medieval Tibeto-Burman Languages*, 1–11. Leiden: Brill.

Taylor, Timothy 2003. A Platform for Studying the Scythians. *Antiquity* 77. 296: 413–415.

Teed, Peter 1992. *A Dictionary of Twentieth Century History, 1914–1990*. Oxford: Oxford University Press.

Tekin, Talat 1968. *A Grammar of Orkhon Turkic*. Uralic and Altaic Series, vol. 69. Bloomington: Indiana University.

Thant Myint-U 2001. *The Making of Modern Burma*. Cambridge: Cambridge University Press.

Thomas, F. W. 1948. *Nam: An Ancient Language of the Sino-Tibetan Borderland*. London: Oxford University Press.

Thomason, Sarah Grey, and Terrence Kaufman 1988. *Language Contact, Creolization, and Genetic Linguistics*. Berkeley: University of California Press.

Thompson, E. A. 1996. *The Huns*. Revised and with an afterword by Peter Heather. Oxford: Blackwell.

Thompson, P. M. 1979. *The Shen Tzu Fragments*. Oxford: Oxford University Press.

Tilly, Charles 1975. Reflections on the History of European State-Making. In Charles Tilly, ed., *The Formation of the National States in Western Europe*, 3–83. Princeton: Princeton University Press.

—— 1990. *Coercion, Capital, and European States, AD 990–1990*. Cambridge, Mass.: Basil Blackwell.

Treadgold, Warren 1997. *A History of the Byzantine State and Society*. Stanford: Stanford University Press.

Tu Yu 1988. 通典 (*T'ung tien*). Peking: Chung-hua shu-chü.

Turnbull, Stephen R. 2003. *Samurai: The World of the Warrior*. Oxford: Osprey. http://www.ospreysamurai.com/samurai_death02.htm.

Turner, Jane, ed. 1996. *The Dictionary of Art*. London: Macmillan.

Twitchett, Denis, and Michael Loewe, eds. 1986. *The Cambridge History of China*, vol. 1: *The Ch'in and Han Empires, 221 B.C.–A.D. 220*. Cambridge: Cambridge University Press.

Twitchett, Denis, and Frederick W. Mote, eds. 1988. *The Cambridge History of China*, vol. 7: *The Ming Dynasty, 1368–1644, Part 1*. Cambridge: Cambridge University Press.

Twitchett, Denis, and Klaus-Peter Tietze 1994. The Liao. In Herbert Franke and Denis Twitchett, eds., *Cambridge History of China*, vol. 6: *Alien Regimes and Border States, 907–1368*, 43–153. Cambridge: Cambridge University Press.

Twitchett, Denis, and Howard J. Wechsler 1979. Kao-tsung (reign 649–83) and the Empress Wu: The Inheritor and the Usurper. In Denis Crispin Twitchett, ed., *The Cambridge History of China*, vol. 3: *Sui and T'ang China, 589–906, Part 1*, 242–289. Cambridge: Cambridge University Press.

Uray, Géza 1960. The Four Horns of Tibet. According to the Royal Annals. *Acta Orientalia Academiae Hungaricae* 10: 31–57.

——— 1961. Notes on a Tibetan Military Document from Tun-huang. *Acta Orientalia Academiae Hungaricae* 12: 223–230.

Valentino, Benjamin A. 2004. *Final Solutions: Mass Killing and Genocide in the 20th Century*. Ithaca: Cornell University Press.

Vallé, S. 1910. Marcianopolis. *The Catholic Encyclopedia*. Vol. IX. New York: Robert Appleton. http://www.newadvent.org/cathen/09645b.htm.

Van de Mieroop, Marc 2004. *A History of the Ancient Near East, ca. 3000–323 BC*. Oxford: Blackwell.

Van Walt van Praag, Michael C. 1987. *The Status of Tibet: History, Rights, and Prospects in International Law*. Boulder: Westview Press.

Vernet, J. 1997. Al-<u>Kh</u>ʷārazmī. *E.I.*₂ IV: 1070–1071.

Vladimirtsov, B. I. 1948. *Le régime social des Mongols: le féodalisme nomade*. Paris: Maisonneuve.

——— 2002. Работы по истории и этнографии монгольских народов. Moscow: Vostočnaja literatura.

Vovin, Alexander 2000. Did the Xiong-nu Speak a Yeniseian Language? *Central Asiatic Journal* 44.1: 87–104.

Vyvyan, J.M.K. 1968. The Approach of the War of 1914. In C. L. Mowat, ed. *The New Cambridge Modern History*, vol. XII: *The Shifting Balance of World Forces, 1898–1945, 2nd ed.*, vol. XII: *The Era of Violence*, 140–170. Cambridge: Cambridge University Press.

Wakeman, Frederic, Jr. 1978. The Canton Trade and the Opium War. In John K. Fairbank, ed., *The Cambridge History of China*, vol. 10: *Late Ch'ing, 1800–1911, Part 1*, 163–212. Cambridge: Cambridge University Press.

——— 1985. *The Great Enterprise: The Manchu Reconstruction of Imperial Order in Seventeenth-Century China*. Berkeley: University of California Press.

Walter, Michael forthcoming. *Buddhism and Politics in the Tibetan Empire*.

Walters, Philip 1993. A Survey of Soviet Religious Policy. In Sabrina P. Ramet, ed., *Religious Policy in the Soviet Union*, 3–30. Cambridge: Cambridge University Press.

Wang Ch'in-jo et al., eds. 1960. 册府元龜 (*Ts'e fu yüan kuei*). Hong Kong: Chung-hua shu-chü.

Watkins, Calvert 1995. *How to Kill a Dragon: Aspects of Indo-European Poetics*. Oxford: Oxford University Press.

—— 2000. *The American Heritage Dictionary of Indo-European Roots*. 2nd ed. Boston: Houghton Mifflin.

Watson, Burton 1961. *Records of the Grand Historian of China: Translated from the Shih chi of Ssu-ma Ch'ien*. 2 vols. New York: Columbia University Press.

Watt, W. Montgomery 1991. Al-Ghazālī. *E.I.₂*, II: 1038–1041.

Wechsler, Howard J. 1979a. The Founding of the T'ang Dynasty: Kao-tsu (reign 618–26). In Denis Twitchett, ed., *The Cambridge History of China*, vol. 3: *Sui and T'ang China, 589–906, Part 1*, 150–187. Cambridge: Cambridge University Press.

—— 1979b. T'ai-tsung (reign 626–49) the Consolidator. In Denis Twitchett, ed., *The Cambridge History of China*, vol. 3: *Sui and T'ang China, 589–906, Part 1*, 188–241. Cambridge: Cambridge University Press.

Weinstein, Stanley 1987. *Buddhism under the T'ang*. Cambridge: Cambridge University Press.

Weiss, Aharon 2000. The Destruction of European Jewry, 1933–1945. In Robert Rozett and Shmuel Spector, eds., *Encyclopedia of the Holocaust*, 46–55. New York: Facts on File.

Whitman, John W. 2001. Fall of the Philippines. In Stanley Sandler, ed., *World War II in the Pacific: An Encyclopedia*, 478–483. New York: Garland.

Willemen, Charles, Bart Dessein, and Collett Cox 1998. *Sarvāstivāda Buddhist Scholasticism*. Leiden: Brill.

Wills, John E., Jr. 1998. Relations with Maritime Europeans, 1514–1662. In Denis Twitchett and Frederick W. Mote, eds., *The Cambridge History of China*, vol. 8: *The Ming Dynasty, 1368–1644, Part 2*, 333–375. Cambridge: Cambridge University Press.

Wittfogel, Karl, and Chia-shêng Fêng 1949. *History of Chinese Society: Liao, 907–1125*. Philadelphia: American Philosophical Society.

Witzel, Michael 2001. Autochthonous Aryans? The Evidence from Old Indian and Iranian Texts. *Electronic Journal of Vedic Studies* 7.3: 1–115.

—— 2003. *Linguistic Evidence for Cultural Exchange in Prehistoric Western Central Asia*. Sino-Platonic Papers No. 129. Philadelphia.

Wolfram, Herwig 1988. *History of the Goths*. Trans. Thomas J. Dunlap. Berkeley: University of California Press.

Wood, Ian 1994. *The Merovingian Kingdoms, 450–751*. London: Longman.

Wyatt, David K. 2003. *Thailand: A Short History*. 2nd ed. New Haven: Yale University Press.

Wylie, Turrell V. 1964. Mar-pa's Tower: Notes on Local Hegemons in Tibet. *History of Religions* 3: 278–291.

Yakubovskii, A. Y., and C. E. Bosworth 1991. Marw al-S̲h̲āhid̲j̲ān. *E.I.*$_2$ VI: 618–621.

Yamada Katsumi, ed. and trans. 1976. 王充. 論衡, 上 (Wang Ch'ung, '*Lun heng*, Part I') Shinshaku Kanbun taikei 68. Tokyo: Meiji shoin.

Yang Chih-chiu 1985. 元史三論 (*Yüan shih san lun*). Peking: Jen-min ch'u-pan she.

Yang Po-chün, ed. 1990. 春秋佐傳注 (*Ch'un ch'iu tso chuan chu*). 2nd rev. ed. Peking: Chung-hua shu chü.

Yarshater, Ehsan, ed. 1983. *The Cambridge History of Iran*, vol. 3: *The Seleucid, Parthian and Sasanian Periods*. 2 vols. Cambridge: Cambridge University Press.

Yoshida, Yutaka, and Takao Moriyasu 1999. ブグト碑文 (Bugut Inscription). In T. Moriyasu and A. Ochir, eds., モンゴル国現存遺蹟・碑文調査研究報告 (*Provisional Report of Researches on Historical Sites and Inscriptions in Mongolia from 1996 to 1998*), 122–125. Osaka: Society of Central Eurasian Studies.

Yü Ying-shih 1967. *Trade and Expansion in Han China: A Study in the Structure of Sino-Barbarian Relations*. Berkeley: University of California Press.

—— 1990. The Hsiung-nu. In Denis Sinor, ed., *The Cambridge History of Early Inner Asia*, 118–149. Cambridge: Cambridge University Press.

—— 1986. Han Foreign Relations. In Denis Crispin Twitchett and Michael Loewe, eds., *The Cambridge History of China*, vol. 1: *The Ch'in and Han Empires, 221 B.C.–A.D. 220*, 377–462. Cambridge: Cambridge University Press.

Zabecki, David T., et al., eds. 1999. *World War II in Europe: An Encyclopedia*. New York: Garland.

Zakeri, Mohsen 1995. *Sāsānid Soldiers in Early Muslim Society: The Origins of 'Ayyārān and Futuwwa*. Wiesbaden: Harrassowitz.

Zlatkin, I. Ja. 1983. История Джунгарского ханства, 1635–1758. Издание второе. Moscow: Nauka.

Zuckerman, Constantine 1997. Two Notes on the Early History of the *Thema* of Cherson. *Byzantine and Modern Greek Studies* 21: 210–222.

INDEX

Aachen, Aix-la-Chapelle, 148–149
Abahai. *See* Hung Taiji
'Abbâs I, Safavid shâh, 209, 230, 245
'Abbâs II, Safavid shâh, 209–210
Abbasid Revolution, 143, 146
Abbasid Caliphate, Abbasids, 143, 145, 147, 153, 157, 161–162, 167. *See also* Arab Empire
'Abd al-Malik, Umayyad caliph, 132
'Abd al-Raḥman, governor of Spain, 136
'Abû al-'Abbâs, first Abbasid caliph, 143
Abû Bakr, first caliph, 121
Abû Ja'far al-Manṣûr, second Abbasid caliph, 147, 152
Abû Sa'îd, last Il-Khan, 195
Abû Yazîd al-Biṣṭâmî, first Sufi mystic, 177
Adrianople, Battle of, 95–96
Aetius, Flavius, Roman general, 98–100
Afghanistan, Afghan, 232, 310, 312; Civil War, 286, 362. *See also* Sur
Afonso de Albuquerque, 212
Agni. *See* Karashahr
Agra, 210, 221, 230
Akbar, Mughal emperor, 221, 230
Ak-Koyunlu, 208–209
Aksu, 130
Al-Akhfash al-Ausaṭ. *See* Al-Mujâshi'î of Balkh
Alamut, 190
Alans, 78, 81–82
Albanian, 34, 365
Albazin, 224, 234
Al-Birûnî, 177
Aleppo, 199
Alexander the Great, 69, 74–75, 77, 83, 329n21
Al-Fârâbî, Avennasar, 177
Al-Farghânî, Alfraganus, 177
Al-Ghazâlî, Algazel, 177–179
Algorithmus. *See* al-Khwârizmî
Al-Ḥajjâj ibn Yûsuf, Umayyad governor-general, 132–133
Alhambra, 206
'Alî, fourth caliph, 123
Al-Khwârizmî, Algorithmus, 153, 179

alliances, Allied Powers, 267, 290; Allies, 275–277; Arab-Chinese, 134–135, 142; Axis, 276–278; Central Powers, 267, 290; Ch'ing-Russian, 234; Mongolian-Soviet, 278; Paekche-Koguryo-Japanese, 134–135; T'ang-Silla, 134–135; Tibetan-Western Turk, 129–131; 133–135
alligators, 7, 389–390n16
Al-Ma'mûn, Abbasid caliph, 25, 152–154, 158, 161
Al-Mujâshi'î of Balkh, actual author of *al-Kitâb*, 154, 413–414n78
Al-Mu'taṣim, Abbasid caliph, 25, 161
Alp Arslan, Seljuk ruler, 168–169, 177
Alpha Male Hierarchy, xi, 323
Alptigin, Samanid-Ghaznavid ruler, 167
Altai Mountains, 9
Altan Khan, 345–346
Alutâr, king of Ferghana, 133
Al-Walîd I, Umayyad caliph, 132–133
Al-Wâthiq, Abbasid caliph, 161–162
Amazons, 58, 70
American Indians, xxiv–xxv, 279n47
Amursana, Junghar leader, 239–240
Anacharsis, Scythian philosopher, 75
Anagai, Avar kaghan, 9, 104
Anatolian, 32, 36, 37–39, 365
Anglo-Saxons, 101
Angora, 271; Battle of, 199
An-hsi, Pacified West Protectorate, 129–130
An Lu-shan, T'ang rebel, 21, 145–146, 171–172
An-nan, Annam, 138n87, 192
Anthony, David W., xvin1
Arab Empire, Arabs, 16, 23–26, 101, 111n50, 113, 118–123, 130–134, 136, 140–147, 149, 151n37, 152–156, 161–164, 167–168, 171, 206, 208, 212, 245–246, 251–252, 256–257, 326, 337n45, 381, 408–409nn62–65, 409n67, 412–413n75, 413–414nn77–78; first civil war, 409n67; Arabs in Spain (*see* Spain, Arabs in)

Germania, 17–18, 79–82, 98–102, 110, 136, 340
Germanic, Germanic peoples 33–34, 100–101, 349, 351, 354, 363, 365
Germany, republics of, 269–271, 284, 285, 309
Ghaznavids, 167–168, 177
Ghazne, 167–168, 210
Glang Darma. *See* Khri U'i Dum Brtsan
Glass, Philip, 297n98
Goa, 212, 220
Godan. *See* Köden
gold, 4, 9nn32–33, 15n47, 16–18, 21–22, 26, 43, 57n106, 58, 63–65, 97, 148, 220, 243, 254, 293, 323, 391–392nn19–20, 405–406n54, 425n107
Golden Horde, 189–190, 196, 198–199, 222
Gorbachev, Mikhail, 305
Goths, Gothones, 82–83, 95–102, 109–110, 331–332, 333, 335, 352–353
Graeco-Roman, xxiii, 39, 111, 257, 323, 332, 340, 350, 353, 357–358
Grand Canal, 124
graphic art, artists. *See* Modernism: in painting; painting
Grassmann, Hermann, 363
Great Khanate, 194. *See also* Mongol Empire
Great Wall of China. *See* walls
Greek, Greeks, 33–35, 42–43, 47, 49, 51, 58–61, 63, 65, 68–70, 74–75, 77, 78–79, 80n5, 83, 102, 109–110, 113, 122, 153–155, 164, 169, 178, 253, 353–354, 357–358, 363, 365, 371, 413n77; texts translated into Arabic, 154. *See also* Byzantine Empire; Mycenaean Greek; Romans
guard corps. *See* comitatus
guerrilla tactics, 68, 339–340
Guge, kingdom of, 169–170
guns. *See* firearms
Gur-e Emir, 200
Gür Khan, 175–176
Gushi Khan, Khoshut ruler, 227–228; ruler of Tibet, 228
Güyük, Great Khan, 189–191

Hafiz, 203–204, 229
hair, of the Franks, 80n5; of the Turks, 80n5
Hami, 235

Han Dynasty, 86–89, 92, 102–103, 257, 332–334, 337–338
Hang-chou, 175
Hârûn al-Rashîd, Abbasid caliph, 25, 152, 158
Hattusa, 39
Heaven, god of, 2, 3, 115
Hellig, Hsieh-li, Eastern Türk kaghan, 125, 126
Hephthalites, 102, 116, 122–123, 132–133, 406n56
Heraclius, Byzantine Emperor, 119–120, 208
Herat, 196, 229
Hideyoshi, Japanese general, 243
Hildebrand, Frankish lord, 136
Hiroshima, 278
Hitler, Adolf, 270, 273, 275, 278
Hittite, 37–38, 371–372, 396–397nn35–36
Hittites, 2, 32–33, 37–39, 260n84; origin myth, 386n4
Ho-lu, Western Turk kaghan, 129
Homs, 199
Hong Kong, 249, 276
Honoria, Roman princess, 97–98
Hormuz, 209, 212, 215, 245
horse: Chinese word for, 402n45; domestication of, 50–52; introduction to China, 396; price of, 393–394n26
Hou Chi, 3
Hsien-pei, Mongolic people, 89–90, 103, 104–105, 113, 257
Hsi-hsia Dynasty. *See* Tangut Empire
Hsining, 237–238
Hsiung-nu, 5–7, 71–73, 84, 86–90, 92, 117, 125, 212, 257, 321, 330–332, 339, 347, 354–355, 357–358, 382–383; invasion by Chinese, 71–72; name, 404–405nn51–52; names and titles, 387nn7–8, 387–388n10; origin myth, 5–6; putative equation with Huns, 72–73, 404–405n51
Hsüan Tsang, Buddhist monk traveler, 21, 123, 409n66
Hsüan-tsung, T'ang emperor, 126–127, 145, 393–394
Huang Ch'ao, Chinese rebel, 171–172
Hui-tsung, Sung emperor and artist, 174–175
Hülegü, first Il-Khan, 190, 192

MAPS

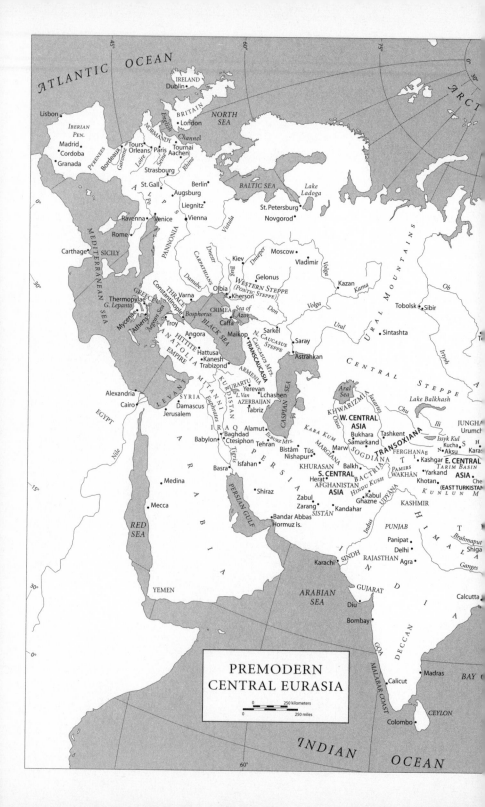

PREMODERN
CENTRAL EURASIA

0 ——————— 250 kilometers
0 ——————— 250 miles

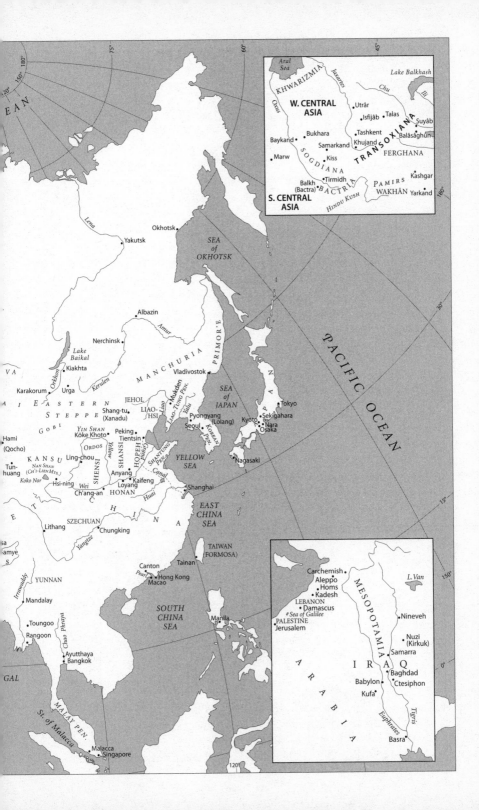

Inset 1 (top right):

Aral Sea

KHWARIZMIA

W. CENTRAL ASIA

Lake Balkhash

Jaxartes

Oxus

Chu

Ili

•Utrâr

•Isfîjâb   •Talas

•Suyâb

Baykand•   •Bukhara   •Tashkent   •Balâsâghûn

Samarkand   Khujand

SOGDIANA   •Kiss

TRANSOXIANA   FERGHANA

Marw•

Balkh •Tirmidh   PAMIRS   •Kashgar

•(Bactra)   BACTRIA   WAKHÂN   •Yarkand

S. CENTRAL ASIA   Hindu Kush

Main map:

EAN

OCEAN (PACIFIC OCEAN)

Lena

Okhotsk•

•Yakutsk

SEA of OKHOTSK

Albazin•

Amur

•Nerchinsk

PRIMOR'E

Lake Baikal

VA

Orkhon

Kerulen

•Kiakhta

MANCHURIA

Vladivostok•

Karakorum•   •Urga

SEA of JAPAN

A I   E A S T E R N

S T E P P E   JEHOL

Shang-tu   LIAO-HSI   Mukden

GOBI   (Xanadu)   LIAO-TUNG PEN.

Hami   YIN SHAN   Köke Khoto•   Peking•   Liao   Yalu

(Qocho)   •   Tientsin•   Pyongyang (Lolang)•   Tokyo•

ORDOS   Seoul•   KOREAN PEN.   •Sekigahara

KANSU   NAN SHAN   Ling-chou•   SHANSI   HOPEH   Peiho   Kyoto• •Nara

(CH'I-LIEN MTS.)   Anyang•   SHANTUNG PEN.   Osaka•

Tun-   •Hsi-ning   Wei   Kaifeng•   YELLOW SEA   •Nagasaki

huang   Koko Nor   Ch'ang-an•   •Loyang HONAN   Canal

C H I N A   Huai   Shanghai•

SZECHUAN   •Chungking   Yangtze   EAST CHINA SEA

Lithang•

amye   TIBET?

s   TAIWAN (FORMOSA)

YUNNAN   Canton•   •Tainan

Irrawaddy   Pearl   •Hong Kong

•Mandalay   Chao Phraya   Macao•   SOUTH CHINA SEA

•Toungoo

Rangoon•   •Manila

GAL   •Ayutthaya
Bangkok•

MALAY PEN.

St. of Malacca

Malacca•
•Singapore

Inset 2 (bottom right):

Carchemish•   L. Van

Aleppo•   MESOPOTAMIA

•Homs

•Kadesh

LEBANON

•Damascus   •Nineveh

Sea of Galilee

PALESTINE   •Nuzi (Kirkuk)

Jerusalem   •Samarra

I R A Q

A R A B I A   •Baghdad

Babylon• •Ctesiphon

Kufa•

Euphrates   Tigris

Basra•

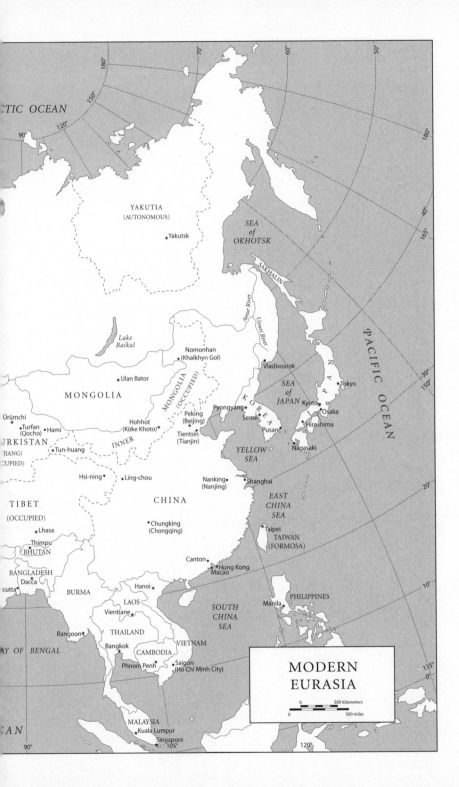

ARCTIC OCEAN

YAKUTIA
(AUTONOMOUS)

★Yakutsk

SEA
of
OKHOTSK

SAKHALIN

Amur River

Ussuri River

Lake
Baikal

Nomonhan
(Khalkhyn Gol)

Vladivostok

★Ulan Bator

MONGOLIA
(OCCUPIED)

MONGOLIA

SEA
of
JAPAN

Tokyo

Kyoto

PACIFIC OCEAN

J A P A N

K O R E A

Pyongyang★

Osaka

Ürümchi

Turfan
(Qocho)

Hami

Hohhot
(Köke Khoto)★

INNER

Peking
(Beijing)

Tientsin
(Tianjin)

Seoul★

Pusan

Hiroshima

TURKISTAN
(XINJIANG)
(OCCUPIED)

Tun-huang

Nagasaki

Hsi-ning

Ling-chou

Nanking
(Nanjing)

Shanghai

YELLOW
SEA

EAST
CHINA
SEA

TIBET
(OCCUPIED)

CHINA

Chungking
(Chongqing)

★Lhasa

Thimpu
BHUTAN

Taipei
TAIWAN
(FORMOSA)

BANGLADESH

Dacca

Calcutta

BURMA

Hanoi

Canton

Hong Kong
Macao

LAOS

Vientiane

PHILIPPINES

SOUTH
CHINA
SEA

Manila

Rangoon★

THAILAND

Bangkok

CAMBODIA

Phnom Penh

Saigon
(Ho Chi Minh City)

VIETNAM

BAY OF BENGAL

MALAYSIA

Kuala Lumpur

Singapore

MODERN
EURASIA

0   500 kilometers
0   500 miles

180° 70° 60° 50°

150°

120°

90°

180°

165°

40°

30°

150°

20°

10°

135°

120°

105°

90°